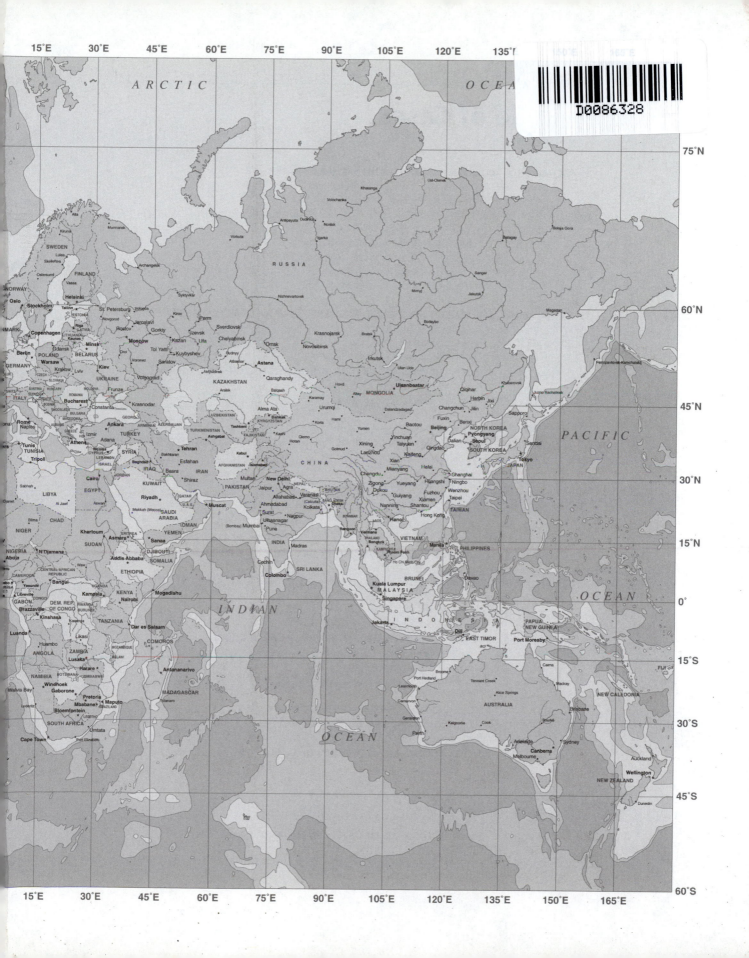

Table of Cases

THE WORLD ECONOMY

OPEN-ECONOMY MACROECONOMICS AND FINANCE

SEVENTH EDITION

Beth V. Yarbrough
Amherst College

Robert M. Yarbrough
Amherst College

THOMSON

SOUTH-WESTERN

Australia · Canada · Mexico · Singapore · Spain · United Kingdom · United States

THOMSON
SOUTH-WESTERN

The World Economy: Open-Economy Macroeconomics and Finance, Seventh Edition
Beth V. Yarbrough and Robert M. Yarbrough

VP/Editorial Director:
Jack W. Calhoun

VP/Editor-in-Chief:
Dave Shaut

Senior Developmental Editor:
Sarah Dorger

Marketing Manager:
John Carey

Senior Production Editor:
Kara ZumBahlen

Production Editor:
Amy McGuire

Manager of Technology, Editorial:
Vicky True

Technology Project Editor:
Peggy Buskey

Web Coordinator:
Karen Schaffer

Senior Manufacturing Coordinator:
Sandee Milewski

Production House:
Stratford Publishing Services, Inc.

Compositor:
Integra

Art Director:
Michelle Kunkler

Internal Designer:
Paul Neff Design

Cover Designer:
Tippy McIntosh

Cover Images:
© Getty Images, Inc.

Printer:
Courier
Kendalville, IN

Library of Congress Control Number:
2005920273

For more information about our products, contact us at:

Thomson Learning Academic Resource Center
1-800-423-0563

Thomson Higher Education
5191 Natorp Boulevard
Mason, OH 45040
USA

Asia (including India)
Thomson Learning
5 Shenton Way
#01-01 UIC Building
Singapore 068808

Australia/New Zealand
Thomson Learning Australia
102 Dodds Street
Southbank, Victoria 3006
Australia

Canada
Thomson Nelson
1120 Birchmount Road
Toronto, Ontario
M1K 5G4
Canada

Latin America
Thomson Learning
Seneca, 53
Colonia Polanco
11560 Mexico
D.F. Mexico

UK/Europe/Middle East/Africa
Thomson Learning
High Holborn House
50/51 Bedford Row
London WC1R 4LR
United Kingdom

Spain (including Portugal)
Thomson Paraninfo
Calle Magallanes, 25
28015 Madrid, Spain

To Y. Y.

Preface

The success of earlier editions of *The World Economy: Trade and Finance* owes much to developments outside the classroom. Specific episodes come and go, but the pace of world events continues to remind us all of the big role international issues play in our economic lives. Zimbabwe slips into economic crisis as Argentina attempts to crawl out, and Japan teeters between economic recovery and continued stagnation. The United States and China make progress on intellectual property rights disputes, while the European Union and the United States bicker and test the World Trade Organization's ability to resolve disputes over U.S. tax and antidumping policies. The global textile and apparel industries scramble to adjust to the January 1, 2005, end of the complex web of import quotas that dominated the industries for 40 years. Ten Central and Eastern European countries, most only recently released from decades of central planning, celebrate their new membership in the European Union; but others, such as Belarus and Turkmenistan, remain mired in isolation, erratic reform, and recurrent political and economic crisis. After decades of hope and years of planning, the euro finally arrives as a real currency, promptly plummets in value relative to the dollar, then reverses course. The entire Iraqi economy needs rebuilding, amid significant turmoil in its major export market—oil. And several of the poorest countries in the world face the daunting and expensive task of recovering from a tsunami that ranks among the worst natural disasters in the past 100 years.

WHAT ARE WE TRYING TO DO IN *THE WORLD ECONOMY: OPEN-ECONOMY MACROECONOMICS AND FINANCE*?

The pace, scale, and scope of such events underscore the widespread perception of the increased importance of international economics for understanding world events. Luckily, just a few simple tools of economic analysis can provide a great deal of insight into the ever-changing world economy. The goals of this seventh edition of *The World Economy* remain unchanged from those of the first six:

- Present the *basic tools* of international economic analysis clearly, consistently, and comprehensively;
- Provide lots of applications to actual events so students can learn to *use* the tools soundly and confidently to analyze the world economy; and
- Give a sense of the broad range of *challenging and exciting issues* (as well as some humorous and quirky ones) that arise in the international economic arena.

Integrated Theory and Applications

By combining up-to-date theory with current events and policy debates, we emphasize learning how to use international economics as a tool for understanding. By the end of the course, students can analyze problems independently, not just those that happen to dominate the headlines at the time of the book's writing. *The World Economy* has never glorified theory for its own sake. The rule we endeavor to follow remains that *any theory worth presenting is worth teaching students to use; if it's not useful in understanding the world economy, it doesn't belong in the book.*

The World Economy is self-contained; it defines all necessary concepts and doesn't rely on students' memories from other economics courses. Frequent data tables tie abstract concepts to their concrete empirical counterparts. *We believe that an international economics course should familiarize students with the empirical reality of the world economy as well as with abstract models of it*, so we present data more frequently than is typical in other texts. We refer often to common errors or misinterpretations in the popular press, because learning how to read the newspaper or listen to the television news with a keen eye and ear is at least as important as learning how to read the scholarly literature.

The integration of clear, concise theory with up-to-date examples and cases has always set *The World Economy* apart from its competitors. One example of this integration is our focus throughout the book on policy's distributional consequences. These consequences represent the crux of most international economic policy controversies, but many texts shortchange them with a flurry of tangency conditions. We make extensive use of examples from diverse areas of the world economy—Iceland, Central Asia, Africa, Singapore, and North Korea, not just the United States and Western Europe. We highlight the relevance of international economic theory for understanding front-page macroeconomic issues such as currency risk and stock markets, the external debt of the U.S., the effect of German unification on the country's banks, creation of a new central bank and currency for Bosnia, the role of capital flows in financial crises, Japan's long economic slump, why countries don't always follow the exchange rate regime that they say they do, Poland's German "tank tourists," the changing character of business cycles, and countries' adoption of the dollar or euro in lieu of their own national currencies.

Careful, Clear Pedagogy

We employ a number of pedagogical devices to assist students in their reading. We number major sections within each chapter of *The World Economy* for easy reference. And to encourage *active* reading, at crucial points in an argument, we ask students in a parenthetic insertion, "*Why?*" These queries stop the reader from moving passively through the argument without confronting its underlying logic. Comments from our students indicate that the queries achieve their goal.[1] *The World Economy's* generous use of graphs, as well as their color format, make the arguments easy to follow. All graphs are fully integrated into the text and accompanied by self-contained legends. We encourage students to practice active translation between graphs and legends (*Can you cover the graph and draw your own, given the legend? Can you cover the legend and write your own explanation of the graph?*). Again, the emphasis is on learning to *use* the graphs as tools for understanding, not on memorization or rote manipulation.

Each chapter contains several cases, a summary, a "Looking Ahead" section that links the chapter to the next one, a list of key terms (boldfaced in the text), review questions and problems (including new ones in every chapter of the seventh edition), and a list of supplementary readings. The cases provide examples of the economic concepts and models developed in the chapter as well as extensive empirical information about the countries that make up the world economy. The end-of-chapter "Problems and Questions for Review" highlight major concepts from the chapter and relate those concepts to current policy debates. Many of the end-of-chapter questions from earlier editions now appear in the *Study Guide* (a new version of which accompanies this new edition). Unlike the bibliographies in many textbooks, the readings suggested in *The World Economy* include short, up-to-date

---

1. Several students have reported making a game of the queries by trying to read each chapter without being "caught" unprepared to answer a query.

articles as well as classic treatises and survey articles; and we note readings as appropriate for introductory, intermediate, or advanced students.

WHAT'S NEW TO THE SEVENTH EDITION?

Our basic goals, philosophy, and pedagogy remain unchanged, but this seventh edition incorporates many improvements. We've thoroughly updated and revised the book, including the text of each chapter as well as figures, tables, and cases. We've also made the language, headings, figure titles, and case titles more student friendly.

New Cases

We've added many new cases to reflect current events and issues. The new cases include:

- Foreign Exchange Market Update
- World Merchandise Trade
- Components of GDP
- Banking on Unification
- Capital Decontrols
- The Truth about Exchange Rate Regimes
- *Tank-Touristen*
- The Ups and Downs of Business Cycles
- Mapping the Euro Zone
- Do Floating Rates Really Float?
- Is Growth Fixed or Flexible?
- Monetary-Policy Transition in China

We've also updated and expanded many of the cases carried over from the sixth edition.

INTENDED AUDIENCE

By presenting the fundamentals of international economics clearly but rigorously, *The World Economy* becomes adaptable for a variety of courses. Our correspondence with adopters of earlier editions indicates that they use the book successfully in many different ways. Students with only a one-semester introductory economics course as background have no trouble mastering the material; in fact, we use the text extensively in classes at that level. Simply omit the appendixes and choose supplementary reading from the articles denoted as appropriate for beginning students. For students who've completed courses in intermediate macro, add the appendixes along with a wider range of supplementary reading. The flexibility of the book also serves beginning graduate students with no specific background in international economics and provides a stepping stone to more advanced texts and the professional literature. The book appeals to students of political science, international relations, and international business by providing economics' unique perspective on international issues.

ALTERNATE COURSE OUTLINES

In a one-semester course, we cover all the chapters of *The World Economy: Open-Economy Macroeconomics and Finance*. For quarter-length courses or to allow for more time for a wider range of outside readings, we recommend omitting some combination of chapters Eight, Nine, Ten, or Eleven. In a course with a focus on developing economies, consider spending extra time on chapters Five, Six, and Eleven and making cuts elsewhere. If you teach both international trade and open-economy macroeconomics in a single course, our combined text *The World Economy: Trade and Finance* includes all the material here plus all the chapters from the companion international-trade text, *The World Economy: International Trade*.

ANCILLARIES BY THE TEXT AUTHORS

Study Guide

The seventh edition of *The World Economy* has its own *Study Guide*, available from Thomson Business and Professional Publishing through your local or college bookstore or from your Thomson Business and Professional Publishing representative. We wrote the *Study Guide* ourselves, coordinating it with the text and using the same careful pedagogy. The *Study Guide* contains:

- A "Quick Quiz" of multiple-choice questions for each chapter, designed to test whether students understood the chapter's main points
- Additional "Problems and Questions for Review" with answers
- Answers to chapter italicized queries
- Matching exercises for key terms in each chapter
- List of key points for each chapter
- Hints for writing a successful term paper on the world economy
- List of source materials for international information and data
- List of Web resources

Instructor's Manual

The *Instructor's Manual*, which we also wrote, contains:

- Answers to the italicized queries in the text
- Suggested test questions for each chapter
- Answers to the end-of-chapter "Problems and Questions for Review," including those new to the seventh edition
- Chapter-by-chapter key points
- Information on alternate course structures

PowerPoint Slides

PowerPoint slides are available for use by instructors for enhancing their lectures. The slides are available for download from the book's Web site at http://yarbrough.swlearning.com.

Online Quizzes

Students can test their comprehension of text readings by taking the online quizzes available at the book's Web site at http://yarbrough.swlearning.com.

e-con @pps

Thomson Business and Professional Publishing has included an innovative technology supplement with this edition: the e-con @pps Web site (http://econapps.swlearning.com). This site provides some valuable Web features: EconNews Online, EconDebate Online, and EconData Online. These features, which are organized by pertinent economic topics, are easy to integrate into classroom discussion. EconNews, EconDebate, and EconData should help motivate students, by taking them out of their usual passive mode and prompting them to analyze the latest economic news stories, policy debates, and data. These features are updated on a regular basis. The e-con @pps Web site is complimentary via an access card included with each new edition of *The World Economy*.

ACKNOWLEDGMENTS

The staffs at Thomson Business and Professional Publishing and Stratford Publishing deserve all the credit for the beautiful book that's emerged at the end of a long production process. The stalwart team of Sarah Dorger, Kara ZumBahlen, and Simone Payment, in particular, cheerfully kept things afloat even when their authors were sinking.

Thanks go also to our reviewers: Basanta Chaudhuri, *Rutgers University*, Tolga Koker, *Hamilton College*, Wetinee Matsathit, *University of Hawaii-Manoa*, Marc Melitz, *Harvard University*, Devashish Mitra, *Syracuse University*, Emanual Ornelas, *University of Georgia*, Raymond Robertson, *Macalester College*, Udayan Roy, *Long Island University*, Jeffery Steagall, *University of North Florida*, and Michael Szenberg, *Pace University*. We're grateful to all, and we appreciate the comments we didn't use as much as those we did. Compliments, suggestions, and criticisms from *The World Economy* users continue to play an essential role in the book's edition-to-edition improvement, so do contact us if you have comments.

Suggestions and questions—and, yes, even occasional blank stares—from students in the Open-Economy Macroeconomics courses at Amherst College constantly help us improve. One of those students, Rajashree Datta, helped compile the original list of Web resources now included in the *Study Guide*. Our long-time friend and administrative assistant, Jeanne Reinle, graciously tolerates us even when a tight production schedule occasionally puts us in a cranky mood.

Beth V. Yarbrough
Robert M. Yarbrough
Amherst, Massachusetts
January 2005

Contents

CHAPTER 6
Short-Run Macroeconomic Policy under Fixed Exchange Rates   162

CHAPTER 7
Short-Run Macroeconomic Policy under Flexible Exchange Rates   203

CHAPTER 8
The Exchange Rate in Long-Run Equilibrium   235

CHAPTER 9
Prices and Output in an Open Economy   268

Introduction to *The World Economy: Open-Economy Macroeconomics and Finance*

1 WHY STUDY OPEN-ECONOMY MACROECONOMICS AND FINANCE?

Chances are at least some of the clothing you're wearing right now bears a "Made in China" label. Software programmers in India probably wrote or debugged parts of the computer software you'll use for your studies this semester. If you ate a banana as a before-class snack, it probably came from Central America, Africa, or the Caribbean. And even if you think you drive a domestic car, at least some of your car's components almost certainly were produced in far-flung locations. So you have lots of day-to-day experience with international trade. But international trade is just one of the more-visible layers of the complex interactions that comprise the world macroeconomy.

Funding for many of the clothing factories in China that produce your "Made in China" clothing came not from within China, but from Taiwan and even from the United States, in the form of foreign direct investment. You pay in your country's domestic currency when you buy the clothes, but the clothing firms in China want to be paid in *yuan*, the Chinese currency. So the prices you pay depend, in part, on the policy that the Chinese government uses to manage the value of China's currency, the yuan, relative to the value of other currencies, including your home country's. Currently, that policy consists of fixing the yuan's value, or the *exchange rate*, at approximately 8.3 yuan per U.S. dollar. For reasons we'll see in later chapters, this policy makes Chinese clothing cheaper in foreign markets and allows Chinese clothing firms to sell more abroad, at least in the short run. But, again for reasons we'll examine later, the policy also encourages Chinese banks to make bad loans and makes it more difficult for Chinese policy makers to control one of the fundamental instruments of macroeconomic policy, the money supply. Some experts fear that the combination of bad bank loans and difficult macroeconomic policy challenges in China could lead to a financial crisis there, with potentially severe consequences for industries and banks throughout the developing and industrialized worlds. So your Chinese shirt or sweater represents your personal point of contact with an intricate set of economic interactions that also include the central tools of macroeconomic policy. We could tell similar stories about computer software, bananas, or automobiles.

The fact that the international macroeconomy tends to be less visible in our day-to-day lives than international trade doesn't make it any less important. Understanding the international macroeconomy—what it is, how it works, and how policy makers can affect it—is absolutely essential to understanding today's world. Discussions of new degrees and even new types of international economic interdependence fill the news, and the increasingly integrated or open macroeconomy is one important reason. The fact that no nation is an economic island has never been more obvious. Citizens of many countries increasingly feel affected by external events—economic and otherwise—over which they, and sometimes their national policy makers, exert less-than-total control. Most of the major economic stories that occupy newspaper headlines are stories about international economic interdependence, its ramifications, and policy makers' and citizens' attempts to come to terms with it.

Sometimes the stories have a long-run focus: How has Japan's decade-long macroeconomic slump affected that country's trading partners? Will the relatively new European euro become an international currency as widely used as the U.S. dollar? How long will it take for the countries in transition from central planning to develop well-functioning and stable macroeconomies? Will the Chinese economy continue to grow rapidly, or will it succumb to financial crisis? Sometimes the stories emerge in an instant: How will the aftermath and implications of the September 11, 2001, terrorist attacks on New York and Washington, D. C., affect the economies of the United States and its trading partners, and for how long? Does Russia's sudden nationalization of oil giant Yukos signal improved economic governance or a shift toward economic authoritarianism? How will the answer affect world oil prices and the performance of the world macroeconomy? How did the December 2004 earthquake and tsunami affect the short-run and long-run prospects for emerging Asian economies such as Indonesia and Thailand?

All these questions make studying open-economy macroeconomics more important than ever before, whether you are (or hope to be) a national policy maker, a business owner planning corporate strategy, or simply an informed citizen, voter, and participant in the world economy. *The World Economy: Open-Economy Macroeconomics and Finance* provides a basic tool kit. It presents simple models to explain how an open macroeconomy works, empirical evidence to evaluate the models' predictions, dozens of case studies and applications from both history and current events around the globe, and lots of useful information and data about the world macroeconomy and the diverse countries that constitute it. When you finish the book, you should feel confident weighing politicians' statements about international macroeconomic policy and analyzing the linkages between the economic policies followed by your home country and those followed by the rest of the world.

2 WHAT DO WE MEAN BY INTERNATIONAL INTERDEPENDENCE?

It's hard to pick up a newspaper or listen to the news these days without hearing about *globalization*. But the term itself usually goes undefined. Does it refer to the fact that consumers in dozens of countries can buy McDonald's Big Macs—although the burgers, in fact, differ according to local tastes and culinary customs? Or that consumers in Mongolia can buy goods from abroad without having to pay any taxes to import them? Or that a British firm can issue bonds denominated in euros and sell those bonds throughout the world? Or that the World Trade Organization can tell the United States that it can't subsidize its cotton producers? Or that Chinese exchange-rate policy affects where the clothing you buy is produced? Or that many citizens in remote corners of the globe admire and strive for "Western" values of individual freedom, democracy, and economic growth? The diversity of these issues suggests that the term *globalization* may be so broad and subject to varying connotations that it loses its ability to communicate effectively. So, marketing considerations aside, most economists prefer to speak instead in terms of **international interdependence** and **international economic integration**. These terms refer to the degree to which economic events in one country affect others and the extent to which markets for goods, services, labor, and capital can operate freely across national boundaries. In other words, to what extent do national boundaries matter; do they block the flow of economic transactions or the effects of economic events and policies?

The term *international interdependence* entered the newspaper-headline vocabulary during the 1970s when the industrialized countries, along with oil-importing developing ones, helplessly endured two rounds of sudden and dramatic oil-price increases by the Organization of Petroleum Exporting Countries (OPEC). By the early 1980s, countries' roles reversed. OPEC watched the price of oil tumble as demand fell because of a policy-induced recession in the industrialized countries. Most industrial and oil-importing developing countries welcomed the fall in oil prices (although not the recession that triggered it); but the decline also heightened the debt problem of several developing-country oil exporters, most notably Mexico. The resulting debt crisis among developing countries, in turn, generated financial uncertainty and a loss of export markets for the developed world and threatened the solvency of major U.S. commercial banks.

By the 1980s, key industries such as steel and automobiles, once dominated by a handful of U.S. firms, spanned the globe. Many U.S. industries struggled against increasingly potent foreign competition, and one by one those industries sought protection in the form of policy barriers against imports. But industries are themselves interdependent; so one industry's import barriers, which raise the price of that industry's output, can make it more difficult for related industries to remain competitive. For example, when the U.S. steel industry won protection from its foreign rivals, U.S. automobile manufacturers had to pay higher prices for steel and became more vulnerable to competition from foreign car producers. As U.S. auto producers lost their dominance in their home market, they pressured policy makers for their own protection from foreign competition.

Policy makers responded to the auto industry's demands by placing a "voluntary" export restraint on Japanese automobiles. The restraint, which limited Japanese firms' ability to export cars produced in Japan to the United States, prompted a dramatic international relocation of the world's auto production. Japanese firms such as Honda and Toyota now produce cars in the United States and export them to Europe, to Asia, and even back to Japan. Figure 1 documents one example: the worldwide pattern of production and sales of Hondas. In fact, it no longer makes much sense to talk about "American" or "Japanese" cars. Auto-industry analysts speak instead of "captive imports" (vehicles such as the Geo, made by a foreign-based company but sold through domestic dealerships) and "transplants" (for example, the Honda Accord, built domestically by a foreign-based company). Today, Chinese factories assemble "German" Volkswagens, "Japanese" Hondas, and "American" Chevrolets.

Even though consumers can no longer easily define cars' nationality, firms recognize that as long as domestic interests dominate the policy-making process, it's to the firms' advantage to appear domestic. So advertising often emphasizes firms' links to the domestic economy. For example, a 1997 Toyota advertisement in *Newsweek* highlighted the firm's "homegrown success" at its U.S. plants, such as the original one in Georgetown, Kentucky, and implicitly linked the firm to a quintessentially American event, the Kentucky Derby horse race.

Figure 1   **Honda Automobiles Produced and Exported by Region, January–September 2004**

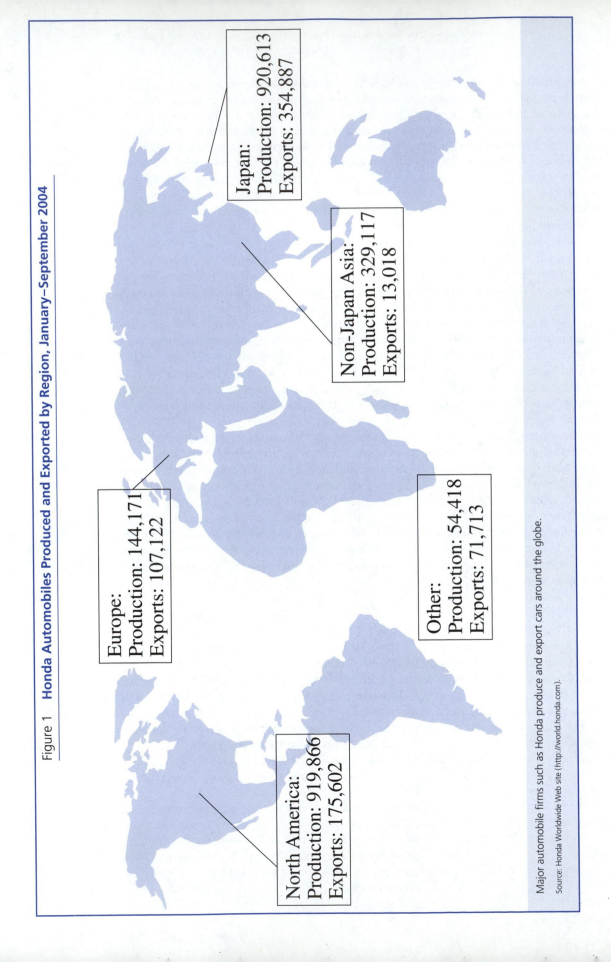

Japan:
Production: 920,613
Exports: 354,887

Non-Japan Asia:
Production: 329,117
Exports: 13,018

Europe:
Production: 144,171
Exports: 107,122

North America:
Production: 919,866
Exports: 175,602

Other:
Production: 54,418
Exports: 71,713

Major automobile firms such as Honda produce and export cars around the globe.

Source: Honda Worldwide Web site (http://world.honda.com).

A product's nationality becomes even more difficult to determine once we recognize that firms assemble their products from components manufactured around the world. Ford, for example, assembles its Escort in Germany from parts produced in 15 countries, from Austria to Canada to Japan. Such production linkages represent one type of economic interdependence, a type increasingly prevalent in the world economy. Occasionally, the result is embarrassment—for policy makers intent on giving preference to domestic products to win favor with domestic special-interest groups. For example, a small town in New York, determined to "buy American," bought a $55,000 John Deere excavator in preference over a comparable $40,000 Komatsu model. Town decision makers soon discovered that Komatsu built its machine in Illinois and that Deere built its in Japan.[1]

The debates over international interdependence that heated up in the 1970s and 1980s haven't cooled, but some of the details have changed. For example, one of the most important trends of recent years is developing countries' expanding involvement with the world economy. After decades of attempting to isolate themselves from world markets, many developing countries have now opened their borders and pursued policies designed to integrate themselves into international economic activity. This trend produces new patterns of international interdependence that bring new debates to the fore. What are the implications for developed countries of trade with developing ones? Is the "common sense" conclusion—that trade with low-wage countries lowers wages for American workers—correct? In other words, as the title of one article put it, "Are Your Wages Set in Beijing?"[2] Most international economists agree, based on mounting empirical evidence, that trade with low-wage countries has *not* lowered U.S. wages significantly. But the debate continues and many of the loudest antiglobalization activists simply ignore the empirical evidence.

International interdependence and the debates it engenders aren't limited to trade in goods and services. In fact, interdependence in financial markets, where firms and governments borrow, lend, and finance investment projects, has grown even more dramatically than that in markets for goods such as oil, steel, and automobiles. Until the mid-1960s, government regulation of financial flows across national borders, combined with the limitations of transportation and communication technologies, kept national financial markets largely separate. Now, with decreased government regulation and improved technologies, financial activity clusters in international centers such as London, New York, Tokyo, Singapore, Hong Kong, Zurich, Frankfurt, and Paris. The result is a 24-hour market in which the push of a computer button shifts funds from one country or currency to another. U.S.-based firms now raise funds for investment by issuing bonds denominated not just in dollars but also in euros, yen, Swiss francs, British pounds, and other currencies and sell those bonds to buyers around the world. Growing numbers of firms based in one country list themselves on foreign stock exchanges to facilitate global finance of their investment projects. International banks have loan portfolios that span the globe.

Despite rapid growth in virtually all international financial markets, the most dramatic growth of all has occurred in the markets for currencies themselves. The most recent statistics from the Bank for International Settlements indicate that in 2004 global turnover in world foreign exchange markets, where national currencies are traded, measured well over $1.9 trillion *per day*, up from around $200 billion per day in 1986, as illustrated in

---

1. *The Economist,* February 1, 1992, p. 26.

2. Richard B. Freeman, "Are Your Wages Set in Beijing?" *Journal of Economic Perspectives,* 1995, pp. 15–32.

Figure 2 **Daily Turnover in Foreign Exchange Markets, 1986–2004 (Trillions $)**

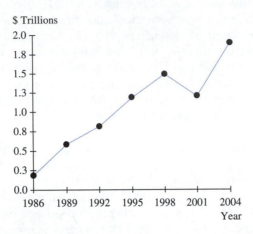

Daily turnover in foreign exchange markets is about a fifth of *annual* trade in goods and services.

Source: Data from Bank for International Settlements (updates available at http://www.bis.org).

Figure 2. This compares with total world merchandise trade of about $6 trillion *per year*. Note, however, the temporary decline in foreign-exchange trading registered between 1998 and 2001. Why the drop? Two primary reasons: (1) As most members of the European Union switched from their national currencies to the euro in 1999, firms no longer needed to use the foreign exchange market to exchange, say German marks for French francs. (2) Financial crises in East Asia, Brazil, and Russia during the late 1990s put many banks out of business, which consolidated foreign exchange trading among a smaller group of players.

All these international financial markets—bonds, stocks, bank loans, foreign exchange—provide mechanisms for **international investment**, which plays a vital role in the world economy. From a lender's perspective, these markets allow individuals, firms, and governments with funds to lend to find the most productive investment projects to fund, regardless of the projects' locations. From a borrower's perspective, international financial markets allow individuals, firms, and governments with promising investment projects to seek lenders willing to fund the projects on attractive terms, regardless of the lenders' nationalities or places of residence. Still, citizens and policy makers in economies hit by economic crises, such as Mexico in 1994, East Asia in 1997, Brazil and Russia in 1998, and Argentina and Turkey in 2001, sometimes ask whether their new financial openness and integration into the world economy caused or contributed to the ensuing crises, in which investment *in*flows turned all too suddenly into investment *out*flows, with painful macroeconomic consequences.

The growth of international flows of goods and services; financial assets such as stocks, bonds, and currencies; and information reflects, in part, declines in international transportation and communication costs. Sea cargo, air transport, and telephone calls all have become dramatically cheaper (see Figure 3), and these trends encourage international economic activity. However, government policies also exert an important influence. Since World War II, more and more governments have recognized the importance of open international markets for goods, services, and investment and have reduced their restrictions on international transactions.

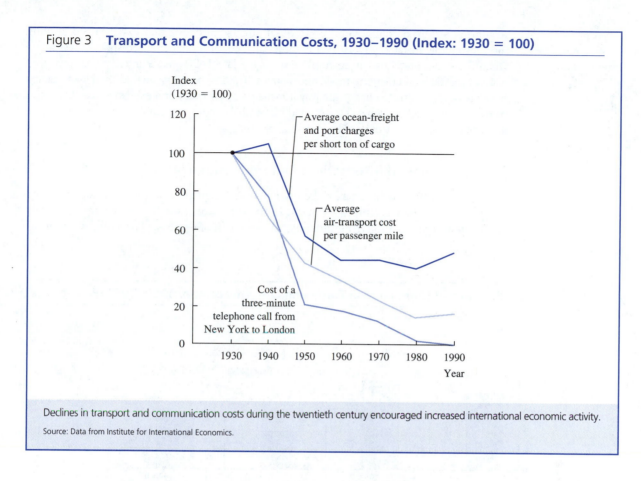

Figure 3   Transport and Communication Costs, 1930–1990 (Index: 1930 = 100)

Declines in transport and communication costs during the twentieth century encouraged increased international economic activity.

Source: Data from Institute for International Economics.

2.1 Policy Implications of International Interdependence

The increase in international economic activity, in turn, has far-flung implications for the world political economy. Policy makers in issue areas once considered domestic—such as antitrust policy, environmental policy, and taxation—now must reckon with those policies' international ramifications. U.S. antitrust policy makers, who approved a merger between General Electric and Honeywell, fumed when the merger failed because European Union antitrust policy makers blocked it. In the North American Free Trade Agreement (NAFTA), U.S. and Canadian environmental activists still fear that firms will exploit Mexico's allegedly lower environmental standards and enforcement by moving to Mexico and exporting goods produced under the laxer standards to U.S. and Canadian markets, although existing empirical evidence doesn't support those fears. With increased international mobility, countries that try to tax their citizens or firms at rates far above those in other nations risk losing some of their most productive citizens and enterprises. In all these cases, "domestic" policies that at first glance appear to have primarily domestic effects turn out to be linked to important international questions as well. Effective economic policy making requires that these international linkages be taken into account.

The implications of interdependence for macroeconomic policy making—that is, for fiscal, monetary, and exchange-rate policy—are at least as dramatic as those for microeconomic policy. In Europe, Germany's tight monetary policy to prevent inflation after the country's unification angered other members of the European Union and temporarily threatened the group's plans to introduce a common currency for Europe. In Asia, despite the Japanese economy's decade-long slump, Japanese policy makers resisted for years lobbying by their foreign counterparts to increase the rate of growth of the money supply. Brazil and

Argentina suffered "hangovers" or "tequila effects" after Mexico experienced serious macroeconomic instability in 1994–1995; the same countries experienced shock waves again when the Asian and Russian financial crises of the late 1990s made international investors wary of the risks of emerging-market economies. Trading partners such as the United States have pressured China to change the way it manages its currency and exchange rate, but some economists argue that such a change could make China more vulnerable to a crisis because of its weak banks, a legacy of decades of central planning.

2.2 Symptoms of International Interdependence

It's not easy to measure international economic interdependence, but we can examine some symptoms. The first is simply the trend in the extent of trade, or the volume of goods exchanged across national boundaries, illustrated in Figure 4. The volume of world

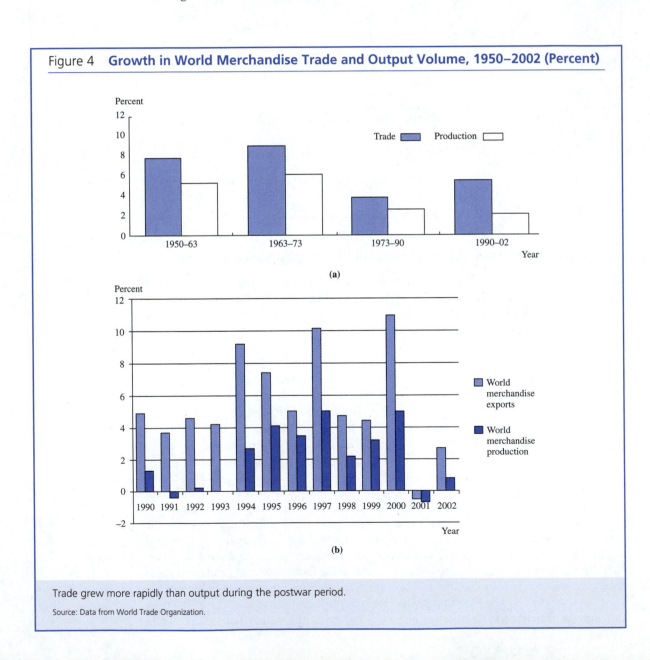

Figure 4 **Growth in World Merchandise Trade and Output Volume, 1950–2002 (Percent)**

Trade grew more rapidly than output during the postwar period.

Source: Data from World Trade Organization.

Figure 5 **Merchandise Exports and Imports, 2002 (Percent of GDP)**

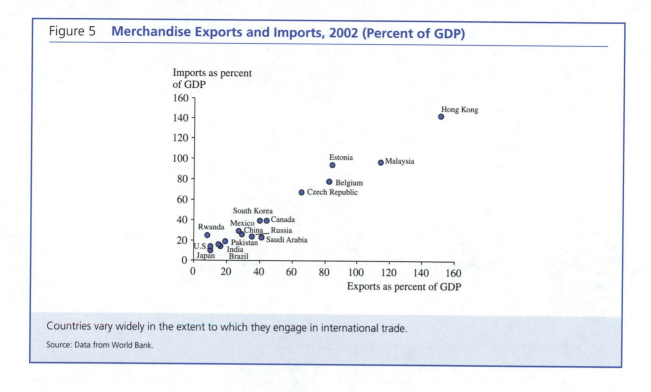

Countries vary widely in the extent to which they engage in international trade.

Source: Data from World Bank.

merchandise trade has expanded rapidly over the past half-century; in fact, since 1950, merchandise *trade* has grown more than twice as fast as merchandise *production*. Panel (b) focuses on the past decade, during which trade volume continued to grow much faster (almost 7 percent per year) than production (about 3 percent per year). These trends indicate an increasingly vital role of international trade in allocating the world's resources. Economics is the study of the allocation of scarce resources among alternative uses, so the importance of international issues in the study of economics also has increased.

Despite dramatic increases in trade worldwide, countries continue to differ significantly in the extent to which they engage in trade. Figure 5 presents some examples; it measures a country's involvement in trade by merchandise exports (horizontal axis) and imports (vertical axis) as shares of total output or gross domestic product (GDP). The 2002 export shares range from a low of 8 percent for Rwanda to a high of 151 percent for Hong Kong, a specialist in trade-middleman services.[3] Import percentages range from Japan's 10 percent to Hong Kong's 142 percent, again reflecting Hong Kong's specialization in assembly and re-export tasks.

Other things being equal, large countries such as the United States tend to engage in less trade, as a share of their production, than do smaller ones. The main reason is easy to see: The size and diversity of the United States mean that domestic markets can efficiently satisfy many needs. On the import side, residents of Rhode Island get corn from Iowa, oil from Alaska, and lettuce from California; they go beachcombing in Florida, mountain climbing in Washington, and bird watching in Hawaii. They execute financial deals in New York and watch Hollywood movies. On the export side, U.S. firms enjoy access to a huge domestic market; historically, very few small and medium-sized U.S. firms exported, but this is slowly changing. Although still modest by world standards, as indicated in Figure 5, U.S. involvement in international trade has increased in recent

---

3. How can a country's trade exceed its production? Economies such as Hong Kong, Malaysia, and Singapore import inputs, assemble them, and then export finished goods. In a multistage production process, measures of output such as GDP and GNP count only the value of the final good, but measures of trade count all imports and exports.

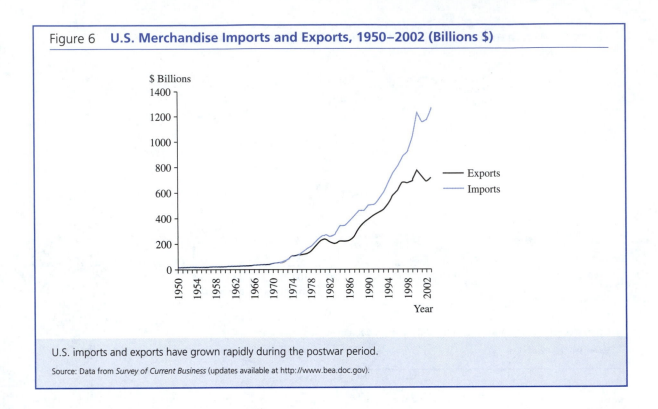

Figure 6   **U.S. Merchandise Imports and Exports, 1950–2002 (Billions $)**

U.S. imports and exports have grown rapidly during the postwar period.

Source: Data from *Survey of Current Business* (updates available at http://www.bea.doc.gov).

years. Figure 6, which reports the dollar value of U.S. merchandise imports and exports through the postwar era, documents this trend. Note, however, that Figure 5 indicates that U.S. imports and exports remain quite small relative to the country's GDP.

As a symptom of international interdependence, the magnitude of trade primarily reflects interdependence among producers and consumers in specific markets. International trade in automobiles makes auto consumers and producers worldwide interdependent, and the same is true in thousands of other markets. But economic interdependence goes much deeper. Synchronized changes in macroeconomic activity across countries represent a second important symptom of interdependence. Figure 7 illustrates the recent paths of industrial production in a set of major industrialized economies. Notice that the countries exhibit a striking tendency toward simultaneous booms and recessions. This historical evidence suggests that it may be difficult for one economy to expand when its trading partners' economies are growing slowly or shrinking. Note also, however, that the correlation of countries' activity is far from perfect. The 1990s provides a clear example of divergence among the major industrial economies: For most of the decade, the United States and Canada boomed, while Western Europe grew very slowly and activity in Japan stagnated.

Like interdependence within specific markets, macroeconomic interdependence often is viewed as a mixed blessing. In general, macroeconomic "spillover effects" create the potential for conflict whenever one country perceives a need to pursue contractionary policies (for example, to fight inflation) while its trading partners want to expand (perhaps to counter unacceptably high unemployment). The 1990s provide plenty of examples. Britain withdrew in 1992 from European Union plans for a common currency, at least in part because of its unwillingness to endure the contractionary spillover effects of German macroeconomic policy on the British economy. Germany hoped to keep Italy out of the new EU common-currency area to insulate the group from a possible replay of Italy's historically inflationary policies. American and European policy makers complained to their Japanese counterparts about the latters' reluctance to address Japan's economic problems, a prerequisite to a Japanese role in helping to resolve the Asian

Figure 7 **Industrial Production in the Major Industrialized Economies, 1979–2003 (Index: 1997 = 100)**

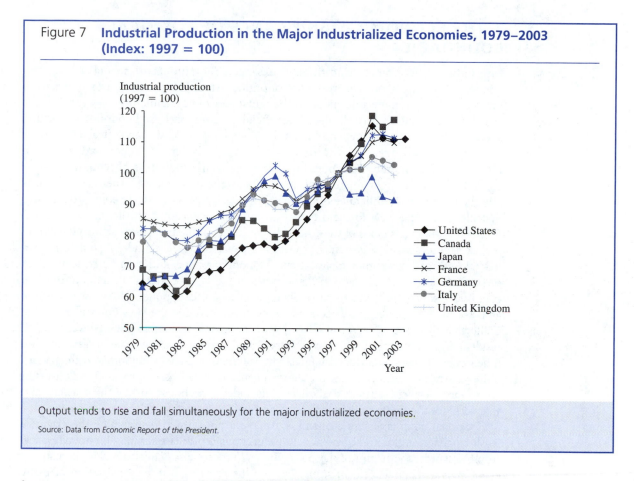

Output tends to rise and fall simultaneously for the major industrialized economies.

Source: Data from *Economic Report of the President.*

financial crisis. And later, already slow-growing Western Europe and Japan despaired over the implications of the 2001 slowdown in U.S. growth.

Despite the clarity of the primary pattern observable in Figure 7, an important cautionary note is in order. Data such as those reported in Figure 7 require careful interpretation. After all, each country's experience may have been totally independent of all the others'. In other words, it's possible either that mere coincidence produced the pattern apparent in Figure 7 or that all the economies responded similarly but independently to outside events. We must take this general caution seriously. Historical evidence can suggest patterns in economic behavior, but can't explain the reasons behind them. Because of the inability of empirical evidence alone to explain observed patterns, we need *theories* of economic behavior to answer questions such as: What are the nature and consequences of the economic ties among the countries of the world economy? How should policy makers respond to particular cases of international macroeconomic interdependence?

This book addresses these fundamental questions from the perspective of economics. Within the sphere of countries' international relationships, political and economic elements are difficult, if not impossible, to separate. However, the basic concepts of economic theory can be surprisingly helpful in untangling the maze of issues that constitutes the world macroeconomy. Millions of firms produce hundreds of thousands of commodities in approximately 200 countries, so we need a systematic framework for analysis—and this is what economic theory can provide. Thus, it is this book's perspective more than its subject matter that marks it as a text in international *economics.* The subjects covered—such as inflation, debt, financial crises, unemployment, and the transition from central planning—are also of direct interest to political scientists, as well as to specialists in international relations, international business, and public policy.

3 THE ECONOMIC SIGNIFICANCE OF POLITICAL BOUNDARIES

International economics traditionally has been the subject of special books and courses, separate from the rest of economics. At the same time, the interaction between international economics and the remainder of economic theory has been rich and, like international trade itself, beneficial to both parties. Economists working specifically on international problems developed many of the analytical techniques now used in all areas of the discipline. Similarly, many recent advances in international economics have built on developments in other areas of economics.

Why does the separate study of international questions persist? The main reason is that the **economic significance of political boundaries** persists. Most people would agree that life in a small New England college town differs radically from life in Los Angeles. From an economist's point of view, however, residents of the two places share a great deal. All use U.S. dollars as a currency or means of payment. All live under a common set of federal laws and a common political and economic system, and many communicate in a common language. All share in the fortunes of the U.S. economy, benefiting from the country's resource endowment and feeling the effects of U.S. policy decisions. Because of all these shared features, most economic transactions between the New Englander and the Californian face a smaller set of barriers than do economic transactions between a U.S. resident and a resident of a foreign country. The Californian can relocate in New England if he or she chooses, and the New Englander is free to migrate to California. If the pattern of interest rates makes deposits in California banks or bonds issued by California firms or government agencies attractive, the New Englander can choose to buy those assets; and vice versa for the Californian buying assets in New England.

National boundaries are economically relevant not only in determining the extent of legal, language, and currency barriers to transactions but in determining economic policy. In other words, the nature of the policy-making process also tends to make international economics a separate field of study. Despite the growing internationalization of many markets, economic policy making remains largely a matter of national sovereignty. In fact, many national governments respond to the perception of increased international interdependence by guarding their sovereign policy-making powers even more jealously. As a result, the policy process typically favors the interests of domestic residents over the interests of the world as a whole. This tendency is easy to understand given the realities of policy making. Decisions on policies that are either universally beneficial or universally harmful are easy—but, unfortunately for policy makers, such easy decisions are rare. The more typical policy decision involves evaluating a policy that benefits some individuals and harms others. In such a situation, we shouldn't be surprised that consideration given to the policy's effect on domestic residents usually outweighs that given to the effect on individuals abroad.

4 STUDYING INTERNATIONAL ECONOMICS

Economists traditionally divide the subject matter of international economics into two parts. This book covers the first, called **open-economy macroeconomics**, which applies *macro*economic analysis to aggregate international problems.[4] Major concerns here

---

4. The second major branch of international economics, called the theory of international trade, applies *micro*economic analysis to international questions and is covered in this book's companion volume, *The World Economy: International Trade*. Major concerns there include the quantities of various goods produced, consumed, and traded by different countries, public policies toward trade, and trade's effect on welfare.

include the level of employment and output in each economy as well as changes in the price level, balance of payments, and **exchange rates** or relative prices of different national currencies. The most basic issue addressed by open-economy macroeconomics is the interaction of international goals and influences with domestic ones in determining a country's macroeconomic performance and policy. Can a country that engages in international transactions (an **open economy**) pursue the same macroeconomic policies as a country that engages in no international transactions (a **closed economy**) and achieve the same results? The answer is no; so, understanding the implications of openness turns out to be essential to effective macroeconomic policy making.

We'll discover that macroeconomic policies have important distributional consequences. Policy choices typically stated in terms of domestic interests versus foreign ones actually involve differences in the interests of various groups *within* each economy. For example, journalists, commentators, and politicians often speak of any currency depreciation (that is, a rise in the exchange rate expressed as the domestic currency price of a unit of foreign currency) as an economic problem in need of a remedy. Indeed, sound economic policy making does require that a country experiencing a chronic currency depreciation consider adjusting its macroeconomic policies. We also must recognize, however, that depreciations *help* some groups within the domestic economy, especially import-competing and export industries. Those same currency depreciations also *hurt* other domestic groups, particularly importers and consumers of imported goods.

We begin our study of open-economy macroeconomics by building a simple model and then elaborate on it and apply it to many historical and current events in the world economy. The models are just road maps to describe the way the world economy works. They may seem overly simple and "unrealistic." However, that's the whole point of building models. After all, a road map would be of little practical use if it faithfully illustrated every bump, anthill, grain of sand, pothole, and roadside sign. We need models like good road maps: as *simple* as possible while still capturing the *key features* necessary to understand the world economy. Once you master the basic models of open-economy macroeconomics covered in this book, you can use them to analyze not only the applications considered in the text but the constantly changing international economic news.

Economists call models that describe in a simplified way how the world economy works *positive models*. For the most part, we'll employ **positive analysis** in this book, using models to understand how the world economy is structured and how it functions. This approach focuses primarily on explanation and prediction. The goal is to understand the world economy well enough to be able to say, "If event X happens, event Y will follow." For example, we might predict that if U.S. policy makers increase the size of the U.S. money supply at a slower rate than European Union policy makers increase the European money supply, the U.S. dollar would tend to gain value (or appreciate) relative to the euro. This prediction *doesn't* depend on whether we, as economists or citizens, believe a particular U.S. or EU monetary-policy stance or a particular value of the dollar–euro exchange rate is desirable. The prediction follows directly from our model of how the world macroeconomy works. We can then look at empirical evidence on U.S. and EU monetary policy and the dollar–euro exchange rate to determine how accurate our prediction is.

Another type of analysis, **normative analysis**, *does* depend on our judgments about what is and isn't desirable. For example, if we thought monetary policy should be used to try to achieve a certain target rate of unemployment or output, we might conclude that EU policy makers should pursue more expansionary monetary policy than U.S. policy makers because of higher European unemployment.[5] Normative analyses rely on our values to determine what types of international economic goals and policies we think policy makers should pursue.

From our discussion of the differences between positive and normative economic analysis, we can see that disagreements over international policy issues can come from at least two sources. First, there may be disagreement about the way the world works. One individual may think that if event X happens, event Y will follow, while another may think that if event X happens, event Z will follow. For example, one person might argue that expansionary EU monetary policy (X) will boost EU growth and increase the value of the euro relative to the dollar (Y), while someone else claims that expansionary EU monetary policy (X) will cause European inflation to rise and decrease the value of the euro relative to the dollar (Z). Analysts usually can resolve such disagreements by conducting further empirical research to determine whether Y or Z follows X.[6]

Disagreements based on normative judgments typically prove more difficult to resolve. Two policy makers may agree that "If we pursue policy X, result Y will follow." But if the two disagree about whether Y is desirable, they will disagree about whether they should pursue policy X. For example, most economists acknowledge that, other things being equal, expansionary monetary policy relative to one's trading partners is likely to lead to a depreciation of the domestic currency in the short run, which helps domestic export industries and import-competing industries and hurts consumers who buy foreign-produced goods. Whether one supports an expansionary monetary policy thus depends on one's evaluation of the desirability of these effects. History suggests that exporting interests are much more likely than consumers of imported goods to support expansionary monetary policy or other policies that depreciate the domestic currency.

Throughout this book, both positive and normative issues arise. Although the distinction isn't always sharp, we must keep in mind the conceptual difference between the two. Debates over the desirability of various international macroeconomic policies can be useful only when it's clear where the disagreement originates—in our views of the way the world works or in our views of how we would like the world to be.

Throughout the book, we present data on many aspects of the world economy, ranging from on-line currency trading, the birth of the Bosnian central bank, the economic effects of German unification, the 1997 Thai baht crisis, Japan's policy dilemmas, dollarization, the transition in Chinese monetary policy, and privatization programs in the formerly centrally planned economies.

A rich variety of sources of additional information about the world economy exists. We've included many in the references at the end of each chapter. In addition, the *Study Guide* written to accompany this book suggests useful leads, including many Web resources, if you want to pursue a particular topic in more detail. If you don't yet have a copy of the *Study Guide*, check with your instructor or bookstore. Along with data sources on the world economy, the *Study Guide* contains study aids and questions with answers for each chapter in the text, helpful hints for writing economics papers, and much more.

---

5. We'll see in later chapters that a large share of the higher unemployment in most of Western Europe than in the United States consists of long-term structural unemployment, which is unlikely to respond to expansionary monetary policy. See, especially, Case One in the chapter on prices and output in an open macroeconomy.

6. Of course, the answer may depend on the time horizon under consideration and on other economic circumstances.

KEY TERMS

international interdependence

international economic integration

international investment

economic significance of political boundaries

open-economy macroeconomics

exchange rates

open economy

closed economy

positive analysis

normative analysis

PROBLEMS AND QUESTIONS FOR REVIEW

1. For each of the types of cost illustrated in Figure 3 (air transport, sea transport, telephone costs), explain why a decline in the cost might lead to an increase in international trade. Why might a decline in the cost lead to an increase in international investment?
2. Look at the data in Figure 5. Why might some countries choose to engage more in international trade than other countries?
3. Name some examples of the economic significance of political boundaries.
4. Explain why the term *international economic integration* communicates the nature of recent changes in the world economy more precisely than *globalization*.
5. Name three recent events in international macroeconomics that you hope to understand better.
6. Some economists have argued that increased liberalization of international trade is allowing geographically smaller countries to be economically viable. The number of recognized independent nation-states rose from 74 in 1946 to 192 in 1995.[7] Why might small countries be especially reliant on the availability of open international trade?
7. Suppose we divided developing countries into two groups: those that have followed policies to integrate themselves into the world economy ("globalizers") and those that have followed policies to insulate themselves from the world economy ("nonglobalizers").[8] How would you expect the groups' economic performances to compare?
8. Suppose that country A is in an economic recession, suffering a high rate of unemployment. Would country A prefer that its trading partner, country B, follow macroeconomic policies that would transmit an expansionary or a contractionary effect to country A? What if, instead of experiencing a recession and high unemployment, country A was experiencing a rapid economic boom and accelerating inflation? Under what conditions would country B be likely to have preferences that matched or opposed those of country A?

REFERENCES AND SELECTED READINGS

Cohen, Tyler. *Creative Destruction: How Globalization is Changing the World's Cultures.* Princeton: Princeton University Press, 2002.
Readable introduction to the cultural effects of international economic integration.

European Bank for Reconstruction and Development. *Annual Transition Report.* Paris: EBRD, annual.
Excellent source of up-to-date information and analysis of the transitional economies.

Fieleke, Norman S. "Popular Myths about the World Economy." *New England Economic Review* (July–August 1997): 17–26.
Introductory overview of popular misconceptions about trade.

Fischer, Stanley. "Globalization and Its Challenges." *American Economic Review Papers and Proceedings* 93 (May 2003): 1–30.
Overview of the challenges of economic integration by the former chief economist of the International Monetary Fund.

International Monetary Fund. *World Economic Outlook.* Washington, D.C.: IMF, semi-annual.
Recent macroeconomic events and analysis by the staff of the Fund.

James, Harold. *The End of Globalization: Lessons from the Great Depression.* Cambridge, Mass.: Harvard University Press, 2001.
Historian's treatment of the end of the earlier era of international economic integration.

Legrain, Philippe. *One World: The Truth About Globalization.* Chicago: Ivan R. Dee, 2002.
Nontechnical introduction to the many aspects of international economic integration.

---

7. See Alberto Alesina et al., "Economic Integration and Political Disintegration," *American Economic Review* 90 (December 2000), p. 1276.

8. See David Dollar and Aart Kraay, "Trade, Growth, and Poverty," World Bank Policy Research Working Paper No. 2199, 2001 (available at http://www.worldbank.org).

Organization for Economic Cooperation and Development. *OECD Economic Outlook.* Paris: OECD, annual.
Macroeconomic outlook and recent macroeconomic events in the OECD member countries, which include the major industrial economies.

Symposium on "The Shape of Global Integration." *Finance and Development* 39 (March 2002): 4–43.
Collection of accessible papers on the meaning and effects of globalization.

United Nations. *World Investment Report.* New York: UN, annual.
Excellent source of data and analysis of recent trends in international capital flows.

World Bank. *Globalization, Growth, and Poverty.* Washington, D.C.: World Bank, 2002.
Easy-to-read overview of what economists know about the relationship between international economic integration and poverty.

World Bank. *World Economic Indicators.* Washington, D.C.: World Bank, annual.
Excellent source of recent economic data, as well as analysis of development-related events by the World Bank staff.

International Macroeconomics

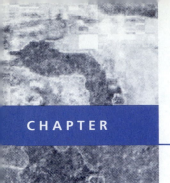

Currency Markets and Exchange Rates

1 INTRODUCTION

From a macroeconomic perspective, one fundamental characteristic distinguishes international economic activity from domestic: International transactions typically involve more than one currency or monetary unit. Whether a Swede buys an Italian sports car, a British airline buys a Boeing airplane, a Korean firm borrows from a Japanese bank, or an American buys stock in a Chinese firm, the transaction requires that one country's currency be exchanged for another's. So, as a first step toward our goal of understanding how the international macroeconomy works, we need to examine the mechanics of currency markets and their role in international trade and financial activity.

2 EXCHANGE RATES AND PRICES

2.1 What Do Prices Tell Us?

Economic models of how individuals and firms decide what to produce, consume, and trade assume that they use relative prices as guides for making these decisions. Relative prices convey information about the opportunity costs of various goods. In day-to-day transactions, however, we rarely see relative prices directly. It would be unusual to walk into a store and find the price of a pound of apples listed as two pounds of bananas or to shop for a car and find a sticker price of 20 personal computers. Instead, we use **money prices**; they tell us how many units of money (dollars in the United States, yen in Japan, baht in Thailand, pesos in Mexico, or yuan in China) we must pay to buy apples, bananas, a car, or a personal computer. If individuals and firms are to make everyday economic decisions efficiently, these money prices must reflect relative prices or opportunity costs.

Suppose that good X sells in the United States for \$10 per unit and good Y for \$5 per unit. The *ratio* of these two money prices (P_X/P_Y = \$10/\$5 = 2 units of Y per unit of X) reveals the opportunity cost or relative price of good X; to obtain a unit of good X, we must forgo 2 units of good Y. Similarly, P_Y/P_X = \$5/\$10 = 0.5 units of X gives the opportunity cost of Y; a consumer must forgo 0.5 units of X to obtain a unit of Y. Economists sometimes refer to the **relative price** of a good as its real price; this means the price is measured in "real" units (that is, other goods) rather than monetary or "nominal" units (such as dollars or yen). The simple relationship between money prices and relative prices allows individuals to enjoy the convenience of using money prices for everyday decisions without losing the information about opportunity costs that relative prices convey.

Notice that money prices can change while relative prices remain unchanged—as long as all money prices change proportionally. If the money prices of goods X and Y doubled from the previous example to $P_X = \$20$ and $P_Y = \$10$, the relative prices of X and Y still would be 2 units of Y and 0.5 units of X, respectively. This will prove important in our analysis of inflation in upcoming chapters where we turn our attention to how the macroeconomy behaves in the long run. After all, inflation is simply a persistent proportional rise in all money prices, so it leaves relative prices unchanged.[1]

2.2 How Can We Compare Prices in Different Currencies?

We've solved the puzzle of the relationship between relative and money prices in a single currency. Now, we need an additional step to compare prices stated in different currency units. How can we compare the price of an item that sells for 10 dollars in the United States ($P^{US} = \$10$) and for 5 pounds sterling in Britain ($P^B = £5$)? We need to know the exchange rate between pounds and dollars. We define the **exchange rate** (e) as the number of units of *domestic* currency required to purchase 1 unit of the *foreign* currency— in our example, the number of U.S. dollars required to buy 1 British pound sterling. In shorthand notation, $e = \$/£$; for example, if the exchange rate (e) is 2, buying 1 pound requires 2 dollars ($e = \$2/£1$).

We could also express the exchange rate as the number of units of *foreign* currency required to buy 1 unit of *domestic* currency, or $e' = £/\$$. Of course, e' just equals $1/e$. Writers use both definitions, and we'll see that the daily *Wall Street Journal* reports both. To avoid confusion, form the habit of checking carefully when reading about exchange rates (as well as while traveling) to see which definition is quoted. Buying 2 dollars with 1 pound ($e = \$2/£1$) is quite a different matter than buying 2 pounds with 1 dollar ($e' = £2/\$1$). In this book, we'll define the exchange rate as the domestic currency ($) price of foreign currency unless specified otherwise.

Suppose the United States and Britain both produce an identical good. At $P^{US} = \$10$, $P^B = £5$, and $e = \$2/£1$, individuals would be indifferent between buying the U.S. good and the British one, ignoring transportation costs. To get the £5 to buy the British good, an American would have to give up $10, or $2 for each pound; this makes the dollar price the same for both the British- and U.S.-made good. Similarly, a British resident would have to give up £5 to buy the $10 necessary to buy the U.S. good; thus, the price of the two goods would also be the same when measured in pounds. If $e > 2$, at $P^{US} = \$10$ and $P^B = £5$, individuals from both countries would have an incentive to buy the U.S.-made good. (*Why?*) If $e < 2$, individuals would have an incentive to buy the British good. (*Why?*)

Now consider goods produced uniquely in one country, say, tickets to the National Football League's Super Bowl, produced only in the United States and priced in dollars, and tickets to the Wimbledon tennis tournament, produced only in Britain and priced in pounds. Assume for simplicity that a Super Bowl ticket costs $125 and a ticket to Wimbledon costs £75. The exchange rate between dollars and pounds allows potential purchasers to compare the *relative prices* of the two tickets, even though their *money prices*

---

1. Don't make the common error of referring to a rise in the price of a single good as inflation, even if the price increase is large and the good is an economically important one, such as housing or oil. Inflation refers to a rise in the overall price level or the prices of all goods, not a rise in the price of one good or a narrow range of goods.

are denominated in different currencies. In 2001, the exchange rate between dollars and pounds was e = $1.45/£. From an American's perspective, a Super Bowl ticket cost $125, while a ticket to Wimbledon cost an amount equal to the dollar price of a pound multiplied by the pound price of a Wimbledon ticket, or ([$1.45/£] · £75) = $108.75. So the relative price of the two sporting events was equal to $125/$108.75 = 1.15. A resident of Britain would compare the prices in pounds; and the pound price of a Super Bowl ticket equals the dollar price of the ticket divided by the dollar price of a pound; so ($125/[$1.45/£])/£75 = 1.15—the same result. From either nationality's perspective, the exchange rate in 2001 made the Super Bowl more expensive than Wimbledon, because the pounds necessary to buy a Wimbledon ticket were relatively cheap compared with the dollars necessary to buy a Super Bowl ticket. But by 2004, the dollar price of a pound had risen from $1.45 to $1.79. The change in the exchange rate lowered the Super Bowl's relative price from an American's perspective to $125/([$1.79/£] · £75) = $125/$134.25 = 0.93. Similarly, a British resident would find that a Super Bowl ticket now cost $125/ ($1.79/£) = £69.83, while a Wimbledon ticket cost £75; and £69.83/£75 = 0.93. The rise in the dollar price of pounds between 2001 and 2004 raised the price of Wimbledon tickets relative to Super Bowl tickets, from either an American or a British perspective.

From these examples, we can see that *a change in the exchange rate, other things equal, changes all foreign prices relative to all domestic prices.* When the dollar price of the pound falls (e decreases), American goods become more expensive relative to British ones. If the dollar price of the pound rises (e increases), American goods become cheaper relative to British ones. This simple observation explains why individuals, firms, and governments care about the value of the exchange rate: Changes in the exchange rate can alter the relative prices of domestic and foreign goods, and this shifts demand away from the goods that become more expensive and toward the ones that become cheaper.[2] When the dollar price of pounds falls, other things equal, American imports and British exports rise while American exports and British imports fall. When the dollar price of pounds rises, other things equal, American imports and British exports fall and American exports and British imports rise.

If exchange rates or the relative prices of various currencies never changed, we wouldn't have much reason to study the effects of using different currencies. Exchange rates would be merely a minor nuisance—like the fact that distances are measured in inches, yards, and miles in the United States and in centimeters, meters, and kilometers in Canada. But what if the "rate of exchange" between miles and kilometers weren't a constant (= 0.62 mile/1 kilometer) but varied over time? Travelers then would need a theory to explain the relationship. Similarly, because exchange rates aren't constant but change over time, we need a theory to explain them. So let's turn to an analysis of foreign exchange markets.

3 FOREIGN EXCHANGE MARKETS

3.1 What Are They?

The **foreign exchange market** is the generic term for the worldwide institutions that exist to exchange or trade different countries' currencies. Most of the approximately 200 countries in the world use a unique currency or monetary unit, from Albania's lek to Zimbabwe's dollar (*not* the same as the U.S. dollar); international trade requires some mechanism for exchanging them. With so many different currencies, there are literally thousands of exchange rates, because each currency has a relative price in terms of every other.

---

2. Note that we've held the prices of the goods themselves constant; we'll relax this assumption later.

Figure 1 **Exchange Rate Quotations**

Exchange Rates
October 1, 2004

The foreign exchange mid-range rates below apply to trading among banks in amounts of $1 million and more, as quoted at 4 p.m. Eastern time by Reuters and other sources. Retail transactions provide fewer units of foreign currency per dollar.

Country	U.S. $ EQUIVALENT Fri	Thu	CURRENCY PER U.S. $ Fri	Thu
Argentina (Peso)-y	.3356	.3355	2.9797	2.9806
Australia (Dollar)	.7262	.7279	1.3770	1.3738
Bahrain (Dinar)	2.6524	2.6524	.3770	.3770
Brazil (Real)	.3526	.3499	2.8361	2.8580
Canada (Dollar)	.7921	.7928	1.2625	1.2614
1-month forward	.7918	.7924	1.2629	1.2620
3-months forward	.7910	.7917	1.2642	1.2631
6-months forward	.7899	.7906	1.2660	1.2649
Chile (Peso)	.001654	.001638	604.59	610.50
China (Renminbi)	.1208	.1208	8.2781	8.2781
Colombia (Peso)	.0003802	.0003811	2630.19	2623.98
Czech. Rep. (Koruna)				
Commercial rate	.03933	.03947	25.426	25.336
Denmark (Krone)	.1668	.1670	5.9952	5.9880
Ecuador (US Dollar)	1.0000	1.0000	1.0000	1.0000
Egypt (Pound)-y	.1604	.1604	6.2352	6.2352
Hong Kong (Dollar)	.1282	.1283	7.8003	7.7942
Hungary (Forint)	.005042	.005056	198.33	197.78
India (Rupee)	.02181	.02177	45.851	45.935
Indonesia (Rupiah)	.0001092	.0001093	9158	9149
Israel (Shekel)	.2235	.2232	4.4743	4.4803
Japan (Yen)	.009055	.009090	110.44	110.01
1-month forward	.009069	.009104	110.27	109.84
3-months forward	.009101	.009136	109.88	109.46
6-months forward	.009153	.009189	109.25	108.83
Jordan (Dinar)	1.4104	1.4104	.7090	.7090
Kuwait (Dinar)	3.3932	3.3932	.2947	.2947
Lebanon (Pound)	.0006603	.0006603	1514.46	1514.46
Malaysia (Ringgit)-b	.2632	.2632	3.7994	3.7994
Malta (Lira)	2.8910	2.8993	.3459	.3449
Mexico (Peso)				
Floating rate	.0882	.0879	11.3340	11.3830
New Zealand (Dollar)	.6748	.6777	1.4819	1.4756
Norway (Krone)	.1496	.1490	6.6845	6.7114
Pakistan (Rupee)	.01688	.01690	59.242	59.172
Peru (new Sol)	.2987	.2994	3.3478	3.3400
Philippines (Peso)	.01775	.01779	56.338	56.211
Poland (Zloty)	.2859	.2846	3.4977	3.5137
Russia (Ruble)-a	.03423	.03422	29.214	29.223
Saudi Arabia (Riyal)	.2666	.2666	3.7509	3.7509
Singapore (Dollar)	.5949	.5936	1.6810	1.6846
Slovak Rep. (Koruna)	.03098	.03104	32.279	32.217
South Africa (Rand)	.1548	.1549	6.4599	6.4558
South Korea (Won)	.0008707	.0008684	1148.50	1151.54
Sweden (Krona)	.1376	.1374	7.2674	7.2780
Switzerland (Franc)	.7996	.8031	1.2506	1.2452
1-month forward	.8005	.8040	1.2492	1.2438
3-months forward	.8023	.8059	1.2464	1.2408
6-months forward	.8053	.8088	1.2418	1.2364
Taiwan (Dollar)	.02944	.02944	33.967	33.967
Thailand (Baht)	.02418	.02417	41.357	41.374
Turkey (Lira)	.00000066	.00000067	1515152	1492537
U.K. (Pound)	1.7983	1.8121	.5561	.5518
1-month forward	1.7939	1.8076	.5574	.5532
3-months forward	1.7857	1.7994	.5600	.5557
6-months forward	1.7744	1.7881	.5636	.5593
United Arab (Dirham)	.2722	.2722	3.6738	3.6738
Uruguay (Peso)				
Financial	.03670	.03650	27.248	27.397
Venezuela (Bolivar)	.000521	.000521	1919.39	1919.39
SDR	1.4690	1.4690	.6807	.6807
Euro	1.2412	1.2436	.8057	.8041

Special Drawing Rights (SDR) are based on exchange rates for the U.S., British, and Japanese currencies. Source: International Monetary Fund.

a-Russian Central Bank rate. b-Government rate. y-Floating rate.

The daily *Wall Street Journal* reports exchange rates (both e and e′) for about 50 widely used currencies.

Source: *The Wall Street Journal*, October 4, 2004.

In practice, many smaller countries' currencies rarely are traded (professional foreign exchange traders call them "exotics"), and some nonmarket and developing economies, such as Cuba, Zimbabwe, Venezuela, and China, don't allow their currencies to trade freely in foreign exchange markets. Figure 1 reproduces a recent set of daily exchange rate quotations from *The Wall Street Journal*. The daily lists include only about 50 of the most heavily traded currencies. The first two columns in Figure 1 report the exchange rate as this book defines it: the number of U.S. dollars required to buy a unit of foreign currency (e). The two columns on the right report the number of units of foreign currency required to purchase a U.S. dollar (e′ = 1/e). (*Verify the relationship between e and e′ for several of the currencies.*) The prices quoted are for the large commercial transactions ($1 million or more) that constitute the bulk of the market activity. For small "retail" transactions, such as those undertaken by individuals or small firms, higher prices prevail to cover banks' costs of handling them.

Each Monday, *The Wall Street Journal* publishes a more complete listing of exchange rates that includes about 200 currencies. This listing quotes rates for the previous two Fridays, so the change in a currency's value over the preceding week can be calculated. Figure 2 reproduces a recent listing. (*Are the quotations e or e′? Can you find currencies on the list for which e = e′? Why?*)

The primary participants in foreign exchange markets include banks (who execute about 90 percent of foreign exchange market transactions), firms, foreign exchange brokers, and central banks and other official government agencies. Most transactions are made by electronic transfer and involve the exchange of large bank deposits denominated in different

Figure 2 Extended Exchange Rate Quotations

World Value of the Dollar

The table below, based on foreign-exchange quotations from Reuters, gives the rates of exchange for the U.S. dollar against various currencies as of Friday, October 1, 2004. Unless otherwise noted, all rates listed are middle rates of interbank bid and asked quotes, and are expressed in foreign currency units per one U.S. Dollar.

Country (Currency)	Value 10/01	Value 09/24
Albania (Lek)	100.500	101.150
Algeria (Dinar)	72.6459	72.2050
Angola (New Kwanza)	86.8174	86.5764
Angola (Readj Kwanza)	86.8174	86.5764
Antigua (East Caribbean $)	2.6700	2.6700
Argentina (Peso)	2.9797	2.9958
Armenia (Dram)	503.00	507.50
Aruba (Florin)	1.7900	1.7900
Australia (Dollar)	1.3770	1.4008
Azerbaijan (Manat)	4908.5	4902.5
Bahamas (Dollar)	1.0000	1.0000
Bahrain (Dinar)	0.3770	0.3770
Bangladesh (Taka)	59.3500	59.4000
Barbados (Dollar)	1.9900	1.9900
Belarus (Ruble)	2172.9	2167.5
Belize (Dollar)	1.9700	1.9700
Benin (CFA Franc)	528.54	534.71
Bermuda (Dollar)	1.0000	1.0000
Bhutan (Ngultrum)	45.9400	45.8700
Bolivia (Boliviano) f.	7.9835	7.9835
Bosnia & Herzeg. (Convertible Mark)	1.6074	1.6074
Botswana (Pula)	4.7393	4.8019
Bouvet Island (Krone)	6.6825	6.8063
Brazil (Real)	2.8361	2.8703
Brunei (Dollar)	1.6856	1.6908
Bulgaria (Lev)	1.5758	1.5949
Burkina Faso (CFA Franc)	528.54	534.71
Burundi (Franc)	1075.2	1075.1
Cambodia (Riel)	3850.0	3850.0
Cameroon (CFA Franc)	528.54	534.71
Canada (Dollar)	1.2625	1.2750
Cape Verde Isl (Escudo)	89.3500	90.4000
Cayman Islands (Dollar)	0.8200	0.8200
Central African Rep (CFA Franc)	528.54	534.71
Chad (CFA Franc)	528.54	534.71
Chile (Peso)	604.59	613.87
China (Yuan)	8.2781	8.2781
Colombia (Peso) o	2630.2	2596.1
Comoros (Franc)	403.000	404.500
Congo Dem Rep (CFA Franc)	528.54	534.71
Congo, People Rep (CFA Franc)	528.54	534.71
Costa Rica (Colon)	448.340	447.480
Croatia (Kuna)	6.1173	6.1413
Cuba (Peso)	1.0000	1.0000
Cyprus (Pound)	0.4635	0.4702
Czech Republic (Koruna)	25.4259	25.7533
Denmark (Krone)	5.9952	6.0680
Djibouti (Franc)	169.750	170.400
Dominica (East Caribbean $)	2.6700	2.6700
Dominican Rep (Peso)	28.4000	34.7000
Ecuador (US $) g	1.0000	1.0000
Egypt (Pound)	6.2352	6.2201
El Salvador (Colon) d	8.7520	8.7520
Equatorial Guinea (CFA Franc)	528.54	534.71
Estonia (Kroon)	12.6069	12.7592
Ethiopia (Birr) o	8.6250	8.6000
European Union (Euro)	0.8057	0.8155
Faeroe Islands (Danish Krone)	5.9959	6.0663
Falkland Islands (Pound)	0.6269	0.6269
Fiji (Dollar)	1.7268	1.7507
French Guiana (Franc)	7.4330	7.4330
Gabon (CFA Franc)	528.54	534.71

Country (Currency)	Value 10/01	Value 09/24
Gambia (Dalasi)	29.5000	29.5000
Ghana (Cedi)	9010	9010
Gibraltar (Pound)	0.5531	0.5563
Greenland (Danish Krone)	5.9959	6.0663
Grenada (East Caribbean $)	2.6700	2.6700
Guadeloupe (Franc)	7.4330	7.4330
Guam (US $)	1.0000	1.0000
Guatemala (Quetzal)	7.8800	7.9125
Guinea Bissau (CFA Franc)	528.54	534.71
Guinea Rep (Franc)	2615.0	2603.0
Guyana (Dollar)	179.000	179.000
Haiti (Gourde)	35.2500	35.2500
Honduras Rep (Lempira)	18.4600	18.4400
Hong Kong (Dollar)	7.8003	7.8003
Hungary (Forint)	198.334	200.240
Iceland (Krona)	70.7550	71.2550
India (Rupee) m	45.8505	45.8295
Indonesia (Rupiah)	9158	9116
Iran (Rial) o	8759	8753
Israel (Shekel)	4.4743	4.4843
Ivory Coast (CFA Franc)	528.54	534.71
Jamaica (Dollar) o	61.2800	61.3000
Japan (Yen)	110.436	110.656
Jordan (Dinar)	0.7090	0.7090
Kazakhstan (Tenge)	134.265	134.660
Kenya (Shilling)	80.9000	80.8000
Kiribati (Australia $)	1.3777	1.4001
Korea, North (Won)	2.2000	2.2000
Korea, South (Won)	1148.5	1148.5
Kuwait (Dinar)	0.2947	0.2947
Laos, People DR (Kip)	7841	7841
Latvia (Lat)	0.5379	0.5400
Lebanon (Pound)	1514.5	1514.0
Lesotho (Maloti)	6.4405	6.5505
Liberia (US $)	1.0000	1.0000
Libya (Dinar)	1.3150	1.3151
Liechtenstein (Swiss Franc)	1.2501	1.2627
Lithuania (Lita)	2.7823	2.8156
Macau (Pataca)	8.0066	8.0066
Macedonia (Denar)	50.1450	50.1500
Madagascar DR (Malagasy Franc)	10372	10381
Malawi (Kwacha)	108.750	108.550
Malaysia (Ringgit) e	3.8000	3.8000
Maldives (Rufiyaa)	12.8500	12.8500
Mali Rep (CFA Franc)	528.54	534.71
Malta (Lira)	0.3459	0.3488
Martinique (Franc)	7.4330	7.4330
Mauritania (Ouguiya)	253.600	253.500
Mauritius (Rupee)	28.5250	28.5250
Mexico (Peso)	11.3340	11.4168
Moldova (Leu)	12.1650	12.0700
Mongolia (Tugrik) m	1202.0	1202.0
Montserrat (East Caribbean $)	2.6700	2.6700
Morocco (Dirham)	8.8791	8.9632
Mozambique (Metical)	20950	21317
Myanmar (Kyat)	6.4200	6.4200
Namibia (Dollar)	6.4593	6.4176
Nauru Island (Australia $)	1.3777	1.4001
Nepal (Rupee)	72.0000	72.0000
Netherlands Antilles (Guilder)	1.7800	1.7800
New Zealand (Dollar)	1.4819	1.4961
Nicaragua (Cordoba Oro)	16.0400	16.0200
Nigeria (Naira) m	132.250	133.250
Norway (Krone)	6.6845	6.8074
Oman (Sul Rial)	0.3850	0.3850
Pakistan (Rupee)	59.2417	59.2066
Panama (Balboa)	1.0000	1.0000
Papua New Guinea		

Country (Currency)	Value 10/01	Value 09/24
(Kina)	3.0534	2.9940
Paraguay (Guarani) d	5945	5940
Peru (Nuevo Sol) d	3.3478	3.3501
Philippines (Peso)	56.3380	56.4016
Pitcairn Island (NZ $)	1.4815	1.4961
Poland (Zloty) o	3.4975	3.5490
Puerto Rico (US $)	1.0000	1.0000
Qatar (Rial)	3.6402	3.6401
Reunion, Ile de la (Franc)	7.4330	7.4330
Romania (Leu)	33158	33560
Russia (Ruble) m, b	29.2141	29.2141
Rwanda (Franc)	561.85	561.82
Saint Christopher (East Caribbean $)	2.6700	2.6700
Saint Helena (Pound)	0.5531	0.5563
Saint Lucia (East Caribbean $)	2.6700	2.6700
Saint Pierre (Franc)	7.4330	7.4330
Saint Vincent (East Caribbean $)	2.6700	2.6700
Samoa, American (US $)	1.0000	1.0000
Samoa, Western (Tala)	2.6918	2.7211
Sao Tome and Principe (Dobra)	8875	8867
Saudi Arabia (Riyal)	3.7509	3.7509
Senegal (CFA Franc)	528.54	534.71
Seychelles (Rupee)	5.4175	5.3350
Sierra Leone (Leone)	2455.0	2455.0
Singapore (Dollar)	1.6810	1.6906
Slovakia (Koruna)	32.2789	32.5945
Slovenia (Tolar)	193.400	195.690
Solomon Islands (Dollar)	7.2727	7.4349
Somalia (Shilling) d	2782.0	2779.0
South Africa (Rand) c	6.4599	6.4185
Sri Lanka (Rupee)	103.500	103.530
Sudan (Dinar) c	258.635	258.635
Sudan Rep (Pound)	2586.4	2586.4
Suriname (Guilder)	2515.0	2515.0
Swaziland (Lilangeni)	6.4550	6.4250
Sweden (Krona)	7.2674	7.3692
Switzerland (Franc)	1.2506	1.2628
Syria (Pound)	51.8500	45.5050
Taiwan (Dollar) o	33.9674	33.8295
Tanzania (Shilling)	1057.5	1066.0
Thailand (Baht)	41.3565	41.3907
Togo, Rep (CFA Franc)	528.54	534.71
Tonga Islands (Pa'anga)	1.9833	1.9912
Trinidad & Tobago (Dollar)	6.2250	6.2250
Tunisia (Dinar)	1.2550	1.2668
Turkey (Lira) h	1515152	1492537
Turks & Caicos (US $)	1.0000	1.0000
Uganda (Shilling)	1740.0	1745.0
Ukraine (Hryvnia)	5.3206	5.3236
United Arab Emir. (Dirham)	3.6731	3.6731
United Kingdom (Pound Sterling)	0.5561	0.5543
Uruguay (Peso) m	27.2480	27.4725
Vanuetu (Vatu)	113.300	113.600
Venezuela (Bolivar) d	1919.4	1919.4
Vietnam (Dong) o	15750	15755
Virgin Islands (US $)	1.0000	1.0000
Yemen (Rial) a	184.500	185.300
Yugoslavia (New Dinar)	60.5571	61.0059
Zambia (Kwacha)	4840.0	4825.0
Zimbabwe (Dollar)	5300	5560

*US $ per national currency unit. a-parallel. b-Russian Central Bank rate. c-commercial. d-freemarket. e-Government rate. f-financial. h-Floating rate as of 2/22/01. m-market. o-official.

Each Monday *Wall Street Journal* reports exchange rates (e') from the previous two Fridays for about 200 currencies.

Source: *The Wall Street Journal*, October 4, 2004.

currencies. There are separate, much smaller markets for the exchange of actual cash or bank notes; this form of foreign exchange is more expensive to buy because banks incur the costs of transporting the cash and guarding it from theft. Just as each country's domestic money supply consists primarily of bank deposits rather than cash, activity in the foreign exchange market consists mainly of transactions in bank deposits denominated in the various currencies.[3] This is important to keep in mind in the discussion that follows: "Selling dollars and buying pounds" really means using funds from a bank deposit denominated in dollars to open or add to a bank deposit denominated in pounds.

3.2 What Types of Transactions Happen in Foreign Exchange Markets?

We'll see that the decisions by actors in the foreign exchange market to buy and sell bank deposits denominated in different currencies determine the equilibrium exchange rates between various currency pairs. But why do those actors buy and sell deposits in different currencies? The basic answer is that each bank, firm, or individual must choose how to allocate its available wealth among various assets. An **asset** is simply something of value, such as a house, a diamond, an acre of land, a bank deposit, a share of Microsoft stock, or a U.S. Treasury bond. An **asset portfolio** is a set of assets owned by a firm or individual. *Portfolio choice* refers to allocating one's wealth among various types of assets, some of which may produce pleasure from consumption (for example, houses, DVD players, sports cars), and some of which produce income (for example, interest from bank deposits or capital gains from shares of stock). We'll assume that each firm or individual already has decided how to split the available wealth between pleasure-producing, consumption-oriented assets such as houses and income-generating wealth such as bank deposits; and we'll focus on allocation *within* the second group. In particular, because the demand for bank deposits denominated in various currencies determines exchange rates, we need to examine what determines that demand.

The primary determinant of any particular asset's desirability is its expected rate of return, or the expected future change in its value expressed as a percent of its purchase price. Maximizing wealth requires that individuals and firms try to add to their portfolios those assets whose value will rise in the future and eliminate from their portfolios those assets whose value will fall. Of course, asset owners can't know perfectly today what will happen to the value of different assets in the future, so portfolio choice involves collecting the available information on different assets and forming expectations about their future rates of return. Before we explore in detail the implications for the demand for bank deposits denominated in different currencies, we can see that maximizing the expected rate of return from an asset portfolio could lead to four basic circumstances in which an individual or firm might make transactions in the foreign exchange market. For now, we restrict our attention to the **spot foreign exchange market**, that is, the market in which participants trade currencies for current delivery.

CLEARING   Suppose a U.S. firm decides to buy a bond issued by a British firm.[4] The U.S. firm typically enters the spot foreign exchange market to buy the pounds in which the British firm issuing the bond wants to be paid. This happens when the U.S. firm instructs

---

3. The bank deposits traded in the foreign exchange market consist of large time deposits or certificates of deposit, not part of the issuing country's money stock.

4. A bond is just an IOU. The U.S. firm lends funds to the British firm in return for a promise of future repayment with interest.

its bank to debit its dollar account and credit the pound bank account of the British firm. This type of transaction provides an example of the **clearing** function of the foreign exchange market. The American firm demands foreign exchange (a bank deposit denominated in pounds) in exchange for domestic currency (a bank deposit denominated in dollars). In fact, it doesn't matter who (buyer or seller) actually conducts the foreign exchange transaction. At some point, if a U.S. firm buys a British bond, a dollar deposit will be exchanged for a pound deposit. The location of the foreign exchange transaction doesn't really matter because arbitrage links foreign exchange markets all over the world. This means that the rate at which dollar deposits exchange for pound deposits will be approximately the same whether the buyer of the bond makes the foreign exchange transaction in New York or the seller of the bond makes the transaction in London.

ARBITRAGE   **Arbitrage** refers to the process by which banks, firms, or individuals (mainly banks in the case of foreign exchange) seek to earn a profit by taking advantage of discrepancies among prices that prevail simultaneously in different markets. For example, suppose $e^{NY} = \$2/£1$ in New York and $e^L = \$2.20/£1$ in London, and you have \$100 to use to arbitrage the foreign exchange market. You could use the \$100 deposit to buy a £50 deposit in New York and then use the £50 deposit to buy a \$110 deposit in London. You'd make a profit of \$10 (or a \$10/\$100 = 0.10 = 10 percent rate of return), ignoring transaction costs—which are close to zero in the foreign exchange market where most trading is done electronically in very large denominations. Of course, you wouldn't be the only person doing this. Not only is the transaction very profitable; it also involves no risk, because the New York and London transactions can be simultaneous. In the process of making your profitable transaction, you increase the demand for pound-denominated deposits in New York (where you supply \$100 to demand £50) and increase the demand for dollar-denominated deposits in London (where you demand \$110 by supplying £50). This places upward pressure on e^{NY} and downward pressure on e^L. Such arbitrage continues to be profitable until the two exchange rates (e^{NY} and e^L) equalize at some value between \$2.00 and \$2.20 per pound.

Arbitrage ensures not only that dollars and pounds exchange at the same rate in New York and London but also that exchange rates will be consistent across currencies. Suppose exchange rates were such that you could buy 1 euro (€) for 1 dollar, 1 pound for 2 euros, and 3 dollars for 1 pound. Such a situation is referred to as *inconsistent* and wouldn't persist in the presence of arbitrage. What if you again had \$100 to use in arbitrage? You could use your \$100 bank deposit to buy a €100 deposit, use the 100 euros to buy £50, and use the 50 pounds to buy \$150—a 50 percent rate of return for your efforts! Of course, the example exaggerates the inconsistency of the rates, and you wouldn't be lucky enough to be the only one seeking to take advantage of the situation. Your efforts, along with those of others, would raise the dollar price of euros, the euro price of pounds, and the pound price of dollars, thereby eliminating the opportunity for profitable arbitrage and ending the **inconsistent cross rates**. Because of the possibility of such **triangular** (three-currency) **arbitrage**, we expect that $\$/£ = \$/€ \cdot €/£$. (*Why?*)

Until recently, cross exchange rates rarely were reported. Most foreign exchange transactions took place through a two-step process with the dollar serving as an intermediary, or vehicle, currency. Someone who wanted to exchange Swiss franc deposits for yen deposits would trade the francs for dollars and the dollars for yen. However, with the growth of international trade and, especially, financial activity in the past few years, more transactions now occur directly between nondollar currencies. *The Wall Street Journal* prints a daily chart of cross exchange rates for seven major currencies, shown in Figure 3. The chart reports both e and e′ for each currency pair. For example, the first column reports the price of a U.S. dollar in terms of each of the other currencies (e′), and the last row reports the

---

Figure 3   **Cross Exchange Rates**

Key Currency Cross Rates   Late New York Trading Friday, October 1, 2004

	Dollar	Euro	Pound	SFranc	Peso	Yen	CdnDlr
Canada	1.2625	1.5670	2.2703	1.0095	.11139	.01143	...
Japan	110.44	137.07	198.60	88.305	9.744	...	87.477
Mexico	11.3340	14.0678	20.382	9.0627	...	.10263	8.9777
Switzerland	1.2506	1.5523	2.2490	...	.11034	.01132	.9906
U.K.	.55610	.6902	...	.4446	.04906	.00504	.44047
Euro	.80570	...	1.4488	.64422	.07108	.00730	.63817
U.S.	...	1.2412	1.7983	.79960	.08823	.00906	.79210

The daily *Wall Street Journal* reports cross exchange rates (both e and e') for seven widely traded currencies.

Source: *The Wall Street Journal*, October 4, 2004.

U.S. dollar price of each of the other currencies (e). (*Use the data in the chart to check the consistency of the cross rates for several currencies. Also, check the relationship between e and e'.*)

For the many currencies for which cross rates still aren't reported, the best guess is the rate that would be consistent in the sense defined earlier. (*Use Figure 2 to predict the cross rates between the Panamanian balboa and the Belizian dollar and between the Angolan readjusted kwanza and the Turkish lira.*) The degree to which consistency holds for a given currency depends on the extent of arbitrage allowed. If government policies restrict purchases and sales of a currency, inconsistent cross rates may persist.

HEDGING   Another reason for making transactions in the spot foreign exchange market is hedging. **Hedging** is a way to transfer the **foreign exchange risk** inherent in all noninstantaneous transactions, such as international trade, that involve two currencies. For example, suppose you're a U.S. importer who just purchased £1,000 of goods from a British exporter. Payment is due in pounds in 30 days. You face two alternatives (we'll see a third later): (1) You can buy a £1,000 deposit now in the foreign exchange market at the current spot exchange rate and earn interest on the deposit for 30 days until payment to the British exporter is due, or (2) you can hold your dollars in a deposit and earn interest for 30 days until the payment comes due, at which time you enter the spot foreign exchange market and buy a £1,000 deposit at what is *then* the spot exchange rate. In other words, you can choose whether to hold a pound deposit or a dollar deposit as an asset in your portfolio over the next 30 days.

If you choose the first option and buy pounds now, you're hedging to avoid the risk that the dollar price of pounds could rise. If you wait (take option 2), the exchange rate might rise during the next 30 days, meaning you'll have to pay more dollars for the £1,000. During the 30-day period under option 2, you're said to hold a **short position** in pounds—that is, you're short of pounds you'll need at the end of the 30 days. Option 1 (buying now the pounds you'll need in 30 days) allows you to avoid this short position and the associated foreign exchange risk. Once you've purchased the pounds, changes in the exchange rate no longer affect you. You're then said to hold a **balanced**, or **closed**, **position** in pounds: You own just as many pounds as you need to cover your upcoming pound payment.

Entering the foreign exchange market to hedge is a way to avoid foreign exchange risk; it insulates your wealth from the effects of adverse changes in the exchange rate. But what if you hedge and buy your pounds now; then, in 30 days, you happen to glance at *The Wall Street Journal* and find that the dollar price of pounds has fallen? You could have bought the pounds now for less than you paid for them 30 days ago. Hedging allowed you to avoid the possibility that pounds would become more expensive, but it didn't allow you to take advantage of the possibility of pounds becoming cheaper.[5]

SPECULATION   Speculation is yet another reason to make transactions on the spot foreign exchange market. In one sense, **speculation** is just the opposite of hedging: It means deliberately making your wealth depend on changes in the exchange rate by either (1) buying a deposit denominated in a foreign currency (taking a long position) in the expectation that the currency's price will rise, allowing you to sell it later at a profit, or (2) promising to sell a foreign-currency deposit in the future (taking a short position) in the expectation that its price will fall, allowing you to buy the currency cheaply and sell it at a profit. When you speculate, changes in the exchange rate affect your wealth. Exchange rate movements in the direction you expected increase wealth, but those in a direction opposite to that anticipated reduce it. The line between hedging and speculation is a fuzzy one; choosing not to hedge is one kind of speculation. However, the term *speculation* often is reserved for cases in which someone buys (sells) an asset denominated in a currency solely because he or she expects the currency's price to rise (fall), with no link to financing another transaction, as in the case of the hedging decision.

3.3 Buying Currency *Now* for Delivery *Later*

The major markets for foreign exchange other than spot markets are forward markets. Here participants sign contracts for foreign exchange deliveries to be made at some specified future date (usually in 30, 90, or 180 days). The important thing is that the price of the foreign exchange is agreed on *now* for *future* delivery. The **30-day forward rate** for pounds is simply the dollar price at which you can buy a contract today for a pound deposit to be delivered in 30 days. The percentage difference between the 30-day forward rate (e^f) on a currency and the spot rate (e) is called the **forward premium** if positive and the **forward discount** if negative.[6] If pounds sell at a 10 percent forward premium against dollars, the dollar price of a pound deposit to be delivered in 30 days is 10 percent higher than the dollar price of a pound deposit delivered today (that is, the spot rate). If a forward pound to be delivered in 180 days costs 5 percent less than a pound delivered today, the pound sells at a 5 percent 180-day forward discount against the dollar. Active forward markets exist in a relatively small number of currencies. Figure 1 reports 30, 90, and 180-day forward rates for the British pound (£), the Canadian dollar (Can$), the Japanese yen (¥), and the Swiss franc (SF). (*In Figure 1, which currencies sell at a forward premium against the dollar? Which sell at a forward discount?*)

As we've already seen, every international transaction that doesn't occur instantaneously involves a foreign exchange risk because the spot exchange rate may change unexpectedly during the transaction's time horizon.[7] The existence of forward markets allows parties to transfer this risk from a party less willing to bear it to a party more willing to do so.

---

5. For a small set of heavily traded currencies, a financial instrument known as an option contract provides still another alternative. Case One at the end of the chapter explains these contracts.

6. A forward premium or discount can be defined for any time horizon; 30 days is only one example. Note that, for any two currencies, a forward premium on one is equivalent to a forward discount on the other. If the pound sells at a forward premium against the dollar ($[e^f - e] > 0$), the dollar sells at a forward discount against the pound ($[e'^f - e'] < 0$). Therefore, when using the term *forward premium* or *forward discount*, you must specify the currency.

7. The appropriate definition and measurement of foreign exchange risk is a matter of controversy. Here we mean simply that changes in the value of the exchange rate during a transaction may alter the rate of return anticipated by the parties at the time they agreed to the terms of the transaction.

Suppose you're a U.S. firm holding $1,000. What if you expect the dollar to lose value against the pound (that is, the dollar price of a pound to rise) over the next 30 days? You can buy a pound deposit now in the spot market, hold it for 30 days, and then sell it in the spot market in exchange for dollars; or you can buy a pound deposit now in the spot market *and* buy a dollar deposit in the 30-day forward market to "freeze" the price at which you can buy dollars in 30 days; or you can simply hold dollars over the entire period. Which alternative will maximize your expected rate of return depends on (1) the forward exchange rate, (2) short-term interest rates available on assets denominated in the two currencies, (3) the spot rate you expect to prevail in 30 days, and (4) the current spot rate. If you choose to buy pounds now in the spot market and sell them in the future spot market, the current and future spot exchange rates and the interest rate on pound-denominated deposits will determine your rate of return. This is a risky strategy—because you can't know now the future spot rate; so whether you would make this choice depends on your attitude toward risk and on your expectation about the future spot rate. If you buy pounds now in the spot market *and* buy dollars in the forward market, your rate of return will depend on the current spot rate, the forward rate, and the interest on the pound-denominated deposit you will hold for 30 days. If you simply hold a dollar-denominated deposit, your rate of return will depend on the interest rate available on dollar-denominated deposits.

The collective decisions of many individuals weighing the alternatives just outlined determine the equilibrium relationships among the spot exchange rate, the forward rate, short-term interest rates on deposits denominated in the two currencies, and individuals' expectations of the future spot rate. The efforts of all individuals in the economy to maximize the expected rates of return on their asset portfolios result in two conditions—called *interest-parity conditions*—that summarize the relationships between spot and forward exchange rates and short-term interest rates on assets denominated in the two currencies.

4 INTEREST PARITY

Uncovered interest parity applies to transactions in which participants don't use forward markets to transfer foreign exchange risk, and covered interest parity applies to transactions in which they do. Let's examine each in turn.

4.1 Uncovered Interest Parity

Suppose the 30-day interest rate on dollar-denominated deposits is 1 percent, the 30-day interest rate on comparable pound-denominated deposits is 2 percent, and the spot exchange rate between dollars and pounds is e = $2/£1. If you have $1,000, should you buy a £500 bank deposit or keep the funds in a dollar deposit over the next 30 days?

If you keep your $1,000 in a dollar-denominated deposit at 1 percent interest, you'll end up with $1,010, or a rate of return of 1 percent (the interest rate on dollar-denominated deposits). If you use your $1,000 in the spot foreign exchange market to buy a £500 deposit, it will mature in 30 days and earn 2 percent interest in pounds. Then, you can take your £510 (£500 of principal plus 2 percent interest) and convert them back into dollars at the then-current spot exchange rate. The rate of return on your deposit measured in dollars will depend on the spot exchange rate at the end of the 30-day period.[8] For example, if the spot rate doesn't change over the 30 days, you'll end up with $1,020. The dollar rate of return on the pound deposit will equal 2 percent, and you'll be

---

8. Note that investors generally care about rates of return in their *domestic* currency and that, when comparing assets' rates of return, they must always be expressed in the *same* currency.

glad you chose the pound deposit over the dollar deposit. But what if the spot rate during the 30-day period falls to e = $1.50/£1? Then, when you convert your £510 back into dollars, you'll get only $765, a dollar rate of return of *negative* 23 percent, consisting of the 2 percent interest on the pound deposit plus a *loss* of 25 percent from holding pounds, which lost 25 percent of their value against the dollar over the 30 days because [$1.50/£1 − $2.00/£1]/($2.00/£1) = −25%. In this case, you'd have been much better off taking the 1 percent interest rate and rate of return on the dollar-denominated deposit.

Obviously, whether there's an incentive to buy the pound-denominated deposit depends not only on a comparison of interest rates but also on what the individual expects to happen to the spot exchange rate during the life of the deposit. There's no way of knowing in advance (before the decision about which deposit to purchase) what the future value of the spot rate will be. The decision maker must form an expectation about the future spot rate and base the asset decision on that. This expectation is called the **expected future spot rate**, e^e (that is, what people expect *today* about the spot rate that will prevail in the future). If the expectation turns out to be correct, the outcome of the decision will please the individual. If the expectation turns out to be wrong, the individual may regret the decision after the fact, even though it was made on the best information available at the time.

When all individuals in the economy choose between purchasing dollar- and pound-denominated deposits in a way to maximize their expected rate of return, the result is a relationship among interest rates, the current spot rate, and individuals' expectations of the future value of the spot rate. The expected dollar rate of return on a dollar-denominated deposit is just the interest rate available on such deposits, $i^\$$. The expected dollar rate of return on a pound-denominated deposit has two components: the interest rate on a pound-denominated deposit, $i^£$, and the expected rate of change in the value of pounds relative to dollars, $([e^e − e]/e)$. Portfolio owners will buy more pound-denominated deposits if the return on dollar-denominated deposits is less than the expected return on pound-denominated ones. Algebraically,

General Case:

If $i^\$ < i^£ + (e^e − e)/e$, purchase pound-denominated deposits.

Numerical Example: [1]
$$1.5\% < 1\% + [(\$2.02/£1 − \$2.00/£1)/(\$2.00/£1)] = 2\%;$$
therefore, purchase pound-denominated deposits,

where $i^\$$ is the interest rate on dollar-denominated deposits, $i^£$ is the interest rate on comparable pound-denominated deposits, e^e is the spot rate individuals *expect* to prevail at the end of the deposit's life, and e is the current spot rate. In the numerical example in Equation 1, the rate of return on dollar-denominated deposits is 1.5 percent. The interest rate on the pound-denominated deposit is only 1 percent, but the dollar price of pounds is expected to rise by ($2.02 − $2.00)/$2.00 = 1%. Therefore, the expected dollar rate of return on the pound-denominated deposit (= 1% + 1% = 2%) exceeds that on the dollar-denominated one (= 1.5%), and portfolio owners will choose to buy pound-denominated deposits to earn the higher expected rate of return. (*What if $i^\$ = 1\%$, $i^£ = 2\%$, $e = \$2/£1$, and $e^e = \$2/£1$?*)

On the other hand,

General Case:

If $i^\$ > i^£ + (e^e − e)/e$, purchase dollar-denominated deposits.

Numerical Example: [2]
$$3\% > 1\% + [(\$2.02/£1 − \$2.00/£1)/(\$2.00/£1)] = 2\%;$$
therefore, purchase dollar-denominated deposits.

In this case, the dollar rate of return on dollar-denominated deposits ($= 3\%$) exceeds that on pound-denominated ones ($1\% + 1\% = 2\%$). The extra interest on dollar deposits is large enough to compensate for the expected foreign exchange loss (1%) in holding dollars. Therefore, portfolio owners will switch out of pounds and into dollars. (*What decision would investors make if $i^\$ = 1\%$, $i^£ = 2\%$, $e = \$2/£1$, and $e^e = \$1.50/£1$?*)

From the rules in Equations 1 and 2, we can see that there will be no incentive to shift from one currency to the other when the expected dollar rates of return on the two types of deposits are equal. This equilibrium condition is known as **uncovered interest parity**. It holds when

General Case:
$$i^\$ = i^£ + [(e^e - e)/e].$$

Numerical Example: [3]
$$2\% = 1\% + (\$2.02/£1 - \$2.00/£1)/(\$2.00/£1) = 2\%.$$

The relationship in Equation 3 is an *equilibrium condition* because if the condition doesn't hold, expected rates of return on the two deposits differ and we expect portfolio owners to reallocate their portfolios between deposits denominated in the two currencies. When the condition does hold, the two assets carry the same expected rates of return and we expect the allocation of deposits between the two currencies to be in equilibrium, with no tendency to change.[9]

An alternative way of writing the uncovered interest-parity condition from Equation 3 puts the **interest differential** ($i^\$ - i^£$) on the left-hand side. The remaining term on the right-hand side is the expected increase (if positive) or decrease (if negative) in the value of pounds against dollars, expressed in percentage terms. Uncovered interest parity holds when $i^\$ - i^£ = [(e^e - e)/e]$, or when the difference in interest rates on deposits denominated in two currencies equals the percentage difference between the expected future spot exchange rate and the current spot rate between those currencies. If the interest differential in favor of dollar-denominated assets is less than the expected increase in value of pounds against dollars ($[i^\$ - i^£] < [(e^e - e)/e]$), portfolio owners have an incentive to sell dollar-denominated deposits and purchase pound-denominated ones; this is equivalent to the situation in Equation 1. On the other hand, if the interest differential in favor of dollar-denominated assets exceeds the expected increase in value of pounds against dollars ($[i^\$ - i^£] > [(e^e - e)/e]$), portfolio owners will sell pound-denominated deposits and purchase dollar-denominated ones; this is just another way of stating the situation in Equation 2.

How do portfolio adjustments bring about the interest-parity equilibrium? Suppose the condition in Equation 1 holds. The interest rate available on dollar-denominated deposits exceeds that on pound-denominated deposits ($i^\$ - i^£ > 0$), but by less than the percentage by which the pound is expected to gain value against the dollar ($[e^e - e]/e$). Portfolio owners will buy pound-denominated deposits because the expected gain in the form of increased value of pounds will more than offset the forgone interest; in other words, because the expected rate of return on pound deposits exceeds that on dollar deposits. As many market participants try to buy pound deposits and few want to sell them, the price of pound deposits relative

---

9. More precisely, uncovered interest parity requires $i^\$ = i^£ + ([e^e - e]/e) \cdot (1 + i^£)$. The second term on the right-hand side appears because the interest earned on a pound-denominated asset, as well as the principal, must be reconverted into dollars and thus is subject to the premium or discount on foreign exchange. Because interest rates typically are less than 10 percent, at least in the major industrialized economies, the extra term is close to 1 and often is dropped, leaving the simplified expression for uncovered interest parity in Equation 3.

to that of dollar deposits rises. In other words, the current spot price of pounds rises.[10] (*Why?*) The increase in e lowers the right-hand side of Equation 1, leading toward interest parity as in Equation 3.

The portfolio-choice activities discussed in this section clearly involve a foreign exchange risk. The total expected return on an asset includes both the interest earned and the expected gain or loss on the value of the currency. Individuals, firms, and banks make decisions based on what they expect to happen to the spot exchange rate. If those expectations turn out to be incorrect, enormous losses can result very quickly. Many banks hesitate to take large open positions in foreign currencies because of the possibility of large losses; most banks' foreign exchange activities focus on transactions central to their customers' day-to-day international trade and financial dealings. There are exceptions, however; Citibank, Deutsche Bank, and Chase Manhattan, for example, actively trade foreign exchange.

For those who want to speculate in foreign currencies beyond the extent of ordinary international trade and finance activities, the International Monetary Market (part of the Chicago Mercantile Exchange) provides a forum for the sale and purchase of foreign exchange futures contracts. Figure 4 presents futures price quotations from *The Wall Street Journal* for seven currencies.

Futures contracts are similar to, but distinct from, forward contracts. Both involve buying or selling currency deposits for future delivery with the price determined today. Futures contracts are for uniform amounts and delivery dates (see Figure 4), while forward contracts can be negotiated for amounts and delivery dates tailored to the parties' specific needs. On September 30, 2004, you could buy a contract for 62,500 British pounds to be delivered in December 2004 for $1.7894 per pound; a similar contract for pounds to be delivered in March 2005 would have cost $1.7779 per pound. (*Does this indicate that most market participants in September 2004 expected the pound to gain value or to lose value against the U.S. dollar between December 2004 and March 2005? How do you know?*) Because of their uniform nature, futures contracts are liquid or tradable. Also, because the futures market imposes significant margin requirements (money put "up front" to guarantee that the buyer will honor the contract), speculators are free to use the market. Forward contracts, on the other hand, usually are arranged between a bank and a customer or between two banks. Most banks engage in forward contracts primarily to provide clearing and hedging services for customers, although in the process they can carry large short or long currency positions for brief periods.[11]

4.2 Covered Interest Parity

Undertaking a transaction in the forward market at the same time the portfolio decision is made can cover foreign exchange risk. A U.S. resident who purchases a pound-denominated deposit in the spot market could buy dollars (by selling pounds) in the forward market at the same time, thereby avoiding the risk that the price of dollars might rise during the deposit's life. For an individual using the forward market to cover foreign exchange risk, the relevant information for choosing between a dollar-denominated deposit and a pound-denominated one still includes a comparison of the rates of return on the two deposits. The rate of return on the dollar deposit is still just $i^\$$. Pound

---

10. In this simple, partial-equilibrium model of the foreign exchange market, we assume that adjustment takes the form of changes in the exchange rate alone, not in interest rates. Later chapters will incorporate the foreign exchange market into a general-equilibrium model of the macroeconomy, which will allow interest rate adjustment as well.

11. Case Three discusses another type of risk banks face in foreign exchange markets.

Figure 4   **Currency Futures Prices**

FUTURES

	OPEN	HIGH	LOW	SETTLE	CHG	LIFETIME HIGH	LIFETIME LOW	OPEN INT
Japanese Yen (CME)-¥12,500,000; $ per ¥								
Dec	.9015	.9072	.9013	.9057	.0043	.9740	.8800	94,094
Mr05	.9089	.9122	.9089	.9108	.0043	.9762	.8873	438
Est vol 29,832; vol Tue 28,151; open int 94,536, +3,771.								
Canadian Dollar (CME)-CAD 100,000; $ per CAD								
Dec	.7857	.7880	.7846	.7855	...	.7880	.6940	95,391
Mr05	.7847	.7866	.7840	.7845	...	.7866	.7150	1,515
Est vol 20,032; vol Tue 20,756; open int 98,326, +1,971.								
British Pound (CME)-£62,500; $ per £								
Dec	1.8024	1.8031	1.7857	1.7894	-.0123	1.8648	1.6850	55,626
Mr05	1.7846	1.7846	1.7740	1.7779	-.0123	1.8200	1.7321	15
Est vol 24,665; vol Tue 15,902; open int 55,643, +1,406.								
Swiss Franc (CME)-CHF 125,000; $ per CHF								
Dec	.7961	.7978	.7931	.7962	-.0003	.8260	.7264	29,698
Mr05	.7996	.8000	.7979	.7989	-.0003	.8245	.7853	16
Est vol 16,269; vol Tue 13,122; open int 29,774, +254.								
Australian Dollar (CME)-AUD 100,000; $ per AUD								
Dec	.7130	.7131	.7078	.7116	-.0006	.7705	.6150	29,347
Mr05	.7065	.7065	.7044	.7061	-.0006	.7505	.6400	136
Est vol 6,384; vol Tue 9,125; open int 29,604, +2,109.								
Mexican Peso (CME)-MXN 500,000; $ per MXN								
Dec	.08645	.08677	.08627	.08647	00005	.08855	.08270	56,427
Mr05	...	...	...	.08522	00005	.08525	.08200	419
Est vol 3,910; vol Tue 6,803; open int 57,174, +1,906.								
Euro/US Dollar (CME)-€125,000; $ per €								
Dec	1.2322	1.2340	1.2283	1.2323	.0003	1.2781	1.0735	106,648
Mr05	1.2320	1.2336	1.2287	1.2324	.0004	1.2720	1.1363	756
Est vol 73,366; vol Tue 75,221; open int 107,544, +9,791.								
Euro/US Dollar (NYBOT)-€200,000; $ per €								
Dec	1.2321	1.2324	1.2321	1.2322	.0003	1.2341	1.2037	482
Est vol 171; vol Tue 337; open int 482, -92.								
Euro/Japanese Yen (NYBOT)-€100,000; ¥ per €								
Dec	136.30	136.30	135.73	136.12	-.53	136.84	131.37	14,071
Est vol 847; vol Tue 2,604; open int 14,071, +2,551.								
Euro/British Pound (NYBOT)-€100,000; £ per €								
Dec	.6857	.6857	.6857	.6888	.0048	.6904	.6824	6,733
Est vol 555; vol Tue 214; open int 6,733, -40.								

Futures markets permit traders to buy uniform contracts of currency for future delivery with the price and delivery date specified today.

Source: *The Wall Street Journal*, September 30, 2004.

deposits' return consists of two components: the interest rate ($i^£$) and the forward premium. Letting e^f represent the *f*orward rate,

General Case:

If $i^\$ < i^£ + [(e^f - e)/e]$, purchase pound-denominated deposits.

Numerical Example: [4]

$1.5\% < 1\% + [(\$2.02/£1 - \$2.00/£1)/(\$2.00/£1)] = 2\%$;

therefore, purchase pound-denominated deposits.

Here, the rate of return on pound deposits exceeds that on dollar deposits, so portfolio owners shift toward pounds. Dollar deposits pay a higher interest rate than pound ones, but pounds sell at a forward premium (or, equivalently, dollars sell at a forward discount). The foreign exchange premium earned by holding pounds over the 30 days more than makes up for the forgone interest.

Just as a high dollar interest rate doesn't necessarily imply that portfolio owners would switch toward dollars, a high pound interest rate needn't imply a shift toward pounds. In Equation 5, the pound interest rate exceeds that on dollars, but the return on dollar deposits still exceeds that on pound deposits because of a large forward discount on pounds.

General Case:

If $i^\$ > i^£ + [(e^f - e)/e]$, purchase dollar-denominated deposits.

Numerical Example: [5]

$1\% > 2\% + [(\$1.50/£1 - \$2.00/£1)/(\$2.00/£1)] = -23\%$;
therefore, purchase dollar-denominated deposits.

In summary, both the interest differential and the forward premium or discount on foreign exchange must be taken into account in choosing among deposits denominated in different currencies based on their rates of return. When individuals in the economy make their decisions based on the relationships in Equations 4 and 5, the resulting equilibrium condition is **covered interest parity**. This condition holds when the rates of return on dollar- and pound-denominated deposits are equal.

General Case:

$i^\$ = i^£ + [(e^f - e)/e]$.

Numerical Example: [6]

$2\% = 1\% + [(\$2.02/£1 - \$2.00/£1)/(\$2.00/£1)] = 2\%$.

When interest parity holds, the rates of return on dollar- and pound-denominated deposits are the same, so no incentive exists to alter the composition of asset portfolios. Therefore, currency markets are in equilibrium.

We can also express covered interest parity as a comparison of the interest differential and the forward premium or discount on foreign exchange (that is, the percentage difference between the forward and spot exchange rates). When $i^\$ - i^£ = [(e^f - e)/e]$, rates of return on the two types of assets are equal, and foreign exchange markets are in equilibrium. If $i^\$ - i^£ > [(e^f - e)/e]$, portfolio owners will shift toward dollar assets; and if $i^\$ - i^£ < [(e^f - e)/e]$, they'll switch toward pounds.

Table 1 summarizes the interest-parity results. The spot exchange rate responds to changes in domestic interest rates, foreign interest rates, the expected future spot rate, and the forward rate. When these changes cause portfolio owners to shift toward domestic-currency deposits, the exchange rate tends to fall. When something happens to cause portfolio owners to shift toward foreign-currency deposits, the spot exchange rate tends to rise.[12]

4.3 Does Interest Parity Hold?

Covered interest parity is one of the most frequently tested relationships in international macroeconomics.[13] The empirical support for the relationship is quite strong, but the results are sensitive to the testing technique. In particular, the parity relationship holds more closely when all deposits used in the test are issued in a single country. For example, a test using dollar-denominated and pound-denominated certificates of deposit (CDs)

---

12. We'll see in section 7 that the government may choose to fix or peg the exchange rate, not allowing the changes implied here.

13. Testing uncovered interest parity is much more difficult because the relationship involves the unobservable expected future spot exchange rate rather than the observable forward rate.

Table 1   INTEREST PARITY AND THE EXCHANGE RATE

Variable	Shift in Expected-Return-Maximizing Asset Portfolio	Effect on Spot Exchange Rate
Domestic interest rate (i):		
Increase	Toward domestic-currency-denominated deposits	e falls (domestic currency appreciates)
Decrease	Toward foreign-currency-denominated deposits	e rises (domestic currency depreciates)
Foreign interest rate (i*):		
Increase	Toward foreign-currency-denominated deposits	e rises (domestic currency depreciates)
Decrease	Toward domestic-currency-denominated deposits	e falls (domestic currency appreciates)
Expected future spot rate (e^e):		
Increase	Toward foreign-currency-denominated deposits	e rises (domestic currency depreciates)
Decrease	Toward domestic-currency-denominated deposits	e falls (domestic currency appreciates)
Forward rate (e^f):		
Increase	Toward foreign-currency-denominated deposits	e rises (domestic currency depreciates)
Decrease	Toward domestic-currency-denominated deposits	e falls (domestic currency appreciates)

both issued by a Zurich bank typically will show a tighter parity relationship than a test using a dollar-denominated CD from a New York bank and a pound-denominated CD from a London bank. This is why, in our discussion of interest parity, we speak of the interest rates on deposits denominated in different *currencies* ($i^\$$ and $i^£$) rather than the interest rates in different *countries* (i^{US} and i^B).

Why the difference? One factor in addition to the expected rate of return that influences individuals' portfolio decisions is the risk that a country might impose restrictions on the movement of funds across national boundaries. A high rate of return on a deposit issued by a London bank would be worth little to an American if Britain imposed controls that prevented the owner from converting the proceeds of the deposit into dollars and moving them back to the United States. In comparing a dollar-denominated CD issued by a New York bank and a pound-denominated CD issued by a London bank, three things differ: (1) the currency, (2) the bank, and (3) the country. The interest-parity relationship addresses factor 1. For major banks in industrialized countries, factor 2 is of little significance, because bank failures are rare and, when they occur, deposits usually are backed by government insurance such as that provided by the U.S. Federal Deposit Insurance Corporation. But factor 3 can interfere with interest parity, especially in times of uncertainty—when market participants might expect changes in government policy.

By testing interest parity using deposits issued in the same country but in different currencies, the risk of government restrictions on movement of funds is equalized across currencies, allowing a purer test of interest parity. Offshore currency markets provide the perfect opportunity for testing interest parity. **Offshore deposits** (or **Eurocurrencies**) are currencies held in deposit outside their country of issue; in other words, a dollar deposit held anywhere outside the United States is a Eurocurrency (or Eurodollar) deposit, regardless of who owns the deposit.[14] Among offshore deposits held in the same country but denominated in different currencies, interest parity holds so tightly and routinely that dealers use the relationship as a shorthand way to calculate the forward rates they offer.

5 DEMAND AND SUPPLY IN THE FOREIGN EXCHANGE MARKET

Up to now our reliance on the standard demand-and-supply framework to analyze the foreign exchange market has been implicit. In this section, we'll develop a simple model of the demand for and supply of foreign exchange based on the interest-parity conditions. We'll see that equilibrium in the foreign exchange market and interest parity are equivalent conditions.

The demand for and supply of foreign exchange are similar in many respects to those for any other asset. The important thing to remember is that the demand for a currency is really the demand for deposits denominated in that currency, not demand for actual paper money. The **demand curve for a foreign currency** shows how many units of the currency individuals want to hold at various exchange rates. In other words, the demand curve summarizes the relationship between the quantity demanded and the price of a foreign currency, holding constant the other economic variables that affect quantity demanded. Similarly, the **supply curve for a foreign currency** shows how many units of foreign-currency deposits are available for individuals to hold at various exchange rates.

The supply-and-demand model of the foreign exchange market is a partial-equilibrium model and, as such, ignores many interconnections among variables. Despite this limitation, the model is a useful first step in understanding the determination of exchange rates and their role in the international macroeconomy. Fuller elaboration of the relationships between exchange rates and the rest of the macroeconomy forms the basis of later chapters.

The interest-parity relationships developed in section 4 suggest that individuals allocate their asset portfolios among deposits denominated in different currencies by comparing expected rates of return, which depend on interest rates, spot exchange rates, expected future spot exchange rates, and forward rates. When the interest-parity conditions are satisfied (as in Equations 3 and 6), individuals are content to hold their existing portfolios; there's no incentive to shift from deposits denominated in one currency toward those denominated in another. So the foreign exchange market is in equilibrium when, given current interest rates, spot and forward exchange rates, and exchange rate expectations, individuals are content to hold in their portfolios the existing supply of deposits in each currency. In other words, interest parity and equilibrium in the foreign exchange market are two ways of looking at the same relationships.

5.1 The Demand for Foreign Exchange

The relationship between the quantity demanded of foreign exchange and the spot exchange rate (expressed as the domestic-currency price of a unit of foreign currency) is a *negative* one: As the exchange rate rises, the quantity of foreign exchange demanded falls. It's easy to see why. As the spot exchange rate rises, each unit of foreign currency becomes more expensive in terms of domestic currency. Given existing interest rates, expected future spot rates, and forward rates, foreign-currency deposits become less attractive assets than domestic-currency ones because the expected return on foreign-currency deposits falls. As a result, individuals choose to hold fewer foreign-currency deposits in their

---

14. Section 9 discusses Eurocurrency markets.

portfolios. (*Use the expressions for interest parity in Equations 3 and 6 to verify that a rise in the value of e, holding the other values constant, changes the situation from interest-parity equilibrium to one in which individuals substitute away from foreign-currency deposits.*) On the other hand, a fall in the exchange rate makes foreign-currency deposits more attractive because their expected rate of return rises, causing individuals to want to hold more in their portfolios. (*Use the expressions for interest parity in Equations 3 and 6 to verify that a fall in the value of e, holding the other values constant, changes the situation from interest-parity equilibrium to one in which individuals demand a larger quantity of foreign-currency deposits.*)

The negatively sloped line in Figure 5 illustrates the negative relationship between the quantity demanded of foreign exchange and the exchange rate. Just as in the markets for other goods or assets, the exchange rate is only one of several determinants of quantity demanded. Each demand curve is drawn for fixed values of the domestic interest rate ($i^\$$), the foreign interest rate ($i^£$), the expected future spot rate (e^e), and the forward rate (e^f). A change in any of these values causes individuals to demand a different quantity of foreign-currency-denominated deposits at each value of the spot exchange rate; this causes the entire demand curve to shift.

If the domestic interest rate rises, the demand curve for foreign exchange shifts to the left. The higher rate of interest paid on domestic-currency deposits causes individuals to shift their portfolios away from foreign-currency deposits and toward domestic-currency ones whose rate of return has risen. A fall in the domestic interest rate shifts the demand curve for foreign exchange to the right. (*Use Equations 1 through 6 to verify.*) In Figure 5, the (−) sign over the domestic interest rate ($i^\$$) term represents this relationship; when the domestic interest rate changes, the demand curve for foreign exchange shifts in the *opposite* direction.

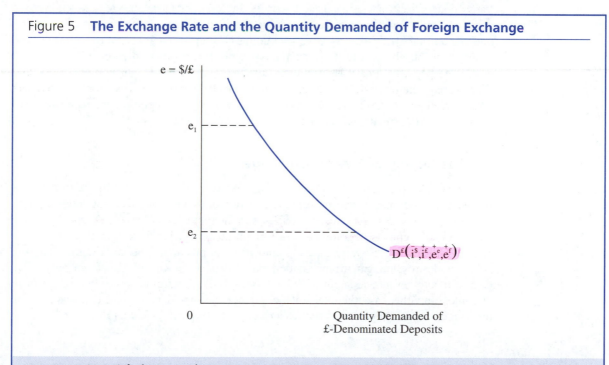

Figure 5 **The Exchange Rate and the Quantity Demanded of Foreign Exchange**

For given values of $i^\$$, $i^£$, e^e, and e^f, a high value of e (such as e_1) makes foreign-currency-denominated deposits less attractive relative to domestic-currency ones. The result is a low quantity demanded. A fall in the exchange rate from e_1 to e_2 makes foreign-currency deposits more attractive to portfolio holders, increasing the quantity demanded. Increases in $i^£$, e^e, or e^f shift the demand curve to the right; increases in $i^\$$ shift it to the left.

A rise in the interest rate on foreign-currency deposits increases the quantity of those deposits demanded at any given value of the exchange rate; the demand curve shifts to the right. (*Why?*) A fall in the foreign-currency interest rate lowers the rate of return on foreign-currency deposits and shifts the demand curve to the left. The (+) sign over the foreign interest rate ($i^£$) term represents the positive relationship between the foreign interest rate and the quantity demanded of foreign-currency-denominated deposits; a change in $i^£$ shifts the demand curve in the *same* direction.

Using Equations 1 through 3, we can see that a rise in the expected future spot exchange rate increases the quantity demanded of foreign exchange. Such a change means that the dollar price of pounds is expected to rise; during such a change, individuals want to hold pounds (that are becoming more valuable), not dollars (that are becoming less valuable). So the expected exchange rate term in Figure 5 has a (+) sign; the demand for pounds shifts in the same direction as any change in e^e.

Similarly, Equations 4 through 6 imply that a rise in the forward exchange rate causes an increase in the quantity demanded of foreign exchange. Converting the proceeds of pound-denominated deposits back into dollars brings more dollars when e^f rises, so holding pound-denominated deposits now becomes more attractive. The sign over e^f in Figure 5 is (+); when the forward rate changes, the demand for pounds shifts in the same direction.

The model of the demand for foreign exchange just developed is an *asset-oriented model*. It focuses on demand for foreign-currency deposits *as assets*. It may be tempting to ask, "What about international trade? Don't Americans demand yen to buy Toyotas, while Japanese demand dollars to buy Boeing 777s?" The answer, of course, is yes. Holding foreign-currency deposits for making trade transactions rather than as interest-bearing assets is called the *liquidity* or *transactions motive*. But in today's world economy, international financial activity dwarfs such considerations. Experts estimate that fewer than 5 percent of foreign exchange transactions reflect trade in goods and services. In 2004, foreign exchange transactions total about $1.9 trillion *per day*, representing about one-third of the value of all world merchandise trade *for an entire year*! Also, as we've seen in this chapter, an international trade transaction, such as the purchase of an imported good, typically involves an asset decision, since immediate payment usually isn't required; the buyer must decide which currency to hold over the payment interval. Since asset-oriented financial transactions have come to dominate actual foreign exchange markets over the last few years, it's only appropriate that economists' models reflect this important change in the nature of the world economy.

5.2 The Supply of Foreign Exchange

Individuals determine the *demand* for foreign exchange through their efforts to earn the highest expected rates of return on their asset portfolios, as reflected in the interest-parity conditions. In contrast, government policies, together with banks' loan decisions, determine the *supply* of deposits denominated in foreign currency. We'll explore this process in some detail later. For now, it suffices to point out that private individuals' transactions can't create or destroy foreign-currency-denominated deposits.[15] An individual can only sell a deposit to another individual, firm, or bank or buy a deposit from another individual, firm, or bank.[16] In either case, the total stock of foreign-currency-denominated deposits remains unchanged; it will simply have been reallocated between portfolio holders.

---

15. In the same sense, individual deposit transactions don't create or destroy domestic bank deposits. If an individual writes a $15,000 check for a new car, his or her account balance falls by $15,000, but the car dealer's account rises by the same amount. Total deposits remain unchanged; they've merely been reallocated between individuals. Cash transactions can affect total deposits but represent such a small share of activity that we can ignore them.

16. We ignore for now the possibility that the individual will buy from or sell to a *central* bank (that is, the country's monetary authority); we'll cover this case in the forthcoming discussion of foreign exchange market intervention.

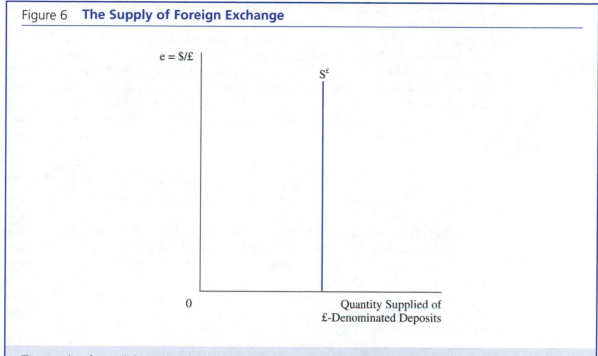

Figure 6   The Supply of Foreign Exchange

The quantity of pound-denominated deposits available is determined by government policies and banks' loan decisions. At each point in time, this quantity is independent of the exchange rate; therefore, a vertical line represents the supply of foreign-currency-denominated deposits.

Because the stock of foreign-currency-denominated deposits available at any time is fixed, we can represent the supply of foreign exchange by a vertical line, S^f, in Figure 6. The supply curve is vertical because the supply of deposits in existence at any time doesn't depend on the exchange rate.

Now we can combine the demand for and supply of foreign exchange to see how they determine exchange rates.

Although we can draw demand and supply curves for foreign exchange, governments choose whether to allow the forces of demand and supply to determine the value of exchange rates for their respective currencies. In each country, the government decides the type of policy to follow regarding the exchange rate. Economists call this policy the **exchange rate regime**. There are four main types of regime: (1) flexible or floating exchange rates, (2) fixed or pegged exchange rates, (3) managed floating (a mixture of flexible and fixed), and (4) exchange controls in which the government maintains monopoly control over the allocation and pricing of foreign currency. In the remaining chapters, we'll discuss all four systems. We begin with the simplest: the flexible or floating exchange rate.

6 HOW ARE EXCHANGE RATES DETERMINED UNDER A FLEXIBLE-RATE REGIME?

Since the early 1970s, most countries have moved toward the use of **flexible**, or **floating**, **exchange rates**. Under such a regime, the demand for and supply of each currency in the foreign exchange market determine the exchange rate. We can treat the market for foreign exchange as a competitive one, because millions of individuals, firms, and banks participate; foreign exchange is a homogeneous commodity; market information is good; and market entry and exit are unrestricted. The market for foreign exchange under a flexible regime works much like the market for any other good: The price (the exchange rate) moves to the level that equates quantity demanded to quantity supplied. In the case of the foreign exchange market, the good in question is an asset in the form of bank deposits denominated in a foreign currency. The exchange rate adjusts until the quantity of foreign-currency-denominated deposits individuals want to hold equals the quantity available, or equivalently, until the expected rates of return on domestic- and foreign-currency-denominated deposits are equal, or until interest parity holds.

Figure 7 shows the equilibrium exchange rate, e_3, between the dollar and the pound. If the exchange rate were *above* the equilibrium (for example, at e_1), individuals would want to hold *fewer* than the existing quantity of pound-denominated deposits. A surplus of foreign exchange would cause the price to fall as individuals offered to sell pound-denominated deposits in exchange for dollar-denominated ones. If the exchange rate were *below* the equilibrium rate (for example, at e_2), individuals would want to hold *more* than the existing quantity of pound-denominated deposits. A shortage of foreign exchange would cause individuals to bid up its price as they offer to buy pound-denominated deposits in exchange for dollar-denominated ones. Only at e_3, where quantity demanded equals the quantity supplied of foreign exchange, is the market in equilibrium. At that exchange rate (given the values of $i^\$$, $i^\pounds$, e^e, and e^f), individuals are content to hold exactly $S^\pounds$ of pound-denominated deposits in their portfolios, and interest parity is satisfied because the expected rates of return on dollar-denominated and pound-denominated assets are equal.

Figure 7   **Equilibrium in the Foreign Exchange Market under a Flexible-Rate Regime**

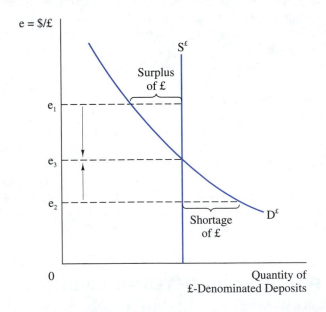

The exchange rate moves to equate the quantity demanded and quantity supplied of pounds. The equilibrium exchange rate is e_3; at that exchange rate, portfolio owners willingly hold the existing quantity of pound-denominated deposits given the values of $i^\$$, $i^\pounds$, e^e, and e^f.

Under a flexible exchange rate regime, the price mechanism equates the quantity demanded of each currency with the quantity supplied; therefore, the foreign exchange market clears. Later chapters will explore the arguments for using a flexible exchange rate regime as well as the implications of such a regime for various macroeconomic policies.

When the exchange rate is flexible, we call a rise in the market-determined rate a **depreciation** of the currency whose price has fallen and an **appreciation** of the currency whose price has risen. In Figure 7, a change in the rate from e_1 to e_3 represents a depreciation of the pound or, equivalently, an appreciation of the dollar. A move from e_2 to e_3 involves a depreciation of the dollar and an appreciation of the pound. Note that in discussing an appreciation or a depreciation we must always refer to a specific currency. A change in any exchange rate always involves an appreciation of one currency *and a depreciation of another*, so saying "the exchange rate between yen and francs appreciated" conveys no information. *Either* the yen appreciated against the franc (implying that the franc depreciated against the yen) *or* the franc appreciated against the yen (implying that the yen depreciated against the franc).

Any change in economic conditions that increases the demand for pounds causes the pound to appreciate (e to rise). Such changes could include a rise in $i^£$, a fall in $i^\$$, or a rise in e^e or e^f, as in Figure 8. A fall in the demand for pounds causes a depreciation of the pound (a fall in e). This could result from a fall in $i^£$, a rise in $i^\$$, or a fall in e^e or e^f.

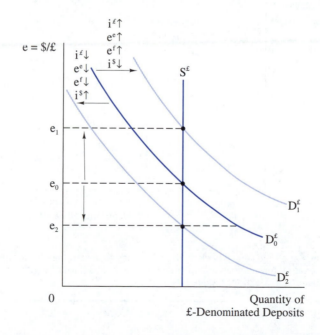

Figure 8   Shifts in the Demand for Foreign Exchange Change the Exchange Rate

Increases in $i^£$, e^e, or e^f increase the demand for pound-denominated bank deposits and cause the pound to appreciate against the dollar. Increases in $i^\$$ decrease the demand for pound-denominated deposits and cause the pound to depreciate against the dollar.

7 HOW ARE EXCHANGE RATES DETERMINED UNDER A FIXED-RATE REGIME?

Exchange rates haven't been flexible through most of modern economic history; in fact, peacetime flexible rates were rare until the early 1970s. Instead, most governments used **fixed** or **pegged exchange rates** for their respective currencies. Such a practice works much like fixing the price of any good. The demand for and supply of foreign exchange still exist, but they don't determine the exchange rate as they would in a flexible-rate system. Central banks (such as the U.S. Federal Reserve, the Bank of England, the European Central Bank, or the Bank of Japan) must stand ready to absorb any excess demand for or supply of a currency to maintain the pegged rate.[17]

Suppose the U.S. government decides to peg the exchange rate between dollars and pounds at e_1^p in Figure 9. At that rate, the quantity supplied of pounds exceeds the quantity demanded. The high dollar price of the pound makes dollar-denominated deposits attractive relative to pound-denominated ones, so the quantity demanded of pounds is low. The surplus of pounds in the foreign exchange market at e_1^p creates a tendency for the exchange rate to fall (that is, for the pound to depreciate against the dollar) as individuals try to sell pound-denominated deposits in exchange for dollar ones.

To keep the exchange rate at e_1^p, the U.S. central bank must step into the market and buy up the surplus pound-denominated deposits. This is called a policy of **intervention**

Figure 9   A Pegged Exchange Rate above the Equilibrium Rate

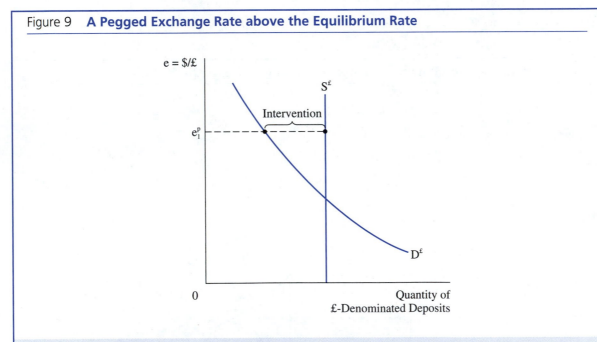

To maintain the exchange rate at e_1^p, the central bank must stand ready to absorb the excess quantity supplied of pounds. The U.S. central bank intervenes by buying pound-denominated deposits at a price of e_1^p; the horizontal distance between $D^£$ and $S^£$ at e_1^p represents the magnitude of the required intervention.

---

17. In some countries, government agencies other than the central bank can also intervene in foreign exchange markets. The U.S. Treasury, for example, sometimes intervenes using its Exchange Stabilization Fund. However, interventions by these agencies typically do not have the important macroeconomic effects (in particular, increasing or decreasing the money supply) that central banks' interventions do; so we'll focus on central banks' role in foreign exchange markets.

in the foreign exchange market. Individuals sell the pound-denominated deposits they don't want to the U.S. central bank in return for dollar-denominated deposits at a rate of e_1^p per pound. The horizontal distance between $D^£$ and $S^£$ at e_1^p in Figure 9 represents the magnitude of the required intervention.

Alternatively, if the central bank chooses to adjust the pegged exchange rate downward from e_1^p, the policy is called a **revaluation** of the dollar. A revaluation under a pegged exchange regime is analogous to an appreciation under a flexible regime; that is, both revaluation and appreciation refer to a rise in the value of the currency (here, the dollar) relative to another currency (the pound).

Suppose, on the other hand, that the U.S. government decided to hold the exchange rate between dollars and pounds at e_2^p, below the equilibrium rate in Figure 10. At e_2^p, the quantity demanded of pounds exceeds the quantity supplied. The low value of the exchange rate makes pound-denominated deposits more attractive and dollar-denominated deposits less so. The forces of supply and demand in the foreign exchange market put upward pressure on the dollar price of pounds. If the exchange rate is to stay at e_2^p, the central bank must intervene in the foreign exchange market to supply enough pounds to cover the difference between the quantity individuals demand and the quantity supplied at e_2^p. For intervention purposes, governments hold stocks of deposits denominated in various foreign currencies, called **foreign exchange reserves**. In our example, the U.S. central bank would sell a portion of its pound reserves by buying dollar-denominated deposits with those pound-denominated reserves, thereby satisfying portfolio owners' demand for pounds.

If a central bank tried to hold the exchange rate between its currency and another at a level below equilibrium for a long period, it eventually would deplete its foreign exchange reserves. Then the policy choices would be to (1) borrow reserves from other central banks or from the International Monetary Fund to continue the intervention, (2) reset the pegged

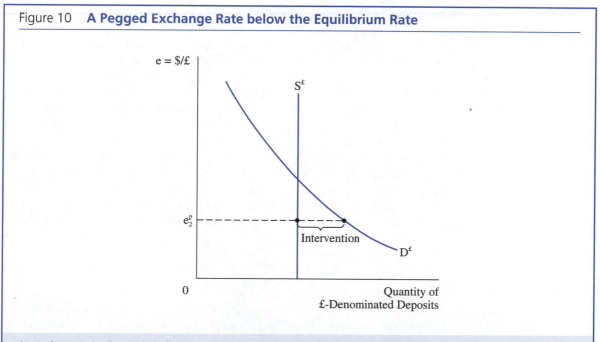

Figure 10 **A Pegged Exchange Rate below the Equilibrium Rate**

At e_2^p, the quantity demanded of pounds exceeds the quantity supplied. The central bank can maintain the rate at e_2^p if it intervenes by supplying pound-denominated deposits to the market from its foreign exchange reserves.

exchange rate at a level more consistent with equilibrium in the foreign exchange market, or (3) allow the exchange rate to float to its equilibrium value.[18] If the central bank chooses to reset the exchange rate at a level higher than e_p^R, the policy is called a **devaluation** of the dollar against the pound, analogous to a depreciation under a flexible exchange regime.

Later we'll discuss at length the implications of a fixed exchange rate regime for the conduct of macroeconomic policy. For now, note that the type of foreign exchange risk analyzed in our earlier discussion of hedging arises from the possibility that the spot exchange rate will *change* over time. If it were possible for governments' monetary authorities to peg e such that everyone was certain exchange rates would never change, there wouldn't be any foreign exchange risk of this type. There would be little need for a forward market, because everyone would know that foreign exchange could be bought in the future at the same price prevailing today. Such fixed exchange rates would eliminate many but not all the roles of private foreign exchange markets—if the exchange rate were fixed within very narrow bands that were permanent and dependable. However, history suggests that no fixed-rate system can provide that degree of certainty, since there always is a possibility that, due to shifts in the demand for and supply of a currency, the government may become unable or unwilling to maintain the pegged rate. We'll see in later chapters that these issues played a big role in the Asian financial crisis of 1997−1998. Banks and other firms in countries such as Thailand and Indonesia took out loans denominated in foreign currencies under the assumption that their governments would keep exchange rates fixed at their current values. Faced with mounting economic problems, governments instead devalued the currencies or, in some cases, abandoned the pegs and allowed the currencies to depreciate. Banks and firms, which had assumed they'd be able to buy foreign currency in the future at the long-standing fixed rates, suddenly faced much higher prices for the foreign currency they needed to repay their loans.

8 THE EFFECTIVE EXCHANGE RATE

An exchange rate is the relative price of two currencies, reflecting the relative demands for and supplies of deposits denominated in those currencies, so a currency may *appreciate* against some currencies at the same time it *depreciates* against others. This means it's not possible, based on a **bilateral exchange rate**, to determine whether a currency generally is appreciating or depreciating in foreign exchange markets. Nonetheless, it often is useful to have an indicator of the trend of a currency's overall movement relative to other currencies "on average." **Effective exchange rates** serve this purpose. The effective exchange rate of the dollar, for example, provides a measure of the dollar's value relative to U.S. trading partners' currencies as a group.

Several government agencies, international organizations, and private financial institutions compute effective exchange rates for the U.S. dollar and other currencies. Table 2 reports one measure of the effective exchange rate of the dollar, calculated by the U.S. Federal Reserve Board, for June of each year since the dollar began to float. This particular measure, called the major-currencies index, includes the euro, Canadian dollar, Japanese yen, Swedish krona, Swiss franc, British pound, and Australian dollar.

Various measures of the effective exchange rate differ primarily in the weights attached to the bilateral exchange rates in the calculation. Over short periods, these

---

18. Central banks enter agreements, called swaps, to lend specified amounts of their currencies to one another for intervention. For example, if the U.S. Federal Reserve ran short of pounds while trying to hold the dollar price of pounds below the equilibrium rate, it could borrow pounds from the Bank of England, to be repaid at a later date after U.S. pound reserves were replenished. The Federal Reserve Bank of New York's quarterly publication, *Treasury and Federal Reserve Foreign Exchange Operations,* reports recent trends in exchange rates and activity in the U.S. swap accounts.

Table 2   MAJOR-CURRENCY INDEX EFFECTIVE EXCHANGE RATE OF THE U.S. DOLLAR, 1973–2004

Year	Effective Exchange Rate (Index: March 1973 = 100)	Year	Effective Exchange Rate (Index: March 1973 = 100)
1973	101.8	1989	102.1
1974	99.7	1990	107.5
1975	99.7	1991	108.3
1976	93.4	1992	116.0
1977	93.6	1993	113.0
1978	101.3	1994	112.5
1979	103.7	1995	112.5
1980	107.3	1996	114.0
1981	93.5	1997	108.1
1982	85.5	1998	99.5
1983	82.9	1999	101.1
1984	79.1	2000	100.1
1985	72.9	2001	91.3
1986	90.7	2002	95.9
1987	102.2	2003	109.6
1988	111.1	2004	114.2

As reported here, the index reports the trade-weighted value of foreign currencies in terms of the U.S. dollar; therefore, an increase in the index represents a depreciation of the dollar.

Source: Data from Board of Governors of the Federal Reserve System (updates are available at http://www.federalreserve.gov).

differences in weighting procedures can cause substantial variation in measures of the effective exchange rate. For example, during the Asian financial crisis of 1997–1998, measures that weighted Asian currencies heavily showed a larger appreciation of the dollar, because the dollar's value rose particularly sharply against the currencies belonging to those trading partners.

9 OFFSHORE CURRENCY MARKETS

Recall that an offshore deposit is simply a bank deposit denominated in the currency of a country *other than* the one in which the deposit is located. A dollar deposit in a London bank or a pound deposit in a Hong Kong bank both constitute offshore deposits, regardless of their owners' nationalities. What makes a deposit part of the offshore currency market is the combination of the bank's location and the deposit's currency of denomination.

One obvious question about offshore currency markets concerns why they exist at all. Why would anyone want to hold a deposit in a country other than the one issuing the currency? There are three answers to this question, two primarily economic and the other political; they are the reasons most often cited for the emergence and rapid growth of offshore currency markets.

Governments regulate banking within their borders. The United States, for example, imposes reserve, disclosure, and insurance requirements and many other restrictions on U.S. banks. Similar regulatory patterns exist in other countries, but the details vary considerably. There are several reasons for regulation of the industry. Smooth functioning of the banking system constitutes an important element in the successful conduct of monetary policy, as we'll see in an upcoming chapter. Confidence in the banking system is critical; and the reserve, insurance, and disclosure requirements that governments impose on banks help ensure stability in banking and promote the public's confidence.

While government banking regulations provide benefits, they also raise banks' costs of doing business. Banks—at least those in the United States—are privately owned, profit-maximizing businesses, so the costs of regulation imply that banks must pay lower interest rates to depositors and charge higher ones to borrowers to operate profitably. Any bank that can partially escape the costly national regulations can lower its operation costs and thus afford to pay higher interest rates to depositors and charge lower rates to borrowers. Offshore markets achieve this goal. The U.S. government, for example, has little control over a bank that accepts deposits denominated in dollars in other countries. Even for overseas branches or subsidiaries of a U.S. bank, a foreign location reduces the government's power to regulate it.

Countries that choose not to regulate banking heavily attract international banking activity. By escaping regulation, banks operating in these countries can offer more attractive interest rates to both depositors and borrowers. Countries that have deliberately fostered the growth of offshore banking include Britain, Switzerland, Panama, Bahrain, the Cayman Islands, Singapore, and Hong Kong. Other countries, including the United States, Germany, and Japan, historically have used regulation to discourage borrowing and lending in foreign currencies within their borders.

With the rapid growth of international trade and financial activity, firms' demand for offshore banking services has grown as well. When a firm buys and sells in many countries around the world, the ability to hold bank deposits in different currencies and locales becomes an important part of doing business. Firms' increased needs for international financial services help explain the rapid growth of offshore markets.

We can trace the third—and political—reason for offshore deposits to 1950s Cold War tensions between the United States and the Soviet Union. As part of its efforts to modernize and develop its economy, the Soviet Union entered into growing trade relations with Western economies, which meant dealing in dollars. However, the Soviet Union and the other Eastern European nonmarket economies were reluctant to hold dollar deposits in the United States, fearing that if hostilities escalated, the United States would seize their assets. To avoid this possibility, the Soviets searched for a bank outside the United States that would accept dollar-denominated deposits and located one in Paris.

Foreign branches and subsidiaries of the largest U.S. banks now dominate the offshore currency market. About half of all offshore deposits are denominated in dollars. In the market's early years, the bulk of activity consisted of dollar deposits held in Europe, which explains why offshore deposits often are called *Eurocurrencies* or *Eurodollars*. As a larger number of currencies have come to be used actively in offshore currency markets, the markets themselves have proliferated throughout the world. Offshore banking activity tends to move to areas of least regulation. Such activity originally centered in Europe, with London still the dominant location (although about 85 percent of the activity there is undertaken by foreign institutions). More recently offshore banking has expanded to a number of Asian centers, such as Tokyo and Singapore, making the term *Eurocurrency* less descriptive of the entire phenomenon.

The primary effect of offshore currency markets has been to increase the mobility of financial capital. Previously it was difficult to buy short-term assets denominated in foreign currencies. Investment abroad took the form of direct investment, purchases of common stock or equity in foreign firms, or purchases of foreign bonds. Now, offshore bank deposits provide a way to hold assets denominated in foreign currencies for very short periods, often only a few days. Most deposits in the offshore market are time deposits with maturities ranging from overnight to a few years.

CASE 1: MULTINATIONALS AND FOREIGN EXCHANGE

The analysis in this chapter makes clear that any noninstantaneous transaction involving more than one currency involves a foreign exchange risk. If the exchange rate between the relevant currencies changes significantly during the transaction, the terms of the transaction will deviate *ex post* from those originally negotiated. As reductions in transportation and communication costs have encouraged firms to become more international in their production, finance, and marketing operations, firms' exposure to foreign exchange risk has grown. Businesses and the financial institutions that serve them have developed several techniques to manage these risks.[19]

For large multinational firms, internal hedging (that is, offsetting one division's long position in a currency against another division's short position) provides the most common way of handling exchange risk. The costs involved in internal hedging often prove less than that of using a bank's forward foreign exchange services. If a firm's chemical division expects to be paid 1 million euros in 30 days for goods exported to Germany while the plastics division owes 1 million euros for imported raw materials, a simple internal transfer of the euros from chemicals to plastics can hedge against foreign exchange risk while avoiding the cost of forward contracts.

For smaller, less internationalized firms, forward markets provide the most widely used method of managing foreign exchange risk. By allowing a firm to contract to buy or sell a currency in the future at a prespecified price, forward markets facilitate planning by eliminating uncertainty about the domestic-currency value of future revenues earned in foreign currencies and about future costs owed in foreign currencies. Forward contracts can be expensive, however, especially during times when foreign exchange market participants perceive exchange risk to be high—exactly when firms would most want to hedge. Also, banks typically offer forward contracts in only a few major currencies and only for relatively short durations (typically less than two years). For other currencies and longer-term risks, firms must pursue other strategies to cover their foreign exchange risk.

One strategy to avoid losses due to currency fluctuations is to design contracts that allow flexibility in the timing of receipts and payments. A U.S. firm importing ¥1 billion of goods from Japan may request contract terms that allow payment at any time within a 180-day period following the delivery date. If the U.S. firm expects the dollar to appreciate against the yen, the firm may postpone payment as long as possible to obtain the best expected price on the yen. If, on the other hand, the firm expects the dollar to depreciate, the firm may pay the bill right away to avoid the possibility that the dollar price of yen will rise. The same idea can be used to alter the timing of foreign-currency-denominated export receipts.

Another strategy involves holding domestic bank deposits denominated in foreign exchange. As of 1990, U.S. firms can hold such accounts, insured by the Federal Deposit Insurance Corporation. The accounts, with minimum deposits of $20,000–$25,000, are invested in foreign time deposits (CDs) with maturities of three months to one year. But, again, a relatively small number of currencies are available.

Still another possibility is a financial instrument called an *option contract.* Buying an option contract guarantees the buyer the right to purchase (or sell) a specified quantity of a currency at a future date for a predetermined price called the *strike price.* The contracts are called *options* because the buyer has the option whether to exercise the contract; forward or futures contracts, in contrast, obligate the buyer to accept delivery at the specified date and price. Option contracts for future purchases of a currency are *calls,* and options for future sales are *puts.* Figure 11 reproduces a set of price quotations for currency options.

A call option guarantees that the holder of the contract won't have to pay a price higher than the contract's strike price, because the owner will exercise the call if the spot price exceeds the strike price. (*Why?*) Note in Figure 11 that call-option prices rise for contracts with lower strike prices. A put option guarantees that the holder won't have to sell currency for a price below the strike price; the owner will exercise the put if the spot price is below the strike price. (*Why?*) For puts, note that prices rise for contracts with higher strike prices. Option contracts therefore provide the opportunity to combine hedging and speculation. The holder of an option contract can still enjoy the benefits of favorable movements in the exchange rate (the speculative

---

19. These techniques can't eliminate foreign exchange risk, but they transfer the risk from one party to another.

Figure 11   **Quotations on Foreign Exchange Futures Option Contracts**

FUTURES OPTIONS PRICES

STRIKE	CALLS-SETTLE			PUTS-SETTLE		

Japanese Yen (CME)

12,500,000 yen; cents per 100 yen

Price	Oct	Nov	Dec	Oct	Nov	Dec
8900	0.00	0.00	2.21	0.12	0.40	0.65
8950	0.00	0.00	1.90	0.20	0.55	0.83
9000	0.90	1.31	1.60	0.33	0.74	1.03
9050	0.62	1.05	1.34	0.55	0.98	1.27
9100	0.41	0.83	1.12	0.84	1.26	1.55
9150	0.26	0.64	0.92	1.19	1.57	1.85

Est vol 641 Tu 346 calls 226 puts
Op int Tues 19,410 calls 14,065 puts

Canadian Dollar (CME)

100,000 Can.$, cents per Can.$

Price	Oct	Nov	Dec	Oct	Nov	Dec
7750	1.17	0.00	1.66	0.12	0.38	0.61
7800	0.77	1.10	1.35	0.22	0.55	0.80
7850	0.43	0.81	1.07	0.38	0.76	1.02
7900	0.24	0.60	0.85	0.69	0.00	0.00
7950	0.00	0.43	0.67	0.00	0.00	0.00
8000	0.06	0.00	0.52	0.00	0.00	0.00

Est vol 1,070 Tu 67 calls 242 puts
Op int Tues 6,464 calls 5,831 puts

British Pound (CME)

62,500 pounds; cents per pound

Price	Oct	Nov	Dec	Oct	Nov	Dec
1780	1.47	2.28	2.96	0.53	1.34	2.02
1790	0.86	1.74	2.44	0.92	1.80	2.50
1800	0.49	1.31	1.98	1.55	0.00	3.04
1810	0.27	0.97	1.58	2.33	0.00	3.63
1820	0.14	0.70	1.25	3.20	0.00	4.30
1830	0.08	0.00	0.98	0.00	0.00	0.00

Est vol 176 Tu 290 calls 135 puts
Op int Tues 4,134 calls 3,610 puts

Swiss Franc (CME)

125,000 francs; cents per franc

Price	Oct	Nov	Dec	Oct	Nov	Dec
7850	1.27	0.00	1.96	0.15	0.51	0.84
7900	0.89	1.31	1.66	0.27	0.69	1.04
7950	0.57	1.03	1.39	0.45	0.91	1.27
8000	0.35	0.79	1.15	0.73	0.00	1.53
8050	0.00	0.00	0.95	0.00	0.00	1.83
8100	0.13	0.46	0.78	1.51	0.00	2.15

Est vol 86 Tu 59 calls 28 puts
Op int Tues 2,473 calls 1,087 puts

Euro Fx (CME)

125,000 euros; cents per euro

Price	Oct	Nov	Dec	Oct	Nov	Dec
12200	1.50	2.09	2.57	0.27	0.86	1.34
12250	1.14	1.78	2.29	0.41	1.05	1.56
12300	0.84	1.50	2.02	0.61	1.27	1.79
12350	0.60	1.26	1.79	0.87	1.53	2.06
12400	0.42	1.05	1.57	1.19	1.82	2.34
12450	0.29	0.86	1.37	0.00	0.00	2.64

Est vol 2,360 Tu 1,520 calls 934 puts
Op int Tues 48,171 calls 26,587 puts

Options contracts give buyers the option to buy or sell currency at a future date at the prespecified strike price.

Source: *The Wall Street Journal*, September 30, 2004.

element) while limiting the effects of unfavorable movements (the hedging element). The Philadelphia Stock Exchange and Chicago Mercantile Exchange dominate currency options markets in the United States.

Some firms follow the ultimate strategy to avoid foreign exchange risk. They insist on being paid in their own currencies even on foreign sales, thereby forcing customers to bear the risk. Such arrangements occur primarily in markets where the selling firm has substantial market power; otherwise, customers can threaten to go to a competitor with more willingness to take on the risk. In 2000–2001, as the British pound appreciated dramatically against the new euro, manufacturers in Britain, including Unilever and Toyota, demanded billing from their suppliers in euros—in order to avoid the painful combination of euro revenues and pound payments. And Airbus, the European commercial aircraft manufacturer, argues that all world trade in commercial aircraft should be denominated in euros (Airbus's home currency) rather than in U.S. dollars (rival Boeing's home currency).

The Asian financial crisis caused many firms that historically had left exchange risk unhedged to reconsider, especially after they were surprised by the dramatic July 1997 devaluation of the Thai baht. But many of the Asian currencies most affected by the crisis—the baht, the Korean won, the Indonesian rupiah, and the Malaysian ringgit, for example—are only thinly traded, so forward contracts are unavailable or very costly. Nonetheless, firms such as computer manufacturer Digital Equipment started to hedge.[20] Dell Computer routinely buys currency options in all currencies in which the company operates. Other firms deliberately took out loans in the Asian currencies in which they expected to earn revenues, so if a devaluation lowered the revenues' dollar value, the firm enjoyed the offsetting benefit of repaying the loan with devalued currency. Avon Cosmetics chose to buy most of its raw materials and do most of the manufacturing for its Asian sales in its biggest Asian markets (China, Indonesia, the Philippines, and Japan); that strategy assured that any devaluation that lowered revenues would also lower costs.[21] The company also denominated its operational loans in local currency and ordered its Asian operations to convert their earnings to dollars weekly rather than monthly.

Traditionally, Asian firms hedged currency risks less than U.S. or European firms, in part because so many Asian countries pegged their currencies to the dollar. Even in November 1997, well into the financial crisis, a survey of 110 chief financial officers (CFOs) at a CFO forum in the Philippines found that only 42 percent hedged their companies' foreign exchange risk. Of those that did, most relied on forward contracts. But as the Asian crisis shook the countries' traditionally pegged exchange rates, more firms began to hedge, using a variety of techniques. Japanese auto manufacturer Mitsubishi responded to the weakness of the Thai baht by boosting production facilities in Thailand and replacing inputs previously imported from Japan with local ones. Since the Asian financial crisis, firms around the world report placing a higher priority on financial market expertise, especially foreign exchange trading, in recruiting for CFO and chief executive officer positions.

CASE 2: PICKING STOCKS MEANS PICKING CURRENCIES

We saw in this chapter that the expected dollar rate of return on a deposit denominated in foreign currency has two components: the interest rate on the deposit plus the expected appreciation or depreciation of the currency relative to the dollar. A similar rule applies to other assets, including stocks. The dollar rate of return on a share of Mexican stock, for example, equals the change in the stock's peso price plus any change in the dollar value of the peso. Table 3 reports rates of return in local currency and in U.S. dollars for 22 countries' stock indexes during 2001.

For most of the countries in the table, the return measured in U.S. dollars differed significantly from the local-currency return. In South Africa, a large depreciation of the rand turned a large positive local-currency return on stocks into a significantly negative dollar return. Mexico, on the other hand, experienced a peso appreciation against the dollar, so dollar stock returns there exceed the local-currency ones. Hong Kong, with its fixed exchange rate relative to the U.S. dollar, exhibited equal returns in both currencies.

Anyone owning stock in a foreign firm experiences a rate of return that reflects both the firm's performance and changes in the value of the foreign currency. Managers of international mutual funds vary widely in the degree to which they hedge to avoid this foreign exchange risk, but funds' policies toward foreign exchange rarely appear in the fund prospectus.[22]

---

20. Darren McDermott, "Asian Turmoil in Currencies Creates Risks," *The Wall Street Journal*, August 15, 1997.

21. Fred R. Bleakley, "How U.S. Firm Copes with Asia Crisis," *The Wall Street Journal*, December 26, 1997.

22. For some examples, see "Fund Managers Disagree on Value of Currency Hedging," *The Wall Street Journal*, February 1, 2001.

Table 3 LOCAL-CURRENCY AND DOLLAR STOCK RETURNS, 2001

Market	Percent		Market	Percent	
	Local Currency	Dollar		Local Currency	Dollar
Canada	−15.00%	−20.09%	Hong Kong	−20.53%	−20.52%
U.S.	−13.09	−13.09	Thailand	+6.75	+4.62
Mexico	+13.15	+19.06	Singapore	−14.60	−19.91
Venezuela	−4.27	−11.67	Malaysia	+3.53	+3.52
Brazil	−9.71	−23.85	Indonesia	−12.01	−18.57
Chile	+10.54	−4.08	Japan	−18.79	−29.47
Britain	−14.37	−16.58	South Korea	+51.10	+45.29
France	−18.99	−23.44	Taiwan	+18.37	+11.51
Germany	−19.84	−24.25	Philippines	−24.93	−27.33
Finland	−34.21	−37.83	Australia	+8.44	−1.30
South Africa	+18.81	−24.81	N. Zealand	+12.96	+6.28

Source: Data from *Wall Street Journal*, January 2, 2002.

CASE 3: HERSTATT RISK

On June 26, 1974, German Bankhaus I. D. Herstatt collapsed after major losses on its foreign currency trading operations. German bank regulators closed Herstatt at 3:30 P.M. Frankfurt time. The bank had already *received* the day's payments on its foreign exchange contracts; but, because of the hour, it hadn't yet *made* its dollar payments to U.S. banks. The episode eventually cost U.S. banks about $200 million, and the risk when a bank on one side of a foreign exchange contract fails to pay up had earned a name: Herstatt risk. It is also called settlement risk, since the problem stems from settling payments for foreign exchange contracts across markets in different time zones. When a bank is victimized by a partner's failure to honor a contract, the victim may become unable to honor its own contracts, lacking the foreign currency to do so; so the problem can spread quickly through the world financial system. Healthy banks may refuse to trade with those in trouble, afraid of themselves falling victim to nonpayment. The size of the average currency trade has grown to over $10 million, so failure of even a single transaction can have a large impact.

A 1994 study of the problem by the Federal Reserve Bank of New York found banks lulled into complacency in dealing with each other. A bank would often settle several contracts with a single partner on consecutive days without having received any payment in return, thereby accumulating significant exposure to Herstatt risk. Central bankers issued stern warnings to banks in 1996: (1) Do something as an industry about Herstatt risk or face increased regulation of currency trading, and (2) don't expect to be bailed out by taxpayers if you suffer Herstatt-type losses.

Banks responded by joining netting pools, which pool trades in a particular currency, net out offsetting ones, and settle any differences at the end of the day. Trading in net rather than gross terms reduces significantly the volume of currency traded and the associated risk. In late 2000, Hong Kong became the first Asian market to offer "real-time, gross settlement" in both local currencies and U.S. dollars. Each transaction, regardless of time of day, is settled immediately and for the full gross amount; participants no longer have to wait until New York markets open to get their dollars, thereby reducing Herstatt risk.

An even larger-scale solution, called CLS Bank for "continuous linked settlement," went live in 2002. Headquartered in London but regulated by the U.S. Federal Reserve, CLS Bank handles settlements in seven currencies—the U.S., Canadian, and Australian dollars, euro, yen, British pound, and Swiss franc—for about 70 banks. At midnight Central European Time each day,

CLS Bank announces to each member bank how much of each currency it needs to provide to settle its payments with other member banks. Each bank sends its currency to CLS Bank between 7 and 9 A.M. Payments by CLS to members are made only when both sides of the transaction are ready. As long as member banks play by the rules, CLS Bank members don't face any Herstatt risk when dealing with other member banks.

CASE 4: FOREIGN EXCHANGE MARKET UPDATE

Every three years, the Bank for International Settlements (BIS), an international organization of central banks, conducts its *Triennial Central Bank Survey of Foreign Exchange Market Activity*. The BIS surveys central banks who report on foreign exchange market activity in their respective countries. The most recent survey, completed in April 2004, includes data from 52 central banks on spot, forward, and simple swap foreign exchange transactions.[23] The data are corrected for the two-sidedness of transactions; that is, the total volume of foreign exchange traded is divided by two to arrive at the figures reported in the study. So, how much foreign exchange is traded, which currencies, and where?

Average *daily* turnover in the foreign exchange market rose to $1.9 trillion in the 2004 survey, a growth rate of 36 percent, measured at constant exchange rates, since the 2001 survey.[24] The BIS attributes this rapid growth to increased interest among portfolio managers in foreign currencies for their own sake, as asset alternatives to bonds and stocks. Figure 12 illustrates the division of the $1.9 trillion in daily market turnover between spot, forward, and swap transactions. The figure also includes the BIS's estimate of activity that escaped measurement in the survey due to gaps in reporting, either by the 52 participating central banks or by banks that did not participate.

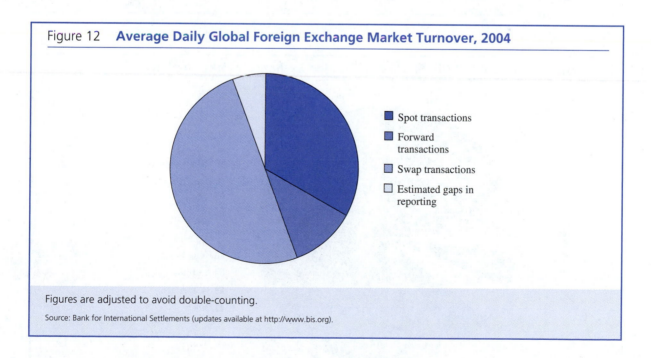

Figure 12   **Average Daily Global Foreign Exchange Market Turnover, 2004**

- Spot transactions
- Forward transactions
- Swap transactions
- Estimated gaps in reporting

Figures are adjusted to avoid double-counting.

Source: Bank for International Settlements (updates available at http://www.bis.org).

---

23. A simultaneous spot and forward transaction comprises a foreign exchange swap. For example, a bank might buy one million pounds with U.S. dollars today in the spot market and simultaneously agree to sell the million pounds back to the seller in exchange for dollars in 30 days.

24. The study reports figures in dollars, so an appreciation or depreciation of the dollar between triennial surveys generates a decline or an increase in the dollar value of market activity. To correct for these changes, the study also reports the figures at constant exchange rates.

Figure 13   **Currency Distribution of Foreign Exchange Market Turnover**

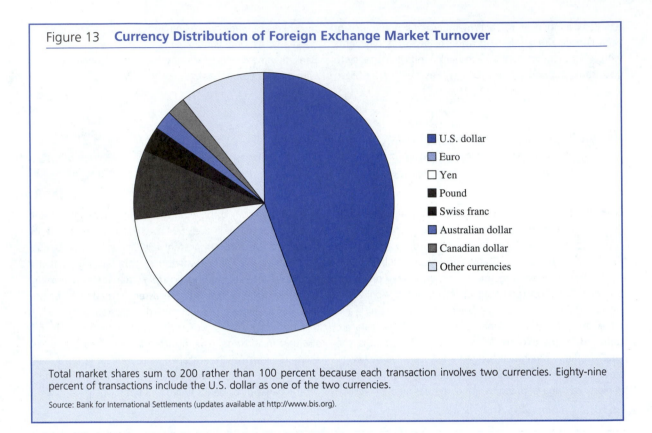

Total market shares sum to 200 rather than 100 percent because each transaction involves two currencies. Eighty-nine percent of transactions include the U.S. dollar as one of the two currencies.

Source: Bank for International Settlements (updates available at http://www.bis.org).

Figure 14   **Geographical Distribution of Foreign Exchange Market Activity**

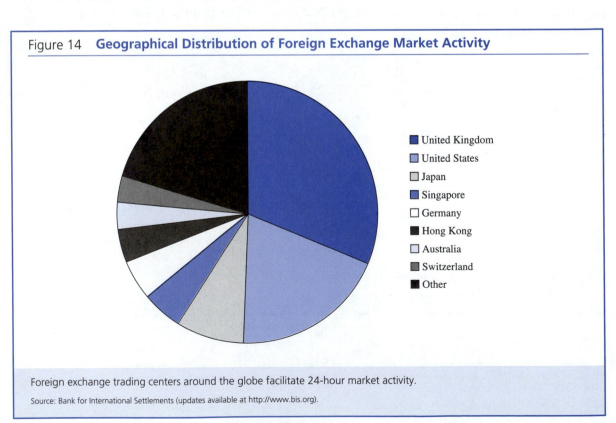

Foreign exchange trading centers around the globe facilitate 24-hour market activity.

Source: Bank for International Settlements (updates available at http://www.bis.org).

Figure 13 divides daily foreign exchange market turnover into the market share attributed to each currency. Note that, because each transaction involves two currencies, the reported shares sum to 200 percent rather than 100 percent. Of that 200 percent, 180 percent is attributable to just 9 currencies. Another 15 currencies, including those of the smaller industrialized economies such as Denmark and New Zealand, along with the major emerging economies such as Korea and Mexico, account for another 15 percent of transactions. All the rest of the world's currencies are represented in just 6.1 percent of transactions. So, despite the growth and spread of international trade and financial activity, turnover in the foreign exchange market still reflects the central roles played by a relatively small number of vehicle currencies.

The fact that foreign exchange transactions can be conducted electronically at very low cost means that market locations throughout the world are tightly linked through arbitrage. The exchange rate between dollars and euros, for example, will be virtually identical in all major market centers. Half of all transactions occur in the United Kingdom or United States. Figure 14 reports other important foreign exchange trading centers. Note that they're arrayed around the globe—so the market can function 24 hours per day.

SUMMARY

This chapter outlined foreign exchange markets' role in the world economy. Transactions involving more than one currency are a hallmark of international trade and finance. Activities in the foreign exchange market include clearing, arbitrage, hedging, and speculation, as portfolio owners choose assets with the highest expected rates of return. These activities create relationships among interest rates, spot and forward exchange rates, and expected exchange rates called *covered* and *uncovered interest parity*. The chapter used a partial-equilibrium demand and supply framework based on interest parity to examine the determination of the spot exchange rate along with the mechanics of the two simplest exchange rate regimes—a flexible-rate system and a fixed-rate system.

LOOKING AHEAD

The next chapter introduces the balance of payments as the summary of all transactions of domestic individuals, firms, and governments with their foreign counterparts. It examines the various accounts of the balance of payments and explores some popular but misleading misconceptions.

KEY TERMS

money price
relative price
exchange rate
foreign exchange market
asset
asset portfolio
spot foreign exchange market
clearing
arbitrage
inconsistent cross rates
triangular arbitrage
hedging
foreign exchange risk
short position
balanced (closed) position
speculation
30-day forward rate
forward premium
forward discount

expected future spot rate
uncovered interest parity
interest differential
covered interest parity
offshore deposits (Eurocurrencies)
demand curve for a foreign currency
supply curve for a foreign currency
exchange rate regime
flexible (floating) exchange rate
depreciation
appreciation
fixed (pegged) exchange rate
intervention
revaluation
foreign exchange reserves
devaluation
bilateral exchange rate
effective exchange rate

PROBLEMS AND QUESTIONS FOR REVIEW

1. Assume that a fixed exchange rate regime is in effect.
   a. Countries A and B have agreed to peg the exchange rate between their currencies (the alpha, α, and the beta, β, respectively) at $\alpha 1/\beta 2$. Initially, this exchange rate corresponds to equilibrium in the foreign exchange market. Illustrate the initial situation in the market for beta-denominated deposits; be sure to label your graph carefully.
   b. Country A undertakes an economic policy that lowers the interest rate on alpha-denominated deposits (i^{α}). Explain and illustrate the effects of the policy in the market for beta-denominated deposits.
   c. If the two countries want to maintain the original exchange rate of $\alpha 1/\beta 2$, what must Alphabank (country A's central bank) do?
   d. Time passes, and the situation remains as described in part (c). Individuals in the two countries begin to anticipate a change in the pegged exchange rate. What type of change (that is, in which direction) would they be likely to expect? Why?
   e. Illustrate how the change in expectations described in part (d) would affect the market for beta-denominated deposits. Would the expectations make a change in the actual exchange rate more likely or less likely? Would the expectations be likely to make any change in the exchange rate larger or smaller? Why?
   f. Can your answers to parts (d) and (e) help explain the observation that policy makers and central bankers in countries facing likely currency devaluations often publicly deny that any devaluation is forthcoming? Why? Might there be a long-run cost to repeating such denials that turn out to be false? Why?

2. In 1998, India marketed $2 billion worth of Resurgent India bonds to Indians living abroad. The five-year bonds are denominated in foreign currency, not Indian rupees. Explain in what sense this transfers the foreign exchange risk from buyers of the bonds to the Indian government.

3. You have $2,000. The current interest rates on dollar- and pound-denominated deposits for 180-day maturity are $i^{\$} = 0.02$ (2 percent) and $i^{£} = 0.03$ (3 percent), respectively. The current spot exchange rate is $e = \$2/£1$.
   a. What are your three basic choices of strategy over the next 180 days?
   b. If you (and everyone else) were certain that the exchange rate between dollars and pounds would not change over the next 180 days, what would you do? What would you have at the end of 180 days?
   c. Assume that you do not mind bearing foreign exchange risk. You expect the spot rate in 180 days to be $1.90/£1. What strategy would you follow, and why? After 180 days, the actual spot rate turns out to be $1.80/£1. Are you pleased with your decision? Why or why not?
   d. Now assume you are risk averse. The 180-day forward rate is $2.02/£1. What strategy do you follow?

4. On July 30, 2002, an article entitled "Yen's Mood Swings Raise Hackles," appeared in the *Financial Times*. The first paragraph in the article read, "Someone, somewhere is always angry about the yen. Either it is too hot or too cold, it seems, but rarely is it at the right temperature." Explain why, given what you learned about exchange rates in the chapter, someone, somewhere is likely always to be angry about the exchange value of every currency.

5. Suppose wheat sells for $3.00 per bushel in the United States and for 90 rubles per bushel in Russia. Ignoring transportation costs, what exchange rate between the dollar and the ruble would make consumers indifferent between buying U.S. and Russian wheat? Explain.

6. On January 31, 2000, *The Wall Street Journal* reported, "The euro's sharp plunge against the U.S. dollar last week has forced Europe's policy makers to confront the question of what, if anything, they should do about it. They have four options: do nothing, talk it up, intervene, or raise interest rates." Explain each of the four options using the basic supply/demand diagram of the foreign exchange market between the dollar and the euro.

7. As of September 8, 1992, the exchange rate between the Swedish krona and the dollar was $1/k5.5. The interest rate on krona-denominated deposits was 0.12 (or 12 percent), and the interest rate on dollar-denominated deposits was 0.03 (or 3 percent).
   a. Assume that the foreign exchange market is in equilibrium given the situation described. Is the *expected* spot exchange rate between the krona and the dollar closer to $1/k5.0, $1/k5.5, or $1/k6.0? (*Hint: There's no need for complicated numerical calculations.*) Explain

how you know, and provide the equation for equilibrium in the foreign exchange market that you used to arrive at your answer. Illustrate the equilibrium in a graph of the foreign exchange market between the dollar and the krona. Be sure to label your graph.

b. On September 9, 1992, the expected future spot rate fell. Illustrate the effects of the change in expectations on the graph of the foreign exchange market. If policy makers did nothing, what would happen to the exchange rate? Explain why.

c. Instead of doing nothing, Swedish policy makers raised interest rates on krona-denominated deposits. Use the equation for equilibrium in the foreign exchange market and your graph of the foreign exchange market to explain and illustrate the effect of the Swedish policy.

d. After several days, Swedish policy makers reduced interest rates on krona-denominated deposits back to about 0.12 (or 12 percent), their original level. Yet the exchange rate between the krona and the dollar remained approximately unchanged in the short run. What could account for this scenario? (*Hint: What effect, if any, might the temporary rise in interest rates have on exchange rate expectations? Why?*)

8. Comment on the following statements.

a. "In 1993, short-term Mexican bonds paid an interest rate of over 17 percent, Argentine bonds over 23 percent, Indonesian certificates of deposit over 15 percent, and Philippine Treasury bills over 12 percent. U.S. interest rates on dollar-denominated assets during the same period ranged from 3 to 6 percent, depending on the type of asset. This is proof that portfolio owners don't pursue high rates of return. Otherwise, no one would have held any dollar assets in 1993."

b. "During 1992, Brazil's currency depreciated by 95 percent against the dollar, Turkey's lira by 46 percent, Peru's new sol by 41 percent, Poland's zloty by 34 percent, and Russia's ruble by 100 percent. Surely no one holds deposits denominated in these currencies, because of their volatility."

REFERENCES AND SELECTED READINGS

Coughlin, Cletus C., and Patricia S. Pollard. "A Question of Measurement: Is the Dollar Rising or Falling?" Federal Reserve Bank of St. Louis, *Review* (July–August 1996): 3–18.
Introduction to measures of the effective exchange rate.

Dominguez, Kathryn M., and Jeffrey A. Frankel. *Does Foreign Exchange Intervention Work?* Washington, D.C.: Institute for International Economics, 1993.
Examination of the ability of intervention to affect exchange rates; for intermediate students.

Frankel, J. A., and A. K. Rose. "Empirical Research on Nominal Exchange Rates." In *Handbook of International Economics*, Vol. 3, edited by G. M. Grossman and K. Rogoff, 1689–1730. Amsterdam: North-Holland, 1995.
Survey of what economists know from empirical work on foreign exchange markets; for intermediate to advanced students.

Giddy, Ian H. *Global Financial Markets*. Lexington, Mass.: D. C. Heath, 1994.
Textbook covering international financial markets; for intermediate students.

International Monetary Fund. *Exchange Arrangements and Foreign Exchange Markets*. Washington, D.C.: IMF, 2003.
How countries' exchange arrangements have changed over time; for all students.

Isard, Peter. *Exchange Rate Economics*. Cambridge: Cambridge University Press, 1995.
Excellent survey for advanced students.

Neely, Christopher J. "Are Changes in Foreign Exchange Reserves Well Correlated with Official Intervention?" Federal Reserve Bank of St. Louis, *Review* 82 (September/October 2000): 17–32.
Empirical investigation of how accurately changes in reserves reflect intervention; for intermediate and advanced students.

Pollard, Patricia S. "The Creation of the Euro and the Role of the Dollar in International Markets." Federal Reserve Bank of St. Louis, *Review* (September/October 2001): 17–36.
How will the euro affect international use of the dollar? For all students.

Tavlas, George S. "The International Use of Currencies: The U.S. Dollar and the Euro." *Finance and Development* (June 1998): 46–49.
Why a few currencies dominate international transactions; for all students.

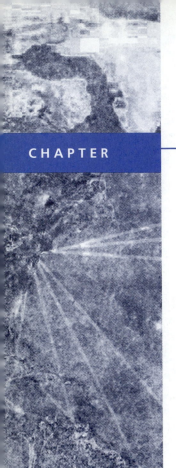

3

The Balance-of-Payments Accounts

1 INTRODUCTION

Countries differ widely in their degree of *openness*, or the extent to which they engage in economic activity across international boundaries. The United States is, by world standards, a relatively closed economy, as measured by its ratio of exports or imports to gross domestic product (GNP), although its degree of openness has increased in recent years. Between 1965 and 2002, U.S. **merchandise exports** (exports of physical goods) rose from 4 to 6.7 percent of GDP and merchandise imports from 3 to 11.6 percent. These trade percentages remain small, but fewer than ten countries have GDPs as large as U.S. merchandise exports!

Table 1 provides a perspective on openness by reporting merchandise exports as a share of GNP for a sample of countries. The ratios range from 10 percent of GNP in India to 98 percent in Malaysia, an economy that specializes in assembly and trade.

Although important, merchandise trade is only one of many types of economic activity that occur internationally. Another significant dimension of openness is trade in **services**—banking, insurance, travel, transportation, consulting, and other economic activities in which the item traded isn't a physical good. Trade in services represents one of the fastest-growing areas in the world economy, although data are difficult to obtain because of measurement problems. The developed economies traditionally have been net exporters of services; that is, the value of their service exports has exceeded that of their service imports, because of their highly developed markets in banking and insurance and their populations of skilled consultants. Table 2 reports commercial service exports for the same sample of countries covered in Table 1.

Financial and investment activities such as purchases and sales of stocks, bonds, and other financial assets and of physical capital such as factories, machines, and land constitute a third major category of international transactions. Reductions in transportation and communication costs have resulted in growing internationalization of both production and financial markets. It's no longer unusual for a U.S.-based firm to buy a plant in Asia financed with bonds sold worldwide and denominated in several currencies. Table 3 summarizes the magnitude of net private international investment flows for our sample countries.

A set of accounts called the country's **balance-of-payments (BOP) accounts** summarizes all these transactions by individuals, firms, and governments of one country with their counterparts in the rest of the world. Like any single set of numbers, the BOP accounts can't capture the full extent of the complex economic interactions among countries. In addition, a number of misconceptions that cause both confusion and bad

Table 1 MERCHANDISE EXPORTS AS A PERCENTAGE OF GNP, 2002 (PERCENT)

Country	Exports as Percent of GNP	Country	Exports as Percent of GNP
India	10%	Mexico	25%
Brazil	13	China[a]	26
Central African Republic	15	Russia	31
Mozambique	19	Hungary	52
Malawi	25	Malaysia	98

[a]Excludes Hong Kong.

Source: World Bank.

Table 2 COMMERCIAL SERVICE EXPORTS, 2002 (MILLIONS $)

Country	Commercial Service Exports	Country	Commercial Service Exports
India	$24,553	Mexico	$12,474
Brazil	8,844	China[a]	39,381
Central African Republic	n.a.	Russia	13,453
Mozambique	249	Hungary	7,726
Malawi	49	Malaysia	14,753

[a]Excludes Hong Kong.

Source: World Bank.

Table 3 NET PRIVATE INVESTMENT FLOWS, 2002 (MILLIONS $)

Country	Net Private Investment Flows	Country	Net Private Investment Flows
India	$4,944	Mexico	$10,261
Brazil	9,861	China[a]	47,107
Central African Republic	4	Russia	8,011
Mozambique	381	Hungary	221
Malawi	6	Malaysia	4,807

[a]Excludes Hong Kong.

Source: World Bank.

economic policy surround the balance-of-payments accounts. This chapter introduces the fundamental definitions and mechanics of the balance-of-payments accounts, explores the associated misconceptions, and relates the accounts to the currency markets and exchange rates we learned about in the previous chapter.

2 WHAT'S IN THE BALANCE-OF-PAYMENTS ACCOUNTS?

The balance-of-payments accounts summarize all the transactions undertaken by residents of one country with the rest of the world, so we can divide them into subaccounts that correspond to the various categories of international transactions in which individuals, firms, and governments participate. The actual balance-of-payments accounts, as reported quarterly for the United States by the Department of Commerce, are quite complex, involving about 70 categories of transactions. Table 4 reproduces a recent report.

For our purposes, a much simpler classification will suffice. Individuals and firms engage in international transactions when they buy or sell goods or services abroad; borrow or lend abroad (that is, sell or buy financial assets); or buy or sell buildings, equipment, or land located abroad. Government agencies also can engage in any of these transactions plus other "official" transactions outside the province of private individuals and firms. We can use this simple classification to define three basic accounts: the current account, the (nonofficial) capital and financial account, and the official settlements account.

As we'll see, the balance-of-payments accounts consist of a **double-entry bookkeeping system**. This means that each international transaction appears twice, because every transaction has two sides. For example, when the United States exports a Boeing plane to Britain, Britain also makes a payment to the United States. The plane flows in one direction, while the payment flows in the other; *both* enter the double-entry bookkeeping system of the balance-of-payments accounts of *both* the United States and Britain. Or, when a U.S. firm buys a factory in China, the title to the factory flows from China to the United States *and* payment for the factory from the United States to China; two entries appear in each country's balance-of-payments accounts. Often the two entries reflecting the two sides of a single transaction occur in different accounts (for example, one in the current account and one in the capital and financial account). But before we can analyze the dual entries for various types of transactions, we must understand the differences among the current, capital and financial, and official settlements accounts.

2.1 What Goes in the Current Account?

The major categories of transactions within the **current account** are (1) merchandise exports and imports, (2) imports and exports of military services, travel and transportation, and other services, (3) current income received and paid on international investments, and (4) unilateral transfers, including worker remittances and pension payments. Table 5 reports the status of the various current-account components for the United States.

Each category of current-account transactions includes both exports by the United States (entered as **credits** [+] in the bookkeeping sense because they generate *receipts from foreigners to U.S. residents*) and imports by the United States from the rest of the world (entered as **debits** [−] because they generate *payments* from U.S. residents to foreigners). A net value entered with a negative sign means that imports (payments by U.S. residents) exceeded exports (receipts) in that category; a positive value represents exports (receipts) in excess of imports (payments).

Table 4   U.S. INTERNATIONAL TRANSACTIONS, 2003 (MILLIONS $)[a]

Line		2003
	Current Account	
1	**Exports of goods and services and income receipts**	**1,314,888**
2	Exports of goods and services	1,020,503
3	Goods, balance of payments basis	713,122
4	Services	307,381
5	Transfers under U.S. military agency sales contracts	12,491
6	Travel	64,509
7	Passenger fares	15,693
8	Other transportation	31,833
9	Royalties and license fees	48,227
10	Other private services	133,818
11	U.S. government miscellaneous services	810
12	Income receipts	294,385
13	Income receipts on U.S.-owned assets abroad	291,354
14	Direct investment receipts	187,522
15	Other private receipts	99,135
16	U.S. government receipts	4,697
17	Compensation of employees	3,031
18	**Imports of goods and services and income payments**	**−1,778,117**
19	Imports of goods and services	−1,517,011
20	Goods, balance of payments basis	−1,260,674
21	Services	−256,337
22	Direct defense expenditures	−25,117
23	Travel	−56,613
24	Passenger fares	−20,957
25	Other transportation	−44,768
26	Royalties and license fees	−20,049
27	Other private services	−85,829
28	U.S. government miscellaneous services	−3,004
29	Income payments	−261,106
30	Income payments on foreign-owned assets in the United States	−252,573
31	Direct investment payments	−68,657
32	Other private payments	−111,874
33	U.S. government payments	−72,042
34	Compensation of employees	−8,533
35	**Unilateral current transfers, net**	**−67,439**
36	U.S. government grants	−21,865
37	U.S. government pensions and other transfers	−5,341
38	Private remittances and other transfers	−40,233
	Capital and Financial Account	
	Capital Account	
39	**Capital account transactions, net**	**−3,079**

(continues)

Table 4   *(continued)*

Line		2003
	Financial account	
40	**U.S.-owned assets abroad, net (increase/financial outflow (−))**	**−283,414**
41	U.S. official reserve assets, net	−1523
42	Gold	
43	Special drawing rights	601
44	Reserve position in the International Monetary Fund	1,494
45	Foreign currencies	−572
46	U.S. government assets, other than official reserve assets, net	573
47	U.S. credits and other long-term assets	−7,279
48	Repayments on U.S. credits and other long-term assets	7,981
49	U.S. foreign currency holdings and U.S. short-term assets, net	−165
50	U.S. private assets, net	−285,474
51	Direct investment	−173,799
52	Foreign securities	−72,337
53	U.S. claims on unaffiliated foreigners reported by U.S. nonbanking concerns	−28,932
54	U.S. claims reported by U.S. banks, not included elsewhere	−10,406
55	**Foreign-owned assets in the United States, net (increase/financial inflow (+))**	**829,173**
56	Foreign official assets in the United States, net	248,573
57	U.S. government securities	194,568
58	U.S. Treasury securities	169,685
59	Other	24,883
60	Other U.S. government liabilities	−564
61	U.S. liabilities reported by U.S. banks, not included elsewhere	49,420
62	Other foreign official assets	5,149
63	Other foreign assets in the United States, net	580,600
64	Direct investment	39,890
65	U.S. Treasury securities	113,432
66	U.S. securities other than U.S. Treasury securities	250,981
67	U.S. currency	16,640
68	U.S. liabilities to unaffiliated foreigners reported by U.S. nonbanking concerns	84,014
69	U.S. liabilities reported by U.S. banks, not included elsewhere	75,643
70	**Statistical discrepancy (sum of above items with sign reversed)**	**−12,012**
70a	*Of which*: Seasonal adjustment discrepancy	
	Memoranda:	
71	Balance on goods (lines 3 and 20)	−547,522
72	Balance on services (lines 4 and 21)	51,044
73	Balance on goods and services (lines 2 and 19)	−496,508
74	Balance on income (lines 12 and 29)	33,279
75	Unilateral current transfers, net (line 35)	−67,439
76	Balance on current account (lines 1, 18, and 35 or lines 73, 74, and 75)	−530,668

[a]Credits (+), debits (−).

Source: U.S. Department of Commerce (quarterly updates are available at the department's Web site, http://www.bea.doc.gov).

Year	Net Merchandise Trade	Net Services Exports	Net Investment Income	Net Unilateral Transfers	Current-Account Balance
1960	$4,892	−$1,382	$3,379	−$4,062	$2,824
1965	4,951	−287	5,350	−4,583	5,431
1970	2,603	−349	6,233	−6,156	2,331
1975	8,903	3,503	12,787	−7,075	18,116
1980	−25,500	6,093	30,073	−8,349	2,317
1985	−122,173	295	20,592	−22,700	−123,987
1990	−109,030	27,901	24,174	−34,669	−91,624
1995	−173,729	73,838	19,275	−34,638	−115,254
2000	−449,468	80,988	−13,656	−53,241	−435,377
2003	−547,552	51,044	33,279	−67,439	−530,668

Table 5 U.S. CURRENT ACCOUNT, 1960–2003 (MILLIONS $)

Source: U.S. Department of Commerce (updates are available at the department's Web site, http://www.bea.doc.gov).

The final column in Table 5 reports the **current-account balance**. This equals the sum of all the other entries and represents the difference between total exports or receipts (credits) by U.S. residents for current transactions and total imports or payments (debits) by U.S. residents for current transactions. Again, a negative value implies that debits exceed credits. To understand better the various categories in Table 5, we can illustrate each with examples of typical entries.

MERCHANDISE TRADE The largest source of credits in the U.S. current account is merchandise exports. This category includes shipments abroad of a variety of items: agricultural products, high-technology goods such as the software exported by Microsoft, and the aircraft exported by Boeing. The sum of the value of all the goods exported by American individuals, firms, and government agencies (excluding the military) equals merchandise exports. Imports of goods include the value of all U.S. merchandise purchases: automobiles from Japan, coffee from Brazil, crude oil from Saudi Arabia, DVD players from South Korea, and apparel from China.

Since the mid-1970s, the value of U.S. merchandise imports has exceeded the value of U.S. merchandise exports; this is called a **deficit** on the **merchandise trade balance**. During the 1950s and 1960s, the United States ran a **surplus** on its merchandise trade balance; that is, the value of exports exceeded the value of imports. For the past few years, the large U.S. merchandise trade deficit (reaching well over $500 billion in 2003) has received much attention.[1] Pundits have proposed many policies for reducing the deficit, often claimed to cause "export of jobs" and "deindustrialization." Unfortunately, many of the policy proposals amount to protectionism, as they attempt to restrict imports from countries with a comparative advantage in the production of items such as steel, automobiles, apparel, and footwear. We'll explore some misconceptions surrounding the effects of a merchandise trade deficit later. For now, note that the merchandise trade balance is only one of several components of the current account, which in turn is only

1. For example, the U.S. government commissioned a 12-member panel to study the issue. You can find their 2000 report (U.S. Trade Deficit Review Commission, *The U.S. Trade Deficit*) at http://govinfo.library.unt.edu/tdrc.

one of several components of the balance-of-payments accounts. A deficit in the merchandise trade balance is *not* the same as a balance-of-payments deficit (a concept we haven't yet defined), although the popular press often confuses the two.

SERVICES   The services category of current-account transactions includes military transactions, travel and transportation, royalties, education, accounting, banking, insurance, and consulting. A U.S. resident vacationing in France or attending Oxford University imports a service; that import enters the U.S. balance-of-payments accounts as a current-account debit because it involves a payment to foreigners. When Mexico hires a U.S. petroleum engineer to work in its oil industry, the United States, in effect, exports the consultant's services to Mexico, a credit in services from the U.S. point of view. The United States typically runs a surplus (credits > debits) in the services account, primarily because U.S. firms provide large shares of the insurance, transportation, and financial services that constitute integral parts of international economic activity.

Net merchandise trade and net services trade often are combined to report the **balance on goods and services,** or the value of U.S. exports of goods and services (credits) minus the value of U.S. imports of goods and services (debits).

INVESTMENT INCOME   The third category of transactions in the current account captures interest, dividends, and other income Americans receive from investments they own abroad (credits) and payments by Americans to foreigners as income earned on foreign-owned investments in the United States (debits). This account does *not* include any flows of new investments but merely the current income from investments made previously. Included as credits are all interest, dividends, and other income earned by American residents on the $7 trillion of foreign assets they own. To remember that these receipts are credits, it helps to recall that they involve payments *to* U.S. residents *from* foreigners, just as U.S. merchandise exports (which are credits) do. Debit entries include all the interest, dividends, and other income paid to owners of the approximately $9 trillion of foreign-owned assets in the United States. Like U.S. merchandise imports, these represent debits on the U.S. current account because they involve payments *from* U.S. residents *to* foreigners. Despite the fact that the value of U.S. assets owned by foreigners exceeds the value of foreign assets owned by U.S. residents, the United States runs a small surplus in the net investment income subaccount.

UNILATERAL TRANSFERS   The final category of current-account transactions, unilateral transfers, covers transactions that aren't purchases or sales of either goods or services. Unilateral debits include U.S. nonmilitary aid to foreign countries (government aid or private charity); worker remittances, or funds sent back to the home country by individuals working in the United States; and pensions paid to former U.S. residents now living abroad. The United States consistently runs a deficit in unilateral transfers.

CURRENT-ACCOUNT BALANCE   The sum of the current-account components—merchandise trade, services, investment income, and unilateral transfers—equals the country's current-account balance. As Table 5 reports, in most years between World War II and the late 1970s the United States had a current-account surplus, although occasionally current-account debits exceeded current-account credits. Since the late 1970s, however, a deficit has characterized the current account, reaching over $500 billion in 2003.

The sum of a country's current-account credits is analogous to the total of an individual's current income, and the total of current-account debits corresponds to the total of an individual's current expenditures. A current-account surplus (credits > debits) is similar to a situation in which an individual's current income exceeds current expenditures. A deficit on the current account (debits > credits) matches the situation of an individual whose current expenditures exceed current income.

Just as current income and expenditures fail to capture all the relevant dimensions of an individual's economic situation, the current account gives an incomplete record of a country's transactions with the rest of the world. In both cases, the primary items missing include borrowing and lending activity, purchases and sales of assets, and changes in money balances. For an individual, if current income exceeds current expenditures, the "excess" income must be used to make new loans, pay off old loans, buy an asset (such as a house or shares of stock), or increase money balances (for example, a checking account). On the other hand, if an individual's current expenditures exceed current income, the difference must be covered by borrowing, selling an asset, or running down money balances. A similar logic applies for a country and carries us beyond the current account to the other balance-of-payments accounts.

2.2 What Goes in the Capital Account?

The **capital account** records international borrowing and lending and purchases and sales of assets.[2] When a U.S. resident (individual, firm, or government agency) purchases a foreign asset or makes a foreign loan, the asset or IOU is imported into the United States and enters as a debit in the U.S. capital account, known as a **capital outflow**. The asset could be a bond issued by a British firm, a house in France, or shares of stock in a Japanese company. The way to remember that a capital outflow is a debit (like the *import* of a good) is to think of it as *importation* of the title to the asset or of the IOU. Capital outflows from the United States represent *increases* in U.S. ownership of foreign assets. The figure reported in the capital account of the balance-of-payments accounts is a net value; it reflects the net increase (if negative) or decrease (if positive) in U.S. ownership of foreign assets, because debits (payments to foreigners) enter the balance-of-payments accounts with a negative sign and credits (receipts from foreigners) with a positive sign.

One effect of using net figures in the balance-of-payments accounts is to make the volumes of capital flows appear much smaller than they actually are. For example, if one U.S. resident purchases $10 million worth of bonds from a British firm and another individual sells $9 million worth of Japanese bonds, the figure in the U.S. capital account will report a net capital outflow of $1 million ($9 million − $10 million), even though $19 million of bonds have changed hands. Also, annual balance-of-payments accounts don't reflect purchases of foreign assets resold within the same year.

Credit transactions in the capital account occur when foreign residents buy assets such as bonds, stocks, or land in the United States. It may help to think of the United States as *exporting* the titles to the assets or IOUs for the loans; thus, these **capital inflows** are credits in the U.S. balance-of-payments accounts, as are *exports* of goods. Capital inflows also are reported in net terms, so the figure reflects the net increase (or decrease, if negative) in foreign ownership of U.S. assets.

The difference between net capital inflows and net capital outflows is the capital-account balance: a surplus if inflows (= credits) > outflows (= debits) and a deficit if inflows < outflows.[3] Until recently, the United States consistently ran a capital-account deficit, buying more assets abroad than the rest of the world bought in the United States.

---

2. Strictly speaking, what we call the *capital account* is now called the *capital and financial account* in government reports. However, both to keep things simple and for consistency with popular usage, we'll call it just the *capital account*.

3. The account as reported by the Department of Commerce includes all borrowing/lending and purchases/sales of assets by individuals, firms, and governments. For our purposes, we exclude transactions by central banks—changes in official reserve assets—and report them separately as the official settlements account to be discussed in the next section. Other borrowing/lending and purchases/sales of assets by governments are part of the (nonofficial) capital account.

Table 6   **U.S. NONOFFICIAL CAPITAL ACCOUNT, 1960–2003 (MILLIONS $)**

Year	Net U.S. Purchases of Assets Abroad (Increase or Capital Outflow [−])	Net Foreign Purchases of U.S. Assets (Increase or Capital Inflow [+])	Nonofficial Capital-Account Balance
1960	−$6,244	$821	−$5,423
1965	−6,941	607	−6,334
1970	−11,818	−550	−12,368
1975	−38,854	10,143	−28,711
1980	−78,813	47,115	−31,698
1985	−36,032	147,501	111,469
1990	−71,853	107,082	35,229
1995	−317,711	355,681	37,970
2000	−553,059	916,521	363,462
2003	−288,016	580,600	292,584

Source: U.S. Department of Commerce (updates are available at the department's Web site, http://www.bea.doc.gov).

The 1980s, however, brought a change in the pattern: The pace of U.S. investment abroad slowed dramatically (though only temporarily), while the growth of foreign investment in the United States accelerated. Table 6 reports the U.S. capital-account balance.[4]

Again, an analogy with an individual helps clarify the role of capital-account transactions in the world economy. At the individual level, net capital outflows represent the net change in the individual's lending plus purchases of other assets. Net capital inflows represent the individual's net change in borrowing plus sales of assets. A surplus in the capital account occurs when net capital inflows exceed net capital outflows. The capital account is in deficit when the overall flow of capital out of a country exceeds the flow coming in. Note the somewhat counterintuitive terminology here: A capital-account *surplus* denotes a *decline* in the net domestic ownership of foreign assets, while a capital-account *deficit* corresponds to an *increase* in such ownership.

2.3   What Goes in the Official Settlements Balance?

Unlike the current and capital accounts, all transactions in the official settlements account are conducted by "official" government authorities, usually central banks, rather than by individuals or firms. The **official settlements balance** reports the net change in a country's stock of foreign exchange reserves (see section 7 in the previous chapter) and official government borrowing.[5] Increases in the level of U.S. reserves or decreases in the

---

4. Official transactions aren't included but are discussed separately in the next section under the official settlements account; therefore, the figures in Table 6 refer to the nonofficial capital account.

5. For simplicity, we assume that all transactions in the official settlements account represent changes in the levels of official foreign exchange reserves resulting from intervention in foreign exchange markets. In reality, several other types of transactions can show up in the account. For example, if a foreign central bank (say, the Bank of Japan) reduces its reserve holdings of a currency (such as the euro) by selling the currency and buying U.S. Treasury bills, the transaction will appear as an increase in foreign official holdings in the United States (a credit in the U.S. official settlements account) even though the purpose was not to intervene in foreign exchange markets to affect the exchange rate between yen and dollars. In addition, government agencies other than the central bank (for example, the U.S. Treasury Department through its Exchange Stabilization Fund) occasionally intervene in foreign exchange markets; but we can ignore such cases.

Table 7	U.S. OFFICIAL SETTLEMENTS BALANCE, 1960–2003 (MILLIONS $)		
Year	Net U.S. Official Reserve Assets (Increase [−])	Net Foreign Reserve Assets in U.S. (Increase [+])	Official Settlements Balance
1960	$2,145	$1,473	$3,618
1965	1,225	134	1,359
1970	2,481	6,908	9,389
1975	−849	7,027	6,178
1980	−8,155	15,497	7,342
1985	−3,858	−1,119	−4,977
1990	−2,158	33,910	31,752
1995	−9,742	109,768	100,026
2000	−290	35,909	35,619
2003	1,523	248,573	250,096

Source: U.S. Department of Commerce (updates are available at the department's Web site, http://www.bea.doc.gov).

level of reserves held by foreign central banks in the United States enter as debits in the U.S. official settlements account. (It may help to think of increases in U.S. foreign exchange reserves as *imports* of foreign exchange.) Decreases in U.S. central bank reserves or increases in foreign central banks' reserves held in the United States represent credits (think of decreases in U.S. reserves as *exports* of foreign exchange and, therefore, as a credit).[6] Table 7 reports the transactions on the U.S. official settlements balance. We'll see later in the chapter that whether governments undertake these transactions depends on whether the exchange rate is fixed or flexible.

The easiest way to see the relationship between the official settlements balance and the rest of the balance-of-payments accounts is through the analogy developed earlier with the transactions of an individual. The balance on the current account represents the relationship between the individual's current income and current expenditures. The capital account represents changes in the individual's borrowing and lending or purchases and sales of assets. Suppose the sum of the individual's current income, borrowing, and revenue from sales of assets exceeds the sum of current expenditures, loans made, and purchases of assets. What happens to the difference? It goes into the individual's cash balances.[7] On the other hand, how does an individual handle a situation in which the sum of current expenditures, loans made, and purchases of assets exceeds the sum of income, borrowing, and revenue from sales of assets? This is possible only if the individual possesses cash balances that can be depleted to cover the shortfall.

---

6. In recent years, it's become increasingly common for foreign central banks to hold a portion of their dollar reserves outside the United States. When central banks undertake intervention using these reserves, the U.S. official settlements account doesn't capture the activity. Because of this phenomenon, changes in the level of reserve assets as reported in the official settlements account have become somewhat less reliable as measures of the extent of intervention to affect the value of other currencies relative to the dollar.

7. Consider a simple numerical example. Suppose that in a given month an individual earns a salary of $2,000, takes out a new-car loan from the bank for $15,000, and sells a used car for $5,000. During the same month, the individual buys a new car for $15,000 and spends $3,000 on routine expenses (rent, food, clothing, and so on). What must be true about the individual's cash balances? They rise by $4,000, or the difference between $22,000 and $18,000.

Table 8	**A COUNTRY'S CURRENT, CAPITAL, AND OFFICIAL SETTLEMENTS BALANCES MUST SUM TO ZERO JUST LIKE AN INDIVIDUAL'S TOTAL RECEIPTS AND TOTAL PAYMENTS**

Balance-of-Payments Accounts	Individual Transactions
Current-account balance	Current income − current expenditures
+Capital-account balance	+Net new borrowing + net revenue from sales of assets
+Official settlements balance	+Change in cash balances
Zero	Zero

Transactions on the official settlements account play the same role as increases or decreases in the individual's cash balances: They cover or compensate for any differences between total payments and total receipts in the other accounts, as summarized in Table 8. For the individual, the sum of income minus expenditures, borrowing minus lending, revenue from sales minus purchases of assets, and changes in cash balances *must* sum to zero. (*Why?*) In the balance-of-payments accounts, the sum of the current-account balance, the capital-account balance, and the official settlements balance must sum to zero. If the combined balance on the current and capital accounts is in deficit (debits > credits), there must be an offsetting surplus (credits > debits) in the official settlements account. With a surplus in the current and capital accounts, the official settlements account must be in deficit.

When the U.S. Department of Commerce collects data for the balance-of-payments accounts, many transactions are missed or unreported. This occurs for a variety of reasons. The United States doesn't closely monitor tourism and imports brought into the United States by travelers, so many goods enter and exit the country unreported. Tax avoidance provides an incentive for some types of capital flows to go undisclosed (and therefore untaxed). These imperfections in data collection are reflected in the **statistical discrepancy**, or the amount by which the sum of the current, capital, and official settlements balances as actually calculated fail to sum to zero. The magnitude of the statistical discrepancy has grown over the last few years along with international trade and financial activity. Over the past few decades, the discrepancy has ranged yearly from several hundred million dollars to around $100 billion, as shown in Table 9.

From one perspective, these numbers are quite large; in fact, in several years since 1960, the U.S. statistical discrepancy was larger than the current-account balance! From another perspective, the statistical discrepancy is remarkably small given the task of accounting for all transactions between U.S. residents and the rest of the world. Once we take the existence of the statistical discrepancy into account, the fundamental relationship that must hold for U.S. transactions with the rest of the world becomes:

$$\text{Current-account balance} + \text{Capital-account balance} + \\ \text{Official settlements balance} + \text{Statistical discrepancy} = 0 \qquad [1]$$

Next, we must address a question that probably has occurred already to the careful reader: If the components of the balance-of-payments accounts always sum to zero, what do we mean by a balance-of-payments surplus or deficit? As a first step toward answering this question, we must recall that each international transaction has two sides and, therefore, enters *twice* in the double-entry bookkeeping system that comprises the balance-of-payments accounts. This guarantees that Equation 1 holds, because any

Table 9	**U.S. STATISTICAL DISCREPANCY, 1960–2003 (MILLIONS $)**			
Year	Current-Account Balance	Capital-Account Balance	Official Settlements Balance	Statistical Discrepancy
1960	$2,824	−$5,423	$3,618	−$1,019
1965	5,431	−6,334	1,359	−457
1970	2,331	−12,368	9,389	−219[a]
1975	18,116	−28,711	6,178	4,417
1980	2,317	−31,698	7,342	20,886[a]
1985	−123,987	111,469	−4,977	17,494
1990	−91,624	35,229	31,752	24,643
1995	−115,254	37,970	100,026	−22,742
2000	−435,377	364,142	35,619	35,616
2003	−530,668	292,584	250,096	−12,012

[a]Small allocations of special drawing rights in 1970 and 1980 are omitted.

Source: U.S. Department of Commerce (updates are available at the department's Web site, http://www.bea.doc.gov).

credit entry automatically generates an equal debit entry somewhere in the accounts. To see the logic of the double-entry system, let's look at a few hypothetical transactions.

2.4 How Double-Entry Bookkeeping Works: Some Illustrative Transactions

The simplest international transaction from a balance-of-payments perspective is barter, or the exchange of two goods without use of money. Suppose Coca-Cola exports $1 million worth of Coke to Poland in exchange for $1 million worth of Polish beer.[8] How would the Department of Commerce record the transaction in the U.S. balance-of-payments accounts? The soft-drink export is a $1 million credit in the merchandise-trade category of the current account, and the beer import is a $1 million debit, also in the merchandise category. Note that, although trade has increased, both the merchandise trade balance and the current-account balance remain unaffected— because both debits and credits have risen by the same amount. This occurs whenever both the debit and credit entries for a given transaction occur in the same account. (*How would the transaction appear in Poland's balance-of-payments accounts?*)

Now suppose Coca-Cola exports $1 million worth of Coke to Britain and the British importer pays with a check for the pound equivalent of $1 million, which Coca-Cola deposits in its London bank. The Coke export is again a $1 million credit entry in the merchandise category of the U.S. current account. But the payment for the Coke— the check—is a capital outflow, a debit in the U.S. capital account, because a U.S. resident now owns an asset (the pound bank deposit in London) previously owned by the British importer.[9] The U.S. merchandise trade balance (as well as the current

---

8. Such transactions are called *countertrade*.

9. Alternatively, Coca-Cola could exchange the pound deposit for a dollar deposit at a New York bank. In this case, the New York bank would now be holding $1 million worth of pounds. For our purposes, this wouldn't affect the way the transaction is recorded in the balance-of-payments accounts.

account) shows a $1 million credit entry (*Why?*), while the U.S. capital account shows a $1 million debit entry (*Why?*). (*How would the transaction appear in Britain's balance-of-payments accounts?*)

Now consider a third possibility. A private charity in the United States ships $1 million worth of Coke to a foreign country as aid following an earthquake that destroyed the sources of pure drinking water. What happens in the U.S. balance-of-payments accounts? The export of Coke is still a $1 million credit in the merchandise subaccount of the U.S. current account, but the United States expects no payment in return for the aid. So what's the second side of the transaction? This is where the unilateral transfer subaccount comes in; the second entry is a $1 million debit under unilateral transfers. The net effect is an increase of $1 million in the merchandise trade balance but no effect on the current-account balance. (*Why?*) (*Show the transaction's effect on the recipient country's balance-of-payments accounts.*)

Finally, consider a transaction that occurs solely in the capital account. Suppose Coca-Cola buys a $1 million building in London to open a production facility there. The firm pays the building's owner with a check for $1 million. The U.S. capital account shows a debit and a credit of $1 million. The debit represents Coca-Cola's "import" of the title to the building, and the credit Coke's "export" of ownership of the asset represented by the check. (*Show the entries in Britain's balance-of-payments accounts.*)

As these transactions illustrate, every transaction creates *both* a credit *and* a debit entry in each country's balance-of-payments accounts, and the two entries always are equal in magnitude. Therefore, total credits always equal total debits (as in any double-entry bookkeeping system), although the debit and credit entries from any given transaction don't necessarily occur within the same account. But if total credits equal total debits, what do we mean by a balance-of-payments surplus or deficit?

3 WHAT ARE BALANCE-OF-PAYMENTS SURPLUSES AND DEFICITS?

The balance-of-payments accounts always "balance" in the sense that total credits equal total debits. Just as for an individual, total receipts must equal total payments once changes in asset holdings and cash balances are taken into account. This type of balance in the balance-of-payments accounts is trivial and arises from accounting and bookkeeping conventions, not from the economics of international trade and finance. The fact that an individual's total receipts must equal total payments tells us very little about that individual's economic circumstances. Likewise, the fact that a country's total receipts from the rest of the world must equal its total payments to the rest of the world reveals little about that country's economic situation.

Examination of the balance (or lack thereof) in the balance of payments in the *nontrivial* sense requires distinguishing between two types of transactions: autonomous and accommodating ones. We refer to transactions that individuals, firms, or government agencies undertake for their own purposes (such as utility maximization by individuals, asset portfolio decisions, profit maximization by firms, and foreign-policy goals by government) and whose goals are unrelated to the balance of payments as **autonomous**, or **independently motivated, transactions**. These transactions represent the routine international trade and finance that constitute world economic activity. A U.S. resident buying a pair of Italian shoes, a U.S. firm selling a bond to a German resident, and the U.S. government sending foreign aid to Afghanistan constitute actions taken for their own sake and independently of their effects on the balance of payments. The transactions may affect the balance of payments, but any such effects would be unintentional and not the goal of the transaction.

For our purposes, we can identify the sum of the current-account balance, the capital-account balance, and the statistical discrepancy as the balance on autonomous transactions.[10] The current and nonofficial capital accounts include all the trade and finance activities undertaken by individuals, firms, and governments without regard for their balance-of-payments effects. The statistical discrepancy measures omitted or mismeasured current- and capital-account transactions.[11] The sum of autonomous transactions is the country's balance of payments (BOP) with the rest of the world:

$$\text{Current-account balance} + \text{Capital-account balance} + \text{Statistical discrepancy} = \text{Balance of payments (BOP)} \qquad [2]$$

If total autonomous credits exceed total autonomous debits, a **balance-of-payments surplus** (BOP > 0) exists. An excess of autonomous debits over credits implies a **balance-of-payments deficit** (BOP < 0). The balance of payments shows whether a country's trade and finance activities (that is, its autonomous transactions) involve receipts from foreigners in excess of payments to foreigners (a surplus) or payments to foreigners in excess of receipts from foreigners (a deficit).

In each of the illustrative transactions discussed previously, the net effect on the balance of payments is zero. In the first, the Coke-for-beer barter transaction, both the debit and the credit sides of the current account rise by $1 million, leaving the current-account balance unchanged. The capital account and the statistical discrepancy remain unaffected; therefore, Equation 2 implies that the transaction doesn't change the country's balance of payments. In the second transaction, in which exported Coke is paid for by a check deposited in a London bank, the current-account balance rises by the $1 million credit while the capital-account balance falls by a $1 million debit; again the two parts of the transaction offset, leaving the overall balance (the left-hand side of Equation 2) unaffected. In the third transaction, the charity shipment of Coke is recorded as a $1 million credit in merchandise exports and a $1 million debit in unilateral transfers within the current account, leaving the current account and the balance of payments unaffected. In the fourth transaction, the purchase of a factory abroad appears as a $1 million debit and the payment by check as a $1 million credit, both in the U.S. capital account. For all four transactions, *both* the debit and credit entries occur on the left-hand side of Equation 2. All the entries are independent or autonomous, undertaken by private parties for reasons unrelated to the balance of payments.

The second class of transactions is **accommodating**, or **compensatory**, **transactions**. These are official government actions taken for balance-of-payments purposes; they correspond to the transactions in the official settlements account—changes in central banks' stocks of foreign exchange reserves. A comparison of Equations 1 and 2 reveals the relationship between the official settlements balance and the balance of payments. Rearranging Equation 1, the sum of the current-account

---

10. As noted in footnotes 2 through 4, official transactions actually are recorded in a separate subaccount *within* the capital and financial account. We treat official transactions separately; when we speak of the capital account, we mean the nonofficial capital account.

11. We attribute the statistical discrepancy to mismeasurement in the current and capital accounts rather than in the official settlements account because the latter includes only official transactions subject to few measurement errors, omissions, or revisions.

balance, the capital-account balance, and the statistical discrepancy equals the *negative* of the official settlements balance:

$$\text{Current-account balance} + \text{Capital-account balance} + \text{Statistical discrepancy} = \\ - \text{Official settlements balance} \quad [3]$$

Combining this with Equation 2, the balance of payments just equals the negative of the official settlements balance:

$$\text{Balance of payments} = -\text{Official settlements balance} \quad [4]$$

The balance of payments represents the difference between credits and debits for autonomous transactions undertaken by individuals, firms, and governments. Any deficit or surplus must be "accommodated," or "compensated for," by official transactions on the official settlements account because a country's total receipts from foreigners must equal its total payments to foreigners (that is, the balance-of-payments accounts must balance in the double-entry bookkeeping sense). To highlight this point, we can rewrite Equation 4 as the explicit relationship between autonomous and accommodating transactions:

$$\text{Balance on autonomous transactions} + \\ \text{Balance on accommodating transactions} = 0 \quad [5]$$

To understand better the significance of the distinction between autonomous and accommodating transactions in defining and interpreting the balance of payments, it's useful to relate the ideas and definitions developed in this chapter back to the previous chapter's model of the demand for and supply of foreign exchange.

4 WHAT'S THE CONNECTION? THE BALANCE OF PAYMENTS AND THE FOREIGN EXCHANGE MARKET

Before introducing more explicitly the demand for and supply of foreign exchange as a way to view the balance of payments, we need to distinguish between the overall, or multilateral, balance-of-payments accounts and the bilateral balance-of-payments accounts. The **overall**, or **multilateral**, **balance-of-payments accounts** are the ones discussed so far; they record all the transactions between U.S. residents and the rest of the world as a whole. The **bilateral balance-of-payments accounts** report receipts and payments between the United States and one other country; there's one set of bilateral balance-of-payments accounts for each country with which the United States interacts. The multilateral balance-of-payments accounts such as the one in Table 4 simply aggregate the bilateral ones. In relating the balance-of-payments accounts to demand and supply in foreign exchange markets, it's convenient to assume that there are only two countries in the world (such as the United States and Britain), so we can give specific names to the currencies involved.

Recall from the previous chapter—Currency Markets and Exchange Rates—that the foreign exchange market is in equilibrium when the quantity of foreign-currency-denominated deposits individuals want to hold in their asset portfolios just equals the quantity of foreign-currency-denominated deposits available. Figure 1 reproduces the previous chapter's Figure 7, the graphical representation of such an equilibrium, using pounds as the foreign currency.

The supply of foreign-currency deposits, represented by the vertical line $S^\pounds$, is determined by government policies and banks' lending decisions, independent of the

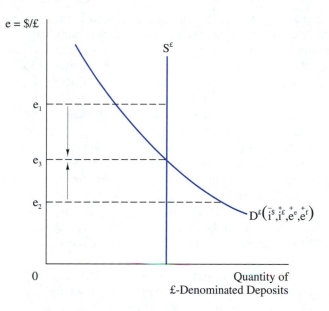

Figure 1   Foreign Exchange Market Equilibrium under a Flexible Exchange Regime

The exchange rate moves to equate the quantity demanded and supplied of pound-denominated deposits. The equilibrium exchange rate is e_3. At e_1, individuals aren't willing to hold the existing supply of pound-denominated deposits. As individuals try to exchange their excess pound-denominated deposits for deposits denominated in dollars, they must accept fewer dollars per pound; and the dollar price of pounds falls toward e_3. At e_2, individuals want to hold more than the existing supply of pound-denominated deposits. Individuals enter the market trying to exchange dollar-denominated for pound-denominated ones, thereby bidding up the dollar price of pounds to e_3.

exchange rate. The demand for foreign-currency deposits reflects the asset-portfolio decisions of individuals and firms based on the interest parity conditions from section 4 in the previous chapter. The higher the value of the spot exchange rate (for given values of $i^\$$, $i^\£$, e^e, and e^f), the higher the expected rate of return on domestic-currency deposits and the more attractive those become relative to foreign-currency deposits. (*Why? For a review, see section 5.1 in the previous chapter.*) Therefore, we represent the demand curve for foreign-currency deposits as a negatively sloped line. Changes in interest rates, the expected future spot rate, or the forward rate shift the demand curve in the directions indicated by the (+) and (−) signs in Figure 1, as portfolio owners respond to changes in the expected rates of return on deposits denominated in the two currencies.

When quantity demanded and supplied of a good aren't equal, what usually happens to bring a market back into equilibrium? If government doesn't interfere with the forces of supply and demand, price adjusts to equate quantity demanded and quantity supplied. This is the case in the foreign exchange market when the exchange rate (the domestic-currency price of foreign currency) is flexible. If the quantity supplied of foreign exchange exceeds the quantity demanded (as at e_1), the domestic currency appreciates (e falls); if the quantity demanded of foreign exchange exceeds the quantity supplied (as at e_2), the domestic currency depreciates. (*Explain why, using the interest parity conditions.*) In contrast, under a fixed exchange rate regime, some other mechanism must equilibrate the foreign exchange market. In the next two sections, we examine the relationship among the balance of payments, demand and supply in foreign exchange markets, and exchange rates, first under a flexible and then under a fixed exchange rate regime.

4.1 The Balance of Payments, Foreign Exchange Markets, and a Flexible Exchange Rate

The demand for foreign exchange as developed in the chapter on currency markets and exchange rates reflects the autonomous transactions in the balance-of-payments accounts. In these transactions, individuals and firms exchange goods, services, and financial assets, paid for with deposits denominated in various currencies.[12] Portfolio owners hold foreign-currency-denominated deposits to buy foreign goods and services, to earn interest on the deposits, to purchase other foreign assets (bonds, factories, and so forth), and to speculate by holding foreign exchange in the hope of an appreciation against the dollar. These transaction categories correspond to the various categories of autonomous transactions in the current and capital accounts of the balance-of-payments accounts. The balance of payments is in equilibrium when individuals are willing to hold as assets any foreign-currency-denominated deposits received in payment for international transactions.

Consider a hypothetical transaction. A resident of Britain uses a £1,000 check to purchase a bond issued by a U.S. firm. The foreign exchange market is in equilibrium at e = $2/£1, as in Figure 2. If the firm selling the bond is content to hold the £1,000 in its asset portfolio and deposits the check in a London bank, the total demand for pound-denominated deposits remains unchanged. The £1,000 deposit simply has been reallocated from the individual who purchased the bond to the firm that sold it.

Figure 2   Balance-of-Payments Equilibrium under a Flexible Exchange Rate

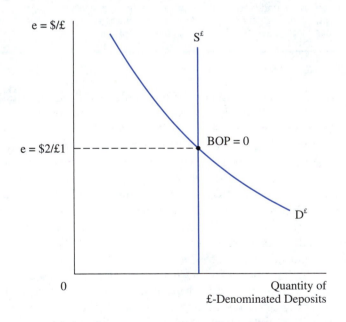

At e = $2/£1, individuals willingly hold the pound-denominated deposits they receive in payment for merchandise exports and other transactions. Autonomous debits match autonomous credits in the balance-of-payments accounts (BOP = 0).

---

12. Of course, some transactions are arranged using barter and others using actual currency rather than payment by check, but the overwhelming majority of international transactions are financed by check or bank deposit.

The transaction appears in the U.S. balance-of-payments accounts as a capital-account credit of $2,000 (= £1,000 · $2/£1) and a capital-account debit of $2,000. (*Why?*)[13] But suppose the bond seller doesn't want to hold the pounds and instead sells the pound-denominated deposit to the firm's New York bank in return for a $2,000 deposit. If e = $2/£1 is the equilibrium exchange rate, then by definition someone *will* be content to hold the pound-denominated deposit, perhaps the New York bank or one of its other customers. (*Why?*) Again the total demand for pound-denominated deposits remains unchanged. Portfolio owners are content to hold $S^£$ pound-denominated deposits (including the £1,000 involved in our hypothetical transaction) at e = $2/£1. The autonomous demand for pound-denominated deposits equals the quantity available. The British resident who buys the U.S. firm's bond makes available the £1,000 deposit, and the U.S. firm or its bank is willing to hold that deposit. The current- and capital-account balances sum to zero.

If, given current interest rates and expected and forward exchange rates, *no one* wants to hold the pound-denominated deposit, e = $2/£1 is *not* the equilibrium exchange rate. The firm that received the pound-denominated deposit in payment for the bond will be willing to sell it for *less* than $2,000, receiving less than $2 for each £1. The pound depreciates against the dollar (see panel (a) of Figure 3). If the equilibrium value of the exchange rate is, say, $1.80/£1, the U.S. balance of payments reports the transaction as a $1,800 capital-account credit for "export" of the bond (= £1,000 · $1.80/£1) and a capital-account debit of $1,800 for "importing" ownership of the deposit. Again autonomous debits equal autonomous credits; the balance of payments is in equilibrium at e = $1.80/£1.

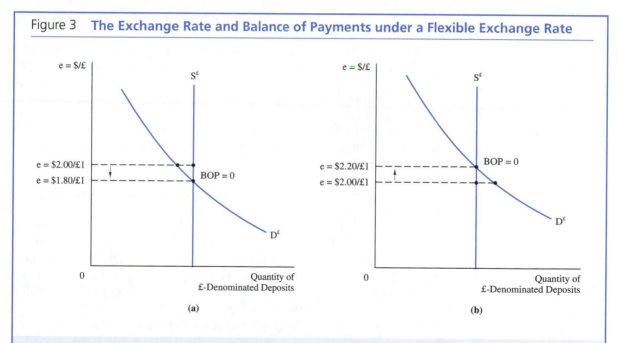

Figure 3 The Exchange Rate and Balance of Payments under a Flexible Exchange Rate

In panel (a), the dollar appreciates from $2/£1 to $1.80/£1 to encourage individuals to hold more pound-denominated deposits in their asset portfolios. The balance of payments is in equilibrium at e = $1.80/£1, where autonomous debits equal autonomous credits. In panel (b), the dollar depreciates from $2/£1 to $2.20/£1 to discourage individuals from holding pound-denominated deposits in their asset portfolios. At e = $2.20/£1, autonomous debits equal autonomous credits and the balance of payments is in equilibrium.

---

13. The bookkeeping for each country's balance-of-payments accounts is conducted in the domestic currency.

On the other hand, if at current interest rates and expected and forward exchange rates, many portfolio owners want to purchase the pound-denominated deposit at a price of e = $2/£1 to add to their portfolios, the price of the deposit will be bid up. Each pound will bring the firm more than $2, and the pound will appreciate against the dollar, as in panel (b) of Figure 3. If the equilibrium exchange rate turns out to be $2.20, the transaction appears in the U.S. balance-of-payments accounts as a $2,200 capital-account credit (for export of the bond) and a $2,200 capital-account debit (for import of the deposit). Autonomous debits and credits in the current and capital accounts remain equal, so the balance of payments is in equilibrium at $2.20/£1.

In both cases (panels (a) and (b) of Figure 3), the exchange rate adjusts until someone becomes willing to hold the pound-denominated deposit at current interest rates, although not necessarily the same firm that originally received it in payment for the bond exported to Britain. This is the essence of a flexible exchange rate regime. Under such a regime, governments allow the market forces of supply and demand to determine the price of foreign exchange, here the exchange rate between dollars and pounds. The exchange rate adjusts until individuals willingly hold the existing supply of pound-denominated deposits in their asset portfolios. As long as individuals and firms are willing to hold the existing supply of deposits at the current exchange rate, autonomous credits equal autonomous debits and the balance of payments balances (BOP = 0). *A perfectly flexible exchange rate guarantees that the equality between autonomous debits and credits will hold and, therefore, that the balance of payments will be neither in surplus nor in deficit.* This adjustment process occurs in each foreign exchange market where the dollar exchanges for a trading partner's currency. Often the dollar appreciates against some currencies (to eliminate a bilateral U.S. balance-of-payments surplus) and depreciates against others (to eliminate a bilateral U.S. BOP deficit).

Another perspective on the balance of payments under a flexible exchange regime focuses on the official settlements account. Recall that the balance of payments equals the negative of the official settlements balance (see Equation 4). The transactions on the official settlements account represent changes in central banks' stock of foreign exchange reserves. The cause of changes in the level of these reserves is intervention in foreign exchange markets to maintain the exchange rate at a level away from equilibrium (see section 7 in the previous chapter).[14] Under a flexible-rate regime, authorities make no effort to hold the exchange rate away from its equilibrium level and, therefore, engage in no foreign exchange intervention that would lead to changes in their foreign exchange reserves. With no changes in official reserves, the official settlements balance equals zero—another way of saying that the balance of payments is in equilibrium (BOP = 0).

Under a perfectly flexible exchange rate regime, the balance-of-payments concept is not very meaningful, since the exchange rate always will move to keep the balance of payments balanced or in equilibrium. "Balance" in the balance of payments is just another way of looking at equilibrium in the market for foreign exchange. Since a perfectly flexible exchange rate, by definition, guarantees foreign exchange market equilibrium, equilibrium in the balance of payments also follows.

This does *not* imply that either the merchandise trade balance or the current account necessarily will be in balance under a flexible exchange rate regime. A current-account deficit (or surplus) merely requires an offsetting surplus (or deficit) on the capital account. There's a widespread misconception, often repeated in the popular press, that the theory of flexible exchange rates claims that such a system will balance either the merchandise trade account or the current account. Since the move away from a fixed exchange rate regime in

---

14. See footnote 5.

the early 1970s, deficits and surpluses have been observed widely in the merchandise trade and current accounts of many countries. This is the basis of frequently heard claims that flexible exchange rates don't work the way economic theory suggests. This argument reveals two misunderstandings. First, as we've noted, the theory of flexible exchange rates does *not* claim that deficits or surpluses in the merchandise trade or current accounts will disappear under flexible exchange rates, only that balance-of-payments deficits or surpluses will. Second, the exchange rate regime in use since the early 1970s, although much more flexible than the earlier system, is *not* a purely flexible exchange rate regime. Monetary authorities still intervene in foreign exchange markets to affect exchange rates, although, as we'll see, the extent and frequency of intervention differ widely over time and across countries.

4.2 The Balance of Payments, Foreign Exchange Markets, and a Fixed Exchange Rate

Under a fixed exchange rate regime, the demand for and supply of foreign exchange still reflect the autonomous transactions in the balance of payments. However, governments don't allow the forces of demand and supply to determine the exchange rate; instead, policy makers peg, or fix, the exchange rate at a certain level by intervening in foreign exchange markets to buy and sell assets denominated in various currencies (for a review, see the discussion in section 7 in the currency markets and exchange rates chapter).

Figure 4 panel (a) reproduces Figure 9 from the previous chapter, which illustrates an exchange rate pegged above the equilibrium rate. Consider again a U.S. firm that sells a £1,000 bond to a resident of Britain and receives payment by a check for £1,000. At the fixed exchange rate, e_1^p, the firm doesn't want to hold the pound-denominated deposit in its portfolio. Overall, at e_1^p, the quantity supplied of pounds in the foreign exchange market exceeds the quantity demanded. Portfolio owners aren't willing to hold the existing supply of pound-denominated deposits because the expected rate of return on dollar deposits is higher than that on pound deposits. With the exchange rate pegged, market forces can't restore equilibrium by bidding down the value of pound-denominated deposits, as happened under a flexible-rate regime in section 4.1. If the dollar price of pounds is to remain at e_1^p, either the U.S. or British central bank, or both, must intervene to eliminate the excess supply of pounds. The intervention consists of permitting individuals or firms holding unwanted pound-denominated deposits to exchange them for dollar-denominated ones with the central bank at a rate of e_1^p.

Under the rules of the fixed exchange rate system that governed the international monetary system from the end of World War II until 1971—called the **Bretton Woods system**—each central bank was responsible for intervening to maintain the value of its currency relative to the U.S. dollar. In other words, with the situation depicted in panel (a) of Figure 4, the Bank of England, the British central bank, intervened. Anyone holding unwanted pound-denominated deposits could take them to the Bank of England and exchange them for deposits denominated in dollars, receiving e_1^p dollars per pound. To purchase the pounds, the Bank of England would use dollar-denominated deposits from its stock of foreign exchange reserves held in the United States. The size of the Bank of England's pound purchase would equal the difference between the quantity demanded and the quantity supplied of pounds at e_1^p. The result would be a decrease in the Bank of England's stock of dollar reserves held in the United States. Recall that such a decrease in British reserves would appear as a debit in the U.S. official settlements balance, because that account records changes in *both* U.S. official reserves and foreign official reserves held in the United States (see section 2.3). The debit in the official settlements balance just matches the surplus (BOP > 0) in the U.S. balance of payments, as indicated by Equation 4.

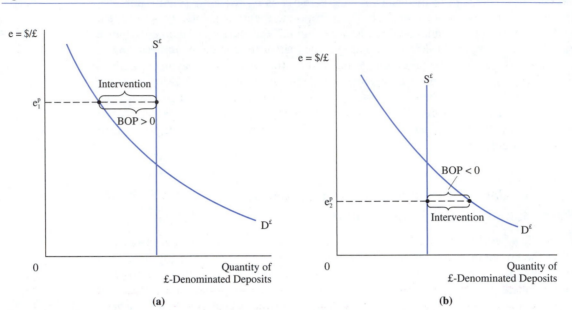

Figure 4 **The Exchange Rate and Balance of Payments under a Fixed Exchange Rate**

At e_1^p in panel (a), individuals aren't willing to hold the existing supply of pounds. To maintain the exchange rate at e_1^p, a central bank must absorb the excess supply of pounds. Individuals holding unwanted pound-denominated deposits can exchange them with the central bank for dollar-denominated deposits at a rate of e_1^p. The intervention enters the U.S. balance-of-payments accounts as a debit in the official settlements account, accommodating the surplus (BOP > 0) in the autonomous current and capital accounts.

At e_2^p in panel (b), the quantity demanded of pounds exceeds the quantity supplied. The exchange rate can be maintained at e_2^p only if a central bank supplies pounds to the market through intervention. Individuals who want pound-denominated deposits can purchase them at the central bank at a price of e_2^p. The U.S. balance-of-payments accounts record the intervention as an accommodating official settlements credit, reflecting the BOP deficit (BOP < 0).

Consider our hypothetical transaction in which a U.S. firm receives a £1,000 check in payment for a bond sold in Britain, and assume that $e_1^p = \$2.50/£1$. The firm sells the pound-denominated deposit to the Bank of England in return for a $2,500 dollar-denominated deposit. The net effect on the U.S. balance-of-payments accounts is an autonomous capital-account credit of $2,500 (= £1,000 · $2.50/£1) for "export" of the bond and an official settlements debit of the same amount for the Bank of England's sale of $2,500 of its dollar reserves. (*Why?*) Using Equation 4, the result is a U.S. balance-of-payments surplus of $2,500. (*What is the corresponding situation in Britain's balance-of-payments accounts?*)

The analysis of a balance-of-payments deficit under a fixed exchange rate proceeds similarly. Panel (b) in Figure 4 repeats Figure 10 from the previous chapter's analysis of an exchange rate fixed below the equilibrium level. At the relatively low dollar price of pounds represented by the fixed exchange rate, e_2^p, portfolio owners want to hold more than the existing stock of pound-denominated deposits. Some individuals who want to buy pound-denominated deposits can't do so at the current exchange rate. The U.S. balance of payments with Britain shows a deficit. With no intervention, the dollar would depreciate against the pound. To prevent depreciation of the dollar, one of the central banks must intervene to supply pound-denominated deposits to the foreign exchange market. The Bank of England may sell pound-denominated deposits in exchange for dollar-denominated deposits and add the dollars to its foreign exchange reserves in the

United States (a credit in the U.S. official settlements account), or the U.S. Federal Reserve may sell pound-denominated deposits from its foreign exchange reserves (also a credit in the U.S. official settlements account). In either case, the balance-of-payments deficit at e_2^p reflected in the excess demand for pounds is just matched by a credit on the official settlements balance of the U.S. balance of payments, as indicated by Equation 4.

Suppose a U.S. resident buys £5,000 worth of stock in a British firm. At the pegged exchange rate (say, $1.50/£1), the individual isn't able to buy a pound-denominated deposit with which to pay for the stock because the quantity demanded of such deposits exceeds the quantity available. But the Bank of England can prevent appreciation of the pound by selling a £5,000 deposit to the individual at the pegged exchange rate (at $e = \$1.50/£1$, the £5,000 deposit will exchange for a $7,500 deposit). The transaction's effect on the U.S. balance of payments will consist of a $7,500 autonomous capital-account debit for the "imported" ownership of the stock and an accommodating $7,500 official settlements credit for the increase in dollar reserves held by the Bank of England. From Equation 4, the United States has a $7,500 balance-of-payments deficit (BOP < 0) with Britain. (*How would the transaction affect Britain's balance-of-payments accounts?*)

Earlier we noted that under flexible exchange rates a currency may simultaneously appreciate against some currencies and depreciate against others. With a fixed exchange regime, a similar phenomenon occurs when the quantity demanded of some currencies exceeds the quantity supplied while for other currencies the opposite holds true. A central bank may find it necessary to intervene by simultaneously purchasing one currency and selling another from its reserves. Suppose, for example, that the United States wants to maintain fixed exchange rates between the dollar and the pound and between the dollar and the euro. If demand and supply in the two foreign exchange markets create pressure for the dollar to depreciate against the pound (excess demand for pounds) and to appreciate against the euro (excess supply of euros), the Federal Reserve can intervene by selling pound deposits from its reserves and purchasing euro-denominated ones. The balance on the multilateral official settlements account shows the net change in U.S. reserves (assuming the Bank of England and the European Central Bank undertake no intervention).

CASE 1: THE U.S.–CHINA TRADE DEFICIT: $10 BILLION OR $40 BILLION?

U.S./China

The U.S. merchandise trade deficit with China is a politically sensitive topic. Many U.S. industries would like protection against Chinese imports; those industries with heavy protection, especially the apparel sector, would like even more. U.S. protectionist forces routinely cite figures on the bilateral trade deficit in their efforts to muster political support to block trade; however, the two countries disagree significantly about the correct figure for the bilateral merchandise trade balance. U.S. figures for 1996 placed the deficit at just under $40 billion, second in size only to the U.S. trade deficit with Japan. China, on the other hand, claimed that the right number for 1996 was less than $10 billion. How could the numbers diverge so dramatically?

One answer is Hong Kong. A big share of China's trade flows through Hong Kong and did so even before the former British colony's 1997 reversion to Chinese sovereignty.[15] Official U.S. trade figures count all China's exports through Hong Kong as imports from China. But China counted that trade as exports to Hong Kong until 1993. In other words, a sweater exported from China to the United States through Hong Kong would appear in U.S. trade statistics as an import from China, but in Chinese trade statistics as an export to Hong Kong, not

---

15. Even after the 1997 Chinese takeover of Hong Kong, the government continues to report the special administrative region's trade statistics separately from those of the rest of China.

the United States. Since 1993, China has begun to identify exports' final destinations; but many transactions go unrecorded or misrecorded. Also, the United States doesn't count its own exports to China that pass through Hong Kong as going to China.

A second statistical problem that Hong Kong introduces concerns its own value-added. Suppose the sweater mentioned earlier is shipped unfinished from China to Hong Kong, where the final manufacturing steps are taken before the finished product goes to the United States. Accurate trade accounts would show part of the sweater's value coming from China and part from Hong Kong. U.S. statistics, however, typically assign the full value as an import from China.

In 1997, the Chinese government shared previously secret trade data with the U.S. Department of Commerce and a team of U.S. academic economists who specialize in international trade. The purpose was to reconcile the two countries' statistics. The economists found that the "correct" merchandise-trade-balance number fell between U.S. and Chinese estimates, somewhere in the $21 billion – $26 billion range.

Similar problems plague data on foreign direct investment. Numbers reported by source countries rarely match those reported by host countries. And, again, the China–Hong Kong case provides a dramatic example. For 2000, Hong Kong reported receiving $64 billion in foreign direct investment, placing behind just the United States and China in the world ranking of FDI recipients. But how could Hong Kong, with a population of 7 million and annual GDP of $162 billion, have absorbed $64 billion of foreign direct investment in a single year? The answer, again, seems to be: China. Experts expect that a large share of Hong Kong's inward foreign direct investment is merely making a temporary stop on its way to China.[16]

United States

CASE 2: THE UNITED STATES AS A DEBTOR

A country's **net foreign wealth**, or **net international investment position**, equals the difference between the value of foreign assets the country's residents own and the value of the country's domestic assets owned by foreigners. Unlike the purchases and sales of assets recorded in a country's capital account, net foreign wealth or international investment position represents asset ownership accumulated over time; in other words, while transactions in the capital account are flows, net foreign wealth or international investment position is a stock. A country's net foreign wealth is negative when foreigners own more assets in that country than the country's residents own abroad. This all seems straightforward. However, controversy surrounds the measurement of U.S. net foreign wealth. What's the value of U.S. assets owned by foreigners, and what's the value of foreign assets owned by Americans? When did the United States become a debtor in the sense of having negative net foreign wealth? And how big is the debt?

There are at least three ways of valuing assets. Until recently, U.S. Department of Commerce statistics valued assets at historical cost, or their original purchase price. In other words, if a U.S. firm bought a factory in Britain in 1950, government statistics still reported the value of that asset in 1980 at the original 1950 purchase price. Economists agree that this is a poor way to measure asset value. Most U.S. purchases of foreign assets occurred in years prior to the bulk of foreign purchases of U.S. assets, so measuring at historical cost tends to understate the value of U.S.-owned foreign assets relative to foreign-owned U.S. assets.

The two alternate methods of valuing assets attempt to estimate their current values rather than relying on historical values at the time of purchase. One current-valuation method estimates assets' current cost, or the cost of purchasing them now. The other method estimates market value, or the price for which each asset could be sold now. Both measures are difficult to estimate, but conceptually superior to the old historical-cost method. When U.S. net foreign wealth became negative and by how much depend on the measure used, as reported in Table 10.

16. "FDI Is Hong Kong's $64 Billion Question," *Financial Times*, March 30, 2001.

Table 10 U.S. INTERNATIONAL INVESTMENT POSITION (BILLIONS $)

Year	Historical Cost			Current Cost			Market Value		
	U.S. Assets Abroad	Foreign Assets in U.S.	U.S. Net Foreign Wealth	U.S. Assets Abroad	Foreign Assets in U.S.	U.S. Net Foreign Wealth	U.S. Assets Abroad	Foreign Assets in U.S.	U.S. Net Foreign Wealth
1982	$838.1	$688.6	$149.5	$1,100.6	$736.6	$364.0	$954.9	$696.4	$258.5
1983	887.5	781.5	106.0	1,169.2	1,068.3	337.4	831.8	800.7	267.6
1984	895.9	892.6	3.3	1,177.5	1,081.8	232.9	944.7	905.9	175.9
1985	949.7	1,061.1	−111.4	1,296.4	1,171.1	125.3	1,288.3	1,159.8	128.5
1986	1,073.3	1,341.1	−267.8	1,468.8	1,434.2	34.6	1,566.4	1,441.3	125.1
1987	1,167.8	1,536.0	−368.2	1,625.4	1,648.2	−22.8	1,709.0	1,650.9	58.1
1988	1,253.7	1,786.2	−532.5	1,841.0	2,002.8	−161.8	2,006.6	2,019.2	−12.6
1989				2,076.0	2,319.8	−243.8	2,348.1	2,418.6	−70.5
1990				2,180.0	2,426.4	−246.4	2,291.7	2,498.7	−207.0
1991				2,285.1	2,611.1	−326.0	2,468.4	2,788.3	−319.9
1992				2,325.0	2,798.0	−473.0	2,464.2	2,993.7	−529.5
1993				2,742.5	3,112.6	−370.1	3,055.3	3,330.2	−274.9
1994				2,899.0	3,310.7	−411.7	3,178.0	3,499.5	−321.5
1995				3,272.7	3,960.4	−687.7	3,700.4	4,337.9	−637.5
1996				3,720.7	4,591.3	−870.5	4,284.5	5,115.8	−831.3
1997				4,237.3	5,460.9	−1,223.6	5,007.1	6,329.6	−1,322.5
1998				5,079.1	6,190.9	−1,111.8	6,045.5	7,453.2	−1,407.7
1999				5,889.0	6,971.5	−1,082.5	7,173.4	8,647.1	−1,473.7
2000				6,167.2	8,009.9	−1,842.7	7,189.8	9,377.2	−2,187.4
2001				6,270.4	8,160.1	−1,889.7	6,898.7	9,206.9	−2,308.2
2002				6,413.5	8,646.6	−2,233.0	6,613.3	9,166.7	−2,553.4
2003				7,202.7	9,633.4	−2,430.7	7,864.0	10,515.0	−2,651.0

Source: U.S. Department of Commerce (updates are available at the department's Web site, http://www.bea.doc.gov).

Although the U.S. international investment position has been negative since some point during the 1980s by all three measures reported in Table 10, the United States continues to earn positive current net income on its foreign investments in most years. That is, U.S. owners of foreign assets earn more income from those assets than foreign owners earn from their U.S. assets (see Table 5).

The United States' negative net foreign wealth position often is compared with the debt of developing countries. U.S. external debt is approximately equivalent in size to the total external debt of all developing economies (which totals about $2.5 trillion)—making the United States by far the world's largest debtor. If the developing-country debt threatened the stability of those economies and the world financial system during the 1980s, mustn't

the same be true of the U.S. external debt? Not necessarily. First, the U.S. debt, though large in absolute terms, remains relatively small compared with the size of the U.S. economy with its annual GDP of more than $10 trillion, while several developing countries' debts equal many times their respective annual GDPs. Second, the U.S. debt is denominated in dollars, the country's own domestic currency, while the developing countries owe debt denominated largely in foreign currencies, which means those economies must run current-account surpluses to earn the foreign exchange to make their debt payments. Finally, whether debt presents a problem depends on the uses to which borrowed funds are put. For countries with a comparative advantage in future production (that is, low current income but plentiful productive investment opportunities), borrowing provides a way to use those opportunities. The projects funded by such borrowing earn returns sufficient to repay the loans and make both debtors and creditors better off by creating gains from intertemporal trade. Borrowing to finance consumption beyond a country's income, on the other hand, fails to generate returns to repay the loans and leads to debt problems.

CASE 3: REST OF GALAXY ENJOYS CURRENT-ACCOUNT SURPLUS

Official statistics indicate that the entire world economy runs an annual current-account deficit of almost a hundred billion dollars. Since Earth doesn't yet conduct interplanetary trade, something must be wrong with the numbers. In principle, the *world's* current-account balance must equal zero, because every transaction generates equal debit and credit entries in the world balance-of-payments accounts. We've seen that each country's balance-of-payments accounts typically include a statistical-discrepancy term to cover unreported or misreported data. But we might expect individual countries' statistical discrepancies to more-or-less offset in any given year, leaving the world accounts in rough balance. Instead, the world current account has shown a deficit every year since the mid-1970s, except for 1997; and the deficit has grown.

Experts have offered several explanations. If exports get recorded before imports because of transportation delays, then during periods of growing world trade, the current account could appear to be in chronic deficit. More flexible exchange rates, in place since the early 1970s, may make it more common for the same good to be recorded at different export and import values if the exchange rate changes during the transaction. Trade liberalization may leave countries with less incentive to count their trade carefully, especially imports, since less tariff revenue is at stake. Trade over the Internet may slip through cracks in the data-collection process. Emerging market economies, which may have fewer data-collection resources and less bookkeeping expertise, account for a growing share of trade. The growth of offshore financial centers and tax havens may make it easier for tax evaders to hide current income on their international asset holdings. And financial crises can create incentives for exporters to understate their exports in order to export the undeclared earnings illegally. No one really knows how much of the observed discrepancy should be attributed to these various possible explanations. But economists and policy makers are actively studying the problem because they realize that good policy making requires good information.

CASE 4: WORLD MERCHANDISE TRADE

In 2002, countries traded internationally approximately $6.5 trillion dollars worth of goods. Figure 5 illustrates the regional breakdown of trade for both exports and imports. In panel (a) of the figure, industrial countries accounted for two-thirds of all merchandise exports, or about $4.2 trillion worth. The remaining one-third of traded goods came from developing countries. Of developing-country exports, just over half originated in Asia. All developing countries in Africa, Europe, the Middle East, and the Western hemisphere combined exported 16 percent of the world total.

On the import side (illustrated in panel (b) of Figure 5), regional shares are similar to those for exports. Almost two-thirds of all traded-good imports went to industrial economies in 2002. Of the remaining one-third, most went to developing countries in Asia. Developing countries in Africa, Europe, the Middle East, and the Western hemisphere absorbed 11 percent of total world imports.

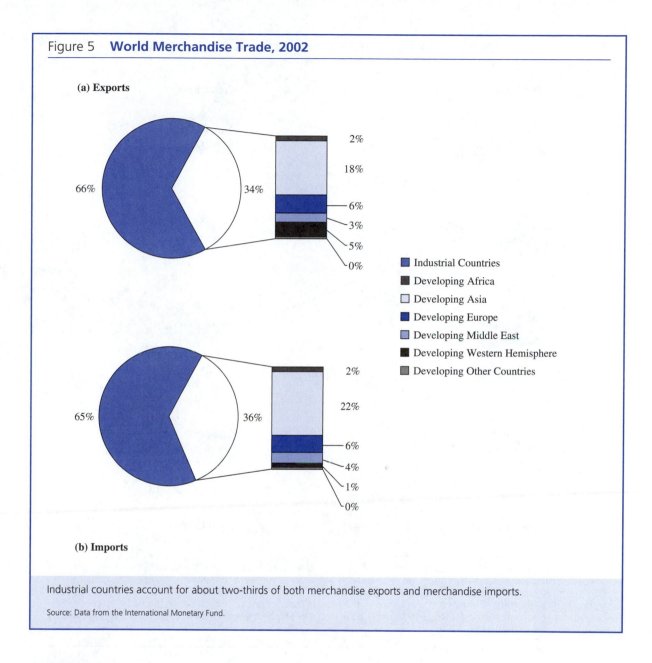

Figure 5 **World Merchandise Trade, 2002**

(a) Exports

66%   34%

2%
18%
6%
3%
5%
0%

■ Industrial Countries
■ Developing Africa
□ Developing Asia
■ Developing Europe
■ Developing Middle East
■ Developing Western Hemisphere
■ Developing Other Countries

65%   36%

2%
22%
6%
4%
1%
0%

(b) Imports

Industrial countries account for about two-thirds of both merchandise exports and merchandise imports.

Source: Data from the International Monetary Fund.

SUMMARY

The balance-of-payments accounts record transactions between residents, firms, and government agencies in one country and those in the rest of the world. Goods, services, loans, and a variety of assets are traded internationally, and a country's balance-of-payments accounts reflect all these transactions.

One of the simplest and most useful schemes for examining the balance-of-payments accounts divides transactions into current, capital, and official settlements accounts. By accounting convention, the accounts must "balance" in the trivial sense, so the sum of the balances on the current and capital accounts (plus the statistical discrepancy) equals the negative of the balance on the official settlements account. The current account, capital account, and statistical discrepancy represent autonomous transactions; when these three entries sum to zero, payments balance in the nontrivial sense. Transactions for which both entries occur in the current or the nonofficial capital account exert no effect on the balance of payments. The official settlements account records changes in the level of official foreign exchange reserves (accommodating transactions) and

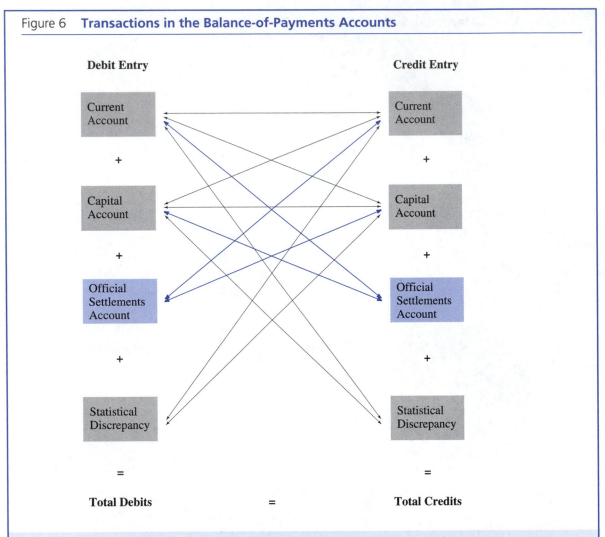

Figure 6   Transactions in the Balance-of-Payments Accounts

The sum of the current-account balance, the nonofficial capital-account balance, the official settlements balance, and the statistical discrepancy must equal zero. Transactions for which both the debit and the credit entry appear in the (autonomous) current or capital accounts don't affect the balance of payments (BOP = CAB + KAB = −OSB). Such transactions are represented by solid black lines in the figure. Transactions for which either the debit or credit entry occurs in the (accommodating) official settlements balance do affect the balance of payments and are represented by solid color lines in the figure.

captures the effects of government intervention in foreign exchange markets when exchange rates aren't completely flexible. Transactions for which one entry occurs in the official settlements balance do alter the balance of payments. Figure 6 summarizes the balance-of-payments accounts and the effect of various classes of transactions.

A number of popular misconceptions surround the balance of payments. Two of the most widespread concern the relationship between the merchandise trade balance and the balance of payments. First, a balance-of-payments deficit (or surplus) is *not* the same as a merchandise trade deficit (or surplus). The merchandise trade balance reflects trade in goods only, while the balance of payments records trade in goods and services as well as borrowing/lending and purchases/sales of assets. Second, a perfectly flexible exchange rate assures balance-of-payments equilibrium, but not balance in either merchandise trade or the current account. A flexible exchange rate moves to equate the quantity demanded and supplied of a currency in the foreign exchange markets. Like the balance-of-payments accounts, the demand for a currency reflects not only trade in goods but trade in services, assets, and loans.

LOOKING AHEAD

A country's international economic relations, including its balance of payments, matter primarily because they affect and are affected by domestic economic performance. The various components of the balance-of-payments accounts can affect domestic output, employment, prices, and interest rates as well as exchange rates. The next chapter begins the process of integrating international considerations—foreign exchange markets and the balance of payments—into a simple model of the macroeconomy.

KEY TERMS

merchandise exports
services
balance-of-payments (BOP) accounts
double-entry bookkeeping system
current account
credit
debit
current-account balance
deficit
merchandise trade balance
surplus
balance on goods and services
capital account
capital outflow

capital inflow
official settlements balance
statistical discrepancy
autonomous (independently motivated)
    transactions
balance-of-payments surplus
balance-of-payments deficit
accommodating (compensatory) transactions
overall (multilateral)
    balance-of-payments accounts
bilateral balance-of-payments accounts
Bretton Woods system
net foreign wealth (net international
    investment position)

PROBLEMS AND QUESTIONS FOR REVIEW

1. For the year 2004, country A has a current-account balance of −1,000 and a (nonofficial) capital-account balance of +1,500 (measured in units of country A's currency).
   a. What's the status of country A's 2004 balance of payments? What happened to country A's net investment position during 2004?
   b. What would happen under a flexible exchange regime? Why?
   c. Now assume that country A operates under a fixed exchange rate regime. If foreign central banks didn't buy or sell any country A deposits during 2004, what happened to the country's central bank's foreign exchange reserves during 2004? How would this be recorded in country A's balance-of-payments accounts?
   d. Continue to assume that country A operates under a fixed exchange rate regime. Foreign central banks sold 500 worth of deposits denominated in country A's currency. How would this be recorded in country A's balance-of-payments accounts?

2. China's dollar foreign exchange reserves rose by over $35 billion during the first three months of 2004 as a result of the Chinese central bank's intervention in the foreign exchange market.
   a. What does this suggest about the relationship between the observed yuan–dollar exchange rate and the yuan–dollar exchange rate that would have prevailed in the absence of the intervention, other things being equal? Why?
   b. Suppose that the Chinese central bank had not intervened in the foreign exchange market *and* that Chinese policy makers had removed the capital controls that prevent Chinese citizens from undertaking many types of investment abroad. Can you predict confidently the relationship between the observed yuan–dollar exchange rate and the rate that would have prevailed in this case? Why, or why not?

3. Under the Bretton Woods system of pegged exchange rates in effect from the end of World War II to the early 1970s, suppose that (then West) Germany had a balance-of-payments deficit with the United States. According to the rules of the Bretton Woods system and ignoring other countries, what would have happened, and how would it have been reflected in the U.S. balance-of-payments accounts?

4. Evaluate the following statements:
   a. "The theory of flexible exchange rates doesn't work. Otherwise, the United States couldn't have a $550 billion merchandise trade deficit."
   b. "Look at Tables 6 and 10. The U.S. capital-account balance and net international investment position never even show the same number for any given year. Obviously, the statistics can't be trusted."

5. Assume that the United States operates under a flexible exchange rate regime. Comment on the following statement: "The U.S. current-account deficit provides a measure of how much the United States must borrow abroad."

6. For each of the following transactions, show the entries in the balance-of-payments accounts for each of the countries involved and the overall effect on each country's balance of payments.
   a. In the 1980s, Pepsico (a U.S.-owned firm) sold $3 billion worth of Pepsi syrup to the Soviet Union in exchange for $3 billion worth of Stolichnaya vodka and ships. The exchange rate between dollars and rubles was $1/ruble0.5.
   b. A U.S. book publisher sells $20,000 of books to China and is paid with a check for 80,000 yuan that the publisher holds in an account in Beijing. The equilibrium exchange rate is $1/yuan4.
   c. A U.S. firm imports SF5,000 worth of goods from Switzerland. In the foreign exchange market, the firm is unable to purchase a Swiss franc deposit (with which to pay for the goods) at the pegged exchange rate of $1/SF2. The firm buys a SF5,000 deposit from the U.S. central bank.
   d. General Motors issues $10 million of new bonds, sells them to residents of Mexico, and uses the proceeds to buy an automobile factory in Mexico. The equilibrium exchange rate is $0.10/P1.
   e. Seagram sells Can$1 million worth of liquor to a U.S. distributor, who pays Seagram with a Can$1 million deposit in a New York bank. Seagram decides to keep the deposit. The equilibrium exchange rate is U.S.$1/Can$1.
   f. A British firm purchases a U.S. supercomputer and pays with a £100,000 deposit in a New York bank. The computer seller doesn't want to hold the pounds and sells them to the U.S. central bank at a pegged rate of $2/£1.
   g. Nissan (a Japanese auto firm) buys a factory in England and pays the British seller for the land and building with a ¥1 billion account in a Tokyo bank. The British seller decides to keep the yen deposit. The exchange rate is £1/¥200.
   h. A German firm hires a British attorney as a consultant. The attorney is paid with a € = 1,000 deposit in a Frankfurt bank, which she sells to the Bank of England (the British central bank) in exchange for a deposit of £350.

7. Briefly explain why equilibrium in the foreign exchange market and equilibrium in the balance of payments are two ways of looking at the same phenomenon.

8. Can a country have a
   a. current-account deficit, capital-account surplus, and flexible exchange rate? Why or why not?
   b. current-account deficit, capital-account deficit, and flexible exchange rate? Why or why not?
   c. merchandise trade deficit, capital-account deficit, and flexible exchange rate? Why or why not?
   d. current-account surplus, capital-account surplus, and fixed exchange rate? Why or why not?
   e. current-account surplus, capital-account surplus, official settlements balance surplus, and fixed exchange rate? Why or why not?

REFERENCES AND SELECTED READINGS

Feenstra, Robert C., et al. "Discrepancies in International Data: An Application to China-Hong Kong Entrepôt Trade." *American Economic Review Papers and Proceedings* 89 (May 1999): 338–343.
Difficulties in measuring countries' trade accurately; more on the subject of Case One.

International Monetary Fund. *Annual Report on Exchange Arrangements and Exchange Restrictions.* Washington, D.C.: International Monetary Fund, annual.
Comprehensive country-by-country report of exchange restrictions.

International Monetary Fund. *Balance of Payments Statistics.* Washington, D.C.: International Monetary Fund, annual. *Official balance-of-payments accounts for all IMF member countries.*

International Monetary Fund. *International Capital Markets.* Washington, D.C.: International Monetary Fund, annual. *Comprehensive survey of recent events in world capital markets.*

Obstfeld, M., and K. Rogoff. "The Intertemporal Approach to the Current Account." In *Handbook of International Economics,* Vol. 3, edited by G. M. Grossman and K. Rogoff, 1731–1800. Amsterdam: North-Holland, 1995. *Survey of the literature on the current account as intertemporal trade; for advanced students.*

U.S. Trade Deficit Review Commission. *The U.S. Trade Deficit: Causes, Consequences, and Recommendations for Action.* Washington, D.C.: U.S. Trade Deficit Review Commission, 2000. *Report of blue-ribbon panel on the trade deficit; available at http://govinfo.library.unt.edu/tdrc.*

World Bank. *Global Development Finance.* Washington, D.C.: World Bank, annual. *Comprehensive report on capital flows to and from developing countries.*

4

The Market for Goods and Services in an Open Economy

1 INTRODUCTION

Thus far, we've examined foreign exchange markets and the balance-of-payments accounts in relative isolation from other elements of the international macroeconomy. The next few chapters integrate exchange-rate and balance-of-payments considerations into a simple model of the macroeconomy. Our goal is to understand better the interactions between international and domestic elements in determining macroeconomic performance and the effectiveness of macroeconomic policy.

This is an area in which one hears many claims and counterclaims in the popular press. Critics of international openness claim that merchandise-trade deficits reduce economic growth and "deindustrialize" the U.S. economy. So-called experts disagree whether the U.S. trade deficit reflects unfair trade practices abroad, an attractive investment environment in the United States, or simply the interplay of domestic and foreign macroeconomic policies. Opponents of NAFTA (the North American Free Trade Agreement) allege that the agreement's opening of the Mexican economy contributed to the country's 1994 peso crisis. Critics of the European Union's macroeconomic integration worry that the lowering of economic barriers between countries lessens national policy makers' control over the macroeconomy. And policy makers the world over worry about catching at least an economic cold—if not pneumonia or worse—from other countries.

These complex issues involve the interaction of many economic variables, including output, price levels, rates of inflation, employment, exchange rates, and interest rates. Therefore, the perspective of this and subsequent chapters will alternate between partial-equilibrium analyses, which focus on a small subset of the interactions, and more general-equilibrium analyses, which, although more complicated, permit a broader view. We'll see that many disagreements and contradictory statements concerning international macroeconomics stem from ignoring or misunderstanding the relationship between partial- and general-equilibrium analyses. Statements that hold true when we consider only one market in isolation may be false once we introduce a more complete set of economic interactions.

Our investigation of the international macroeconomy will focus on three key markets: that for domestically produced goods and services (the subject of this chapter) and those for money and for foreign exchange (the subjects of the next chapter). Along the way, we'll mention several common sources of confusion and disagreement that have important effects on public opinion and on the policy-making process.

2 HOW DO WE MEASURE A COUNTRY'S OUTPUT?

The market for goods and services produced by the domestic economy provides the first building block of our model of an open macroeconomy. The most commonly used measures of an economy's goods and services output are **gross national product (GNP)** and **gross domestic product (GDP)**. Both measure the sum of the market values of all final goods and services produced by the economy in a given period (typically a year, although most governments report figures quarterly). Several features of this definition deserve note.

First, GNP and GDP exclude most goods and services not transacted through markets. Thus, both measures fail to reflect items such as homegrown food and housekeeping by family members—even though those goods and services contribute to society's economic welfare. Both measures also ignore the economy's production of "bads," such as pollution and congestion, because these costs aren't transacted in markets. Therefore, GDP and GNP don't necessarily accurately reflect residents' economic well-being.[1]

Second, calculation of GNP or GDP involves adding the *values* of all goods and services produced in the economy, evaluated at market prices. This step facilitates the aggregation of many diverse goods and services into a single measure. We can't simply add in physical units (bushels, dozens, and so forth) the automobiles, bananas, and computers produced, because each good is measured in different units. But market prices can translate the quantity of each good and service into a dollar value; and we can add the dollar values because they're measured in a common unit.

Third, GNP and GDP include only production of *final* goods and services, not intermediate ones; this convention avoids double-counting. If we included the values of silicon production, semiconductor-chip production, and computer production in GNP, we would count the value of the silicon three times, because the values of both chips and computers include the value of the silicon used as an input.

Finally, GNP and GDP refer to production within a specified period. For example, consider an economy with a GDP of $11 trillion. With no time period specified, this figure conveys little information. If the figure were a daily one, the economy would be enormous (approximately 365 times the size of the U.S. economy in 2003). If the figure referred to a decade, the economy would be much smaller (approximately one-tenth the size of the 2003 U.S. economy).

The difference between GNP and GDP lies in their definitions of "the economy." Gross *national* product refers to the output produced by a country's factors of production—regardless of where in the world the production takes place. Gross *domestic* product refers to output produced within a country's geographical boundaries—regardless of the resources' nationality. The output of a U.S. resident temporarily working in Germany, for example, is a part of U.S. GNP but not U.S. GDP, and a part of German GDP but not German GNP. Beginning with a country's GDP, we can arrive at its GNP by adding the country's receipts of factor income from the rest of the world and subtracting the country's payments of factor income to the rest of the world. Table 1 performs this exercise for the United States for a sample of years.

Until recently, most countries emphasized GDP in their economic reporting, while the United States emphasized GNP. In late 1991, the U.S. Department of Commerce announced that it would begin to focus more on GDP as its primary measure of output, although both figures would continue to be collected and reported. For the United States,

---

1. Despite this disclaimer, empirical evidence suggests that many important measures of well-being (for example, life expectancy and infant-mortality rates) are highly correlated with countries' GNP and GDP.

Table 1   **U.S. GDP AND GNP, 1960–2003 (BILLIONS $)**

Year	GDP	Plus: Receipts of Factor Income from the Rest of the World	Less: Payments of Factor Income to the Rest of the World	Equals: GNP
1960	$ 536.6	$ 5.0	$ 1.8	$ 529.8
1965	719.1	8.1	2.7	724.5
1970	1,035.6	13.0	6.6	1,042.0
1975	1,630.6	28.2	14.9	1,643.9
1980	2,784.2	81.8	46.5	2,819.5
1985	4,180.7	108.1	87.7	4,201.0
1990	5,743.8	177.5	156.4	5,764.9
1995	7,265.4	222.8	217.5	7,270.6
2000	9,963.1	370.6	374.9	9,958.7
2003	11,004.0	329.0	273.9	11,059.2

Source: U.S. Department of Commerce (updates are available at http://www.bea.doc.gov).

differences between the two measures are tiny. For countries with a greater divergence between factor-income receipts from the rest of the world and factor-income payments to the rest of the world, the GNP versus GDP distinction makes a bigger difference. For example, in 2002, GNP was 8 percent greater than GDP for Bangladesh, but 34 percent less than GDP for Ireland. Countries, such as Bangladesh, that are net providers of factor services to the rest of the world have GNPs that exceed their respective GDPs. Countries, such as Ireland, that are net importers of factor services have GNPs smaller than their GDPs. International factor payments include not only wages and salaries, but also interest and dividends and firms' profits.

3 WHAT DETERMINES OUTPUT AND INCOME IN AN OPEN ECONOMY?

One useful way to think about the market for goods and services at the macroeconomic level is to imagine the entire economy as composed of one giant firm, Nation Inc. This firm earns revenue by producing output that it sells at market prices. The firm's revenue equals the value of its output (the economy's GDP); this revenue, in turn, goes to pay the owners of the firm's inputs. Households in the economy own these inputs (labor services, raw materials, factories, and so on); so the revenue earned by Nation Inc. is paid out as income to households. Therefore, the economy's GDP (represented by Nation Inc.'s revenue) also equals **national income** or the total income of households in the economy (represented by Nation Inc.'s payments to inputs).[2] This equality between the value of output or GDP and the value of national income is important for understanding the determination of the equilibrium level of GDP.

---

2. In the national-income accounts, two entries preclude exact equality between GDP and national income: the capital consumption allowance, or depreciation, and indirect business taxes. Neither is a part of national income. For simplicity, we assume both to be zero to create exact equality between GDP and national income. This simplification doesn't affect the basic results of the analysis.

The next step involves analyzing the sources of demand for Nation Inc.'s output. Nation Inc. can sell its output to four basic groups: individuals, the firm Nation Inc. itself, government agencies, and foreigners. When individuals buy goods and services such as food, automobiles, books, and medical care, the spending is referred to as **consumption expenditure (C)**. When Nation Inc. retains a portion of the goods and services it produces (for example, machine tools, hammers, and personal computers) to use to produce next year's output, this spending is **investment expenditure (I)**.[3] Local, state, and federal government agencies purchase a variety of goods and services (such as file cabinets, missiles, and telephone service); these are called **government purchases (G)**. Government purchases refer only to government spending on goods and services and exclude government spending that simply transfers income between groups within the economy, such as Social Security, unemployment-insurance, and public-assistance benefits. Finally, **export expenditures (X)** represent spending by foreigners on the domestic economy's output.

We must make one adjustment before we can add consumption, investment, government purchases, and exports to arrive at total expenditure on Nation Inc.'s output. Consumption expenditure by individuals, investment expenditure by firms, and government purchases each may include some purchases of foreign-produced goods, or **import expenditures (imp)**, which we must subtract to obtain a measure of total expenditure on *domestic* economy's output. After this adjustment, we can write total expenditures (E) on Nation Inc.'s output as:

$$E = C + I + G + X - imp \qquad [1]$$

Equilibrium in the market for domestically produced goods and services requires that this expenditure just equal GDP, or the value of the economy's output of goods and services (denoted by Y):

$$Y = C + I + G + X - imp \qquad [2]$$

In words, the value of the economy's output (the left-hand side of Equation 2) must equal total expenditures made on that output (the right-hand side of Equation 2).[4] If we think of the economy as a single firm, the value of Nation Inc.'s output must equal the amount of revenues it takes in from selling that output. Table 2 reports GDP, consumption, investment, government purchases, exports, and imports for the United States for a sample of years, illustrating the relationships from Equations 1 and 2.[5]

Equation 2 provides the basic framework for our analysis of the market for goods and services, but it can't reveal much until we understand how its various terms are determined as well as which economic variables are held constant in the analysis. Remember that the Y on the left-hand side of Equation 2 represents the value of the economy's output, or GDP; however, Y also represents the total income of the individuals

---

3. Without our simplifying assumption of only one firm, investment includes one firm's purchases of other firms' outputs.

4. Equation 2 can be either an identity (a relationship that's always true—by definition) or an equation true only in equilibrium. If we define expenditure as including even unplanned changes in inventories (that is, accumulations of unsold output by firms), Equation 2 holds as an identity. If we define expenditure as excluding unplanned changes in inventories, Equation 2 holds only when no such changes occur. We use the second interpretation here.

5. In Table 2, the categories of expenditure include unplanned changes in firms' inventories so that the equality of income and expenditure holds as an identity in each period (see footnote 4).

Table 2   COMPONENTS OF U.S. GDP, 1960–2003 (BILLIONS $)

Year	Y	=	C	+	I	+	G	+	X	−	imp
1960	$ 526.2		$ 332.2		$ 78.8		$ 113.2		$ 25.3		$ 22.8
1965	719.1		444.3		118.0		153.0		35.4		31.5
1970	1,035.6		648.1		150.2		236.1		57.0		55.8
1975	1,630.6		1,029.1		225.4		362.6		136.3		122.7
1980	2,784.2		1,760.4		465.9		572.8		278.9		293.8
1985	4,180.7		2,704.8		715.1		875.0		303.0		417.2
1990	5,743.8		3,839.3		799.7		1,176.1		557.3		628.6
1995	7,265.4		4,957.7		1,038.2		1,355.5		818.4		904.5
2000	9,963.1		6,757.3		1,832.7		1,743.7		1,097.3		1,468.0
2003	11,004.0		7,760.9		1,665.8		2,075.5		1,046.2		1,544.3

Source: U.S. Department of Commerce (updates are available at http://www.bea.doc.gov).

in the economy (also known as *national income*).[6] This must hold true because Nation Inc. pays out the total value of its revenues to the owners of the resources it uses; these payments represent income to the recipients.

The amount of consumption expenditure (C) depends on income. In the case of one individual, the proposition that consumption depends positively on that individual's income seems intuitively appealing. The same relationship holds for the economy as a whole: Higher incomes coincide with higher consumption expenditures, and lower incomes with lower consumption expenditures, other things held constant. We can represent this relationship in shorthand form with $C(\overset{+}{Y})$, where the plus sign represents the positive relationship between income and consumption. When income rises, consumption rises, but by less than the increase in income; the remainder of the additional income goes into saving. Economists call the share of the increase in income consumed the **marginal propensity to consume (mpc)**, a fraction between 0 and 1. For example, if a $1,000 increase in national income causes consumption to rise by $800, the marginal propensity to consume equals $\Delta C/\Delta Y = \$800/\$1,000 = 0.8$, where we use the uppercase Greek letter delta, Δ, to denote the change in a variable.

Investment includes firms' purchases of new capital equipment (machines, factories, and so on) to produce future output, along with changes in firms' inventories. The level of investment expenditure in the economy depends primarily on the interest rate, i, which measures the opportunity cost of using funds in a particular investment project.[7] If a firm borrows funds to finance an investment project, it's easy to see that the interest rate represents the opportunity cost of the borrowed funds. At first, it may seem less obvious that the interest rate also measures the relevant opportunity cost when the firm uses internal (nonborrowed) funds. But remember that opportunity cost always measures forgone opportunity. A firm that undertakes an investment project using $1,000 of its own funds forgoes the opportunity to lend out those funds and earn interest.

---

6. GDP excludes factor income earned abroad, but includes payments to foreign factors employed in the domestic economy.

7. If individuals in the economy expect inflation, we must distinguish between real and nominal interest rates, with real rates determining investment behavior. We assume temporarily that expected inflation equals zero so that real and nominal rates of interest are equal.

Therefore, the interest rate measures the opportunity cost of the funds used for investment—regardless of whether the funds are borrowed or not. When the interest rate is low, so is the opportunity cost of funds with which to undertake investment projects; and firms undertake a relatively large number of projects. With a higher interest rate, the higher opportunity cost of funds makes fewer investment projects worthwhile. We can represent this negative relationship between the rate of interest and investment by $I(\bar{i})$.

Explaining the determinants of the level of government purchases is an important but complex and elusive goal. Two subfields within economics, public finance and public-choice theory, address this question directly. For our macroeconomic purposes, it suffices to assume that the level of government purchases of goods and services is determined exogenously, that is, outside our model. We'll take government purchases as a policy variable, one of policy makers' fiscal policy tools; and we can examine the effects of changes in fiscal policy on the economy's performance.

Exports, or purchases of domestically produced goods and services by foreigners, depend primarily on income in trading-partner countries and on the relative prices of domestic and foreign goods. To keep things simple by examining one country at a time, we'll assume that foreign income is just a constant, Y^*. (Whenever possible, we'll let a^* denote a magnitude for the foreign country; for example, if Y refers to domestic income, Y^* refers to foreign income.) Higher foreign incomes imply higher levels of foreign spending on all goods and services, including imports from the domestic economy. Therefore, foreign income and the domestic economy's exports are positively related. As in the case of government purchases, we can investigate the effects of changes in the level of foreign income even though we won't build an explicit model of its determinants.

Demand for exports also depends on their prices relative to the prices of their foreign-produced counterparts. The price of domestically produced goods is P, the domestic price level, measured in the domestic currency.[8] The domestic-currency price of foreign-produced goods equals their foreign-currency price (P^*) multiplied by the exchange rate, or the domestic-currency price of a unit of foreign currency. (*Why?*)[9] Therefore, we can define R, the *relative price of domestically produced goods and services*, as:

$$R \equiv P/eP^* \qquad\qquad [3]$$

The higher the relative price, R, the more expensive are domestic goods relative to foreign ones and the lower the domestic economy's ability to export. The lower the relative price, the less expensive are domestic goods compared with foreign ones and the higher the level of domestic exports. In other words, exports depend positively on foreign income and negatively on the relative price of domestic goods, or $X(\overset{+}{Y}{}^*, \bar{R})$.

The relative price of domestic and foreign goods, R, also is known as the **real exchange rate**. The domestic country's currency undergoes a real appreciation whenever R rises and a real depreciation when R falls. A real appreciation decreases the country's ability to export, and a real depreciation increases that ability. Note that a nominal appreciation of a country's currency (that is, a fall in e) leads to a real appreciation *if* there's no offsetting change in the domestic or foreign price level. Similarly, a nominal depreciation (that is, a rise in e) with no change in either price level implies a real depreciation as well.

The determinants of imports simply mirror the determinants of exports. Imports depend on domestic income and on the relative prices of domestic and foreign goods, or the real

---

8. The price level measure that takes into account prices of all the goods and services included in GDP is the *GDP deflator*. The deflator measures changes in prices over time by comparing the value of a given level of production at two sets of prices, one from a base year and the other from the current year.

9. Whenever we compare two prices, we must express them in a common currency. This is why we compare P with eP^*, not P with P^*. For a review, see section 2 in the Currency Markets and Exchange Rates chapter.

exchange rate. Imports rise with domestic income and with the relative price of domestic goods, $imp(\overset{+}{Y}, \overset{+}{R})$. (*Why?*) The share of any rise in income that goes to increased imports is the **marginal propensity to import (mpi)**, which, like the marginal propensity to consume, is a fraction between 0 and 1. If an increase in income of $1,000 leads to a $100 increase in imports, the marginal propensity to import equals $\Delta imp/\Delta Y = \$100/\$1,000 = 0.1$.

We now have the tools to depict graphically the relationship between national income and total expenditure on the economy's output of goods and services. The panels of Figure 1 combine consumption, investment, government purchases, exports, and

Figure 1 **Expenditure on Domestically Produced Goods and Services Depends on Income**

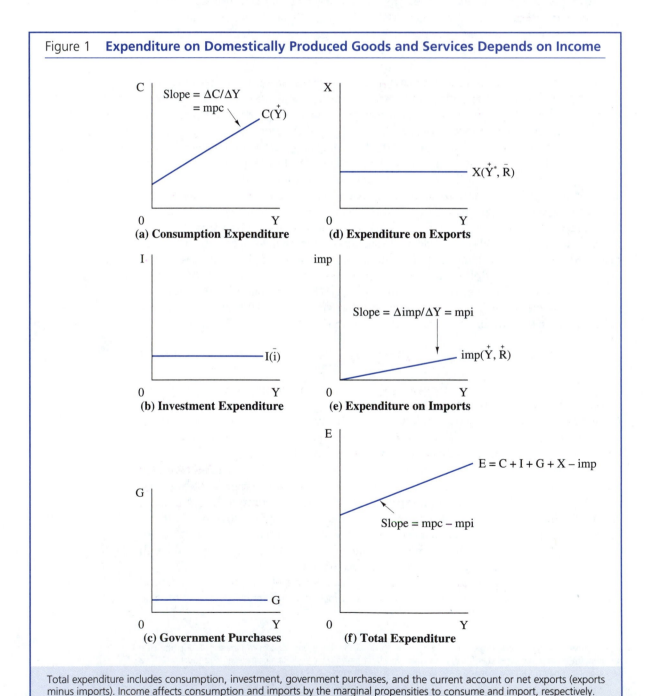

Total expenditure includes consumption, investment, government purchases, and the current account or net exports (exports minus imports). Income affects consumption and imports by the marginal propensities to consume and import, respectively.

imports to construct total expenditure. Panel (a) illustrates the positive relationship between consumption and income; the slope of the consumption line equals the marginal propensity to consume, or $\Delta C/\Delta Y$. The consumption line doesn't go through the origin but has a positive vertical intercept. This intercept captures the fact that if some disaster reduced national income to zero in one period, consumption wouldn't fall to zero but would continue at a positive level financed out of accumulated saving.

Panel (b) shows a horizontal line because we've assumed, for simplicity, that investment doesn't depend on income. The height of the investment line depends on the interest rate. The government purchase and export lines (panels (c) and (d), respectively), also are horizontal, since we assume that both spending categories are independent of income. Panel (e) exhibits a positive slope to capture the positive relationship between domestic income and expenditures on imports; the slope of the line measures the marginal propensity to import.

Total expenditure (panel (f)) is simply the sum of the various expenditure components (note that imports enter with a *negative* sign). The slope of the total expenditure line gives the effect of a change in income on total expenditure ($\Delta E/\Delta Y$). A rise in income causes two of the expenditure components to increase: consumption by the marginal propensity to consume and imports by the marginal propensity to import. The slope of the expenditure line equals the sum of these effects, where the change in imports again enters with a negative sign. Therefore, the slope of the total expenditure line equals (mpc − mpi).

Panel (f) of Figure 1 illustrates the relationship between the economy's national income or GDP (measured on the horizontal axis) and total expenditure on domestically produced goods and services (measured on the vertical axis). The market for goods and services will be in equilibrium when national income or GDP equals total expenditure (see Equation 2). We can easily find the point that satisfies this condition—by sketching in a 45-degree line, as in Figure 2. Recall that along any 45-degree line, the quantity measured on the horizontal

Figure 2   Equilibrium in the Market for Domestically Produced Goods and Services Requires That National Income (GDP) Equal Total Expenditure

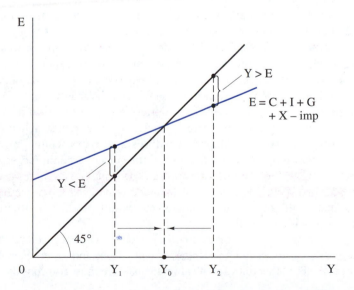

The market for goods and services is in equilibrium at Y_0. At incomes below Y_0 (such as Y_1), expenditure exceeds income, inventories decline, production increases, and income rises. At incomes greater than Y_0 (such as Y_2), income exceeds expenditure, inventories accumulate, production decreases, and income falls.

axis equals the quantity measured along the vertical axis; here this implies that national income equals total expenditure. The equilibrium level of income or GDP is Y_0.

At income levels below Y_0 (such as Y_1), expenditure exceeds the value of the economy's output of goods and services. When firms sell more goods and services than they produce, they see their inventories decline unexpectedly and respond by producing more. As a result, the value of output rises, moving Y toward Y_0. On the other hand, at levels of income above Y_0 (such as Y_2), income exceeds expenditure. The value of goods and services produced exceeds the expenditures made to buy them. Inventories begin to accumulate, and firms respond by reducing production. Income falls toward Y_0. The equilibrium at Y_0 is based on the assumption that i, Y^*, G, and R are fixed at the levels in Figure 1. A change in any of these variables will *shift* the expenditure line, resulting in a different equilibrium income; we'll explore the details of such changes later.

Now that we've seen how to determine the equilibrium level of income or GDP, we turn to investigations of international trade's effects and of events that alter the economy's equilibrium income.

4 HOW DOES INTERNATIONAL TRADE AFFECT THE MARKET FOR GOODS AND SERVICES?

The current account is one component of the market for domestically produced goods and services.[10] The other balance-of-payments accounts discussed in the previous chapter don't enter directly into the market for goods and services. Although simple, this point is important to remember to avoid confusion and spot common errors. The model of the market for goods and services presented in section 3 often is used to draw sweeping conclusions concerning the relationship between a country's income or output and its balance of payments. This is obviously inappropriate, since the model contains only a small subset of the transactions recorded in the balance-of-payments accounts. The model does, however, produce some useful insights into the interaction between the current account and national income.

The most important lesson to be learned is that the relationship between national income and the current account is an interactive one; that is, income affects the current account *and* the current account affects income. We can see this interaction clearly in Figure 3, which combines the export and import panels from Figure 1. Recall that exports are independent of the level of domestic income, while imports rise with income.

Holding constant foreign income (Y^*) and the relative prices of domestic and foreign goods or real exchange rate (R), the current account will be in balance (neither in surplus nor in deficit) at only one income, denoted Y_{ca} in Figure 3. When income falls below Y_{ca}, the resulting decline in imports produces a current-account surplus (X > imp). When income rises above Y_{ca}, imports rise and the current account moves into deficit (imp > X). *The level of income at which the market for goods and services is in equilibrium (Y_0 in Figure 2) and the level of income at which the current account balances (Y_{ca} in Figure 3) generally aren't the same*. Only an unlikely coincidence would produce a situation in which the two income levels coincided.

So far we've focused on income's effect on the current account: *Other things equal*, higher incomes are associated with current-account deficits and lower incomes with current-account surpluses. But other things aren't always equal. We must also consider the effect of changes in

---

10. In fact, the market for domestically produced goods and services includes only part of the current account—that is, net exports of goods and services.

Figure 3   **The Current Account and National Income**

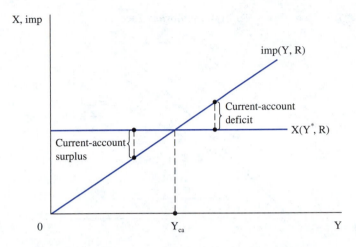

Because imports increase with income, other things equal, increases in income lead to current-account deficits, and decreases in income to surpluses. Income Y_{ca} represents the income at which the current-account balance equals zero. There's no necessary relationship between Y_{ca} and the level of income at which the market for goods and services is in equilibrium.

the current account on income. Suppose, for example, that an increase in foreign income from Y_0^* to Y_1^* increases the demand for exports, shifting up the total expenditure line, as in panel (a) of Figure 4. (You may want to review the effect of a change in exports on total expenditure in Figure 1.) The increased expenditures on domestic output run down inventories and cause firms to increase their production. The equilibrium level of domestic income rises from Y_0 to Y_1. The current account moves toward a surplus, but by *less* than the initial increase in exports would indicate. The increased exports lead to increased domestic income, which in turn raises imports and partially offsets the initial positive effect on the current account.[11] Once adjustment is complete, income is higher than in the initial equilibrium, and the current account will have moved toward a surplus. Similarly, a decrease in exports will move the current account toward a deficit and lead to a decrease in income that partially offsets that deficit. (*Illustrate the effects of a decrease in exports in a graph similar to Figure 4.*)

These results are simple but important, because they point out a common error. Earlier we argued that, other things equal, an increase in income leads to a current-account deficit (through an increase in imports) and a decrease in income to a current-account surplus (through a decrease in imports). But Figure 4 illustrates a rise in income accompanied by a move toward a surplus in the current account. There's no contradiction between the two lines of reasoning; in Figure 4, we can illustrate them by distinguishing between *movements along* the expenditure curves and *shifts* in the curves.

---

11. You may wonder whether imports might rise by more than exports, leading to a deficit on the current account. The answer is no, and the logic goes like this: Suppose Y* rises by $1, causing foreign imports to rise by mpi* · ΔY* = mpi* · $1. With only two countries in the world, foreign imports equal domestic exports, so ΔX = mpi* · $1. Domestic income rises by the increase in domestic exports multiplied by the spending multiplier (defined in section 5.1), so ΔY = mpi* · $1 [1/(1 − mpc + mpi)]. This causes domestic imports to rise by mpi · ΔY = mpi · mpi* · $1 [1/(1 − mpc + mpi)]. Because the marginal propensity to consume must lie between zero and one, we can show that the increase in domestic exports (ΔX = mpi* · $1) exceeds the increase in domestic imports (mpi · mpi* · $1 [1/(1 − mpc + mpi)]). Therefore, the rise in Y* must move the domestic current account toward a surplus.

Figure 4   **Interaction between Changes in the Current Account and Changes in Income**

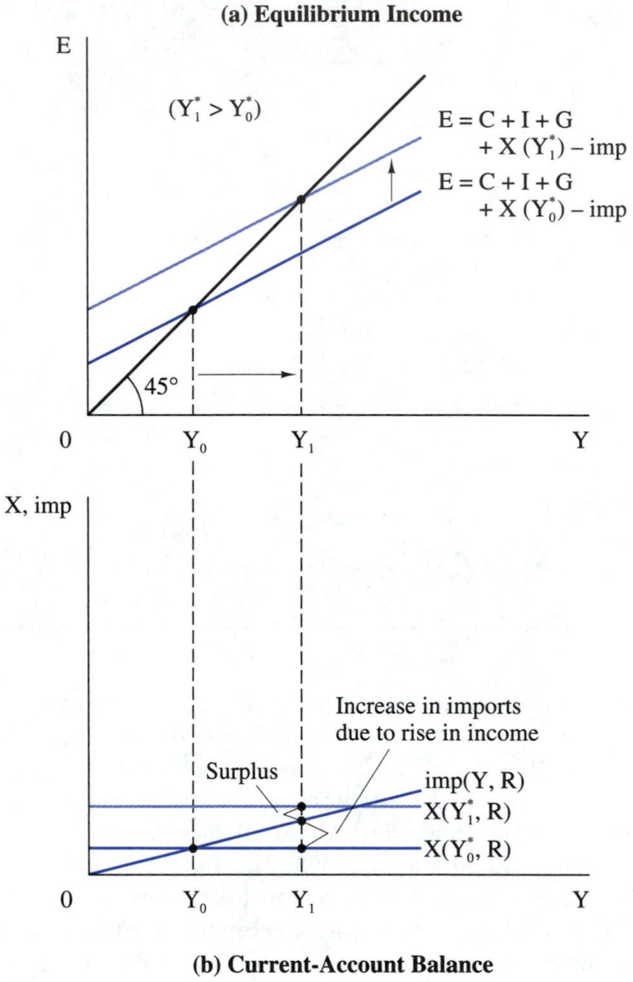

(a) Equilibrium Income

$(Y_1^* > Y_0^*)$

$E = C + I + G + X (Y_1^*) - imp$

$E = C + I + G + X (Y_0^*) - imp$

45°

$0 \qquad Y_0 \qquad Y_1 \qquad\qquad\qquad Y$

X, imp

Increase in imports due to rise in income

Surplus

$imp(Y, R)$

$X(Y_1^*, R)$

$X(Y_0^*, R)$

$0 \qquad Y_0 \qquad Y_1 \qquad\qquad\qquad Y$

(b) Current-Account Balance

The net effect of an increase in exports (caused here by an increase in foreign income) on the current account is smaller than the original increase in exports. Domestic income rises, producing a partially offsetting increase in imports.

A change in income (represented by a horizontal *movement along* an expenditure curve in Figure 4) changes imports in the same direction. As a result, any rise in income causes a move toward a deficit in the current account, while a fall in income causes a move toward a current-account surplus. But a change in exports or imports caused by something *other than* a change in domestic income (such as a change in foreign income) *shifts* the expenditure curve in panel (a) of Figure 4 and changes the equilibrium level of income. The new level of income is reflected in panel (b) in a new current-account value read from the intersection of the import line and the *new* export line at the new equilibrium income. The increase in imports causes the current-account surplus to be smaller than it would be otherwise, but the rise in income nonetheless accompanies a move toward a surplus in the current account.

Because of the two-way interaction between income and the current account, we must draw conclusions with care. In some situations, income may rise while the current account moves toward a deficit; in others, income may rise while the current account moves toward a surplus. The relationship depends on what causes the initial change.

4.1 A Note on Terminology

A move toward a surplus in the current account commonly is referred to as an *improvement* and a move toward a deficit a *deterioration* or *worsening* of the current account. Although this terminology is convenient in the sense that it is easier to say "the current account improved" than to say either "the current account moved toward a surplus" or "the current-account deficit declined," it also is potentially misleading. Speaking of a move toward a surplus as an improvement implies that such a move is desirable—which isn't necessarily the case.

Surpluses aren't necessarily good, just as deficits aren't necessarily bad. In fact, economies that grow rapidly relative to the rest of the world and provide many profitable investment opportunities tend to run current-account deficits. Those deficits are matched by capital inflows (capital-account surpluses) as foreign investors take advantage of the profitable opportunities provided by the growing economy. Similarly, a surplus may (but doesn't always) reflect a stagnant economy in which imports fall with declining income and foreign investors see few profitable investment opportunities. We can judge the desirability of a surplus or a deficit only in light of the country's overall economic situation.

There's another reason to avoid words with positive or negative connotations when describing economic events or situations: Such phenomena typically affect different individuals or groups in the economy differently. An entertaining editorial in *The Economist* noted this problem:

> It is bound to end in tears: some economists are trying to give their dismal science sex appeal. To make dry numbers more alluring, economic and financial commentators add emotive adjectives or nouns: gloom, worsening, cheer, improved. But the next time you spot the word gloom in a headline or read that a trade balance has deteriorated, ask this question: gloom for whom? The answer may be surprisingly cheery. . . . Economic commentators take note. Trade surpluses and deficits increase, rise, grow, widen or swell, but they never improve.[12]

Make it a habit to avoid terminology with inappropriate positive or negative connotations.

5 WHAT CAUSES CHANGES IN THE MARKET FOR GOODS AND SERVICES?

Variables held constant so far in our analysis include government purchases (G), the relative price of domestic and foreign goods or the real exchange rate (R), and the interest rate (i). We can determine the effects of each of these variables on income and the current account using the graphical framework developed in the preceding sections.[13] When we refer to "the" equilibrium level of income in the economy, we really mean the particular level of income that represents equilibrium in the market for goods and services *given* the values of other variables, including G, i, Y*, P, P*, and e, as well as the marginal propensities to consume and import. A change in any of these variables changes the income at which the value of goods and services produced (Y) equals expenditure on goods and services (E).

---

12. *The Economist,* August 31, 1991, p.16.

13. Other variables also can be changed, including the marginal propensities to consume and import; we leave these analyses to the reader.

5.1 Fiscal Policy and the Spending Multiplier

A change in government purchases of goods and services provides one example of a **fiscal policy**, a policy that uses changes in government spending or taxation to affect the macroeconomy's performance. Government purchases constitute one category of total expenditure on domestically produced goods and services (see Equation 2), so the *initial effect of a change in government purchases* is an equal change in total expenditure. Figure 5 depicts such a change as an increase from G_0 to G_1. Equilibrium income rises as a result, and the current account moves toward a deficit.

The magnitude of fiscal policy's effect on income depends on the **spending multiplier**. A $1 increase in government purchases generates an income increase of $1 times the spending multiplier. The value of the multiplier is given by $1/(1 - mpc + mpi)$, where mpc denotes the marginal propensity to consume and mpi denotes the marginal propensity to

Figure 5 **A Rise in Government Purchases Raises Equilibrium Income and Moves the Current Account toward a Deficit**

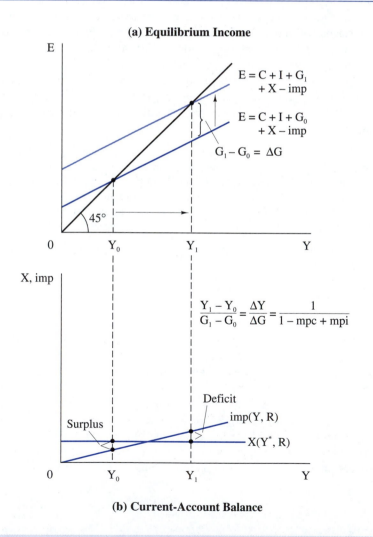

(a) Equilibrium Income

$$E = C + I + G_1 + X - imp$$

$$E = C + I + G_0 + X - imp$$

$$G_1 - G_0 = \Delta G$$

$$\frac{Y_1 - Y_0}{G_1 - G_0} = \frac{\Delta Y}{\Delta G} = \frac{1}{1 - mpc + mpi}$$

Deficit

imp(Y, R)

Surplus

$X(Y^*, R)$

(b) Current-Account Balance

The amount of the increase in income per unit increase in government expenditure is known as the spending multiplier and is equal to $1/(1 - mpc + mpi)$.

import. A high marginal propensity to consume increases the value of the multiplier by causing a larger share of the additional income to be passed along in the form of increased consumption expenditure. A high marginal propensity to import decreases the value of the multiplier, because income spent on imports "leaks" out of the domestic economy.

Suppose, for example, that the initial increase in government purchases ($G_1 - G_0$) equals \$1,000. Income immediately rises by \$1,000. The \$1,000 rise in income increases spending on domestic output by \$1,000(mpc − mpi). (*Why?*) This second round of increased spending is passed on as additional income out of which the recipients spend \$1,000(mpc − mpi)(mpc − mpi) on domestic output. This process—often called the **round-by-round effect**, because additional spending gets passed on in the next "round" as an increase in income—continues until the initial \$1,000 in government purchases has increased income by \$1,000(1/[1 − mpc + mpi]).[14] Therefore, the total change in the equilibrium level of income caused by a change in government purchases is:

$$\Delta Y = Y_1 - Y_0 = [1/(1 - mpc + mpi)]\,(G_1 - G_0) = \text{spending multiplier} \cdot \Delta G \qquad [4]$$

Because a rise in government purchases increases income, imports rise and the current account moves toward a deficit, as represented in panel (b) of Figure 5.

5.2 Relative Prices of Domestic and Foreign Goods: The Real Exchange Rate

Changes in the relative price of domestic and foreign goods or real exchange rate, R, also alter equilibrium income and the current account. A real appreciation of the domestic currency, or a rise in R, reflects domestic goods becoming more expensive relative to foreign ones. Exports fall (shown as a downward shift in the export line in Figure 6), and imports rise (shown as an upward shift in the import line).[15] These responses result from individuals shifting their purchases from now-more-expensive domestic goods to now-cheaper foreign goods.

Total expenditure on domestically produced goods and services falls, and the total expenditure line shifts down. As expenditure on domestically produced goods declines, inventories accumulate and domestic firms cut their production. Income falls by an amount equal to the magnitude of the shift down in total expenditure multiplied by the spending multiplier, (1/[1 − mpc + mpi]). Because of the decline in income, individuals curtail their spending, including spending on imports. The current account moves toward a deficit, but by somewhat less than the initial impact of the change in R, because of the partially offsetting effect of the decline in income and imports.[16]

Relative price or real exchange rate changes sometimes stem from deliberate economic policies. Economists call these policies, designed to alter the allocation of expenditure between domestic and foreign goods, **expenditure-switching policies**. The nominal exchange rate enters into the relative price of domestic and foreign goods or real exchange rate ($R \equiv P/eP^*$),

---

14. This follows from the fact that \$1 + \$1(mpc − mpi) + \$1(mpc − mpi)(mpc − mpi) + \$1(mpc − mpi)(mpc − mpi)(mpc − mpi) + . . . = \$1/(1 − [mpc − mpi]) = \$1/(1 − mpc + mpi). Each term corresponds to an increase in income of which a share equal to (mpc − mpi) is spent on domestic goods and therefore passed on as an increase in income to another individual in the economy.

15. For simplicity, we assume that the demands for imports and exports are price elastic. A rise in the relative price of domestic goods increases the quantity of imports and decreases the quantity of exports. The effects on the *value* of imports and exports depend on the cause of the change in relative price (P, e, or P*) and on the elasticities of demand. See the section on the J curve and footnote 17.

16. We know that the *net* effect on the current account is a move toward a deficit, because otherwise a net move toward a surplus would *increase* expenditure on domestically produced goods and services and *raise* income. But it is the *fall* in income that causes the secondary move toward a surplus on the current account to begin with. Hence, a net surplus on the current account from a rise in R produces a contradiction. We can show this algebraically using the technique from footnote 11.

Figure 6   **A Domestic Real Appreciation Reduces Income and Moves the Current Account toward a Deficit**

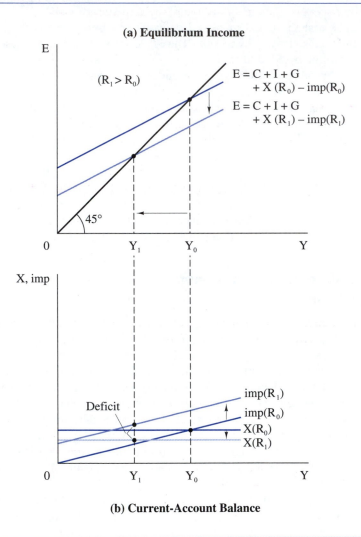

(a) Equilibrium Income

(b) Current-Account Balance

If domestic goods become relatively more expensive, demand shifts to imports, income falls, and the current account moves toward a deficit.

so changes in the nominal exchange rate under either fixed or flexible exchange rate regimes can alter relative prices, at least in the short run. Under a fixed exchange rate regime, a nominal devaluation (a rise in the domestic currency price of foreign currency, e) will lower the relative price of domestic goods (or, equivalently, generate a real devaluation) as long as price levels, P and P*, don't respond to offset completely the effect of the rise in e. A similar statement holds for a depreciation under a flexible exchange rate regime. We'll see in later chapters that there are good reasons to doubt that a devaluation or depreciation will leave P and P* unaffected in the long run.

This short-run effect of the exchange rate on relative prices historically has played an important role in international economic policy making. During the Depression of the 1930s, countries desperately tried to increase export markets for their goods as a means of combating unemployment. Country after country devalued its currency in an effort to achieve a real devaluation and a competitive advantage at the expense of its trading partners. Like other policies designed to benefit one country at the expense of others, such **competitive devaluations** are known as **beggar-thy-neighbor policies**. The nominal devaluations often failed to achieve the desired results because as soon as one country devalued its currency against its trading partners', the trading partners retaliated by devaluing their own currencies, leaving the initial exchange rate and relative prices little changed. At the same time, protectionist policies such as the Smoot-Hawley tariff in the United States were on the rise, effectively eliminating the possibility that international trade could help pull the world economy out of its depression.

Movements in nominal exchange rates, unless accompanied by offsetting price-level movements, always have distributive consequences within the domestic economy. Export-oriented and import-competing industries lose and domestically oriented (nontradable) industries gain from currency appreciations. Domestic consumers also gain as the domestic-currency price of imported goods falls, lowering the cost of living. Currency depreciations have the opposite effects, helping industries involved in international trade at the expense of nontrade industries and domestic consumers. These distributive effects help explain why the exchange rate never is perceived by everyone as being at the "right" level. During the 1970s, the dollar depreciated heavily against other major currencies, and the politicians seen as responsible lost public support. The early 1980s provided an example of the opposite phenomenon: The dollar appreciated substantially against other currencies, and support grew for policies designed to depreciate the dollar as well as for protectionism aimed at reducing the U.S. current-account deficit. The late 1980s and early 1990s produced substantial depreciations of the dollar against trading-partner currencies, especially the yen and Deutsche mark, a trend policy makers sought to interrupt through foreign exchange market intervention. By the late 1990s, dollar appreciation again made the headlines, especially against the depreciating Asian currencies during the Asian financial crisis and against the euro during that new currency's debut years. Headlines changed again early in the new century as the dollar lost value relative to currencies such as the euro and yen.

A CAVEAT: J-CURVE EFFECTS   We just argued that a real depreciation (or real devaluation) of the domestic currency lowers the relative price of domestically produced goods and services, increases exports, reduces imports, and thus moves the current account toward a surplus. This adjustment process, however, may not occur immediately. In fact, in the short run, a depreciation or devaluation of the domestic currency can even push the domestic current account toward a further *deficit*. To see why, it helps to write out the expression for the current-account balance, as in Equation 5:

$$\text{Current-account balance} = (\text{Price of exports} \cdot \text{Quantity of exports})$$
$$- (\text{Price of imports} \cdot \text{Quantity of imports}) \qquad [5]$$
$$= (P \cdot Q_X) - ([e \cdot P^*] \cdot Q_{imp}),$$

where Q_X and Q_{imp} represent the *quantities* of exports and imports, respectively. When e rises, the price of imports rises immediately, but the quantity of imports may take some time to adjust downward in response to the price change, because current imports and exports typically occur based on orders placed months in advance—before the devaluation or depreciation. If so, the *value* of imports will rise in the short run. Similarly, the domestic currency depreciation makes exports more attractive to foreign buyers, but those buyers may not adjust immediately to the price change. The result of quantities' slow adjustment to the relative price changes caused by a domestic currency depreciation or devaluation can be a short-run move toward a further deficit in the current account. (*Use Equation 5 to explain why.*)

Figure 7   The J Curve

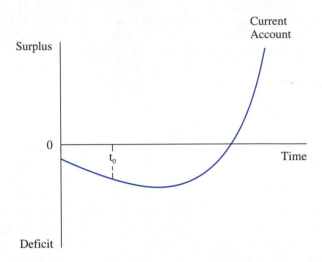

Policy makers devalue the domestic currency at time t_0. The devaluation immediately raises the domestic-currency price of imports. The quantities of imports and exports don't adjust right away, so the current-account deficit grows in the short run. As time passes, the quantity of imports falls and the quantity of exports rises. Eventually, the current account moves toward a surplus. The time path of the devaluation's effect on the current-account balance traces out a pattern similar to the letter *J*.

As time passes, import and export quantities do adjust. The quantity of imports falls, and the quantity of exports rises. This distinction between the effects of a real depreciation or devaluation depending on whether export and import quantities have had time to adjust is called the **J-curve** phenomenon. Figure 7 illustrates the logic behind the name. The horizontal axis measures time; the vertical axis measures the current-account balance. As the story opens, the current account is in deficit. The devaluation or depreciation of the domestic currency occurs at time t_0. Initially the current-account deficit grows because the domestic-currency price of imports rises. (*To test your understanding, explain what would happen to the J-curve analysis if contracts for imports were written in domestic currency, that is, if the prices paid for imports were set in terms of domestic rather than foreign currency.*) As time passes, export and import quantities begin to adjust. Export receipts rise, and expenditures on imports fall. The deficit stops growing, and the current account moves toward a surplus. The time path of the current account following the rise in e traces out a shape similar to the letter *J*.

Is the J curve just a theoretical curiosity, or is there evidence that it accurately describes the actual effects of exchange rate changes? Unfortunately, this question doesn't have a simple or definitive answer. The presence or absence of the J curve hinges on the demand elasticities for imports and exports.[17] These elasticities differ across historical periods and countries, so we observe the J curve in some cases and not in others. Recent experience suggests that industrial countries often experience J-curve effects for six months to a year following currency devaluations or depreciations. But even in cases with a pronounced J curve caused by low short-run elasticities, evidence shows longer-run elasticities high enough for real currency depreciations or devaluations to move the current account toward a surplus.

---

17. Letting ε_{imp} and ε_x represent the elasticities of demand for *imports* and exports, respectively, the effect of a domestic currency depreciation on the current-account balance equals $\varepsilon_x + \varepsilon_{imp} - 1$. Therefore, the more elastic the demands, the more a depreciation will shift the current account toward a surplus. If $(\varepsilon_x + \varepsilon_{imp}) > 1$, the current account does move toward a surplus; this is known as the *Marshall-Lerner condition*.

5.3 Interest Rates

Changes in interest rates alter equilibrium income by changing investment expenditure. A rise in interest rates discourages investment (see section 3). Investment expenditure is one component of total expenditure on the economy's output, so a fall in investment reduces total expenditure and causes a decline in income. This is illustrated in Figure 8, in which the interest rate rises from i_0 to i_1. The decline in income equals the change in investment expenditure multiplied by the spending multiplier ($1/[1 - \text{mpc} + \text{mpi}]$). The decline in income reduces imports and moves the current account toward a surplus. We

Figure 8   A Rise in the Interest Rate Reduces Income and Moves the Current Account toward a Surplus

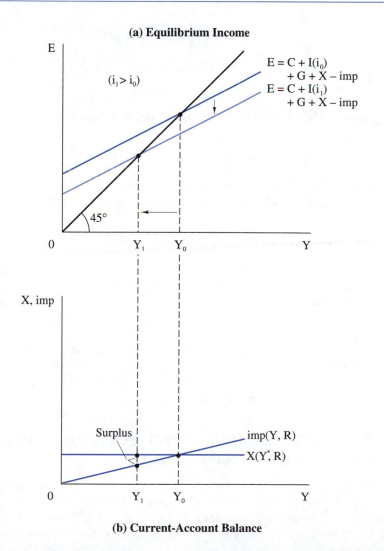

(a) Equilibrium Income

$$E = C + I(i_0) + G + X - \text{imp}$$

$$E = C + I(i_1) + G + X - \text{imp}$$

$(i_1 > i_0)$

(b) Current-Account Balance

A rise in the interest rate increases the opportunity cost of funds for investment. Investment expenditure falls, reducing total expenditure and the equilibrium level of income. The fall in income reduces imports, and the current account moves toward a surplus.

Table 3 EFFECTS ON EQUILIBRIUM INCOME AND THE CURRENT ACCOUNT

Variable	Effect on Equilibrium Income	Effect on Current-Account Balance
Increase total expenditure (E):		
Increase in G	+	−
Increase in Y*	+	+
Decrease in R	+	+
Decrease in P	+	+
Increase in P*	+	+
Increase in e	+	+
Decrease in i	+	−
Decrease total expenditure (E):		
Decrease in G	−	+
Decrease in Y*	−	−
Increase in R	−	−
Increase in P	−	−
Decrease in P*	−	−
Decrease in e	−	−
Increase in i	−	+

don't yet have a theory of what causes changes in the interest rate but will develop one in the next chapter, where we add money to our model of the macroeconomy.

5.4 Summary of Effects on Income and the Current Account

Changes in variables that increase total expenditure on domestically produced goods and services increase the income consistent with equilibrium in the market for goods and services. Such changes include increases in government purchases or foreign income and decreases in the relative price of domestic goods and services or in the domestic interest rate. Table 3 summarizes these effects.

Increases in government purchases and decreases in interest rates move the current account toward a deficit. Increases in foreign income or decreases in the relative price of domestic goods and services (whether caused by a fall in P, or a rise in P* or e) move the current account toward a surplus.

6 INTERDEPENDENCE: PROTECTIONISM, INCOME, AND THE CURRENT ACCOUNT

Despite protectionism's popularity as a response to a current-account deficit, economic analysis suggests that imposing tariffs and quotas to restrict imports is ineffective at best and damaging to the world economy at worst. Problems with protection include repercussions from the adverse effect of protectionism on trading partners' economies, the possibility of retaliation, and the economic inefficiencies introduced by trade barriers.

Just as exports provide a source of demand for domestic products, imports provide a source of demand for trading-partner economies. Protectionism by one country, to the extent it succeeds in reducing that country's demand for foreign goods, reduces foreign incomes. The reduction in foreign incomes then feeds back into the domestic economy through a reduction in foreign demand for exports. Because of these linkages among economies, artificial reductions in imports through protectionism result in reductions in exports.

The history of protectionist legislation makes clear that protectionism by one country in the world trading system leads to similar protectionism by other countries. Beggar-thy-neighbor policies of any type, by their very nature, spread quickly from one country to another. Each country's exports constitute its trading partners' imports, so successful efforts by one country to alter its current account always produce consequences for trading partners' current accounts. Retaliation adds one more reason why the belief that protectionism can reduce imports while leaving exports unchanged is naive. In fact, if protectionism simultaneously switches expenditure from foreign- to domestically produced goods for all countries, current-account balances remain unchanged, other things equal, because exports simply decline by the same amount as imports.

Finally, the most important reason for avoiding protectionist policies is that unrestricted international trade allows the world's scarce resources to produce the maximum quantity of goods and services. By interfering with the efficient allocation of resources, barriers to trade reduce the world economy's ability to produce goods and services. The result: fewer goods available for consumption and higher prices.

7 THE "TWIN DEFICITS"

In the popular- or business-press coverage of the U.S. economy one of the most commonly encountered subjects is the **"twin deficits"**. The term refers to the combination of a government budget deficit and a current-account deficit. In what sense are the two deficits "twins"? After all, the government budget deficit equals the amount by which government purchases of goods and services exceed the net tax revenues government takes in (G − T), while the current-account deficit refers to the amount by which the value of a country's imports exceeds the value of its exports.[18] Given these definitions, a direct connection between the two isn't immediately obvious.

Repeating the information from Equation 2, we know that national income equals the sum of consumption expenditure, investment expenditure, government purchases, and the current-account balance or net exports of goods and services (CA = X − imp):

$$Y = C + I + G + X - imp = C + I + G + CA \qquad [6]$$

Rearranging Equation 6, we can see that Y − (C + I + G) = CA, or that a country's current account reflects the difference between the country's national income (Y) and its residents' spending on goods and services (C + I + G). If residents buy more goods and services than the country produces, the country runs a current-account deficit (imports more goods and services than it exports), and the country must borrow from foreigners to cover its excess spending. From a balance-of-payments perspective, this is just another way of saying that a current-account deficit must be covered by a capital-account surplus, or a decline in the country's net foreign wealth. A country that

---

18. Note the other components of current account discussed in section 2.1 of the previous chapter.

produces more goods and services than its residents buy, on the other hand, runs a current-account surplus, and sells the excess to foreigners. The current-account surplus is matched by a capital-account deficit, or an increase in the country's net foreign wealth.

From the standpoint of the households that earn national income, there are three outlets for that income: It can be spent on consumption (C), paid to the government in taxes (T), or saved (S):[19]

$$Y = C + T + S \qquad [7]$$

Combining and rearranging Equations 6 and 7, we get an expression that highlights the relationship between the government budget and the current account:

$$S - I = (G - T) + (X - \text{imp}) = (G - T) + CA \qquad [8]$$

The difference between saving and investment in the economy $(S - I)$ must equal the sum of the government budget surplus $(G - T < 0)$ or deficit $(G - T > 0)$ and the current-account surplus $(CA > 0)$ or deficit $(CA < 0)$. The two terms on the right-hand side of Equation 8 are "twins" in the sense that, for given values of saving and investment, a change in one necessarily accompanies an offsetting change in the other. The larger the budget deficit (that is, the larger $G - T$), the larger the current-account deficit. Given private saving and investment in the economy, when government spends more than the revenue it takes in, the country must borrow abroad to finance that spending. (Recall that a current-account deficit implies a capital-account surplus or net borrowing from abroad.)

We can rearrange Equation 8 to note that:

$$I = S + (T - G) - CA \qquad [9]$$

An open economy has three sources of funds to finance investment: domestic private saving, a government budget surplus, or borrowing from abroad. Saving represents individuals in the economy forgoing current consumption and using the income not consumed to fund investment projects that increase future output. A government budget surplus occurs when government doesn't spend all the tax revenue it takes in $(T - G > 0)$; we can think of this as public saving by the government, and the excess funds can finance investment projects. The sum of private saving (S) and public or government saving $(T - G)$ is called national saving. Finally, the country can import more goods and services than it exports $(CA < 0)$, use the net imports for investment purposes, and borrow from foreigners.

To take yet another perspective, we can rearrange Equation 8 to focus on private saving in the economy:

$$S = I + (G - T) + CA \qquad [10]$$

When individuals in the economy save, that saving can go into any of three channels: domestic investment projects (I), purchases of bonds issued by the domestic government to cover its spending in excess of tax revenues $(G - T)$, or purchases of foreign assets and loans to foreigners (CA).

---

19. By definition, saving equals income minus consumption expenditures and net taxes.

Equation 10 also suggests why many analysts proposed policies to increase domestic private saving as a means of reducing the twin deficits. Higher saving raises the left-hand side of Equation 10, allowing any given budget deficit to coincide with a smaller current-account deficit. But evaluating policy proposals for dealing with the twin deficits requires more than the information provided in Equation 10. In particular, we need to understand how the variables in the equation are related, both to each other and to other important macroeconomic variables—tasks for the next three chapters. Before undertaking those tasks, we can summarize this chapter's results in a form handy for later use.

8 A CONCISE GRAPHICAL SUMMARY: THE IS CURVE

Our goal is to combine the insights from this chapter's examination of the market for goods and services with an understanding of the markets for money and foreign exchange. To help accomplish that goal, a graphical technique called an IS curve will prove useful. An **IS curve** summarizes the relationship between income and the interest rate that must hold for the market for goods and services to be in equilibrium. When we use IS curves, we'll assume that the price level (P) is fixed so that changes in nominal GDP (or Y, in our notation) translate directly into changes in real GDP, which we denote as Q, where $Y \equiv Q \cdot P$.

In section 5.3, we argued that a rise in the interest rate would, by discouraging investment, lower the income at which the market for goods and services was in equilibrium. Figure 9 repeats panel (a) of Figure 8, showing the effect of an increase in the interest rate on the income (now real GDP) at which the market for goods and services is in equilibrium. When the interest rate rises from i_0 to i_1, firms face an increased opportunity cost of funds for investment and investment expenditure falls from $I(i_0)$ to $I(i_1)$. Investment expenditure is one component of total expenditure on the goods and services produced by the domestic economy, so total expenditure falls. Firms find their inventories accumulating and respond by cutting their output, so GDP falls from Q_0 to Q_1. Similarly, a fall in the interest rate would require an increase in income for the market for goods and services to remain in equilibrium.

We can summarize the *negative* relationship between income and interest rate necessary to maintain equilibrium in the market for goods and services by a downward-sloping line as in panel (b) of Figure 9. We call this an *IS curve*, so named because in a closed economy the market for goods and services is in equilibrium when investment equals saving. In an open economy the relationship becomes more complex, making the IS terminology less descriptive. Nevertheless, we'll use the standard term, keeping in mind that the IS curve shows the combinations of income and interest at which the market for goods and services is in equilibrium.

An IS curve is drawn assuming that government expenditure (G), exports (X), and the marginal propensity to import are fixed. Changes in any of these variables shift the entire IS curve. In fact, a change in any variable, *other than the interest rate*, that shifts the total expenditure line also shifts the IS curve.[20] Any change that shifts the total expenditure line *up* shifts the IS curve to the *right*, and any change that *lowers* the total expenditure line shifts the IS curve to the *left*. For example, a rise in either government expenditure or exports raises total expenditure and therefore raises income at each level of the interest rate (see Equation 1). An increase in G or X thus shifts the

---

20. Changes in the interest rate cause movements along an IS curve rather than shifts in the curve, because the interest rate is the variable graphed on the diagram's vertical axis.

Figure 9   **The IS Curve**

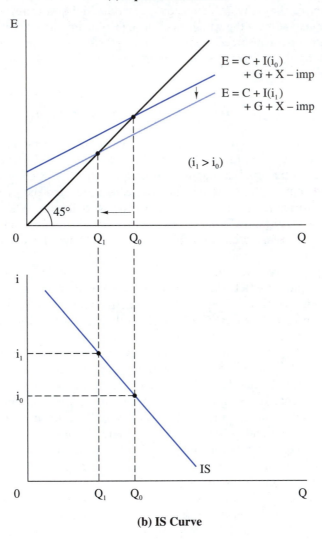

(a) Equilibrium Income

(b) IS Curve

An increase in the interest rate raises the opportunity cost of funds for investment, discourages investment, and lowers total expenditure on goods and services. The IS curve in panel (b) represents all combinations of domestic income and interest rate consistent with equilibrium in the market for goods and services. The IS curve is negatively sloped; a rise in the interest rate lowers investment expenditure and the equilibrium level of income.

IS curve to the right. An exogenous increase in imports reduces total expenditure and, given the interest rate, reduces income, shifting the IS curve to the left. Figure 10 summarizes these changes.

The IS curve summarizes the requirements for equilibrium in the market for goods and services in a single line, a convenient way to carry this chapter's results forward and to integrate them with other elements of the world macroeconomy.

Figure 10   Variables That Shift the Total Expenditure Line Also Shift the IS Curve

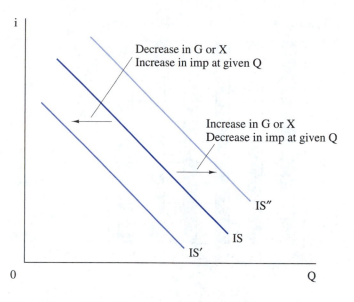

Changes that increase total expenditure (for example, an increase in G) shift the IS curve to the right. Changes that decrease total expenditure (for example, a decrease in G) shift the IS curve to the left. However, changes in the interest rate, i, shift the expenditure line but cause movements along the IS curve.

CASE 1: COMPONENTS OF GDP

The definition of gross domestic product as the sum of consumption expenditure, investment expenditure, government purchases of goods and services, and exports minus imports of goods and services applies to all countries. But the components' relative contributions to overall GDP vary significantly across countries, especially in the short run. Figure 11 provides some examples.[21] For each of the six countries in the table, the way the bar is divided represents the division of that country's GDP among the four components.

Consumption expenditure's share of GDP ranges from just under 40 percent in Saudi Arabia to almost 70 percent in Argentina. In three of the six countries, the consumption share exceeds half of GDP, and in three it falls short of half. For most countries, investment comprises 15–25 percent of

GDP. But two countries stand out as exceptions in Figure 11. Argentina, in the midst of a severe economic crisis in 2002, saw investment virtually halted. In China, on the other hand, investment expenditure took up approximately one-third of the country's overall output as the process of economic liberalization and integration with the world economy—which started in the late 1970s—continued.

Government purchases of goods and services vary widely with the different roles societies assign to government. Shares of 15–25 percent—similar to the investment shares—are common. But, again, there are exceptions. Of the countries included in Figure 11, Hong Kong, an economy with a tradition of a limited role for government predating its 1997 reversion to Chinese control, devotes the smallest share of its GDP to

---

21. You can find data for the United States in Table 2.

Figure 11   Components of GDP, 2002

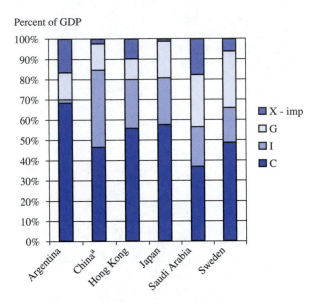

GDP equals the sum of consumption expenditure, investment expenditure, government purchases, and net exports; but the components' relative shares vary across countries.
aData for Mainland China refer to 2001.

Source: Data from International Monetary Fund.

---

government purchases. Saudi Arabia and Sweden, in contrast, while very different societies and economies, both assign government a much broader role in the economy; and these broad roles are reflected in higher shares of government purchases in GDP.

Finally, the net share of output sold to foreigners (that is, the difference between exports of goods and services and imports of goods and services) varies. Notice that this doesn't reflect the overall roles of trade in the respective economies. China, for example, exhibits a tiny contribution of trade to GDP in Figure 11, although both its exports and imports are very large. This follows from the fact that the similarity in the sizes of the country's exports and imports generates a small *net* effect of trade in GDP.

U.S./Mexico

CASE 2: THE PESO AND MEXICO–U.S. TRADE

Between November 1994 and March 1995, the peso price of a dollar almost doubled (see Figure 12, panel (a)), from about three and one-half pesos per dollar to almost seven. Mexican exports to the United States became much cheaper as a result, and Mexican imports from the United States much more expensive. Mexico's bilateral trade balance with the United States moved from a small deficit to a sizable

surplus (see Figure 12, panel (b)) in response to the sudden change in relative prices. Adding to the shift in trade patterns was a large decline in Mexico's national income brought about by some of the same economic conditions that led to the peso depreciation.

We'll see more about the 1994–95 Mexican episode in later chapters. But we can already understand part of what

Figure 12   Peso–Dollar Exchange Rate and Mexico–U.S. Trade Balance, 1992–2002

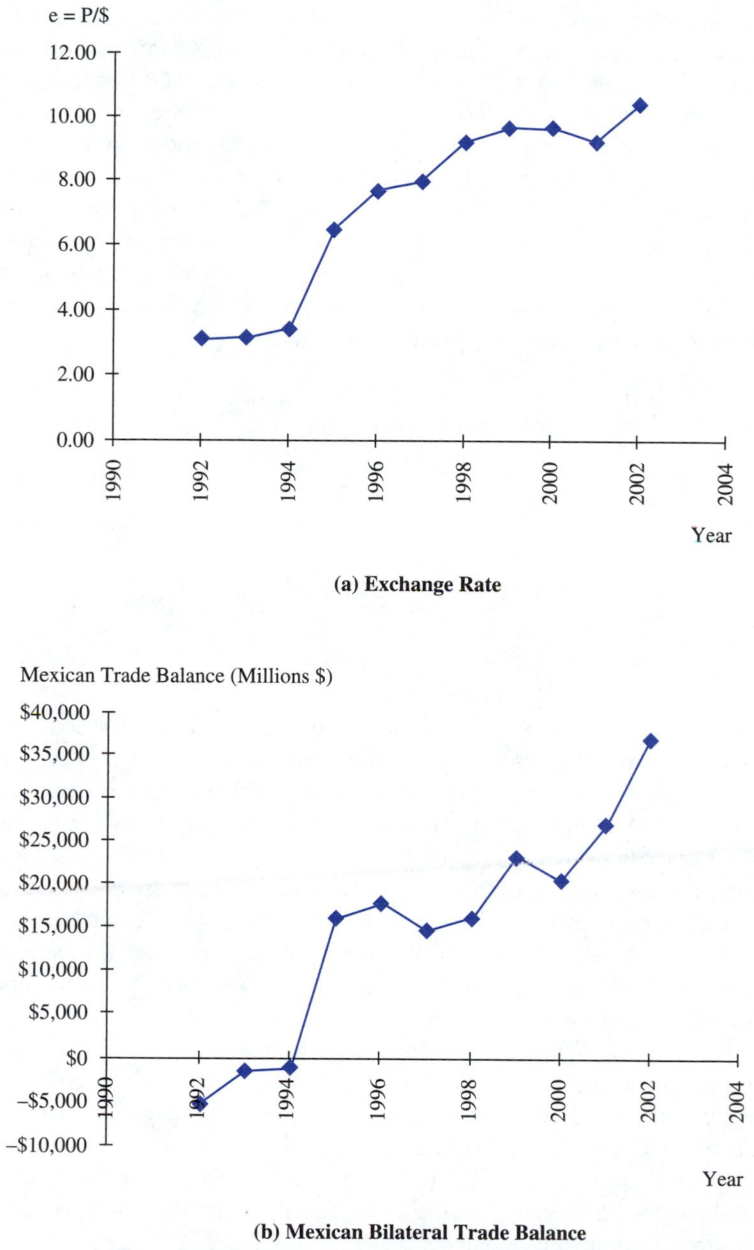

e = P/$

(a) Exchange Rate

Mexican Trade Balance (Millions $)

(b) Mexican Bilateral Trade Balance

The large peso depreciation against the dollar in December 1994 lowered the relative price of Mexican goods and services and moved Mexico's bilateral trade balance with the United States from a small deficit to a large surplus.

Source: Data from International Monetary Fund.

happened leading up to the 1994 crisis and devaluation. Mexico undertook a broad and successful program of economic liberalization starting in 1987 and culminating with the signing of NAFTA with the United States and Canada. But, despite the impressive liberalization, problem areas remained—a weak and largely unreformed financial and banking system and potential political instability related to alleged government corruption, for example. In 1994, an economic downturn was magnified by two political assassinations and a rebellion in the southern part of the country. Foreign-exchange market participants started to expect a peso devaluation; that is, the expected future spot peso price of dollars (e^e) rose. The expected rate of return on peso-denominated assets fell; and both Mexican and foreign investors started to move funds out of pesos in anticipation of a peso devaluation. The Mexican government pegged the peso–dollar exchange rate; so the Mexican interest rate rose substantially, from about 10 percent in early 1994 to almost 20 percent by the end of the year, to maintain interest parity. This rise in i discouraged investment expenditures and further reduced national income, as this chapter's model predicts. Finally,

the Mexican central bank ran short of dollar reserves with which to buy pesos in the foreign exchange market and had to devalue on December 20, 1994.

By the end of 1995, the worst of the crisis had ended. The post-crisis period has, so far, been one of relative stability in Mexico. Even the 2000 election generated few economic jitters, unusual in a country with a dramatic history of election-related economic crises. The peso, now floating in foreign exchange markets, has depreciated against the dollar.[22] Mexico maintains a bilateral trade surplus with the United States as the two economies continue to experience increased trade and economic integration under the North American Free Trade Agreement (NAFTA).

CASE 3: THE MACROECONOMICS OF GERMAN UNIFICATION

Germany

In 1990, the Federal Republic of (West) Germany and the (East) German Democratic Republic unified into a single economic and political entity. The act carried dramatic macroeconomic implications, as we'll see at several points over the next few chapters. Table 4 highlights a few key macroeconomic variables for Germany and how they were affected by unification and the policies that accompanied it.

Prior to unification, the Federal Republic of Germany ran a surplus on its current account, and the Deutsche mark price of a U.S. dollar stood at e = DM1.88/$1.[23] Fiscal policy exerted little net effect on the macroeconomy as the government budget surplus equaled less than one-half of 1 percent of GDP. With unification in 1990, government spending soared, the Deutsche mark appreciated dramatically against the dollar as well as other currencies, and the interest rate rose.[24] The current-account surplus

shrank, and the growth rate of real GDP accelerated, just as this chapter's model would lead us to expect. The expansionary fiscal policy continued for several years, and the DM price of the dollar remained low. The German current account shifted into deficit, reflecting reduced demand for German goods and services. At the same time, the rising interest rate reduced domestic investment in Germany. The combination of these two forces pushed the German economy into recession, and real output actually fell in 1993.

German policy makers' responses included reducing the government budget deficit and lowering the interest rate by pursuing somewhat more expansionary monetary policies. By 1994, real GDP was growing again, but the Deutsche mark hadn't reversed its appreciation relative to the dollar, and the German current account remained in deficit.

---

22. We'll see later, when we relax the assumption of a fixed price level, that currencies of high-inflation countries tend to depreciate against currencies of low-inflation countries. Throughout the period, Mexico's inflation rate exceeded the U.S. inflation rate.

23. Since we focus in this case on the German economy, we report the exchange rate, e, as the German (domestic) currency price of U.S. (foreign) currency, or the Deutsche mark price of a dollar.

24. We'll see in later chapters that there are reasons to expect a currency appreciation and a rise in the interest rate to follow expansionary fiscal policy.

Table 4 **GERMAN MACROECONOMIC INDICATORS, 1989–1994**[a]

Year	Current-Account Balance (Billions $)	Structural Fiscal Balance (Percent of GDP)[b]	e = DM/$	Percent Change in Real GDP	Interest Rate (Percent)
1989	$57.3	−0.4%	1.88	3.6%	6.6%
1990	46.9	−3.5	1.62	5.7	8.0
1991	−19.2	−5.3	1.66	2.9	8.9
1992	−21.0	−3.6	1.56	2.2	9.4
1993	−14.8	−2.0	1.65	−1.1	7.4
1994	−22.6	−1.0	1.62	2.3	5.3

[a]Figures through 1990 refer to Federal Republic only.
[b]Government budget surplus (+) or deficit (−) evaluated at potential output and expressed as a percent of GDP.

Source: International Monetary Fund, *World Economic Outlook; Economic Report of the President.*

SUMMARY

The current account's effect on equilibrium in the market for goods and services is one important avenue by which international trade affects the performance of the domestic macroeconomy. But the relationship between income and the current account is more complex than is often recognized. Changes in the current account do affect national income, but changes in national income affect both the current account and the incomes of trading-partner countries. Other important considerations determining equilibrium in the market for goods and services include fiscal policy, the relative prices of domestic and foreign goods or real exchange rate, and interest rates.

LOOKING AHEAD

In section 5.3, we saw that for every possible interest rate there exists a different equilibrium income. This implies that to determine actual equilibrium income, we need to know the interest rate. This chapter focused solely on the market for goods and services, so we don't yet have a way to determine the interest rate. In the next chapter, we'll combine the market for goods and services developed here with the markets for money and foreign exchange. Using a general-equilibrium approach with all three markets will allow us to examine income, the interest rate, and the balance of payments (or the exchange rate) simultaneously.

KEY TERMS

gross national product (GNP)
gross domestic product (GDP)
national income
consumption expenditure (C)
investment expenditure (I)
government purchases (G)
export expenditures (X)
import expenditures (imp)
marginal propensity to consume (mpc)
real exchange rate

marginal propensity to import (mpi)
fiscal policy
spending multiplier
round-by-round effect
expenditure-switching policy
competitive devaluation
beggar-thy-neighbor policy
J curve
"twin deficits"
IS curve

PROBLEMS AND QUESTIONS FOR REVIEW

1. Beginning from a position of equilibrium in the market for goods and services and in the current account, government expenditure rises by 100. The marginal propensity to consume is 0.6, and the marginal propensity to import is 0.1. *Ignoring the effects on other countries*, by how much will equilibrium GDP change? What happens to exports? To imports? To the current account?

2. Between 1992 and 1998, the U.S. government budget moved from a large deficit to a small surplus, and the current-account deficit grew. What do you think happened to the relationship between saving and investment in the United States over the same period? Explain.

3. Assume that the United States and Japan are the only countries in the world. Beginning from a position of equilibrium in the U.S. and Japanese markets for goods and services, suppose Japan increases government spending by 1,000.
   a. If the Japanese marginal propensity to consume equals 0.7 and the Japanese marginal propensity to import equals 0.2, what will happen to Japanese income (Y^J) as a result of the fiscal expansion?
   b. What will happen to U.S. exports of goods and services because of the Japanese fiscal expansion?
   c. Assume that the U.S. marginal propensity to consume is 0.9 and the U.S. marginal propensity to import is 0.1. What will happen to U.S. income (Y^{US}) as a result of the Japanese fiscal expansion?
   d. What is the net effect of the Japanese fiscal policy on the U.S. current-account balance?
   e. Illustrate the U.S. results of the Japanese policy. (Don't worry about the numerical precision of your graph; just illustrate the qualitative effects.)

4. Suppose the government institutes a tax cut. What would be the effects on equilibrium income and the current-account balance?

5. State how you would expect each of the following groups to feel about a real depreciation of the U.S. dollar. Briefly explain your reasoning.
   a. Boeing (one of the largest U.S. exporters)
   b. The United Auto Workers Union
   c. The owner of a small U.S. shop that sells foreign-made handicrafts
   d. A dedicated American consumer of fine French wines

6. Explain: "Other things equal, a high marginal propensity to import reduces the macroeconomic impact of fiscal policy."

7. If country A has a government budget deficit of $400 billion and a current-account deficit of $500 billion dollars, what is the relationship between investment and saving in the economy? Assuming no change in investment or saving, if the government budget deficit fell to $200 billion, what would happen to the current-account balance?

8. Suppose an auto producer obtains all its components in Britain, with their costs denominated in pounds. The firm sells most of its cars in the euro zone of Europe. How would a 20 percent appreciation of the pound against the euro affect the firm?

REFERENCES AND SELECTED READINGS

Baxter, M. "International Trade and Business Cycles." In *Handbook of International Economics*, Vol. 3, edited by G. M. Grossman and K. Rogoff, 1801–1864. Amsterdam: North-Holland, 1995.
Survey of research on the relationship between international trade activity and macroeconomic cycles; for intermediate and advanced students.

Boskin, Michael J. "Economic Measurement: Progress and Challenges." *American Economic Review Papers and Proceedings* 90 (May 2000): 247–252.
Accessible overview of issues in measuring countries' GDP and trade.

Obstfeld, M., and K. Rogoff. "The Intertemporal Approach to the Current Account." In *Handbook of International Economics*, Vol. 3, edited by G. M. Grossman and K. Rogoff, 1731–1800. Amsterdam: North-Holland, 1995.
Survey of research on the current account from the perspective of intertemporal trade; for advanced students.

Obstfeld, Maurice, and Kenneth Rogoff. *Foundations of International Macroeconomics.* Cambridge, Mass.: MIT Press, 1996.
Advanced textbook on international macroeconomics.

Pollard, Patricia S., and Cletus C. Coughlin. "Going Down: The Asian Crisis and U.S. Exports." Federal Reserve Bank of St. Louis, *Review* 81 (March/April 1999): 33–46.
Accessible overview of how the early stages of the Asian financial crisis affected U.S. exports.

U.S. Trade Deficit Review Commission. *The U.S. Trade Deficit: Causes, Consequences, and Recommendations for Action.* Washington, D.C.: U.S. Trade Deficit Review Commission, 2000.
Report of blue-ribbon panel on the trade deficit; available at http://govinfo.library.unt.edu/tdrc.

5

Money, the Banking System, and Foreign Exchange

1 INTRODUCTION

This chapter constructs the second and third building blocks of our basic model of an open macroeconomy: the markets for money and foreign exchange. The previous chapter explored the effect of openness on the market for goods and services. We saw that an economy that engages in international trade has an additional source of demand for its output (exports) and an additional leakage of domestic expenditure out of the domestic economy (imports). The current account—or, more precisely, the difference between the value of goods and services exports and the value of goods and services imports—provides one avenue through which the exchange rate and events in trading-partner economies affect the domestic economy.

An economy's openness also affects its money market, but in a more subtle way than it does the market for goods and services. At first glance the money market in an open economy appears identical to that in a closed one, which you may remember from introductory economics or other courses in macroeconomics. Later in this chapter, we'll see that the effect of openness on the money market, though subtle, is perhaps the most important key to understanding policy options in the world macroeconomy.

Of course, the most obvious effect of openness on the macroeconomy involves the introduction of a foreign exchange market. We examined the essentials of this market in an asset-oriented demand/supply framework in the chapter on currency markets and exchange rates and then related it to the balance-of-payments accounts. Later in this chapter, we'll translate our findings from those chapters into a form more convenient for combining with what we learned in the last chapter about the market for goods and services.

2 MONEY IN THE WORLD ECONOMY

2.1 What's Money?

As an important first step in studying money's role in the world economy, we must recall economists' definition of money, which differs somewhat from the popular usage. To an economist, money is an asset that its owner can use directly as a means of payment. Currency (coins and paper notes) held by the public plus checkable deposits, or deposits on which checks can be written, constitute a country's money stock.[1]

---

1. Traveler's checks also are included. The large time deposits transacted in the foreign exchange market *don't* constitute part of a country's money stock. Be careful not to confuse the foreign exchange market with the money market.

Either form of money, currency or checks, can be used directly (that is, without an intermediate exchange) to pay for goods and services.

Nonmoney assets, such as stocks, bonds, real estate, certificates of deposit, and diamonds, also represent purchasing power to their owners, but those assets typically can't be used directly as a means of payment. If an owner of shares of Microsoft stock, a U.S. Treasury bond, or a diamond ring decides to use that asset's purchasing power to buy a new car, the transaction requires two steps, or exchanges. First, the individual must find someone to buy the asset; this involves exchanging the asset for money. Second, the individual uses the money obtained in the first step to buy the car. Only an unlikely coincidence would find two individuals directly exchanging Microsoft stock for a car. Such **barter** exchanges—transactions that don't use money as an intermediate step—are rare, because they require a *double coincidence of wants*. The owner of Microsoft stock may find it difficult to locate an individual who both has the desired type of car for sale and wants to buy Microsoft stock. Money eliminates the need for this double coincidence of wants by allowing monetary exchange to separate the car-stock transaction into two pieces.

Note that the economist's definition of money is narrower than the popular one, which identifies money with purchasing power, income, or wealth. A statement such as, "I want to take a vacation, but don't have enough money," usually means that the individual has chosen not to spend a portion of his or her limited income or purchasing power on a vacation. The individual might have $5,000 in his or her checking account—more than enough money, by the economist's definition, for a vacation—but have higher-priority uses for those funds. The shortage, then, isn't really one of *money* but one of *purchasing power* or *income*. Another way to view the distinction between money and income is to realize that a shortage of money, by the economist's definition, rarely is a problem. As long as an individual owns some nonmoney assets, he or she can obtain more money simply by selling a nonmoney asset. In discussing the market for money, we'll need to keep in mind the distinction between money and purchasing power or income.

Money serves its purpose primarily because individuals expect that it will continue to do so. A music store owner doesn't hesitate to accept a $20 bill in payment for a compact disk, because the owner believes that he or she, in turn, can use the $20 bill to buy some other good or service. It's this confidence in money's acceptability as a means of payment—rather than any intrinsic value of the paper itself—that allows money to facilitate transactions effectively. Historically, many curious items have functioned as money, including beads, seashells, beer, and cigarettes. The specific physical form of money is relatively unimportant as long as it is commonly accepted as payment.[2]

We denote a country's **nominal money stock**, or the money stock measured in current dollars, as M.[3] The term *money stock* denotes the quantity of money *at a point in time* in the same way the term *housing stock* refers to the number of houses that exist at a given time.[4] Table 1 reports the U.S. nominal money stock from 1960 through 2002. The reported measure, called M1, includes currency and checkable deposits as well as minor items such as traveler's checks. The government also reports several broader measures of money, but for our purposes M1 will suffice. U.S. M1 has increased by a factor of about 8 since 1960; but its annual rate of change has been erratic, ranging from a decline of more than 4 percent in 1996 to an increase of almost 17 percent in 1986.

Before going on to discuss money demand, we'll make one adjustment. Economists traditionally analyze money demand in real rather than nominal terms, so it's convenient to translate the money stock into real terms as well. As always, we can make this translation

---

2. It's helpful if money is durable and easily measured and transported, conditions satisfied by paper currency.

3. Each country's money stock is measured in current units of *that country's* currency.

4. The alternative type of measure is a *flow*, which refers to a quantity (such as GDP) per unit of time.

Table 1	U.S. NOMINAL AND REAL MONEY STOCKS (M1), 1960–2002				
Year	M1 ($ Billions)	M1/P (2000 $ Billions)	Year	M1 ($ Billions)	M1/P (2000 $ Billions)
1960	$140.7	$668.7	1985	$ 619.1	$ 888.1
1965	167.8	744.6	1990	824.1	1,010.1
1970	214.3	778.3	1995	1,126.7	1,223.3
1975	286.8	754.7	2000	1,084.7	1,084.7
1980	408.1	755.1	2002	1,210.4	1,164.5

Source: Data from Board of Governors of the Federal Reserve System (updates are available at http://www.federalreserve.gov).

easily by dividing the nominal money stock by a price index. The **real money stock** at any time equals the nominal money stock, M, divided by a price index, here the GDP deflator, P:

$$\text{Real money stock} = \text{Nominal money stock/Price index} = M/P \qquad [1]$$

The real money stock is measured in constant dollars or at the price level in effect during the base year on which the price index is calculated. Over periods of rising prices, the nominal money stock grows faster than the real money stock. During periods of falling prices, the real money stock grows faster than the nominal one. Table 1 also reports the U.S. real money stock for 1960–2002. Because prices rose each year, the nominal money stock exceeds the real money stock after the base year—2000 in Table 1—and the real money stock stated in 2000 dollars exceeds the nominal money stock for each year before 2000. (*Verify these relationships in Table 1.*)

2.2 The Demand for Money

Money is defined as assets that can be used directly as a means of purchase, so individuals choose to hold a portion of their total wealth in the form of money primarily for its convenience in making transactions. The demand for money reflects the quantity of currency and checkable deposits the public wants to hold to make purchases.[5] In 2000, money holdings in the United States averaged over $4,000 per person (including children!), with almost $1,900 per person in the form of currency.[6]

Studies of individuals' money-demand behavior suggest that they care primarily about how many goods and services they can buy with their money balances. In other words, individuals don't choose the number of *dollars* to hold in the form of money but rather the amount of *purchasing power* over goods and services to hold in that form. This explains why economists usually formulate their models of money demand in terms of **real money balances**, or nominal money balances divided by the price level. These models recognize that if the price level in the economy suddenly doubled while nothing

---

5. This discussion concentrates on the transactions demand for money, that is, the demand for money based on its convenience as a means of payment. Other reasons for holding money include precautionary and speculative motives. Standard macroeconomics texts discuss these; including them here would add little to the discussion.

6. In fact, no one really knows the location of a large portion of the U.S. currency in circulation. Experts think that much of the currency facilitates illegal transactions (for example, the drug trade) and circulates in foreign countries that lack reliable domestic currencies.

else changed, individuals would choose to double the number of dollars held in money balances, to maintain the original purchasing power of their money balances.[7]

If individuals choose to hold money for its transactional convenience, the quantity of money held should vary with the volume of transactions. We can incorporate this relationship into our model by assuming that the demand for real money balances depends on real income, Q.[8] When real income is high, individuals undertake more and larger transactions and therefore demand a larger quantity of real money balances. Low levels of real income, on the other hand, are associated with fewer and smaller transactions and correspondingly lower real money balances. Letting L (for liquidity) represent the demand for real money balances, we can express the positive relationship between real income and money demand as $L(\overset{+}{Q})$.

If money provides convenience for making transactions, why don't individuals choose to hold all their assets in this form? Because an individual holding money incurs a cost: the forgone interest the individual could have earned on other assets, such as bonds. Typically, money balances earn little or no interest. Even though some forms of money, such as interest-bearing checking accounts, do earn some interest, the rates paid remain much lower than those on nonmoney assets such as bonds. Therefore, the difference between the interest paid on interest-bearing checking accounts and the interest paid on bonds still represents an **opportunity cost of holding money**.

When the interest rate is high, the opportunity cost of holding money assets also is high, and individuals choose to hold a smaller fraction of their assets in money; in other words, they demand a relatively small quantity of money. At a lower interest rate, the opportunity cost of holding money is smaller and the quantity demanded of money is higher. We can combine the negative relationship between money demand and the interest rate with the earlier result for income and summarize the two as $L(\overset{+}{Q},\overset{-}{i})$.

Figure 1 depicts the relationship among the quantity of real money balances, the interest rate, and income. We measure the interest rate, which represents the opportunity cost of holding money, on the vertical axis and the quantity of real money balances on the horizontal one. The downward-sloping demand curve for money shows the negative relationship between the interest rate and the quantity demanded of money. Each money-demand curve assumes a fixed level of real income, for example, Q_0. Changes in real income shift the money-demand curve, just as a change in income shifts the demand curve for other goods. An increase in real income to $Q_1 > Q_0$ shifts the money-demand curve to the right, because at any given interest rate individuals demand a larger quantity of money than before. The higher real income is associated with a desire to undertake more economic transactions; this makes it worthwhile to forgo interest on more funds in order to have enough money to make those additional transactions conveniently.

2.3 Where Does Money Come From, and What Determines How Much There Is?

In a modern economy, the nominal money stock is the outcome of a process involving the government central bank (often called a country's *monetary authority*), commercial banks, and the public. While this process seems a bit mysterious at first, it will become clearer if you make sure to keep the definition of money in mind: Money is simply a type of asset, one that can be used directly as a means of payment.

---

7. If a portion of the goods and services that individuals purchase are imported, real money balances are more appropriately measured as nominal balances divided by a price level that's a weighted average of the domestic and foreign price levels, with the weights reflecting the shares of domestic goods and services and imports in total spending. Nonetheless, the real money stock typically is reported as the nominal money stock divided by the domestic price level.

8. Real income, Q, equals nominal income or GDP (Y) divided by the price level (P): $Q \equiv Y/P$.

Figure 1   **The Demand for Real Money Balances Depends Negatively on the Interest Rate and Positively on Real Income**

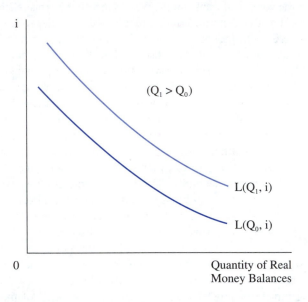

The negative slope of each demand curve (drawn for a fixed level of Q) represents the negative relationship between the interest rate (i) and the quantity demanded of real money balances (L). Changes in income shift the demand curve for real money balances. Here a rise in income from Q_0 to Q_1 shifts the demand curve to the right; individuals want to hold more real money balances at any given value of the interest rate.

The central bank creates the base for a country's money stock by buying nonmoney assets—in particular, government bonds or foreign exchange—from the public, using checks written by the central bank and drawn on itself.[9] These central-bank checks are unique because they *create* money rather than merely *transfer* money from one person to another. When a party other than the central bank writes a check, that check can only transfer funds from the person writing the check to the person receiving it, leaving no effect on the total quantity of checkable deposits and, therefore, no effect on the money stock. In contrast, when the central bank buys a bond from the public using one of the central bank's checks, the seller exchanges a nonmoney asset (the bond) for money. The check written by the central bank represents money because the recipient can either cash the check and receive currency or deposit the check in a checkable bank deposit. In either case, the funds represent an addition to the country's money stock because, by definition, the money stock includes both currency and checkable deposits (see section 2.1). To see more concretely how this money-creation process works, it helps to look at the balance sheets both for the country's central bank and for its commercial banks. These balance sheets are often called "T accounts," for a reason that will become obvious when we examine them.

---

9. To avoid confusion, it's important to distinguish between two different types of bond transactions: (1) issuance of a new government bond that may be sold to the public and (2) the central bank's purchase of an outstanding (previously issued) bond from the public. Bonds are just IOUs, so issuance of a new government bond constitutes a loan from the bond purchaser to the government. In the United States, the Department of the Treasury handles this type of transaction. The central bank (the Federal Reserve in the United States) doesn't issue new bonds (that is, borrow from the public); rather, it purchases bonds from the public that the public had purchased earlier from the Treasury. In so doing, the central bank exchanges money for nonmoney assets, thereby "creating money."

THE CENTRAL-BANK BALANCE SHEET   Any organization's balance sheet records the assets owned by the organization as well as its liabilities, or what the organization owes to others. Balance sheets are governed by the principles of double-entry bookkeeping, which we encountered already in the balance-of-payments accounts. Traditionally, assets appear on the left side of a balance sheet and liabilities on the right, giving the balance sheet a structure reminiscent of the letter *T*. Table 2 provides a simplified balance sheet for country A's central bank, which we'll call Alphabank. We can call the situation in Table 2 the Stage I balance sheet because it presents the initial situation from which we'll later initiate some changes.

On the asset side, Alphabank owns two main types of assets. The first consists of foreign exchange reserves—the stocks of foreign currencies that we've already learned the central bank holds in case it decides to intervene in the foreign exchange market. We assume that Alphabank holds foreign currencies in an amount with a domestic-currency value of $1,000.[10] The second type of assets is domestic ones. This category can include many different items, but for our purposes the most important is domestic government bonds. We assume that Alphabank holds $2,500 in such bonds, the accumulation of the bank's earlier bond purchases. Alphabank's total assets equal $3,500, or the $1,000 of foreign exchange reserves plus the $2,500 of domestic government bonds.

Central banks also have two main types of liabilities. First, commercial banks hold deposits at the central bank, much as individuals and firms hold deposits at commercial banks. In fact, a central bank often is described as a "bank for banks." The commercial banks' deposits at the central bank belong to their commercial bank owners and can be withdrawn; therefore, from the central bank's perspective, these deposits are liabilities. In our Table 2 example, these liabilities equal $500. Currency held by the public, $2,000 in our example, also appears as a central bank liability.[11] In our example, Alphabank's total liabilities equal $2,500, or $500 in commercial bank deposits plus $2,000 in publicly held currency.

The difference between an organization's total assets and its total liabilities equals its net worth. For our purposes, the central bank's net worth isn't important, so we can simply ignore it in our example in Table 2. The balance sheet is a double-entry bookkeeping system; so any time assets change, liabilities plus net worth change by the same amount. Suppose the central bank buys an asset, either a domestic government bond or some foreign exchange. The bank pays for its purchase either with a check or with currency. If it pays by check, the seller of the asset will deposit the central bank's check in a commercial bank, after which the commercial bank will deposit the check in its own account at the central bank. Therefore, the first category of Alphabank's liabilities—commercial banks' deposits—rise by the amount of the central bank's asset purchase. If Alphabank pays instead with currency, then currency held by the public rises by the amount of the

---

Table 2   CENTRAL-BANK BALANCE SHEET FOR ALPHABANK (STAGE I)

Assets		Liabilities	
Foreign exchange reserves (FXR)	$1,000	Commercial banks' deposits in Alphabank	$500
Domestic government bonds (GB)	$2,500	Currency held by the public	$2,000

---

10. Just as in the balance-of-payments accounts, the foreign-currency value of foreign exchange reserves is multiplied by the exchange rate to record the reserves' value in domestic-currency units.

11. This seems odd in a modern banking system, but it made sense for the historical period when banks developed their accounting conventions. At the time, currency was "backed" by gold or silver, which meant that if someone took paper currency to the central bank and demanded gold or silver in exchange, the central bank was required to meet the request. Therefore, currency was a liability from the viewpoint of the central bank.

purchase. So any increase in Alphabank's assets is matched by an equal increase in one of its liabilities. Using the same logic, if Alphabank sells an asset, its liabilities also fall by an equal amount. This happens because the buyer of the asset pays for it either with a check (which causes commercial banks' deposits at the central bank to fall when the check "clears") or with cash (which causes currency held by the public to fall).

The process just described captures the key steps in how the central bank conducts monetary policy, that is, how the central bank increases or decreases the country's money stock. Whenever the central bank expands its assets by buying either domestic government bonds or foreign exchange, its liabilities also expand. Those liabilities consist of commercial banks' deposits at the central bank and currency held by the public. We already know that currency held by the public constitutes one of the two components of the money stock; the other component is checkable deposits. So our next job is to discover the relationship between commercial banks' deposits at the central bank, which appear as a liability in the central bank's balance sheet, and the amount of checkable deposits in the economy. To do this, we need another balance sheet—this time that of commercial banks.

THE COMMERCIAL-BANKS' BALANCE SHEET Each commercial bank, like any other firm or organization, has its own balance sheet. However, we're interested in the macroeconomy and, in particular, in the banking system's role in determining the size of country's money stock. We aren't interested in the performance of individual banks. Therefore, rather than looking at a single commercial bank's balance sheet, we examine in Table 3 the "consolidated" balance sheet of all commercial banks as a group. Again, assets appear on the left side and liabilities on the right side of the T.

Commercial banks hold many types of assets. We can focus on just three. First, consider commercial banks' reserves (not to be confused with the central bank's *foreign exchange* reserves). Modern economies operate under a **fractional reserve banking system**. Under such a system, banks can lend funds from the deposits they accept, because government regulation requires banks to hold only a fraction (say, 10 percent) of their deposits on hand to cover customers' possible withdrawals.[12] When you deposit $5,000 in a commercial bank, the bank must hold $500 (10 percent of $5,000) in reserves in case you want to make a withdrawal.[13] The bank holds these reserves in a deposit at the central bank, and they are an asset from the commercial bank's perspective. Note in Table 2 that they're also a liability from the central bank's point of view.

The second category of commercial bank assets is loans. Once the bank satisfies its reserve requirement, it can loan out the remainder of the funds you deposit. These loans ($4,500 in

Table 3	**CONSOLIDATED BALANCE SHEET FOR COUNTRY A'S COMMERCIAL BANKS (STAGE I)**		
Assets		**Liabilities**	
Reserves	$500	Deposits	$5,000
Loans	$4,500	Borrowing	$1,000
Other assets	$1,500	Net worth	$500

---

12. Banks would choose to hold reserves even without government regulation, because a bank that lent out all its deposits and couldn't meet its depositors' requests for withdrawals wouldn't stay in business very long.

13. Unfortunately, both the funds banks hold to cover withdrawals and the central bank's stock of foreign currencies are called "reserves." To minimize confusion, we'll refer to the foreign currencies as *foreign exchange*, or *international, reserves*.

Table 3) are also a bank asset, because they represent something that the borrowers owe to the bank. Commercial banks earn most of their revenue from making loans on which they charge interest. The third asset category—other assets—can include many different items. Banks may own office buildings, other real estate, government bonds, or (in some countries) corporate stock. We assume in the example that commercial banks own $1,500 worth of such assets.

Commercial bank liabilities come in two main types. Customers' deposits (here, $5,000) are liabilities from the banks' perspective (although assets from the customers') because customers own the deposits and can withdraw them. Commercial banks may also owe other commercial banks or the central bank if they've borrowed funds; our example assumes that banks have borrowed $1,000.

The net worth of country A's commercial banks (here, $500) equals the value of their total assets ($6,500) minus the value of their total liabilities ($6,000). Net worth must be positive or the banking system is insolvent; that is, if net worth were negative, banks couldn't pay off what they owe to depositors and other creditors. In fact, international standards followed by the internationally active banks based in most industrial economies require net worth equal to at least 8 percent of assets. The other requirement that commercial banks' balance sheet must meet is that banks' reserves must satisfy the government's reserve requirement, which we assumed to be 10 percent. Banks typically don't want to hold more reserves than necessary because doing so involves forgoing making loans, which, again, provide the primary source of banks' revenues. In Table 3, banks have made as many loans as they can. They hold $500 in reserves, which equals the required 10 percent of their $5,000 in deposits.

OPEN MARKET OPERATIONS: CHANGING THE MONEY STOCK BY BUYING OR SELLING GOVERNMENT BONDS
Now we can use the central- and commercial-bank Stage I balance sheets to see exactly how and by how much a central bank asset purchase or sale changes the country's money stock. Suppose, beginning from the Stage I situation represented in Tables 2 and 3, that Alphabank buys a $1,000 government bond from an individual using one of its special checks. The bond seller exchanges a $1,000 nonmoney asset (the bond) for $1,000 of money. The $1,000 Alphabank check represents money because the recipient can either cash the check at his or her commercial bank and receive $1,000 in currency (which is money) or deposit the check in a checkable bank deposit (which is also money). To take the empirically more important case, let's assume the latter. The bond seller deposits the $1,000 Alphabank check in his or her commercial bank. That bank, in turn, sends the check to Alphabank, which credits the commercial bank's account there for $1,000.

What's happened in our balance sheets? In Table 4's Stage II balance sheets, Alphabank's holdings of domestic government bonds have risen by $1,000, as have Alphabank's liabilities in the form of commercial banks' deposits there. In Table 4's commercial bank balance sheet, deposits have risen by $1,000. Reserves also have risen by $1,000 because the commercial bank sent Alphabank's check back to the central bank and the check was credited to the commercial bank's account. What's happened to the money stock so far? The amount of currency held by the public ($2,000) hasn't changed, and checkable deposits have risen by $1,000; so the central bank's purchase of a government bond has increased the country's money stock by the amount of the bond purchase, or $1,000.

However, Alphabank's purchase of a $1,000 bond from the public actually increases the money stock by considerably more than this initial $1,000. The additional money-stock expansion happens because of the fractional-reserve banking system. When the seller of the government bond deposits the $1,000 Alphabank check in a commercial bank, the bank need hold only $100 (10 percent of $1,000) in reserves in case depositors want to make a withdrawal. The other way to think about the situation is to note that in Table 4 commercial banks now hold $1,500 in reserves and $6,000 in deposits. Only $600 (10 percent of $6,000) in reserves is required for this level of deposits, so the banking

Table 4 BALANCE SHEETS FOR ALPHABANK AND FOR COMMERCIAL BANKS (STAGE II)

Alphabank's Assets		Alphabank's Liabilities	
Foreign exchange reserves (FXR)	$1,000	Commercial banks' deposits in Alphabank	$500
			+$1,000
Domestic government bonds (GB)	$2,500	Currency held by the public	$2,000
	+$1,000		

Commercial Banks' Assets		Commercial Banks' Liabilities	
Reserves	$500	Deposits	$5,000
	+$1,000		+$1,000
Loans	$4,500	Borrowing	$1,000
Other assets	$1,500	Net worth	$500

system can make more loans. But how many more? The key to answering this question lies in seeing that additional loans made by the banking system increase deposits at commercial banks by the amount of the new loans.

To see why, suppose an individual borrows $900 from the bank to buy a computer. The bank credits the borrower's account with the $900. Once the individual buys the computer, the $900 deposit moves into the computer dealer's bank account as a deposit.[14] The computer dealer's bank must then hold 10 percent of the new $900 deposit, or $90, in reserves and can lend the remaining $810, which in turn ends up as an additional deposit. This "round-by-round" process, called **deposit expansion**, ends when the commercial banking system can no longer make any additional loans because it's required to hold all available funds as reserves. At the end of this process, the money stock will have grown by a multiple, called the **money multiplier**, of Alphabank's original $1,000 purchase of the government bond. The money multiplier, or the relationship between the size of the original central bank purchase and the size of the total change in the money stock, depends on the fraction of deposits that banks hold as reserves and on how much money the public chooses to hold in currency rather than in checkable deposits.[15] So the answer to the question, "How many more loans can the commercial banking system in Table 4 make?" is that it can expand loans until the corresponding increase in deposits brings total deposits to the maximum level supportable by the existing reserves. In Table 4, the reserves of $1,500 could support up to $15,000 in deposits with our assumed required reserves of 10 percent. In the Stage II balance sheet, commercial banks have $6,000 in deposits; so they can make $9,000 (= $15,000 − $6,000) in new loans. Those new loans will find their way into commercial bank deposits, bringing total deposits up to the allowable $15,000. At that point, commercial banks can't expand loans further. Table 5 updates the balance sheets to Stage III in order to take account of the final results of the deposit-expansion process.

Stage III is the end of the process. What's happened to country A's money stock as a result of Alphabank's purchase of a $1,000 government bond? Currency held by the public

---

14. Recall that we care what happens at the macroeconomic level, not at particular banks. We're working with commercial banks' consolidated balance sheet, so it doesn't matter if the computer buyer and computer seller bank at different commercial banks.

15. We can write the *money* multiplier as mm = (c + 1)/(c + d), where c denotes the ratio of currency to deposits held by the public and d the reserve-to-deposit ratio of banks. If we make the simplifying assumption that there's no cash in the economy (that is, that c = 0), then the money multiplier simplifies to mm = 1/d. For a more extensive discussion of the money multiplier and the money creation process, see any intermediate macroeconomics or money and banking text.

Table 5	**BALANCE SHEETS FOR ALPHABANK AND FOR COMMERCIAL BANKS (STAGE III)**

Alphabank's Assets		Alphabank's Liabilities	
Foreign exchange reserves (FXR)	$1,000	Commercial banks' deposits in Alphabank	$500
			+$1,000
Domestic government bonds (GB)	$2,500	Currency held by the public	$2,000
	+$1,000		

Commercial Banks' Assets		Commercial Banks' Liabilities	
Reserves	$500	Deposits	$5,000
	+$1,000		+$1,000
			+$9,000
Loans	$4,500		
	+$9,000	Borrowing	$1,000
Other assets	$1,500	Net worth	$500

hasn't changed, but checkable deposits have risen by a total of $10,000. This increase has two components: (1) the initial $1,000 increase from the bond seller's deposit of Alphabank's check into a commercial bank, and (2) the secondary $9,000 increase from the deposit-expansion process that the initial increase in commercial banks' reserves made possible.

Policies by which the central bank changes the nominal money stock by buying or selling government bonds are called **open market operations**. As we just learned, a central bank purchase of bonds increases the money stock. The same type of policy in reverse, in which case the central bank *sells* government bonds to the public rather than buying them, decreases the money stock. Open market sales cause bank deposits to shrink as individuals exchange their deposits (money) for bonds (nonmoney assets).

INTERVENTION: CHANGING THE MONEY STOCK BY BUYING OR SELLING FOREIGN EXCHANGE   The central bank can achieve exactly the same effect on the money stock in another way: It can buy or sell foreign exchange rather than domestic government bonds.[16] Suppose the quantity supplied of foreign-currency-denominated assets exceeds the quantity demanded in the foreign exchange market. Individuals currently hold foreign exchange in excess of the amount they want to hold in their asset portfolios; they want to exchange the excess foreign-currency assets for domestic-currency ones. The central bank can buy the excess foreign-currency-denominated assets from the public just as it did the government bond in the earlier open-market-operation example. The central bank purchases the foreign-currency assets with its special check. The deposit-expansion process operates again, increasing the money stock by a multiple of the central bank's purchase. In fact, a central bank's purchase of $1,000 of foreign-currency-denominated assets from the public has exactly the same effect on the money stock as did the $1,000 open market purchase of a government bond. (*Beginning from the situation in Tables 2 and 3, explain the effects of central bank intervention to buy $500 of foreign exchange; show your analysis in tables like Tables 4 and 5.*)

If the quantity demanded of foreign exchange in the economy exceeds the quantity supplied, the central bank can sell foreign exchange from its international reserves.

---

16.   Other policy options through which the central bank can alter the money stock include changes in the required reserve ratio for banks and changes in the discount rate, or the interest rate at which the central bank lends reserves to commercial banks.

Table 6 **MONEY STOCK EXPANSION AND CONTRACTION**	
Central Bank Operation	**Effect on Money Stock (ΔM)**
Open Market Operations:	
Purchases of government bonds from the public	$\Delta M = mm \cdot \Delta GB > 0$
Sales of government bonds to the public	$\Delta M = mm \cdot \Delta GB < 0$
Foreign Exchange Market Intervention:	
Purchases of foreign-currency assets	$\Delta M = mm \cdot \Delta FXR > 0$
Sales of foreign-currency assets	$\Delta M = mm \cdot \Delta FXR < 0$

The effect is identical to that of the central bank's open market sale of government bonds; that is, the money stock falls by the amount of foreign exchange reserves sold times the money multiplier.

SUMMING UP   The size of a country's money stock is the outcome of the processes just outlined. The money stock rises whenever the central bank purchases either government bonds or foreign exchange and falls whenever it sells either government bonds or foreign exchange, so the money stock's size at any time is determined by the quantity of government bonds and foreign exchange currently held by the central bank. We've seen, however, that each purchase or sale has a multiplier effect on the money stock, so the current money stock (M) equals the money multiplier (mm) times the government bonds (GB) and foreign exchange reserves (FXR) held by the central bank:[17]

$$M = mm\,(GB + FXR) \qquad [2]$$

Table 6 summarizes the effects of central bank open market operations and foreign exchange intervention on the domestic money stock. In each case, the change in the central bank's asset holdings changes the money stock in the same direction and by more than the asset purchase or sale.

2.4 Money Market Equilibrium

Equilibrium in the money market requires that the real money stock, the outcome of the central bank operations just described, equal the quantity of real money balances demanded by the public:

$$M/P = L(\overset{+}{Q}, \overset{-}{i}) \qquad [3]$$

The nominal money stock, M, depends on the actions of the central bank, as we just saw. In the remainder of this chapter, we'll assume that the price level, P, is fixed. (Later chapters will explore the importance of price flexibility in the long run.) Other variables, in particular the interest rate and income, must adjust to equate the quantity demanded of money (the right side of Equation 3) to the stock of money created by the central bank (the left side of Equation 3).

---

17.   With minor adjustments, the term in parentheses in Equation 2 represents what's known as *high-powered money*, or the *monetary base*. This is the determinant of the money stock that the central bank can affect directly through its policy choices. The money multiplier depends on the willingness of banks to lend, the central bank's regulated minimum reserve requirement imposed on banks, and the public's currency/deposit ratio (see footnote 15). Together, high-powered money and the money multiplier determine the money stock. In Equation 2, foreign exchange reserves are measured in units of domestic currency.

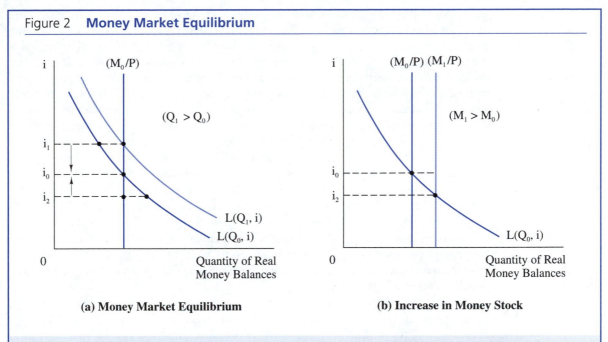

Figure 2 Money Market Equilibrium

(a) Money Market Equilibrium

(b) Increase in Money Stock

The equilibrium interest rate is the opportunity cost of holding money at which individuals willingly hold the existing stock of real money balances. Increases in income raise the demand for money and increase the equilibrium interest rate, as in panel (a)—where a rise in income from Q_0 to Q_1 raises the interest rate from i_0 to i_1. Increases in the money stock produce a fall in the equilibrium interest rate, inducing individuals to hold the new higher level of real money balances, as in panel (b)—where the nominal money stock rises from M_0 to M_1 and reduces the equilibrium interest rate from i_0 to i_2.

Panel (a) of Figure 2 combines the money-demand curves from Figure 1 with a vertical money-supply curve that represents the size of the money stock (M_0/P) created by the central bank. If the current level of income in the economy is Q_0, the money market will be in equilibrium only if the interest rate equals i_0, the rate at which the quantity of real money balances individuals want to hold equals the quantity of real money balances the central bank has created.

What would happen at other interest rates? Suppose the interest rate were i_1. Panel (a) suggests that, at that relatively high interest rate, individuals choose to hold little of their wealth as money because of its high opportunity cost. The quantity of money individuals want to hold falls short of the quantity the central bank has created. Individuals try to eliminate their unwanted money balances by buying other assets, such as interest-bearing bonds. This process bids up the price of bonds or, equivalently, pushes down the interest rate.[18] Once the interest rate falls to i_0, individuals are content to hold (M_0/P) in real money balances, because the opportunity cost of doing so is lower than at i_1.

18. The simplest form of bond is an IOU promising to pay the owner (lender) the face value (say, $1,000) on a certain future date. Such a bond sells for less than its face value, because the purchaser (lender) must wait until the future date to receive the $1,000, and $1,000 received in the future has a value today of less than $1,000 even if future receipt is certain. The seller of the bond (borrower) willingly pays the difference between the face value and the purchase price to borrow funds over the bond's life. In other words, the seller willingly pays, and the purchaser demands, interest on the loan. When the demand for bonds is high (such as when individuals are holding a larger-than-desired portion of their assets in money), the price of bonds gets bid up. The mirror image of this price increase is the fact that bond sellers need pay only a relatively low rate of interest because individuals are eager to lend (buy bonds). When the demand for bonds falls, so does the purchase price. Sellers must then pay higher rates of interest (that is, accept lower purchase prices for a given face value of a bond).

Suppose the interest rate initially were i_2. At such a low interest rate, individuals want to hold a large portion of their wealth in the form of money—more money than the central bank has created, because money provides convenience for making transactions and at i_2 the opportunity cost of holding money rather than bonds is low. As individuals try to sell bonds to increase their money holdings, the price of bonds falls or, equivalently, the interest rate rises. When the interest rate reaches i_0, the opportunity cost of holding money has risen sufficiently to make individuals content to hold only (M_0/P) in real money balances.

Changes in income shift the demand for money, as we saw in section 2.2. When income rises from Q_0 to Q_1, individuals undertake more transactions and need more real money balances to do so conveniently. The demand curve shifts to the right, as in Figure 2, panel (a). At the old equilibrium interest rate, i_0, individuals now want to hold more than the existing quantity (M_0/P) of real money balances. They try to sell bonds to reach the desired level of money balances and, in the process, push up the interest rate to i_1.

The demand for money also can shift for other (exogenous) reasons. For example, the widespread availability of automatic teller machines reduces the demand for money by providing easier access to nonmoney assets such as savings accounts. Such an institutional innovation shifts the demand for money to the left and, other things being equal, results in a lower interest rate.

Panel (b) of Figure 2 illustrates the effect of a change in the size of the money stock.[19] If the central bank buys government bonds or foreign-currency assets, the money stock rises from (M_0/P) to (M_1/P). At the old equilibrium interest rate, i_0, the existing money stock now exceeds the quantity of real money balances individuals want to hold given their income, Q_0. To reduce their money holdings, individuals try to purchase bonds, and the interest rate falls to i_2. If the central bank were to cut the money stock by selling government bonds or foreign-currency assets, individuals would respond by trying to sell bonds, and the interest rate would rise.

Table 7 summarizes the key relationships required for money-market equilibrium. An increase in income, a decrease in the nominal money stock, a rise in the price level, or an exogenous increase in money demand raises the equilibrium interest rate. A fall in

Table 7 SUMMARY OF MONEY-MARKET EFFECTS ON THE INTEREST RATE	
Variable	**Effect on Equilibrium Interest Rate**
Income (Q):	
Increase	+
Decrease	−
Nominal Money Stock (M):	
Increase	−
Decrease	+
Price Level (P):	
Increase	+
Decrease	−
Demand for Money (L):	
Exogenous increase	+
Exogenous decrease	−

19. For now, we continue to assume that the price level remains unchanged, but note that a rise in the price level reduces the real money stock, while a decline in the price level raises the real money stock.

income, an increase in the nominal money stock, a fall in the price level, or an exogenous decline in money demand lowers the interest rate at which individuals are content to hold the existing real money stock.

To make it easier to combine our insights from the money market with those from the markets for goods and services and foreign exchange, we can summarize the money-market results in an LM curve.

2.5 A Concise Graphical Summary: The LM Curve

Panel (a) of Figure 3 illustrates one point of equilibrium in the money market, point I. The real money stock equals M_0/P. Real money demand is given by $L(Q_0, i_0)$, because income equals Q_0 and the interest rate equals i_0. Panel (b) marks the combination of income (Q_0, measured on the horizontal axis) and interest rate (i_0, measured on the vertical axis) that corresponds to the equilibrium at point I.

Now suppose income rises to Q_1. Panel (a) shows that at the original interest rate (i_0) and the new, higher level of income (Q_1), the new quantity demanded of money exceeds the unchanged money stock; that is, $M_0/P < L(Q_1, i_0)$. In panel (b), the (Q_1, i_0) point corresponds to a quantity demanded of money that exceeds the money stock. Given this situation, individuals attempt to obtain the additional desired cash balances by selling other assets, particularly bonds. Increased bond sales lower the price of bonds, and a fall in the price of bonds is equivalent to a rise in the interest rate. The interest rate will continue to rise until individuals are content to hold the quantity of money available (M_0/P). Point II represents the new equilibrium, and we mark the corresponding combination of income and interest (Q_1, i_1) in panel (b). The original rise in income required a rise in the interest rate to reequate the quantity demanded of money with the money stock. The rise in income increased the demand for money, and the rise in the interest rate raised the opportunity cost of holding money, causing an offsetting decline in quantity demanded. Note that throughout the process, the stock of money remained constant at M_0/P.

Beginning again at the original equilibrium, point I, suppose events in the economy cause the interest rate to rise from i_0 to i_1. With income at Q_0, the rise in the interest rate causes the quantity demanded of money to fall below the level of the money stock. In panel (b) of Figure 3, the point (Q_0, i_1) corresponds to a situation in which the quantity demanded of money is less than the money stock. The money market can be in equilibrium at an interest rate of i_1 only if income rises to Q_1, raising the demand for money and restoring equilibrium at point II. Again, the real money stock doesn't change between points I and II.

The upward-sloping curve in panel (b) of Figure 3, called an **LM curve**, shows the various combinations of income and interest rate at which the money market is in equilibrium. The term *LM curve* refers to the fact that, at every point on the curve, the quantity demanded of money (L) equals the fixed money stock (M/P). At points to the right of the LM curve, the quantity demanded of money exceeds the money stock; at points to the left, the opposite holds. (*Why?*)

When the real money stock changes, the LM curve shifts. Since we assume for now that the price level is fixed, only a change in the nominal money stock, M, can cause a change in the real money stock. As illustrated in Figure 4, increases in the nominal money stock shift the LM curve to the right. In panel (a), the nominal money stock rises to M_1, shifting the money stock line to the right. At income Q_0, equilibrium now requires an interest rate of i_2 at point III. A lower interest rate ($i_2 < i_0$) induces individuals to hold the larger stock of money.

The same argument holds at income Q_1. When the real money stock rises, the interest rate must fall from i_1 to i_3 for the quantity demanded of money to rise. At i_1,

Figure 3   **The LM Curve Represents Equilibrium in the Money Market**

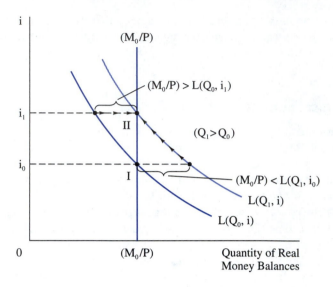

(a) Money Market Equilibrium

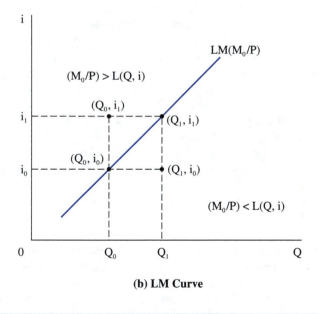

(b) LM Curve

A rise in income from Q_0 to Q_1 increases the demand for real money balances. To reequate quantity demanded with the fixed stock of money, the interest rate must rise. Similarly, a rise in the interest rate lowers the quantity demanded of money. With the stock of money fixed, income must rise to increase the demand for money. Therefore, the interest rate and income combinations consistent with equilibrium in the money market are *positively* related. The curve summarizing this positive relationship between equilibrium i and Q is called an LM curve, because at each point on it the quantity demanded of money (L) equals the money stock (M/P). To the right of the LM curve, the quantity demanded of money exceeds the money stock; to the left of it, the quantity demanded of money is less than the money stock.

Figure 4   Effect of an Increase in the Real Money Stock on the LM Curve

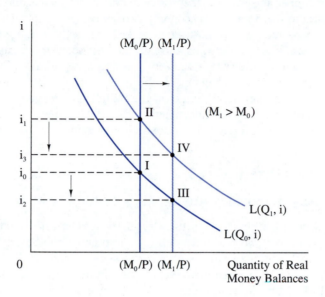

(a) Money Market Equilibrium

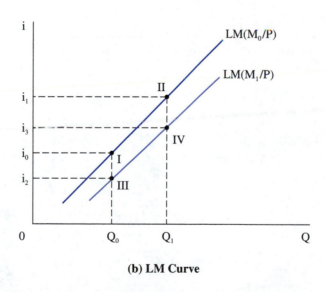

(b) LM Curve

An increase in the real money stock (caused here by an increase in the nominal money stock from M_0 to M_1 with the price level constant) shifts the LM curve to the right. Any given level of income now requires a lower interest rate for money market equilibrium.

the opportunity cost of holding money was too high for the public to willingly hold the new, larger money stock. Panel (b) of Figure 4 marks the new combinations of income and interest that result in money market equilibrium given the new money stock. (As a reminder, we label each LM curve with the real money stock on which that curve is based.)

2.6 Money in Open versus Closed Economies

As mentioned in section 1, the money market in an open economy at first glance appears identical to that in a closed economy. Money demand depends on domestic income and the interest rate, which must adjust to keep money demand equal to the money stock. The effects of openness enter through the additional mechanism by which the central bank can create or destroy money, that is, purchases or sales of foreign exchange. In fact, we'll see later in the chapter that the nature and extent of a central bank's ability to control the money stock hinge on the nature of the country's international linkages, particularly the exchange rate regime under which it operates. But first we investigate the banking system as a potential source of macroeconomic instability.

3 BANKING CRISES

3.1 How Important Are Banking Problems?

A country's banking system usually gets relatively little attention as long as it works well. However, most countries do, at one time or another, experience banking-sector problems. The aftermath of Argentina's severe financial crisis and Japan's economic malaise, both problems rooted in the countries' banks, have dominated recent headlines; but the International Monetary Fund reports that 130 of its member countries, approximately three-quarters of all IMF members, experienced "significant banking sector problems" between 1980 and 1996. Figure 5 locates those countries

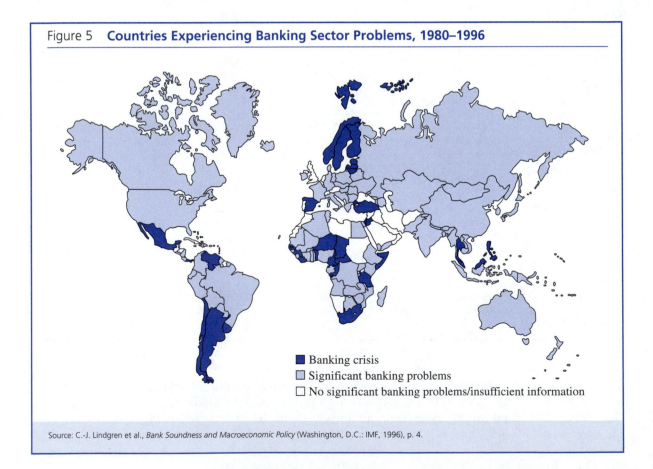

Figure 5   **Countries Experiencing Banking Sector Problems, 1980–1996**

■ Banking crisis
■ Significant banking problems
□ No significant banking problems/insufficient information

Source: C.-J. Lindgren et al., *Bank Soundness and Macroeconomic Policy* (Washington, D.C.: IMF, 1996), p. 4.

and reveals that they included all regions of the world economy and developed as well as developing economies.

For reasons we'll examine shortly, banking crises can impose large costs on an economy. To give just one example, when banks fail and become unable to pay back their depositors, governments often step in and either provide the failed banks with resources to continue to function or directly compensate depositors for their losses. Several banking crises have cost the respective governments the equivalent of significant shares of the country's annual GDP. For example, Argentina's 1980–1982 crisis ended up costing the Argentine government almost 60 percent of annual GDP; and this cost estimate includes only the direct fiscal cost to the government but excludes the cost to the economy of lost output during the crisis. Figure 6 provides a summary of the effects of more recent banking crises and includes information on both direct costs to the government and costs due to lost output, both measured as a percent of the country's GDP.

3.2 What Does It Mean for a Bank to Be "Unsound"?

Recall from our discussion of commercial banks' balance sheet that banks' total assets, by definition, equal their total liabilities plus their net worth. A useful way to think about net worth (also called *bank capital*) is as what would be left over for the bank's owners if they used the bank's assets to pay off all its liabilities. Net worth also represents the funds that the bank's owners or stockholders have at stake.

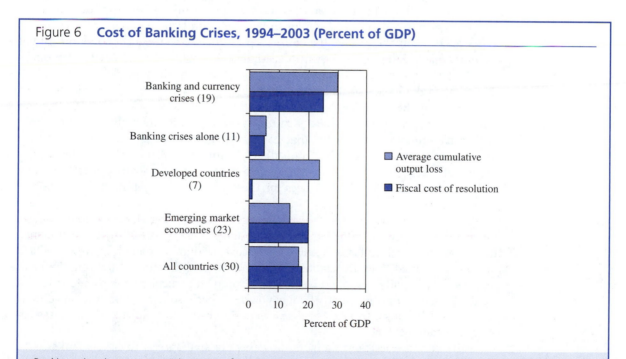

Figure 6   Cost of Banking Crises, 1994–2003 (Percent of GDP)

Banking crises impose two major types of cost on an economy: the direct fiscal cost to the government of resolving the banking crisis and the output lost during the crisis. Each type of cost can amount to a substantial percent of GDP, especially when a loss of confidence in the country's currency accompanies the banking crisis. Numbers in parentheses refer to the number of crises during 1994–2003. Average cumulative output loss is measured as the shortfall from trend growth during the three years following a crisis.

Source: Data from Agustin G. Carstens, et al. "Avoiding Banking Crises in Latin America." *Finance and Development* 41 (September 2004), p. 31.

A bank can be unsound in one of two ways, both serious but one more so than the other. Illiquidity occurs when a bank's assets are sufficient to cover its liabilities, but there is a time-horizon mismatch. Liabilities are due *now*; revenue from the assets isn't available until *later*. For example, in January 1998, South Korean banks announced that they couldn't repay the approximately $20 billion in short-term borrowing that they owed to foreign banks. The creditors postponed repayment (called *restructuring* or *rolling over the debt*), hoping to be paid when the economic situation in South Korea improved.

If a situation of short-term illiquidity fails to improve, it can turn into the long-term, often fatal problem of insolvency. This occurs when the value of a bank's assets is insufficient to cover the value of its liabilities. Net worth is negative. The bank must then be "recapitalized" (for example, by merging with a healthy bank), bailed out by the government at taxpayers' expense, nationalized by the government, or allowed to fail. In late 2003, the Japanese government declared regional bank Ashikaga insolvent after regulators found the bank's assets to be less than its liabilities by $930.5 million; policy makers nationalized the bank.[20] China's banks, all state-owned, are viewed by most banking experts as insolvent; and the big four Chinese banks have received more than $30 billion in government bailouts in recent years.[21]

3.3 What Are Some Recipes for Banking-System Problems?

A RUN ON AN INDIVIDUAL BANK A bank's health always depends on depositors' confidence in the value of its assets. After all, the bank uses depositors' funds to buy the assets, so depositors' ability to get their funds back hinges on the bank's assets maintaining their value. If a bank's depositors lose confidence in the integrity of its assets, each depositor will want to withdraw his or her funds. But all depositors can't get their funds simultaneously—even from a healthy bank. The reason is that many of the bank's assets can't be sold quickly to pay off depositors. Suppose, for example, that the bank has used its deposits to make a 30-year mortgage loan on a family's new home. If depositors suddenly want to withdraw all their funds, the bank can't simply call the family that bought the new house and tell them that they must repay the entire $250,000 immediately! Moreover, if the bank suddenly tries to sell off large quantities of its assets to meet depositor withdrawals, it may end up having to accept lower prices for those assets, thereby further damaging the bank's health.

In terms of the balance sheet, a sudden run by depositors seeking to withdraw their funds initially causes both the bank's deposits and its reserves to fall by equal amounts. It will have to curtail its loans or sell assets to cover withdrawals and bring reserves back up to the required level. Depending on the severity and duration of the run, the bank may become illiquid or even insolvent. Still, a run on a particular bank shouldn't have a significant effect on the country's money supply, because depositors will move their funds to other banks, so *total* checkable deposits in the consolidated banking system should remain the same.

A bank run does pose dangers, however. It may spread to other banks, with consequences we'll investigate in a minute. One bank's sudden large-scale asset sales may

---

20. "Japan Begins Cleanup of Regional Lenders," *Wall Street Journal*, December 1, 2003; and "Japan Faces Up to Banking Reality," *Financial Times*, December 1, 2003.

21. "China's Shaky Banks Suffer a Blow," *Wall Street Journal*, June 27, 2003.

reduce the value of other banks' assets if, for example, all own large quantities of local real estate. Finally, in an economy with only a few banks and other financial institutions, a single bank's stoppage of loans may curtail the flow of credit to firms in the economy and slow overall economic activity.

Policy makers can help stop a bank run by promising to lend the bank funds to cover depositors' withdrawals. In the balance sheet, this policy intervention shows up as a rise in the bank's borrowing on the liability side and in reserves on the asset side. These increases offset the decline in deposits on the liability side and in reserves on the asset side caused by the run itself. With prompt intervention to restore depositors' confidence, a basically sound bank is likely to survive the run. For example, Vietnam's largest private bank, Asia Commercial Bank, fell victim to a run in late 2003 when rumors spread that its general director had fled the country. Policy makers responded promptly by lending the bank $61.2 million to cover all withdrawals, keeping branches open all night to reassure depositors that they could retrieve their funds, and making sure the bank's general director put in public appearances to demonstrate the lack of factual basis in the rumor that started the run. Within a day, deposits began to trickle back into the bank.[22]

ECONOMY-WIDE BANK RUNS When many or all of a country's banks fall victim to a run, the consolidated banking system's total deposits and reserves fall. All banks must curtail their loans or sell other assets to try to cover the withdrawals and bring reserves back up to their required levels. Unlike the case of a run on a single bank, the country's money stock falls unless policy makers act, because the banking system's total deposits fall. If policy makers fail to act and allow the money stock to decline, this can cause a further loss of confidence or trigger a recession.[23] Central bank policy makers can help prevent this by promptly lending banks reserves (often called the central bank's *lender-of-last-resort function*) or conducting open-market purchases to boost reserves.

Russia's banking system suffered a severe crisis in 1998, which left depositors nervous. In 2004, when regulators used a money-laundering law to close Sodbiznesbank, a private bank long suspected of regulatory violations, panic spread quickly through the banking system, moving from small banks to larger ones, including Alfa, the country's largest private bank. Both the banks themselves and Russia's central bank responded promptly. Banks cancelled employee vacations, extended hours of operation, and packed extra cash into automated teller machines. The central bank cut the required level of reserves, thereby providing banks with more liquidity to meet customers' withdrawal demands. In the end, most banks survived the run intact. The episode exposed continuing weaknesses of Russia's banking system, but also demonstrated banks' and policy makers' ability to handle a growing crisis much more capably in 2004 than had been the case in 1998.[24]

BAD LOANS Banks are in the business of making loans. This both provides banks themselves a source of income—interest on the loans—and provides households and firms in the economy with a source of borrowed funds with which to buy goods and services and fund investment projects. But a loan's value as an asset to the lending bank depends on the loan's being repaid. When banks make loans that end up "not performing" (banking jargon for not being repaid), the value of the banks' loan assets declines.

If widespread loan nonperformance is a temporary problem, banks become illiquid and unable to make timely payments on their own borrowing. If widespread loan

---

22. "Jitters that Started Run on Vietnamese Bank," *Financial Times*, October 29, 2003.

23. We'll see in detail in the next two chapters how and why a contraction of the money supply can reduce a country's GDP.

24. "Russia Passes a Banking Test," *Wall Street Journal*, July 21, 2004.

nonperformance is a long-term problem, then banks become insolvent. In November 1997, Hokkaido Takushoku Bank, Japan's tenth largest, failed because of its bad loans. The bank's losses exceeded its net worth, so all of the owners' equity stake in the bank went to pay creditors; Japan's Deposit Insurance Corporation, run by banks themselves rather than the Japanese government, absorbed the rest of the losses.

Estimates of bad loans still on surviving Japanese commercial banks' balance sheets range from $265 billion to $1,900 billion. China's four big state-owned banks hold bad loans estimated at between $240 billion and $600 billion. Most analysts agree that these lingering bad loans, which reduce confidence in the banks, interfere with firms' ability to obtain loans for promising investment projects, and place a huge drain on government budgets, represent the biggest hurdle to full recovery of the Asian economies.

DECLINES IN VALUE OF NONLOAN ASSETS   As we mentioned earlier, banks can hold many types of assets other than loans. The macroeconomic effects of declines in the value of nonloan bank assets are similar to the effect of bad loans. If banks hold corporate stocks in their portfolios, for example, stock-market declines reduce the value of the banks' assets.[25] If banks hold long-term bonds in their portfolios, increases in interest rates reduce the market value of those assets by pushing down bond prices. If banks hold inflation-hedge assets such as real estate in their portfolios, reductions in the rate of inflation or increases in interest rates reduce the market value of those assets. All these problems are especially likely if government banking regulators restrict banks' asset purchases to the domestic market, thereby limiting banks' ability to diversify risk. During Argentina's recent economic crisis, for example, banks' assets included a large amount of government bonds on which the government had defaulted.

Loss of value of banks' nonloan assets contributed heavily to the 1997–1998 financial crisis in Asia. It's easy to see why. Many banks held large shares of their total asset portfolios in a very narrow class of assets, such as local real estate. When banks encountered problems and started to sell assets, their actions caused local real estate prices to drop, further damaging banks' balance sheets. For example, Hong Kong property values fell by about 40 percent during 1997–1998. In addition to the countries most directly affected by the financial crisis, Japan experienced an 80 percent decline in the value of commercial real estate between 1991 and 1998, with dramatic consequences for Japanese banks' balance sheets.

As we mentioned earlier, in many Asian economies, banks rather than individuals or other firms own most corporate stock. When stock prices plummeted in 1997 and 1998, so did the value of these bank assets. Stock market losses, along with bad loans, also caused much of Japan's decade-long banking problems. Accounting rules changed in late 2001 so that banks had to report on their balance sheets their stock-portfolio assets at current market value rather than historical value (that is, the value of the shares at the time they were purchased, often well before the 1990 stock market collapse). This new "mark-to-market" rule reduced the banks' stock assets, as shown on their balance sheets, by ¥4.7 trillion.

FRAUD, CORRUPTION, AND POLITICAL FAVORS   Poorly managed and inadequately supervised banks may make loans to insiders or to politicians, spend the banks' income on lavish salaries and perquisites for employees, or undertake overly risky investments. After all, most of the funds that banks spend ultimately belong to someone else—depositors. So bank managers may not be as careful as they would be if all the funds they spent were their own. This is why regulators require a minimum level of net worth. Recall that net worth is what the bank owners have at stake in the operation; it's the amount owners

---

25. Because of stocks' price volatility, U.S. banking regulators restrict stock ownership by U.S. banks; but most corporate stock in Asia is owned by banks, a fact that contributed to the area's late-1990s banking crisis.

stand to lose if they run the bank unwisely. Regulators want to keep that amount high enough to provide an adequate incentive for bank managers to act prudently with depositors' funds. However, banks in many developing economies, including in Asia, receive lax supervision and regulation.

When corruption affects a banking system, the economy's most productive firms may have trouble getting loans, which go instead to the politically well connected. This reduces economic output and growth. Taxpayers often bear the cost of bailing out corrupt and politically influential bankers, even in countries without formal deposit insurance programs. Table 8 lists countries with formal deposit insurance at the time of the Asian financial crisis; note the absence of the key Asian economies. The Indonesian and South Korean governments did pledge, well into the crisis, to provide deposit insurance. Such moves can avert political instability, since without deposit insurance the public can perceive bank bailouts as help for the rich while small savers lose their life savings. Individuals may hesitate to save unless the government guarantees their deposits against loss. But if the government provides such guarantees, they may reduce bankers' incentives to be prudent, since taxpayers will pick up the tab for any losses.

Fraud, corruption, and banks run on a political rather than an economic basis played important roles in the Asian financial crisis. At the time of the onset of the crisis, Indonesian banks held an estimated $700 million in loans to the former president's son for his "national car" project. Indonesian authorities have made progress in cleaning up the banking sector, but problems remain; in 2003, regulators discovered a $200 million fraud at Bank Negara Indonesia, the second largest bank.[26] No single region, however, has a monopoly on corruption. In 2003, fraud led to the collapse of the Dominican Republic's second largest bank, Banco Intercontinental. Depositor nervousness then caused a run at the country's third largest bank, Banco Nacional de Credito; and, in the

Table 8 COUNTRIES WITH EXPLICIT DEPOSIT INSURANCE SYSTEMS

Africa	Asia	Europe		Middle East	Western Hemisphere
Kenya	Bangladesh	Austria	Italy	Bahrain	Argentina
Nigeria	India	Belgium	Luxembourg	Kuwait	Brazil
Tanzania	Japan	Bulgaria	Netherlands	Lebanon	Canada
Uganda	Marshall Is.	Czech Rep.	Norway	Oman	Chile
	Micronesia	Denmark	Poland		Colombia
	Philippines	Finland	Portugal		Dominican Rep.
	Taiwan	France	Spain		El Salvador
		Germany	Sweden		Mexico
		Greece	Switzerland		Peru
		Hungary	Turkey		Trinidad/Tobago
		Iceland	United Kingdom		United States
		Ireland			Venezuela

Source: Morris Goldstein, *The Asian Financial Crisis: Causes, Cures, and Systemic Implications* (Washington, D.C.: Institute for International Economics, 1998), p. 48.

---

26. "Indonesia's Groucho Marx Lenders," *Financial Times*, November 7, 2003.

Figure 7   **Corruption Index, 2004**

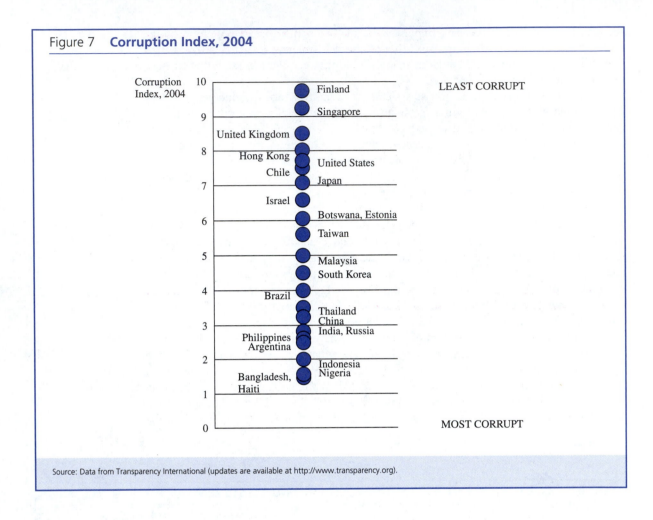

Source: Data from Transparency International (updates are available at http://www.transparency.org).

process of cleaning up the aftermath of the run, regulators discovered fraud there as well.[27] Since 1997, Turkish authorities have seized 22 banks and tried their owners and managers for embezzlement. The largest single case in Turkey involves the Uzan family, accused of using a specially designed computer program to steal $6 billion from a bank they owned.[28]

A Berlin-based organization called Transparency International collects data on the perceived level of government and business corruption in various countries; Figure 7 presents some of their findings. Countries near the top of the figure have low levels of corruption, and those near the bottom have high levels.

FOREIGN-EXCHANGE PROBLEMS   Often banks borrow in foreign currency (usually U.S. dollars), sell it for local currency, and then buy assets denominated in the local currency. For example, an Argentine bank might take out a dollar-denominated loan from a U.S. bank, sell the dollars for pesos, and use the pesos to make a loan to an Argentine firm. If the domestic currency is devalued or depreciates against the foreign currency (here, the peso against the dollar), the bank may not be able to repay its

27. "Banking Sector Hit by Arrest Warrants," *Financial Times*, November 14, 2003.

28. "Turkey's Uzan Dynasty Accused of $6bn Bank Fraud," *Financial Times*, October 6, 2003.

loan—because the domestic-currency price of buying the necessary dollars rises. In terms of the bank's balance sheet, the domestic-currency value of liabilities (borrowing) rises with no corresponding increase in the value of the bank's assets, leading to insolvency.

In 2002, Argentine banks and other firms had high levels of dollar-denominated liabilities, both deposits and loans, when Argentina's government suddenly stopped pegging the value of the peso to the dollar at e = P1/$1. The peso's value fell immediately by 30 percent and then continued to decline until the currency had lost more than two-thirds of its value relative to the dollar. To make matters even worse for Argentine banks, the government promised to cushion the devaluation's effect on Argentine households by forcibly converting all of households' dollar-denominated bank loans smaller than $100,000 into pesos; in other words, the government allowed households to repay their dollar-denominated loans to Argentine banks with now heavily devalued pesos rather than dollars. As a result, Argentine banks were caught in a squeeze: left with balance sheets filled with dollar-denominated liabilities and assets that either had originally been denominated in pesos or had arbitrarily been transformed into pesos by government decree. Later, the government tried to provide some relief to banks—at depositors' expense—by forcibly converting the banks' deposit liabilities from dollars into devalued pesos; but the Argentine Supreme Court overturned the policy as unconstitutional in early 2003. Eighteen months later, the court reversed itself, leaving open the question of banks' ability to recover the dollars they'd paid out to depositors under the earlier ruling.

3.4 Why Do Banking Problems Spread?

Once one or a few banks encounter problems of the types just discussed, those problems often spread to other banks in the same country and even to those across the region and around the world. This *contagion* happens in part simply because of the nature of the banking business. All banking systems are based on confidence—depositors' confidence that they can safely place funds in a bank. Any event that shakes this fundamental confidence can have wide-ranging effects. For example, a run on one weak bank can easily spread to healthy ones, especially if ignored or mishandled by policy makers.

We've seen that one bank's liabilities often comprise another bank's assets. So if Bank A borrows from Bank B and becomes unable to repay its loan, Bank B may itself be forced into illiquidity or even insolvency.[29] And if Bank B had borrowed from Bank C, then the value of C's assets also decline. In Asia, many banks own stock in other banks. When Hokkaido Takushoku bank failed, for example, its major stockholders included Long-Term Credit Bank of Japan and Nippon Credit Bank; so those banks suffered a decline in the value of assets.

If one bank experiences a run and has to sell off assets quickly to cover withdrawals and rebuild its reserves, its asset sales may lower the market value of other banks' similar assets, especially if banks hold regionally or sectorally undiversified portfolios, as is often the case. Asian banks, for example, held large shares of their asset portfolios in local real estate at the onset of the Asian financial crisis.

Once a banking crisis gets started, fixing the underlying problems becomes much more difficult. Foreign banks start to charge banks in the troubled country a premium to borrow because of the increased default risk. Japanese banks, for example, had to pay

---

29. On the related counterparty or Herstatt risk, see Case Three in the chapter on currency markets and exchange rates.

a "Japan premium" of up to 1 percent to borrow from foreign banks during much of the 1990s. Often, weak banks need to be closed, but doing so during a crisis can further erode the public's confidence. Governments tend to bail out banks, especially big ones judged "too big to fail," and force taxpayers to bear the cost. In the long run, such policies can encourage reckless lending behavior by bankers, who assume that the government will save them if they run into difficulties because of overly risky loans.

3.5 Why Do Banks Matter So Much?

Why can trouble in a single sector—banking—cause such multifaceted microeconomic and macroeconomic problems? The answer lies in recognizing the many crucial roles that banks play in an economy.

In market-oriented economies, banks allocate capital; that is, they channel savers' funds to firms to finance investment projects. When a banking system works well, the most economically promising firms get funding, and their productive investment projects help the economy grow. When the banking system works poorly, politically connected or bureaucratically targeted firms get funding, and their unproductive projects become a drain on the economy. If the public perceives corruption in the banking system, that perception can discourage saving. To prevent this from happening, the government may have to provide full deposit insurance to reassure potential depositors; but the insurance, in turn, can discourage bankers' prudence by shifting the cost of bank failure from bank owners to taxpayers who typically fund the deposit insurance.

Banks also play a key role in monetary policy. We've seen in this chapter how banks interact with the central bank and the public to determine the size of the money stock. In the next few chapters we'll see how changes in the size of the money stock, in turn, can affect the economy's macroeconomic performance. A banking system with too many bad loans on its books may hesitate to extend additional loans, thereby reducing the central bank's ability to alter the size of the money stock through the deposit-expansion process described in section 2.3. Many experts see this problem as the major continuing problem in the Japanese economy. In addition to hampering monetary policy, a weak banking system carries important fiscal implications. Figure 6 revealed that government bailouts of failed banks often involve large costs to the government; and this can limit governments' ability to provide needed spending for other sectors of a struggling economy.

Weak banks also constrain policy makers' ability to carry out the macroeconomic policies needed by the rest of the economy. We'll see much more about this in later chapters, but we can already understand the basic reason why. Suppose that macroeconomic conditions were such that a devaluation of the domestic currency seemed the appropriate policy, but the countries' shaky banks hold large amounts of foreign-currency-denominated liabilities and domestic-currency-denominated assets. Policy makers might find themselves unwilling or unable to devalue for fear of pushing the banks into illiquidity or insolvency. Or, suppose a history of high inflation has led to high prices for real estate, an asset whose price tends to rise during expected inflation. Normally, policy makers would pursue policies to reduce inflation. But if banks, already weak, hold large amounts of real estate in their asset portfolios, policy makers may hesitate to reduce inflation, because to do so would likely cause a substantial drop in real-estate prices.

Banks play key economic roles in virtually all economies, but their role is more crucial in some than in others because the availability of other, nonbank financial institutions varies widely. In developed industrial economies, for example, there may be a large number of commercial banks, plus investment banks, active government and corporate bond markets, and stock markets in which firms can issue stock to raise funds to finance investment projects. In some developing economies, on the other hand, there may be a mere handful of

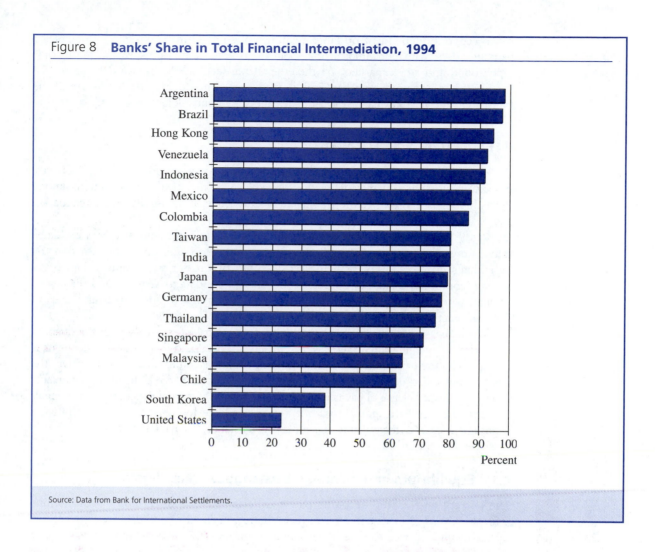

Figure 8   **Banks' Share in Total Financial Intermediation, 1994**

Source: Data from Bank for International Settlements.

banks, no bond markets, and no stock markets. The few banks constitute firms' only source of investment funds. Figure 8 shows banks' share of financial intermediation for a sample of countries in 1994. *Financial intermediation* refers to channeling saving to investors. In the United States, commercial banks accounted for only 23 percent of this activity. Note that banks dominated financial intermediation in the Asian economies included in the figure, with the exception of South Korea. For Hong Kong, Indonesia, Japan, Malaysia, Singapore, Taiwan, and Thailand, banks' share on the eve of the Asian financial crisis ranged from 64 to 94 percent. This high level of dependence on the banking system for financial intermediation made bank soundness even more important than in countries such as the United States. In addition, some of these economies had a small number of banks, so trouble at even a few significantly affected firms' ability to obtain investment funds and, therefore, the growth of the overall economy.

Governments in developing economies, including the newly industrializing ones in Asia, sometimes deliberately concentrate financial intermediation in the hands of banks because it allows government policy makers—who supervise, regulate, and sometimes own the banks—to influence the allocation of credit. Favored sectors, including heavy industry such as cars, steel, chemicals, and semiconductors in Asia, get plentiful credit at low interest rates. Firms are discouraged from issuing bonds or raising investment funds through other financial markets that would dilute the government's role in capital allocation. The result can be an economy dependent on large quantities of short-term bank debt, vulnerable to banking crises, with poor information about the true economic prospects of most firms. Open bond and stock markets, on the other hand, facilitate long-term debt, make the economy less dependent on banks, and encourage firms to provide disclosure of the transparent and reliable financial statistics demanded by nonbank lenders.

4 FOREIGN EXCHANGE[30]

We've now seen the basic mechanics and roles of the markets for goods and services, money, and foreign exchange. Before we can explore the details of the interactions among these three markets, we need to translate our knowledge of the foreign exchange market and balance of payments into a more convenient form.

Recall that the balance-of-payments accounts classify autonomous foreign exchange transactions (that is, those arising in the course of day-to-day economic transactions by individuals, firms, and government agencies) into two major subaccounts: the *current account*, composed mainly of purchases and sales of goods and services, and the *capital account*, which reflects international borrowing and lending or purchases and sales of financial assets and direct investment.[31]

When the sum of the current- and capital-account balances equals zero, the quantity demanded of foreign exchange equals the quantity supplied and the balance of payments is in balance. When the sum of the current- and capital-account balances is negative, the quantity demanded of foreign-currency-denominated deposits exceeds the quantity available and the domestic balance of payments is in deficit. A positive sum of the current- and capital-account balances corresponds to a quantity of available foreign-currency-denominated deposits that exceeds the quantity demanded and a balance-of-payments surplus.

4.1 Equilibrium in the Foreign Exchange Market, Again

The current and capital accounts reflect different classes of economic transactions (purchases/sales of goods and services versus borrowing/lending and direct investment), so each account responds to different economic variables. The current account depends on domestic and foreign incomes and on the relative prices of domestic and foreign goods and services. A rise in foreign income increases exports and moves the current-account balance toward a surplus. Increased domestic income has the opposite effect by raising imports. A rise in the relative price of domestic goods or real exchange rate ($R \equiv P/eP^*$) reduces exports and increases imports, moving the current account toward a deficit.[32] Letting CAB denote the *current-account balance*, a plus sign denote a move toward a surplus, and a minus sign denote a move toward a deficit, we can summarize the effects on the current account:

$$\text{CAB}(\overset{+}{Q}^*, \overline{Q}, \overline{R})$$ [4]

The capital account depends on relative interest rates on domestic and foreign assets and on the spot exchange rate, the forward rate, and the expected future spot rate. Other things being equal, a rise in the foreign interest rate, i^*, makes foreign assets more attractive, resulting in a capital outflow and a move toward a deficit in the domestic capital account.

---

30. The following discussion assumes that the reader is familiar with the material covered earlier in the chapter on currency markets and exchange rates; if not, we suggest a review at this point.

31. In the actual government accounts, what we refer to as the *capital account* is the *financial and capital account*.

32. For a review, see sections 4 and 5.2 in the preceding chapter on the market for goods and services.

A rise in the domestic interest rate, i, has the opposite effect, generating a capital inflow and a capital-account surplus. A rise in the spot exchange rate lowers the expected return on foreign assets and causes a capital inflow, while a rise in the forward rate raises the expected return on foreign assets and produces a capital outflow. Given domestic and foreign interest rates, an expectation that the domestic currency will depreciate in the future makes foreign assets more attractive and produces a capital-account deficit. Letting KAB denote the capital-*account balance* (since K has symbolized capital throughout this book):

$$KAB(\overset{-}{i^*}, \overset{+}{i}, \overset{+}{e}, \overset{-}{e^f}, \overset{-}{e^e}) \qquad [5]$$

When the sum of the current- and capital-account balances equals zero, the overall balance of payments is in equilibrium. The market for foreign exchange also is in equilibrium, because the quantity demanded of foreign-currency-denominated assets equals the quantity available:

$$CAB + KAB = 0 \text{ for BOP equilibrium} \qquad [6]$$

We can rearrange Equation 6 slightly:

$$CAB = -KAB \text{ for BOP equilibrium} \qquad [7]$$

Figure 9 represents graphically this requirement for equilibrium in the balance of payments or the foreign exchange market by a negatively sloped 45-degree line along which Equation 7 holds. At points above and to the right of the line, the balance of payments shows a surplus (BOP > 0) because either (1) the current-account surplus

---

Figure 9 Balance-of-Payments Equilibrium Requires That the Current-Account Balance (CAB) and the Capital-Account Balance (KAB) Sum to Zero

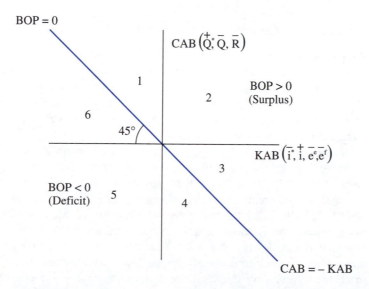

Along the negatively sloped 45-degree line, the balance of payments is in equilibrium. Below and to the left of the line, there is a deficit; above and to the right of the line, the balance of payments is in surplus.

exceeds the capital-account deficit (in area 1), (2) both the current and capital accounts are in surplus (in area 2), or (3) the capital-account surplus exceeds the current-account deficit (in area 3). Below and to the left of the line, the balance of payments is in deficit (BOP < 0). In area 4, the current-account deficit exceeds the capital-account surplus. Area 5 represents combinations at which both the current and capital accounts are in deficit. In area 6, the current-account surplus is too small to offset the deficit in the capital account.

In the remainder of this section, we'll assume that foreign income, relative prices of domestic and foreign goods and services, foreign interest rates, the spot exchange rate, the forward exchange rate, and the expected future spot exchange rate are fixed, so we can concentrate on the relationship between domestic income and interest rate that must hold for equilibrium in the foreign exchange market. Figure 10, panel (a), repeats Figure 9 with these simplifications.

Beginning at any point on the 45-degree line in panel (a) of Figure 10 (such as point I), let domestic income rise, say, from Q_0 to Q_1. The fact that point I lies *on* the balance-of-payments line implies that the interest rate equals i_0 such that $CAB(Q_0) = -KAB(i_0)$, as required for balance-of-payments equilibrium. The increase in income moves the current-account balance toward a deficit, because $CAB(Q_1) < CAB(Q_0)$ as Equation 4 implies. This is represented graphically as a move downward to point II, at which the balance of payments is in deficit because $CAB(Q_1) < -KAB(i_0) = CAB(Q_0)$. Restoring balance-of-payments equilibrium requires that the interest rate rise by enough to generate an increased capital inflow sufficient to offset the current-account move toward a deficit.[33] We denote the new interest rate as i_1, where $CAB(Q_1) = -KAB(i_1)$. Point III in panel (a) of Figure 10 represents this new equilibrium.

Generally, any rise in domestic income moves the CAB toward a deficit; therefore, maintaining foreign exchange market equilibrium requires a rise in the interest rate to generate an offsetting move toward a surplus in the KAB. Similarly, a fall in the interest rate moves the KAB toward a deficit (as individuals want to hold more foreign-currency-denominated assets) and requires a fall in income to reduce imports and move the CAB toward a surplus.

4.2 Another Concise Graphical Summary: The BOP Curve

We can summarize the relationship among income, the interest rate, and the balance of payments by stating that the various combinations of domestic income and interest rate that result in foreign exchange market equilibrium lie along an upward-sloping line as illustrated in panel (b) of Figure 10. We label this line a **BOP curve**, because it reflects all combinations of income and interest rates that correspond to *balance-of-payments* (and foreign exchange market) equilibrium.

Although the balance of payments is in equilibrium at every point along the BOP curve, each point reflects a different situation for the current and capital accounts. Points on the lower left end of the BOP curve correspond to low levels of income and interest rate, implying current-account surpluses and capital-account deficits. At the upper right end of the BOP curve, high income results in a current-account deficit and a high interest rate produces an offsetting capital-account surplus. The BOP curve alone can't determine at which point the economy will operate; but once we combine the markets for goods and services, money, and foreign exchange we can determine the point at which all three markets are in equilibrium. First, we need to know what shifts the BOP curve.

---

33. We'll see that the magnitude of the rise in the interest rate depends on the degree of capital mobility. The more mobile is capital, the smaller the rise in i required to generate a capital inflow sufficient to restore balance-of-payments equilibrium.

Figure 10 **Effects of Domestic Income and Interest on the Market for Foreign Exchange**

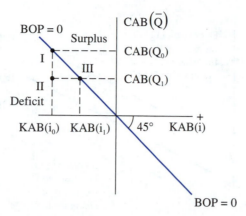

(a) Balance-of-Payments Equilibrium

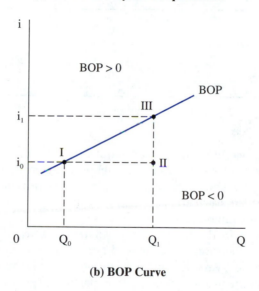

(b) BOP Curve

Starting from a point of balance-of-payments equilibrium, point I, in panel (a), an increase in domestic income from Q_0 to Q_1 moves the current-account balance toward a deficit, resulting in a balance-of-payments deficit at an unchanged interest rate (point II). To generate increased capital inflows with which to offset the decreased current-account surplus, the interest rate must rise from i_0 to i_1 (point III). At point III, the balance of payments is again in equilibrium, but with a smaller current-account surplus and capital-account deficit than at the original equilibrium, point I. The BOP curve in panel (b) represents all the combinations of domestic income and interest rate at which the balance of payments and the foreign exchange market are in equilibrium. Increases in income move the CAB toward a deficit while increases in interest rates move the KAB toward a surplus, so the BOP line is upward sloping. Points I and III in panel (b) refer to those combinations of income and interest that correspond to equilibrium points I and III in panel (a).

The BOP curve is drawn for given values of foreign income (Q^*), relative foreign and domestic prices or real exchange rate (R), foreign interest rate (i^*), forward rate (e^f), and expected exchange rate (e^e). Changes in any of these variables shift the entire BOP curve. At any given level of domestic income, a rise in foreign income or a decline in the relative price of domestic goods moves the CAB toward a surplus. Balance-of-payments equilibrium then requires a lower interest rate to produce an offsetting KAB move toward

---

Figure 11   **Shifting the BOP Curve**

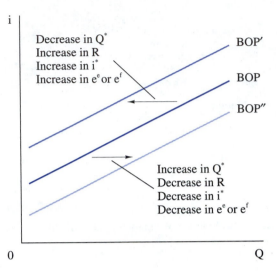

A decrease in Q*, or an increase in R, i*, e^e, or e^f shifts the BOP line to the left. An increase in Q*, or a decrease in R, i*, e^e, or e^f shifts the BOP line to the right.

---

a deficit. Since BOP equilibrium requires a lower interest rate at any given level of income, the BOP curve shifts to the right. A similar analysis in the other direction implies that a fall in foreign income or a rise in the relative price of domestic goods shifts the BOP curve to the left; each level of domestic income requires a higher interest rate for balance-of-payments equilibrium.

Increases in the foreign interest rate, expected depreciations of the domestic currency, or increases in the forward rate encourage capital outflows, moving the KAB toward a deficit. An offsetting move toward a surplus in the current account requires a fall in domestic income to reduce imports. Because a lower level of domestic income is required at each domestic interest rate, the BOP curve shifts to the left. Figure 11 summarizes these results and lists the causes of shifts to the left and to the right of the BOP curve.

TWO SPECIAL CASES: CAPITAL MOBILITY AND THE BOP CURVE   We just argued that balance-of-payments equilibrium requires a *positive* relationship between income and the interest rate. A rise in income increases imports and moves the current account toward a deficit, so BOP equilibrium requires a rise in the interest rate to generate an offsetting move toward surplus in the capital account. How big an increase in the interest rate is required depends on how sensitive international capital flows are to changes in interest rates. If asset owners don't respond strongly to changes in international interest rate differentials, then a large increase in the interest rate may be necessary to induce a capital inflow sufficient to offset the current-account deficit. In such circumstances, the BOP curve will be steeply upward sloping. (*Why?*) On the other hand, asset owners may be highly sensitive to even small changes in the international pattern of interest rates. If so, only a tiny rise in the domestic interest rate will bring about a capital inflow sufficient to restore balance-of-payments equilibrium. Graphically, this implies that the upward-sloping

BOP curve will be relatively flat. (*Why?*) In other words, the *slope* of the BOP curve indicates the degree of capital mobility, or how sensitive international capital flows are to changes in domestic and foreign interest rates. Low capital mobility implies a steep BOP curve, and high capital mobility a flat one.

We'll see in the next two chapters that the degree of capital mobility exerts an important influence on the macroeconomy and on the effectiveness of macroeconomic policies. To examine the effects of differing degrees of capital mobility, it often proves useful to focus on two extreme cases: that of perfect capital immobility (or zero mobility) and that of perfect mobility.

Under perfect capital immobility, the nonofficial capital account, as described in the chapter on the balance-of-payments accounts, contains no transactions, because both capital inflows and outflows equal zero by definition. No autonomous international borrowing and lending occurs, regardless of the interest rate differentials among countries. With no capital-account transactions, the balance of payments (normally BOP = CAB + KAB) consists solely of the current account (BOP = CAB). If the current account is in deficit, the balance of payments is in deficit; with a current-account surplus, a balance-of-payments surplus exists. The requirement for balance-of-payments equilibrium reduces to the requirement that the current-account balance equal zero.

Recall from section 4 of the chapter on the market for goods and services that there exists only one level of income at which the current-account balance equals zero. The interest rate becomes irrelevant to balance-of-payments equilibrium with no capital mobility; thus, the BOP line becomes vertical, as in Figure 12, panel (a). To the right of the BOP line, the balance of payments lies in deficit; to the left of the line, a BOP surplus exists. A rise in foreign income (Q*) or a fall in the relative price of domestic goods and

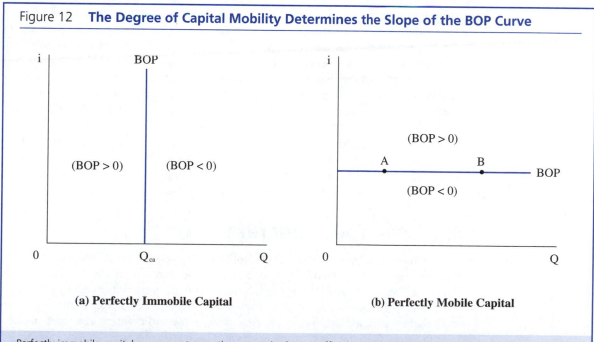

Figure 12   **The Degree of Capital Mobility Determines the Slope of the BOP Curve**

(a) **Perfectly Immobile Capital**

(b) **Perfectly Mobile Capital**

Perfectly immobile capital means no transactions occur in the nonofficial capital account in response to changes in i or i*. The balance of payments includes only the current-account balance, which equals zero at a single level of income, Q_{ca}, in panel (a). Perfectly mobile capital means that infinitesimal changes in the interest rate generate large international capital flows, implying a horizontal BOP curve as in panel (b).

services (R) increases exports at each level of domestic income and causes the income consistent with balance in the current account to rise, so the BOP curve shifts to the right. A decline in foreign income or a rise in the relative price of domestic goods and services decreases exports at each level of income and shifts the BOP curve to the left. (*Why?*)

We now move to the opposite assumption, that of perfect capital mobility. The assumption of perfect capital mobility simply means that investors, in deciding which assets to hold, consider only interest rates and exchange rates, including the forward rate and the expected future spot rate. In other words, investors have no inherent preferences for assets denominated in one currency versus those denominated in another, and government policies don't restrict capital flows. Under perfect capital mobility, the balance-of-payments line becomes horizontal, as illustrated in panel (b) of Figure 12. Recall that in the presence of an active capital account we draw each BOP line for given values of the foreign interest rate, the exchange rate, and forward and expected spot exchange rates. This implies that any rise in the domestic interest rate causes a capital inflow and a move toward a surplus on the capital account.[34]

How does the assumption of perfect capital mobility imply a horizontal BOP line? In Figure 12, panel (b), the balance of payments is in equilibrium at point A; this is true because A lies on the BOP line, which, by definition, represents points of balance-of-payments equilibrium. Beginning at A, suppose a disturbance in the economy raises income. Imports rise with income, and the current account moves toward a deficit. To maintain balance-of-payments equilibrium, the capital account must generate an offsetting move toward surplus. With perfectly mobile capital, how large an increase in the domestic interest rate is required to generate this capital-account surplus? The answer is that an infinitesimal—essentially zero—rise in the interest rate will suffice. The reason is that investors will respond to the slightest rise in domestic rates by moving their funds into the domestic economy.

In terms of the interest parity condition, massive capital flows in response to even minute changes in relative interest rates maintain the equilibrium or parity condition. Therefore, the balance of payments is in equilibrium at B, with a larger current-account deficit and capital-account surplus than at A. All points above the BOP line correspond to situations of balance-of-payments surplus, and those below the line represent balance-of-payments deficits. (*Why?*) An increase in the foreign interest rate, the forward exchange rate, or the expected future spot rate raises the expected return on foreign-currency-denominated assets and shifts the BOP line up, because a higher domestic interest rate is required to induce asset owners to hold domestic-currency assets. A fall in the spot exchange rate has a similar effect. (*Use interest parity to explain why a fall in i^*, e^e, or e^f or a rise in e would shift the BOP curve down.*)

Our models of the goods and services, money, and foreign exchange markets are now complete and summarized in the IS, LM, and BOP curves, respectively, each of which represents the combinations of domestic income and interest rates at which quantity demanded equals quantity supplied in the respective market.

5 BRINGING IT ALL TOGETHER

General equilibrium refers to simultaneous equilibrium in several related markets. General-equilibrium analysis of an open macroeconomy examines how the interaction of the goods and services, money, and foreign exchange markets determines the economy's performance. We've summarized the requirement for each market's equilibrium with a curve relating domestic income and interest rates, so we can combine the three markets easily to facilitate a general-equilibrium analysis.

---

34. For a review, see the discussion of interest parity in section 4 in the chapter on currency markets and exchange rates.

Figure 13   **Combining the IS, LM, and BOP Curves**

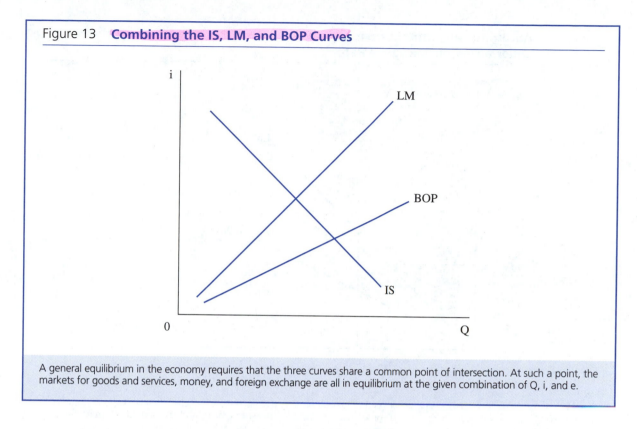

A general equilibrium in the economy requires that the three curves share a common point of intersection. At such a point, the markets for goods and services, money, and foreign exchange are all in equilibrium at the given combination of Q, i, and e.

Figure 13 brings together the IS, LM, and BOP curves that represent equilibrium in the markets for goods and services, money, and foreign exchange, respectively. The IS curve is downward sloping and the LM and BOP curves upward sloping, reflecting our assumption of an intermediate degree of capital mobility.

A point at which all three curves intersect represents a general equilibrium in the economy. No such intersection occurs in Figure 13. In fact, there appears to be no reason to expect such an intersection to occur; the figure suggests that perhaps only a coincidence would result in a common IS-LM-BOP intersection and general equilibrium. This somewhat pessimistic-sounding situation disappears, however, once we recognize several linkages among the three markets. These linkages guarantee that (in the absence of interference) the IS, LM, and BOP curves will move to a point of common intersection and that the economy will reach a general equilibrium. This is an important and somewhat surprising result, especially since we've assumed throughout this chapter that the price level is fixed, thereby ruling out one of the economy's most powerful self-adjustment mechanisms.

The exact nature of the linkages among the three markets depends on the exchange rate regime under which the economy operates. Flexible exchange rates imply linkages that are somewhat easier to see than those under fixed rates. So, let's begin with a flexible-rate regime and then move on to adjustment under a fixed-rate regime.

6 HOW A FLEXIBLE EXCHANGE RATE REGIME WORKS

Under a perfectly flexible exchange rate regime, the exchange rate continually adjusts to keep the balance of payments in equilibrium and, equivalently, to keep the quantity demanded of foreign exchange equal to the quantity supplied. These changes in the exchange rate shift both the IS and BOP curves until they reach a general equilibrium on the LM curve.

Figure 14   **Automatic Adjustment from a Position of Balance-of-Payments Surplus under a Flexible Exchange Rate**

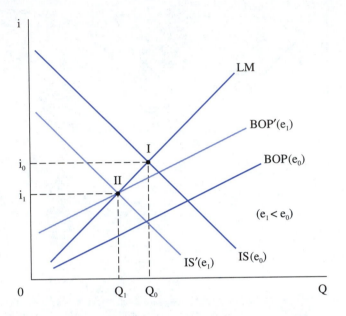

The balance-of-payments surplus at point I causes the domestic currency to appreciate, which shifts the BOP and IS curves to the left. Point II represents equilibrium with income equal to Q_1, the interest rate at i_1, and the domestic-currency price of foreign currency at e_1.

Note that because of the negative slope of the IS curve and the positive slopes of the LM and BOP curves, the IS curve will intersect each of the other two, but not necessarily at the same point. Point I in Figure 14 illustrates a case in which the markets for goods and services and for money are in equilibrium, but with a balance-of-payments surplus with the exchange rate at e_0.[35] The surplus in the BOP at point I is evident from I's position above and to the left of the BOP curve drawn with $e = e_0$ (see section 4.2). The quantity supplied of foreign exchange exceeds the quantity demanded (by the definition of a balance-of-payments surplus), so the domestic currency appreciates, or the domestic currency price of foreign currency falls from e_0 to e_1. The appreciation raises the relative price of domestic goods, because $R \equiv P/eP^*$. Exports fall and imports rise, shifting the IS curve to the left from IS to IS'.[36]

An appreciation of the domestic currency also shifts the BOP curve to the left. The currency appreciation affects both balance-of-payments accounts. The current-account balance moves toward a deficit as exports fall and imports rise. (*Why?*) The capital account also moves toward a deficit.[37] Since the balance of payments initially was in

---

35. We wouldn't actually observe a point such as I under a perfectly flexible exchange rate, because the exchange rate adjusts instantaneously. Nonetheless, an examination of point I proves useful for understanding the nature of the adjustment process.

36. Recall from our analysis of the market for goods and services in the preceding chapter (section 8) that events that lower total expenditure on domestic goods and services (other than a rise in i) shift the IS curve to the left.

37. If you've forgotten why the exchange rate has this effect on the capital account, you may want to review section 4 on interest parity in the chapter on currency markets and exchange rates.

Table 9	**HOW DOES THE ECONOMY ADJUST FROM A BOP SURPLUS UNDER A FLEXIBLE EXCHANGE RATE?**[a]
Variable	
Domestic income (Q)	Falls
Domestic interest rate (i)	Falls
Exchange rate (e)	Falls (domestic currency appreciates)
Money stock (M/P)	None

[a]Here we assume an intermediate level of capital mobility. A later chapter will focus on the implications of different degrees of capital mobility for the adjustment process and for macroeconomic policy under a flexible exchange rate.

Table 10	**HOW DOES THE ECONOMY ADJUST FROM A BOP DEFICIT UNDER A FLEXIBLE EXCHANGE RATE?**[a]
Variable	
Domestic income (Q)	Rises
Domestic interest rate (i)	Rises
Exchange rate (e)	Rises (domestic currency depreciates)
Money stock (M/P)	None

[a]See note in Table 9.

surplus at point I, the changes in both accounts move it toward equilibrium. The new BOP line (BOP′) represents the combinations of income and interest that place the balance of payments in equilibrium given the new, lower value of the exchange rate, e_1. The IS and BOP curves come to a rest once they share a common intersection with the LM curve. At that point (point II in Figure 14), all three markets are in equilibrium simultaneously at income Q_1, interest rate i_1, and exchange rate e_1. Table 9 reports the automatic adjustments in response to the balance-of-payments surplus.

We can use a similar analysis to show that if the IS and LM curves intersect below and to the right of the BOP curve, indicating a BOP deficit, the domestic currency will depreciate. The IS curve will shift to the right (*Why?*), as will the BOP line (*Why?*). Again, general equilibrium occurs when income, the interest rate, and the exchange rate have adjusted such that all three markets are in equilibrium simultaneously, as reported in Table 10.

In the process of shifting the IS, LM, and BOP curves, it's important to keep in mind the major results obtained so far. First, a general equilibrium in the economy requires a combination of income, interest rate, and exchange rate such that all three markets are in equilibrium simultaneously. Second, even with prices held fixed, the economy contains self-adjusting mechanisms for bringing the three major markets into equilibrium. We call these mechanisms *self-adjusting*, or *automatic*, because they require no explicit policy actions. Under a flexible exchange rate regime, the currency appreciates in response to a balance-of-payments surplus and depreciates in response to a deficit as a result of market forces, not government action. Once the exchange rate adjustment begins, individuals respond by altering their relative purchases of foreign and domestic goods, services, and assets. This process brings income, the interest rate, and the exchange rate to levels that clear all three markets, although the adjustment may be gradual.

Notice that the model highlights the pitfalls of drawing conclusions from analysis of only one market. If we consider only the market for goods and services or only the market for money, point I in Figure 14 appears to be an equilibrium. Imagine a situation in which output Q_0 corresponds to an acceptable level of employment (or unemployment) such that policy makers want the economy to operate at point I. If we ignore the balance of payments, the tendency of the economy to move to point II will be difficult to understand. By taking into account the balance of payments, however, it becomes easy to see why the economy ends up at point II. If point II is unacceptable, moving the economy away from it will require some type of active macroeconomic policy. We'll analyze such policies in the next two chapters. There we'll see that a general-equilibrium framework is essential not only for understanding where the economy tends to move independently but also for predicting accurately the effects of the various economic policies available. Just as a model that includes only the market for goods and services can wrongly imply that the economy will be in equilibrium at Q_0 and i_0, so can it produce misleading results concerning economic policies' effects on an open economy.

7 HOW A FIXED EXCHANGE RATE REGIME WORKS

It may seem obvious that the economy can adjust to reach a general equilibrium under a flexible exchange rate regime, since the exchange rate provides an automatic adjustment mechanism. But what about an economy under a completely fixed exchange rate regime in which even policy-induced changes in the pegged rate (that is, devaluations and revaluations) are ruled out? Do we have any reason to expect the economy to self-adjust and reach general equilibrium under such circumstances? The answer is yes, because a direct link exists between the nominal money stock and the balance of payments under a fixed-rate regime.

With a flexible exchange rate, a currency appreciation or depreciation corrects any balance-of-payments surplus or deficit. In terms of the IS-LM-BOP diagram, the change in the exchange rate shifts the IS and BOP curves until they intersect on the LM curve, which remains stationary throughout the adjustment process. Under a fixed exchange rate regime, the IS and BOP curves no longer handle the adjustment. Instead, the LM curve moves to the intersection of the stationary IS and BOP curves, because surpluses or deficits in the balance of payments automatically cause changes in the money stock. (It may prove useful to review Figure 4's analysis of the effect of a change in the nominal money stock on the LM curve.) To understand this process, we need to examine the link between the balance of payments and the money stock under a fixed exchange rate.

7.1 Fixed Exchange Rates and the Nominal Money Stock

Recall that within a fixed exchange rate regime, the central bank maintains the pegged exchange rate by intervening to buy any excess supply of foreign exchange or to sell foreign exchange to cover any excess demand. As we'll see, such intervention by the central bank restores foreign exchange market equilibrium at the pegged exchange rate. The mechanics of foreign exchange market intervention are quite simple. When the balance of payments is in surplus, the central bank must purchase from the public the excess of quantity supplied over quantity demanded of foreign exchange. These purchases raise the central bank's stock of foreign exchange reserves (FXR). As Equation 2 indicates, the money stock rises by the amount of the FXR purchase multiplied by the money multiplier.

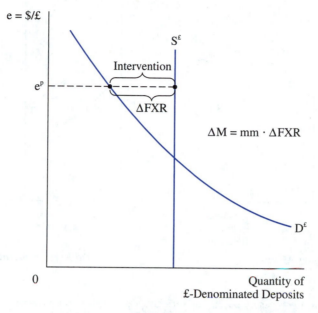

Figure 15 **Effect of Intervention on the Money Stock under a Fixed Exchange Rate**

At the pegged rate, e^p, the quantity of foreign exchange supplied exceeds the quantity demanded. To prevent the dollar from appreciating, the U.S. central bank must intervene to buy the excess pounds. The central bank adds the purchased pounds to its foreign exchange reserves. The central bank check with which the pounds are bought creates the basis for an expansion of the U.S. money stock. The money stock rises by mm · ΔFXR.

Figure 15 ties the analysis of the foreign exchange market to intervention's effect on the money stock (from the chapter on currency markets and exchange rates), using pounds to represent foreign exchange. To maintain the exchange rate at e^p, the central bank must buy the excess supply of foreign exchange at that rate. It makes this purchase with one of its special checks. The central bank's foreign exchange reserves rise by ΔFXR; the money stock rises by mm · ΔFXR through the money-creation process discussed in section 2.3.[38]

Figure 16 illustrates how the rise in the money stock restores foreign exchange market equilibrium at the pegged exchange rate, e^p. Panel (a) traces events in the money market. Prior to the central bank's intervention, the money stock is (M_0/P) and the equilibrium interest rate is i_0. Panel (b), representing the foreign exchange market, shows that the foreign exchange market is *not* in equilibrium at e^p and i_0. Given those values of the exchange rate and the domestic interest rate (along with i^*, e^e, and e^f), portfolio owners want to hold less than the existing stock of pound-denominated assets. The central bank must step in to buy up the excess supply, adding the pounds to its international reserves and expanding the domestic money stock by mm · ΔFXR. The rise in the domestic money stock shifts the money supply line in panel (a) to the right, from (M_0/P) to (M_1/P), where $(M_1/P) = (M_0/P) + (mm · \Delta FXR)$. At the old equilibrium

---

38. In the upcoming chapter, we'll see that this result hinges on an assumption that the central bank doesn't *sterilize* or engage in open market operations designed to offset intervention's effect on the domestic money stock. As Equation 2 makes clear, if central bank purchases or sales of government bonds cancel out the effect of purchases or sales of foreign exchange (ΔGB = $-\Delta$FXR), the money stock will remain unchanged.

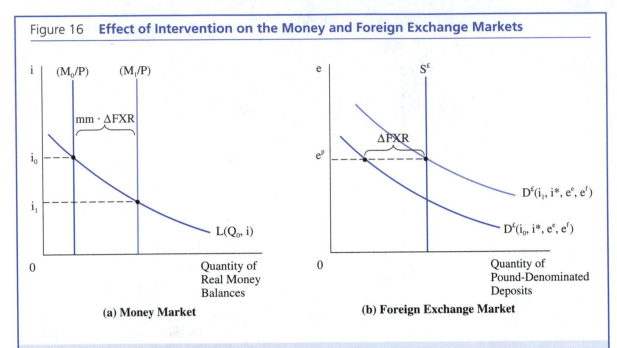

Figure 16   Effect of Intervention on the Money and Foreign Exchange Markets

(a) Money Market

(b) Foreign Exchange Market

When the central bank intervenes by buying the excess supply of foreign-currency-denominated deposits in the foreign exchange market (panel (b)), the domestic money stock rises (panel (a)). The larger domestic money stock pushes down the equilibrium interest rate in panel (a), lowers the rate of return on domestic-currency deposits, and raises the demand for foreign-currency deposits in panel (b). The intervention restores interest parity at the original exchange rate (e^p) and a lower domestic interest rate.

interest rate, i_0, individuals don't want to hold the new, higher level of real money balances. They try to buy bonds to lower real money balances to the desired level and, in the process, push the interest rate down to i_1. At i_1, individuals are content to hold the new, larger domestic money stock. The lower interest rate also affects the foreign exchange market. Because i has fallen, asset owners want to shift their portfolios toward more pound-denominated deposits, since dollar-denominated ones now pay a lower rate of return. This shifts the demand for pound deposits to the right, achieving interest parity and foreign exchange market equilibrium at e^p.

To retrace the argument, the initial excess supply of pound deposits at e^p and i_0 necessitated central bank intervention to buy foreign-currency assets. The intervention increased the domestic money stock and lowered the domestic interest rate, thereby making asset owners content to hold the existing quantity of foreign-currency assets.

If the exchange rate is fixed at a level below the equilibrium rate, the quantity demanded of foreign exchange exceeds the quantity supplied.[39] The central bank intervenes to sell foreign exchange from its reserves. Because the central bank's foreign exchange reserves fall by the amount of the excess demand at e^p, the domestic money stock falls by mm · ΔFXR. The decline in the domestic money stock pushes up the domestic interest rate and restores equilibrium in the foreign exchange market by decreasing demand for foreign-currency-denominated deposits. Interest parity holds at the pegged exchange rate and the new, higher domestic interest rate.

---

39. See, for example, Figure 10 in the chapter on currency markets and exchange rates.

7.2 **The Money Stock and Automatic Adjustment**

As long as a balance-of-payments surplus exists, the central bank's foreign exchange market intervention will cause the money stock to expand, shifting the LM curve to the right. A balance-of-payments deficit, on the other hand, will shrink the money stock, shifting the LM curve to the left. These adjustments ensure that the LM curve will move to the point of intersection with the IS and BOP curves, resulting in a general equilibrium in the economy.

Figure 17 traces the economy's adjustment from a position of surplus in its balance of payments. At the intersection of the IS and LM curves (point I), the balance of payments is in surplus, because the point lies above and to the left of the BOP curve. In the foreign exchange market, there's an excess supply of foreign-currency-denominated deposits. To restore balance-of-payments equilibrium, the central bank must buy the excess foreign exchange, causing the domestic money stock to rise from M_0 to M_1 and shifting the LM curve to the right. The adjustment process is complete when the LM curve reaches a point of intersection with both the IS and BOP curves (point II). There, all three markets are in simultaneous equilibrium at the existing income, interest rate, and exchange rate.

Table 11 summarizes the economy's automatic adjustment from a point of balance-of-payments surplus under a fixed exchange rate regime.

Figure 18 illustrates adjustment from a position of balance-of-payments deficit. At the intersection of the IS and LM curves (point I), the balance of payments is in deficit. To restore balance-of-payments equilibrium, the central bank must sell foreign exchange, causing the money stock to fall from M_0 to M_1 and shifting the LM curve to the left.

Figure 17   **A Surplus in the Balance of Payments Causes the Money Stock to Rise and Shifts the LM Curve to the Right**

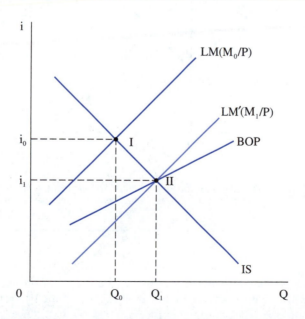

A balance-of-payments surplus corresponds to an excess supply of foreign exchange. To maintain the pegged exchange rate, the central bank must intervene to buy foreign exchange and add it to the bank's reserves. The increase in reserves raises the domestic money stock from M_0 to M_1.

Table 11 **HOW DOES THE ECONOMY ADJUST FROM A BOP SURPLUS UNDER A FIXED EXCHANGE RATE?**[a]

Variable	
Domestic income (Q)	Rises
Domestic interest rate (i)	Falls
Exchange rate (e)	No change
Money stock (M/P)	Rises

[a]Here we assume the degree of capital mobility to be intermediate. In the upcoming chapter, we'll look in detail at the importance of the extent of capital mobility for the automatic adjustment process and for fiscal and monetary policies under a fixed exchange rate.

Figure 18 **A Deficit in the Balance of Payments Causes the Money Stock to Fall and Shifts the LM Curve to the Left**

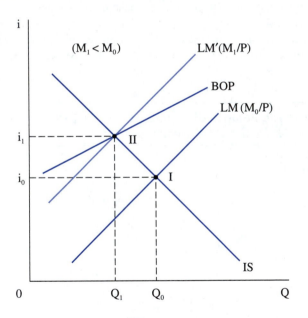

A BOP deficit corresponds to an excess demand for foreign exchange. To maintain the pegged exchange rate, the central bank must intervene to supply foreign exchange from its reserves. The loss of reserves lowers the domestic money stock from M_0 to M_1.

The adjustment process is complete when the LM curve has shifted to a point of intersection with both the IS and BOP curves (point II). Table 12 lists each variable's contribution to the adjustment process.

We've demonstrated that linkages among the goods and services, money, and foreign exchange markets ensure that the economy can reach a point of general equilibrium even if the price level is fixed. The exact mechanism by which adjustment occurs depends on the exchange rate regime in operation. Under a flexible-rate regime, the *exchange rate*

Table 12	**HOW DOES THE ECONOMY ADJUST FROM A BOP DEFICIT UNDER A FIXED EXCHANGE RATE?**[a]
Variable	
Domestic income (Q)	Falls
Domestic interest rate (i)	Rises
Exchange rate (e)	No change
Money stock (M/P)	Falls

[a]See note in Table 11.

adjusts to equilibrate the balance of payments. Graphically, changes in the exchange rate shift the IS and BOP curves to a common intersection with the LM curve. Under a fixed-rate regime, the *money stock* adjusts through the central bank's foreign exchange intervention policies. Graphically, this is reflected in a shift of the LM curve to a common intersection with the IS and BOP curves. Note that the mechanism by which adjustment occurs carries important implications for the macroeconomy. For example, comparing Tables 9 and 11, we can see that automatic adjustment from a balance-of-payments surplus reduces income under a flexible exchange rate (because the currency appreciation raises the relative price of domestic goods and services relative to foreign ones) but increases income under a fixed exchange rate (because the money-stock growth lowers the interest rate and encourages investment).

Under either exchange rate system, the adjustment is automatic in the sense that the only policy required is that the central bank follow the "rules" of the exchange regime in effect. The rules of a flexible-rate regime are to allow the forces of demand and supply to determine the exchange rate. The rules of a fixed-rate regime are to intervene to buy and sell foreign exchange from international reserves to maintain the pegged exchange rate.

CASE 1: TRYING TO GET THE BEST OF BOTH WORLDS

Deposit-insurance systems, under which the government guarantees that bank depositors won't lose their deposits in the event of a bank failure, present policy makers with a dilemma. On the one hand, such plans deepen much-needed confidence in the banking system. This confidence can encourage saving and help get saving into banks, where lenders can channel it to investors to finance productive investment projects that help the economy grow. On the other hand, if lenders and depositors believe that the government will cover any losses that occur because of overly risky loans or other bad management decisions, bankers may lose the incentive to behave prudently with depositors' funds and depositors may lose their incentive to monitor bankers' behavior. Economists

call this problem *moral hazard*. Awareness of this deposit-insurance dilemma has grown since financial crises in Latin America, Mexico, and Asia—all of which involved huge bad-loan problems in the banking system.

So what's a policy maker to do? The answer is to try to tailor a deposit-insurance system in such a way to get the maximum confidence-building benefits while minimizing the moral-hazard problem. One approach is to limit the amount of insurance coverage per depositor to a set amount, say $100,000 (a per-account limit is less effective, because large depositors just open multiple accounts to get full coverage). This ensures that small depositors don't lose their life savings; but it leaves large depositors, presumably those most capable of monitoring the prudence of banks' lending decisions, with uninsured funds, thereby providing an incentive for them to police bank managers' behavior. Almost all of the explicit deposit-insurance systems in effect contain a ceiling or cap on the amount covered; for example, Russia's deposit insurance, introduced in 2003 after the country's devastating 1998 banking crisis, limits coverage to 100,000 rubles (then equal to $3,400) per household. Most governments with unlimited systems in effect plan to introduce limits. Japan had a deposit-insurance ceiling in effect until 1996, when the country's severe financial-sector problems generated political pressure to suspend the ceiling for five years, supposedly to increase depositors' confidence in the banking system. That same political pressure led to a two-year postponement of the scheduled reinstitution of the insurance ceiling. In April 2002, the Japanese government did impose a ¥10 million cap (then equal to $84,000) on savings-deposit coverage, and a parallel move for checking deposits was scheduled to follow in April 2003. But the cap on savings-account coverage caused depositors promptly to shift $353 billion out of savings accounts at Japanese banks, and policy makers responded by delaying once more reimposition of the insurance cap on checking accounts—to April 2005. The proposed Japanese deposit-insurance cap also contains two important loopholes: Individuals can open special checking accounts that earn zero interest and remain eligible for unlimited deposit insurance; and, should the government declare a financial crisis because of a bank failure, all deposits at the failing institution would be fully guaranteed.[40]

A second element of an optimal deposit-insurance system involves making participation compulsory for banks. Otherwise, banks that plan to make overly risky loans will participate, while more-prudently run banks won't. Ideally, the banks themselves can fund the insurance system, with the premium charged each bank dependent on the riskiness of that bank's asset portfolio. Again, this creates an incentive for banks to be careful; by creating a prudent asset portfolio, the bank can reduce its insurance premiums (just as you can reduce your life- and health-insurance premiums by not smoking, or your home insurance premium by installing burglar alarms and smoke detectors). Finally, to work effectively, the deposit-insurance system should be established—with clear and explicit rules—*before* a banking crisis. Governments must beware of implicit or murky deposit-insurance promises that passively encourage depositors and bank owners to count on being bailed out in a crisis. Such a situation encourages risky banking behavior that can itself help bring on a crisis; and, once a crisis develops, the government will face strong political pressure to deliver on even the most implicit or vague promises.

CASE 2: WHERE THE FOREIGN EXCHANGE RESERVES ARE

Central banks hold foreign exchange reserves in case they want to intervene in the foreign exchange market. These reserves are a central bank asset and determine, along with the central bank's domestic assets and the money multiplier, the size of the country's money stock. The quantity of reserves that countries hold varies widely. Of the countries included in the International Monetary Fund's *International Financial Statistics Yearbook 2003*, Liberia held the smallest amount of foreign exchange reserves ($2.72 million) and Japan the largest ($451.62 billion). Figure 19 reports the six countries with the largest foreign exchange reserve holdings in 2002.[41]

Japan accumulated $390 billion in additional reserves between 1992 and 2002 as it intervened periodically to lower the dollar price of yen in response to a sluggish Japanese economy. Of all foreign exchange held in reserves in 2003, dollars make up about two-thirds of the total. For historical reasons, some industrial countries' central banks hold substantial gold reserves. Countries that held the largest quantities of gold in 2002 were the United States, Germany, France, Italy, and Switzerland.

---

40. "Koizumi to End State Guarantee on Deposits," *Financial Times*, October 13, 2004.

41. Note that, because China still reports economic data for Hong Kong separately from that for the mainland, both China and Hong Kong make the list of top holders of foreign exchange reserves even after China's 1997 takeover of Hong Kong.

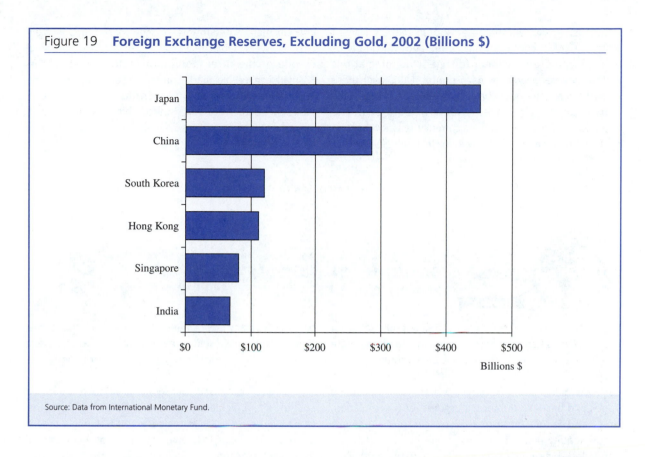

Figure 19 **Foreign Exchange Reserves, Excluding Gold, 2002 (Billions $)**

Source: Data from International Monetary Fund.

CASE 3: BIRTH OF A CURRENCY

Germany

The 1995 Dayton Peace Accord created a new Bosnian state after three years of war among Serbs, Croats, and Bosnian Muslims in Bosnia and Herzegovina. Terms of the settlement included creation of a new central bank and currency, the Bosnian convertible mark (Km).[42] Since the breakup of the former state of Yugoslavia, three currencies had been widely used in the war-ravaged territory: the German mark, the Yugoslavian dinar, and the Croatian kuna. But participants at the Dayton talks thought a new currency could help reunite Bosnia.

The Bosnian constitution created a central bank that works as a currency board. This means that the bank can't buy government bonds, but can only buy and sell foreign exchange reserves to keep the convertible mark's exchange rate pegged, originally to the German

Deutsche mark at an exchange rate of Km1/DM1 and then to the euro at a rate of Km1/€ 0.51. Such a system was designed to develop confidence in the new currency by maintaining a fixed value relative to the trusted foreign currency of an important trading partner. The new Bosnian constitution also embodied other confidence-building rules. For example, it specified that until at least 2003 the central bank had to be run by someone *not* from Bosnia or any neighboring state. A Frenchman did the early groundwork for the new currency; the next governor of the Central Bank of Bosnia hailed from New Zealand.

Not everything went smoothly in introducing the new currency. Serbs, Croats, and Bosnian Muslims argued for months about the design of the new bank

42. See "Building Bosnia on Banknotes," *The Economist*, May 1, 1999, and "Euro Changeover Reveals a Lot of Hidden Cash," *Financial Times*, November 12, 2002.

notes, especially whether they should feature Roman script or Cyrillic script (they have both) and which famous writers would adorn them (different denominations feature writers favored by each group). Once over these initial hurdles, the new currency fared well. Convertible marks quickly circulated widely in Sarajevo. The population's trust in the new currency was symbolized by the fact that shopkeepers didn't even separate

Bosnian mark notes from Deutsche mark notes in their cash drawers. Outside Sarajevo, in areas dominated by one of the three dominant factions, use of the Bosnian convertible mark spread more slowly. Areas of Bosnia with large Croat populations favored the Croatian kuna; and Serb areas still used the dinar, although that currency's dramatic loss of value discouraged even its Serb users.

CASE 4: **BANKING ON UNIFICATION**

Germany

Germany is unusual among the developed industrial countries in its heavy reliance on banks to fund corporate investment. More than 95 percent of corporate funding in Germany takes the form of bank loans. The corresponding figure is around 40 percent in the United States and between 60 and 80 percent for Britain, Japan, Italy, and France.[43] Nonbank sources of investment funds—equity markets and corporate bond markets, in particular—play much smaller roles in Germany than in the other industrial economies. Germany's private "universal" banks are permitted to hold equity in other firms, so banks' performance can be affected by stock-market swings.

German banks' unique position as near-sole financiers of firms' investment projects means that when banks perform poorly, the drag on the economy's overall performance can be significant. And German banks have been performing poorly. Most experts agree the country has far too many banks, with a branch for approximately every 1,700 people. And many banks are heavily burdened by bad loans, especially in the commercial and real-estate sectors. As the value of these loans sinks, banks face the prospect of insolvency if the value of assets falls below that of liabilities. Experts place the likely value of bad loans at approximately $325 billion, but no one knows for sure

because Germany's banks are notoriously secretive. Some German banks have sold some of their loans as distressed assets, usually at prices below 50 percent of the loan's face value.[44]

Why so many bad loans in a developed industrial country with a regulatory apparatus in place? Most of the worst loans were made in the early 1990s during a period of great exuberance following unification of the then-East and West Germanys. Government policy provided generous tax breaks and subsidies for projects in the "new states"—former Communist East Germany; for example, investors could take tax deductions equal to 50 percent of investments made in the East. The projects were speculative in the sense that business parks, hospitals, office buildings, and shopping malls were built just on the assumption that there would be demand for them; after all, many Germans expected the East to rapidly catch up economically with the West upon unification. Many of these projects now stand either half-completed or finished but empty.[45] HVB Bank, Germany's second largest, left its real-estate business in 2002 after a single-year loss of almost $1 billion, bringing an end to a commercial real-estate business that dated back to the original German "unification" in 1871.[46]

43. See "Trust Me, I'm a Banker: A Survey of International Banking," *The Economist*, April 17, 2004, p. 10. Figure 8 earlier in this chapter provides similar figures for other countries.

44. "German Banks Send Distress Signal," *Financial Times*, September 4, 2003.

45. "A Basket Case—Or Worse," *Financial Times*, March 28, 2003.

46. "A Big Bet on Land in the East Haunts Germany's Banks," *Wall Street Journal*, August 5, 2003.

SUMMARY

An economy is in general equilibrium when the markets for goods and services, money, and foreign exchange all clear at a common income, interest rate, and exchange rate. The economy contains self-adjusting mechanisms for reaching a general equilibrium under both fixed and flexible exchange rate regimes.

Under a flexible-rate regime, imbalances in the balance of payments cause *exchange rate* changes. These changes alter the relative price of domestic and foreign goods, which affects both the market for goods and services and the current account. Under a fixed-rate regime, imbalances in the balance of payments cause changes in the *money stock*. The central bank must intervene in foreign exchange markets to maintain the pegged exchange rate in the face of a deficit or a surplus. This intervention causes changes in the stock of foreign exchange reserves and in the money stock. Since 1973, the major currencies have operated under a mixed exchange regime involving some flexibility of rates in response to market forces and some intervention by central banks.

LOOKING AHEAD

This chapter argued that an economy contains self-adjusting mechanisms that bring the markets for goods and services, money, and foreign exchange into equilibrium under either a fixed or flexible exchange rate regime. However, these automatic mechanisms may operate slowly or produce side effects that conflict with other goals. For this reason, policy makers may choose to conduct a variety of policies that attempt to either speed up or hinder the adjustment process. These policies are the subject of the next chapter.

KEY TERMS

money	fractional reserve banking system
barter	deposit expansion
nominal money stock	money multiplier
real money stock	open market operation
real money balances	LM curve
opportunity cost of holding money	BOP curve

PROBLEMS AND QUESTIONS FOR REVIEW

1. Mr. Imnot Competent, country A's Assistant Minister for Monetary Policy, never can remember if country A has a fixed or a flexible exchange rate. He claims it doesn't matter for his job, since he runs monetary policy, not exchange-rate policy. Do you agree? Why?
2. Explain the following statement: "Macroeconomic policy makers can control either the money stock or the exchange rate, but not both."
3. Begin with the situation reported in the consolidated banking system's balance sheet in Table 3. A bank run causes the banking system to lose $500 in deposits. If individuals hold the $500 that they withdraw from banks in currency, what is the run's effect on the money stock? Explain.
4. Explain the following statement: "The central bank can have the same effect on the domestic money stock by buying (or selling) either government bonds or foreign exchange."
5. Use a diagram similar to Figure 16 to predict the effect of an increase in the domestic money stock on the exchange rate under a flexible exchange rate regime. Explain.
6. Country A keeps its exchange rate fixed. Currently, the markets for goods and services and for money are in equilibrium, but country A's balance of payments is in deficit.
   a. Assume that capital is perfectly immobile. Once automatic adjustment eliminates the balance-of-payments deficit, will country A's income be higher or lower than before? Why?
   b. Assume that capital is perfectly mobile. Once automatic adjustment eliminates the balance-of-payments deficit, will country A's income be higher or lower than before? Why?

7. a. Draw a diagram of the domestic money market in equilibrium.
    b. Draw a diagram of the foreign exchange market in which the quantity demanded of foreign exchange exceeds the quantity supplied at the current fixed exchange rate.
    c. Illustrate the effects of intervention by the central bank to supply foreign exchange.
    d. Explain how the intervention restores interest parity at the original exchange rate.
8. Using the framework from problem 7, explain the following comment: "Central bank intervention is more successful when it affects market participants' expectations."

REFERENCES AND SELECTED READINGS

Ahearne, Alan G., et al. "Countering Contagion: Does China's Experience Offer a Blueprint?" Federal Reserve Bank of Chicago *Economic Perspectives* (Fourth Quarter 2001): 38–52.
The costs of China's attempts at financial insulation from crises in neighboring economies.

Aninat, Eduardo, et al. "Combating Money Laundering and the Financing of Terrorism." *Finance and Development* 39 (September 2002): 44–47.
Introduction to how authorities can and can't control money laundering and terrorism finance.

Burnside, Craig, et al. "Prospective Deficits and the Asian Currency Crisis." *Journal of Political Economy* 109 (December 2001): 1155–1197.
Argues that the expected fiscal costs of dealing with banks' insolvency played an important role in causing the Asian financial crisis; for intermediate and advanced students.

Carstens, Agustin, et al. "Avoiding Banking Crises in Latin America." *Finance and Development* (September 2003): 30–33.
History, causes, and lessons of Latin America's numerous banking crises; for all students.

DeLong, J. Bradford. "Financial Crises in the 1890s and the 1990s: Must History Repeat?" *Brookings Papers on Economic Activity* 2 (1999): 253–294.
Commonalities and differences between the two end-of-century financial crises.

Dominguez, Kathryn M., and Jeffrey A. Frankel. *Does Foreign Exchange Intervention Work?* Washington, D.C.: Institute for International Economics, 1993.
Examines intervention's ability to affect exchange rates and the money stock; for intermediate students.

Fischer, Stanley. "On the Need for an International Lender of Last Resort." *Journal of Economic Perspectives* 13 (Fall 1999): 85–104.
The pros and cons of international lending to banks in the midst of financial crises.

Goldstein, Morris. *The Asian Financial Crisis.* Washington, D.C.: Institute for International Economics, 1998.
Accessible overview of the origins and implications of the Asian financial crisis.

Hardy, Daniel C. "Are Banking Crises Predictable?" *Finance and Development* (December 1998): 32–35.
Introduction to the early indicators of banking-sector problems.

Helfer, Ricki Tigert. "What Deposit Insurance Can and Cannot Do." *Finance and Development* 36 (March 1999): 22–25.
The benefits and costs of deposit insurance in financial crises.

Hoshi, Takeo, and Anil K. Kashyap. "Japan's Financial Crisis and Economic Stagnation." *Journal of Economic Perspectives* 18 (Winter 2004): 3–26.
The role of banking-system weakness in Japan's continuing economic problems; for all students.

Hume, David. "On the Balance of Trade." In *Essays, Moral, Political, and Literary,* Vol. 1. London: Longmans, Green, 1898 [1752].
The classic work on automatic adjustment of the balance of payments, including the original statement of the specie-flow mechanism; for all students.

Kester, Anne Y. "Improving the Framework for Reporting on International Reserves." *Finance and Development* 37 (June 2000): 49–52.
How reporting standards could improve market participants' information about central banks' reserves.

Lindgren, Carl-Johan, et al. *Bank Soundness and Macroeconomic Policy.* Washington, D.C.: International Monetary Fund, 1996.
Interrelationship between the banking system and macroeconomic policy; for all students.

Neely, Christopher J. "The Practice of Central Bank Intervention: Looking under the Hood." Federal Reserve Bank of St. Louis *Review* 83 (May/June 2001): 1–10.
Accessible overview of the mechanics of foreign exchange market intervention.

Peek, Joe, and Eric Rosengren. "Implications of the Globalization of the Banking Sector: The Latin American Experience." Federal Reserve Bank of Boston *New England Economic Review* (September/October 2000): 45–62.
How has internationalization affected the performance of Latin American banks?

Proceedings of a Conference on "Beyond Pillar 3 in International Banking Regulation: Disclosure and Market Discipline of Financial Firms." Federal Reserve Bank of New York *Economic Policy Review* (September 2004).
Papers on how to improve supervision of international banks to lower the risks of banking crises; for advanced students.

Quirk, Peter J. "Money Laundering: Muddying the Macroeconomy." *Finance and Development* (March 1997): 7–10.
Macroeconomic effects of money laundering; for all students.

Rogoff, Kenneth S. "The Surprising Popularity of Paper Currency." *Finance and Development* 39 (March 2002): 56–57.
The continuing popularity of paper over electronic alternatives; for all students.

Sarno, Lucio, and Mark P. Taylor. "Official Intervention in the Foreign Exchange Market: Is It Effective and, If So, How Does It Work?" *Journal of Economic Literature* (September 2001): 839–868.
Survey of the empirical evidence on sterilized intervention's effectiveness.

Summers, Lawrence H. "International Financial Crises: Causes, Prevention, and Cures." *American Economic Review Papers and Proceedings* 90 (May 2000): 1–16.
Accessible discussion by the former U.S. Treasury Secretary, now president of Harvard University.

Symposium on "Reform and Restructuring in Asia." *Finance and Development* 38 (March 2001): 2–28.
Policy changes instigated by the crisis.

CHAPTER

6

Short-Run Macroeconomic Policy under Fixed Exchange Rates

1 INTRODUCTION

Among the many purposes of studying an open macroeconomy is to understand better the implications of openness for macroeconomic policy. The effectiveness of various policies depends, often in crucial ways, on the nature and extent of a country's linkages with the larger world economy. These linkages include the magnitude of trade in goods and services, the integration of financial markets reflected in capital flows, and the type of exchange rate regime used for facilitating currency transactions.

These linkages vary across countries as well as over time, so the effectiveness of different macroeconomic policies also varies across these dimensions. For example, during the 1950s and 1960s the degree of international capital mobility and the magnitude of capital flows were limited. Most governments regulated international borrowing and lending to limit the flows of funds into and out of their economies. The absence of highly developed institutions through which to facilitate international capital flows, such as Eurocurrency markets[1] and bonds issued in multiple currencies, also contributed to a relatively low degree of international capital mobility. During the past quarter-century, the growth of a truly international capital market has been one of the major developments on the world scene. Governments of the major industrial economies and of many developing ones have loosened their regulation of capital flows, and elaborate institutions have evolved to handle the resulting transactions.

These developments carry major implications for businesses, which can now conduct production, marketing, and borrowing and lending operations on a worldwide scale. Less recognized but equally important are the implications for macroeconomic policy. For many countries, increased international capital mobility along with a move to a more flexible exchange rate have made fiscal policy a less effective tool for managing the economy than in the 1950s. In general, changes in either the degree of capital mobility or the exchange rate regime will alter the expected effectiveness of the basic tools of macroeconomic policy.

This chapter examines the goals of macroeconomic policy in an open economy; defines some general principles useful in designing policies to meet those goals; and explores the effectiveness of the three major types of macroeconomic policy: fiscal,

---

1. Eurocurrencies are offshore deposits denominated in the currency of a country other than the one in which the deposits are located. Section 9 in the earlier chapter on currency markets and exchange rates discusses Eurocurrencies.

162

monetary, and exchange rate policy, under a fixed exchange rate using the IS-LM-BOP model from the preceding chapter. Why analyze a fixed exchange rate regime when the United States and most other industrial economies shifted to more flexible-rate regimes in the early 1970s? First, exchange rates for most currencies have been fixed throughout most of modern macroeconomic history. To understand that history, including its lessons for today and the future, we must understand the basic functioning of a fixed exchange rate system. Second, as reported in Table 1, two important groups of countries continue to

---

Table 1 IMF MEMBERS WITH DE FACTO PEGGED EXCHANGE RATES, DECEMBER 31, 2003

Exchange Rate Regime (Number of Countries)	
Exchange arrangements with no separate legal tender[a] (41)	*Another currency as legal tender*: Ecuador, El Salvador, Kiribati, Marshall Islands, Micronesia, Palau, Panama, San Marino, Timor-Leste *East Caribbean Common Market*: Antigua & Barbuda, Dominica, Grenada, St. Kitts & Nevis, St. Lucia, St. Vincent & the Grenadines *CFA Franc Zone*: Benin, Burkina Faso, Cameroon, Central African Republic, Chad, Republic of Congo, Côte d'Ivoire, Equatorial Guinea, Guinea-Bissau, Gabon, Mali, Niger, Senegal, Togo *Euro area*: Austria, Belgium, Finland, France, Germany, Ireland, Italy, Luxembourg, Netherlands, Portugal, Spain
Currency board arrangements[b] (7)	Bosnia & Herzegovina, Brunei Darussalam, Bulgaria, Hong Kong, Djibouti, Estonia, Lithuania
Other conventional fixed peg arrangements[c] (41)	Aruba, The Bahamas, Bahrain, Barbados, Belize, Bhutan, Botswana, Cape Verde, China (Mainland), Comoros, Eritrea, Fiji, Guinea, Jordan, Kuwait, Latvia, Lebanon, Lesotho, Libya, Macedonia FYR, Malaysia, Maldives, Malta, Morocco, Namibia, Nepal, Netherlands Antilles, Oman, Qatar, Samoa, Saudi Arabia, Seychelles, Suriname, Swaziland, Syrian Arab Republic, Turkmenistan, Ukraine, United Arab Emirates, Vanuatu, Venezuela, Zimbabwe
Pegged exchange rates within horizontal bands[d] (4)	Cyprus, Denmark, Hungary, Tonga
Crawling pegs[e] (5)	Bolivia, Costa Rica, Nicaragua, Solomon Islands, Tunisia
Exchange rates within crawling bands[f] (5)	Belarus, Honduras, Israel, Romania, Slovenia

[a]The currency of another country circulates as the sole legal tender or the member belongs to a monetary or currency union in which the same legal tender is shared by the members of the union.
[b]A monetary regime based on an implicit legislative commitment to exchange domestic currency for a specified foreign currency at a fixed exchange rate, combined with restrictions on the issuing authority to ensure the fulfillment of the legal obligation.
[c]The country pegs its currency (formally or de facto) at a fixed rate to a major currency or a basket of currencies where the exchange rate fluctuates within a narrow margin of at most ±1 percent around a central rate.
[d]The value of the currency is maintained within margins of fluctuation around a formal or de facto fixed peg that are wider than ±1 around a central rate.
[e]The currency is adjusted periodically in small amounts at a fixed, preannounced rate or in response to changes in selective quantitative indicators.
[f]The currency is maintained within certain fluctuation margins around a central rate that is adjusted periodically at a fixed preannounced rate or in response to changes in selective quantitative indicators.

Source: International Monetary Fund.

maintain less-flexible exchange rates. Countries that adopt a common currency, such as the euro used by most members of the European Union, operate under the ultimate fixed exchange rate system (the exchange rate between a "German euro" and a "French euro" always equals one, by definition), although the currency floats against nonmember currencies. Also, many developing economies continue either to fix their exchange rates relative to a major currency (for example, Hong Kong) or to use the currency of a major trading partner as their domestic money (for example, Ecuador). Thus, policy decisions by EU members and by many developing economies remain bound by the structure and rules of a fixed-rate regime. Third, even the governments of economies such as the United States, which operate under flexible exchange rates, engage in foreign exchange market intervention on occasion. When they do, knowledge of how a fixed exchange rate system works is an important prerequisite to understanding the intervention's impact on the macroeconomy.

2 MACROECONOMIC GOALS IN AN OPEN ECONOMY

2.1 Internal and External Balance

A complete list of economic goals would constitute a book in itself. The main goals for an economic system include the efficient allocation of resources to produce goods and services wanted by society, an acceptable rate of economic growth, and an acceptable distribution of income. The study of each of these goals and the interrelationships among them constitutes economics as a discipline.

Here we focus on the two primary macroeconomic goals of an open economy—usually referred to as *internal* and *external balance*. **Internal balance** involves the full use of the economy's resources, or full employment, along with a stable price level. We'll examine directly not the level of employment or unemployment but the corresponding level of output or income. At income levels below that consistent with internal balance, the employment rate is too low or the unemployment rate too high. Unemployed resources indicate that the economy fails to produce as many goods and services as it can, a situation that clearly makes society worse off. If output rises above the level consistent with internal balance, the unemployment rate is too low to maintain stable prices and inflation may emerge as a problem.[2]

But what exactly does a "too low" or "too high" rate of unemployment mean? We can't define full employment as a specific percentage of unemployment measured by governments' official statistics (for example, 2, 4, or 6 percent). The percentage of measured unemployment properly identified with "full employment" depends on many factors, such as the pattern of wages in the economy, demographics—the population's age, gender, health, and educational characteristics, and citizens' tastes for income versus leisure. We can, however, rule out a zero rate of unemployment as a reasonable or desirable policy goal. For an economy to function efficiently, workers must sometimes spend time searching for the employment in which they'll be most productive. During that search, workers may be unemployed, but such temporary unemployment ultimately raises productivity through a better match between workers and jobs. In the remainder of this chapter, we'll assume that there exists a desired

---

2. So far, we've ignored inflation, or a sustained rise in the price level, through our assumption of fixed prices. The upcoming two chapters will relax that assumption and raise questions about macroeconomic policies' ability to alter real income, especially in the long run. For now, we merely note that attempts to use macroeconomic policy to increase real output above a level sustainable given the economy's resources will promote inflation. Inflation poses problems for an economy, so avoidance of inflation constitutes a major goal of macroeconomic policy making, as does avoidance of unemployment.

output for the economy that corresponds to "full" employment, given the society's resources, technology, and tastes for leisure, and that the goal of internal balance consists of maintaining that level of output.

At first glance, the external-balance goal appears more easily definable. We might argue that an economy achieves **external balance** when the quantity demanded of foreign exchange equals the quantity available; that is, when the foreign exchange market is in equilibrium. Under a fixed exchange rate regime, such external balance occurs when the balance of payments balances (BOP = 0). The analogous definition of external balance under a flexible exchange rate regime corresponds to a situation in which the domestic currency neither appreciates nor depreciates against other currencies. However, we'll see that in reality the goal of external balance is subtle and complex.

Policy makers often have preferences for the status of particular subcategories within the balance-of-payments accounts (for example, a balanced merchandise trade account or current account) along with a goal of overall balance. But those preferences may differ across time and across countries. The current account provides no clear value to serve as a policy goal analogous to full employment or low inflation on the internal-balance side. A current-account balance of zero, for example, may make sense as a policy goal in some circumstances, but not as a general rule. We've seen at several points that international borrowing and lending (or intertemporal trade) can provide gains from trade to both the borrowing and the lending country by allowing them to be net importers and net exporters, respectively, of current goods and services. In such circumstances, policy makers who pursue a current-account balance of zero needlessly forgo the gains from intertemporal trade. Temporary disasters, such as earthquakes or wars, provide a second reason for tolerating current-account imbalances. A country that suffers a sudden but temporary reduction in its productive capacity can borrow from foreigners to "smooth" or spread the disaster's negative effect on consumption over several years rather than bearing the entire burden in a short period.

Nonetheless, large and persistent current-account deficits or surpluses cause policy makers concern. Large deficits, which imply large-scale foreign borrowing, raise the risk that some of the borrowed funds may go not to fund worthwhile investment projects but rather to either excessive current consumption or unproductive "white-elephant" investments. If this happens, the funds will fail to earn a rate of return sufficient to repay the loans, and the debtor may be forced to either default or undergo costly adjustment policies to avoid default. Countries that borrow heavily abroad also must worry about foreigners' perceptions of their economic policies and performance. Foreign investors who begin to suspect unwise use of borrowed funds may become unwilling to lend, forcing the debtor to suffer through a sudden reduction in its ability to borrow to finance its current-account deficit.[3]

Large and persistent current-account surpluses pose more subtle concerns for policy makers. They correspond to large and persistent capital-account deficits, or accumulation of foreign assets, and to lower levels of domestic investment than would occur in the absence of the current-account surplus. Policy makers must wonder why foreign investments appear so much more attractive than domestic ones, when a higher rate of domestic investment might foster domestic economic growth, as well as a larger tax base on which to collect government revenue. In addition, the accumulation of foreign lending runs the risk that some borrowers may be unable to repay their obligations. Countries with large current-account surpluses also often receive intense political pressure from the corresponding deficit countries to reduce exports, accept protectionist policies against exports, or endure accusations of unfair trade practices.

---

3. Mexico's situation in 1994, reported in Case Three, provides one example. The Asian crisis, discussed in Cases Two, Four, and Five, provides another.

Market forces, combined with governments following the rules of the exchange rate regime in effect, will produce external balance in the sense of balance-of-payments equilibrium, but not necessarily external balance by other definitions governments may have in mind, such as target levels for the current account. Therefore, in our analysis of macroeconomic policies' effects, we'll track not only their impact on the macroeconomy as a whole, but also their effects on the current-account balance.

2.2 Targets and Instruments

The overall goal of macroeconomic policy making in an open economy is to help the economy achieve the desired performance. We've defined this objective as achievement of internal and external balance. The word *objective* is subtly deceptive here, because there actually are two objectives: internal balance *and* external balance. In the terminology of the theory of economic policy, these objectives are **targets**, that is, the desired consequences of policy.

Instruments, on the other hand, are the policy tools available to pursue the targets. Possible policy instruments include fiscal policy (changes in government expenditure or taxation), monetary policy (changes in the money stock), and exchange rate policy (devaluation or revaluation). However, not all these instruments will always be accessible to the policy maker; for example, according to the discussion of automatic balance-of-payments adjustment under fixed exchange rates in section 7 of the preceding chapter, monetary policy vanishes as an instrument under a fixed-rate regime. One of the major tasks of open-economy macroeconomics is to determine under what circumstances each potential instrument will be both available and effective.

The definitions of targets and instruments appear straightforward and may seem to do little more than give labels to common sense: Policy makers have goals (targets) and tools (instruments) to pursue them. However, the targets and instruments concepts yield important insights, and the distinction between targets and instruments is less clear than common sense may suggest.

The major insight gleaned from the targets and instruments view concerns the important relationship between the number of targets and the number of available instruments. A rule of successful policy making is that at least one instrument must be available for each target. Simple physical analogies prove useful in considering this point. The game of bowling, for example, involves aiming a single instrument (a bowling ball) at multiple targets (10 pins). The object of the game, to hit multiple targets with a single instrument, is feasible only because the prearrangement of the pins makes it possible (but not easy!) to down them all with a single ball. Only when multiple targets are closely related—so that the requirement for achieving one is similar to that for achieving another—is the multiple-target/single-instrument game possible; after all, bowling wouldn't work if the pins were scattered over an area the size of a football field rather than arrayed in the usual tight pattern. Macroeconomic policy makers rarely are lucky enough to have their multiple targets placed in such a convenient pattern; so, in macroeconomics, reaching N targets typically requires at least N instruments.

Despite its useful insights, the distinction between targets and instruments is less sharp than it first appears. Additional targets tend to appear on closer examination. For example, exchange rate policy is one of the previously mentioned instruments. Under a flexible exchange rate regime, exchange rate changes automatically achieve external balance, defined as balance-of-payments equilibrium. In the United States, this process produced a substantial appreciation of the dollar against most other currencies during the early 1980s. The flexibility of the exchange rate did facilitate external balance; but, many individuals in the United States and abroad expressed dissatisfaction with the dollar's value relative to other currencies. U.S. farmers blamed the dollar's high value for their inability to export agricultural products. U.S. automobile producers and firms in other import-competing sectors of the economy blamed the dollar for a "flood of imports" that "exported jobs." Some commentators worried that large-scale capital inflows meant foreign investors, especially those from Japan, were "buying up" the United States. Debt-ridden developing countries blamed the worsening of their already severe debt problems on their currencies' depreciation against the dollar.

Each of these elements of dissatisfaction reflected an additional target. Farmers wanted a value of the dollar that enhanced their ability to export; import-competing industries wanted a value of the dollar that lessened their import competition; opponents of foreign investment in the United States wanted a value of the dollar that discouraged such investment; and debtor countries wanted a stable value of their currencies against the dollar because of their dollar-denominated debts. In other words, the exchange rate, because of its distributional effects, became a target as well as, or rather than, an instrument.

In spite of these pitfalls, the targets-and-instruments terminology proves useful in examining the prospects for macroeconomic policy in an open economy. Achievement of any number of targets requires at least an equal number of instruments. This means that policy makers must be on the lookout for hidden targets and for instruments that may be unavailable or ineffective in some circumstances.[4] Additional targets and missing instruments present problems for policy makers. The primary determinants of effective instruments for the policy maker are: (1) the degree of international capital mobility and (2) the nature of the exchange rate regime. We'll explore the effects of each combination in turn, beginning with macroeconomic policy under a fixed exchange rate and immobile capital.

3 MACROECONOMIC POLICY WITH IMMOBILE CAPITAL

Economists developed their early analyses of macroeconomic policy in an open economy using the assumption of capital *immobility*, that is, the absence of private international capital flows. From a twenty-first-century perspective, this assumption seems quite unrealistic; however, until the 1970s capital immobility was a more reasonable supposition than a glance at today's active capital markets suggests. Most governments heavily regulated private capital flows, because most policy makers viewed such flows as a source of instability and therefore something to avoid. Further, many of the institutions that facilitate private capital flows today had not yet developed. The markets for Eurocurrencies didn't exist, nor did today's extensive international linking of bond and stock markets. Today, the degree of capital mobility varies widely across countries; and most still maintain some restrictions on nonofficial capital-account transactions; but increased capital mobility is one of the major international economic trends of the last three decades.

Under perfect capital immobility, no private capital flows occur to enter the nonofficial capital account as described in the chapter on the balance-of-payments accounts. Since private capital inflows and outflows equal zero, the capital-account balance simply equals a constant, which we can set arbitrarily at zero for simplicity. No private international borrowing and lending occurs, regardless of the interest rate differentials among countries. With no capital account (KAB = 0), the balance of payments (BOP = CAB + KAB) consists solely of the current account. If the current account is in deficit, the balance of payments is in deficit; with a current-account surplus, a balance-of-payments

---

4. For example, for monetary and fiscal policy to constitute two instruments, the central bank must pursue a policy *independent* of the expenditure and taxing patterns of the fiscal authority. This isn't the case in countries whose central banks are expected to expand the money supply to offset any interest rate rise generated by expansionary fiscal policies.

surplus exists. The requirement for external balance reduces to the requirement that the current-account balance equal zero. The variables that ordinarily affect the capital account—domestic and foreign interest rates and forward and expected future exchange rates (i, i*, e^f, and e^e)—no longer play a role in determining the country's balance of payments, because private capital flows don't respond to changes in those variables.

Recall from section 4 of the chapter on the market for goods and services that only one level of income exists at which the current-account balance (and therefore, with no capital mobility, the balance of payments) equals zero. We'll denote that level of income as Q_{EB}, for *external balance*. Capital immobility renders the interest rate irrelevant to balance-of-payments equilibrium, so the BOP line becomes vertical, as in Figure 1, rather than upward sloping.[5] The degree of capital mobility doesn't affect the IS and LM curves, which represent equilibrium in the markets for goods and services and for money, respectively.

In Figure 1, Q_{IB} denotes the income consistent with internal *balance*, or full employment. All three key markets—goods and services, money, and foreign exchange—are in equilibrium at the intersection of the IS, LM, and BOP curves, and that equilibrium income satisfies the requirements of both internal and external balance (that is, $Q_{IB} = Q_{EB}$). But so far, we have no reason to expect the incomes consistent with internal balance (full employment) and external balance (balance-of-payments equilibrium) to coincide.[6] If the lucky coincidence illustrated in Figure 1 held, there'd be little need for macroeconomic policy.

Figure 1   Internal and External Balance with Immobile Capital

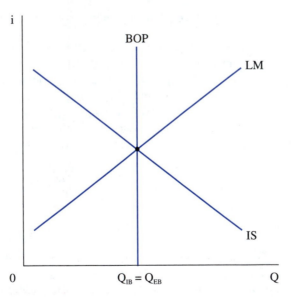

The economy is in equilibrium at the intersection of the IS, LM, and BOP curves, which represent the three major markets: goods and services, money, and foreign exchange. As drawn, the equilibrium income satisfies both internal balance (full employment, represented by Q_{IB}) and external balance (balance-of-payments equilibrium, represented by Q_{EB}).

---

5. For a review of why this is the case, see section 4.2 of the preceding chapter.

6. Once we introduce price flexibility, in a later chapter, the economy will contain an adjustment mechanism with which to equate the incomes required for internal and external balance, at least in the long run.

We've seen that the economy does contain a self-adjustment mechanism for reaching external balance under a fixed exchange rate regime.[7] If the balance of payments is in deficit (at a point to the right of the BOP curve), the quantity demanded of foreign exchange exceeds the quantity available. To prevent the domestic currency from depreciating, the central bank intervenes to supply foreign exchange from its international reserves. The resulting loss of reserves causes the money stock to fall and the domestic interest rate to rise. Graphically, the reduction in the money stock shifts the LM curve to the left until it intersects the IS and BOP curves at Q_{EB}. The new equilibrium level of income is lower, because the higher interest rate discourages investment expenditure; the reduction in income curtails imports and eliminates the current-account deficit. The higher interest rate also reduces the quantity of real money balances individuals in the economy choose to hold, making them content with the new lower money stock.

Similarly, a balance-of-payments surplus (at any point to the left of the BOP curve) requires central bank intervention to buy foreign exchange. Reserves rise, and the money stock increases. The LM curve shifts to the right until it intersects IS and BOP at Q_{EB}. The lower rate of interest in the economy induces greater investment and higher income, as well as making portfolio owners content to hold the larger stock of money balances now available in the economy. The increased income encourages imports and eliminates the balance-of-payments surplus.

With the price level fixed (an assumption we've not yet relaxed), no analogous mechanism exists to enable the economy to reach internal balance if the income required for internal balance differs from that for external balance, as is generally the case. The primary role of macroeconomic policy under such circumstances would be to bring the economy into internal balance. The menu of possible policy instruments includes fiscal, monetary, and exchange rate policies. We now consider each in turn. For each analysis, we begin with the economy in external balance at a level of income below that required for internal balance, or full employment. (*In each case, you should test your understanding by constructing the reasoning that would apply if the economy found itself in external balance at an income level above that required for internal balance, thereby creating a threat of inflation.*)[8]

3.1 Fiscal Policy

Expansionary fiscal policy can take the form of increased government spending on goods and services or of decreased taxes. The expansionary impact of a tax cut works through the effect on consumption: Lower taxes leave a larger share of income available for consumption.[9] Either form of expansionary fiscal policy shifts the IS curve to the right.[10]

In Figure 2, we selected the magnitude of the fiscal policy to shift the IS curve from IS^0 to IS^1—just enough to cause it to intersect the LM^0 curve at the income corresponding to internal balance. Initially the economy moves into internal balance. The interest rate rises because the increased income raises the demand for money, requiring a rise in the interest rate to lower money demand to match the constant money stock. The rise in income also causes a current-account deficit as imports rise with income. The deficit requires intervention by the central bank to maintain the fixed value of the exchange rate, so the money supply falls, shifting the LM curve back to LM^1. Income falls back to its original level, eliminating the current-account deficit, but with a higher interest rate at the new equilibrium.

---

7. For a review, see section 7 of the preceding chapter.

8. See footnote 2.

9. Tax cuts may also encourage production if they take the form of lower marginal tax rates. These effects are referred to as the *supply-side impact* of tax cuts.

10. For a review, see section 8 of the chapter on the market for goods and services.

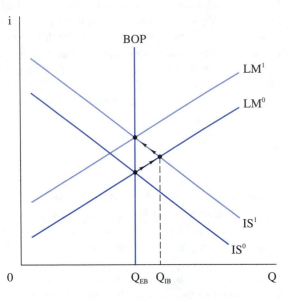

Figure 2   **Short-Run Effects of Fiscal Policy with Immobile Capital**

An increase in government purchases raises total expenditure and shifts the IS curve to the right. Income rises as the economy moves to the intersection of the new IS curve with the LM curve. The rise in income increases imports, producing a balance-of-payments deficit. The central bank must intervene to supply foreign exchange, reducing foreign exchange reserves and the money stock. The LM curve shifts to the left and restores equilibrium at the original income, but at a higher interest rate. Complete crowding out renders fiscal policy ineffective for achieving internal balance.

Although income ultimately remains unchanged by the fiscal policy, the pattern of spending in the economy does change. The new equilibrium involves a higher level of government spending. The overall level of spending can't be higher, however, since output both begins and ends at Q_{EB}; therefore, the higher interest rate has curtailed the level of private investment spending, a phenomenon known as **crowding out**. When capital is immobile, increased government spending completely crowds out private investment; that is, private investment spending falls by the full amount of any rise in government purchases. This outcome follows from the rise in the interest rate caused by the combination of the increased government spending and the reduction in the money stock generated by the current-account deficit. Fiscal policy proves unsuccessful in expanding the economy to achieve internal balance; in fact, it leaves income completely unaffected.

3.2 Monetary Policy

Monetary policy also turns out to be incapable of achieving internal balance under fixed exchange rates and immobile capital. The reason for the failure here is even more apparent than in the case of fiscal policy. Under fixed exchange rates, the central bank must intervene in the foreign exchange market to maintain external balance; otherwise, the fixed exchange rate can't be maintained. This intervention alters the domestic money stock. In other words, policy makers must allow the domestic money stock to grow and shrink according to the requirements for *external* balance, so the size of the money stock can't be manipulated in pursuit of *internal* balance.

Figure 3   **Short-Run Effects of Monetary Policy with Immobile Capital**

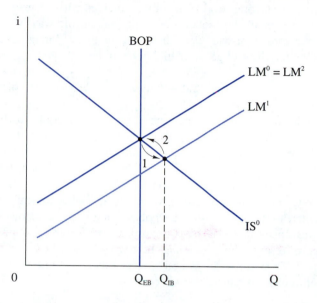

Monetary policy can't achieve internal balance under a fixed exchange rate and perfect capital immobility. Any attempt to increase the money stock (LM^0 to LM^1) raises income and imports, causing a balance-of-payments deficit. The deficit requires intervention in the foreign exchange market to supply foreign exchange. Reserves fall, offsetting the initial increase in the money stock (LM^1 to LM^2).

Figure 3 illustrates the basic problem. Beginning from equilibrium at the intersection of IS^0, LM^0, and BOP, expansionary monetary policy shifts the LM curve to LM^1 in an effort to reach internal balance at Q_{IB}. The increase in the money stock lowers the interest rate; investment rises, and the increase in total expenditure raises income. But the rise in income increases imports and causes a balance-of-payments deficit. Intervention in the foreign exchange market to maintain the pegged value of the exchange rate then causes a loss of reserves, shrinking the money stock and shifting the LM curve back to its original position. The interest rate returns to its original level, the temporary increases in investment and income disappear, and imports fall. These adjustments restore external balance but leave the goal of internal balance unachieved.

3.3 Sterilization

The monetary authority's primary means for expanding the money stock involves open market operations, or purchases of government bonds from the public.[11] The money stock equals the product of the money multiplier (mm) and the central bank's assets. These assets, in turn, include the central bank's stock of government bonds (GB) accumulated through open market operations plus its foreign exchange reserves (FXR). The central bank accomplishes the move from LM^0 to LM^1 in Figure 3 by a purchase of government bonds that increases the money stock by $\Delta M = mm \cdot \Delta GB$. The resulting balance-of-payments

---

11. For a review, go to section 2.3 of the preceding chapter.

deficit and intervention then cause the money stock to fall by $\Delta M = mm \cdot \Delta FXR$, where $\Delta FXR < 0$ because the central bank must *sell* reserves.

Since only one level of income coincides with external balance with completely immobile capital, the money stock must fall all the way back to its original level—the only one consistent with Q_{EB}. Therefore, the loss of foreign exchange reserves must fully offset the purchase of government bonds so that

$$\text{Total } \Delta M = mm\,(\Delta GB + \Delta FXR) = 0 \quad \text{or} \quad -\Delta FXR = \Delta GB \qquad [1]$$

The central bank loses foreign exchange reserves equal to the amount of government bonds it purchased. Monetary policy's only lingering effect is a change in the central bank's portfolio of assets. After its intervention, the bank holds a larger quantity of government bonds and a smaller quantity of foreign exchange reserves, but its total assets and the money stock remain unchanged.

Policy makers hardly can expect monetary policy to achieve internal balance if it can't even increase the money stock! A policy that appeals to many central bankers under these circumstances is a **sterilization policy**. The idea is to prevent the loss of foreign exchange reserves from affecting the money stock, thereby maintaining LM^1 and Q_{IB} in Figure 3. To sterilize, the central bank simply buys more government bonds to offset any loss of foreign exchange reserves, or:

$$\Delta GB = -\Delta FXR \qquad [2]$$

The incentive to pursue sterilization is obvious. Policy makers typically are much more sensitive to problems of internal imbalance (that is, unemployment) than to those of external imbalance. Sterilization attempts to prevent the realities of external requirements from interfering with domestic economic priorities. But, as we'll see, such attempts aren't likely to succeed.

Equations 1 and 2 make clear the mechanics of sterilization policy: As the loss of foreign exchange reserves reduces the central bank's assets, the bank offsets the loss with additional open market operations that raise GB. But such a policy isn't viable in the long run.[12] As long as the government pursues sterilization policy, the economy fails to reach external balance—because sterilization blocks the necessary downward adjustment in the size of the money stock. A balance-of-payments deficit persists, requiring continued sales of foreign exchange reserves to maintain the exchange rate. However, the central bank's stock of such reserves is finite, and eventually the reserves will run out. Then policy makers face a choice: cease sterilization and allow the money stock to shrink back to LM^2 or alter the exchange rate with a devaluation, the policy to which we now turn.

3.4 Exchange Rate Policy with Immobile Capital

Under fixed exchange rates with capital immobility, exchange rate policy has the power to remove the fundamental barrier to simultaneous internal and external balance. This barrier is the fact that each target requires a unique level of income, that is, Q_{IB} for internal balance and Q_{EB} for external balance. If the two income levels differ, as they generally do, the two targets must conflict. Neither fiscal nor monetary policy, alone or used together, can resolve this conflict. The advantage of exchange rate policy is that it can *change* the level of income required for external balance; in other words, changes in the exchange rate can alter Q_{EB}, making it equal to Q_{IB}.

---

12. In the case of mobile capital, sterilization may affect the perceived riskiness of foreign and domestic assets, thereby altering portfolio decisions and rendering sterilization somewhat effective, at least in the short run. See section 4.2.

Recall that a government fixes its exchange rate by announcing the price at which it will buy and sell foreign exchange and then following through on the promise to exchange foreign for domestic currency at that price as demanded by participants in the foreign exchange market. To devalue or revalue its currency, the government simply announces a change in the price at which it will trade foreign exchange.

Figure 4 illustrates the use of exchange rate policy—in particular, a devaluation—to solve the same problem we've been examining: $Q_{EB} < Q_{IB}$. With fixed domestic and foreign price levels, a devaluation of the domestic currency lowers the relative price of domestic goods ($R \equiv P/eP^*$), encourages exports, and discourages imports.[13] The devaluation shifts both the IS and BOP curves to the right. By lowering the relative price of domestic goods, the devaluation raises exports relative to imports at each level of income. Therefore, the income at which exports equal imports (Q_{EB}) rises, which shifts the BOP curve to the right.[14] The increase in net exports due to the devaluation also shifts the IS curve to the right by raising total expenditure on domestic goods and services. To achieve the goal of simultaneous internal and external balance, the devaluation must be just enough to shift the BOP curve such that $Q_{IB} = Q_{EB}$.

Figure 4  **Short-Run Effects of a Devaluation with Immobile Capital**

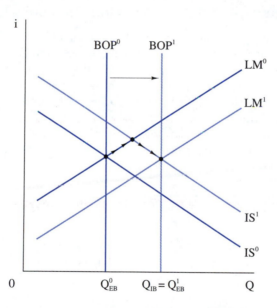

A devaluation of the domestic currency lowers the relative price of domestic goods and services. Exports rise relative to imports, shifting the IS and BOP curves to the right. The initial effect is to create a balance-of-payments surplus. Intervention in the foreign exchange market then increases the money stock. This increase restores equilibrium at a point that satisfies both internal and external balance. The key to this result is the devaluation's ability to alter the income consistent with external balance to match that required for internal balance.

---

13. The assumption of fixed domestic and foreign price levels proves important because, once we relax it, changes in the exchange rate may not affect the relative prices of foreign and domestic goods. Since $R \equiv P/eP^*$, it remains unaffected if P rises proportionally with e or P* falls proportionally with a rise in e. In other words, changes in the nominal exchange rate (e) imply corresponding changes in the real exchange rate (R) only if price levels are somewhat sticky.

14. Recall that the change in the exchange rate exerts no influence on the capital account when capital is completely immobile.

The devaluation shifts the BOP curve from BOP^0 to BOP^1 and the IS curve to IS^1. Initially the economy moves to the intersection of the new IS curve with the original LM curve, LM^0. The effect on income is positive, but income remains below the full-employment level. The balance of payments moves into surplus temporarily, causing central bank intervention to buy foreign exchange. The money stock rises with the stock of foreign exchange reserves, which shifts the LM curve to the right. The new equilibrium occurs at the intersection of IS^1, LM^1, and BOP^1, which satisfies both the internal- and external-balance goals. By shifting the income required for external balance from Q_{EB}^0 to Q_{EB}^1, equal to the level consistent with internal balance, the devaluation eliminates the basic policy conflict that prevented both fiscal and monetary policies from achieving the two targets.

Our analysis makes clear why governments might choose to devalue their currencies. The policy is simple in the sense that it requires merely an announcement of the government's intention to buy or sell foreign exchange at a different price; therefore, the policy change can be accomplished quickly. We've seen that governments with fixed exchange rates and immobile capital can't use fiscal or monetary policy effectively to influence the economy's performance. Exchange rate policy, by generating changes in the size of the money stock indirectly, provides an alternative policy. And, if the central bank is running short of reserves, a devaluation can replenish them.

3.5 Summary of Policy Effects with Immobile Capital

Under conditions of perfectly immobile capital and a fixed exchange rate, exchange rate policy is policy makers' only effective tool for altering domestic income in the short run. Neither fiscal nor monetary policy is effective, because attempts to use either generate offsetting changes in the money stock through foreign exchange market intervention. The money stock must adjust to achieve external balance (equivalent to current-account balance). Only exchange rate policy has the power to change the income consistent with external balance to match that consistent with internal balance, thereby permitting policy makers to achieve both targets. Table 2 summarizes these results.

Table 2 SHORT-RUN POLICY EFFECTS WITH IMMOBILE CAPITAL

Policy	Effect on Equilibrium Q	Effect on Equilibrium Current-Account Balance	Effect on Equilibrium Money Stock
Fiscal Policy:			
Increase in G	0[a]	0[b]	−
Decrease in G	0[a]	0[b]	+
Monetary Policy:			
Increase in M	0	0[b]	0[c]
Decrease in M	0	0[b]	0[c]
Exchange Rate Policy:			
Devaluation	+	0[b]	+
Revaluation	−	0[b]	−

[a]Effect completely crowded out by offsetting impact of interest rate on investment.
[b]With completely immobile capital, only a current-account balance of zero is consistent with balance-of-payments equilibrium.
[c]Effect of initial monetary policy completely offset by foreign exchange market intervention.

4 MACROECONOMIC POLICY WITH PERFECTLY MOBILE CAPITAL

As mentioned earlier, the assumption of international capital immobility has grown increasingly unrealistic in recent years. To see the effect of changing degrees of capital mobility, we now move to the opposite assumption: **perfect capital mobility**. This simply means that investors, in deciding which assets to hold, consider only interest rates and exchange rates, including the forward rate and the expected future spot rate. In other words, investors have no built-in preferences for assets denominated in one currency versus those denominated in another, and government policies don't restrict capital flows.

Under perfect capital mobility, the capital account plays the dominant role in foreign exchange markets. Recall that the balance-of-payments or BOP line depicts all the combinations of income and interest rate consistent with foreign exchange market equilibrium, or with interest parity. We draw each BOP line for given values of the foreign interest rate, exchange rate, and forward and expected spot exchange rates.[15] This implies that any rise in the domestic interest rate causes a capital inflow and a move toward a surplus on the capital account.[16]

How does perfect capital mobility produce a horizontal BOP line? In Figure 5, the balance of payments is in equilibrium at point A; this is true because A lies on the BOP line that, by definition, represents points of balance-of-payments equilibrium. Beginning at A, suppose

Figure 5 Perfect Capital Mobility and the Slope of the BOP Line

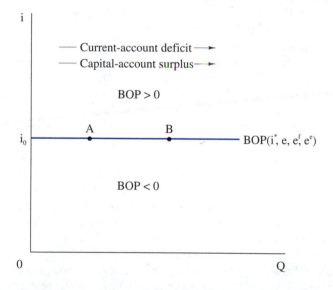

The BOP line is horizontal in the case of perfect capital mobility. A BOP line is drawn for given values of the foreign interest rate and of spot, forward, and expected future spot exchange rates. Given these values, even a tiny increase in the domestic interest rate causes capital inflows. Moving to the right along the BOP line (such as from point A to point B), the current account moves toward a deficit as a result of rising income and imports, and the capital account moves toward a surplus. Above the BOP line, the balance of payments is in surplus; below it, the balance is in deficit.

---

15. See section 4.2 in the preceding chapter.

16. For a review, see the discussion of interest parity in section 4 of the chapter on currency markets and exchange rates.

income rises. Imports rise with income, and the current account moves toward a deficit. To maintain balance-of-payments equilibrium, there must be an offsetting move toward surplus on the capital account. With perfectly mobile capital, how large an increase in the domestic interest rate is required to generate this capital-account surplus? An infinitesimal rise will suffice because under perfect capital mobility, investors respond immediately to the slightest rise in domestic rates by moving funds into the domestic economy.[17]

In terms of the interest parity condition, massive capital flows in response to even minute changes in relative interest rates maintain the equilibrium or parity condition. Therefore, the balance of payments is in equilibrium at B, but with a larger current-account deficit and capital-account surplus than at A. All points above the BOP line correspond to situations of balance-of-payments surplus, and those below the line represent balance-of-payments deficits. (*Why?*)

We now turn to the question of the ability of fiscal, monetary, and exchange rate policies to achieve internal and external balance with perfect capital mobility. We'll continue to assume that the problem the economy faces is one of unemployment.

4.1 Fiscal Policy

The change in assumption from perfectly immobile to perfectly mobile capital carries radical implications for fiscal policy's effectiveness under fixed exchange rates. Recall that with no capital mobility, fiscal policy results in complete crowding out and leaves income unaffected. However, with perfect capital mobility in response to international interest differentials, fiscal policy is highly effective in raising income and achieving simultaneous internal and external balance.

Figure 6 traces the effects of an expansionary fiscal policy. Beginning in equilibrium at the intersection of IS^0, LM^0, and BOP, an increase in government spending shifts the IS curve to IS^1. Initially the economy moves to the intersection of the new IS curve with LM^0. The rise in income increases the demand for money. The money stock doesn't change, so the interest rate must rise to bring the quantity demanded of money back down to equality with the existing money stock. The rise in the domestic interest rate generates capital inflows and a balance-of-payments surplus. Note that the balance of payments is in surplus even though imports have risen with income; this occurs because, under perfect capital mobility, the capital flows made in response to interest rate changes dominate changes in the current account. To maintain the fixed exchange rate in the face of the BOP surplus, the central bank must purchase foreign exchange; this intervention raises the domestic money stock and shifts the LM curve to LM^1. A new equilibrium occurs at the intersection of IS^1, LM^1, and BOP.

Fiscal policy has achieved internal balance (assuming that the policy shifts the IS curve to the right by an amount sufficient to ensure that the new IS curve intersects BOP at Q_{IB}). The interest rate remains at its original level; the balance of payments is again in equilibrium, but with a larger current-account deficit and capital-account surplus. (*Why?*) The central bank also holds a larger stock of foreign exchange reserves, acquired through its intervention.

The key to understanding capital mobility's crucial role in the success of fiscal policy is the policy's effect on the balance of payments. With no capital mobility (see Figure 2), expansionary fiscal policy causes a balance-of-payments *deficit*. It (temporarily) raises income and moves the current account into deficit, and there is no possibility of offsetting capital flows. The balance-of-payments deficit, through the automatic adjustment mechanism, *reduces* the money stock. The fall in the money stock counteracts the fiscal policy's expansionary effect (see fiscal policy's impact on the money stock in Table 2).

---

17. This assumes that the country can't affect world interest rates. Although called the *small-country assumption*, this condition holds true for most countries.

Figure 6   **Short-Run Effects of Fiscal Policy with Perfectly Mobile Capital**

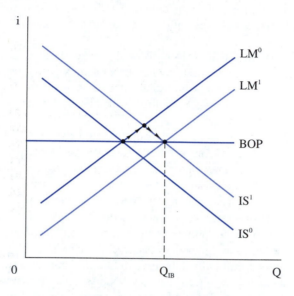

An expansionary fiscal policy, by raising income, causes the interest rate to rise. The response is a capital inflow that more than offsets the move toward deficit on the current account. Because the balance of payments is in surplus, foreign exchange market intervention increases the domestic money stock. This increase prevents crowding out; thus, the expansionary fiscal policy raises total expenditure and income. This contrasts with the case under immobile capital, in which expansionary fiscal policy causes a balance-of-payments deficit and a decrease in the domestic money stock.

Perfectly mobile capital reverses the effect of fiscal policy on the balance of payments. Although an expansionary policy still moves the current account toward a deficit, this effect is more than offset by the capital inflow in response to the rise in the domestic interest rate. The net effect is a balance-of-payments *surplus*, which, through the automatic adjustment mechanism, results in an *increase* in the money stock. Thus, capital mobility causes expansionary fiscal policy to generate an accompanying increase in the money stock, rather than a decrease as under capital immobility. The expansion of the money stock prevents the interest rate from rising and short-circuits the crowding-out mechanism. The increase in government spending doesn't cause an offsetting decrease in private spending (that is, investment), and total expenditure and income rise.

An alternative way to view fiscal policy's success with mobile capital focuses more directly on the requirements for internal and external balance. With no capital mobility, external balance requires a unique income—the one consistent with a balanced current account. With capital mobility, *any* income can be consistent with external balance (represented graphically by a horizontal BOP line). Because capital mobility guarantees that external balance can occur at any income level, the policy problem reduces to one of reaching internal balance.

4.2 Monetary Policy

Capital mobility greatly enhances fiscal policy's ability to alter the economy's equilibrium level of income. However, this isn't true for monetary policy. Monetary policy can't affect income under a fixed exchange rate regardless of the degree of capital mobility.

Expansionary monetary policy (represented by Figure 7's shift from LM^0 to LM^1) initially lowers the domestic interest rate and raises income, resulting in capital outflows as well as a current-account deficit. The balance-of-payments deficit requires sales of foreign exchange reserves until the money stock falls back to its original level.

STERILIZATION, ONCE AGAIN Recall that to sterilize, the central bank simply buys government bonds to offset any loss of foreign exchange reserves caused by intervention (see section 3.3). As the loss of foreign exchange reserves reduces the central bank's assets (GB + FXR), the sterilizing central bank offsets the loss with additional open market operations that raise GB.

Could policy makers permanently prevent the shift of LM back to LM^2 in Figure 7 through sterilization? Given the model developed so far, the answer is no. Sterilization isn't viable, because as long as the central bank pursues such a policy, the interest rate remains below the rate consistent with interest parity and the economy can't reach external balance. The persistent balance-of-payments deficit requires continued sales of foreign exchange reserves to maintain the fixed exchange rate. But each central bank's stock of such reserves is finite and eventually would be depleted, forcing policy makers to choose between a currency devaluation and the reduction in the money stock represented by the leftward shift of the LM curve to LM^2 in Figure 7.

An alternate way to recognize sterilization's futility is to recall that a balance-of-payments deficit reflects excess demand for foreign-currency deposits in the foreign exchange market, such as the one depicted in panel (a) of Figure 8. A fall in the domestic money stock, through foreign exchange market intervention to supply foreign currency, can eliminate such excess demand because, as the money stock falls, the domestic interest rate rises (shown in panel (b)). The increase in the domestic interest rate increases the expected return on

---

Figure 7 **Short-Run Effects of Monetary Policy with Perfectly Mobile Capital**

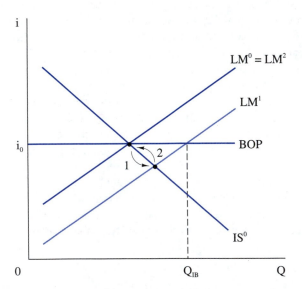

Beginning from a point of equilibrium, expansionary monetary policy causes a fall in the interest rate and a capital outflow. The resulting balance-of-payments deficit requires intervention to sell foreign exchange from reserves. The loss of reserves reduces the money stock; this process continues until M is back at its original level.

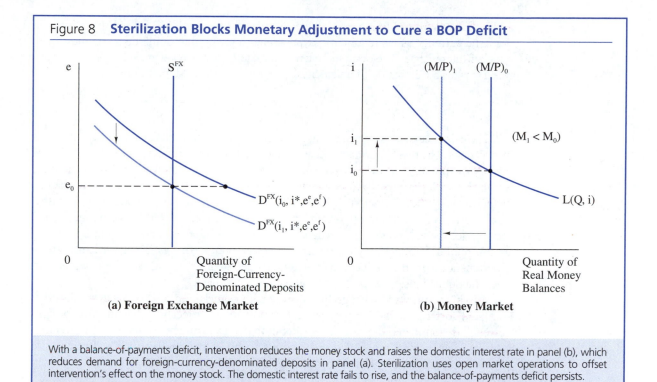

Figure 8   Sterilization Blocks Monetary Adjustment to Cure a BOP Deficit

(a) Foreign Exchange Market

(b) Money Market

With a balance-of-payments deficit, intervention reduces the money stock and raises the domestic interest rate in panel (b), which reduces demand for foreign-currency-denominated deposits in panel (a). Sterilization uses open market operations to offset intervention's effect on the money stock. The domestic interest rate fails to rise, and the balance-of-payments deficit persists.

domestic-currency-denominated deposits, reduces the demand for foreign-currency-denominated ones in panel (a), and restores equilibrium in the foreign exchange market at e_0.[18] Sterilization, by preventing the decline in the money stock and the increase in the interest rate, blocks this adjustment process and keeps the economy out of external balance—because the excess demand for foreign-currency deposits at the fixed exchange rate persists.

Empirical evidence, however, suggests that many central banks do sterilize. In fact, popular discussions of monetary policy often ignore completely the link between a country's balance of payments and its money stock, because they assume that sterilization automatically accompanies any foreign exchange market intervention. Questions regarding the viability of sterilized intervention have become the subject of active research by both academic economists and policy makers. Two considerations, when integrated into the model developed so far, suggest channels through which sterilized intervention—that is, intervention that doesn't affect the money stock—might alter the demand for foreign-currency-denominated deposits to restore equilibrium in the foreign exchange market at the fixed exchange rate.

Suppose that in allocating their asset portfolios between foreign-currency- and domestic-currency-denominated deposits, investors care about the perceived riskiness of each type of deposit as well as its expected return.[19] To hold an asset perceived as risky, investors will demand a higher expected rate of return in compensation, and they will be willing to hold an asset carrying little risk at a lower expected rate of return. If assets denominated in different currencies vary in their perceived riskiness, the interest parity condition will contain a **risk premium**, σ, which represents the extra return investors require to compensate them for the

---

18. Figure 17 in the preceding chapter illustrates the corresponding case of monetary adjustment to eliminate a balance-of-payments surplus.

19. This condition is known as *imperfect asset substitutability*, in contrast to *perfect asset substitutability*, in which investors care only about expected rates of return in choosing among assets.

additional risk in holding a particular currency.[20] In Equation 3, σ will be positive if domestic-currency assets require a risk premium, implying that domestic assets must carry a higher interest rate. The domestic interest rate can be lower relative to the foreign interest rate if σ is negative, that is, if foreign-currency assets require a risk premium.

$$i - i^* = [(e^e - e)/e] + \sigma \qquad [3]$$

The existence of a risk premium in the interest parity condition carries several important implications. The most important is that, as the quantity of the domestic government's bonds held by the public rises, the risk premium on domestic assets may rise because a large share of such bonds in investors' portfolios makes the investors' wealth more vulnerable to changes in the exchange rate. Under such conditions, expansionary domestic monetary policy (that is, a central bank purchase of government bonds that expands the domestic money stock) may reduce the risk premium by reducing the number of domestic government bonds held by the public. Similarly, contractionary monetary policy (that is, a central bank sale of government bonds that reduces the domestic money stock) may increase the risk premium since the public must hold the bonds sold by the central bank.

A risk premium that changes in this way with domestic monetary policy implies that sterilized foreign exchange market intervention might affect the demand for foreign-currency-denominated deposits. How? Recall that a government sterilizes its intervention by purchasing or selling government bonds to offset the intervention's effect on the domestic money supply, as summarized in Equation 2. With no risk premium, sterilized intervention leaves the domestic money stock and interest rate unchanged. However, with a risk premium, if the central bank sterilizes a sale of foreign exchange by buying bonds, the quantity of government bonds that the public must hold falls, and this may cause the risk premium on domestic-currency assets to fall. If so, the domestic interest rate consistent with interest parity falls, as indicated in Equation 3.

Figure 9 illustrates the implications for a country with a balance-of-payments deficit. To hold the exchange rate fixed, the central bank intervenes to supply foreign exchange but also sterilizes by buying government bonds so that the money stock remains unchanged in panel (b). The central bank's bond purchase leaves fewer bonds to be held by the public, reduces the perceived riskiness associated with holding domestic bonds, and lowers the risk premium, σ. The reduction in risk makes investors more willing to hold domestic-currency-denominated assets and less willing to hold foreign-currency-denominated ones at any given interest rate. The demand for foreign-currency assets in panel (a) shifts to the left and restores balance-of-payments equilibrium at the fixed exchange rate of e_0. With the variable risk premium, sterilization doesn't block foreign exchange market equilibrium, as it does in the absence of a risk premium. In other words, a risk premium may allow even sterilized intervention to shift the demand for foreign-currency assets.

The second channel through which sterilized intervention may be able to shift the demand for foreign-currency assets, even in the absence of a risk premium, relies on market participants using intervention as a source of information, or a **signal**, about future macroeconomic policy. When a government intervenes, even on a sterilized basis, market participants may interpret the intervention as a sign that future government policies will push the exchange rate in the direction indicated by the intervention. For example, if a central bank sells foreign exchange and buys domestic bonds, market participants may expect future macroeconomic policies aimed at reducing the domestic-currency price of foreign currency. If so, the expected future exchange rate (e^e) may fall,

---

20. In the economics literature, the lowercase Greek letter *sigma* (σ) constitutes the standard notation for variability or risk in a variable.

Figure 9   Sterilized Intervention with a Risk Premium

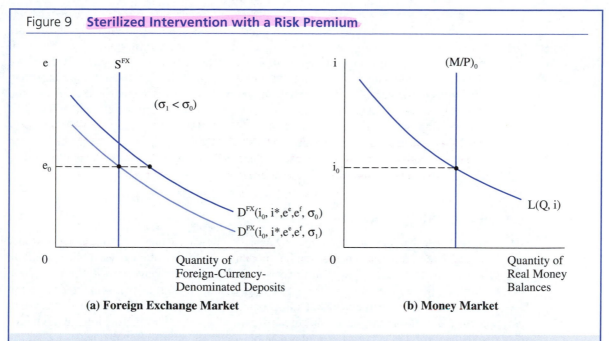

(a) Foreign Exchange Market

(b) Money Market

With a balance-of-payments deficit, sterilized intervention reduces the quantity of government bonds held by the public. If this reduces the risk premium (σ) demanded by market participants, the demand for foreign-currency deposits falls, and the balance-of-payments deficit is eliminated in panel (a), even though sterilized intervention fails to alter the size of the money stock or the interest rate in panel (b).

which would shift the demand for foreign-currency-denominated assets to the left, even though the domestic money stock remained unchanged.

Governments that attempt to use such signaling too often, however, will suffer a loss of credibility. Unlike the risk-premium effect, the signaling effect of sterilized intervention requires that market participants take such intervention as a credible indication of future government policies. Too many episodes of faulty signals lead market participants to ignore future signals.

Several empirical studies have found that sterilized intervention can alter the demand for foreign-currency-denominated assets, but often only insignificantly. Generally, however, studies of sterilized intervention's effectiveness lead to mixed results for several reasons. First, detailed intervention data often are kept secret by central banks, so many studies rely on somewhat unreliable data. Second, statistical studies suffer from observers' lack of knowledge of what would have happened in the absence of intervention. Third, the risk-premium and signaling hypotheses rest on effects that we might expect to vary across time and across countries. Investors may demand risk premiums for some currencies and not others or during some periods and not others; some risk premiums may respond to factors other than the quantity of government bonds held by the public. Similarly, market participants may accept sterilized intervention as a policy signal from some governments and not from others. Therefore, there may be no single correct answer to whether sterilized intervention "works."

Many economists remain skeptical, for several reasons, of sterilized intervention's ability to alter the exchange rate.[21] First, they point out that intervention is most likely when exchange rates reach extreme values; such episodes, however, correspond to times

---

21. The Obstfeld article in the chapter references contains a useful discussion.

when exchange rate trends are most likely to reverse themselves even without intervention. Therefore, attributing such trend reversals to sterilized intervention runs the risk of interpreting something that would have happened anyway as an effect of intervention. Second, central banks may choose to intervene only when they believe market conditions are such that intervention could alter the path of the exchange rate. Finally, if central banks continue intervention until the exchange rate trend changes, then intervention will, by definition, be followed by trend reversal and will appear to "work."[22] Most economists agree that sterilized intervention, while it may exert some small short-run influence in foreign exchange markets in some circumstances, *cannot* be used to overcome trends in the foreign exchange market or to avoid the fundamental monetary adjustment necessary to achieve external balance under a fixed exchange rate.

4.3 Exchange Rate Policy

As with fiscal policy, changes in the exchange rate can achieve internal balance under a fixed-rate regime with perfect capital mobility. The devaluation doesn't affect the BOP curve as long as the forward and expected future spot exchange rates move in tandem with e. This will be the case when foreign exchange market participants expect the devaluation to be permanent but don't expect it to lead to further devaluations. When these assumptions are met, the forward premium (or discount) on foreign exchange and the expected rate of future devaluation (or revaluation) remain unchanged during the actual devaluation. Therefore, for any given value of the foreign interest rate, the same domestic interest rate that was consistent with balance-of-payments equilibrium before the devaluation is still consistent with equilibrium after the devaluation.

A devaluation shifts the IS curve in Figure 10 to the right by lowering the relative price of domestically produced goods and services. The economy moves to the intersection of the new IS curve with LM^0. The interest rate rises because the rise in income raises money demand, and the rise in the interest rate reequates the quantity demanded of money with the money stock. The balance of payments moves to surplus because of increased capital inflows brought on by the higher interest rate.

The BOP surplus requires central bank intervention to buy foreign exchange, swelling the money stock and moving the LM curve from LM^0 toward LM^1. Equilibrium is restored at the intersection of IS^1, LM^1, and BOP. The devaluation raises income by generating an increase in the money stock through the automatic adjustment mechanism. The devaluation also moves the current account toward a surplus and raises the central bank's stock of foreign exchange reserves. While devaluations can serve as an important tool of macroeconomic policy, they do run certain risks. In particular, a devaluation may lead market participants to anticipate further devaluations. If so, a devaluation can precipitate a balance-of-payments crisis, along the lines suggested in the following section.

4.4 Changes in Exchange Rate Expectations

Even under a pegged exchange rate, participants in foreign exchange markets may come to believe that a government will be unwilling or unable to maintain its current pegged value. For example, individuals might come to expect a devaluation of the domestic currency because the central bank is running short of foreign exchange reserves, because of prolonged domestic unemployment, or because of a large chronic current-account deficit. Figure 11 depicts the effects of such a change in expectations.

---

22. This is akin to the old saying that you always find a lost object in the last place you look for it—because when you find it you stop looking in additional places.

Figure 10 **Short-Run Effects of a Devaluation with Perfectly Mobile Capital**

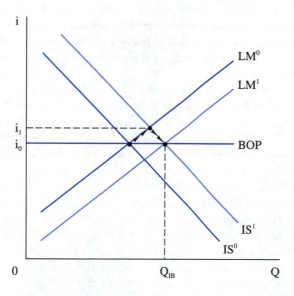

A devaluation of the domestic currency shifts the IS curve to the right. At first, the balance of payments moves to a surplus because of an increased capital inflow. Intervention in the foreign exchange market increases the domestic money stock and shifts the LM curve from LM^0 to LM^1. The interest rate returns to i_0.

Figure 11 **Short-Run Effects of an *Expected* Devaluation with Perfectly Mobile Capital**

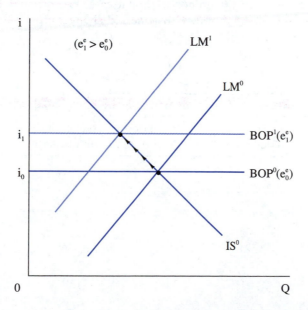

An expected devaluation of the domestic currency (a rise in e^e) shifts the BOP line from BOP^0 to BOP^1. At i_0, the domestic balance of payments is in deficit. As the central bank intervenes to supply foreign exchange, the domestic money stock falls and the LM curve shifts from LM^0 to LM^1. A new equilibrium occurs at the intersection of IS^0, LM^1, and BOP^1.

Initially the economy is in equilibrium at the intersection of IS^0, LM^0, and BOP^0. Suddenly e^e rises from e_0^e to e_1^e, which causes the BOP line to shift up to BOP^1. The actual exchange rate hasn't changed, so the rise in e^e requires a higher domestic interest rate to make portfolio owners content to hold the existing stock of domestic-currency-denominated deposits in the face of the expected devaluation. (*Explain why, using the interest parity condition from section 4.1 of the chapter on currency markets and exchange rates.*)

At the intersection of IS^0 and LM^0, the balance of payments is in deficit with $e^e = e_1^e$ because of the low domestic interest rate. Intervention by the central bank to hold the exchange rate at its peg lowers the domestic money stock and shifts the LM curve to the left to LM^1. The capital flight in response to the expected devaluation requires a rise in the domestic interest rate, thereby reducing investment and income. Maintaining the exchange rate in the face of the expected devaluation also causes the central bank to expend part of its foreign exchange reserves. This loss of reserves may cause foreign exchange market participants to anticipate a further devaluation, which can set the entire process in motion again. The result can be a vicious circle in which the loss of reserves creates expectations that require further central bank intervention to protect the exchange rate, further reducing its reserves. The possibility of such vicious circles has led many analysts to question the viability of fixed but adjustable exchange rates under perfect capital mobility, especially for governments that lack a reputation for conducting sound macroeconomic policies and keeping their policy promises.

4.5 Summary of Policy Effects with Perfectly Mobile Capital

With perfectly mobile capital, fiscal policy and exchange rate policy can alter the level of income in the domestic economy. Monetary policy, in contrast, remains ineffective, as in the immobile-capital case. Fiscal policy and exchange rate policy work through their ability to generate changes in the domestic money stock, as reported in Table 3.

Table 3 **SHORT-RUN POLICY EFFECTS WITH PERFECTLY MOBILE CAPITAL**

Policy	Effect on Equilibrium Q	Effect on Equilibrium Current-Account Balance	Effect on Equilibrium Money Stock
Fiscal Policy:			
Increase in G	+	−	+
Decrease in G	−	+	−
Monetary Policy:[a]			
Increase in M	0	0	0^b
Decrease in M	0	0	0^b
Exchange Rate Policy:			
Devaluation	+	+	+
Revaluation	−	−	−

[a]Foreign exchange market intervention unsterilized.
[b]Effect of initial monetary policy completely offset by foreign exchange market intervention.

5 MACROECONOMIC POLICY WITH IMPERFECTLY MOBILE CAPITAL

The two assumptions we've used so far concerning the capital market—zero capital mobility and perfect capital mobility—represent extremes. Although such extremes rarely are observed in the world economy, they provide useful benchmarks to understand capital mobility's role in determining the effectiveness of macroeconomic policies. We now turn to the case in which the degree of capital mobility falls between the two extremes: Investors do respond to international changes in interest rates by altering the compositions of their portfolios; however, the responses may not be instantaneous, investors may prefer assets denominated in certain currencies, and government policies may restrict mobility.

In this section, we examine the effectiveness of fiscal, monetary, and exchange rate policy in achieving internal balance under this intermediate degree of capital mobility. As we might expect, the results lie between those of the two extreme cases. Fiscal policy is effective in raising income (as in the perfect capital mobility case), but some degree of crowding out occurs (as in the perfect capital immobility case). Monetary policy remains ineffective, and a devaluation can still achieve internal balance.

When capital is imperfectly mobile, a question arises concerning the relative slopes of the LM and BOP curves. The more mobile is capital, the flatter the BOP curve. (*Why?*) We'll examine the case in which the BOP curve is flatter than the LM curve—that of high capital mobility. (*For each policy discussed, the reader should test his or her understanding by constructing a similar analysis under the assumption that capital is somewhat less mobile and the BOP curve thus is steeper than the LM curve.*)

5.1 Fiscal Policy

Fiscal policy raises income through the following chain of events, illustrated in Figure 12. The initial expansionary policy shifts the IS curve from IS^0 to IS^1 and raises income, increasing the demand for money. The money stock doesn't change, so the interest rate must rise to cause an offsetting decline in the quantity demanded of money. The rise in the interest rate implies increased capital inflows and a balance-of-payments surplus. The surplus raises the money stock through the automatic adjustment mechanism under a fixed exchange rate. The rise in the money stock shifts the LM curve to the right, from LM^0 to LM^1.

The new equilibrium involves a higher income and a higher interest rate. The two must occur together because the higher income moves the current account toward a deficit. External balance, then, requires an increased capital inflow, which occurs with imperfect capital mobility only in response to a higher domestic interest rate.

5.2 Monetary Policy

Regardless of the degree of capital mobility, monetary policy can't raise income under a fixed exchange rate regime. This is because the money stock must vary with the requirements of external balance through foreign exchange market intervention.

The more mobile capital is, the more futile are attempts to use expansionary monetary policy to raise income, even in the short run. The more sensitive capital flows are to interest rate changes, the larger and more rapid is the capital outflow in response to the temporary drop in the domestic interest rate that follows an open market purchase (see arrow 1 in Figure 13). A larger and more rapid capital outflow implies a larger, more immediate balance-of-payments deficit and greater, more rapid losses of foreign exchange reserves (represented by arrow 2 in Figure 13).

Figure 12   Short-Run Effects of Fiscal Policy with Imperfectly Mobile Capital

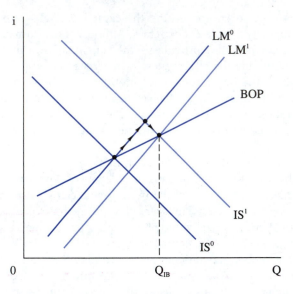

Expansionary fiscal policy shifts the IS curve to the right. The rise in the interest rate generates capital inflows, and foreign exchange market intervention increases the money stock. The new equilibrium occurs at a higher income and interest rate.

Figure 13   Short-Run Effects of Monetary Policy with Imperfectly Mobile Capital

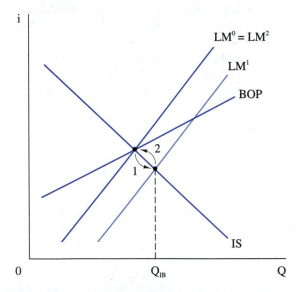

Expansionary monetary policy shifts the LM curve to the right and lowers the interest rate. Capital outflows cause a balance-of-payments deficit; the central bank must intervene to sell foreign exchange. The decline in foreign exchange reserves cuts the money stock to its original level. The new equilibrium occurs at the original income and interest rate.

Figure 14   **Short-Run Effects of a Devaluation with Imperfectly Mobile Capital**

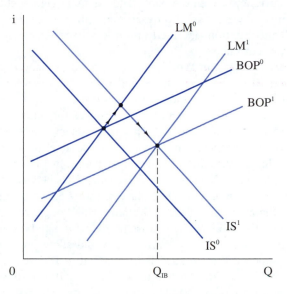

A devaluation of the domestic currency shifts both the IS and BOP curves to the right by lowering the relative price of domestic goods and services. The balance-of-payments surplus results in an increase in the domestic money stock. The new equilibrium occurs at a higher income level and a lower interest rate.

5.3 Exchange Rate Policy

A devaluation raises income when capital is imperfectly mobile. The change in the exchange rate lowers the relative price of domestically produced goods and services, which shifts both the IS and BOP curves to the right.[23] The resulting balance-of-payments surplus leads to a rise in the stock of foreign exchange reserves and in the domestic money stock, shifting the LM curve from LM^0 to LM^1 (see Figure 14). The devaluation succeeds in raising income to a level consistent with internal balance.

6 A SPECIAL CASE: THE RESERVE-CURRENCY COUNTRY

Thus far, we've examined the case of a single country that fixes its currency's value against the currency of a single trading partner by intervening in the foreign exchange market to exchange domestic-currency deposits for foreign-currency ones as demanded by participants in the foreign exchange market. In practice, hundreds of currencies exist in the world economy, but fixed exchange rate regimes typically don't involve each country intervening in hundreds of separate foreign exchange markets to fix their respective currencies against each of the other currencies. Instead, countries agree,

---

23. If the devaluation is expected to be permanent, but doesn't generate expectations of further devaluations, then e and e^e move together, the original interest rate remains consistent with interest parity, and the BOP line shifts solely because of e's impact on the current account through the relative price of domestic goods and services (R ≡ P/eP*). If the devaluation alters market participants' expectations of the future exchange rate, those changes must be taken into account in shifting the BOP line. Devaluation-induced changes in expectations can have dramatic consequences, as in Mexico in 1994 and Asia in 1997; see Cases Two and Three.

either implicitly or explicitly, on a single currency to act as the **reserve currency**. Each central bank announces a fixed exchange rate between its domestic currency and the reserve currency, which the bank holds as its foreign exchange reserves. The system of fixed rates between each nonreserve currency and the reserve currency, maintained through intervention, indirectly produces fixed exchange rates between each pair of nonreserve currencies.

Under the **Bretton Woods** system of fixed exchange rates, in effect from the end of World War II until 1973, the U.S. dollar served as the reserve currency. Non-U.S. central banks held most of their foreign exchange reserves in dollars, and each bank intervened as required to hold the exchange rate between its currency and the U.S. dollar at the agreed rate.[24] Private arbitrage kept cross exchange rates between nondollar currencies fixed, because whenever an exchange rate became inconsistent with the two respective dollar exchange rates, the situation created a profitable arbitrage opportunity.[25] Suppose, for example, that in 1967 the fixed exchange rates between the dollar and the pound and between the dollar and the Deutsche mark were $2.75/£1 and $0.275/DM1, respectively, and that the Bank of England and Bundesbank bought or sold dollars from their reserves to maintain those rates. The consistent exchange rate between pounds and marks would be DM10/£1; any other exchange rate would allow profitable arbitrage. Consider what would happen if the cross exchange rate fell to DM9/£1. Arbitrageurs could use $2.75 to buy DM10, use the 10 marks to buy £1.11, and turn those pounds into $3.05, earning a riskless profit of $0.30. The impact of the arbitrage would raise the mark price of a pound back toward the consistent rate of DM10/£1.

Existence of a reserve currency creates a special situation for policy makers in the reserve-currency country, the United States in the case of the Bretton Woods system. The reserve-currency country never has to intervene in the foreign exchange market, because each nonreserve central bank handles the task of keeping its exchange rate fixed relative to the reserve currency. Another way of noting this special situation is to realize that a world of N countries and N currencies has $N - 1$ exchange rates against the reserve currency. For example, if Britain, Germany, and the United States constituted the entire world economy ($N = 3$), there would be only two ($N - 1 = 3 - 1 = 2$) exchange rates relative to the dollar ($2.75/£1 and $0.275/DM1). Consistency determines the third rate, so that £/DM = £/$ · $/DM.

This asymmetry carries an important implication: The reserve-currency country *can use monetary policy to pursue internal balance even under a fixed exchange rate*. Recall that monetary policy fails for nonreserve countries because they must intervene to cover any balance-of-payments surpluses or deficits, and such intervention offsets the effect of their initial monetary policy. The reserve country, in contrast, never has to intervene, so it can use monetary policy. In fact, it can conduct monetary policy not only for itself, but also for the entire set of countries in the fixed exchange rate system. Figure 15 shows why. Panel (a) represents the situation in the reserve country. We omit the BOP line from the diagram because, as we just argued, the reserve-country central bank needn't intervene to offset any balance-of-payments surplus or deficit that might arise. In effect, the reserve country is unconstrained by external balance, because other countries adjust to keep the reserve country in balance-of-payments equilibrium. Panel (b), which illustrates events in a representative nonreserve economy, does contain a BOP line, because the nonreserve-country central bank has the responsibility to intervene to keep its currency's exchange rate fixed against the reserve currency.

---

24. Under Bretton Woods, exchange rates could fluctuate within bands of plus or minus 1 percent of the central rate.

25. The same logic applies to the case of triangular arbitrage in section 3.2 of the chapter on currency markets and exchange rates.

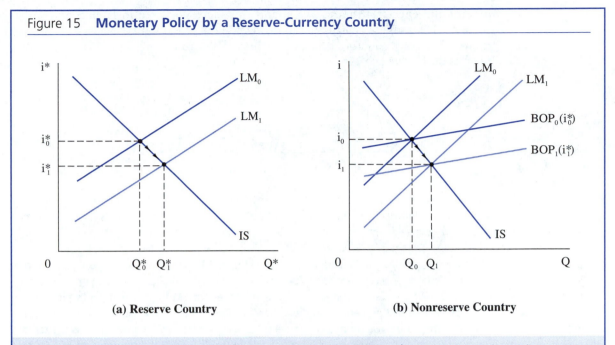

Figure 15 Monetary Policy by a Reserve-Currency Country

(a) Reserve Country

(b) Nonreserve Country

The reserve-currency country, in panel (a), doesn't face the usual balance-of-payments constraint on its monetary policy. Expansionary monetary policy by the reserve country shifts its LM curve to the right and lowers its interest rate. In the nonreserve country (panel (b)), the decline in the reserve-country interest rate shifts the BOP line down, because the fall in i* lowers the expected return on deposits denominated in the reserve currency and makes portfolio owners content to hold nonreserve-currency deposits at a lower interest rate than before. At i_0, the nonreserve country has a balance-of-payments surplus. It intervenes by purchasing reserve-currency deposits in the foreign exchange market. The domestic money stock rises and shifts the LM curve to the right. Expansionary monetary policy by the reserve country expands not only its own money stock, but that of the nonreserve country as well.

Suppose the reserve country conducts an expansionary monetary policy that shifts its LM curve to the right. The domestic interest rate falls, and the balance of payments moves into deficit. In the nonreserve country, the BOP line shifts down. This occurs because the lower interest rate in the reserve country generates a capital outflow from the reserve country into the nonreserve country and makes a lower interest rate in the nonreserve country consistent with interest parity. As the nonreserve country's BOP line shifts down, the economy experiences a balance-of-payments surplus from the capital inflow. To prevent its currency from appreciating against the reserve currency, the nonreserve central bank must buy foreign exchange (that is, reserve-currency-denominated deposits) in the foreign exchange market. This increases the nonreserve country's money stock and shifts its LM curve to the right. At the new equilibrium, both the reserve and nonreserve economies have higher levels of income and lower interest rates.

Policy makers in the reserve country clearly enjoy an advantage from their ability to conduct monetary policy under a fixed exchange rate regime. Put another way, the reserve country avoids responsibility for financing its own balance-of-payments surpluses or deficits; other countries must do so. Other countries will likely view the spillover effects of reserve-country policy as a mixed blessing. If reserve and nonreserve countries tend to experience similar economic situations (for example, simultaneous booms or recessions), then the across-border effects of reserve-country policy may cause no problem and even be welcomed. However, if economic situations in the two countries differ, making expansionary policy appropriate for one and contractionary policy appropriate for the other, tensions are likely to rise as the nonreserve country inherits the effects of the reserve country's policy. We'll see in later chapters that tensions such as these contributed to the demise of the Bretton Woods system of fixed exchange rates, as countries became unwilling to absorb the impact of U.S. inflationary policies during the late 1960s.

Germany

CASE 1: MORE ON GERMAN UNIFICATION

The unification of the Federal Republic of Germany and the German Democratic Republic in 1990 occurred in the context of a fixed exchange rate regime among the (then 12) member countries of the European Community (EC), now the European Union. Within the group, the German Deutsche mark served as the unofficial reserve currency; and other member countries adjusted their policies to maintain the values of their currencies relative to the mark. This implied that Germany could conduct effective monetary policy while other member countries could not, as we saw in section 6. This exchange rate regime played an important role in the economic impact of German unification on other EC members. In particular, the fixed-rate system caused

Germany's unification-based economic boom to exert a contractionary effect on the country's European trading partners.

To keep our analysis simple, let's let Britain represent all non-German EC members. Figure 16 illustrates pre-unification economic conditions in Germany and Britain, where all three markets in both countries are in equilibrium. Recall that the absence of a BOP^G curve reflects Germany's monetary independence as the reserve-currency country. The unification process caused German consumption, investment, and especially government expenditure to rise, so the IS^G curve shifted substantially to the right. German central bankers, fearful that too much

Figure 16   The Macroeconomics of German Unification

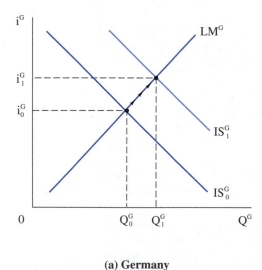

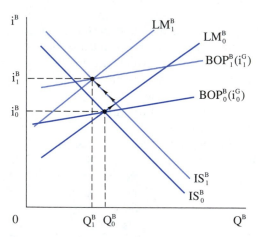

(a) Germany

(b) Britain

The accelerated expenditure and tight monetary policy that accompanied unification in Germany (panel (a)) exerted two influences on trading partners, represented here by Britain (panel (b)). First, increased demand for their exports shifted IS to the right and exerted an expansionary influence on trading-partner economies. Second, the increased German interest rate shifted trading partners' BOP lines upward. To keep their currencies from depreciating against the mark, trading partners had to intervene to supply marks, shifting their LM curves to the left and exerting a contractionary influence on the economy. The net effect on trading-partner economies—expansionary or contractionary—depends on the relative sizes of the two effects.

expansion might cause inflation to rise, kept the money stock constant. Upward pressure on German interest rates shifted BOP^B up and caused a capital flow from Britain to Germany, resulting in a British balance-of-payments deficit and a German surplus. Increased German demand for imports also shifted the IS^B curve to the right.

To prevent the pound from depreciating against the mark, the Bank of England had to supply marks to the foreign exchange market. This shifted the LM^B curve to the left until it intersected the new BOP$^B_1$ and IS$^B_1$. Note that the *net* effect of German unification on Britain depends on the relative sizes of the shifts in IS^B and LM^B. The greater the increase in German demand for foreign goods and services, the bigger the rightward shift in Britain's IS curve and the more likely Germany's unification boom would be transmitted as a boom to Germany's European trading partners. The smaller the increase in German demand for foreign goods and services, the smaller the shift in Britain's IS curve and the more likely Germany unification would push its partners into economic slumps through the monetary contraction transmitted by the fixed exchange rate system.

How did the scenario actually play out? Following unification, Germany pursued tight monetary policy to avoid unification-induced inflation. As the German LM curve shifted to the left, European trading partners were forced to do likewise to maintain their exchange rates against the mark. (*Illustrate in a diagram similar to Figure 16.*) Germany entered a recession—along with most of the other economies of Europe.

By late 1992, Germany's ability to force its partners to follow the Bundesbank's monetary policy threatened the whole process of monetary integration within the European Community. Participants in the foreign exchange market started to doubt the resolve of countries such as Britain and France to carry through with contractionary monetary policies when their economies were already in recession. Portfolio owners began to expect devaluations of the pound, franc, and other non-mark EU currencies. As e^e (defined as pounds or francs per DM) rose, the BOP lines of the nonreserve countries shifted further up—in September 1992, November 1992, and again in July 1993—requiring even more monetary contraction to maintain the exchange rate pegs against the mark. France continued to engage in large-scale intervention to support the franc. By the time the dust settled, the French franc was one of only a few EU currencies to survive with its pre-crisis exchange rate intact.

We'll see in the next chapter that Britain removed the pound from the EU's fixed exchange rate system in September 1992 and allowed the currency to float against the mark, permitting a more expansionary British monetary policy than would otherwise have been feasible. (*Illustrate in a diagram similar to Figure 16.*) The pound depreciated by more than 10 percent against the mark, but Britain began to move out of its recession, unlike France and Germany, whose unemployment rates continued to rise until 1995.

CASE 2: BETTING AGAINST THE BAHT

Thailand

For 13 years, the Thai government pegged the country's currency, the baht, to an international currency basket composed of 80 percent U.S. dollars and the rest German marks and Japanese yen. After a decade of rapid growth of around 8 percent per year, the Thai economy fell into a slump in 1997. Demand for electronics exports dropped. The appreciation of the dollar, which carried the baht with it, hurt other Thai export industries. (*Why?*) The banking system struggled under billions of dollars' worth of bad loans, many to the domestic real-estate sector, financial institutions, and inefficient manufacturers. The Stock Exchange of Thailand index had dropped 60 percent from its high in early 1996.

In the midst of these myriad economic problems, keeping the baht pegged required monetary contraction and higher interest rates. The Bank of Thailand repeatedly announced its plans to maintain the peg, but foreign exchange market participants started to wonder. (*Illustrate in an IS-LM-BOP diagram the combination of a slump in export demand and an* expected *currency devaluation. What would the central bank need to do to maintain the fixed exchange rate?*) The central bank held about $30 billion in foreign exchange reserves; but no one knew how much of that total the bank had already committed in the forward market to buy baht in 3, 6, 9, or 12 months. (Later, the answer would turn out to be more than $23 billion of the $30 billion, although fulfilling the forward contracts would reduce reserves by much less than the full $23 billion.)

A devaluation could devastate the country's already-shaky banks and other firms that had borrowed heavily in dollars and lent in baht. Thai private firms owed over $67 billion in foreign debt, much of it with unhedged foreign exchange risk. On the other hand, the monetary restraint and high interest rates (initially around 13 percent) necessary to maintain the baht peg also took their toll. Interest rates continued to rise with expectations of an impending devaluation. The government imposed capital controls that prohibited foreigners from buying baht except as required for trade transactions. (*Illustrate the effects in your IS-LM-BOP diagram.*) Capital outflows slowed, but so did capital inflows, because the controls prevented potential foreign investors from hedging the foreign exchange risk of buying Thai assets. More and more of the still-functioning Thai firms found themselves unable to get credit to cover their day-to-day operating needs.

The devaluation came on July 2, 1997. The government abandoned its peg and allowed the baht to float. It dropped over 16 percent against the dollar and 12 percent against the yen on the first day. Within a month, the Bank of Thailand and the Finance Ministry sought an IMF loan assistance package to finance the country's payments and replenish the Bank of Thailand's foreign exchange reserves. The IMF granted $4 billion in loans, contingent on the country meeting IMF-approved policy plans and economic targets.

Additional assistance came from Japan, Australia, China, Hong Kong, Malaysia, Singapore, Indonesia, South Korea, the World Bank, the Asian Development Bank, and the Bank for International Settlements (the bank for central banks). As of August 1997, experts estimated that Thailand had spent over $32 billion in its failed effort to defend the baht's peg.

As we saw in the preceding chapter, economic crises with their roots in the banking sector tend to spread, and Thailand's certainly did. Soon Indonesia, South Korea, and Malaysia succumbed, as did Hong Kong, the Philippines, and even Japan and China—albeit to a lesser extent. In the year after the baht devaluation, Thai manufacturing production, private investment, and exports all fell between 10 and 20 percent, and imports by 40 percent. Analysts estimated that between 30 and 40 percent of all loans by Thai banks and finance companies were nonperforming. In January 1998, the government moved to explicitly guarantee all bank liabilities, including debts owed to foreigners. This amounted to a promise that the Thai government would, if necessary, use its foreign exchange reserves to service Thai banks' debts.

CASE 3: **PESOS AND TEQUILA**

Mexico

In 1987, after years of ineffective economic policies, failed efforts at reform, and a major external debt crisis, Mexico instituted a set of economic reforms that promised growth, stable prices, open trade, reduction of government's intrusive role in the economy, and a stable peso. Policy makers in other countries and participants in world markets viewed the reforms as evidence of Mexico's strong commitment to shift to a market-based economy as a means of supporting economic growth and development.

In 1994, events external and internal to Mexico interfered with the reforms. U.S. monetary policy shifted from expansionary to contractionary and pushed the U.S. interest rate sharply higher. Capital flows, which had rushed into Mexico in response to the country's reforms and growth prospects, slowed. Policy makers had to intervene to supply dollars from their foreign exchange reserves to keep the peso within its promised exchange-rate band against the dollar (*Illustrate using an IS-LM-BOP diagram for Mexico.*) Internal political disturbances—including an uprising in Chiapas and

the assassination of a leading presidential candidate—added to the political and economic uncertainty. Expectations of a pending devaluation mounted. (*Illustrate the impact of such expectations.*) By late December 1994, the Bank of Mexico's foreign exchange reserves had fallen by almost two-thirds from their March level. On December 22, after a December 20 devaluation failed to stabilize the currency, the new government abandoned its promise to peg the peso and allowed the currency to float. Market participants took the government's reneging on its peso commitment as a signal that the country's economic reforms and ability to make payments on its external debt were at risk. By the end of January, the peso had depreciated by more than 40 percent.

Adding to the pressure was the fact that the Mexican government had borrowed a large quantity of dollar-denominated short-term debt, called *tesobonos*, which were coming due.[26] The upcoming payments on the government's *tesobono* debt exceeded the country's foreign exchange reserves by several times. Lenders lost

---

26. The government had started issuing *tesobonos*, which promised repayment in dollars, to avoid paying the high interest rates lenders were demanding on *cetes*, bonds denominated in pesos. In effect, *tesobonos* placed the foreign exchange risk on the Mexican government, while *cetes* placed it on the lenders.

confidence in the country and its policies, leaving the government unable to borrow fresh funds to make its *tesobono* payments. Mexico received emergency loans and loan guarantees from several sources: $20 billion from the U.S. Treasury Exchange Stabilization Fund, $18 billion from the IMF, $10 billion from the Bank for International Settlements, and $1 billion from Canada.

Economists and policy makers have performed many "autopsies" on the Mexican crisis in hopes of understanding what went wrong and how it could have been avoided. Most analysts agree that several factors contributed to Mexico's rapid descent from promising emerging market to developing country on the verge of economic collapse. First, Mexico routinely sterilized its intervention in early 1994 in an attempt to prevent a contraction in the domestic economy prior to the upcoming presidential election. But, as we've seen, sterilized intervention can interfere with necessary macroeconomic adjustments, leading to a crisis. As foreign interest rates rose, especially in the United States, a decline in the Mexican money stock could have facilitated international adjustment; but sterilization foreclosed that adjustment. Second, Mexico by 1994 ran a current-account deficit of almost $30 billion because of the real peso appreciation caused by continuing inflation in excess of the nominal peso depreciation. The current-account deficit required financing by private capital inflows (that is, a capital-account surplus) or by intervention (that is, an official-settlements-balance surplus), which reduced the Bank of Mexico's reserves. At least part of the current-account deficit and associated international borrowing, no doubt, produced intertemporal gains from trade, but a portion went to consumption expenditure rather than investment. And the size of the deficit and the associated international borrowing rendered the Mexican economy vulnerable to a loss of confidence by international investors. The Chiapas rebellion and the political assassination contributed to just such a loss of confidence. Note, however, that Mexicans faced the same incentives as foreign investors to move funds out of the country in response to an expected devaluation.

Mexico and its foreign investors weren't the only ones affected by the peso experience. In what came to be known as the *tequila effect*, financial markets throughout Latin America, only recently recovered from their own 1980s debt crisis, became more volatile. Governments throughout the region, especially those of Argentina and Brazil, had to intervene to prevent their currencies from depreciating in foreign exchange markets, the result of market participants' expectations of devaluations similar to Mexico's.

The Mexican government made the Bank of Mexico, the central bank, formally independent in 1994 in an effort to reduce the political-business-cycle problem, in which overly expansionary pre-election policies cause post-election economic crises. The crisis-induced recession continued until mid-1996, when the Mexican economy began to grow. Once again able to borrow in international capital markets, Mexico in early 1997 paid off its 1995 emergency borrowing from the United States and the International Monetary Fund.

A weak banking system, the risk of political business cycles (especially overly expansionary monetary policy in pre-election periods), vulnerability to oil-price changes (especially since 35 percent of government revenues come from oil products), poor contract enforceability, and the country's delicate political stability continue to constrain Mexico's economic performance. Unlike 1994, the 2000 election passed without an economic crisis. More recently, stalled reforms have raised concern, because experts agree that the high oil prices of the past few years provided an important opportunity for Mexico to move forward on economic reforms, which are much easier to accomplish during periods of relative prosperity.

CASE 4: THE TWO FACES OF CAPITAL FLOWS

In the wake of what have been dubbed the "first financial crises of the 21st century"—Mexico and Asia—a debate emerged about the appropriate role of and policy toward capital mobility, especially in developing economies. When most developing countries followed import-substitution policies during the 1950s and 1960s, they discouraged foreign direct investment, fearful that former colonial powers would simply buy up the developing economies to replace lost political control. Private portfolio capital flows at the time were minimal; even industrial economies imposed capital controls, and many of the technologies and markets that exist today to facilitate such flows hadn't yet developed.

As import substitution failed and developing countries opened up to the world economy, they were encouraged to liberalize their capital markets. Figure 17 illustrates that countries did move toward more liberal policies toward capital-account transactions, although many restrictions remain in place.

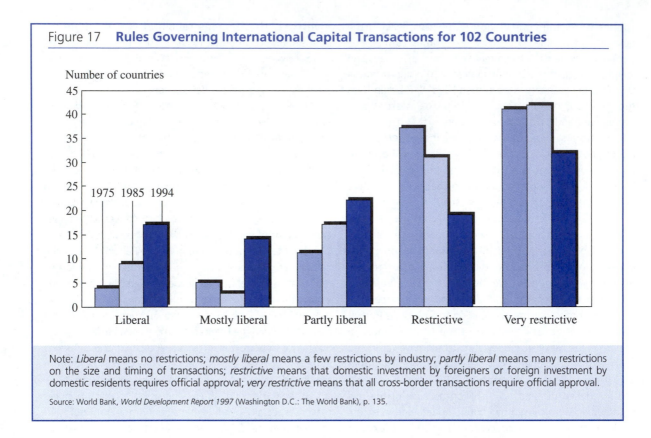

Figure 17 **Rules Governing International Capital Transactions for 102 Countries**

Number of countries

1975 1985 1994

Liberal   Mostly liberal   Partly liberal   Restrictive   Very restrictive

Note: *Liberal* means no restrictions; *mostly liberal* means a few restrictions by industry; *partly liberal* means many restrictions on the size and timing of transactions; *restrictive* means that domestic investment by foreigners or foreign investment by domestic residents requires official approval; *very restrictive* means that all cross-border transactions require official approval.

Source: World Bank, *World Development Report 1997* (Washington D.C.: The World Bank), p. 135.

Evidence indicates strongly that foreign direct investment plays complex and multifaceted roles in providing new technology, management skills, and other sources of enhanced productivity and growth to developing economies. Along with foreign direct investment, many developing economies allowed or encouraged private portfolio capital flows. Such flows allow savers around the world to seek the highest expected rates of return on their saving and permit investors with promising projects to borrow in international markets. Free flows of funds also permit markets to "judge" countries' policies by moving funds into countries with policies perceived as sound and out of countries whose economic policies seem problematic. Such capital movements can provide policy makers, especially those in developing economies, with early information about the perceived quality of their policy choices. Capital controls, in contrast, provide an opening for corruption, because policy makers can grant exemptions to special interests. For all these reasons, economists generally encourage countries to eliminate controls on capital flows.

However, large-scale and sudden capital flows can contribute to financial crises. If market participants lose confidence in a country's prospects and suddenly withdraw funds, even a basically sound economy can find itself in trouble, just as a basically sound bank can be rendered illiquid by a run, as we learned in the previous chapter. For economies with deep-rooted economic problems, sudden capital flows can turn painful episodes into genuine financial crises. When capital-market participants in Mexico, Thailand, and Indonesia began to expect currency devaluations, they pulled funds from the countries and contributed to the deep economic crises that followed.

How does one weigh these two faces of capital mobility? Recently, some economists have suggested that *temporary* controls on *short-term* capital *inflows*, especially foreign borrowing by domestic banks, may have a role to play in developing economies that as yet lack well regulated, well supervised, and transparent financial systems. Permanent capital controls are judged unlikely to work, because the longer controls remain in place, the more adept market participants become at circumventing them. So long-term capital controls simply introduce distortions and corruption. Efforts to control capital outflows send a bad signal to potential foreign investors: You can put funds into the economy but you may not be able to get them out. Hardly a recipe for confidence! Any positive role for capital controls centers on short-term flows (pejoratively called *hot money*) because they're the ones more likely to contribute to crises by suddenly shifting direction. Long-term foreign direct investment, on the other hand, can't abandon a country quickly and brings needed technology and know-how.

Large-scale short-term capital inflows to banks can bring particular risks. Banks play such a vital role in a well-functioning economy that allowing them to engage in risky behavior puts the entire macroeconomy in jeopardy. When banks overborrow abroad and become unsound, governments tend to bail them out in an effort to insulate the rest of the economy from damage. But such bailouts, in turn, cause banks to be less than prudent in their choices, because they count on future bailouts.

Can a country really have too much capital flowing in? In a world of perfect information, such a thing couldn't happen. Market participants would know the true productivity of all potential assets and investment projects; no one would shift funds to a country that wouldn't invest them prudently and productively. In practice, especially in developing economies, information can be highly imperfect. Banks can be poorly supervised and regulated, allowed to borrow abroad and to lend to overly risky projects, counting on public bailouts if they get in trouble. A big capital inflow can quickly turn into a big capital outflow. However, it's important to recognize that evidence suggests that in financial crises—including those in Mexico and Asia—*domestic residents'* capital typically flees in advance of that of *foreign* investors, presumably because locals are more attuned to early signs of trouble.

Capital-control proponents typically point to Chile as a success story. Chile required that a percentage of any non-equity capital entering the country be placed in a non-interest-paying deposit at the central bank for one year. This *encaje* policy acted as a tax on capital inflows, and the effective tax rate was higher the shorter the capital flow's time horizon. In addition, any foreign investment had to stay in the country for at least one year. Fans of the Chilean system claim it maintained overall capital inflows and shifted them from less-desirable short-term portfolio flows toward more-desirable long-term foreign direct investment. They also point to the fact that Chile suffered relatively little from the tequila effect after Mexico's 1994 devaluation. But capital-control opponents ask whether Chile's tequila immunity really came from its controls on capital inflows. Or did the immunity result from Chile's

strong bank reform of 1986, which gave it one of the best-regulated banking systems in Latin America?[27] In any event, Chile surprised fans of its capital controls by eliminating the *encaje* in September 1998, after economic problems in Russia disturbed international financial markets. In 2000, Chile dropped the one-year-stay rule for direct investment, fearful that such requirements were pushing valuable foreign investment funds into other countries with more accommodating policies.

Part of the disagreement over capital controls stems from varying definitions of the term. Most economists agree that a sound banking system *requires* government supervision and prudential regulation of banks. For example, banks in the United States are restricted in their ownership of corporate stock, because the values of such stock are viewed as inappropriately volatile to form a major part of banks' asset portfolios. The prohibition extends to stock in foreign firms, so the rule is, in some sense, a capital control. But it is a very specific, narrowly defined control targeted at a very specific potential problem. Such prudential regulations are very different from, for example, the across-the-board currency and capital controls imposed by Malaysia after the height of that country's financial crisis. Malaysia abruptly outlawed trading of its ringgit abroad, restricted Malays' holdings of foreign currencies, and dictated that the proceeds of any foreigner's sales of any Malay asset or property had to remain in the country for a year unless the Bank of Negara (the central bank) granted an exemption.

An important risk posed by even temporary capital controls is that policy makers will view them as a substitute for needed policy changes. The most important lessons of recent financial crises are simple: (1) there's no substitute for sound, consistent macroeconomic policies or for prudent regulation of a transparent banking system, (2) a fixed exchange rate can't provide macroeconomic stability if policy makers pursue policies inconsistent with the mandated peg, (3) protecting local banks from competition by foreign ones tends to generate a bloated, inefficient, and vulnerable banking sector, and (4) a lack of information (for example, markets not knowing in May 1997 that the Bank of Thailand had already committed many of its reserves to buy forward baht or how much short-term debt South Korea's private sector had accumulated) may postpone a crisis but not avoid one and is highly likely to make the eventual crisis more severe.

27. The evidence for this view is that Chilean controls on capital inflows failed to prevent a major banking and currency crisis in the early 1980s, before the banking reform. At the time, Chile's banking system resembled that of many Asian countries during the 1990s—poor regulation, rampant real-estate speculation, and questionable loans to bank insiders.

CASE 5: PAYING THE BILLS

Economists rarely have the opportunity to run laboratory experiments of the kind conducted by chemists or physicists. More often, we have to learn what we can from "experiments" that the world economy provides. The Mexican and Asian crises represent excellent examples. Economists and policy makers have scoured data about the two crises in search of insights. One question of particular interest is: What are the signs of an impending crisis? In other words, what variables might we monitor in order to spot potential trouble?

One answer seems to be the relationship between a country's short-term foreign borrowing and its international reserves. After all, short-term foreign borrowing represents debt that must be repaid in foreign currency within a year or less. If this debt exceeds available foreign exchange reserves, then the country is at least illiquid even if not insolvent, making it reliant on its ongoing ability to borrow in capital markets to meet its existing payment obligations. An excess of reserves

over short-term debt, in contrast, means a country has a cushion to weather any temporary interruption to its capital-market access—for example, one due to a brief lapse of confidence.

In early 1998, economists Steven Radelet and Jeffrey Sachs analyzed a sample of 22 developing countries and computed their short-term foreign debt to reserve ratios, which we report in Table 4. Radelet and Sachs found that in eight of the nine countries that had experienced a recent financial crisis, the ratio exceeded 0.8; the only exception was Malaysia.

With hindsight, another of their results proves even more revealing. Radelet and Sachs note that "This [0.8] value is exceeded by only three of the thirteen noncrisis economies: Russia, South Africa, and Zimbabwe. It is possible to have a high level of short-term debt without entering a crisis . . . but it does seem to indicate vulnerability" (p. 46). Shortly after Radelet and Sachs wrote this statement, all three countries they mentioned *did* experience financial crises.

Table 4 PRELUDE TO CRISIS? RATIO OF SHORT-TERM DEBT TO FOREIGN EXCHANGE RESERVES

Country	Period	Short-Term Foreign Debt/ Foreign Exchange Reserves
Noncrisis:		
Brazil	1994–1997	0.71
Chile	1994–1997	0.50
Colombia	1994–1997	0.68
Hungary	1994–1997	0.40
India	1994–1997	0.36
Jordan	1994–1997	0.35
Peru	1994–1997	0.49
Poland	1994–1997	0.19
Russia	1994–1997	3.33
South Africa	1994–1997	3.17
Sri Lanka	1994–1997	0.24
Taiwan	1994–1997	0.22
Zimbabwe	1994–1997	1.40

(continues)

Table 4 (*continued*)

Country	Period	Short-Term Foreign Debt/ Foreign Exchange Reserves
Crisis:		
Argentina	1995	1.57
Indonesia	1997	1.70
Korea	1997	2.06
Malaysia	1997	0.61
Mexico	1995	5.28
Philippines	1997	0.85
Thailand	1997	1.45
Turkey	1994	2.06
Venezuela	1994	0.81

Source: Data from Steven Radelet and Jeffrey D. Sachs, "The East Asian Financial Crisis: Diagnosis, Remedies, Prospects," *Brookings Papers on Economic Activity* (1998), p. 47.

CASE 6: PEGGED, BUT TO WHAT?

Choosing a fixed exchange rate isn't the end of policy makers' exchange-rate decisions. A fixed rate involves pegging the currency's value relative to the value of something else. This something else can be the currency of a major trading partner (such as Hong Kong's peg to the U.S. dollar), an accounting unit created by an international organization (such as Saudi Arabia's use of the International Monetary Fund's special drawing right, or SDR), or a "basket" containing several currencies (such as Thailand's pre-crisis peg to a basket containing 80 percent dollars and 20 percent yen and Deutsche marks).

The choice of "pegged to what" can be important because a pegged currency moves in lockstep with its "anchor" against all other currencies. For example, when the U.S. dollar appreciated against most other currencies during the 1990s, it carried the Thai baht with it because of the heavy dollar weight (80 percent) in Thailand's currency-basket peg. The resulting real appreciation of the baht against nondollar currencies cut Thailand's overall ability to export at the same time demand for its electronics exports was falling for other reasons. To minimize this effect, many countries that use a fixed exchange rate choose to peg either to the currency of the predominant trading partner or to a currency basket representative of the country's pattern of trade.

Sometimes countries change their peg anchor. Following years of triple- and quadruple-digit inflation, Argentina in 1991 introduced its Convertibility Plan, which pegged the peso to the U.S. dollar at a one-to-one exchange rate (e = P1/$1). The Argentine monetary authority (a currency board) pledged not to create more pesos than it could back with its dollar reserves. This effectively took away the government's ability to conduct monetary policy, the inflationary consequences of which had repeatedly wrecked the country's economy. After 1991, inflation fell dramatically, and the Convertibility Plan formed the bedrock of residents' confidence in the economy. But Argentina traded more with Europe than with the United States. So, when the dollar appreciated by about 30 percent against the new euro between 1999 and 2001, the dollar carried the peso with it. Argentina, already in recession, experienced a sharp real appreciation of the peso relative to both its neighbor currency, the Brazilian real, and the euro. As the country's economic situation grew worse, Argentina decided in 2001 that a peg against a currency basket containing half dollars and half euros would help. But changing from a dollar peg to a dollar-euro-basket peg at prevailing exchange rates would have amounted to a devaluation. Residents' confidence in the Convertibility Plan would have been lost. And, because most public and private debt in Argentina was denominated in dollars, any devaluation would threaten the country's already shaky ability to pay its debts.

So Argentina passed a law that switched from a dollar peg to a dollar-euro-basket peg, but also delayed the switch for everyone except exporters and importers until the dollar-euro exchange rate reached $1/ €1—in an effort to avoid charges of a clandestine devaluation. International investors worried that the de facto devaluation for international trade represented a step toward a general devaluation, and they responded to the move by selling peso-denominated assets. As expectations of either debt default or a devaluation (or both) rose, so did the interest rates the country had to pay to rollover its outstanding loans. Analysts agreed that getting Argentina's economy back on track would require politically difficult moves: getting government spending, especially that by provincial governments, under control; making labor markets more flexible; deregulating markets; and making the economy more hospitable to foreign investors. The economic situation shifted from bad to worse. Before the end of 2001, the government announced the largest sovereign debt default in history. The end of the Convertibility Plan soon followed. Several successive governments resigned amid a growing economic crisis.

CASE 7: **CAPITAL DECONTROLS**

The term *capital controls* encompasses many different types of restrictions that governments can impose on capital flows. Because the restrictions themselves differ, the process of liberalizing or decontrolling capital flows also differs between countries. The following recent policy changes provide examples of the concrete policies involved in decontrolling a country's capital account.

India. In 2003, India doubled the ceiling on Indian mutual funds' holdings of foreign-listed firms from $500 million to $1 billion and now permits Indian firms and individuals to hold foreign equities.

South Africa. In 2003, the government doubled the amount South African firms are permitted to invest outside of Africa to 1 billion rand per project. Foreign dividends no longer are taxed. Emigrants, who were prohibited from taking their savings with them when they left the country during capital controls, can now access their funds and move them out of South Africa. New emigrants and South African nationals can move up to 750,000 rand each out of the country.

China. In 2004, China altered rules for Chinese firms that want to invest abroad. Existing rules required the government to assess the feasibility of each proposed project; new rules allow on-line application and approval. Tourists can also carry more foreign exchange outside of China, and Chinese firms can retain a larger share of any foreign currency they earn from exports. Chinese authorities also announced their intentions to further liberalize capital flows over the next few years.

SUMMARY

With the price level and the exchange rate fixed, self-adjustment mechanisms exist for reaching external balance (balance-of-payments equilibrium) but not for attaining internal balance (full employment) in the short run. The effectiveness of short-run macroeconomic policy in achieving internal balance under fixed exchange rates depends on the degree of international capital mobility.

With completely immobile capital, neither fiscal nor monetary policy can bring the economy into internal balance. Only a change in the exchange rate can alter the income consistent with external balance to match that required for internal balance.

Increased capital mobility enhances fiscal policy's ability to alter income. Monetary policy remains ineffective even in the presence of capital mobility, and exchange rate policy retains its ability to affect income. Table 5 summarizes these results.

LOOKING AHEAD

Capital mobility strongly influences the effectiveness of various tools of macroeconomic policy. Likewise, a change in the exchange rate regime alters the ability of fiscal and monetary policy to achieve simultaneous internal and external balance. Policy makers can choose the type of

Table 5	SHORT-RUN POLICY EFFECTIVENESS UNDER FIXED EXCHANGE RATES		
	Ability to Affect Income under a Fixed Exchange Rate		
Policy	**Immobile Capital**	**Imperfectly Mobile Capital**	**Perfectly Mobile Capital**
Fiscal	0	Effective	Effective
Monetary	0	0	0
Exchange rate	Effective	Effective	Effective

exchange rate regime under which their currencies operate (in fact, individual countries can—and do—choose different systems), so understanding the implications of the type of exchange rate regime for macroeconomic policy is particularly important. The upcoming chapter explores the move to a more flexible exchange rate system made by the major industrial economies in the early 1970s and its implications for fiscal and monetary policy and for internal and external balance.

KEY TERMS

internal balance   perfect capital mobility
external balance   risk premium
targets   signal
instruments   reserve currency
crowding out   Bretton Woods
sterilization policy

PROBLEMS AND QUESTIONS FOR REVIEW

1. Consider an open market *sale* of 500 under a fixed exchange rate regime. Assume the money multiplier is 10 and the economy is at a general equilibrium before the policy.
   a. Explain carefully what action by the central bank would constitute such a policy.
   b. *Ignoring the foreign exchange market for a moment*, what would be the initial or direct effect of the open market sale on the domestic money stock (that is, by how much would M increase or decrease)? Explain.
   c. What would be the effect of such a policy on the domestic balance of payments? Why? Does your answer depend on the extent of capital mobility? Explain.
   d. To maintain the pegged exchange rate, what action would the central bank need to undertake, if any? What would be the effect on the domestic money stock (that is, by how much would this action increase or decrease M)?
   e. What is the total net effect of the open market operation on the domestic money stock (taking into account the effects in parts (b) and (d))?
   f. What are the implications of your answer to part (e) for discretionary or activist monetary policy under a fixed exchange rate?
2. Assume that the exchange rate is fixed and capital is perfectly mobile.
   a. *Scenario 1*: Country A's central bank devalues the domestic currency, the alpha (α); but the citizens of A do *not* expect the devaluation to be permanent. Illustrate the effect of the exchange rate policy on income and the interest rate.
   b. *Scenario 2*: Country A's central bank devalues the domestic currency, the alpha (α), by the same amount as in Scenario 1; but the citizens of A *do* expect the devaluation to be permanent. Illustrate the effect of the exchange rate policy on income and the interest rate.

   c. *Scenario 3*: Country A's central bank devalues the domestic currency, the alpha (α), by the same amount as in Scenario 1; but the citizens of A expect the devaluation to be permanent *and* it causes them to expect a further devaluation. Illustrate the effect of the exchange rate policy on income and the interest rate.

   d. Explain why you drew the graphs in parts (a), (b), and (c) as you did, and compare the policy effects in the three scenarios.

3. Comment on the following statement by the head of a central bank of a small country that has a fixed exchange rate and strict capital controls that prohibit capital inflows and outflows: "The reason for our capital controls is to prevent external events from affecting our domestic economy. For the same reason, we will not alter the pegged value of our currency by devaluing or revaluing, but rather we will rely on domestic monetary and fiscal policies to achieve our economic goals."

4. Hong Kong maintains a fixed exchange rate of its Hong Kong dollar against the U.S. dollar, managed by a currency board. During the Asian financial crisis, the currencies of most of Hong Kong's Asian trading partners depreciated sharply against the U.S. dollar. What would be the effect on Hong Kong? Why might this have caused market participants to expect a devaluation of the Hong Kong dollar? Why might Hong Kong policy makers have been eager to convince market participants that there would be no devaluation?

5. It is common for countries to complain about one another's interest rates. Assume that the domestic country operates under a fixed exchange rate regime, and capital is completely mobile. Illustrate and explain the effect on the domestic economy of a *decline* in the *foreign* interest rate (i^*), beginning from a point of general equilibrium, using the IS-LM-BOP framework.

6. One effect of a one-time devaluation is to allow a central bank to replenish its foreign exchange reserves. Explain how this happens. Sometimes, a devaluation causes foreign exchange market participants to expect another devaluation in the future. When this happens, would you expect the initial devaluation to increase the central bank's reserves? Why, or why not?

7. Historically, it has been common for a country to pressure its trading partners to follow expansionary macroeconomic policies. Assume that the domestic country operates under a fixed exchange rate regime, and capital is completely mobile. Illustrate and explain the effect on the domestic economy of an *increase* in *foreign* income, beginning from a point of general equilibrium, using the IS-LM-BOP framework.

8. Use an IS-LM-BOP diagram to explain how the following might have contributed to Argentina's economic crisis of 2001–2002.

   a. Argentina, under the Convertibility Plan, pegged its peso to the U.S. dollar at e = P1/$1. In 1998, Argentina's major trading partner, Brazil, during its own economic crisis, devalued its currency, the *real*, against the dollar.

   b. In 2001, the Argentine government proposed changing the peso peg from a fixed exchange rate against the dollar alone to a fixed rate against a basket of half dollars and half euros. At the time, the euro had depreciated against the dollar by approximately 30 percent since its introduction in 1999.

REFERENCES AND SELECTED READINGS

Baldacci, Emanuele, et al. "Using Fiscal Policy to Spur Growth." *Finance and Development* 40 (December 2003): 28–31.
Evaluating fiscal spending and taxation as a tool of macroeconomic policy; for all students.

Burnside, Craig, et al. "Prospective Deficits and the Asian Currency Crisis." *Journal of Political Economy* 109 (December 2001): 1155–1197.
Argues that the expected fiscal costs of dealing with banks' insolvency played an important role in causing the Asian financial crisis; for intermediate and advanced students.

Cooper, Richard N. "Should Capital Controls be Banished?" *Brookings Papers on Economic Activity* 1 (1999): 89–142.
A sympathetic view of capital controls to prevent or manage crises.

Cooper, Richard N., and Jane Sneddon Little. "U.S. Monetary Policy in an Integrating World: 1960 to 2000." In *The Evolution of Monetary Policy and the Federal Reserve System over the Past Thirty Years,* edited by R. W. Kopcke and L. E. Browne, 77–130. Boston: Federal Reserve Bank of Boston, 2000.
History of international influences on U.S. monetary policy.

Corden, W. Max. *Too Sensational: On the Choice of Exchange Rate Regimes.* Cambridge, Mass.: MIT Press, 2002.
Excellent overview of the pros and cons of various exchange rate regimes, covering both theory and cases; for all students.

Desai, Padma. "Why Did the Ruble Collapse in August 1998?" *American Economic Review Papers and Proceedings* 90 (May 2000): 48–52.
What caused the ruble crisis and what, if anything, might have prevented it?

Dominguez, Kathryn M., and Jeffrey A. Frankel. *Does Foreign Exchange Intervention Work?* Washington, D.C.: Institute for International Economics, 1993.
Study of the effect of sterilized intervention; for intermediate students.

Dornbusch, Rudiger, et al. "Currency Crises and Collapses." *Brookings Papers on Economic Activity* 2 (1995): 219–293.
Lessons from four currency crises; for intermediate students.

Dueker, Michael J., and Andreas M. Fischer. "The Mechanics of a Successful Exchange Rate Peg: Lessons for Emerging Markets." Federal Reserve Bank of St. Louis, *Review* (September/October 2001): 47–56.
Why did Austria's peg to the Deutsche mark work while Thailand's peg to the dollar failed?

Edwards, Sebastian. "How Effective Are Capital Controls?" *Journal of Economic Perspectives* 13 (Fall 1999): 65–84.
What capital flows can and cannot do to prevent or manage financial crises.

Eichengreen, Barry. *Globalizing Capital.* Princeton: Princeton University Press, 1996.
Readable account of the history of capital flows and macroeconomic policy.

Eichengreen, Barry, and Michael Mussa. "Capital Account Liberalization and the IMF." *Finance and Development* (December 1998): 16–19.
How to manage capital-account liberalization to obtain its benefits and control its risks.

Fleming, J. M. "Domestic Financial Policies under Fixed and Floating Exchange Rates." *IMF Staff Papers* 9 (November 1962): 369–380.
A classic paper on macroeconomic policy effectiveness in an open economy; for advanced students.

Ghosh, Atish R., et al. *Exchange Rate Regimes: Choices & Consequences.* Cambridge, Mass.: MIT Press, 2002.
A careful look at the empirical evidence on the performance of alternate exchange rate regimes; for intermediate students.

Goldstein, Morris. *The Asian Financial Crisis.* Washington, D.C.: Institute for International Economics, 1998.
Overview of the causes, cures, and implications; for all students.

Hemming, Richard, et al. "Fiscal Vulnerability and Financial Crises in Emerging Market Economies." IMF Occasional Paper No. 218 (2003).
Good source of data, case studies, and background on recent financial crises in emerging market economies.

Hume, David. "On the Balance of Trade." In *Essays, Moral, Political, and Literary,* Vol. 1. London: Longmans, Green, 1898 [1752].
The original statement of the automatic adjustment process under fixed exchange rates; for all students.

International Monetary Fund. *Exchange Arrangements and Foreign Exchange Markets.* Washington, D.C.: IMF, 2003.
Rich source of data and case studies; for all students.

Isard, Peter. *Exchange Rate Economics.* Cambridge: Cambridge University Press, 1995.
Excellent survey of the literature on fixed exchange rates; for intermediate and advanced students.

Kaminsky, Graciela, and Sergio Schmukler. "Short- and Long-Run Integration: Do Capital Controls Matter?" *Brookings Trade Forum* (2000): 125–178.
Short- and long-run implications and effects of controls on capital flows.

Kharas, Homi, et al. "An Analysis of Russia's 1998 Meltdown: Fundamentals and Market Signals." *Brookings Papers on Economic Activity* (2001): 1–68.
Interaction of fixed exchange rate and fiscal policy in Russia's crisis.

Kose, M. Ayhan, and Eswar Prasad. "Liberalizing Capital Account Restrictions." *Finance and Development* 41 (September 2004): 50–51.
Short overview of the pros and cons of capital liberalization; for all students.

Meltzer, Allan H. "U.S. Policy in the Bretton Woods Era." Federal Reserve Bank of St. Louis, *Review* 73 (May–June 1991): 53–83.
Excellent, readable survey of the functioning of the Bretton Woods system of pegged exchange rates.

Mundell, Robert A. "Capital Mobility and Stabilization Policy under Fixed and Flexible Exchange Rates." *Canadian Journal of Economics and Political Science* 29 (November 1963): 475–485.
The original presentation of capital mobility's impact on macroeconomic policy effectiveness in an open economy; for intermediate and advanced students.

Neely, Christopher J. "An Introduction to Capital Controls." Federal Reserve Bank of St. Louis, *Review* 81 (November/December 1999): 13–30.
What are capital controls, and what are their effects?

Noland, Marcus, et al. *Global Economic Effects of the Asian Currency Devaluations.* Washington, D.C.: Institute for International Economics, 1998.
Estimates of the Asian crisis's effects on the rest of the world economy; for intermediate students.

Obstfeld, Maurice. "The Global Capital Market: Benefactor or Menace?" *Journal of Economic Perspectives* (Fall 1998): 9–30.
More on the two faces of capital flows.

Reinhart, Carmen M., et al. "Debt Intolerance." *Brookings Papers on Economic Activity* 2003 (1): 1–74.
How much debt can countries accumulate without triggering a crisis? For intermediate and advanced students.

Rogoff, Kenneth S. "Rethinking Capital Controls." *Finance and Development* 39 (December 2002): 55–56.
Accessible summary of what we know about capital controls after recent crises.

Schuknecht, Ludger. "A Trade Policy Perspective on Capital Controls." *Finance and Development* 36 (March 1999): 38–41.
Uses the basic trade model to illustrate the benefits of open international capital flows.

Session on "Debt, Equity, and Financial Openness." *American Economic Review Papers and Proceedings* 93 (May 2003): 85–101.
Series of short papers on how the structure of economies' borrowing, together with their degree of openness, affects performance; for intermediate and advanced students.

Summers, Lawrence H. "Distinguished Lecture on Economics in Government: Reflections on Managing Global Integration." *Journal of Economic Perspectives* 13 (Spring 1999): 3–18.
An overview of international financial integration by the former U.S. Treasury secretary, now president of Harvard University.

Symposium on "Facing Crises." *Finance and Development* 39 (December 2002): 4–25.
Series of short papers on various aspects of what countries can do once a crisis breaks out; for all students.

Taylor, Alan M. "Global Finance: Past and Present." *Finance and Development* 41 (March 2004): 28–31.
The trilemma presented by countries' inability to have a fixed exchange rate, mobile capital, and an independent monetary policy.

Tinbergen, Jan. *On the Theory of Economic Policy*. Amsterdam: North-Holland, 1952.
An early influential work on the theory of macroeconomic policy making in an open economy; for advanced students.

Tornell, Aaron, et al. "Liberalization, Growth, and Financial Crises: Lessons from Mexico and the Developing World." *Brookings Papers on Economic Activity* 2003 (2): 1–112.
What can the crises of the last decade teach developing countries about how to liberalize and grow without triggering a crisis? For intermediate and advanced students.

Short-Run Macroeconomic Policy under Flexible Exchange Rates

1 INTRODUCTION

After World War II, the world economy operated under the **Bretton Woods system** of fixed, or pegged, exchange rates. The Bretton Woods agreement consisted of a commitment by each member country's central bank to intervene in foreign exchange markets to keep the value of its currency, in terms of U.S. dollars, within a certain range or band. If a currency's value threatened to rise above the upper limit of its band, the central bank would sell the currency for dollars in the foreign exchange market. If a currency's value sank to the lower limit of its band, the central bank would use dollars from its foreign exchange reserves to buy the excess supply of the domestic currency from the foreign exchange market. These intervention activities pegged each currency's value within its agreed-upon band relative to the U.S. dollar.[1]

By the late 1960s, the Bretton Woods system came under stress and threatened to disintegrate for two basic reasons. First, governments of the major industrial economies faced increasing domestic political pressure to pursue short-run macroeconomic policies that maintained full employment; as we saw in the preceding chapter, however, fixed exchange rates prevent countries other than the reserve-currency country from conducting independent monetary policies aimed at domestic targets such as full employment. Second, as we saw in section 6 of the last chapter, the reserve country under a fixed exchange rate regime conducts monetary policy not only for itself, but for all the countries in the system. During the 1960s, the United States, the reserve-currency country under Bretton Woods, pursued increasingly expansionary monetary policies that generated inflation at home; and the rules of the Bretton Woods system transmitted that inflation to other countries.

By early 1973, after several years of gradual disintegration, the Bretton Woods system collapsed, and the major industrial countries allowed their currencies to float against the dollar.[2] The move to flexible exchange rates, viewed as unthinkable by most economists and policy makers only a decade before, occurred primarily as a response to the collapse of the Bretton Woods system and a lack of agreement on an alternative. The move was met with relief in some circles and dismay in others. Gradually the idea of a flexible

---

1. A later chapter provides more detail on the mechanics of the Bretton Woods system.

2. In the post–Bretton Woods world, most central banks still intervene at least occasionally in foreign exchange markets. In other words, the current system is not a perfectly flexible one but a "managed" float (pejoratively called a "dirty" float). The extent of "management" or intervention varies over time and across countries. We'll examine the strengths and weaknesses of such a system later; for now, we focus on the effectiveness of macroeconomic policy under a perfectly flexible exchange rate regime.

Table 1 IMF MEMBERS WITH DE FACTO FLEXIBLE EXCHANGE RATES, DECEMBER 31, 2003

Exchange Rate Regime
(Number of Countries)

Managed floating with no preannounced path for exchange rate[a] (50)	Afghanistan, Algeria, Angola, Argentina, Azerbaijan, Bangladesh, Burundi, Cambodia, Croatia, Czech Republic, Dominican Republic, Egypt, Ethiopia, Gambia, Georgia, Ghana, Guyana, Haiti, India, Indonesia, Iran, Iraq, Jamaica, Kazakhstan, Kenya, Kyrgyz Republic, Lao PDR, Mauritania, Mauritius, Moldova, Mongolia, Mozambique, Myanmar, Nigeria, Pakistan, Paraguay, Peru, Russia, Rwanda, São Tomé and Principe, Serbia and Montenegro, Singapore, Slovak Republic, Sudan, Tajikistan, Thailand, Trinidad and Tobago, Uzbekistan, Vietnam, Zambia
Independently floating[b] (34)	Albania, Armenia, Australia, Brazil, Canada, Chile, Colombia, Democratic Republic of Congo, Guatemala, Iceland, Japan, Korea, Liberia, Madagascar, Malawi, Mexico, New Zealand, Norway, Papua New Guinea, Philippines, Poland, Sierra Leone, Somalia, South Africa, Sri Lanka, Sweden, Switzerland, Tanzania, Turkey, Uganda, United Kingdom, United States, Uruguay, Yemen

[a]The monetary authority influences the movements of the exchange rate through active intervention in the foreign exchange market without specifying, or precommitting to, a preannounced path for the exchange rate.
[b]The exchange rate is market determined, with any foreign exchange intervention aimed at moderating the rate of change and preventing undue fluctuations in the exchange rate, rather than at establishing a level for it.

Source: International Monetary Fund.

---

exchange rate system gained support, though far from unanimous. Today, many countries, including the United States, Japan, Canada, Brazil, and Mexico, operate under flexible exchange rate regimes (see Table 1). However, since the early 1970s, each disruption to the world macroeconomy has generated renewed skepticism regarding a flexible-rate regime; and a vocal constituency continues to support a return to some type of fixed exchange rate system, at least among the world's major currencies. The arguments on both sides of this issue form the subject of a later chapter. Before we can evaluate those arguments, though, we must understand how a flexible exchange rate system works and its implications for macroeconomic policy.

We'll continue to assume, as we did in the preceding chapter's analysis of fixed exchange rates, that policy makers' goal is to bring the economy into internal balance, and that domestic and foreign price levels are fixed.[3] With flexible exchange rates, the economy contains an automatic adjustment mechanism for effecting external balance.[4] The adjustment takes the form of currency appreciations that relieve balance-of-payments surpluses and depreciations that relieve BOP deficits. However, policy makers may not be satisfied with this

---

3. We'll relax the fixed price level assumption in later chapters. Price flexibility has two important implications. First, the economy will contain an automatic adjustment mechanism for reaching internal as well as external balance. Second, attempts to use macroeconomic policy to alter the economy's path may result in price level changes in addition to or instead of changes in real income or employment.

4. The economy also contains an automatic adjustment mechanism for reaching external balance under fixed exchange rates: changes in the money stock through foreign exchange market intervention.

outcome. We've seen that changes in the nominal exchange rate with fixed price levels cause changes in the real exchange rate, or the relative price of domestic goods and services. This implies that different values of the nominal exchange rate carry different implications for the fortunes of various sectors of the economy—exporters, import-competing industries, consumers of imported goods, and users of imported inputs—as well as for the current-account balance. Therefore, the value of the exchange rate consistent with external balance or balance-of-payments equilibrium may prove unacceptable because of its distributional ramifications or its implications for the current account. In addition, the income at which the automatic adjustment mechanism produces external balance may prove unacceptable in terms of policy makers' internal-balance goal; for example, the unemployment rate may be unacceptably high. We'll begin our analysis of each policy at a point of external balance that reflects the outcome of the automatic adjustment mechanism. The question then becomes whether the policy under scrutiny can bring the economy into internal balance while allowing exchange rate changes to continue maintaining external balance. We'll also track the policies' implications for the current account.

A perfectly flexible exchange rate regime allows the supplies of and demands for different currencies to determine exchange rates. Central banks don't intervene in the foreign exchange market. The exchange rate moves to equate the quantity demanded and the quantity supplied for each currency; therefore, external balance is achieved through automatic adjustment in the form of exchange rate movements. The fact that achieving external balance with a flexible exchange rate doesn't require foreign exchange market intervention has important implications for macroeconomic policy.

Recall that under fixed exchange rates, a major determinant of the effectiveness of any macroeconomic policy is that policy's consequence for the balance of payments and, through intervention, for the domestic money stock. A flexible exchange rate breaks this link between a country's balance of payments and its money stock. By giving up the power to determine the exchange rate, the central bank gains the ability to affect the nominal money stock without causing offsetting changes through international reserves. Graphically, under a flexible exchange rate, the central bank's monetary policies, primarily open market operations, determine the position of the LM curve.[5] As long as the central bank doesn't purchase bonds from or sell bonds to the public, the money stock remains unchanged and the LM curve remains stationary.[6]

Exchange rate flexibility's role in breaking the link between the balance of payments and the domestic money stock was the primary argument used by early supporters of a move to flexible exchange rates. Proponents of flexible rates argued that freeing the domestic money stock from the constraint imposed by the balance of payments would allow policy makers to use monetary policy more effectively to pursue internal balance, or full employment.[7] We'll see in a later chapter that, after the inflationary 1970s, opponents of flexible exchange rates reversed the argument and claimed that freeing monetary authorities to pursue internal balance permitted overly expansionary monetary policies that caused a dramatic increase in inflation rates.[8]

---

5. Open market operations refer to central bank sales of government bonds to the public or purchases of government bonds from the public. Other tools of monetary policy include changes in the required reserve ratio, the percentage of their deposits that banks are required to hold in reserves, and changes in the discount rate, the interest rate that the central bank charges banks to borrow reserves.

6. For now, we ignore the possibility of changes in money demand other than those arising from changes in Q or i.

7. Note, however, that policy makers lose their ability to dictate the exchange rate. A fixed exchange rate regime allows control of the exchange rate but not the money stock. A flexible exchange rate allows control of the money stock but not the exchange rate.

8. These arguments will play prominent roles in later chapters in which we relax the fixed-price-level assumption.

2 MACROECONOMIC POLICY WITH IMMOBILE CAPITAL

Recall that with zero capital mobility, the balance of payments simply equals the current-account balance. For each value of the exchange rate, a unique income coincides with a zero current-account balance. Because the unique income that corresponds to external balance varies with the exchange rate, any policy capable of affecting the exchange rate has the potential to bring the economy into simultaneous internal and external balance—by altering the income required for external balance to match that required for internal balance.

2.1 Fiscal Policy

In Figure 1, a rise in government purchases or a cut in taxes shifts the IS curve from IS^0 to IS^1 by raising total expenditure on domestically produced goods and services.[9] The initial effect raises income, because total expenditure has risen, and the interest rate. The rise in the interest rate is necessary to offset the effect of increased income on the demand for money, because the money stock remains fixed at all points along LM^0.[10] At the new

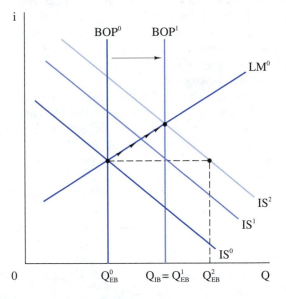

Figure 1   **Short-Run Effects of Fiscal Policy with Immobile Capital**

An expansionary fiscal policy shifts the IS curve from IS^0 to IS^1, raising income and the interest rate. The current-account balance moves into deficit, and the domestic currency depreciates. The depreciation raises the income consistent with external balance (shifting the BOP curve to the right) and lowers the relative price of domestic goods (shifting the IS curve from IS^1 to IS^2). At the new equilibrium, income, the interest rate, and the exchange rate are higher. The domestic crowding-out effect of the rise in the interest rate prevents income from rising to Q_{EB}^2.

---

9. See section 8 of the chapter on the market for goods and services for a review.

10. See section 2.5 of the chapter on the markets for money and foreign exchange for a review.

higher income, imports rise and the balance of payments shifts into deficit.[11] The exchange rate responds to the excess demand for foreign exchange by a domestic currency depreciation. The rise in the exchange rate lowers the relative price of domestic goods and services ($R \equiv P/eP^*$) and, therefore, raises the current-account balance at each income. The current-account balance now equals zero at a higher income, so the BOP curve shifts to the right from BOP^0 to BOP^1. The same fall in the relative price of domestic goods and services shifts expenditure toward those goods and moves the IS curve still further to the right to IS^2. In other words, the depreciation shifts both the BOP and IS curves to the right until they intersect on the original LM curve.

At the new equilibrium, income, the interest rate, and the exchange rate all are higher. The rise in the interest rate that accompanies an expansionary fiscal policy prevents an even larger rise in income by crowding out a portion of private investment expenditure. In terms of Figure 1, crowding out causes income to rise to only Q^1_{EB} rather than to Q^2_{EB}.

Fiscal policy brings the external-balance requirement into harmony with that for internal balance *by generating a depreciation of the currency*.[12] However, governments often seem reluctant to permit their currencies to depreciate. This reluctance has at least two sources. First, a currency depreciation raises the price of imported goods to consumers and the cost of imported inputs to domestic firms. Both groups will lobby against policies that would cause a currency depreciation, although exporters and import-competing firms will lobby for them. Second, an increase in the exchange rate often is called a "weakness" of the currency and thus interpreted as a sign of weakness of the economy.[13] The combination of these two factors may cause governments to intervene in foreign exchange markets to prevent a currency depreciation—even under a supposedly flexible-rate regime. Should this occur, the fiscal policy's expansionary effect disappears, and the appropriate analysis becomes that under a fixed exchange rate as discussed in section 3.1 of the preceding chapter. This possibility calls for a certain amount of caution in evaluating fiscal policy's likely effects.

A second cautionary note in evaluating the effect of fiscal policy centers on the assumption of capital immobility. We'll see that fiscal policy's effectiveness under flexible exchange rates hinges on capital immobility. As capital becomes more internationally mobile, the prospects for fiscal policy restoring internal balance fade because, as we'll see, such a policy tends to cause a currency appreciation rather than depreciation. As the world economy becomes more integrated, capital tends to become more mobile. Efforts to achieve capital immobility often take the form of capital controls that are costly to administer, interfere with the efficient allocation of capital, lead to black markets and other means of circumvention, and tend to be ineffective at least in the long run.[14]

2.2 **Monetary Policy**

The most important effect of a move to a flexible exchange rate is the elimination of foreign exchange market intervention and its effect on the domestic money stock.

---

11. To work step-by-step through the policy's effects, we say that the balance of payments moves into deficit, which causes the currency to depreciate. In fact, the depreciation of the currency prevents the deficit from actually arising; such a deficit is an *incipient* one. An incipient surplus would be a balance-of-payments surplus that would occur in the absence of a currency appreciation.

12. Of course, internal balance doesn't happen automatically in response to *any* expansionary fiscal policy. Policy makers must calibrate the magnitude of the policy to the increase in income required to reach internal balance.

13. See section 4.1 of the chapter on the market for goods and services for a discussion of the dangers of identifying a balance-of-payments surplus (deficit) or a currency appreciation (depreciation) with improvement (deterioration) of the economy.

14. See Cases Four and Seven in the preceding chapter.

Once changes in the central bank's foreign exchange reserves are eliminated, the money stock changes in response to open market operations:[15]

$$\Delta M = mm \cdot (\Delta GB + \Delta FXR) \qquad [1]$$

Thus, $\Delta FXR = 0$ implies that:

$$\Delta M = mm \cdot \Delta GB \qquad [2]$$

The requirement of external balance no longer constrains the size of the domestic money stock, although its size will affect the exchange rate. The central bank can choose any value for the money stock, but it must be willing to accept the implied exchange rate.[16]

The initial effect of a money stock expansion through an open market purchase is a drop in the domestic interest rate and a rise in income, as illustrated in Figure 2 by the shift from LM^0 to LM^1. The lower interest rate encourages private investment spending, which raises total expenditure and income. The change in the interest rate has no direct

---

Figure 2   Short-Run Effects of Monetary Policy with Immobile Capital

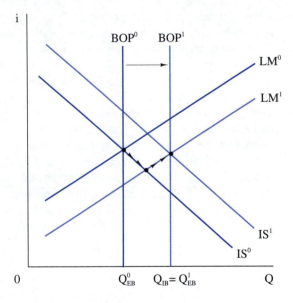

An increase in the money stock causes income to rise and interest rates to fall to equalize the quantity of money demanded with the new, higher stock. As income rises, the current account moves toward a deficit and the currency depreciates. The depreciation lowers the relative price of domestic goods, shifts spending toward domestic and away from foreign goods, and raises the income consistent with external balance.

---

15. The central bank can also alter the money stock by using other policy tools, including changes in the discount rate and in the required reserve ratio. The introduction of these additional tools wouldn't alter the basic conclusion that the move to a flexible exchange rate breaks the link between the balance of payments and the money stock and places control over the nominal money stock in the central bank's hands.

16. Note that under a fixed exchange rate, the central bank could choose the level at which to peg the exchange rate but would have to accept the implied money stock.

Policy	Effect on Equilibrium Q	Effect on Equilibrium Exchange Rate[a]	Effect on Equilibrium Current-Account Balance
Fiscal Policy:			
Increase in G	+	+	0[b]
Decrease in G	−	−	0[b]
Monetary Policy:			
Increase in M	+	+	0[b]
Decrease in M	−	−	0[b]

Table 2   SHORT-RUN POLICY EFFECTS WITH IMMOBILE CAPITAL

[a]A plus sign denotes a rise in e (domestic currency depreciation); a minus sign denotes a fall in e (domestic currency appreciation).
[b]With completely immobile capital, only a current-account balance of zero is consistent with balance-of-payments equilibrium.

effect on the balance of payments when capital is completely unresponsive to changes in the international pattern of interest rates. The higher income leads to more imports and a current-account deficit, so the domestic currency depreciates. The depreciation shifts both the BOP and IS curves to the right, to BOP[1] and IS[1] (*Why?*), until they intersect on the new LM curve at a higher income.

In fact, monetary policy raises income precisely *because* it generates a currency depreciation that lowers the relative price of domestically produced goods and services. Again, depreciation may prove unpopular with consumers, who face higher prices for imported goods, and with producers who face higher prices for imported inputs. On the other hand, exporters and firms that sell import-competing products tend to view a currency depreciation favorably. Monetary policy therefore not only changes the level of income but also redistributes income among sectors of the domestic economy.

2.3 Summary of Policy Effects with Immobile Capital

With a flexible exchange rate and immobile capital, either fiscal or monetary policy can raise the economy's level of income or GDP in the short run. Both expansionary policies work through their ability to depreciate the domestic currency and shift expenditure toward domestically produced goods and services. Table 2 summarizes fiscal and monetary policies' effects on income, the exchange rate, and the current account. (*Compare Table 2 with Table 2 in the preceding chapter, and make sure you can explain the reasons behind any differences.*)

3 MACROECONOMIC POLICY WITH PERFECTLY MOBILE CAPITAL

The years since the move to more flexible exchange rates have also brought increased integration of world capital markets. The world's major trading economies now engage in extensive trade in stocks, bonds, and other financial assets as well as goods and services. These trends make the analysis of macroeconomic policies under flexible exchange rates and mobile capital particularly important. Of course, a number of smaller economies remain largely outside the growing world capital market and have tended to remain under some form of fixed exchange rate system (see Table 1 in the preceding chapter).

3.1 Fiscal Policy

Highly mobile capital reduces fiscal policy's effectiveness under flexible exchange rates.[17] Recall that fiscal policy works to alter income with immobile capital because of the accompanying currency depreciation. With highly mobile capital, expansionary fiscal policy no longer causes a depreciation of the domestic currency but an appreciation. The appreciation causes a second form of the **crowding-out** phenomenon: As the domestic currency appreciates (e falls), the relative price of domestic goods rises because $R \equiv P/eP^*$, and individuals shift their expenditure toward the now relatively cheaper foreign goods.[18] This decline in private expenditure on domestic goods partially or totally offsets the increased government purchases, depending on whether asset holders perceive the fiscal policy as temporary or permanent.

POLICY EXPECTED TO BE TEMPORARY In Figure 3, panel (a), expansionary fiscal policy initially raises spending on domestic goods and services and shifts the IS curve from IS^0 to IS^1. Income rises, and the interest rate must rise to keep the quantity demanded of money equal to the fixed money stock. As the domestic interest rate rises, capital flows into the economy and the balance of payments moves into surplus at point 2. The surplus causes the domestic currency to appreciate. If participants in the foreign exchange market perceive the increased government spending as temporary, they also will expect the accompanying currency appreciation to be temporary, keeping their expected future spot exchange rate, e^e, unaffected. The spot appreciation coupled with an unchanged expected future spot rate shifts the BOP line up to BOP^1. (*Explain why, using uncovered interest parity.*)[19]

The currency appreciation also shifts the IS curve leftward to IS^2 as the relative price of domestic goods and services rises. The temporary rise in government spending moves the economy to the intersection of IS^2, LM^0, and BOP^1 at point 3, with income and the interest rate higher than before the expansionary fiscal policy. The domestic currency has appreciated, and the current-account balance has shifted toward a deficit.

Panel (b) of Figure 3 allows us to view events in the foreign exchange market more explicitly. In the diagram, we denote the foreign currency simply as FX. We saw in panel (a) that the initial shift to the right in the IS curve due to increased government spending on domestic goods and services pushes up the domestic interest rate from i_0 to i_1. This raises the expected rate of return on domestic-currency-denominated deposits relative to that on foreign-currency ones. In the foreign exchange market in panel (b), the demand for foreign-currency deposits shifts to the left in response to the decline in their expected rate of return. At the original exchange rate of e_0, market participants now want to hold fewer foreign-currency deposits in their asset portfolios. Market participants' efforts to rid themselves of the extra foreign-currency deposits bids down the domestic price of foreign currency; that is, the domestic currency appreciates to e_1 at point 3.

---

17. Capital is highly mobile when small changes in international interest rate differentials generate large capital flows.

18. The first, or domestic, form of crowding out is the decline in private investment spending caused by a rise in government purchases.

19. Market participants expect the currency appreciation to be reversed; in other words, they expect a depreciation of the domestic currency. To compensate them for holding deposits denominated in the domestic currency during its expected depreciation, asset holders require a higher domestic interest rate (i_1 rather than i_0 in Figure 3).

Figure 3 Short-Run Effects of Fiscal Policy with Perfectly Mobile Capital

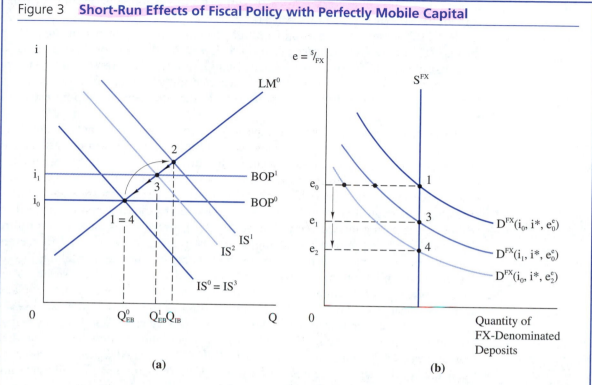

(a) **(b)**

In panel (a), the initial direct effect of an expansionary fiscal policy (illustrated by the movement of the IS curve from IS^0 to IS^1) is to raise income and interest rates. The higher domestic interest rate (at point 2) generates a capital inflow and appreciation of the domestic currency. If the fiscal policy is perceived as temporary, the BOP line shifts to BOP^1. As the exchange rate falls, domestic goods and services become more expensive relative to foreign ones. Individuals respond to the change in relative prices by shifting expenditure to foreign goods. The fall in private expenditure shifts the IS curve back to IS^2, at point 3. If the policy is perceived as permanent, the appreciation doesn't shift the BOP line but shifts the IS curve all the way back to IS^3, and equilibrium is restored at the original income level at point 4. Panel (b) traces the corresponding events in the foreign exchange market.

POLICY EXPECTED TO BE PERMANENT If participants in the foreign exchange market expect the rise in government purchases to be permanent, they also will expect the accompanying appreciation of the domestic currency to persist, so e^e will fall along with e. In panel (a) of Figure 3, the currency appreciation no longer shifts the BOP curve because, as long as $e = e^e$, i_0 is consistent with foreign exchange market equilibrium for the given foreign interest rate. (*Show why, using the interest parity condition.*) With the BOP line unchanged at BOP^0, the balance-of-payments surplus at point 2 is larger than in the case of a temporary policy discussed earlier. The larger surplus requires a larger currency appreciation to restore balance-of-payments equilibrium on BOP^0. The larger appreciation shifts the IS curve further to the left, since the appreciation raises the relative price of domestic goods and shifts spending toward imports.

Equilibrium is restored when the IS and BOP curves again intersect on the LM curve, but this can't happen until income falls all the way back to its original level. As long as income remains above Q_{EB}^0, the demand for money exceeds the money stock at i_0; thus, the interest rate must be above i_0. Perfect capital mobility implies that capital will flow into the economy and cause the currency to appreciate as long as the interest rate remains above i_0. The IS curve continues to shift to the left until the appreciation stops. This can happen only when the interest rate has fallen back to i_0, restoring balance-of-payments equilibrium at point 4 in Figure 3, panel (a).

Panel (b) of Figure 3 focuses on adjustments in the foreign exchange market. When the expected future spot exchange rate drops below e_0^e, the demand for FX-denominated deposits shifts to the left as their expected rate of return falls. The result is a larger spot appreciation of the domestic currency than occurred in the case in which expansionary fiscal policy was expected to be temporary; e_2 denotes the new equilibrium exchange rate at point 4.

Expansionary fiscal policy that's expected to persist can't bring the economy into internal balance when capital is very responsive to interest rates because it generates a large appreciation of the domestic currency. The currency appreciation, acting through the current-account balance, crowds out enough private expenditure on domestic goods and services to offset the expansionary effect of the increased government spending. Although the expansionary fiscal policy leaves total income unchanged, it reallocates spending toward the public sector. It also reallocates income away from export-oriented and import-competing sectors of the economy and toward sectors insulated from the effects of foreign trade, such as construction and retailing. Just as depreciations prove unpopular with consumers and with firms that use imported inputs, currency appreciations are unwelcome in sectors of the economy tightly linked to international trade. For example, the appreciation of the dollar in the early 1980s proved unpopular with trade-oriented sectors of the U.S. economy and led to increased pressure for protectionism. What was the most commonly cited reason for that dramatic rise of the dollar during the early 1980s? The United States' expansionary fiscal policy, dramatically represented by the federal government's rapidly growing budget deficit.[20]

3.2 Monetary Policy

Although fiscal policy is largely or completely ineffective under a flexible exchange rate with mobile capital because of the resulting currency appreciation, monetary policy becomes effective in the same circumstances because it produces a currency depreciation. The depreciation lowers the relative price of domestic goods, which stimulates spending and income. Also unlike the fiscal-policy case, expectations that monetary policy changes are permanent rather than temporary enhance the policy's effectiveness.

POLICY EXPECTED TO BE TEMPORARY An open market purchase of government bonds increases the money stock by an amount equal to the money multiplier times the magnitude of the purchase (from Equation 2) and shifts the LM curve in Figure 4, panel (a), from LM^0 to LM^1. As the money stock rises, income and the interest rate must adjust to keep the quantity demanded of money equal to the growing stock. Income rises, and the interest rate falls, both of which increase the quantity of money that individuals in the economy choose to hold at point 2. The fall in the interest rate causes capital to flow out of the country and moves the balance of payments toward a deficit. The deficit depreciates the domestic currency.[21]

---

20. Case Four in this chapter investigates the relationship between the government budget deficit and the exchange rate.

21. Recall that the deficit is an incipient one. The actual deficit is prevented by the depreciation, but it is helpful in understanding the logic of the adjustment process.

If the expansionary monetary policy is expected to be temporary, the accompanying depreciation will be perceived as temporary as well, implying that e^e remains unchanged at e_0^e. The spot depreciation shifts the BOP line down to BOP^1. (*Why?*)[22] The depreciation also lowers the relative price of domestic goods and shifts the IS curve to the right (to IS^1) until it intersects the new BOP^1 curve on the new LM^1 curve at point 3. The expansionary monetary policy's overall effect is to raise income, depreciate the currency, and move the current-account balance toward a surplus.

Panel (b) of Figure 4 highlights adjustments in the foreign exchange market. Beginning from point 1, the increase in the money stock puts downward pressure on the domestic interest rate, originally at i_0. The decline in the interest rate to i_1 lowers the

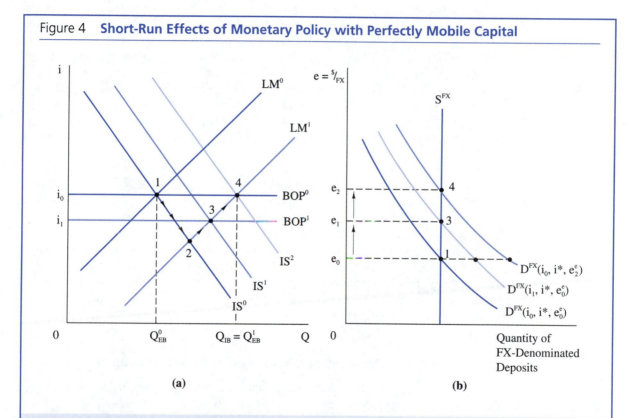

Figure 4   Short-Run Effects of Monetary Policy with Perfectly Mobile Capital

An open market purchase of government bonds by the central bank moves the LM curve from LM^0 to LM^1. Income rises and the interest rate falls to make individuals willing to hold the new, larger stock of money. Because capital flows are very sensitive to interest rate changes, the fall in the domestic interest rate causes a large capital outflow at point 2. The resulting balance-of-payments deficit causes the domestic currency to depreciate. As the exchange rate rises, domestic goods become less expensive compared to foreign ones and spending shifts in favor of domestic goods. The IS curve moves to the right. If the monetary policy is perceived as temporary, e^e doesn't change and the depreciation shifts the BOP line down to BOP^1; the new equilibrium is at point 3. If the policy is perceived as permanent, e^e rises along with e and the BOP line doesn't shift in response to the (now larger) depreciation, but the IS curve shifts further to IS^2, restoring equilibrium at point 4. Panel (b) illustrates the corresponding adjustment in the foreign exchange market.

---

22. This follows directly from uncovered interest parity. If the currency depreciates with no change in e^e, the currency is expected to appreciate. Because of the expected appreciation, portfolio owners are content to hold the existing quantity of domestic-currency deposits at a lower interest rate (i_1) than they would if the currency were not expected to appreciate (i_0).

expected rate of return on domestic-currency-denominated deposits and, therefore, increases demand for foreign-currency ones. At the original exchange rate, e_0, market participants now want to hold more than the existing quantity of foreign-currency deposits. As portfolio owners try to accumulate such deposits, they bid up their price. In other words, the domestic currency depreciates from e_0 to e_1, the new exchange rate at which participants in the foreign exchange market willingly hold the existing stock of deposits in each currency. As the exchange rate rises, the expected future exchange rate doesn't change from e_0^e, because market participants perceive the current depreciation as temporary. The new equilibrium occurs at point 3.

POLICY EXPECTED TO BE PERMANENT If participants in the foreign exchange market expect the expansionary monetary policy to be permanent, they'll expect the currency depreciation to be permanent as well. The expected future exchange rate then rises with e. In this case, in panel (a), the depreciation does *not* shift the BOP curve, which remains at BOP^0. (*Why?*) The large balance-of-payments deficit at point 2 (larger than in the case of the temporary monetary policy) causes a larger currency depreciation, and shifts the IS curve further to the right to IS^2. At the new equilibrium at point 4 in panel (a), income is high enough to make individuals willing to hold the higher stock of money balances at the old interest rate. Only when this is true can the interest rate return to its original level at i_0, halting capital outflows and the currency depreciation.

In panel (b) of Figure 4, when the expected future exchange rate rises above e_0^e, the demand for foreign-currency-denominated deposits shifts to the right as their expected rate of return increases. (*Why?*) The result is a larger spot depreciation of the domestic currency than occurred in the case in which monetary policy was expected to be temporary; e_2 denotes the new equilibrium exchange rate at point 4.

Monetary policy—temporary or permanent—raises income because it causes the domestic currency to depreciate, and the depreciation again alters the distribution as well as the level of income. Export and import-competing sectors of the economy gain relative to nontraded-goods sectors, consumers of imported goods, and firms that are heavy users of imported inputs. The current-account balance moves toward a surplus.

3.3 Summary of Policy Effects with Perfectly Mobile Capital

Table 3 summarizes fiscal and monetary policies' short-run effects on the macroeconomy. Perfectly mobile capital reduces fiscal policy's effectiveness under flexible exchange rates. With highly mobile capital, expansionary fiscal policy causes a currency appreciation, rather than a depreciation as in the zero capital mobility case. The currency appreciation generates a second type of crowding out: As the domestic currency appreciates, the relative price of domestic goods rises, and expenditure shifts toward now-cheaper foreign goods. This shift of expenditure away from domestic goods partially or totally offsets the increased government spending, depending on whether participants in the foreign exchange market perceive the fiscal policy as temporary or permanent. (*Compare Table 3 below with Table 3 in the preceding chapter, and make sure you understand the source of any differences.*)

Although fiscal policy generates partial or complete crowding out because of the accompanying appreciation, monetary policy becomes highly effective in the same circumstances because it produces a currency depreciation. The depreciation stimulates spending on domestic goods by lowering their relative price. Also unlike the fiscal-policy case, expectations that monetary policy changes are permanent rather than temporary enhance the policy's effectiveness because they generate a larger currency depreciation.

Table 3 **SHORT-RUN POLICY EFFECTS WITH PERFECTLY MOBILE CAPITAL**

Policy	Effect on Equilibrium Q	Effect on Equilibrium Exchange Rate[a]	Effect on Equilibrium Current-Account Balance
Fiscal Policy:			
Perceived as temporary			
Increase in G	+	−	−
Decrease in G	−	+	+
Perceived as permanent			
Increase in G	0[b]	−	−
Decrease in G	0[b]	+	+
Monetary Policy:			
Perceived as temporary			
Increase in M	+	+	+
Decrease in M	−	−	−
Perceived as permanent			
Increase in M	+	+	+
Decrease in M	−	−	−

[a]A plus sign denotes a rise in e or currency depreciation; a minus sign denotes a decline in e or currency appreciation.
[b]Completely crowded out through change in the real exchange rate.

4 MACROECONOMIC POLICY WITH IMPERFECTLY MOBILE CAPITAL

Most countries operate under an intermediate degree of capital mobility represented by an upward-sloping BOP curve. If income rises, the current account moves into deficit, and a rise in the domestic interest rate is needed to bring about an offsetting capital inflow. The more sensitive capital flows are to the interest rate, the smaller the required rise in the interest rate and the flatter the BOP curve. As in the preceding chapter, we'll concentrate on the case in which capital is very sensitive to interest rates and the BOP curve thus is flatter than the LM curve. (*A good way to test your understanding of the following analyses: Construct analogous analyses for the low-mobility case in which the BOP curve is steeper than the LM curve.*)

4.1 Fiscal Policy

Fiscal policy may raise income with imperfectly mobile capital, but the expansionary effect is at least partially offset by an appreciating currency that induces a shift toward foreign goods and away from domestic ones. In Figure 5, the expansionary fiscal policy's initial effect is a shift of the IS curve from IS^0 to IS^1. Income rises because of the increased spending on domestic output. The interest rate too must rise to keep the quantity demanded of money equal to the unchanged money stock. In response to the rise in the domestic interest rate, capital flows into the economy.

The balance of payments moves into surplus, and the currency appreciates. The BOP curve shifts to the left (BOP^0 to BOP^1) as a result of the appreciation. Because of the movement from domestic to foreign goods, at each interest rate

---

Figure 5   **Short-Run Effects of Fiscal Policy with Imperfectly Mobile Capital**

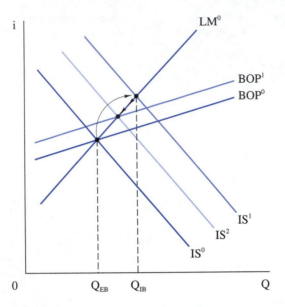

A rise in government purchases shifts the IS curve to the right and raises income and the interest rate. With high capital mobility, capital flows into the economy and the currency appreciates. As the exchange rate falls, the relative price of domestic goods rises. A shift in expenditure to now relatively cheaper foreign goods at least partially offsets the policy's initial expenditure-increasing effect by shifting IS back to the left. Perceptions that the policy is permanent rather than temporary make the policy less effective in raising income.

---

balance-of-payments equilibrium requires a lower income. (*Why?*)[23] The IS curve also shifts to the left as individuals respond to the fall in e by switching spending from domestic to foreign goods. The new equilibrium occurs where the IS^2 and BOP^1 curves intersect on the LM curve.

The precise effects on income, the interest rate, and the exchange rate depend on whether the policy is perceived as temporary or permanent. If temporary, the leftward shift of the BOP line is relatively large because of the expected future depreciation, and the leftward shift of the IS curve is relatively small because of the relatively small BOP surplus; expansionary fiscal policy can then substantially raise income. However, if the policy is perceived as permanent, the leftward shift of the BOP line is small and that of the IS line is large (*Why?*), leaving income little affected by the fiscal policy.

Regardless of whether the fiscal policy is perceived as temporary or permanent, income rises by less than it would were the policy not accompanied by a currency appreciation. The appreciation makes domestically produced goods more expensive relative to foreign ones, and the resulting shift away from spending on domestic goods at least partially offsets the expansionary effect of the fiscal policy. The more mobile capital, the larger the currency appreciation and the smaller the fiscal policy's impact on income. Likewise, the more permanent the policy is perceived as being, the larger the currency appreciation and the smaller the effect on income.

---

23. For a review, see section 4.2 of the chapter on the markets for money and foreign exchange.

The crowding-out effect through the real exchange rate was the center of much attention in the United States during the early 1980s. Fiscal policy was expansionary, and the dollar appreciated dramatically against many trading partners' currencies. The dollar's appreciation, in turn, contributed to rising imports in industries such as steel, automobiles, textiles, and footwear, and to reduced exports of agricultural products. The expansionary fiscal policy's net effect was to increase income, but the accompanying appreciation dampened the policy's impact on income and adversely affected trade-sensitive U.S. industries.

4.2 Monetary Policy

Capital mobility contributes to monetary policy's effectiveness in raising income under a flexible exchange rate regime. This follows from the fact that the currency depreciation that accompanies an expansionary monetary policy gives the economy an extra boost through its effect on domestic and foreign relative prices. The more mobile is capital, the larger the depreciation that follows a given monetary expansion and the greater the fall in the relative price of domestic goods. Similarly, the more permanent the expansionary monetary policy is perceived to be, the larger is the currency depreciation.

Figure 6 traces the effect of an expansionary monetary policy. The initial rightward shift of the LM curve from LM^0 to LM^1 lowers the domestic interest rate and creates a capital outflow. The outflow moves the balance of payments toward a deficit and generates a depreciation of the domestic currency. The depreciation shifts the BOP curve to the right to BOP^1. The more permanent the policy is perceived as being, the smaller will be the

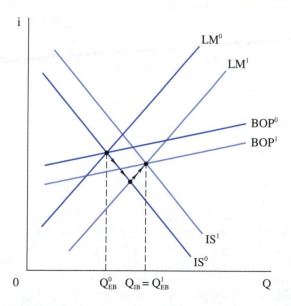

Figure 6   Short-Run Effects of Monetary Policy with Imperfectly Mobile Capital

An increase in the money stock raises income and lowers the interest rate. A capital outflow depreciates the currency, lowering the relative price of domestic goods. Spending switches to domestic goods, and the IS curve shifts to the right. The depreciation of the currency makes monetary policy an effective instrument for reaching internal balance. Perceptions that the policy is permanent rather than temporary (resulting in a smaller shift in the BOP curve and a larger shift in the IS curve) make it more effective in raising income.

rightward shift in the BOP line and the larger will be the depreciation. (*Why? See footnote 22.*) As a result of the depreciation, the relative price of domestic goods falls and demand shifts toward domestic goods, moving the IS curve to the right to IS^1. Again, the more permanent the policy, the larger the deficit and the depreciation, and the larger the shift in the IS curve. The new equilibrium occurs at the income at which the IS^1 and BOP^1 curves intersect on the LM^1 curve. Through the accompanying currency depreciation, the expansionary monetary policy favors export and import-competing sectors of the domestic economy.

5 THE POLICY MIX

The analysis in the preceding section suggests that fiscal and, to a greater extent, monetary policy can be used to pursue internal balance under a flexible exchange rate with imperfectly mobile capital. Which combination of the two available policies should policy makers use, or does it matter? The choice of fiscal and monetary **policy mix** does matter, because each combination results in a different domestic interest rate and exchange rate which, as we've noted all along, can dramatically affect distribution in different sectors of the domestic economy.

5.1 Examples of Policy Mixes

Figure 7 illustrates three policy mixes that policy makers could use to reach internal balance beginning from a point of external balance with unemployment, $Q_{EB} < Q_{IB}$. The economy begins at an identical point in each case. In panel (a), fiscal policy alone is used; panel (b) represents the use of monetary policy alone; and panel (c) illustrates the use of one of many possible combinations of fiscal and monetary policy. Each scenario is designed to achieve the same level of output: the one corresponding to internal balance, Q_{IB}. However, each policy mix has different implications for the allocation of expenditure between the private and public sectors, for the performance of various industries within the economy, and for the status of the current and capital accounts of the balance of payments.

In panel (a) of Figure 7, expansionary fiscal policy raises both income and the interest rate and appreciates the domestic currency. The rise in the interest rate reduces private spending in those sectors most sensitive to interest rates—consumer durables such as automobiles and appliances, firms' investment in new plants and equipment, and construction. The currency appreciation switches expenditure from domestically produced to foreign-produced goods by causing a change in relative prices. Export and import-competing industries suffer from this change in the expenditure pattern. Both effects of fiscal policy—crowding out by a rise in the interest rate and crowding out by currency appreciation—reduce private expenditure on domestic output, partially offsetting the policy's expansionary effect on income. The net effect is an increase in income, a rise in the share of spending accounted for by the public rather than the private sector, and a decline in both interest-sensitive and trade-oriented sectors of the economy.

Panel (b) of Figure 7 represents an expansionary monetary policy intended to have the same net effect on income as the fiscal policy illustrated in panel (a). The other effects of the two policies are quite different, however. The expansionary monetary policy lowers the domestic interest rate, and private investment expenditure rises. Interest-sensitive sectors, such as consumer durables and construction, benefit. The domestic currency depreciates, and trade-oriented sectors find their performances improved. Consumers with a taste for imported goods and firms that use imported inputs, on the other hand, face higher prices for those products as a result of the rise in the exchange rate.

The use of either expansionary fiscal policy or expansionary monetary policy obviously has important domestic implications. Each allows some groups to gain

Figure 7   Use of Various Policy Mixes to Achieve Internal Balance

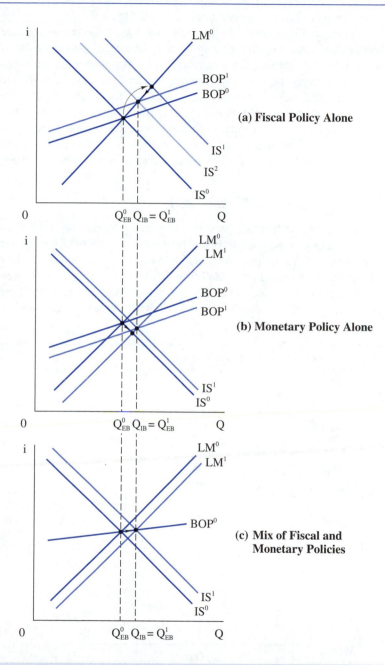

Policy makers can use many fiscal/monetary policy combinations to increase income to Q_{IB}. Each combination results in different values of the interest rate and the exchange rate. Expansionary fiscal policy alone (panel (a)) produces the highest interest rate, monetary policy alone the lowest (panel (b)), and a policy mix an intermediate value (panel (c)). Expansionary fiscal policy appreciates the domestic currency; monetary policy alone depreciates it; and the illustrated policy mix leaves the exchange rate unchanged.

relative to others. One way to limit the extent of these distributional effects is to use a combination of both types of expansionary policy. A large number of such mixes exist that would move the economy to Q_{IB} in Figure 7.

Panel (c) illustrates a policy mix that leaves the exchange rate unchanged. The interest rate rises slightly, causing a small amount of crowding out of interest-sensitive industries. But teaming the expansionary fiscal policy with an expansionary monetary policy moderates the rise in the interest rate and reduces the magnitude of crowding out from the fiscal-policy-only case in panel (a). The accompanying monetary policy also keeps the currency from appreciating; this prevents a rise in the relative price of domestically produced goods. At the same time, the combination keeps the exchange rate from depreciating and prevents a rise in the domestic price of imported goods and inputs, as would happen if policy makers used monetary policy alone (panel (b)).

5.2 Responding to Disturbances

The policy mix with which policy makers choose to pursue internal balance depends on, among other things, the nature of the disturbance that pushed the economy below full employment.[24] Such disturbances fall into two broad categories: shifts in tastes away from domestically produced goods and increases in the demand for real money balances.

Beginning from a position of internal balance (point 1 in Figure 8), suppose the economy experiences a shift in consumer tastes away from domestically produced goods

---

Figure 8   **Policy Responses to a Spending Disturbance**

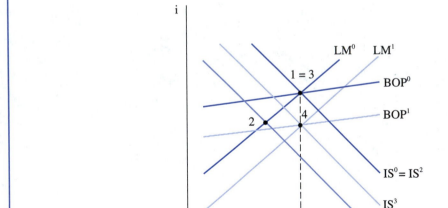

Policy makers can respond to a contractionary spending disturbance with an expansionary fiscal or monetary policy. A fiscal policy restores full employment at the original interest rate and exchange rate (point 3). A monetary policy restores full employment but magnifies the disturbance's effect on the interest rate and exchange rate (point 4).

---

24. Of course, the economy can experience expansionary disturbances that push income above the full-employment level. We concentrate on contractionary disturbances, which call for expansionary policy responses, because we've focused on the impact of expansionary policies.

and services. Potential causes of such a shift could include pessimism about the future, leading to an overall reduction in consumption or investment spending, or a shift in consumer preferences in favor of foreign goods and services rather than domestic ones.[25] We can represent such a spending disturbance by a shift to the left of the IS curve, from IS^0 to IS^1. Income falls below the level consistent with internal balance, and the domestic currency depreciates because of the decline in the domestic interest rate at point 2.

Policy makers might respond to a temporary shortfall in consumption or investment spending in one of two ways. An expansionary fiscal policy shifts IS back to the right to IS^2 and restores full employment at the same interest rate and exchange rate as before the disturbance (point 3). The alternative is an expansionary monetary policy. By shifting LM to the right to LM^1, such a policy puts further downward pressure on the interest rate and causes a further currency depreciation, which shifts the IS curve and BOP curve to the right, to IS^3 and BOP^1. Monetary policy restores full employment, but with a lower interest rate and a depreciated value of the domestic currency at point 4. As noted in section 5.1, the different values of the interest rate and the exchange rate implied by fiscal and monetary policies carry important implications for the performance of specific sectors of the economy, even though either can restore overall full employment.

A second type of contractionary economic disturbance consists of a rise in the demand for real money balances for a given value of income and the interest rate. Beginning from a point of full employment (point 1), such a shock shifts the LM curve to the left, as in Figure 9.[26]

Figure 9   Policy Responses to a Money-Demand Disturbance

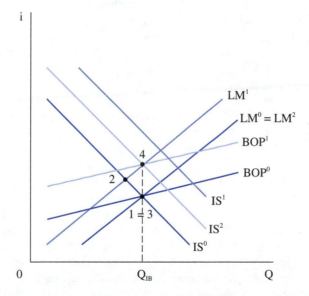

Possible policy responses to a contractionary monetary disturbance include expansionary fiscal or monetary policy. An expansionary fiscal policy restores full employment but exacerbates the rise in the interest rate and the currency appreciation (point 4). Monetary policy restores full employment at the pre-disturbance interest rate and exchange rate (point 3).

---

25. The exogenous spending disturbances under consideration here do *not* include changes in response to the domestic interest rate, domestic income, or the relative price of domestic goods and services, but rather shifts in spending for given levels of those variables.

26. Section 2.5 of the chapter on the markets for money and foreign exchange explains why.

Again, output falls below the full-employment level. The disturbance raises the domestic interest rate and causes a currency appreciation (at point 2).

If policy makers respond with an expansionary monetary policy, LM shifts back to the right, restoring full employment at the original interest rate and exchange rate (point 3). If, instead, policy makers respond with expansionary fiscal policy, the IS curve shifts to the right to IS^1. This puts further upward pressure on the interest rate and causes further currency appreciation. As the domestic currency appreciates, the IS and BOP curves shift to the left to IS^2 and BOP^1. The economy returns to full employment at point 4, with a higher interest rate and a lower value of the exchange rate than prior to the disturbance to money demand.

5.3 Constraints on the Policy Mix

Several considerations not obvious in our analysis of Figures 8 and 9 considerably complicate policy makers' choice of policy mix. For example, we assumed that the level of output consistent with full employment is known, as is how the actual level of output compares with full employment (often called the *output gap*). However, as we saw in the last chapter, defining the full-employment level of output for an economy is a complex task, as is judging whether the current level of output is consistent with, above, or below full employment. Policy makers may disagree among themselves or with the public about the current state of the economy and, therefore, about the need for macroeconomic policies and the appropriate magnitudes of those policies.

We also assumed in our analysis that policy makers know the source of the disturbance to the economy, that is, whether the disturbance originates in the market for goods and services or in the money market. In fact, the nature of disturbances to the economy may be difficult to discern, particularly in the short run, during which policy makers must formulate their response. As Figures 8 and 9 make clear, responding to a spending disturbance with monetary policy or to a monetary disturbance with fiscal policy can exacerbate swings in the interest rate and the exchange rate and the accompanying distributional impacts on the economy.

Policy makers also must judge a disturbance's time horizon in order to make an appropriate policy response. If the decline in spending or increase in money demand is short-lived, then no response may be required, as the economy will return to full employment automatically as soon as the disturbance ends. If policy makers respond aggressively to a short-lived disturbance, they risk pushing output above the full-employment level and generating inflation. On the other hand, an overly passive response that relies too heavily on the temporary nature of the disturbance risks a prolonged period of unemployment if the disturbance turns out to be longer lived than policy makers expected. These timing decisions are complicated by the fact that macroeconomic policies typically affect the economy with lags that can be both long and variable.

Finally, policy makers may face political pressures that constrain their ability to use some macroeconomic policy tools. We've already mentioned one source of such pressure: the distributional implications of changes in interest rates and exchange rates. A second source of pressure comes from policy targets beyond internal and external balance. For example, the ability to use expansionary fiscal policy may be constrained by concerns over the implications of existing government budget deficits or debt. If a government accumulates a large debt during times of economic prosperity, it may find itself constrained against using fiscal policy to respond to a slump. Along similar lines, a government facing reelection may find it difficult to cut public spending—even if macroeconomic conditions point to the appropriateness of a contractionary fiscal-policy stance.

5.4 International Transmission and the Policy Mix

Domestic political considerations aren't the only constraints on macroeconomic policy makers. Different domestic macroeconomic policy mixes exert different effects on trading-partner economies, a phenomenon known as **transmission**; so the governments of those economies often attempt to influence the course of domestic macroeconomic policy.

With a high degree of capital mobility, if domestic policy makers respond to a contractionary disturbance with an expansionary fiscal policy, trading-partner economies typically experience an expansion as well. This happens because the fiscal policy appreciates the domestic currency or, equivalently, depreciates the foreign currency. The depreciation makes foreign-produced goods and services relatively cheaper, so expenditure on them rises. In contrast, if domestic policy makers respond to a contractionary disturbance with an expansionary monetary policy, trading partners are likely to feel the contraction. The domestic currency depreciates, or the foreign one appreciates. Foreign goods and services become more expensive relative to domestic ones, and consumers shift away from spending on foreign goods. Of course, how trading partners feel about these transmitted policy effects depends on the current state of their economies. A country fighting inflation may welcome a contractionary effect transmitted from abroad, while a country suffering from excessive unemployment would resent the same effect.

6 SUMMARY OF SHORT-RUN POLICY EFFECTIVENESS UNDER A FLEXIBLE EXCHANGE RATE

The short-run effectiveness of fiscal and monetary policy in pursuing a goal of internal balance under a flexible exchange rate regime critically depends on the degree of capital mobility. As capital mobility rises, monetary policy becomes more effective than fiscal policy because of its different impact on the exchange rate. Policy-induced changes in the exchange rate are important because, with the assumption of fixed domestic and foreign price levels, they're reflected directly in changes in the real exchange rate or relative prices of domestic and foreign goods. In such circumstances, any policy that can alter the exchange rate can shift expenditure between domestic and foreign goods.

Table 4 summarizes the effects of fiscal and monetary policy under flexible exchange rates with differing degrees of capital mobility. Because of the importance of changes in the exchange rate that accompany each policy, the table reports those as well.

Table 4 SHORT-RUN POLICY EFFECTIVENESS UNDER FLEXIBLE EXCHANGE RATES

Policy	Ability to Affect Income under a Flexible Exchange Rate		
	Immobile Capital	Highly Mobile Capital	Perfectly Mobile Capital
Fiscal	Effective (currency depreciates)	Somewhat effective[a] (currency appreciates)	Ineffective[a] (currency appreciates)
Monetary	Effective (currency depreciates)	Effective[b] (currency depreciates)	Very effective[b] (currency depreciates)

[a]Less effective if perceived as permanent than if perceived as temporary.
[b]More effective if perceived as permanent than if perceived as temporary.

CASE 1: THE JAPAN SLUMP

Japan

After years of envy-inspiring growth, the Japanese economy has struggled since the early 1990s. Growth has averaged only about 1 percent a year. Figure 10 traces the history of Japan's output gap, the percent difference between the country's actual real GDP and its full-employment, or potential, real GDP. The positive output gap of 3.7 recorded for 1990, for example, means that actual output that year exceeded full-employment output by 3.7 percent, a situation that, had it persisted, we would expect to lead to inflation. The gap of –3.5 for 2002, on the other hand, indicates that real GDP fell short of its full-employment level by 3.5 percent, an indication of sluggish macroeconomic performance. Since 1982, Japan has experienced 14 years of negative output gaps and only 8 years of above-potential output; since 1993, there have been nine years with negative output gaps and only two years with positive ones.

Japanese property and stock markets declined precipitously during the 1990s, as illustrated in Figure 11.

Figures 10 and 11 make clear that when the Asian financial crisis hit, in 1997, the Japanese economy already was weak.

Japanese policy makers repeatedly used expansionary fiscal policy in an attempt to get the economy moving. Nine separate fiscal-stimulus packages were enacted during the 1990s. By the time of the Asian financial crisis, Japan hesitated to use further expansionary fiscal policy because of the heavy government debt already accumulated during 1992–1996. Much of that government spending had gone toward public construction programs, notoriously expensive and inefficient in Japan. The country is known for its highways and bridges to nowhere, built in response to political pressure from rural special-interest groups. So, while the number of yen spent on government purchases looked impressive, their actual macroeconomic impact was limited. In 1996, when policy makers sensed a small upturn in the economy,

---

Figure 10   Japanese Output Gap, 1982–2003

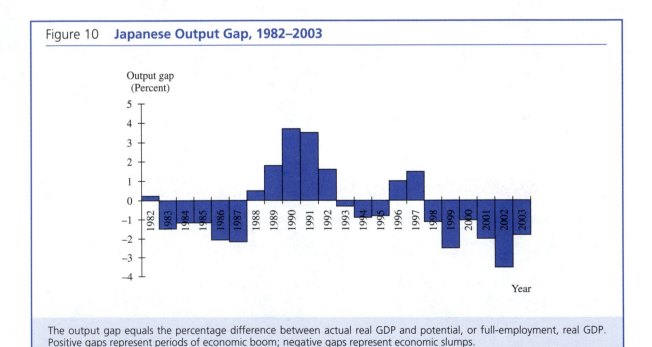

The output gap equals the percentage difference between actual real GDP and potential, or full-employment, real GDP. Positive gaps represent periods of economic boom; negative gaps represent economic slumps.

Source: Data from Organization for Economic Cooperation and Development.

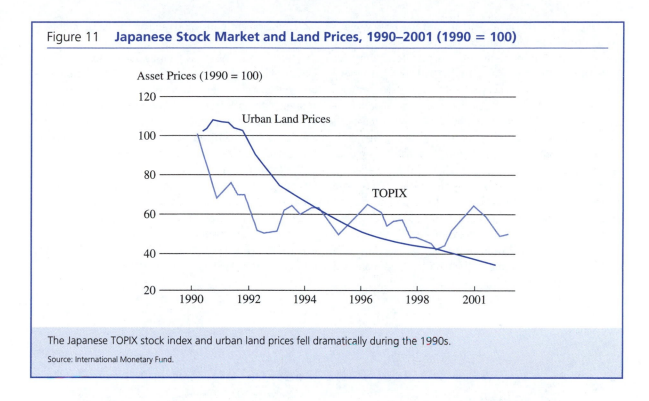

Figure 11   Japanese Stock Market and Land Prices, 1990–2001 (1990 = 100)

Asset Prices (1990 = 100)

Urban Land Prices

TOPIX

1990   1992   1994   1996   1998   2001

The Japanese TOPIX stock index and urban land prices fell dramatically during the 1990s.

Source: International Monetary Fund.

fiscal policy quickly turned contractionary as the government tried to reduce its budget deficit by cutting public spending and instituting a tax increase. The quarter immediately following the tax increase, GDP fell at an annual rate of 11 percent. Policy makers from other countries pressured Japan to postpone its government debt and budget concerns and to use expansionary fiscal policy—in particular, permanent tax cuts—to stimulate the economy. (*If Japan suffered from a negative spending shock, why might fiscal rather than monetary policy be a recommended response?*)

Interest rates in Japan were at historic lows (around 0.5 percent) when the Asian crisis hit, but the rate of growth of the money stock was relatively low. Japanese banks held many bad loans, both domestically and in the rest of Asia, making them less-than-willing lenders, especially to small and medium-sized borrowers. Housing and business investment, two sectors through which expansionary monetary policy traditionally works, declined.

At first, trading partners (especially the United States, with its large trade deficit) criticized Japan's reliance on depreciating the yen and stimulating exports (X)

to the neglect of policies to stimulate the domestic components of demand (C and I). Also, while the yen depreciated against the dollar, the Japanese currency appreciated against the Asian-crisis countries, whose demand for Japanese exports fell. This made currency depreciation a less effective way of stimulating demand because over 40 percent of Japanese exports typically went to Asia. By early 1999, anxious for Japanese growth to accelerate and support recovery in the Asian-crisis countries, the United States switched gears and pushed Japan toward expansionary monetary policy, despite that policy's likely effect of enlarging the politically sensitive U.S. trade deficit.

Regardless of the government's fiscal and monetary policies, Japanese consumers worried about their jobs and curtailed expenditure. They saved rather than spent most of the temporary tax cuts provided by government fiscal policy makers.[27] Businesses found it harder to borrow as banks slowed their loans to comply with the higher bank-capital standards applied in 1998. Firm bankruptcies, failures of several big financial institutions, and corruption scandals, both public and private, further dampened confidence.

---

27. Both macroeconomic theory and experience in other countries indicate that temporary tax cuts tend to increase saving while permanent tax cuts tend to increase consumption expenditure.

Overall, both fiscal and monetary policy were expansionary in Japan through the 1990s, but only erratically so. The nominal interest rate fell from over 8 percent in 1991 to near zero in 1999, but the money stock often grew only slowly. In 2000, at the slightest hint of economic recovery, the Bank of Japan tightened monetary policy, sending the economy back toward recession and requiring a quick policy reversal. A new governor at the Bank of Japan instituted more expansionary monetary policies in 2003. On the fiscal side, the government budget deficit, corrected for business-cycle effects, rose by about 6 percent of GDP over the same period, and the government's debt grew to almost 150 percent of GDP—the highest among industrial economies.[28] The economy's sluggish performance reduced tax revenues, so even a constant rate of government spending required more and more government borrowing, adding to the government's growing debt.

Many economists, as well as some Japanese policy makers, think that more fundamental structural reforms will be required before the Japanese economy really recovers. Those reforms include deregulating many industries, making the economy more open to new firms and new competitors, creating a more competitive and innovative banking and financial sector, reducing firms' reliance on banks as the main source of finance, and stopping the long-standing tendency for the government to insure special-interest groups against losses in return for the groups' political support. All these reforms would prove politically difficult even during a period of strong economic performance; accomplishing them during a long-running slump will challenge Japanese policy makers, their constituents, and their trading partners.

Japan

CASE 2: POLICY SQUEEZES: TO DO, OR NOT TO DO?

Japan's situation over the past fifteen years provides excellent examples of several common dilemmas that confront policy makers. First, let's consider the country's fiscal policy; how expansionary should it be? Given the recessionary conditions prevailing during most of the period, expansionary fiscal policy seemed appropriate from a short-run policy perspective. The United States, a major trading partner, encouraged Japan's expansionary fiscal policy, in part because the resulting yen appreciation helped mitigate the growing U.S. trade deficit. But, of course, that same yen appreciation made the fiscal policy less expansionary for Japan. The main reason for Japanese policy makers' reluctance to continue such expansionary fiscal policy lies in the country's accumulating government debt. That debt quickly passed 100 percent of GDP and, while still modest by developing-country standards, eventually surpassed the debt of infamously profligate developed countries such as Italy. Policy makers feared, with some justification, that holders of Japanese assets would lose confidence in the country's ability to manage and repay its debt. Such a loss of confidence would push up interest rates and hurt already-shaky banks. Fiscal

matters were further complicated by Japan's rapidly aging population, which implies an approaching responsibility, shared by firms and government, to support millions of pensioners. So fiscal policy makers have been squeezed—between a short-run need for fiscal expansion and longer-run pressures for fiscal consolidation and debt reduction.

Japan's monetary policy makers haven't had life much easier. Again, the recessionary conditions suggested a need for expansionary monetary policy. But the United States was slower to support such a move because it risked a sharp yen depreciation and a big spurt in the already-large U.S. trade deficit. Japanese domestic politics also played a role. The central bank, the Bank of Japan, had won formal independence from the Ministry of Finance only in 1998 and was eager to demonstrate that independence. So pressure from politicians, including the Ministry of Finance, to follow expansionary monetary policy to alleviate the fiscal expansion's upward pressure on interest rates encountered resistance at the Bank of Japan. Monetary policy makers also worried that too much expansionary policy would let banks off the hook too easily after years of bad management and bad loans.

---

28. "Fiscal Balance Elusive as Japan Lives Beyond Its Means," *Financial Times,* January 8, 2003.

Again, short-run policy considerations (getting out of the recession) conflicted with longer-term policy goals (getting banks to reform in ways that would support a more efficient economy in the long run).

Other reforms and policy decisions involved similar dilemmas. Most analysts agreed that Japanese banks' large-scale ownership of stock in firms discouraged efficient channeling of saving to the most productive investment projects. The stock "cross-holdings" also presented risks for the banks' own balance sheets. So long-run considerations indicated that banks should sell (or "unwind") those assets. But with the stock market falling for much of the 1990s, large-scale sales by banks could simply exacerbate the short-run problem. Similarly, forcing banks to abide by international regulatory standards in their accounting and capital provisions seems essential

if Japan's financial sector is to better support the country's economy. But forcing those stricter standards on struggling banks with huge bad-loan problems risked forcing even more banks into bankruptcy, with the resulting loss of public confidence.

So what's the lesson from all these dilemmas—other than the fact that it isn't easy being an economic policy maker? The importance of fixing structural weaknesses in the economy when times are good. Policy changes that have distributional consequences (for example, telling banks they're responsible for their own bad loans, or telling depositors that government will insure only part of their bank deposits) is never easy. But politically difficult decisions need to be made when the economy is strong enough to absorb any bad side effects with minimal loss of confidence.

CASE 3: FLOATING THE POUND

Great Britain

The policy dilemmas posed by fixed exchange rates and capital flows didn't arise first in the Mexican or Asian financial crises. Case One in the preceding chapter analyzed the effect of German unification on the country's European trading partners in the early 1990s. The combination of Germany's expansionary fiscal policies to finance unification and tight monetary policies to deter inflation kept the interest rate on Deutsche mark–denominated assets high and shifted trading partners' BOP curves upward. Fellow members of the European Union's Exchange Rate Mechanism of fixed exchange rates had to intervene to sell Deutsche marks from their foreign exchange reserves to prevent their currencies from depreciating against the mark. That intervention lowered trading partners' money stocks and placed contractionary pressures on their economies, where unemployment already was high.

In September 1992, a period of increased uncertainty about the future of monetary integration in Europe, participants in the foreign exchange markets started to expect devaluations of several EU currencies, including the

British pound. The expected devaluations implied that, to prevent actual devaluations, central banks would have to conduct even more intervention and monetary contraction. (*Why?*) But those policies posed political risks in countries such as Britain, already entering its third year of recession.

On September 16, 1992 (dubbed "Black Wednesday" by opponents of the move), rather than pursue further monetary contraction, the British government pulled the pound out of the fixed exchange rate system and allowed the pound to float against the Deutsche mark and other EU currencies. Britain's monetary policy became more expansionary, and interest rates on pound-denominated assets fell. The pound depreciated in foreign exchange markets from the fixed rate of DM2.85/£1 to a low of DM2.34/£1 in February 1993. The pound depreciation lowered the relative prices of British goods and services, and Britain's current-account deficit shrank. By 1994, the British economy was growing faster than EU economies such as France that remained in the Exchange Rate Mechanism (see Figure 12).[29]

29. An obvious question is why more EU member countries didn't abandon their fixed exchange rates. There are at least two reasons. First, several economies had histories of excessively expansionary monetary policies, inflation, and currency devaluations. Those countries feared that escaping the discipline imposed by the Exchange Rate Mechanism would generate expectations of further currency depreciations. Second, countries that pulled out of the system ran the risk of having less voice in the process of European monetary integration.

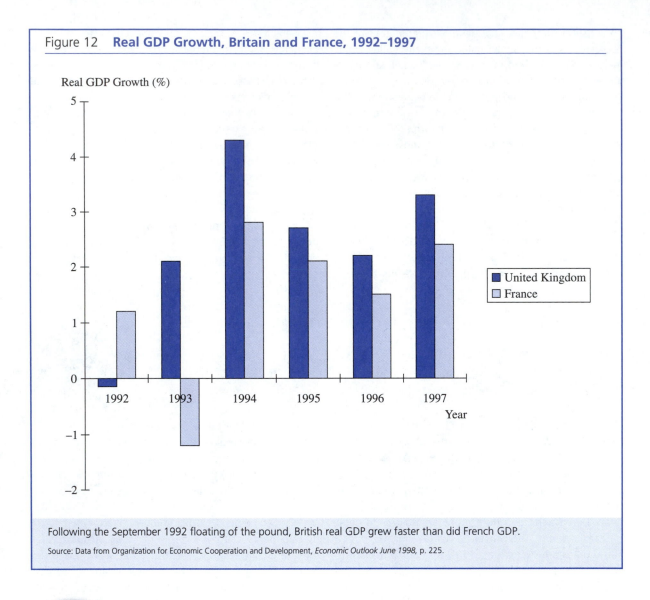

Figure 12 **Real GDP Growth, Britain and France, 1992–1997**

Following the September 1992 floating of the pound, British real GDP grew faster than did French GDP.

Source: Data from Organization for Economic Cooperation and Development, *Economic Outlook June 1998*, p. 225.

CASE 4: THE BUDGET AND THE DOLLAR

United States

During the early 1980s, when the dollar *appreciated* dramatically against the currencies of most U.S. trading partners, many commentators blamed the U.S. government budget deficit, which grew to 5.1 percent of GDP by 1985.[30] Overly expansionary fiscal policy, they argued, pushed up U.S. interest rates, encouraged capital inflows, and caused the dollar to appreciate. (*Illustrate in the IS-LM-BOP framework.*) The period between 1985 and 1996 was one of dollar *depreciation*. Yet some commentators still blamed the U.S. government budget deficit, even though the deficit shrunk during that period from 5.1 percent to 1.4 percent of GDP. From 1996 through 2001, the

---

30. The exchange rates cited in this case refer to the real effective value of foreign currencies relative to the dollar. See section 8 in the chapter on currency markets and exchange rates.

government budget gradually moved from deficit into surplus, and the dollar appreciated. Since 2002, the budget deficit has reappeared and grown from 1.5 percent to 4.5 percent of GDP; the dollar has depreciated. The result has been a lively debate about the likely impact on the dollar of a reduction in the budget deficit.

The link between a budget deficit and currency *appreciation* shows up clearly in the model developed in this chapter. Why, then, would anyone link the deficit to the dollar *depreciation* after 1985 or after 2002? There are three possibilities. First, prolonged, large, and growing budget deficits might cause market participants to anticipate

more expansionary future monetary policies to mitigate the deficit's effect on the interest rate. If so, a future currency depreciation might be expected to follow from the monetary expansion. Those expectations could reduce the demand for domestic-currency-denominated deposits and cause the currency to depreciate. A second possibility also relies on expectations, but in a more general way. If a persistent budget deficit weakened overall confidence in the U.S. economy, it might reduce the demand for dollardenominated deposits. However, note that the resulting depreciation would increase demand for U.S. goods and services and thereby tend to offset the lack

---

Figure 13 The U.S. Government Budget and the Exchange Rate, 1977–2004

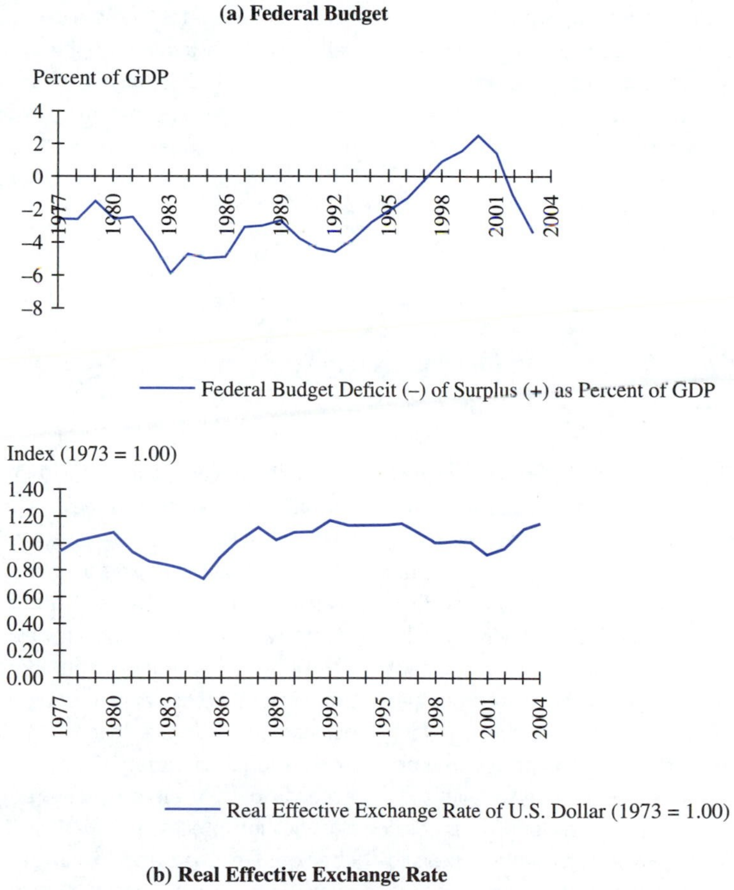

(a) Federal Budget

Percent of GDP

—— Federal Budget Deficit (–) of Surplus (+) as Percent of GDP

Index (1973 = 1.00)

—— Real Effective Exchange Rate of U.S. Dollar (1973 = 1.00)

(b) Real Effective Exchange Rate

The basic open economy macroeconomic model predicts that a government budget deficit would be associated with a domestic currency appreciation and a budget surplus with a depreciation. Several major trends during the 1977–2004 period in the United States conform to the expected pattern, but there are exceptions.

Source: U.S. Department of the Treasury and Board of Governors of the Federal Reserve System.

of confidence in the economy's future performance. The third possibility involves a risk premium.[31] Recall that portfolio owners may demand a risk premium to hold assets denominated in a particular currency if such assets constitute a large portion of their portfolios, making the portfolios' value vulnerable to exchange rate changes. If the U.S. government budget deficit, by requiring individuals to hold a large stock of dollar-denominated government bonds, generated a higher risk premium on dollar assets, then the U.S. BOP line would shift upward and the dollar would depreciate. As we noted in the earlier discussion of risk premiums, the empirical evidence on their importance is mixed.

The basic short-run model of an open macroeconomy suggests a currency appreciation would accompany budget deficits. But several expectations-based arguments may generate effects in the opposite direction. Figure 13 looks at the recent empirical evidence for the United States. Panel (a) reports the federal budget surplus (if positive) or deficit (if negative) as a percent of GDP. Panel (b) illustrates the real effective exchange rate, expressed as an index of the dollar price of foreign exchange; increases represent dollar depreciations, and decreases dollar appreciations.

The two dramatic trends of the 1980s in Figure 13 suggest a positive relationship between the size of the government budget deficit and the value of the dollar. During the early 1980s, the deficit grew dramatically and the dollar appreciated. During the late 1980s, the deficit shrank and the dollar depreciated. This supports the analysis based on the model presented in the chapter. However, the late 1990s appear to exhibit a different pattern. First, the deficit shrank (and, in fact, the government budget moved into surplus), and the dollar appreciated. Later, as the budget moved back into deficit and the deficit grew larger relative to GDP, the dollar began to depreciate.

The large government budget deficits of the 1980s were a relatively new phenomenon for the United States, at least in peacetime. It's possible that had the deficit continued to grow, its impact on expectations could have become more significant. Perhaps market participants perceived the late-1990s disappearance of the budget deficit as just a temporary phenomenon generated by the extraordinary U.S. economic boom of the 1990s. And it's too early to tell the extent to which the recent budget deficits will continue to grow.

CASE 5: THE TRUTH ABOUT EXCHANGE RATE REGIMES

We began this chapter by relating the story of the 1971 collapse of the Bretton Woods system of fixed exchange rates and the more recent move many countries have made toward more flexible exchange rate regimes. Both points are important to an understanding of modern macroeconomic history and policy, but they're not the whole story. Another important fact about the recent evolution of exchange rate regimes is that some countries state that they follow a flexible-rate regime when, in fact, the empirical evidence suggests that policy makers intervene to limit the extent of exchange rate flexibility.

The exchange regime a country claims to follow is called the *de jure* regime, and the framework the country appears to actually follow is called the *de facto* regime. Why might the two differ? As we've seen at many points in our discussion, changes in the exchange rate can have important

distributional consequences within the domestic economy and important consequences for the performance of the banking sector. Both effects can generate potent political pressures on policy makers to limit exchange rate flexibility— even in countries that self-report to the International Monetary Fund as following a flexible exchange rate regime.

Figure 14 documents both the shift away from pegged exchange rate regimes in recent years as well as the smaller percentage of *de jure* than *de facto* pegged regimes. The International Monetary Fund, which classifies countries according to their *de facto* regime, admits that the classification process is imperfect. Experts rely on data on changes in foreign exchange reserves and actual movements in exchange rates, among other information, to determine whether a country should be classified as operating under a *de facto* pegged or flexible regime.

---

31. See section 4.2 in the preceding chapter.

Figure 14 **_De Jure_ versus _De Facto_ Pegged Exchange Rate Regimes, 1990–1998 (Percent of IMF Membership)**

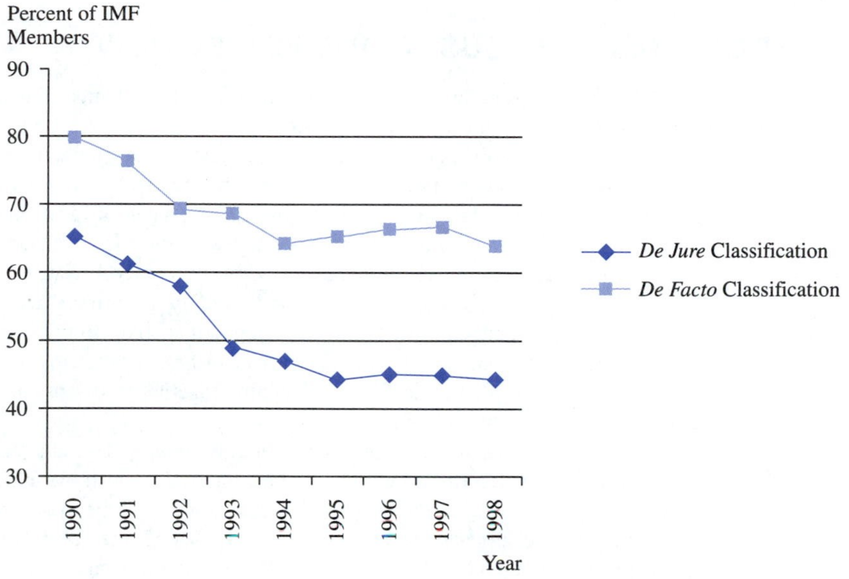

The percent of International Monetary Fund member countries stating that they follow a pegged exchange rate regime fell from 65.4 percent to 44.5 percent between 1990 and 1998. Corresponding figures for *de facto* pegged regimes, as classified by the IMF, fell from 79.9 percent to 64 percent over the same period.

Source: International Monetary Fund, *Exchange Arrangements and Foreign Exchange Markets: Developments and Issues*, 2003, p. 8.

SUMMARY

The switch from a fixed to a flexible exchange rate regime carries important implications for the effectiveness of various types of macroeconomic policy. Unlike a fixed exchange rate, a flexible rate allows the monetary authority to control the domestic nominal money stock through open market operations. Changes in the money stock, however, alter the exchange rate, and policy makers must tolerate these changes—with their distributional implications and their impact on the current-account balance—as a side effect of monetary policy. With high degrees of capital mobility, monetary policy becomes very effective in altering domestic income and fiscal policy loses its effectiveness. The choice of fiscal and monetary policy mix for pursuing internal balance affects the allocation of spending between the private and public sectors as well as the relative performances of various domestic industries and of trading partners' economies.

LOOKING AHEAD

Throughout our discussion of macroeconomic policy in an open economy, we've assumed that the domestic and foreign price levels are fixed. This assumption implies that, despite the economy's automatic adjustment mechanisms for reaching external balance, no analogous mechanism ensures internal balance; that is, the market for goods and services may be in equilibrium at a level of income above or below the level consistent with full employment or internal balance. In the upcoming chapter, we relax the fixed-price assumption and concentrate on long-run macroeconomic behavior, especially that of the exchange rate.

KEY TERMS

Bretton Woods system   policy mix
crowding out   transmission

PROBLEMS AND QUESTIONS FOR REVIEW

1. Countries A and B are trading partners. Both have a flexible exchange rate and highly but not
    perfectly mobile capital. Both want to pursue expansionary policies to raise the level of income.
    a. Country A pursues an expansionary fiscal policy and a tight monetary policy (that is, zero
        growth of the domestic money stock). Illustrate the effects of such a policy mix.
    b. Country B pursues a tight fiscal policy (that is, no change in government purchases or
        taxes) and an expansionary monetary policy. Illustrate the effects of such a policy mix.
    c. What would you expect to happen to the interest rate in country A relative to that in country B?
        What would happen to the exchange rate between country A's currency and country B's?
    d. What distributional effects would your results in part (c) have in the two economies?
    e. Use your answers to construct a brief argument in favor of international macroeconomic
        policy coordination (that is, for countries getting together to discuss and coordinate their
        macroeconomic policy actions).
2. A country hires you as its minister of macroeconomic policy. The country maintains strict
    capital controls that make any nonofficial capital inflows or outflows impossible. Up until
    now, the country has operated under a fixed exchange rate regime. The day you take office,
    exchange rate policy changes to a perfectly flexible exchange rate regime. Your first order of
    business is to give seminars for your subordinates, the assistant minister of fiscal policy and the
    assistant minister of monetary policy, to outline the implications of the change in exchange
    rate policy. Summarize the main points of your seminar presentations on the implications of
    the new policy, using the appropriate tools of analysis.
3. It is common for countries to complain about one another's interest rates. Assume that the
    domestic country operates under a flexible exchange rate regime, and capital is completely
    mobile. Illustrate and explain the effect on the domestic economy of a *decline* in the *foreign*
    interest rate (i*), beginning from a point of general equilibrium, using the IS-LM-BOP
    framework. (Compare your answer with that of Question 5 in the preceding chapter.)
4. Historically, it has been common for a country to pressure its trading partners to follow
    expansionary macroeconomic policies. Assume that the domestic country operates under
    a flexible exchange rate regime and that capital is completely mobile. Illustrate and explain the
    effect on the domestic economy of an *increase* in *foreign* income, beginning from a point of
    general equilibrium, using the IS-LM-BOP framework. (Compare your answer with that of
    Question 7 in the preceding chapter.)
5. You've just been hired by the International Monetary Fund to classify countries' *de facto*
    exchange rate regimes. The only information that you have for each country is the yearly level
    of its foreign exchange reserves and the value over time of its exchange rate. How would you
    use this information to create a rough classification of countries into those that follow *de facto*
    pegged and floating exchange rate regimes?
6. This chapter distinguishes between the effects under a flexible exchange rate regime of
    macroeconomic policies perceived to be temporary and those perceived to be permanent. The
    analysis in the preceding chapter of macroeconomic policy under a fixed exchange rate regime
    made no such distinction. Explain why.
7. Suppose everyone expects a country's new government to follow much more expansionary
    monetary policy, although policy hasn't actually changed yet. How might these expectations
    affect the country's exchange rate? Why?
8. Country A operates under a flexible exchange rate regime and is characterized by a high degree of
    capital mobility. The country is beginning to experience inflationary pressure, and policy makers
    decide that a contractionary macroeconomic policy is appropriate. They consider three policy
    packages, all of which would be designed to generate the same overall effect on income:
    Policy package 1: Contractionary fiscal policy combined with neutral monetary policy.
    Policy package 2: Contractionary monetary policy combined with neutral fiscal policy.

Policy package 3: A combination of contractionary fiscal and contractionary monetary policy such that the exchange rate will remain the same.

a. Suppose you own a residential construction firm. How might you rank your preferences for the three policy packages? Explain.

b. Suppose you own a large soybean farm and typically export a large portion of your crop. How might you rank your preferences for the three policy packages? Explain.

c. Suppose you own a small retail shop that sells handicrafts imported from developing countries. How might you rank your preferences for the three policy packages? Explain.

REFERENCES AND SELECTED READINGS

Browne, L. E. "Does Japan Offer Any Lessons for the United States?" Federal Reserve Bank of Boston, *New England Economic Review* (2001), No. 3: 3–18.
Similarities and differences between Japan's economic downturns of the 1990s and the U.S. downturn of 2001.

Cooper, Richard N. "Is the U.S. Current Account Deficit Sustainable? Will It Be Sustained?" *Brookings Papers on Economic Activity* (2001): 217–226.
The role of capital flows into the United States as a source of the U.S. current-account deficit.

Cooper, Richard N., and Jane Sneddon Little. "U.S. Monetary Policy in an Integrating World: 1960 to 2000." In *The Evolution of Monetary Policy and the Federal Reserve System over the Past Thirty Years,* edited by R. W. Kopcke and L. E. Browne, 77–130. Boston: Federal Reserve Bank of Boston, 2000.
History of international influences on U.S. monetary policy.

Corden, W. Max. *Too Sensational: On the Choice of Exchange Rate Regimes.* Cambridge, Mass.: MIT Press, 2002.
Excellent overview of the pros and cons of various exchange rate regimes, covering both theory and cases; for all students.

Eichengreen, Barry. *Globalizing Capital.* Princeton: Princeton University Press, 1996.
Readable account of the history and implications of international capital flows.

Fleming, J. M. "Domestic Financial Policies under Fixed and Floating Exchange Rates." *IMF Staff Papers* 9 (November 1962): 369–380.
A classic paper on macroeconomic policy effectiveness in an open economy; for advanced students.

Friedman, Milton. "The Case for Flexible Exchange Rates." In *Essays in Positive Economics,* 157–203. Chicago: University of Chicago Press, 1953.
One of the first serious calls for a change to flexible exchange rates; for all students.

Ghosh, Atish R., et al. *Exchange Rate Regimes: Choices & Consequences.* Cambridge, Mass.: MIT Press, 2002.
A careful look at the empirical evidence on the performance of alternate exchange rate regimes; for intermediate students.

Hetzel, Robert L. "Japanese Monetary Policy: A Quantity Theory Perspective." Federal Reserve Bank of Richmond, *Economic Quarterly* 85 (Winter 1999): 1–26.
Introduction to monetary policy's role in Japan's weak economic performance during the 1990s.

Hondroyiannis, George, et al. "Is the Japanese Economy in a Liquidity Trap?" *Economics Letters* 66 (2000): 17–23.
Argues that more rapid money growth would pull the Japanese economy out of its decade-long slump; for advanced students.

Hoshi, Takeo, and Anil K. Kashyap. "Japan's Financial Crisis and Economic Stagnation." *Journal of Economic Perspectives* 18 (Winter 2004): 3–26.
The role of the financial system in Japan's long-term poor macroeconomic performance; for all students.

International Monetary Fund. *Exchange Arrangements and Foreign Exchange Markets.* Washington, D.C.: IMF, 2003.
Rich source of data and case studies; for all students.

Krugman, Paul R. "It's Baaack: Japan's Slump and the Return of the Liquidity Trap." *Brookings Papers on Economic Activity* 2 (1998): 137–206.
Argues that Japan is experiencing a liquidity trap similar to that exhibited during the Great Depression.

Kuttner, Kenneth N., and Adam S. Posen. "The Great Recession: Lessons for Macroeconomic Policy from Japan." *Brookings Papers on Economic Activity* 2001 (2): 93–186.
Japan's macroeconomic policy experience during the 1990s; for intermediate and advanced students.

Lincoln, Edward J. "Japan's Financial Problems." *Brookings Papers on Economic Activity* 2 (1998): 347–385.
The financial-sector basis of Japan's continuing macroeconomic malaise.

Mann, Catherine L. "Perspectives on the U.S. Current Account Deficit and Sustainability." *Journal of Economic Perspectives* 16 (Spring 2002): 131–152.
Accessible discussion of the current-account deficit and its implications for the exchange rate.

McCallum, Bennett T. "Japanese Monetary Policy, 1991–2001." Federal Reserve Bank of Richmond *Economic Quarterly* 89 (Winter 2003): 1–32.
Argues that Japanese monetary policy should have been more expansionary; for advanced students.

Meltzer, Allan H. "U.S. Policy in the Bretton Woods Era." Federal Reserve Bank of St. Louis *Review* (May–June 1991): 53–83.
Excellent survey of the Bretton Woods era; for all students.

Mühleisen, Martin, and Hamid Faruqee. "Japan: Population Aging and the Fiscal Challenge." *Finance and Development* 38 (March 2001): 10–13.
How can Japan reduce its fiscal deficit when it faces pension liabilities for an old and rapidly aging population?

Mundell, Robert A. "Capital Mobility and Stabilization Policy under Fixed and Flexible Exchange Rates." *Canadian Journal of Economics and Political Science* 29 (November 1963): 475–485.
The original presentation of capital mobility's impact on macroeconomic policy effectiveness in an open economy; for intermediate and advanced students.

Olivei, Giovanni P. "The Role of Saving and Investment in Balancing the Current Account: Some Empirical Evidence from the United States." Federal Reserve Bank of Boston, *New England Economic Review* (July/August 2000): 3–14.
The relationship among saving, investment, and the current-account deficit.

Rogoff, Kenneth S. "Why Are G-3 Exchange Rates So Fickle?" *Finance and Development* 39 (June 2002): 56–57.
Overview of reasons for the volatility of exchange rates between the dollar, euro, and yen; for all students.

8

The Exchange Rate in Long-Run Equilibrium

1 INTRODUCTION

Thus far, we've examined macroeconomic behavior in the short run, during which the price level remains fixed. Exchange rates sometimes move dramatically even in the short run. For example, the Indonesian rupiah's value declined from Rp7,750/\$1 to Rp10,550/\$1 on January 8, 1998, in the midst of the Asian financial crisis. On August 26, 1998, the Russian ruble depreciated by more than 69 percent against the German mark, in response to Russia's debt default and general concern about Russian economic and political reform. During Argentina's recent financial crisis, the peso's value dropped from P1/\$1 in early January 2002 to P2.35/\$1 just one month later.[1]

Longer run exchange-rate trends in the world economy can be just as dramatic. In 1973, the dollar price of yen stood at \$1/¥360. By early 1995, the price had risen to \$1/¥80, a dollar depreciation of almost 80 percent. A reversal of trend brought the exchange rate to \$1/¥147 on June 17, 1998, when the U.S. Federal Reserve intervened by buying \$833 million worth of yen in an effort to slow the yen's depreciation. By 2003, Japanese policy makers feared that the yen's appreciation would halt recovery from Japan's decade-long economic slump. So the Bank of Japan bought approximately \$300 billion in foreign exchange reserves during 2003 and early 2004 in an effort to stop the dollar price of yen from rising above about \$1/¥110. To understand such events and their macroeconomic significance, we must take into account the fact that in the long run prices *do* respond to macroeconomic policy, as well as to other events in the economy. This chapter and the next extend our basic open-economy macroeconomic model to incorporate those price-level changes. It's useful to proceed in two stages. In this chapter, we turn our attention to long-run equilibrium under a flexible exchange rate and explore the relationships we expect to observe among key macroeconomic variables *once the price level has adjusted completely to any change in the economy*. The upcoming chapter focuses on the relationship between the short-run results and the long-run results, or on what happens in the economy *as* the price level adjusts.

In **long-run equilibrium**, the economy satisfies two related conditions: First, output reaches its full-employment level, determined by how much capital and labor

---

1. The P2.35/\$1 value occurred in the black market, while the government kept legal foreign exchange markets closed because of the crisis.

the economy contains, as well as by the available technology and by how much individuals in the economy choose to work. Second, all prices in the economy, including the wage rate and the exchange rate, reach levels consistent with equilibrium in their respective markets. We call this a long-run *equilibrium*, because once the economy reaches it, economic variables won't change—until some new shock to the system disturbs them.

In this chapter, we examine how the exchange rate behaves in long-run equilibrium. This requires an understanding of the long-run relationships among the country's money stock, price level, and exchange rate.

2 MONEY IN LONG-RUN EQUILIBRIUM

2.1 How Does the Money Stock Affect Real Output?

What effect does a one-time permanent change in the size of the money stock have on the economy's long-run equilibrium real output? The answer is none. A simple thought experiment can help us understand why. Suppose that, beginning from a position of long-run equilibrium, the government announced that, as of January 1, the money stock would double. Each individual's bank balances would double, as would each worker's nominal wage rate, and the money price of every good and service.

Such a policy would have no effect on real output. No one would be any wealthier or poorer in *real* terms. And the *relative* prices of all goods in the economy would remain the same, because the relative price of two goods equals the ratio of the two goods' money prices, both of which would have doubled with the doubled money stock.[2] Output would remain at its full-employment level, determined by the economy's endowment of resources, its technology, and residents' tastes for income and leisure. Therefore, we can conclude that *a one-time permanent change in the money stock has no effect on the economy's long-run equilibrium real output*. This important result has a name: the **neutrality of money**.

2.2 How Does the Money Stock Affect the Interest Rate?

Just as a one-time change in the money stock leaves long-run output unaffected, such a change also has no effect on the long-run equilibrium interest rate. To understand why, recall that the equilibrium interest rate in the economy represents the rate of return a lender must receive to lend funds to a borrower. A lender lends $1 today in return for a promised repayment of $1(1 + i)$ next year.

Suppose that, at the time the money supply doubled, the equilibrium interest rate in the economy equaled 5 percent, so lending a dollar for one year brought a repayment of $1.05, or a rate of return of 5 percent. A bank willing to lend a firm $1 million to build a new factory (in return for $1,050,000) before the doubling of the money stock should be willing to lend the firm $2 million for the same project after the doubling (in return for $2,100,000), because the bank's rate of return still would equal 5 percent. All borrowing and lending decisions in the economy should remain

---

2. Section 2.1 in the earlier chapter on currency markets and exchange rates covers the relationship between money prices and relative prices.

unchanged, so we can conclude that *a one-time permanent change in the size of the money stock doesn't alter the long-run equilibrium interest rate.*

2.3 How Does the Money Stock Affect the Price Level?

If one-time changes in the money stock don't change real output or the interest rate in long-run equilibrium, such changes in the money stock must cause proportional changes in the price level. For example, if the money stock doubles, the long-run equilibrium price level must double as well. We can see why by recalling the condition required for equilibrium in the money market.[3] The real money stock must equal the demand for real money balances, which depends positively on real income and negatively on the interest rate:

$$M/P = L(\overset{+}{Q}, \overset{-}{i}) \qquad [1]$$

If, in long-run equilibrium, one-time permanent changes in the nominal money stock (M) don't alter either real income (Q) or the interest rate (i), then Equation 1 implies that one-time permanent changes in M must generate proportional changes in P to maintain money-market equilibrium. In other words, if changes in the nominal money stock don't lead to changes in real money demand (L), then the price level must adjust to keep the *real* money stock (M/P) constant. So, *in long-run equilibrium, one-time changes in the money stock lead to proportional changes in the price level.* If the money stock doubles, for example, the price level doubles as well.

We can examine empirically the relationship between changes in countries' money stocks and changes in their respective price levels. Our theory implies that, in the long run, changes in the money stock should lead to proportional changes in the price level. Actual data, of course, come from a world economy constantly bombarded by shocks of various kinds, not from one constantly in long-run equilibrium, so we shouldn't expect the predicted relationship to hold exactly. Nonetheless, countries with larger increases in their money stocks should experience larger increases in their price levels than countries whose money stocks exhibit smaller changes, especially if we focus on averages over a relatively long period to lessen the impact of short-run disturbances.

Figure 1 reports the average adjusted rates of money-stock growth (horizontal axis) and price-level growth (vertical axis) for a subset of industrial economies from 1960 through 1995.[4] If our predicted relationship held exactly, all points would fall along the upward-sloping 45-degree line in the figure. While few of the points actually lie on the 45-degree line, most are close to it, implying a close relationship between long-run changes in countries' money stocks and price levels. Countries such as Iceland and Greece, with high rates of money growth, experienced higher rates of inflation than did countries such as Switzerland and the United States, whose money stocks grew at much slower rates.

---

3. See section 2.4 of the chapter "Money, the Banking System, and Foreign Exchange" for a review.

4. To account for the fact that, over such a long period, the full-employment level of output grows, we reduced the money-stock growth rates in the figure by 3 percent per year to cover real output growth.

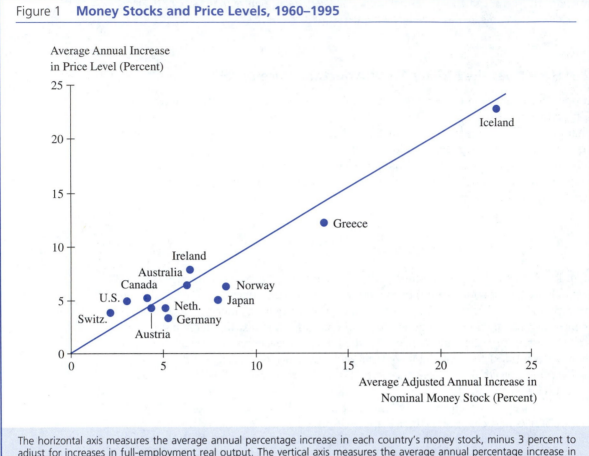

Figure 1 **Money Stocks and Price Levels, 1960–1995**

The horizontal axis measures the average annual percentage increase in each country's money stock, minus 3 percent to adjust for increases in full-employment real output. The vertical axis measures the average annual percentage increase in each country's price level (CPI). In the long run, countries with high rates of money growth experience higher rates of inflation than countries with lower rates of money growth.

Source: Data from Organization for Economic Cooperation and Development.

We can use the graph of money-market equilibrium to summarize the long-run equilibrium relationship among M, P, Q, and i, as in Figure 2.[5] Equilibrium requires that the real money stock (M/P) equal the public's demand for real money balances (L[Q, i]). If changes in M don't change Q or i from their long-run equilibrium values of Q_0 and i_0, the money demand function remains stationary. To maintain equilibrium, the money-stock line must remain stationary as well, and this requires that the *real* money stock (M/P) not change. Therefore, the ratio of the new money stock and price level (M_1/P_1) must equal the ratio of the original money stock and price level (M_0/P_0). In other words, the nominal money stock and price level must change proportionally.

2.4 How Does the Money Stock Affect the Exchange Rate?

We've argued that in long-run equilibrium, all prices in the economy change proportionally with the money stock, while real output and the interest rate remain

---

5. For a review, see section 2.4 in the chapter on money, the banking system, and foreign exchange.

Figure 2   Long-Run Equilibrium in the Money Market

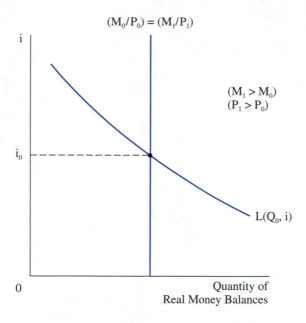

$(M_0/P_0) = (M_1/P_1)$

$(M_1 > M_0)$
$(P_1 > P_0)$

i_0

$L(Q_0, i)$

Quantity of
Real Money Balances

In long-run equilibrium, a change in the nominal money stock exerts no effect on real output or the interest rate. Money demand remains unchanged; and the price level must change proportionally with the nominal money stock to maintain equilibrium.

unchanged. The nominal exchange rate, e, is just the domestic-currency price of a unit of foreign currency. Therefore, under a flexible exchange rate regime, we would expect the exchange rate to move proportionally with any change in the money stock.[6]

Returning to our thought experiment in which a country's money stock doubled, we would expect the domestic-currency price of a unit of each foreign currency to double, implying that each foreign good or service would cost twice as much in domestic currency as before. Again, individuals would be no better and no worse off in real terms. They would earn twice as much, but every item they bought—including imports—would also cost twice as much.

Therefore, *in long-run equilibrium, one-time increases in the money stock lead to proportional nominal depreciations of the domestic currency, and one-time decreases in the money stock lead to proportional nominal appreciations.* Figure 3 depicts equilibrium in the foreign exchange market. Beginning from a long-run equilibrium at point I, a rise in the nominal money stock leaves the domestic and foreign interest rates unchanged at i_0 and i_0^*. But the expected future spot exchange rate rises proportionally with M, because market participants expect a proportional increase in all money prices, including the nominal exchange rate. The rise in e^e lowers the expected rate of return on deposits denominated in the domestic currency and shifts the demand for foreign-currency-denominated deposits to the right. This causes a spot

---

6. Recall that, under a fixed exchange rate, monetary policy fails to alter the nominal money stock, because the necessary foreign exchange market intervention offsets the policy's impact.

Figure 3   **Long-Run Equilibrium in the Foreign Exchange Market**

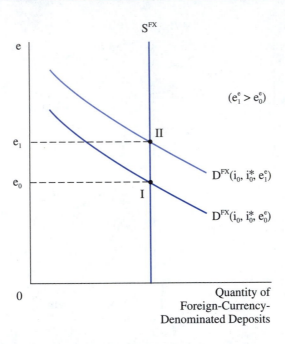

In long-run equilibrium, an increase in the nominal money stock doesn't change the interest rate. However, market participants anticipate proportional increases in all money prices, including the nominal exchange rate. The rise in e^e increases the demand for foreign-currency-denominated deposits and causes a proportional spot depreciation of the domestic currency.

---

depreciation of the domestic currency proportional to the original increase in the domestic money stock.

Note that the *real* exchange rate, $R \equiv P/eP^*$, doesn't change. If a change in the money stock leads to proportional changes in both the domestic price level, P, and the nominal exchange rate, e, then the real exchange rate remains at its original value. This is simply another case of the long-run neutrality of money: One-time money stock changes don't change relative prices. After all, the real exchange rate represents the relative price of domestic goods and services compared with foreign ones. Just as a rise in the price level fails to change relative prices because all money prices change proportionally, a proportional rise in both the price level and the nominal exchange rate leaves the real exchange rate unaffected.

2.5 Summary: How Does the Money Stock Affect the Economy in Long-Run Equilibrium?

A one-time permanent change in the nominal money stock changes all money prices, including the nominal exchange rate, proportionally and leaves real output, the interest rate, relative prices, the real exchange rate, and the real money stock unchanged. Table 1 summarizes these results.

Table 1 **SUMMARY OF THE MONEY STOCK'S EFFECTS IN LONG-RUN EQUILIBRIUM**		
Variable	Effect of One-Time Permanent Increase in Nominal Money Stock	Effect of One-Time Permanent Decrease in Nominal Money Stock
Real output (Q)	0	0
Interest rate (i)	0	0
Price level (P)	$+^a$	$-^a$
Nominal exchange rate $(e)^b$	$+^a$	$-^a$
Real exchange rate (R)	0	0
Real money stock (M/P)	0	0

[a]Proportional to change in nominal money stock.
[b]A plus sign denotes a rise in e or domestic currency depreciation; a negative sign denotes a fall in e or domestic currency appreciation.

3 PURCHASING POWER PARITY

We've seen that changes in countries' money stocks, in the long run, affect both price levels and nominal exchange rates. The interaction between these two relationships suggests a link between a country's price level and its nominal exchange rate. This link forms the basis for a view of long-run exchange rate behavior known as purchasing power parity (PPP), which focuses on exchange rates' role in defining the relative prices of domestic and foreign goods and services. The key building block for purchasing power parity is the law of one price.

3.1 The Law of One Price

The **law of one price** states that identical goods sell for an equivalent price regardless of the currency in which the price is denominated. Arbitrage ensures that, with no transportation costs, barriers to trade, monopolies, or other restrictions, the law of one price will hold. Suppose, for example, that a stereo selling for £200 in London were priced at $500 in New York with the exchange rate equal to $2 per pound (e = $2/£1). This would violate the law of one price, because the pound price of the stereo would be £200 in London and £250 in New York. *(Why?)* Or, equivalently, the dollar price would be $400 in London and $500 in New York. *(Why?)* Arbitrageurs would find it profitable to buy stereos in London and sell them in New York; in fact, their profit would equal £50, or $100, per stereo. Arbitrage would raise the price of stereos in London by increasing demand there and lower the price of stereos in New York by increasing supply there.

Algebraically, we can represent this scenario as follows, letting P^{NY}_S and P^L_S denote the price of stereos in New York and London, respectively. Initially,

$$P^{NY}_S > e \cdot P^L_S, \text{ or } \$500 > (\$2/£1) \cdot (£200) = \$400.$$

Arbitrage causes P^{NY}_S to fall and P^L_S to rise until

$$P^{NY}_S = e \cdot P^L_S. \tag{2}$$

Equation 2 states the law of one price: The dollar price of a stereo must equal the dollar price of a pound multiplied by the pound price of the stereo. *(State the law of one price for stereos in terms of pounds.)*[7]

Complications such as transport costs or trade barriers can prevent the law of one price from holding. Nevertheless, the possibility of arbitrage links prices of homogeneous traded goods expressed in different currencies. Even when we include a consideration such as transport costs, the prices in different currencies of a homogeneous good should differ by only a constant—equal to the amount of transport cost involved in arbitrage. In other words, the prices still should move in tandem.

The degree to which the law of one price holds will differ depending on the characteristics of the good in question. Prices of identical, freely traded goods exhibit the tightest links. Equation 2 will hold more closely if stereos are identical than if their brands, qualities, or technical characteristics differ. But empirical evidence indicates that, even for identical traded goods, surprisingly large deviations from the law of one price do occur.[8] For differentiated products (for example, three automobiles made by Chevrolet, Volkswagen, and Toyota), small differences among them can result in persistent price differences even with no transport costs or trade barriers. We wouldn't expect the dollar price of a Chevrolet to be equivalent to the dollar price of a Volkswagen or a Toyota—because consumers don't perceive the automobiles as identical.

Trade barriers introduce artificial price differences across countries and can cause the law of one price not to hold. Japan, for example, maintains strict import quotas on rice to protect domestic rice farmers, who hold a special place in traditional Japanese culture and wield considerable political clout. Imported rice would be much cheaper for Japanese consumers than domestically produced rice. *(Write out the relationship among the dollar price of rice imported from the United States, the yen price of Japanese-grown rice, and the dollar price of yen.)* But import quotas effectively rule out the kind of arbitrage we used to argue for Equation 2 in the stereo-arbitrage example.

For nontraded items (that is, products not traded internationally) the law of one price may hold even more loosely. Many services are only traded infrequently because the buyer and seller must be in the same location; examples include health-care services, haircuts, and retailing. Even if the dollar price of a tonsillectomy exceeded the pound price of a tonsillectomy multiplied by the dollar price of a pound, few Americans needing a tonsillectomy would travel to London to get it. The inconvenience of some types of transactions limits the process of arbitrage in the case of these services. This implies that price differences may persist; that is, we wouldn't expect the law of one price to hold for such items.

3.2 Going from the Law of One Price to PPP

Purchasing power parity (PPP) carries the law of one price one step further by applying the logic not to the price of a single good such as stereos, but to countries' overall price levels. The simplest version of purchasing power parity states that the price level in one

---

7. If e' denotes the pound price of a dollar, we can write the law of one price as $e' \cdot P_S^{NY} = P_S^L$. This is simply Equation 2 divided through by e because, by definition, $e' = 1/e$. In words, the pound price of a stereo must equal the pound price of a dollar times the dollar price of the stereo.

8. The most commonly cited sources of such deviations include imperfect competition and segmented markets. In particular, firms that face different amounts of competition in different submarkets may charge different prices in those markets if they can prevent resale between low-price and high-price markets.

country (such as the United States) equals the price level in a second (for example, Britain) multiplied by the exchange rate between the countries' currencies:

$$P^{US} = e \cdot P^{B} \qquad [3]$$

The U.S. price level measures the dollar price of a basket of goods and services, and the British price level measures the pound price of a basket of goods and services. Therefore, purchasing power parity holds when the two countries' price levels are equal once translated into a common currency using the exchange rate.

Equations 2 and 3 appear similar. Going from the law of one price to PPP represents only one small step for a typesetter, but a giant leap for economists. The apparently simple move from the law of one price's link between the prices of a good expressed in two currencies to purchasing power parity's link between two countries' price levels actually entails a number of important economic considerations. If the law of one price held perfectly for every good and service, and if the baskets of goods and services used to compute the two countries' price levels were identical, then purchasing power parity would follow. But we've argued that considerations such as transport costs, product differentiation, and trade barriers can render the law of one price ineffective for some goods and services. And the baskets of goods and services produced or consumed in various countries differ.

Still, the forces of arbitrage that underlie the law of one price should keep price levels and exchange rates from deviating too far from the purchasing-power-parity relationship, at least in the long run. If goods and services in the United States become more expensive than those in Britain ($P^{US} > e \cdot P^{B}$), the demand for dollars and for U.S. goods and services should fall, while the demand for British goods and services should rise. This would lower P^{US} and raise both e and P^{B}, leading back toward purchasing power parity. Similarly, if goods and services in the United States become cheaper than those in Britain, market forces should place upward pressure on the U.S. price level and downward pressure on Britain's, as well as generating a dollar appreciation against the pound.

3.3 Absolute and Relative PPP

Economists call the version of purchasing power parity in Equation 3 **absolute purchasing power parity**. Absolute parity represents the strongest form, because it requires the parity relationship between the two countries' price levels to hold continually. In terms of the model of the macroeconomy we developed earlier, absolute purchasing power parity requires that the relative price of domestic and foreign goods or the real exchange rate ($R \equiv P/eP^{*}$) continually equal 1. Suppose R rose above 1. The dollar price of domestic (U.S.) goods would exceed the pound price of foreign (British) goods multiplied by the dollar price of pounds. Arbitrage would result in some combination of a fall in the dollar price of U.S. goods, a rise in the pound price of British goods, and a dollar depreciation. If the relative price of domestic and foreign goods fell below 1, the same types of adjustments would occur, but in the opposite direction. (*Why?*)

Under a weaker form of parity, **relative purchasing power parity**, the percentage change in the domestic country's price level equals the percentage change in the foreign country's *plus* the percentage change in the exchange rate between the two countries' currencies—or, letting "hats" over variables represent percentage rates of change in those variables:[9]

$$\hat{P} = \hat{e} + \hat{P}^{*} \qquad [4]$$

---

9. For example, a P with a "hat" equals the percentage change in P, or $\hat{P} \equiv \Delta P/P$; so $\hat{P}$ denotes the inflation rate.

Equation 4 says that the inflation rate in the domestic country (the percentage rate of change in its price level) equals the rate of its currency's depreciation against that of the foreign country plus the latter's inflation rate. Relative PPP may hold when absolute PPP fails. In particular, if the factors such as transport costs and trade barriers that cause deviations from absolute PPP remain more or less constant across time, then the relative PPP relationship between inflation rates and changes in exchange rates will hold.

3.4 How Can PPP Not Hold?

We've already considered several factors that can cause purchasing power parity not to hold. The most obvious is the presence of transport costs or trade barriers. These cause the law of one price—and therefore absolute purchasing power parity—not to hold, and they may do the same with relative PPP if transport costs or trade barriers change over time.

Suppose two countries produce and consume identical baskets of goods. We would then expect relative purchasing power parity to hold quite closely for them. But most countries produce and consume unique combinations of goods, partly as a result of specialization according to comparative advantage and partly as a result of taste differences. Many items are nontraded; others are heterogeneous (such as Chevrolets, Volkswagens, and Toyotas). All these considerations imply that each country's price level, whether a production-based measure such as the GDP deflator or a consumption-based measure such as the consumer price index (CPI), measures the price of a unique combination of goods. The goods produced and consumed in the United States differ from those produced and consumed in Britain, which can cause either version of PPP to fail to hold. After all, the logic of PPP rests ultimately on the arbitrage that leads to the law of one price. But if each country's basket of goods and services is different, we shouldn't expect arbitrage to equalize the various baskets' prices.

PPP is more likely to hold for traded goods or services than for nontraded ones, so the evidence in its favor tends to be stronger in tests that use wholesale rather than consumer prices. The wholesale (or producer) price index measures changes in the prices of goods bought by firms and includes mainly intermediate traded goods. The consumer price index, on the other hand, measures changes in the prices of items bought by typical consumers. This includes many services, such as housing and health care, for which the law of one price may be only a very weak long-term tendency.

Relative purchasing power parity links inflation rates among countries. The implied relationship between inflation rates assumes that *relative* prices of various goods *within* each country don't change. When relative prices within countries do change, purchasing power parity may not hold, because the baskets of goods that countries produce and consume contain different amounts of the goods whose relative prices have changed. An increase in the relative price of rice, for example, would raise the price levels of many Asian economies relative to those of non-Asian economies, because rice constitutes the main staple of many Asian diets and is, therefore, weighted relatively heavily in the computation of those economies' price levels. Empirically, the PPP relationship holds more closely in periods of rapid inflation. This occurs because high inflation rates tend to overwhelm any changes in the pattern of relative prices that may occur simultaneously. During periods of low inflation, changes in relative prices may conceal any tendency toward PPP.

3.5 Does PPP Hold?

Evidence from many countries and time periods shows conclusively that the absolute form of purchasing power parity doesn't hold reliably. Nor does the law of one price hold for many goods, including some traded ones. The evidence provides more support for relative PPP. Generally it's true that when one country's rate of inflation exceeds another's, the first country's currency depreciates against the second's. Of course, the precise relationship in Equation 4 doesn't always hold, but a trend toward relative purchasing power parity does, at least over the long run. For most country pairs, relative PPP held more closely prior to 1971, during the Bretton Woods system of fixed exchange rates. Since 1973, and particularly since 1979, even relative PPP has failed to explain short- and medium-run movements in exchange rates and price levels. Short-run deviations from PPP often are large, volatile, and persistent. Deviations disappear at a rate of as little as 15 percent per year, and their half-life runs about one to five years (that is, only half of a typical deviation from PPP will have disappeared one to five years after its appearance).

However, for the post-1973 flexible-exchange-rate period as a whole, relative purchasing power parity performs reasonably well in explaining the long-run behavior of industrialized countries' exchange rates against the dollar. Figure 4 demonstrates this relationship over the thirty years after the breakdown of Bretton Woods, using changes in countries' consumer price indices to measure their rates of inflation relative to that of the United States. If relative purchasing power parity held perfectly, all points would lie on the upward-sloping 45-degree line, along which the currency's depreciation or appreciation

Figure 4   Relative Purchasing Power Parity, 1973–2003 (Percent)

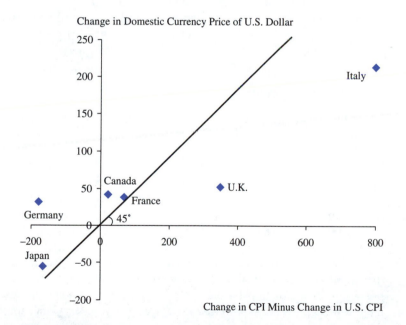

Relative purchasing power parity implies that the rate of change in the exchange rate between two countries' currencies equals the countries' inflation differential. The horizontal axis measures the percentage change in each country's price level minus the percentage change in the U.S. price level between 1973 and 2003. The vertical axis measures the percentage change in the price of the dollar measured in each country's currency over the same 30-year period. If purchasing power parity held perfectly, all points would lie on the 45-degree line. Deviations from the 45-degree line represent real depreciations of the yen, mark/euro, Canadian dollar, and franc/euro, along with real appreciations of the pound and lira/euro.

Source: Data from *Economic Report of the President*.

relative to the dollar (measured along the vertical axis) equals the country's inflation rate minus U.S. inflation (measured along the horizontal axis).

The countries below the 45-degree line in Figure 4—the United Kingdom and Italy—experienced real currency appreciations relative to the dollar between 1973 and 2003. In the case of the United Kingdom, for example, the inflation rate over the 30-year period exceeded the U.S. rate by 349 percent, but the pound depreciated against the dollar by only 51 percent. Therefore, the price of U.K. goods and services relative to U.S. ones rose by about 298 percent between 1973 and 2003 ($\hat{R} \equiv [\hat{P}^{UK} - \hat{P}^{US}] - (\hat{£/\$}) = 349\% - 51\% = 298\%$). Real appreciations of a foreign currency always make the foreign country's goods and services more expensive relative to U.S. goods and services. Note that in the cases of both the United Kingdom and Italy, the currencies *de*preciated in nominal terms but *ap*preciated in real terms. In other words, the nominal depreciations over the 1973–2003 period were smaller than the amount by which U.K. and Italian inflation exceeded that of the United States.

Countries above the 45-degree line in Figure 4 experienced real currency depreciations; changes in their nominal exchange rates more than offset any excess of their inflation rates relative to that of the United States. Canada, for example, experienced inflation 22 percent above that in the United States between 1973 and 2003, while the Canadian dollar depreciated by 41 percent against its U.S. counterpart. Therefore, the relative price of Canadian goods and services fell by approximately 19 percent ($\hat{R} \equiv [\hat{P}^{C} - \hat{P}^{US}] - (\hat{C\$/\$}) = 22\% - 41\% = -19\%$). Real depreciations of a foreign currency always make the foreign country's goods and services cheaper relative to U.S. goods and services. Japan experienced a nominal appreciation of its yen, but a real depreciation.

Now that we've defined the basic concepts of purchasing power parity and examined them empirically, we add a few cautionary notes about what purchasing power parity does and doesn't imply, because the concept often is misinterpreted.

3.6 Cautionary Notes on PPP

Economist Gustav Cassel elaborated the concept of purchasing power parity following World War I. The gold standard of fixed exchange rates had broken down during the war, leaving economists and policy makers with the problem of how to choose new levels at which to peg exchange rates after the war. Cassel suggested using PPP as a guide in selecting the new rates. Purchasing power parity, according to Cassel, would capture the underlying equilibrium level of exchange rates, even if shocks temporarily drove rates away from their PPP levels.

Today, interpretation of purchasing power parity ranges from positive to normative.[10] Some economists perceive PPP as a positive statement of how the economy works. Others attach more normative significance to PPP, arguing that it *should* hold and that, if it fails, policy makers should take action to restore it. We've argued that the possibility of international arbitrage creates a linkage among various prices that drives them toward purchasing power parity, at least over the very long run. However, we have little reason to expect PPP to hold over the short or medium term, nor any justification for using PPP as a policy goal.

Arguments that a currency is under- or overvalued based on purchasing power parity rest on a misunderstanding of PPP. In fact, under a perfectly flexible exchange rate regime, the terms *undervalued* and *overvalued* carry little meaning, because supply and demand in foreign exchange markets determine exchange rates. A currency can be

---

10. The Isard book in the chapter references contains a useful discussion.

"wrongly" valued only if intervention by central banks holds the rate away from its equilibrium level. This *doesn't* imply that all individuals and firms in the economy will be happy with the exchange rate's value. We've repeatedly discovered that different exchange rate values benefit different groups within the economy. Export and import-competing industries benefit from currency depreciations, while consumers and nontraded-goods industries prefer currency appreciations, at least over the short run when changes in the nominal exchange rate imply changes in the relative prices of domestic and foreign goods.

A second caution deals with the cause-and-effect implications of PPP. Purchasing power parity can be interpreted as a theory of exchange rate behavior that attributes changes in the nominal exchange rate between two currencies to differences in the countries' inflation rates. We can make this view of PPP more explicit by rewriting Equation 4 with the exchange rate on the left-hand side and the inflation differential on the right-hand side:

$$\hat{e} = \hat{P} - \hat{P}* \qquad\qquad [5]$$

This view of PPP treats inflation rates as exogenous and assumes that they determine changes in the exchange rate. For example, if the domestic inflation rate equals 10 percent per year and the foreign inflation rate 5 percent per year, Equation 5 predicts that the domestic currency will depreciate by 5 percent.

Alternatively, purchasing power parity sometimes is viewed as a theory of price-level determination. Given the foreign inflation rate and the rate of change in the exchange rate, we can solve the PPP expression for the domestic inflation rate ($\hat{P} = \hat{e} + \hat{P}*$). If the foreign inflation rate is 5 percent and the domestic currency is depreciating by 5 percent per year, the domestic inflation rate must equal 10 percent. (*Could you distinguish empirically between this case and the previous one, in which inflation rates determined the change in the exchange rate?*)

However, neither of these interpretations is really correct. Purchasing power parity does not imply that inflation rates determine exchange rates or vice versa. Domestic and foreign price levels and the exchange rate are determined jointly and simultaneously along with other variables within the macroeconomy. All three values result from the interrelationships among many variables. Neither the price level nor the nominal exchange rate is under policy makers' direct control, although their macroeconomic policy choices certainly affect both prices and exchange rates.

Another caution concerns "tests" of PPP frequently reported in the popular press. One of the most popular is the "hamburger standard" published each year since 1986 by *The Economist*. The *Economist* staff (1) collects the local-currency price of a Big Mac in several dozen of the more than 110 foreign countries in which McDonald's sells the burgers, (2) translates this price into dollars at the current exchange rate, and (3) reports that the foreign currency is overvalued (undervalued) against the dollar by the amount by which the dollar price of the foreign burger exceeds (falls short of) the dollar price of the U.S. burger. For example, in the 2004 survey, the U.S. burger cost $2.90. A Big Mac in Switzerland cost SF6.29, and the spot exchange rate was SF1.28/$1. Converting the price of the Swiss burger into dollars at that exchange rate yields a dollar price of $4.90, or about 69 percent higher than the $2.90 dollar price of the U.S. burger. For the law of one price to hold would have required an exchange rate of SF2.17/$1. So, the market exchange rate made Swiss goods about 69 percent more expensive than comparable U.S. goods, or the franc was "overvalued" by about 69 percent relative to the dollar.[11] At the other end of the spectrum, consider a Big Mac in the Philippines. Converting the price of

---

11. *The Economist*, May 29, 2004, pp. 71–72.

that burger (P69.02) into dollars at the market rate (P56/$1) yields a dollar price of $1.23, or 57 percent lower than the $2.90 dollar price of the U.S. burger. So the market exchange rate made Philippine goods about 57 percent cheaper than comparable U.S. goods, or the peso was "undervalued" by 57 percent.

Our discussion of the law of one price and purchasing power parity suggests at least two potential problems with the burger-based PPP test. First, the use of a single good, the Big Mac, means that the test can at best evaluate the law of one price, *not* purchasing power parity. Second, even as a test of the law of one price, the Big Mac represents a poor choice, because as a restaurant meal it isn't a traded good. The Big Mac market is difficult to arbitrage, although the availability of cheap restaurant meals might serve as a small inducement to tourism. Also, Big Macs differ around the world as a concession to local tastes. It may seem harsh to criticize the Big Mac survey, which was, after all, introduced as a lark (even though studies by economists have found that it predicts remarkably well). But many so-called tests of PPP use inappropriate goods. For example, another PPP test included a deluxe single hotel room, a hotel room-service American-style breakfast, the ubiquitous Big Mac, a one-mile taxi ride, a man's haircut, a drink of Johnnie Walker Black Label scotch on the rocks, a local phone call from a pay phone, and a first-run movie. *(Evaluate each good and service for inclusion in a test of PPP.)*[12]

We're now ready to combine our results on the long-run neutrality of money with those from purchasing power parity to develop a simple but very useful theory of long-run exchange rate behavior, known as the *monetary approach* because the model focuses exclusively on the role of monetary factors in explaining long-run movements in exchange rates.

4 THE MONETARY APPROACH TO THE EXCHANGE RATE

4.1 The History and Intuition Behind the Monetary Approach

The **monetary approach to the exchange rate** assumes that the exchange rate's primary role in the macroeconomy is to equate the quantities supplied and demanded of various monies or currencies.[13] Any event that alters either the quantity of money balances demanded or the money stock will alter the exchange rate according to the monetary approach.

The modern version of this view of the exchange rate dates from the 1970s and work by economists Robert Mundell, Harry Johnson, and Jacob Frenkel. Despite the monetary approach's relatively short modern history, its roots reach back to David Hume's 1752 elaboration of the specie-flow mechanism. Much of the monetary approach's renewed appeal rests on its simplicity. Unlike other models of exchange rate behavior, the monetary approach relies on the fundamental definition of an exchange rate as the relative price of two monies. Just as the supplies of and demands for, say, corn and wheat determine the relative price of those goods, so the supplies of and demands for dollars and yen determine their relative price. When the quantity demanded of a money exceeds the quantity supplied, its relative price rises—that is, the currency appreciates. When the quantity supplied exceeds the quantity demanded, the money's relative price falls, or the currency depreciates.

---

12. Additional information you might find useful: A large portion of the price of liquor in most countries consists of taxes; phone service typically is either government owned or a regulated private monopoly; and most countries subject movies to import restrictions.

13. The analogous theory under a fixed exchange rate regime is known as the *monetary approach to the balance of payments*.

The monetary approach assumes that real output equals its full-employment level and that output and input prices adjust quickly to their long-run equilibrium levels. Therefore, we take the monetary approach as a long-run theory of exchange rate behavior, with little to say about short-run exchange rate fluctuations that occur before prices in the economy have time to adjust to shocks.

4.2 A Simple Monetary Model of the Exchange Rate

We already know that equilibrium in the money market requires that the real money stock, defined as the nominal money stock divided by the price level, equal the quantity demanded of real money balances. The demand for real money balances depends positively on real income and negatively on the nominal interest rate. Equation 6 repeats the money-market equilibrium condition for the domestic country:

$$M/P = L(\overset{+}{Q}, \overset{-}{i}) \qquad [6]$$

Equation 7 presents the corresponding condition for the foreign country:

$$M^*/P^* = L^*(\overset{+}{Q^*}, \overset{-}{i^*}) \qquad [7]$$

We're interested in the causes of *movements* in the exchange rate rather than the particular *level* of the exchange rate, so it's convenient to translate Equations 6 and 7 into relationships among the percentage rates of change of money stocks, price levels, and money demands. Letting "hats" continue to denote percentage rates of change:[14]

$$\hat{M} - \hat{P} = \hat{L} \text{ and } \hat{M}^* - \hat{P}^* = \hat{L}^* \qquad [8]$$

Equation 8 says simply that the rate of growth of the real money stock (the left-hand side of each equation) must match that of the demand for real money balances (the right-hand side of each equation) for the country's money market to remain in equilibrium.

Subtracting the second expression in Equation 8 from the first and rearranging highlights the fundamental relationship central to the monetary approach to the exchange rate:

$$\hat{P} - \hat{P}^* = (\hat{M} - \hat{M}^*) - (\hat{L} - \hat{L}^*) \qquad [9]$$

The difference between two countries' inflation rates depends on the relative growth rates of their money stocks and money demands.

How can the monetary approach provide a theory of exchange-rate behavior when the exchange rate doesn't even appear in Equation 9? The answer is that the monetary approach assumes that relative purchasing power parity holds. This implies that, in the long run, the inflation differential on the left-hand side of Equation 9 will equal the percentage rate of change in the exchange rate (from Equation 5), so that

$$\hat{e} = (\hat{M} - \hat{M}^*) - (\hat{L} - \hat{L}^*) = (\hat{M} - \hat{L}) - (\hat{M}^* - \hat{L}^*) \qquad [10]$$

This statement makes a simple but powerful prediction about the exchange rate: *The relative rates of growth of the supplies of and demands for different monies determine long-run*

---

14. The percentage rate of change of a ratio such as M/P equals the percentage rate of change of the numerator ($\hat{M}$) minus the percentage rate of change of the denominator ($\hat{P}$).

Table 2 **IMPLICATIONS OF THE MONETARY APPROACH TO THE EXCHANGE RATE**	
Variable	Effect on the Exchange Rate[a]
Domestic Nominal Money Stock (M):	
Increase	+
Decrease	−
Foreign Nominal Money Stock (M*):	
Increase	−
Decrease	+
Domestic Money Demand (L):	
Domestic real output (Q)	
Increase	−
Decrease	+
Domestic interest rate (i)	
Increase	+
Decrease	−
Foreign Money Demand (L*):	
Foreign real output (Q*)	
Increase	+
Decrease	−
Foreign interest rate (i*)	
Increase	−
Decrease	+

[a]Plus signs denote increases in e or domestic currency depreciations. Minus signs denote decreases in e or domestic currency appreciations.

movements in the exchange rate. If the domestic money stock grows more rapidly than the foreign money stock and if money demands remain constant, the domestic currency will depreciate. If the stock of each money grows at the same rate as the demand for it, the exchange rate will remain stable. We can also use the simple monetary-approach expression for the exchange rate to highlight the inherent interdependence of exchange rate policies. Equation 10 makes clear that the exchange rate between two currencies depends on money supply and demand in *both* economies. Even a country with rapid money growth can experience an appreciation—if the other country's money stock grows even more rapidly.

4.3 What Does the Monetary Approach to the Exchange Rate Tell Us?

As a theory of long-run exchange rate behavior, the monetary approach summarized in Equation 10 predicts the long-term effects of changes in domestic and foreign money stocks, real outputs, and interest rates on the exchange rate. Table 2 summarizes these results. *Other things being equal,* a one-time permanent rise in the domestic money stock causes a proportional increase in the domestic price level (from Equation 6) and, through PPP, a proportional depreciation of the domestic currency.[15] Similarly, a one-time

---

15. Recall from section 2 that a one-time change in M doesn't affect Q or i and, therefore, doesn't affect the demand for real money balances. For the money market to stay in equilibrium, P must rise to keep the real money stock constant.

permanent increase in the foreign money stock raises the foreign price level (from Equation 7) and appreciates the domestic currency proportionally in the long run.

The monetary approach in Equation 10 also predicts that economic events that raise the domestic demand for money ($\hat{L} > 0$) will cause a domestic appreciation; examples include a rise in domestic income or a fall in the domestic interest rate. If domestic real output rises, for given levels of the nominal money stock and the interest rate, Equation 6 implies that the domestic price level must fall. According to purchasing power parity, a decline in the domestic price level causes the domestic currency to appreciate.

A rise in the domestic interest rate lowers the domestic demand for money according to Equation 6 and, for given values of M and Q, raises the domestic price level. Therefore, the domestic currency must depreciate to maintain purchasing power parity. Note that this seems to contradict the predictions of our short-run model from earlier chapters, in which a rise in the domestic interest rate always caused a currency *appreciation*. Here, the monetary approach argues instead that a rise in the domestic interest rate should cause a domestic currency *depreciation*. Despite first appearances, the two predictions don't contradict one another; they simply rest on different assumptions about the relevant time horizon.

The short-run model of earlier chapters assumed that the price level was fixed. This allowed one-time changes in the money stock to alter the interest rate.[16] The monetary approach, with its long-run equilibrium focus, assumes that the price level adjusts to any monetary disturbance. As we saw in section 2.2, this implies that one-time changes in the money stock don't alter the interest rate. Therefore, when the monetary approach makes predictions about the impact of an interest rate change on the exchange rate, the cause of the change in the interest rate must be something *other than* a simple one-time increase in the money stock. If the interest rate changes for different reasons in the two models, we shouldn't be surprised that the interest rate's effect on the exchange rate also differs between the short-run model and the long-run monetary-approach model. To understand better the relationship between the two models' predictions, we must find the fundamental cause of interest rate changes in long-run equilibrium.

4.4 PPP and Long-Run Interest Parity with Inflation

If permanent one-time changes in the nominal money stock don't alter the interest rate in the long run, what kind of monetary disturbance would cause a change in the long-run equilibrium interest rate? The answer is a change in the *rate of growth* (as opposed to the *level*) of the money stock. Virtually all economies experience more-or-less continual growth in their money stocks. Actual monetary policy decisions typically concern the money stock's rate of growth, not one-time increases or decreases in its level. Table 3 reports recent percentage rates of growth of the money stocks for the major industrial economies. Notice that the growth rates exhibit substantial variation, both across years for a single country and across countries, and that growth rates are positive in most years for most countries.

When the money stock grows continually, prices in the economy must continually adjust. The result is **inflation**, which simply means a continuing rise in the price level. In long-run equilibrium, the money stock's growth rate doesn't affect real output, and the price level rises at the same rate as the money stock. We can incorporate inflation into our theory of the long-run relationship among prices, interest rates, and the exchange rate simply by combining interest parity and purchasing power parity.

---

16. With P fixed, changes in M change the real money stock and, therefore, i.

Table 3	ANNUAL GROWTH OF NOMINAL MONEY STOCKS, 1992–2002 (PERCENT)										
Country	1992	1993	1994	1995	1996	1997	1998	1999	2000	2001	2002
U.S.	11.7	9.7	0.1	−0.9	1.4	3.5	3.5	10.3	−1.7	11.4	3.1
Japan	3.9	7.0	4.2	13.1	9.7	8.6	5.0	11.7	3.5	13.7	23.5
Euro area	5.2	5.3	4.2	37.1	10.6	12.0	10.2	10.7	5.8	6.4	9.6
U.K.	4.3	9.9	0.8	16.7	9.3	25.7	9.4	11.1	14.1	11.3	13.3
Canada	7.1	8.3	6.6	10.2	12.7	9.2	5.7	10.9	13.0	12.7	5.8

Source: Data from International Monetary Fund.

Recall that interest parity summarizes the relationship between interest rates and exchange rates required for portfolio owners to willingly hold the existing quantities of deposits in various currencies.[17] The interest parity relationship, written as

$$i - i^* = (e^e - e)/e = \hat{e}^e,$$ [11]

holds whenever the expected rates of return on deposits denominated in the domestic and foreign currencies are equal, so portfolio owners have no incentive to reallocate their portfolios between the two types of deposits.[18] This requires the interest differential (the left-hand side of Equation 11) to equal the expected rate of domestic currency depreciation (the right-hand side of Equation 11).

But, in the long run, what determines the expected rate of domestic currency depreciation? If relative PPP describes the behavior of the exchange rate in the long run, the *actual* rate of depreciation will equal the difference between the two countries' rates of inflation, as in Equation 5. And if individuals in the economy know that this is how the exchange rate behaves, they will *expect* the domestic currency to depreciate by whatever amount they *expect* domestic inflation to exceed foreign inflation. To summarize the argument algebraically, if relative purchasing power parity implies that

$$\hat{e} = (\hat{P} - \hat{P}^*),$$

then market participants will form their expectations using that same relationship, so

$$\hat{e}^e = (\hat{P}^e - \hat{P}^{*e}).$$ [12]

Combining Equations 11 and 12 tells us that in the long run, if relative purchasing power parity holds and market participants expect it to hold, the interest differential between deposits denominated in two currencies equals the expected inflation differential between the two countries, or:

$$i - i^* = (\hat{P}^e - \hat{P}^{*e})$$ [13]

---

17. Section 4 of the chapter on currency markets and exchange rates develops the theory of interest parity.

18. The expected nominal rate of return on domestic-currency-denominated deposits equals the domestic interest rate. The expected nominal rate of return on foreign-currency-denominated deposits (expressed in terms of domestic currency) equals the foreign interest rate plus any expected rate of domestic currency appreciation/depreciation. Equality between the two expected rates of return requires $i = i^* + \hat{e}^e$, an expression equivalent to Equation 11.

This implies that *differences in countries' nominal interest rates, in long-run equilibrium, reflect differences in their expected inflation.* If the domestic country's expected inflation rate rises relative to the foreign country's, the interest rate on deposits denominated in the domestic currency must rise proportionally to maintain interest parity.[19] To understand why, we need to distinguish between two measures of an asset's rate of return.

REAL AND NOMINAL RATES OF RETURN   The nominal interest rate, i, measures an asset's rate of return measured in units of the domestic currency. Suppose an individual purchases a \$1,000 bond that promises to pay \$1,100 in one year. The interest rate equals (\$1,100 − \$1,000)/\$1,000 = 10%, because the individual earns 10 percent in dollars on the funds invested in the bond. This interest rate gives the **nominal rate of return** on the investment, or the rate of return measured in current dollars.

If the rate of inflation equals zero over the year the bond is held, the individual's purchasing power, or ability to purchase goods and services, also will increase by 10 percent. This increase in purchasing power represents the bond's **real rate of return**, or its return measured in real terms (that is, purchasing power over goods and services) rather than in dollars. Whenever the price level remains constant or the rate of inflation equals zero, the nominal and real rates of return on any asset are equal.

Suppose, instead, that the rate of inflation is 10 percent during the year of the investment. At the end of the year, \$1,100 will buy the same quantity of goods and services that \$1,000 would buy at the beginning. The investment still earns a nominal return (i) of 10 percent measured in dollars—but now earns a real return (r) of 0 percent measured in purchasing power over goods and services; the difference just equals the rate of inflation ($\hat{P}$). Generally, the real return on any asset equals the nominal rate of return minus the rate of inflation, a relationship known as the **Fisher equation**:

$$r = i - \hat{P} \tag{14}$$

Of course, an individual making an asset-portfolio decision can't know in advance what the actual inflation rate will be over the asset's life. Asset decisions must be made on *expected* real rates, or the difference between the observable nominal rate of return and the expected rate of inflation:

$$r^e = i - \hat{P}^e \tag{15}$$

To keep the expected *real* rate of return on domestic-currency-denominated deposits constant, Equation 15 makes clear that the domestic nominal interest rate must rise by the amount of any expected inflation. This is exactly what Equation 13 predicts will happen in the long run. In long-run equilibrium, any inflation-induced interest rate increase doesn't make portfolio owners any better off or any worse off in real terms; it simply compensates them for inflation's expected erosion of the domestic currency's purchasing power.

INTEREST AND EXCHANGE RATES IN THE MONETARY APPROACH   Now we can see more clearly the reasons for the monetary approach's surprising long-run prediction: An increase in the domestic nominal interest rate causes a domestic-currency *depreciation*. In the long run on which the monetary approach focuses, the nominal interest rate increases only in response to a rise in the money stock's rate of growth. Such a rise causes inflation, and market participants expect that inflation. They demand higher *nominal* rates of return in

---

19. The relationship between expected inflation and the interest rate is known as the *Fisher effect*, after Irving Fisher, an economist who did important work on interest rates and their role in the economy.

order to maintain a constant *real* rate of return as inflation erodes the domestic currency's purchasing power. We know that money growth leads to currency depreciations, so the monetary approach's link between increases in interest rates and currency depreciations makes perfect sense—once we understand that increases in the long-run equilibrium interest rate come only from inflation-inducing increases in the rate of money growth.

The monetary approach's link between inflation, the exchange rate, and the nominal interest rate suggests that, other things equal, high-inflation countries should have higher nominal interest rates than low-inflation countries and that a single country's nominal interest rate should vary positively with the country's rate of inflation. We can investigate these relationships empirically by illustrating recent interest rates and inflation for a sample of three industrialized economies, as in Figure 5. Within each economy, periods of higher inflation are associated with higher nominal interest rates. Comparing across economies, the higher inflation rate in the United States and Germany than in Japan in most years translated into a higher nominal U.S. and German interest rate as well.

4.5 What's Missing from the Monetary Approach?

Purchasing power parity and the monetary approach to the exchange rate provide only one piece of a complete explanation of exchange rate behavior—albeit a very important piece. We've seen that even relative purchasing power parity doesn't hold in the short run, making the monetary approach, which relies on PPP, an inappropriate model for predicting short-run behavior of the exchange rate or any other macroeconomic variable. The fixed-price model from earlier chapters provides a better guide to the macroeconomy in the short run, and in the upcoming chapter we'll turn our attention to the economy's adjustment from short-run to long-run results.

But even in long-run equilibrium, elements beyond PPP may play an important role. Purchasing power parity explains how exchange rates respond to price-level changes caused by changes in the money stock. Similarly, the monetary approach focuses exclusively on the long-run equilibrium effect of changes in the money stock or its rate of growth. When *nonmonetary* shocks hit the economy, the exchange rate may behave in ways not explained well by purchasing power parity and the monetary approach, even in long-run equilibrium. In other words, the *real* exchange rate may change.

5 THE REAL EXCHANGE RATE

5.1 Changes in the Real Exchange Rate

The monetary approach to the exchange rate does a reasonably good job of explaining exchange rate movements in the long run if all the disturbances to the economy come from the money market. However, to understand exchange rates better, we must be able to analyze disturbances that are nonmonetary in nature. Such shocks cause purchasing power parity not to hold. In other words, they cause changes in the *real* exchange rate. Recall that the real exchange rate or, equivalently, the relative price of domestic goods and services, equals the ratio of the domestic price level to the foreign price level expressed in terms of domestic currency:

$$R \equiv P/eP^* \qquad [16]$$

A decline in the real exchange rate constitutes a **real depreciation** of the domestic currency. When price levels are fixed, a nominal depreciation (a rise in e) leads directly to a real depreciation. We saw in earlier chapters that a real depreciation causes consumers to shift their spending from foreign to domestic goods. A rise in the real exchange rate represents

Figure 5   Inflation and Nominal Interest Rates, 1991–2002 (Percent)

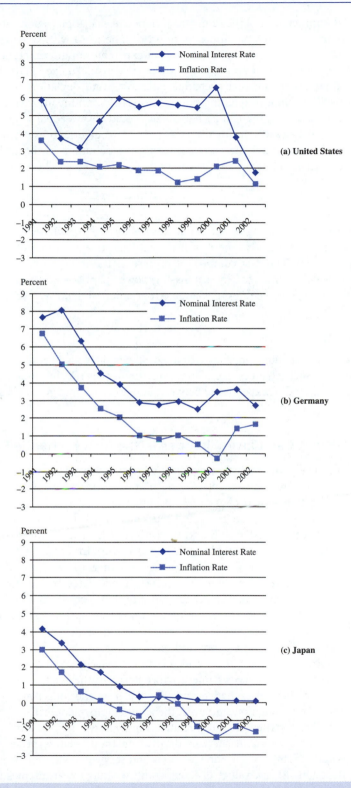

To maintain assets' real rates of return, nominal interest rates must incorporate changes in the rate of inflation. Within each country, nominal interest rates rise and fall with inflation. Across countries, those with higher inflation exhibit higher nominal interest rates.

Source: Data from International Monetary Fund.

a **real appreciation** of the domestic currency. A real appreciation can be caused by, among other things, a nominal appreciation (a decline in e) with price levels fixed. The major impact of a real appreciation is a shift of expenditure from domestic to foreign goods and services. But, as we've seen, price levels can't be assumed fixed in the long run.

Changes in the real exchange rate constitute deviations from purchasing power parity. If absolute purchasing power parity held continually in the long run ($P = e \cdot P^*$ from Equation 3), the real exchange rate would always equal 1. Or, if relative purchasing power parity held continually ($\hat{P} = \hat{e} + \hat{P}^*$ from Equation 4), the real exchange rate would be a constant, because expressing the definition of the real exchange rate (from Equation 16) in rates of change shows that

$$\hat{R} = (\hat{P} - \hat{P}^*) - \hat{e}, \tag{17}$$

so relative purchasing power parity implies that $\hat{R} = 0$. Or, we can rearrange Equation 17 to express changes in the nominal exchange rate in terms of two components as in Equation 18. The first component represents the inflation differential between the two countries—as predicted by purchasing power parity—and the second captures changes in the real exchange rate—deviations from purchasing power parity:

$$\hat{e} = (\hat{P} - \hat{P}^*) - \hat{R} \tag{18}$$

Real exchange rates can change dramatically, and trends in real exchange rates can last for decades. Such changes exert important influences on the international macroeconomy because they shift expenditure between domestic and foreign goods and services.

5.2 What Can Cause Changes in the Real Exchange Rate?

Unfortunately, economists don't yet understand as well as we would like all the causes of real exchange rate movements. Work to understand real exchange rates is in its relatively early stages in part because real exchange rates have exhibited much more volatility during the flexible-exchange-rate years since 1973 than they did during the fixed-rate years between World War II and the early 1970s. A full understanding of real exchange rates presents a formidable task because they involve the interaction of so many macroeconomic variables. However, we can gain substantial insight into several important causes of changes in real exchange rates by noting simply that the real exchange rate represents the relative price of domestic goods and services compared with foreign ones. This focuses our attention on *output markets*, because the relative prices of domestic and foreign goods and services should be determined by the relative demands for and supplies of those goods and services.

Figure 6 illustrates how the relative demands for and supplies of domestic and foreign goods and services interact to determine the relative price of those goods and services, or the real exchange rate. We focus on the long run, so the supplies of both domestic and foreign output are at their full-employment levels, Q_0 and Q_0^*, respectively. This implies a vertical long-run *relative supply* curve, RS_0. Relative demands for domestic and foreign goods and services depend on their relative price. At high values of R, expenditures shift toward foreign goods and services, so the relative demand for domestic goods is low. At low values of R, expenditure shifts toward domestic goods and services, so the relative demand is high. Therefore, the *relative demand* curve, RD_0, exhibits a negative slope in Figure 6. Just as in other product markets, the equilibrium price in Figure 6 is the one at which the relative supply of domestic goods equals the relative demand for them, or R_0.

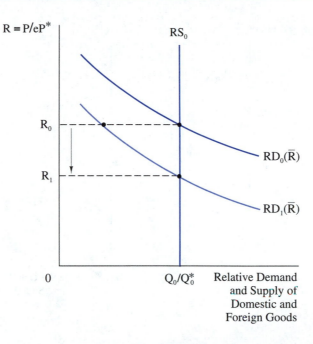

Figure 6   **Relative Output Demand Affects the Real Exchange Rate**

The real exchange rate ($R \equiv P/eP^*$) represents the relative price of domestic and foreign goods and services. When demand for foreign goods rises relative to demand for domestic goods, RD shifts to the left. At the old real exchange rate, R_0, there is excess supply of domestic goods and excess demand for foreign ones. The domestic currency depreciates in real terms to make domestic goods relatively cheaper, increase relative demand for domestic goods, and bring it back into equality with relative output supply at a real exchange rate of R_1.

Disturbances that shift either the relative supply curve or the relative demand curve change the real exchange rate. Suppose consumers' tastes shift in favor of foreign goods and services. RD shifts to the left, from RD_0 to RD_1 in Figure 6. At the original real exchange rate, excess relative supply of domestic goods and services exists, or, equivalently, excess relative demand for foreign ones. This causes the relative price of domestic goods and services to fall to R_1. The foreign currency appreciates in real terms, and the domestic currency depreciates. This makes foreign goods and services relatively more expensive, shifts expenditure toward domestic ones, and reequates relative demands to the unchanged relative supplies of the two countries' outputs. (*Illustrate and explain why an increase in relative demand for domestic goods would lead to a domestic real appreciation.*)

Changes in relative output supplies also influence the real exchange rate. Suppose the foreign economy enjoys an increase in its productivity due to a technological innovation. The long-run, or full-employment, level of foreign output rises relative to domestic output, shifting RS to the left to RS_1 in Figure 7. At the original real exchange rate, R_0, excess relative demand now exists for domestic goods. Their relative price rises to R_1. This constitutes a real domestic-currency appreciation, or a real foreign-currency depreciation. The change in the real exchange rate makes domestic goods relatively more expensive, shifts expenditure away from those goods, and reequates relative demands to the new lower relative supply of domestic goods. (*Illustrate that a rise in domestic relative supply leads to a domestic real depreciation and a foreign real appreciation.*)

Figure 7 **Relative Output Supply Affects the Real Exchange Rate**

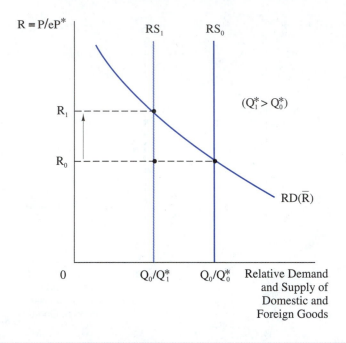

A rise in the long-run equilibrium level of foreign output (Q*) relative to domestic output (Q) shifts RS to the left. At the original real exchange rate, R_0, there is excess demand for domestic goods and excess supply of foreign ones. The domestic currency appreciates to make domestic goods relatively more expensive, reduce relative demand for domestic goods, and bring it back into equality with relative output supply at a real exchange rate of R_1.

6 LONG-RUN EQUILIBRIUM EXCHANGE RATES

We've now seen through the monetary approach how *monetary* disturbances affect nominal exchange rates and through our theory of the real exchange rate how *nonmonetary* disturbances affect real exchange rates. We can combine these two insights to see how the long-run equilibrium exchange rate responds to various shocks to the economy; Table 4 summarizes these responses.

To examine the effect of a one-time change in the size of the domestic money stock, we need only the monetary approach to the exchange rate. Changes in the level of the money stock don't affect long-run equilibrium real output or the interest rate. Therefore, our money market equilibrium condition in Equation 6 implies that the price level moves in proportion to the change in the money stock. The domestic currency depreciates (appreciates) in nominal terms in proportion to the increase (decrease) in the domestic money stock. All *relative* prices in the economy, including the real exchange rate, remain unaffected.

The monetary approach also suffices to understand the effect of a change in relative money growth rates. If the domestic money growth rate rises relative to foreign money growth, we saw in section 4.4 that the rate of domestic inflation rises proportionally. Purchasing power parity requires a proportional nominal domestic currency depreciation. Again, relative prices remain unchanged, including the real exchange rate.

A change in relative demand for domestic output (RD) doesn't change the long-run equilibrium price level, which is determined by the money market equilibrium condition in

Table 4 LONG-RUN EQUILIBRIUM NOMINAL AND REAL EXCHANGE RATES					
Shock	Effect on $\hat{e}$[a]	=	Effect on $(\hat{P} - \hat{P}*)$	−	Effect on $\hat{R}$[b]
Relative Money Stock Levels *(M/M*):*[c]					
Increase	+		+		0
Decrease	−		−		0
Relative Money Growth Rates *($\hat{M}/\hat{M}*$):*[c]					
Increase	+		+		0
Decrease	−		−		0
Relative Output Demands (RD):[d]					
Increase	−		0		+
Decrease	+		0		−
Relative Output Supplies *(RS = Q/Q*):*[d]					
Increase	?		−		−
Decrease	?		+		+

[a]A plus sign denotes a domestic nominal depreciation, and a minus sign a nominal appreciation.
[b]A plus sign denotes a domestic real appreciation, and a minus sign a real depreciation.
[c]Purchasing power parity holds.
[d]Purchasing power parity does not hold.

Equation 6.[20] However, section 5.2 implies that changes in relative output demands do alter the *real* exchange rate. In particular, a rise in relative demand for domestic output causes a domestic real appreciation, and a fall in relative demand causes a domestic real depreciation. But long-run price levels don't change, so nominal currency appreciations and depreciations are the mechanisms through which the real exchange rate changes occur.

Unlike changes in relative output demands, changes in relative output supplies (RS) do change the long-run equilibrium price level. Recall that the price level is determined by the money market equilibrium condition in Equation 6. If the relative supply of domestic output rises, the increase in full-employment Q increases the demand for domestic money. With a fixed nominal money stock, this requires a fall in the price level to maintain money market equilibrium. Through purchasing power parity, the fall in the domestic price level pushes the nominal exchange rate down (a nominal appreciation). But the change in relative output supplies also alters the equilibrium *real* exchange rate. The domestic currency depreciates in real terms as domestic output becomes relatively more plentiful. Therefore, the supply shock's effects through the money and output markets push the nominal exchange rate in opposite directions, and we can't be sure of the net effect.

7 MORE ON WHY INTEREST RATES DIFFER

At any time, the nominal interest rates paid on assets denominated in different currencies generally differ substantially. We encountered one reason why back in our introduction to

---

20. Note that the Q term in Equation 6 isn't affected by a rise in demand for domestic output because, in long-run equilibrium, real output must be at its full-employment level, as determined by the supply side of the economy.

the foreign exchange market: Interest parity suggests that interest-rate differences reflect market participants' expectations about future currency appreciations and depreciations. To hold assets denominated in currencies expected to appreciate, portfolio owners willingly accept lower nominal interest rates. For assets denominated in currencies expected to depreciate, portfolio owners demand higher nominal interest rates as compensation.

The monetary approach to the exchange rate in section 4 carried us one step further toward understanding international interest rate differences. Purchasing power parity implies that long-run equilibrium nominal exchange rate movements reflect differences in countries' rates of inflation. Hence, in long-run equilibrium, *expected* exchange rate movements should equal *expected* inflation differentials. This implies that long-run equilibrium differences in nominal interest rates equal differences in countries' expected inflation rates (see Equation 13).

We can take a further step by building in what we now know about changes in real exchange rates, or deviations from purchasing power parity. If, in long-run equilibrium, changes in the nominal exchange rate include both relative inflation rates (as in the monetary approach) *and* changes in the real exchange rate, then changes in the *expected* nominal exchange rate should include both *expected* relative inflation rates and changes in the *expected* real exchange rate:

$$\hat{e}^e = (\hat{P}^e - \hat{P}^{*e}) - \hat{R}^e \qquad [19]$$

Interest parity says that the interest differential equals the expected rate of change in the nominal exchange rate, or the left-hand side of Equation 19, so we can conclude that:

$$i - i^* = (\hat{P}^e - \hat{P}^{*e}) - \hat{R}^e \qquad [20]$$

Now we can see that international nominal interest-rate differences contain two components. The first reflects expected inflation differentials. The second reflects expected changes in the real exchange rate. Higher expected domestic inflation, lower expected foreign inflation, or an expected real domestic depreciation leads to a higher nominal interest rate differential.

We distinguished earlier between nominal interest rates, which measure an asset's rate of return in nominal or currency units, and real interest rates, which measure an asset's rate of return in real units of purchasing power. Equation 15, repeated here, indicated that the expected real interest rate equaled the nominal interest rate minus any expected inflation:

$$r^e = i - \hat{P}^e$$

We can combine the expressions for the domestic and foreign real interest rates to see what determines the difference between them:

$$r^e - r^{*e} = (i - i^*) - (\hat{P}^e - \hat{P}^{*e}) \qquad [21]$$

Simply plugging the expression for the nominal interest differential from Equation 20 into Equation 21 reveals that *international differences in expected real interest rates reflect expected real currency appreciations or depreciations:*

$$r^e - r^{*e} = (\hat{P}^e - \hat{P}^{*e}) - \hat{R}^e - (\hat{P}^e - \hat{P}^{*e}) = -\hat{R}^e \qquad [22]$$

Note that Equation 22 is simply a *real* form of interest parity. While *nominal* interest parity equates the *nominal* interest differential to the expected change in the *nominal* exchange rate, **real interest parity** equates the *real* interest differential to the expected change in the *real* exchange rate. This suggests that when all disturbances are monetary, implying that purchasing power parity is expected to hold (and, therefore, $\hat{R}^e = 0$), real expected interest rates should be equal across countries. But if nonmonetary shocks are expected to cause deviations from purchasing power parity, real interest rates can differ, *even in long-run equilibrium.*

CASE 1: *TANK-TOURISTEN*

European Union

In 2004, the European Union welcomed 10 new members along a north-south strip through Central and Eastern Europe, from Estonia to Slovenia. With EU enlargement came a significant lessening of transaction-cost barriers to trade and increased movement across national borders. Shoppers and tourists from Italy, Austria, and Germany, along the EU's former eastern border, find it much easier to travel east to Poland, the Czech Republic, the Slovak Republic, Hungary, and Slovenia, now all part of the enlarged EU. Why would shoppers make such a trek? One answer: to tank up with gasoline and cigarettes.

Even before the formal EU enlargement on May 1, 2004, observers estimated that 80–90 percent of business at Czech filling stations within a few miles of the German border consisted of Germans crossing the border to buy gas at about $3.66 per gallon and avoid paying the $5.23 per gallon typical on the German side of the border.[21] The flow of *Tank-Touristen* has grown since the May 1 abolition of customs controls reduced border queues. Even German police crossed the border to gas up their cruisers in Poland until German

officials banned such trips.[22] Drivers also stocked up on products such as cigarettes for which prices differ significantly across countries, often due to differences in national taxes. Cigarettes in Poland, for example, cost about a quarter of what they do in Germany—worth a daytrip for many smokers.

Which of the across-border price differences will last, and for how long? It depends. For products whose price differences reflect variation in the profit-maximizing prices set by firms in different markets rather than tax differences, the variation has already started to disappear. For example, most car companies raised prices in Poland in 2004 after German car-buyers rushed there to save approximately 20 percent on new cars. For products such as gasoline and cigarettes, for which much of the price differences reflect governments' tax policies, the answer depends in part on politics. High-tax EU members such as Germany hope that EU policies will push the new members to raise their tax levels, allowing Germany to maintain its high gasoline and cigarette taxes—without losing business to lower-tax new members such as Poland and the Czech Republic.

CASE 2: **PURCHASING POWER PARITY AT HOME?**

United States

Section 3 cited many possible reasons for a failure of purchasing power parity—trade barriers, nontraded goods, changes in relative prices, and differences in countries' production and consumption patterns among them. With so many possible causes of failure, it can be difficult to sort out empirically which are really important. A recent test took an unusual approach to testing purchasing power parity in order to circumvent this problem.[23]

The study tested whether PPP held among consumer price indices for Philadelphia, Chicago, New York, and Los Angeles. The four U.S. cities use the same currency, so exchange rate fluctuations could be ruled out as the explanation of any intercity price differences. Along the same lines, macroeconomic policies could be assumed to exert similar influences on the four cities. And, while consumption patterns may differ somewhat regionally, the

---

21. "German 'Tank Tourists' Drive Off For Cheap Gas Across Borders," *Wall Street Journal*, January 21, 2004.

22. "Polish Prices Lure Germans Across New Open Border," *Financial Times*, June 7, 2004.

23. Information for this case comes from the Tootell article in the chapter references.

consumer-price-index data reflected the prices of similar consumption baskets.

The study found that purchasing power parity failed to hold in tests based on cities' overall consumer price indices.[24] However, when nontraded goods were excluded, purchasing power parity held. These results indicate that the presence of nontraded goods—such as housing, which contains a large real estate component—may explain much of the observed deviations from purchasing power parity. We can apply these insights in an international context. Suppose, for example, that each country's price level includes two components: one captures prices of *traded* goods and services (P_T) and one reflects prices of *nontraded* goods and services (P_{NT}):

$$P = (\alpha_T \cdot P_T) + (\alpha_{NT} \cdot P_{NT}) \text{ and}$$
$$P^* = (\alpha_T^* \cdot P_T^*) + (\alpha_{NT}^* \cdot P_{NT}^*), \qquad [23]$$

where α_T and α_{NT} represent the weights of *t*raded and *n*ontraded goods in the domestic country's consumption basket, while α_T^* and α_{NT}^* denote the corresponding weights for the foreign country's consumption. If the law of one price

holds for traded goods but not for nontraded ones, because arbitrage works for the former but not for the latter, then $P_T = e \cdot P_T^*$. This allows us to write the real exchange rate by plugging Equation 23 into the definition, $R \equiv P/eP^*$:

$$R = [(\alpha_T \cdot e \cdot P_T^*) + (\alpha_{NT} \cdot P_{NT})]/$$
$$[(\alpha_T^* \cdot e \cdot P_T^*) + (\alpha_{NT}^* \cdot e \cdot P_{NT}^*)]. \qquad [24]$$

Recall that absolute purchasing power parity holds if R equals 1, and relative purchasing power parity holds if R equals a constant. Equation 24 will equal 1 only if two conditions hold. First, the two countries' consumption weights for traded and nontraded goods must be equal ($\alpha_T = \alpha_T^*$ and $\alpha_{NT} = \alpha_{NT}^*$). Second, the prices of nontraded goods must be equal, or the law of one price must hold for those goods (that is, $P_{NT} = e \cdot P_{NT}^*$). Equation 24 will remain constant only if the two countries' weights remain constant relative to one another *and* if nontraded-goods prices in the two countries remain constant relative to one another. The next case examines the importance of across-country changes in nontraded-goods prices for PPP and real exchange rates.

CASE 3: NONTRADED GOODS AND THE REAL EXCHANGE RATE

In most countries, workers exhibit higher degrees of mobility between industries within the domestic economy than across international borders. This characteristic of world markets plays an important role in international trade theory. If workers are more mobile within than across countries, then similarly skilled workers in different sectors of the same economy will tend to earn similar wages, while even similarly skilled workers in different countries may earn very different wages (unless the countries follow free-trade policies, which tend to equalize wages across countries).[25] In such a world, differences in countries' rates of productivity growth can cause changes in real exchange rates, or deviations from purchasing power parity. This link between differential productivity growth and the real exchange rate constitutes what economists call the **Balassa-Samuelson effect**.

Suppose the domestic country enjoys rapid productivity growth limited to its traded-goods sector. Wages will rise with productivity in that sector. And

because workers are mobile between the domestic traded- and nontraded-goods sectors, wages will rise in the nontraded-goods sector as well, even though it hasn't shared in the productivity growth. The combination of rising wages and no productivity growth in the nontraded-goods sector leads to rising prices for nontraded goods (P_{NT}) relative to the prices of traded ones ($P_T = e \cdot P_T^*$) in the domestic economy. With no productivity growth in the foreign economy, the price of domestic nontraded goods rises relative to the price of foreign nontraded ones ($e \cdot P_{NT}^*$) as well. As Equation 24 indicates, such relative price changes cause purchasing power parity to fail in both its absolute and relative forms.

The Balassa-Samuelson effect often is cited as one possible explanation for the yen's dramatic real appreciation relative to the U.S. dollar from 1960 through the late 1990s. Suppose that U.S. and Japanese nontraded-goods sectors enjoyed productivity growth at about the same rate, but productivity growth in Japan's traded-goods sector

24. The *Economist* Big Mac test reported in section 3.6 finds different burger prices in U.S. cities; the U.S. price used in the test is actually the average of the New York, Chicago, San Francisco, and Atlanta prices.

25. This result is known in international trade theory as the factor price equalization theorem.

Figure 8 Rich Countries' Price Levels Are Higher Than Those of Poor Countries

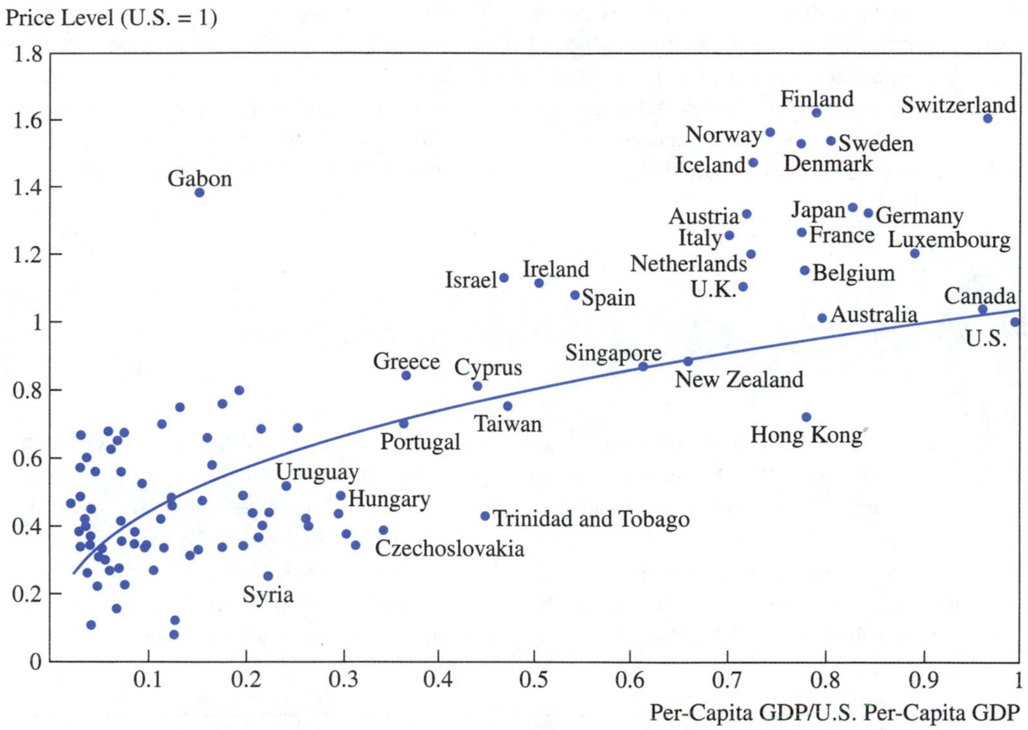

One implication of the Balassa-Samuelson theory is that countries' price levels should be positively related to their per-capita incomes. The evidence clearly supports this implication for the entire country sample, although the theory proves less successful in explaining variation either within rich countries as a group or within poor countries as a group.

Source: Kenneth Rogoff, "The Purchasing Power Parity Puzzle," *Journal of Economic Literature* (June 1996), p. 660.

(for example, autos) outpaced that in the U.S. traded-goods sector. Enhanced productivity in the traded-goods sector raised Japanese wages, and labor mobility within Japan transmitted that wage increase to the nontraded-goods sector. The price of Japanese nontraded goods rose relative to the price of U.S. nontraded goods, and the yen appreciated in real terms against the dollar.

The patterns of traded-goods and nontraded-goods productivity and prices in the United States and Japan since 1960 suggest that the Balassa-Samuelson effect may explain much of the yen's real appreciation. Japanese productivity in tradable goods grew much more quickly than that of the United States, but not in nontradables. And the price of nontradables relative to tradables rose several times as fast in

Japan as in the United States. From Equation 24, we can see the predicted result: a real yen appreciation.

More generally, the Balassa-Samuelson story implies that rich countries' price levels should be higher than those of poor countries.[26] Again, the empirical evidence is broadly supportive. Figure 8 plots each country's per-capita GDP relative to that of the United States on the horizontal axis and each country's price level relative to that of the United States on the vertical axis. Across the entire sample, countries with high per-capita GDPs clearly tend to have higher price levels. However, in samples limited to just poor countries or just rich ones, income doesn't do as good a job at explaining the price-level variation within the group.

---

26. This explains why GDP at market exchange rates tends to be lower (higher) than GDP at PPP exchange rates for low- (high-) income countries.

The Balassa-Samuelson effect also carries another potentially important implication: It may explain why nontraded goods tend to be much cheaper in relatively poor countries than in more affluent ones. If poor countries have lower labor productivity than rich countries in traded goods, but roughly equal productivity with rich countries in nontraded goods and services, then nontraded goods will be cheaper in poor countries. This follows because the low productivity in traded goods implies low wages in poor countries, and low wages imply low prices for nontraded goods. India may provide a classic example:

> A meal at a roadside diner costs the equivalent of about 35 U.S. cents, while lunch at a downtown Delhi cafeteria costs $1. A full-time housekeeper earns $25 a month; a private driver charges $80 a month. Monthly rent for a two-bedroom apartment in New Delhi is about $130.[27]

CASE 4: DRY CLEANING IN OSLO AND KARACHI

The Balassa-Samuelson theory indicates that services would be cheaper in relatively poor countries. Is this true? We can get a rough idea by investigating the relationship between the prices of a basket of 19 services in 70 cities on 5 continents (compiled by Swiss financial-services firm UBS) and the per-capita GNPs in the corresponding countries. The services basket includes items such as the cost of a house cleaner, a visit to the hairdresser, dry cleaning, monthly phone bills, a restaurant meal, a movie ticket, a daily newspaper, and a postage stamp. The price of the entire basket of 19 items varied from $140 in Karachi, Bucharest, Mumbai, and Buenos Aires up to $558 in Oslo, $552 in London, and $514 in Tokyo. Figure 9 reveals that, on average, low-income countries do have cheaper services.

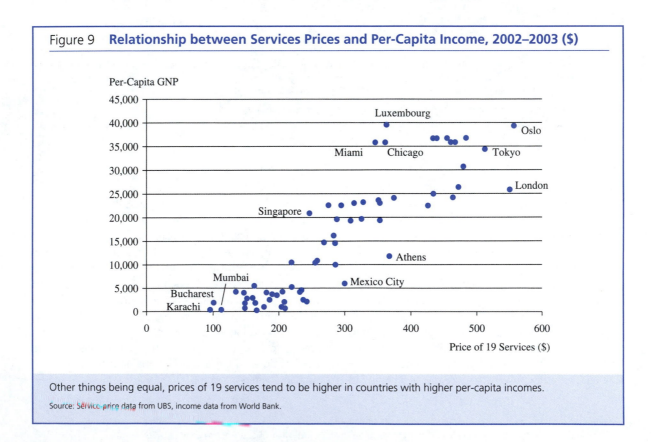

Figure 9   **Relationship between Services Prices and Per-Capita Income, 2002–2003 ($)**

Other things being equal, prices of 19 services tend to be higher in countries with higher per-capita incomes.

Source: Service price data from UBS, income data from World Bank.

---

27. Miriam Jordan, "In India, Luxury Is within Reach of Many," *The Wall Street Journal*, October 17, 1995.

There are also outliers. At the time the data were gathered in early 2003, services were cheaper in Singapore than one might have expected, given the country's relatively high per-capita income. The same was true for Miami and Luxembourg. On the other hand, consumers in Mexico City, Athens, and London paid more for services than Mexico's, Greece's, or the United Kingdom's per-capita incomes would have led us to expect.

SUMMARY

In long-run equilibrium, money has a neutral effect on the macroeconomy. In other words, changes in the money stock can affect nominal variables such as the price level and the nominal exchange rate, but not real variables such as real output, the real rate of interest, or the real exchange rate. The monetary approach to the exchange rate describes how the macroeconomy behaves in the long run when all shocks to the economy are monetary and purchasing power parity holds, at least in its relative form. When shocks can disturb the output market as well as the money market, even relative purchasing power parity can fail, resulting in long-run real currency appreciations and depreciations.

LOOKING AHEAD

So far, we've examined how the macroeconomy behaves in the short run and in long-run equilibrium. In the upcoming chapter, we focus on how the economy adjusts as it moves from its short-run response to a shock to its new long-run equilibrium. We'll see that economic policies may generate short-run effects that differ substantially from their long-run ones.

KEY TERMS

long-run equilibrium	nominal rate of return
neutrality of money	real rate of return
law of one price	Fisher equation
purchasing power parity (PPP)	real depreciation
absolute purchasing power parity	real appreciation
relative purchasing power parity	real interest parity
monetary approach to the exchange rate	Balassa-Samuelson effect
inflation	

PROBLEMS AND QUESTIONS FOR REVIEW

1. A study of prices in 70 cities around the world by UBS found that apartment rents differed much more across cities than did the prices of home electronics and household appliances.[28] Is this what you would have expected based on what you know about the law of one price? Why, or why not?

2. The following data are for 1983–1997.

Country	Percent Increase in Price Level (CPI)	Percent Change in Exchange Rate (e = $/FX)
United States	61%	—
United Kingdom	85%	−8%
Canada	56%	+18%
France	52%	−23%
Germany	37%	−32%
Italy	114%	+12%

28. UBS, "Prices and Earnings: A Comparison of Purchasing Power Around the Globe," 2003 (available at http://www.ubs.com).

    a.   Generally, do the data seem to support purchasing power parity? Be sure to define purchasing power parity.

    b.   Briefly outline three reasons why purchasing power parity might not hold between a particular pair of countries over a particular period.

3. Suppose the law of one price held for all goods and services. Would purchasing power parity necessarily hold? Why or why not?

4. For several decades in the United States, productivity grew more rapidly in traded-goods sectors such as manufacturing than in nontraded sectors such as services. Some analysts recently have argued that the "computer revolution" may finally be changing that trend, as automation raises productivity growth in many nontraded services.

    a.   If increased productivity in the nontraded sector were *unique* to the United States, how would you expect it to affect the real exchange rate? Explain.

    b.   Services (many of which are nontraded) typically comprise a larger share of economic activity in advanced industrial economies than in developing ones. If so, how might a *worldwide* rise in productivity in the service sector affect real exchange rates between advanced industrial economies and developing economies?

5. According to the monetary approach to the exchange rate, what would happen to the nominal exchange rate if:

    a.   the domestic money stock grew at 10 percent, the foreign money stock grew at 10 percent, the demand for domestic money balances grew at 10 percent, and the demand for foreign money balances grew at 10 percent?

    b.   the domestic money stock grew at 10 percent, the foreign money stock grew at 10 percent, the demand for domestic money balances grew at 5 percent, and the demand for foreign money balances grew at 5 percent?

    c.   the domestic money stock grew at 5 percent, the foreign money stock grew at 10 percent, the demand for domestic money balances grew at 5 percent, and the demand for foreign money balances grew at 10 percent?

6. "If country A's nominal interest rate rises because everyone expects a higher real interest rate, A's currency will depreciate. If country A's nominal interest rate rises because everyone expects higher inflation, A's currency will depreciate." Do you agree or disagree? Why?

7. Suppose a developing country pegs its currency, the alpha (α), to the U.S. dollar at an exchange rate $e = (\alpha/\$)$ that rises by a pre-announced amount each month. Such an arrangement is called a crawling peg. If the country's inflation rate exceeds that of the United States by more than the rate at which the α is devalued, what happens to the country's real exchange rate? What effect, if any, would you expect this to have on demand for the country's goods and services?

8. When policy makers in an economy with a history of high inflation rates attempt to change their macroeconomic policies to lower inflation, they often cite declining long-term nominal interest rates as evidence that the policy change is working. Explain. How might policy makers use changes in the exchange rate as an additional source of information about the success of their policy change? Explain.

REFERENCES AND SELECTED READINGS

Engel, Charles, and John H. Rogers. "How Wide Is the Border?" *American Economic Review* (December 1996): 1112–1125.
A study of PPP in U.S. and Canadian cities; for intermediate and advanced students.

Frenkel, Jacob A., and Harry G. Johnson, eds. *The Economics of Exchange Rates.* Reading, Mass.: Addison-Wesley, 1978.
A classic collection on exchange rate theory's major developments during the 1970s, especially the monetary approach; for advanced students.

Frenkel, Jacob A., and Harry G. Johnson, eds. *The Monetary Approach to the Balance of Payments.* London: Allen and Unwin, 1976.
The classic collection on the monetary approach; for intermediate and advanced students.

Goldberg, Pinelopi Koujianou, and Michael M. Knetter. "Goods Prices and Exchange Rates: What Have We Learned?" *Journal of Economic Literature* (September 1997): 1243–1272.
Imperfect competition, market segmentation, and pricing to market; for intermediate to advanced students.

Isard, Peter. *Exchange Rate Economics.* Cambridge: Cambridge University Press, 1995.
Survey of the state of knowledge about exchange rates; level of different sections of the book varies.

Johnson, Harry G. "The Monetary Approach to the Balance of Payments: A Nontechnical Guide." *Journal of International Economics* 7 (August 1977): 251–268.
An introduction to the monetary approach by one of its originators; for all students.

Meltzer, Allan H. "Real Exchange Rates: Some Evidence from the Postwar Years." Federal Reserve Bank of St. *Louis, Review* (March–April 1993): 103–117.
Theoretical and empirical overview of real exchange rates; for intermediate students.

Obstfeld, Maurice. "International Currency Experience: New Lessons and Lessons Relearned." *Brookings Papers on Economic Activity* 1 (1995): 119–220.
Excellent survey of recent currency experience, including purchasing power parity; for intermediate students.

Pakko, Michael R., and Patricia S. Pollard. "Burgernomics: A Big Mac Guide to Purchasing Power Parity." Federal Reserve Bank of St. Louis *Review* (November/December 2003): 9–28.
Examination of The Economist's *burger-based PPP test; for all students.*

Rogoff, Kenneth. "The Purchasing Power Parity Puzzle." *Journal of Economic Literature* (June 1996): 647–668.
Excellent, accessible survey of what we know and what we don't about PPP.

Szapáry, György. "Transition Countries' Choice of Exchange Rate Regime in the Run-Up to EMU Membership." *Finance and Development* 38 (June 2001): 26–29.
Application of the Balassa-Samuelson effect to transition economies.

Taylor, Alan M., and Mark P. Taylor. "The Purchasing Power Parity Debate." *Journal of Economic Perspectives* 18 (Fall 2004): 135–158.
Accessible overview of the theoretical and empirical literatures on PPP.

Tootell, Geoffrey M. B. "PPP within the United States." Federal Reserve Bank of Boston *New England Economic Review* (July–August 1992): 15–24.
Tests find purchasing power parity fails to hold within the United States; for all students.

9

Prices and Output in an Open Economy

1 INTRODUCTION

We examined earlier how fiscal, monetary, and exchange rate policies affect an open macroeconomy in the *short run*—the time horizon over which the price level remains fixed. In the preceding chapter, we turned our attention to the *long run,* when output reaches its full-employment level and the price level adjusts fully to any shocks or policy changes in the economy. Now it's time to explore how the economy behaves *between* the short run and the long run. In other words, what happens *as the price level adjusts* to economic shocks and policy changes?

A quick examination of basic macroeconomic data for a sample of countries reveals that this medium-run period—during which both output and the price level adjust—fits the situation in which most economies find themselves most of the time. This should come as no surprise. After all, economic shocks of all kinds constantly impinge on economies, and policy makers continually adjust their policy instruments. Long-run equilibrium, when all macroeconomic variables have reached states of rest, provides a useful conceptual benchmark; but it's unlikely to be observed often in the world economy, where new shocks and policy changes occur before the economy has adjusted fully to earlier events.

Countries rarely have a stable, unchanging price level. Typically, the price level rises in most years, but at variable and sometimes highly erratic rates. A sustained rise in the overall price level defines **inflation**; a sustained fall in the price level, rarely observed, represents **deflation**. Table 1 reports recent price-level behavior for a sample of countries. Note two patterns. First, inflation rates vary widely across countries. Second, inflation rates often change dramatically within a single country, even over a short period, confirming as we noted previously that economies constantly are adjusting to shocks and policy changes that influence their price levels.

A third pattern related to the rate of inflation constitutes one of the most dramatic and important macroeconomic trends over the past quarter century: a global disinflation. *Disinflation* refers to a sustained decline in the rate of inflation. Unlike deflation, in which the price level falls, disinflation means that the price level continues to rise, but at a decreasing rate. Table 2 documents the disinflation since 1980, which spans all regions of the globe. For the first time in decades, since 2000 no region of the world has experienced inflation at a rate high enough to constitute a grave threat to macroeconomic performance. Of course, the regional averages presented in Table 2 hide a few high-inflation countries. Most are involved in or recovering from civil or international wars. Countries with annual inflation rates averaging over 40 percent for 2000–2004 include

Table 1   ANNUAL CHANGE IN CONSUMER PRICES, 1994–2003 (PERCENT)

Country	1994	1995	1996	1997	1998	1999	2000	2001	2002	2003
United States	2.6	2.8	2.9	2.3	1.5	2.2	3.4	2.8	1.6	2.3
Canada	0.2	1.9	1.6	1.6	1.0	1.7	2.7	2.5	2.3	2.7
Japan	0.7	−0.1	0.1	1.7	0.6	−0.3	−0.6	−0.8	−0.9	−0.2
France	1.7	1.8	2.1	1.3	0.7	0.6	1.8	1.8	1.9	2.2
Germany	2.7	1.7	1.2	1.5	0.6	0.7	2.1	1.9	1.3	1.0
Italy	4.1	5.2	4.0	1.9	2.0	1.7	2.6	2.3	2.6	2.8
United Kingdom	2.4	2.8	3.0	2.8	2.7	2.3	2.1	1.2	1.3	1.4
China	24.1	17.1	8.3	2.8	−0.8	−1.4	0.4	0.7	−0.8	1.2
Thailand	5.1	5.8	5.9	5.6	8.1	0.3	1.5	1.7	0.6	1.8
India	10.2	10.2	9.0	7.2	13.2	4.7	4.0	3.8	4.3	3.8
Turkey	106.3	93.7	82.3	85.7	84.6	64.9	54.9	54.4	45.0	25.3
Mexico	7.0	35.0	34.4	20.6	15.9	16.6	9.5	6.4	5.0	4.5
Uganda	6.5	6.1	7.5	7.8	5.8	−0.2	6.3	−2.0	5.7	5.1
Poland	32.2	27.9	19.9	14.9	11.8	7.3	10.1	5.5	1.9	0.8
Indonesia	8.5	9.4	7.9	6.2	58.0	20.7	3.8	11.5	11.8	6.8
Argentina	4.2	3.4	0.2	0.5	0.9	−1.2	−0.7	−1.1	25.9	13.4
Peru	23.7	11.1	11.5	8.5	7.3	3.5	3.8	−0.1	1.5	2.5
Brazil	2,075.8	66.0	15.8	6.9	3.2	4.9	7.0	6.8	8.4	14.8
D. R. of Congo[a]	23,760.5	541.8	616.8	198.5	29.1	284.9	555.7	357.3	25.3	12.8

[a]Formerly Zaire.

Source: International Monetary Fund, *World Economic Outlook*.

Table 2   AVERAGE ANNUAL CHANGE IN CONSUMER PRICES, 1980–2004 (PERCENT)

	1980–1984	1985–1989	1990–1994	1995–1999	2000–2004
World	14.1%	15.5%	30.4%	8.4%	4.1%
Industrial countries	8.7	3.9	3.8	2.0	2.0
Developing countries	31.4	48.0	53.2	13.1	5.7
Africa	16.8	17.9	39.8	20.6	11.8
Asia	9.0	11.5	10.5	7.3	2.3
Latin America	82.4	185.9	232.6	17.2	8.2
Middle East	18.6	22.5	30.4	29.6	16.4
Transitional economies	6.2	7.7	363.2	53.9	14.5

Source: Data from International Monetary Fund.

Angola (165 percent), Belarus (75 percent), Democratic Republic of Congo (236 percent), Serbia and Montenegro (49 percent), Turkey (45 percent), and Zimbabwe (181 percent).

Just as changes in countries' inflation rates differ, both across countries and across time, so do changes in their outputs. If an economy were perpetually in long-run equilibrium, of the type we examined in the preceding chapter, we would expect its real output to grow fairly smoothly over time, at a rate determined by growth in the country's resource endowment and improvements in its technology. Instead, in Table 3 we see output growth speeding up, slowing down, and occasionally even turning negative, mirrored by changes in unemployment. This provides further evidence that we observe economies primarily in the process of adjusting to more-or-less constant economic shocks and policy changes.

To augment our model of the macroeconomy to incorporate price-level adjustment, we need to distinguish between the *supply*, or production, side of the economy and the *demand*, or expenditure, side, and then combine the two. Our fixed-price model of earlier chapters focused on the demand side alone. In fact, the IS, LM, and BOP curves that we used there together constitute the demand side of the economy. We assumed implicitly that firms willingly supplied at unchanged prices all the output demanded. If this condition were met, the quantity of output demanded, or what we've called *total expenditure on domestic goods and services*, would determine the level of output. However, once we introduce an independent supply side of the economy to represent firms' production decisions and workers' labor-supply decisions, things become more complex—and more realistic.

Table 3 ANNUAL CHANGE IN REAL GDP, 1994–2003 (PERCENT)

Country	1994	1995	1996	1997	1998	1999	2000	2001	2002	2003
United States	4.0%	2.7%	3.6%	4.4%	4.4%	4.2%	5.0%	0.8%	1.9%	3.0%
Canada	4.7	2.8	1.5	4.4	3.3	4.5	4.7	1.8	3.4	2.0
Japan	1.0	1.6	3.3	1.9	−1.1	0.8	1.7	0.4	−0.3	2.5
France	1.8	1.9	1.0	1.9	3.3	3.2	3.2	2.1	1.1	0.5
Germany	2.3	1.7	0.8	1.4	2.1	1.6	3.0	0.8	0.1	−0.1
Italy	2.2	2.9	1.1	2.0	1.8	1.6	2.9	1.8	0.4	0.3
United Kingdom	4.4	2.8	2.6	3.5	2.6	2.3	3.0	2.3	1.8	2.2
China	12.6	10.5	9.6	8.8	7.8	7.1	8.0	7.5	8.3	9.1
Thailand	9.0	9.3	5.9	−1.4	−10.8	4.2	4.3	2.1	5.4	6.8
India	6.7	7.6	7.1	4.9	6.0	6.6	6.4	3.9	5.0	7.2
Turkey	−4.7	8.1	6.9	7.5	3.1	−4.7	7.2	−7.5	7.9	5.8
Mexico	4.4	−6.2	5.2	6.8	4.9	3.8	6.9	−0.2	0.8	1.3
Uganda	6.4	11.9	8.6	5.1	4.6	7.6	4.6	4.9	6.8	4.7
Poland	5.2	6.8	6.0	6.8	4.8	4.1	4.1	1.0	1.4	3.8
Indonesia	7.5	8.2	8.0	4.5	−13.1	0.8	4.8	3.5	3.7	4.1
Argentina	5.8	−2.8	5.5	8.1	3.8	−3.4	−0.5	−4.4	−10.9	8.8
Peru	13.1	7.3	2.5	6.8	−0.4	1.4	3.6	0.3	4.9	4.1
Brazil	5.9	4.2	2.7	3.3	0.2	0.8	4.2	1.3	1.9	−0.2
D. R. of Congo[a]	−3.9	0.7	0.9	−8.2	−3.5	−14.0	−4.9	−2.1	3.5	5.6

[a]Formerly Zaire.

Source: International Monetary Fund, *World Economic Outlook*.

2 APPLES VERSUS GDP: SUPPLY IN MICRO- AND MACROECONOMICS

A microeconomic analogy with a market for a single good, such as apples, is useful here. For the price of apples to remain fixed and for demand alone to determine the equilibrium quantity of apples requires a horizontal supply curve for apples, as depicted in panel (a) of Figure 1. Changes in the demand for apples would then cause quantity to change in the same direction and leave the price of apples unchanged. But the horizontal supply curve in panel (a) of Figure 1 doesn't depict how microeconomic markets typically operate.

In microeconomics, changes in demand typically generate changes in *both* price and quantity. Figure 1 shows this in panel (b), where we draw the supply of apples as an upward-sloping line. The positive slope of the supply curve represents the role of price increases (that is, increases in the price of apples *relative* to the prices of other goods) in drawing resources into apple production and of price decreases in driving resources out of it. These resource movements in response to *demand*-induced price changes cause changes in the quantity *supplied* of apples. When the demand for apples rises, the relative price of apples rises and resources flow out of other endeavors (that is, production of goods whose prices have declined relative to the price of apples) and into apple-growing. This resource movement allows the quantity of apples supplied to fluctuate in response to changes in consumers' demand for apples.

Moving our attention back to the macroeconomy, changes in the economy's overall output, or GDP, also require changes in the quantity of resources employed. Increased production requires more inputs. However, when we want to model changes in real GDP, or the economy's *total* output of goods and services, we can't explain increases and decreases in terms of resource movements among industries in response to relative price changes, as we did in the apple-market example. For the quantity of total output

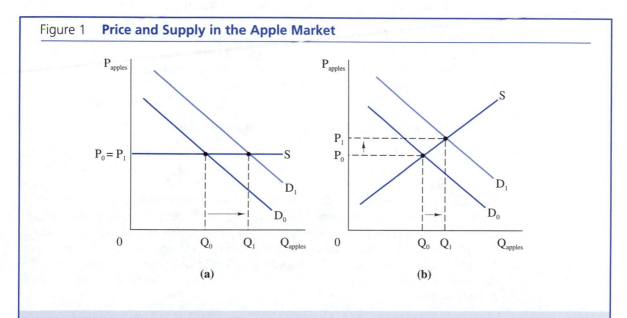

Figure 1   Price and Supply in the Apple Market

In panel (a), the supply curve for apples is perfectly horizontal. The price of apples is fixed, and demand for apples determines quantity. In panel (b), the supply curve for apples is upward sloping, reflecting the movement of resources into and out of apple production in response to relative price changes.

supplied to increase, either resources previously unemployed must come into use or resources must be used more intensively (such as workers' overtime or running machines two shifts per day). *If* a rise in the price level causes these types of adjustments, the economy's macroeconomic or aggregate supply curve (the relationship between the quantity of real output produced and the price level) will slope upward.

The relevant question then becomes: Will an increase in the price level cause resource utilization to rise? Economists' answer to this question has evolved with our understanding of the macroeconomy. In fact, the question represents one of the most fundamental and enduring issues of macroeconomics. A hundred years ago, most economists would have answered no. Fifty years ago, most would have answered with a resounding yes. Today only a few would give such an unequivocal reply. Most would answer, "Yes, but not in the long run, and only if the economy hasn't experienced continual increases in its price level."

With this introduction to the problems at hand, let's proceed to translate our model of an open macroeconomy into a form more convenient for analyzing the economy's adjustment from short-run to long-run equilibrium. We must develop an aggregate demand curve and a more complete understanding of the aggregate, or macroeconomic, supply curve. We can continue to use the microeconomic concepts of demand and supply as analogies, but we must also distinguish the features that make an *aggregate* demand or supply curve unique to macroeconomics.

3 AGGREGATE DEMAND UNDER FIXED EXCHANGE RATES

An economy's **aggregate demand curve** represents the relationship between the quantity demanded of domestic goods and services and the domestic price level. Note that this definition closely resembles that of a market demand curve for a single good in microeconomics. The differences in the case of the aggregate demand curve are that (1) the relevant quantity represents the economy's total output of goods and services, or real GDP, rather than output of a single good or service, and (2) the relevant price represents the overall domestic price level, the GDP deflator, rather than the relative price of a single good. The exact form of the aggregate demand curve differs slightly depending on whether the economy operates under a fixed or flexible exchange rate regime, so we begin with the analysis under a fixed exchange rate.

3.1 The Slope of the Aggregate Demand Curve[1]

The aggregate demand curve slopes downward like a microeconomic demand curve, but for different reasons. Two reasons account for its negative slope. First, a rise in the domestic price level, P (with the foreign price level, P*, and the exchange rate, e, held constant), raises the price of domestic goods and services relative to that of foreign ones because $R \equiv P/eP^*$. Individuals respond by shifting their expenditure from domestic to foreign goods. Thus, the quantity demanded of domestic goods and services falls, resulting in a negative relationship between the domestic price level and the quantity demanded of domestic goods. (*To test your understanding, outline the effect of a* fall *in the price level on relative prices and on the quantity demanded of domestic goods.*)

---

1. The appendix to this chapter derives the aggregate demand curve from the IS-LM-BOP framework used in earlier chapters.

The second reason for the aggregate demand curve's negative slope comes from the money market.[2] Recall that individuals demand real money balances to make transactions conveniently. The quantity demanded of real money balances (L) depends positively on real income (Q)—because the number and size of transactions depend positively on income—and negatively on the interest rate (i), which measures the opportunity cost of holding money balances rather than interest-bearing bonds.

In equilibrium, the quantity of real money balances demanded by the public (L[Q, i]) must equal the stock of real money balances, which equals the nominal money stock (M) divided by the price level (P). Figure 2 illustrates such an equilibrium, along with the effects of a rise in the price level. Given a value for the nominal money stock (M_0), a rise in the price level from P_0 to P_1 reduces the real money stock and shifts the money stock line to the left. At the original interest rate (i_0), the quantity demanded of money exceeds the new, smaller stock. Individuals try to sell bonds to raise their real money balances to the desired level. The price of bonds falls, which is reflected in a rise in the interest rate to i_1. At the new, higher interest rate, individuals are satisfied holding the new, smaller stock of real money balances.

The rise in the interest rate produced by adjustments in the money market discourages investment expenditure.[3] So total expenditure on domestic goods and services falls. This chain of events—from a rise in the price level to a decline in total expenditure—provides the second reason why the aggregate demand curve slopes downward. Again, a higher price level corresponds to a smaller quantity demanded of

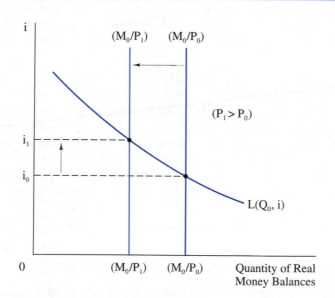

Figure 2 Effect of a Rise in the Price Level on the Money Market

A rise in the price level from P_0 to P_1 reduces the real money stock (M/P), assuming that the nominal money stock (M) is held constant. The equilibrium interest rate rises to reduce the quantity demanded of real money balances to equal the new, smaller stock.

---

2. See section 2 in the chapter on money, the banking system, and foreign exchange to review the money stock and the demand for money.

3. For a review, see the discussion of investment in section 5.3 of the chapter on the market for goods and services.

Figure 3   **Shifts in the Aggregate Demand Curve Under a Fixed Exchange Rate Regime**

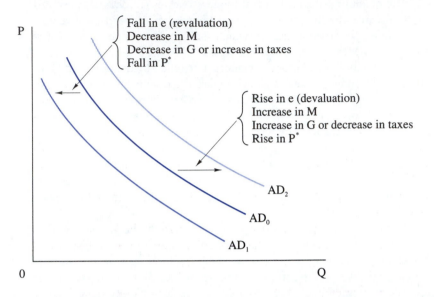

The demand for domestically produced goods and services is reduced at each domestic price level by a revaluation of the domestic currency, a decline in the domestic nominal money stock, a decrease in government purchases, a rise in taxes, or a fall in the foreign price level. The demand for domestically produced goods and services increases at each domestic price level due to a devaluation of the domestic currency, a rise in the domestic money stock, an increase in government purchases, a reduction in taxes, or a rise in the foreign price level. Changes in the domestic price level itself, other things equal, cause movements along a single aggregate demand curve rather than shifts.

domestic goods and services. (*To test your understanding, go through the effects of a fall in the price level on the money market and total expenditure.*)

The effects of a change in the domestic price level on the relative price of domestic goods and on the real money stock both contribute to the negative relationship between the quantity demanded of domestic goods and services and the domestic price level that's represented by the downward-sloping aggregate demand curve in an open economy.[4] Besides its slope, we need to know what variables cause the aggregate demand curve to shift. Just as with a market demand curve in microeconomics, we draw an aggregate demand curve assuming that certain variables are held constant; when the value of any of these variables changes, the entire aggregate demand curve shifts.

3.2 Shifts in the Aggregate Demand Curve

For our purposes, the important variables held fixed along a given aggregate demand curve include the nominal money stock, fiscal policy variables such as government purchases and taxes, the nominal exchange rate, and the foreign price level. A change in any one of these variables alters the demand for domestic goods *at each domestic price level* and, therefore, shifts the entire aggregate demand curve. Figure 3 summarizes the effects of changes in each variable on the aggregate demand curve.

---

4. Note that the second effect, but not the first, exists in a closed economy; therefore, the aggregate demand curve in an open economy tends to be flatter than that in an otherwise comparable closed economy.

Changes in the nominal money stock can arise through either open market operations or foreign exchange intervention in response to a balance-of-payments surplus or deficit (recall that we're examining aggregate demand under a *fixed* exchange rate regime). In either case, an increase in the nominal money stock raises the real money stock for a given price level. The interest rate must fall to make individuals willing to hold the new, larger stock of real money balances. The fall in the interest rate raises the investment component of expenditure on domestic goods and services, and the aggregate demand curve shifts to the right. A decrease in the nominal money stock shifts the aggregate demand curve to the left, for the same reason. Note that a change in the real money stock can cause *either* a movement along a single aggregate demand curve *or* a shift of the entire curve, depending on whether the change in (M/P) was caused by a change in the price level (P) or in the nominal money stock (M).[5]

By raising total expenditure, expansionary fiscal policy (such as an increase in G, government purchases of goods and services) increases demand for domestically produced goods and services at each price level and shifts the aggregate demand curve to the right. Expansionary fiscal policy can consist of either increased government purchases or tax cuts, which work by raising households' disposable income and increasing consumption expenditure. Contractionary fiscal policy lowers demand and shifts the AD curve to the left.

A devaluation of the domestic currency (a rise in the nominal exchange rate, e) lowers the relative price of domestic goods ($R \equiv P/eP^*$) because it now takes fewer units of foreign currency to buy a domestic good and more units of domestic currency to buy a foreign good. This increases demand for domestic goods and services at each level of the domestic price level, P. The aggregate demand curve shifts to the right. A revaluation of the domestic currency has the opposite effect. It raises the relative price of domestic goods and shifts the aggregate demand curve to the left.

Changes in the foreign price level (P^*) also shift the aggregate demand curve because, for given values of the domestic price level and the nominal exchange rate, they alter the relative price of domestic goods. A rise in P^* switches expenditure toward domestic goods and shifts the domestic aggregate demand curve to the right. A fall in the foreign price level switches spending toward now-cheaper foreign goods and shifts the domestic aggregate demand curve to the left. Note that changes in R can lead to either a movement along the AD curve (if R changes through P) or to a shift of the AD curve (if R changes through e or P^*).

3.3 Aggregate Demand Alone Can't Determine Output

The fixed-price model of an open macroeconomy we considered in earlier chapters constitutes a model of aggregate demand. It tells us, *given* the price level, the quantity of domestic goods and services demanded by individuals, firms, government agencies, and foreigners. However, goods and services don't appear magically; they must be produced by firms, using labor and capital inputs and the available technology. The economy's aggregate supply curves contain information about this production process.

4 LONG-RUN AGGREGATE SUPPLY

Aggregate supply refers to the relationship between an economy's price level and the total quantity of goods and services produced. As in a microeconomic context, the theory of aggregate supply reflects the use of inputs and technology to produce output and the responses by firms and input suppliers to changes in the prices they face.

---

5. This seemingly peculiar state of affairs arises because the price level is the variable plotted on the vertical axis in drawing an aggregate demand curve.

The quantity of available resources and the existing technology constrain the total quantity of output an economy can produce. Changes in employment, the capital stock, natural resource inputs, or technology alter an economy's ability to produce goods and services. Macroeconomists typically assume that a country's capital stock, natural resource inputs, and technology are fixed over the time horizon under analysis. Over a long period, capital stocks grow or shrink, natural resources are discovered or exhausted, and new technologies permit the same resources to generate larger quantities of output. These changes usually, but not always, occur gradually and largely outside macroeconomic policy makers' control; so macroeconomic analysis tends to focus on changes in the quantity of output produced holding constant the quantity of available resources and technology. Changes in output then must come from changes in employment or in the intensity with which firms use the given capital stock.

4.1 Time Horizon Matters: The Short, Medium, and Long Runs

When we examine the supply or production side of the economy, we must distinguish among behavior in the short, medium, and long runs. Production inherently takes time, and firms can't adjust instantaneously to changes in their economic environment. For example, firms often hire workers at wage rates fixed contractually for a set period, such as a year or longer; and the cost of adjusting the wage rate during the contract period may be prohibitive. Firms also make contracts with raw-material suppliers, often well before actual input delivery. Toy makers must decide how many of the hottest toys to make for the Christmas season long before they can determine whether the toys' popularity will even last until Christmas. Auto makers must commit to produce a certain number and size of cars before knowing next year's gasoline prices. All these factors force firms to make hiring and production decisions based on less-than-perfect information and limit their ability to adjust quickly as new information becomes available.

The limited availability of information and firms' restricted ability to adjust speedily to new information create an important distinction between their medium- and long-run responses to changes in the price level. We define the **short run** as we did in earlier chapters—the period during which the price level remains fixed in response to economic shocks or policy changes, so aggregate demand alone determines real output. The **medium run** is the period during which the price level begins to respond to shocks or policy changes, but individuals and firms may remain unaware of some price changes or may find it too costly because of contracts or other rigidities to adjust their behavior fully in response to those changes. The **long run**, on the other hand, denotes the time horizon over which everyone in the economy knows the price level and has had time to adjust production decisions accordingly.

Economists can't attach concrete time periods, such as a month, six months, or a year, to the concepts of the short, medium, and long runs, because the time required to learn about and adjust to price changes depends on the nature of the economy and on the past history of the price level. Generally, the more volatile prices have been in the recent past, the shorter will be the short and medium runs. When past price movements have been dramatic, individuals know that they have an economic incentive to monitor and anticipate price-level changes to avoid the large losses that unexpected changes could impose. On the other hand, when prices have been stable historically, individuals have less incentive to monitor prices closely and may be slow to perceive or react to price-level changes when they do occur.

4.2 The Vertical Long-Run Aggregate Supply Curve

Because the theory of aggregate supply in the long run is a bit simpler than that in the medium run, let's begin with the long run. The **long-run aggregate supply curve** is

Figure 4 **Long-Run Aggregate Supply**

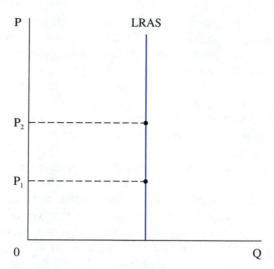

In the long run (when the price level is known and individuals and firms have time to adjust their decisions to any changes in it), the quantity of output supplied doesn't depend on the price level. The economy's quantity of resources and technology determine the horizontal placement of the LRAS curve—at the "full-employment" output.

a simple vertical line at the economy's full-employment output. This implies that changes in the price level don't affect the quantity of output supplied in the long run. Remember that a *long-run aggregate* supply curve (LRAS in Figure 4) represents the behavior by individuals and firms when they know about and have adjusted fully to any change in the price level.

The vertical long-run aggregate supply curve reflects the way individuals and firms make their economic decisions. Firms decide how much to produce and workers how much labor to supply in response to relative prices. If the price a firm receives for its product rises *relative to* the prices the firm must pay for its inputs, the profit-maximizing firm increases production. But if the price a firm receives for its product rises while the prices of all its inputs rise in the same proportion, the profit-maximizing firm finds it not worthwhile to boost production. Similarly, if workers' wages rise *relative to* the prices of the goods workers buy, they will supply a larger quantity of labor to take advantage of the higher real wages. But a similar wage increase wouldn't encourage additional work if the prices of all the goods workers purchase rose in the same proportion as wages, leaving real wages unchanged.

A change in the overall price level on the vertical axis of Figure 4 implies that *all* money prices in the economy (prices of all goods and services, nominal wages, and so on) change proportionally, leaving all relative prices unaffected. Real economic decisions (that is, how much to produce or how much labor to supply) depend on relative prices, so those decisions remain unaffected. Therefore, real output, on the horizontal axis in Figure 4, doesn't vary with the price level: *The long-run aggregate supply curve is vertical.*

Resource availability and technology determine the horizontal position of the long-run aggregate supply curve. As resource supplies increase or as technological progress allows given quantities of resources to produce larger quantities of output, the economy grows and the LRAS curve shifts to the right. This movement usually happens quite slowly and outside the direct control of macroeconomic policy makers; so we'll ignore the effects of growth by assuming a fixed position for the LRAS curve through most of our analysis.[6]

One final note about the LRAS curve is in order. The full-employment output corresponding to the position of the LRAS curve *doesn't* represent the maximum output the economy can produce. In fact, more output can be—and often is—produced for short periods. But, given the pattern of relative prices in the economy, the equilibrium output in the long run (when all firms and workers have made their chosen adjustments to price changes) is given by the LRAS curve. This represents full-employment output, or the output firms can produce without resorting to overtime for workers, overtime for machines (which raises maintenance costs), and other short-term arrangements that put upward pressure on prices.[7]

Consider an economy operating at full employment. Could it produce a still higher output? Yes—for example, workers could work 45 hours per week rather than the 35 to 40 hours typical in modern industrial economies, and output clearly would rise. Societies settle for a smaller output in order to work fewer hours per week, because individuals value leisure as well as income. Given the wage rate, individuals choose how to allocate their time between work (to earn income) and leisure, a decision reflected in the position of the LRAS curve. *(What would happen to the long-run aggregate supply curve if everyone in the economy suddenly wanted to take more leisure and work less? If everyone suddenly wanted to take less leisure and work more?)* Similarly, firms could raise output by running machines for longer periods or using double shifts. When temporary considerations cause individuals to alter their decisions about how to divide time between work and leisure or firms to alter their decisions about how intensively to use their equipment, the economy temporarily moves off the LRAS curve.

5 MEDIUM-RUN AGGREGATE SUPPLY

The **medium-run aggregate supply curve** captures the behavior of individuals and firms when lack of information about the price level, stickiness of some prices, or inability to adjust quickly to a change in the price level causes behavior to differ from what it would be with full information and instantaneous adjustment. Macroeconomic policy decisions tend to center on medium-run considerations, so understanding supply behavior in the medium run is critical.

5.1 The Slope of the Medium-Run Aggregate Supply Curve

The medium-run aggregate supply curve slopes upward, somewhat like the letter *J*. If the price level rises but individuals and firms don't fully perceive or adjust to that event, output increases. Of course, at some output the economy reaches an absolute resource constraint (for example, when all workers are working 100 hours per week and all machines are running 24 hours per day) that prohibits further production. At that point, the *medium-run aggregate supply* curve (MRAS in Figure 5) becomes vertical, since further price increases can't generate further production. However, the upward-sloping portion of the MRAS curve is of interest here; thus, we'll ignore the vertical section in the following discussion and figures.

---

6. Section 10's analysis of supply shocks is an exception.

7. This long-run equilibrium level of real output often is called the *natural rate of output,* or *potential real output.*

Figure 5   **Medium-Run Aggregate Supply**

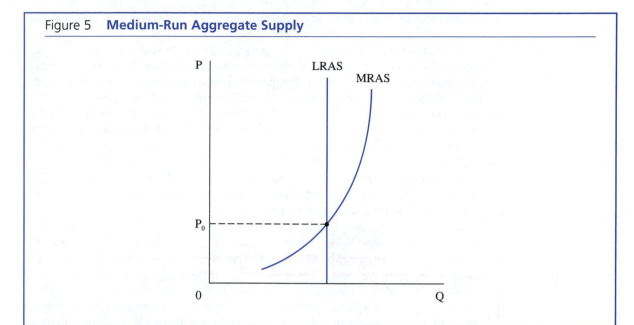

When individuals in the economy aren't fully aware of changes in the price level or able to adjust quickly to them (because of contractual rigidities, for example), a rise in the price level causes an increase in the quantity of output supplied. This is captured by the upward-sloping portion of the MRAS curve. At some point the economy reaches the absolute constraint of resources and technology, causing the medium-run aggregate supply curve to become vertical.

Given the economic arguments for the vertical shape of the long-run aggregate supply curve, why would a rise in the price level ever cause output to increase? Economic theory and empirical evidence from many economies suggest several possible answers to this question. The key definitional differences between the medium-run and long-run supply curves are (1) the information available to individuals and firms and (2) their ability to adjust to that information. We'll focus on the roles these two factors play in explaining the positive medium-run relationship between the price level and quantity supplied.

Even if firms and workers always had complete information about events throughout the economy, contractual rigidities still might prevent instantaneous adjustment. Consider, for example, the case of an industry that sets its wages in nominal terms in year-long contracts. If the price level rises during the year, the price the firm can charge for its product rises, while the contractually fixed wage rate stays constant. The firm responds to the rise in the price of its output relative to the price of its labor input by producing more. Graphically, we illustrate this response by a movement up along the economy's medium-run supply curve; a higher price level has led the firm to produce more. We'll see later that once the firm's wage contract expires and must be renegotiated, the nominal wage will tend to rise to compensate workers for the higher prices of the goods they buy. When this happens, the firm's relative price falls back to its original level, as does its output. This places the economy back on the long-run aggregate supply curve. Before we see more about this adjustment process, let's look at the role of limited information in causing workers' and firms' medium-run behavior to differ from their long-run behavior.

Firms base production decisions on information about the prices received for their products relative to the prices of their inputs. There are two main sources of information about these prices: government statistics and firms' own experience in selling their products and buying inputs. Each of these sources is subject to lags. Governments publish some price statistics monthly and others quarterly; all are subject to periodic revision that continues long after initial publication. Likewise, a firm's own experience can't provide full, up-to-date information on the state of all prices throughout the economy. Suppose an automobile producer sees its sales rise, signaling an increase in demand. How should the producer interpret this information? There are two basic possibilities, and the appropriate (that is, profit-maximizing) response by the firm depends on which one occurs. If the increase in demand occurs *only* in the automobile industry or *only* for the output of that particular automobile producer, the price of the firm's output rises *relative to* those of other goods in the economy (including the firm's inputs) and the firm should increase output. The second possibility is that the increase in demand for the firm's output is part of a general increase in demand for *all* products (that is, in aggregate demand). In this case, the firm can charge a higher price for its product but also must pay proportionally higher prices for its inputs. The firm's *relative* price remains unchanged, and the profit-maximizing response keeps output at its original level.

In the medium run, the firm may be unable to tell which of these two possibilities has occurred. If firms mistakenly interpret a rise in the overall price level as a rise in the relative prices of their respective outputs and respond by raising output, the economy moves up along the medium-run aggregate supply curve. In other words, a rise in the price level, if misperceived by firms as an increase in their relative prices, causes output to increase. But eventually firms will discover their mistake—for example, when they go to buy additional inputs and find that input prices have risen by the same percentage as the prices of their products. When this happens, output falls back to its original level and the economy moves back onto the long-run aggregate supply curve. We'll examine this adjustment from the medium run to the long run by considering the causes of shifts in the medium-run aggregate supply curve.[8]

5.2 Shifts in the Medium-Run Aggregate Supply Curve

Each medium-run aggregate supply curve is drawn for given values of input prices and of firms' expectations about prices other than those of their own products. If the price level rises but contractual rigidities keep some input prices constant and firms don't immediately alter their expectations about other prices throughout the economy, firms will perceive the relative prices of their outputs as having risen and will increase output. This causes the economy to move up along a given MRAS curve.

Figure 6 depicts this situation, in which W denotes nominal *wages* and P^e denotes firms' *expectations* about the price level. Beginning at point 1, the price level rises but input prices and firms' price expectations don't adjust immediately. Output rises, and the economy moves to point 2. Output is above the full-employment level, labor markets are tight, and the price level (P_2) is higher than the one that firms had expected (P_0). Gradually, input prices adjust upward, firms detect the rise in the price level, the expected price level rises, and the economy moves to point 3, back on the long-run aggregate supply curve. (*What would happen to output in the medium run if the price level suddenly fell to $P_2 < P_0$? In the long run?*)

Of course, not every rise in the price level necessarily leaves input prices temporarily untouched or fools firms into thinking their relative prices have risen. If all input prices respond immediately and if firms immediately recognize a proportional rise in all prices, the economy moves directly from point 1 to point 3, leaving output completely unaffected by the rise in prices.

---

8. Several types of shifts in the medium-run aggregate supply curve can occur. We concentrate here on those caused by changes in input prices or perceptions of the price level. Both the medium- and long-run supply curves may shift because of changes in the quantity of available resources or in technology (called *supply shocks*), as we'll see in section 10.

Figure 6   **Shift in the Medium-Run Aggregate Supply Curve Due to a Rise in Input Prices or in the Expected Price Level**

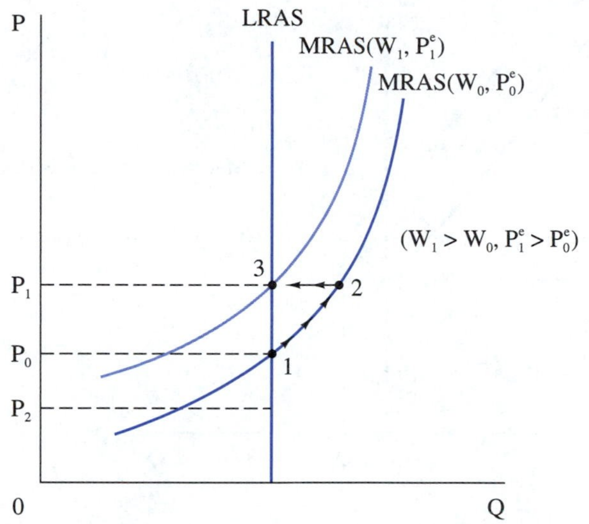

Each MRAS curve is drawn for given input prices (W) and expectations about the price level (P^e). A rise in input prices or in the expected price level shifts the MRAS curve.

When the economy operates at a point to the right of the LRAS curve, two things happen. First, output is above the full-employment level, so wages and other input prices tend to rise, shifting the MRAS upward. Second, if the actual price level exceeds the expected price level ($P > P^e$), the expected price level will rise, again shifting the MRAS curve upward. When the economy operates at a point to the left of the LRAS curve, output is below the full-employment level and the expected price level may be higher than the actual price level ($P^e > P$). As input prices fall and information about the lower-than-expected price level spreads, the expected price level falls and the medium-run aggregate supply curve shifts downward.

6 COMBINING AGGREGATE DEMAND AND AGGREGATE SUPPLY

The simultaneous determination of output and the price level requires that we combine the aggregate demand curve with the aggregate supply curves, as in Figure 7. In the medium run, the economy can operate at any intersection of an aggregate demand curve and a medium-run aggregate supply curve. In the long run, there's the additional requirement that the aggregate demand and medium-run aggregate supply curves intersect at a point *on* the long-run aggregate supply curve. This means that individuals and firms must know the price level and must have adjusted their pricing and output decisions accordingly.

To analyze various policies' effects on output and prices, we must make an assumption about the degree of capital mobility for the country in question. Since the degree of capital mobility has increased in recent years, we choose the assumption of **perfectly mobile capital**. Recall that this means that portfolio owners, in deciding where

Figure 7   **Medium-Run and Long-Run Equilibrium**

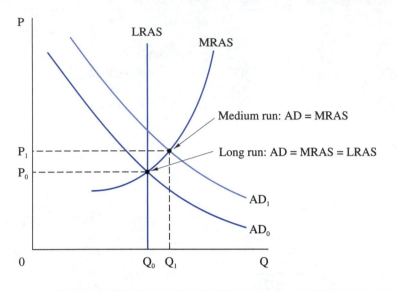

In the medium run, the economy must be at a point of intersection of an aggregate demand curve and a medium-run aggregate supply curve. In the long run, there is an additional requirement: The intersection of the aggregate demand and medium-run aggregate supply curves must occur on the long-run aggregate supply curve.

to place their funds, consider only interest rates, exchange rates, and expected changes in exchange rates. Individuals have no inherent preferences for investments in one currency over those in another, and no government regulations restrict capital flows among countries. With perfectly mobile capital, the interest parity conditions determine the pattern of international interest rates.

7 MACROECONOMIC POLICY UNDER FIXED EXCHANGE RATES

Once we relax the assumption of a fixed price level, the economy contains **automatic adjustment mechanisms** (that is, mechanisms that don't require an active response from policy makers) for reaching a long-run equilibrium in which (1) the quantity demanded of domestic goods equals the quantity supplied *at full employment* and (2) balance-of-payments equilibrium prevails. Changes in input prices and in the expected price level move the economy onto the long-run aggregate supply curve by shifting the medium-run supply curve until it intersects the aggregate demand curve at a point on the long-run supply curve. Changes in the money stock due to intervention in the foreign exchange market handle any imbalance in the country's international payments. A balance-of-payments surplus (deficit) causes a rise (fall) in the money stock that shifts the aggregate demand curve to the right (left) to restore balance-of-payments equilibrium. Therefore, the economy reaches long-run equilibrium once these automatic adjustment mechanisms have resolved problems of output, employment, and balance of payments.

The primary shortcoming of the automatic adjustment mechanisms is their lack of speed. The price level, in particular, may adjust only slowly, leaving the economy off the long-run supply curve for relatively long periods. Given this possibility, an obvious question arises as to whether macroeconomic policies can speed up the adjustment process. In an earlier chapter, we saw that, with a *fixed* price level, fiscal policy can affect domestic output with a fixed exchange rate and perfectly mobile capital. Monetary policy, on the other hand, proved completely incapable of affecting output. How does the introduction of price flexibility alter these results? The already pessimistic conclusion about monetary policy remains unchanged, but the previously optimistic view of fiscal policy becomes a bit more pessimistic. In the medium run, fiscal policy can alter income, but monetary policy can't. Neither policy can affect real output in the long run, although fiscal policy continues to affect the price level. Because price flexibility is important primarily in assessing a policy's medium- and long-run effectiveness, we focus on permanent changes in the level of government spending and the money stock.

7.1 Fiscal Policy

We begin our initial analysis of fiscal policy from a point of long-run equilibrium (point 1 in Figure 8). In long-run equilibrium, the markets for goods and services, money, and foreign exchange are in equilibrium and everyone in the economy has adjusted fully to the actual price level (P_1).[9] A one-time permanent expansionary fiscal policy shifts the aggregate demand curve to the right from AD_1 to AD_2.[10] The price level begins to rise.

Figure 8   Expansionary Fiscal Policy with Flexible Prices, Fixed Exchange Rates, and Perfectly Mobile Capital

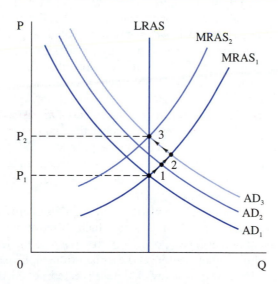

Beginning from a long-run equilibrium at point 1, an expansionary fiscal policy temporarily raises output. As firms and individuals adjust to the rise in the price level, the increase in output is offset, and the long-run effect is merely a rise in the price level (at point 3).

---

9. Recall that the AD curve incorporates the IS, LM, and BOP lines, as shown in more detail in the chapter appendix.

10. See section 3.2.

If some input prices don't adjust quickly, or if some individuals or firms mistake the rise in all prices for a rise in a specific relative price, the quantity of output supplied increases, as illustrated by point 2. However, the economy can't remain at point 2 in the long run for two reasons: (1) balance of payments disequilibrium, which implies additional movement of AD, and (2) lack of full adjustment to the new price level, which places the economy off the long-run aggregate supply curve.

The balance of payments is in surplus at point 2, because the rise in income raises the demand for money with a fixed nominal money stock, implying a rise in the interest rate and a capital inflow. The resulting intervention increases the nominal money stock and shifts AD further to the right from AD_2 to AD_3. As individuals and firms in the economy gradually come to realize that the price level has risen, and as input prices rise in response to the above-full-employment level of output, the MRAS curve shifts upward until long-run equilibrium is restored on the LRAS curve at point 3. *The net long-run effect of the expansionary fiscal policy is a rise in the price level with no effect on real output.*

If government purchases of goods and services increase while total output remains unchanged, some sectors of the economy must shrink. The growth of the public sector comes at the expense of other components of expenditure on goods and services. In this case, it's the trade-oriented sectors of the economy that shrink. The rise in the domestic price level from P_1 to P_2 makes foreign goods more attractive by raising the real exchange rate $(R \equiv P/eP^*)$, so both export and import-competing industries in the domestic economy contract.[11]

Perhaps it isn't surprising to find that an expansionary fiscal policy that begins from a point of long-run equilibrium and attempts to expand output beyond full employment fails in the long run. In fact, it's unclear why policy makers would pursue expansionary policies when output already is at full employment and can be raised further only by generating a rise in the price level that firms and individuals in the economy misinterpret or respond to slowly.[12] A less-demanding test of fiscal policy's effectiveness might be its ability to bring the economy into long-run equilibrium from a point of less-than-full employment. In other words, if an exogenous disturbance pushed the economy below full employment, could fiscal policy help restore output to its long-run equilibrium in a timely fashion?

Suppose policy makers executed an expansionary fiscal policy beginning at a point to the left of the LRAS curve. Could the policy then raise real output? The answer is yes, but the policy would still result in a rise in the price level. *(We leave the graphical demonstration to the reader.)* The domestic economy still experiences a real currency appreciation caused by the price-level increase, and the trade-oriented sectors still contract, but by less than the initial increase in government purchases.

However, this more optimistic result requires a proviso. With flexible prices, the economy contains a mechanism with which to move *automatically* to the LRAS curve without using expansionary policies. At any point to the left of the LRAS curve, output is below its full-employment level. Less-than-full employment puts downward pressure on input prices. And as a lower-than-expected actual price level (including input

---

11. The capital inflow maintains balance-of-payments equilibrium in the face of a move toward a deficit in the current account. Note that the real appreciation under a fixed exchange rate comes through a rise in P, with the nominal exchange rate and foreign price level fixed. We'll see in section 9 that, under a flexible exchange rate, the real appreciation comes through a nominal currency appreciation with the domestic and foreign price levels fixed.

12. Political-business-cycle theory suggests that politicians, prior to elections, have an incentive to engage in overly expansionary policies to generate higher employment and output in the short run. The long-run effect is inflation, but only *after* the election.

prices) becomes known, the expected price level falls and the medium-run supply curve shifts downward to restore a long-run equilibrium on the LRAS curve. Unfortunately, this process may unfold slowly, leaving output and employment at a low level for extended periods. This presents a possible role for fiscal policy in speeding up adjustment by shifting AD to the right rather than waiting for MRAS to shift downward.

Figure 9 compares the two alternative paths to long-run equilibrium. Beginning at point 1, with low output and employment, automatic adjustment through a reduction in input prices and the expected price level would gradually shift the MRAS curve down, bringing the economy into long-run equilibrium at point 2a. If, instead, policy makers pursue expansionary fiscal policy in an effort to speed up the return of output to its long-run level, the aggregate demand curve would shift rightward to AD_2 and the price level would rise to P_2 at point 2b. Both scenarios would end with the same level of real output, but the final price level would be higher under the expansionary fiscal policy (P_2) than under automatic adjustment (P_0).

The primary reason for using expansionary fiscal policy in such a situation is that empirical evidence suggests that sometimes the automatic adjustment mechanism may work slowly, leaving output and employment low for a long period. The fiscal-policy solution might be faster, at least ideally. However, as anyone who follows congressional debates on tax and spending policy knows, fiscal policy is hardly an instantaneous cure. In fact, many economists believe that by the time policy makers realize the need for an expansionary fiscal policy and implement it, the economy is likely to be well on the way to correcting itself through the admittedly slow process of price adjustment. If the expansionary policy arrives too late (that is, when the

---

Figure 9 **Expansionary Fiscal Policy versus Automatic Adjustment**

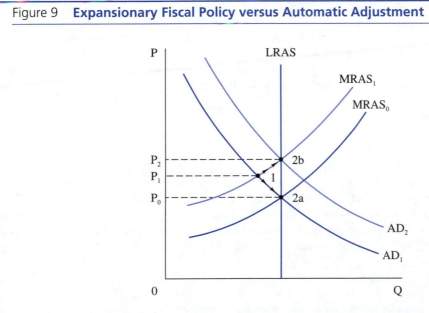

Beginning at point 1, automatic adjustment leads to a long-run equilibrium at point 2a. Expansionary fiscal policy brings the economy to a new long-run equilibrium at point 2b. In either case, the location of the long-run aggregate supply curve determines output. The equilibrium price level is higher in the case of expansionary fiscal policy (P_2) than in that of automatic adjustment (P_0).

economy has already moved from point 1 to point 2a in Figure 9), the rightward shift of AD will push output above full employment and the price level will rise, as we saw in Figure 8.[13]

Automatic adjustment and expansionary fiscal policy lead the economy to the same level of real output in Figure 9, but the two alternatives imply different outcomes for other macroeconomic variables besides just the price level. Automatic adjustment lowers the price level to P_0, generates a real currency depreciation, improves the competitiveness of the country's export goods in world markets and its import-competing goods in domestic markets, and leads toward a surplus on the current account. Expansionary fiscal policy, on the other hand, raises the price level to P_2. The current account moves toward a deficit as the real currency appreciation makes domestic goods less competitive in world markets; public expenditure rises to offset the decline in net exports of goods and services. These effects imply that various interest groups within the economy are likely to disagree about the appropriate policy.

7.2 Monetary Policy

We learned earlier that monetary policy can't affect income with a fixed price level, a fixed exchange rate regime, and perfectly mobile capital. This conclusion continues to hold when we introduce price flexibility. Recall that the economy's aggregate demand curve is drawn for a given value of the nominal money stock.[14] An open market purchase that attempts a one-time permanent expansion of the nominal money stock puts downward pressure on the interest rate and causes a capital outflow. The resulting balance-of-payments deficit requires foreign exchange market intervention by the central bank to supply foreign exchange. Foreign exchange reserves fall, and the money stock returns to its original level. Graphically, an open market purchase can shift the aggregate demand curve to the right (raising output and prices) only for the brief interval between the initial expansionary policy and the offsetting loss of foreign exchange reserves.

Unlike the fiscal policy case, the pessimistic outlook for monetary policy with perfectly mobile capital doesn't depend on the output at which we begin the policy experiment. Even if current output lies to the left of the LRAS curve, where the economy operates at less-than-full employment, the balance-of-payments constraint on the money stock still prevents monetary policy from affecting income. This *doesn't* mean, however, that the economy remains stuck at low levels of output and employment indefinitely.

Again, price flexibility eventually restores output to its long-run, full-employment level. Output remains below that level only as long as input prices fail to decline or the actual price level remains below the expected price level. As information about the price level spreads and input-price adjustments occur, the medium-run aggregate supply curve shifts downward to restore a long-run equilibrium. Therefore, as long as the price level is flexible, the **price adjustment mechanism** pushes output toward its long-run level, though not necessarily quickly. As for the balance of payments, the fixed exchange rate implies that the money stock adjusts—through changes in foreign exchange reserves—to equate the balance of payments.

---

13. We ignore some economists' even more fundamental argument that fiscal policy cannot shift the AD curve. The simplest version of this view (known as *Ricardian equivalence*) is that increased government expenditures must imply eventual increased taxes to pay for them. When individuals in the economy realize that a rise in government spending means higher future taxes, they reduce consumption expenditures to save to cover their expected tax liability. The reduction in consumption expenditures offsets the rise in government purchases, leaving total expenditures and aggregate demand unchanged.

14. See section 3.2.

Figure 10   **Devaluation with Flexible Prices, Fixed Exchange Rates, and Perfectly Mobile Capital**

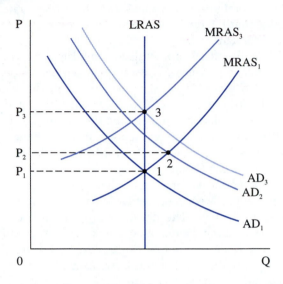

Beginning at point 1, a devaluation of the domestic currency lowers the relative price of domestic goods and services and switches expenditure toward them. The aggregate demand curve shifts to the right from AD_1 to AD_2. At point 2, the balance of payments is in surplus due to the devaluation. Intervention in the foreign exchange market increases the domestic money supply, and the aggregate demand curve shifts further to the right. The medium-run aggregate supply curve moves upward; long-run equilibrium is restored at point 3.

7.3 Exchange Rate Policy

A third type of possible macroeconomic policy under a fixed exchange rate involves a permanent change in the exchange rate, such as a devaluation. Figure 10 illustrates the medium- and long-run effects of a devaluation.

The story begins at point 1 with the economy in long-run equilibrium. A devaluation shifts the aggregate demand curve to the right from AD_1 to AD_2.[15] At point 2, the rise in the price level from P_1 to P_2 has reduced the real money stock, placed upward pressure on interest rates, and generated a capital inflow. The combination of the capital inflow and the move toward a surplus on the current account due to the devaluation implies that the balance of payments exhibits a surplus at point 2. In the medium run, export- and import-competing sectors gain from the decline in the relative price of domestically produced goods and services.[16]

Under the fixed exchange rate regime, the central bank must intervene to buy foreign exchange, and the money stock rises with the accumulation of foreign exchange reserves. Aggregate demand shifts further to the right to AD_3. Above-full-employment output puts upward pressure on input prices, and the expected price level adjusts upward as information about rising prices spreads. These developments shift MRAS upward from

---

15. See section 3.2 for a review of the reasons why.

16. Don't make the mistake of concluding that the relative price of domestic goods ($R = P/eP^*$) has risen at point 2 just because P has. A devaluation of the domestic currency (a rise in e) caused the initial shift of AD. At point 2, both P and e have risen, but e has risen by more.

MRAS$_1$ to MRAS$_3$. The new long-run equilibrium is at point 3. The domestic nominal money stock and the domestic price level have risen proportionally with the exchange rate. The real money stock remains unchanged (*Why?*), as do the relative price of domestic and foreign goods (*Why?*) and the interest rate (*Why?*). In the long run, distribution within the domestic economy as well as the overall level of output returns to its original configuration.[17]

What about the effects of a devaluation implemented when the economy's output has fallen below full employment? A devaluation can restore output to its full-employment level, but only by generating a rise in the price level. The devaluation shifts the AD curve to the right by lowering the relative price of domestic goods and services, or causing a short-run real devaluation, and shifting the current account toward a surplus. As the price level begins to rise, the real money stock falls, putting upward pressure on the domestic interest rate. Capital inflows add to the balance-of-payments surplus and require the central bank to intervene by buying foreign currency. The resulting increase in the domestic nominal money stock shifts the aggregate demand curve further to the right. The process ends when output is back at its full-employment level, on the long-run aggregate supply curve. The devaluation's long-run effects include restoring full employment, increasing the domestic money stock, increasing the central bank's foreign exchange reserves, and a long-run real devaluation, because the price level rises less than proportionally with the initial nominal devaluation.[18]

The economy's response to a currency devaluation depends in part on the economy's history. When past policy has been overly expansionary and currency devaluations have been common responses to balance-of-payments crises, then a devaluation may cause foreign exchange market participants to expect further devaluations and inflation. If so, the medium-run aggregate supply curve may shift up further and more quickly following a devaluation, as input suppliers and firms try to protect themselves from losses due to future price increases. In this case, the response to the devaluation will be a bigger price increase and a smaller increase in real output. However, if a country has a history of stable prices and past devaluations have been rare, a devaluation is likely to have less effect on price expectations, keeping the medium-run aggregate supply curve more stable. Such conditions lead to a longer-lasting effect on real output from a currency devaluation.

7.4 Summary of Long-Run Policy Effects under Fixed Exchange Rates

Table 4 summarizes the long-run effects of one-time permanent fiscal, monetary, and exchange rate policies under a fixed exchange rate with perfectly mobile capital. The table assumes that the policies pursued are expansionary ones. Just switch the signs of all nonzero entries in the table to evaluate the effects of the corresponding contractionary policies. Note that whether the policy is initiated from a point of full employment affects the long-run impact of fiscal and exchange rate policies. Monetary policies, in contrast, have no long-run impact on any economic variable reported in the table regardless of whether the economy is initially operating at full employment. This result reflects the fact that in the long run, policy makers can't alter the size of the domestic money stock under a fixed exchange rate regime from the size consistent with balance-of-payments equilibrium.

---

17. We'll see that devaluations and revaluations under a fixed exchange rate regime have identical effects, respectively, as increases and decreases in the nominal money stock under a flexible exchange rate regime (section 9). This shouldn't come as a surprise, because a fixed exchange rate requires policy makers to surrender their ability to control the nominal money stock in order to control the exchange rate, while a flexible rate requires that they surrender control over the exchange rate to gain control over the nominal money stock.

18. See footnote 16.

Table 4 **LONG-RUN EFFECTS OF EXPANSIONARY POLICIES UNDER A FIXED EXCHANGE RATE**

Policy	Effect on					
	Q	P	i	e	R	CAB
Fiscal:						
Initiated on LRAS	0	+	0	0	+	−
Initiated to left of LRAS	+	+	0	0	+	−
Monetary:						
Initiated on LRAS	0	0	0	0	0	0
Initiated to left of LRAS	0	0	0	0	0	0
Exchange Rate:						
Initiated on LRAS	0	+[a]	0	+	0	0
Initiated to left of LRAS	+	+	0	+	−	+

[a]Proportional to initial policy.

8 AGGREGATE DEMAND UNDER FLEXIBLE EXCHANGE RATES

Just as under a fixed exchange rate regime, the aggregate demand curve under a flexible-rate regime captures the negative relationship between the domestic price level and the quantity demanded of domestic goods and services.[19] Due to differences in how the economy adjusts to disturbances under the two types of regime, however, there are minor differences in the aggregate demand curve for each system, primarily in the variables held constant along a given aggregate demand curve. We continue to assume that capital is perfectly mobile among countries.

8.1 The Slope of the Aggregate Demand Curve

The aggregate demand curve under a flexible exchange rate slopes downward for the same reasons that the aggregate demand curve under a fixed exchange rate does. First, a rise in the price level raises the relative price of domestic goods and shifts expenditure toward foreign goods. Second, a rise in the domestic price level (given the nominal money stock) lowers the real money stock, raises the domestic interest rate, lowers investment, and causes capital inflows and a currency appreciation.[20] Both mechanisms cause a rise in the price level to correspond with a fall in the quantity demanded of domestic goods and services. The difference in the aggregate demand curve under a flexible exchange rate arises because any change in the price level may result in a change in the exchange rate.[21] Each aggregate demand curve is drawn taking these exchange rate changes into account; thus, the exchange rate isn't held constant along an aggregate demand curve, as was the case under a fixed exchange rate system, but adjusts to maintain balance-of-payments equilibrium.

---

19. In both cases, the aggregate demand curve incorporates the requirements for equilibrium in the goods, money, and foreign exchange markets; that is, the aggregate demand curve is derived from the IS, LM, and BOP curves. The chapter appendix illustrates the derivation.

20. Since we continue to operate under the assumption of perfectly mobile capital, changes in the interest rate are incipient just as under a fixed exchange rate.

21. For details, see section A.2 in the chapter appendix.

8.2 Shifts in the Aggregate Demand Curve

Although a number of variables are held constant along each aggregate demand curve, we'll focus on the effects of changes due to monetary policy and fiscal policy.

A one-time permanent increase in the nominal money stock (holding the price level constant) raises the real money stock and lowers the interest rate. The fall in the interest rate causes a capital outflow, which depreciates the domestic currency and lowers the relative price of domestic goods. This implies a larger quantity demanded of domestic goods *at each price level,* represented graphically by a rightward shift in the aggregate demand curve. (*Go through the logic in the opposite direction, beginning with a fall in the nominal money stock, to see why the result would be a leftward shift in AD.*)

It's tempting to conclude that a one-time permanent rise in government purchases would shift the AD curve to the right in a manner similar to the effect of a rise in the money stock. However, this conclusion would be incorrect: Changes in government purchases have *no* effect on aggregate demand under a flexible exchange rate and perfect capital mobility. When government purchases rise, any expansionary effect on income raises the quantity demanded of money. But the money stock remains fixed, so the interest rate must rise to make individuals content with the available stock of real balances. With perfectly mobile capital, the rise in the interest rate brings in capital flows that appreciate the domestic currency and raise the relative price of domestic goods. Net exports respond to the rise in relative prices by falling enough to offset the initial increase in government purchases. Total demand remains unchanged, but spending shifts from the trade-oriented sector (export and import-competing industries) to the public sector.

9 MACROECONOMIC POLICIES UNDER FLEXIBLE EXCHANGE RATES

9.1 Automatic Adjustment Mechanisms

With both a flexible price level and a flexible exchange rate, the economy contains automatic adjustment mechanisms for bringing it into equilibrium on the long-run supply curve with balanced payments. The price level adjusts to equate the quantity demanded of domestic goods and services with the quantity supplied at full employment, and the exchange rate adjusts to bring the balance of payments into equilibrium.

As in the case of fixed exchange rates, the automatic adjustment mechanisms may work slowly, especially the price adjustment mechanism. This can be particularly troublesome when shocks push the economy to the left of the long-run aggregate supply curve, to low output and employment levels. In such a situation, the question again arises whether an expansionary macroeconomic policy can speed up the economy's movement toward long-run equilibrium, minimizing the loss of output and the costs of unemployment.

9.2 Macroeconomic Policy

Within the aggregate demand–aggregate supply framework, a policy clearly must shift the aggregate demand curve if that policy is to affect income.[22] Section 8.2 argued that monetary but not fiscal policy can shift the aggregate demand curve under a flexible exchange rate and perfectly mobile capital. In fact, this is just another way of saying that with a fixed price level,

---

22. We ignore the possibility of "supply-side" policies that alter the position of the medium-run and/or long-run aggregate supply curve. Monetary and fiscal policy don't affect the supply curves directly, although they may shift the MRAS curve indirectly through their effects on the expected price level.

Figure 11 **Expansionary Monetary Policy with Flexible Prices, Flexible Exchange Rates, and Perfectly Mobile Capital**

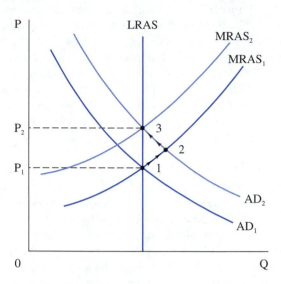

Beginning from a point of long-run equilibrium such as 1, expansionary monetary policy can raise output, but only temporarily. As individuals and firms recognize and adjust to the accompanying rise in the price level, output falls back to its original level at point 3. The policy's long-run effect consists solely of a proportional rise in the price level and a proportional depreciation of the domestic currency.

monetary policy can affect income but fiscal policy can't. Recall that when the price level is fixed, aggregate demand completely determines income; so any policy that can shift aggregate demand can affect income as long as the price level is fixed. A one-time permanent fiscal expansion fails because it generates a nominal and real appreciation of the domestic currency that fully offsets the policy's potential effect on output.[23]

Fiscal policy is ruled out by its inability to shift the aggregate demand curve, so we'll concentrate on the possibility of using monetary policy. Beginning from a point of long-run equilibrium, consider the impact of an open market purchase that raises the nominal money stock and shifts the AD curve to the right, as illustrated in Figure 11. The rise in aggregate demand pushes up the price level. In the medium run, contractual rigidities may prevent some prices (for example, nominal wages) from adjusting quickly, and firms or individuals may mistake the price increase for a change in relative prices. Output climbs along MRAS$_1$.

What causes the quantity demanded of domestic goods to rise to match the temporarily higher output? Domestic goods become temporarily cheaper relative to foreign goods—even though the domestic price level has risen. This is caused by the depreciation of the domestic currency. The relative price of domestic goods is defined as $R \equiv P/eP^*$, so a rise in e can more than offset a rise in P, lowering the relative price of domestic goods. We know from the preceding chapter (section 2) that in the long run, P and e must rise proportionally with M; in the short and medium runs, the price level lags behind, so the rise in e temporarily represents a real as well as a nominal depreciation.

---

23. Note that under a fixed exchange rate, the real appreciation caused by a fiscal expansion works through a rise in P with no change in e. Under a flexible exchange rate, the real appreciation caused by a fiscal expansion works through a nominal appreciation with no change in P. See footnote 11.

The rise in output occurs either because of confusion over a change in the price level versus a change in the relative price that a firm receives for its output or because input prices fail to rise immediately. When firms and labor suppliers realize that the price level (including input prices) has risen and adjust their behavior accordingly, the medium-run supply curve shifts upward and output returns to its original level. As the price level rises to P_2, the relative price of domestic goods returns to its original level, with the total rise in P just matching the overall depreciation of the domestic currency and leaving R unchanged. The domestic interest rate also returns to its original level as the price level catches up with the increase in M. In the long run, the sole remaining effects of the expansionary monetary policy are a proportionally higher price level and a proportionally depreciated domestic currency. Note that these policy results match those of a currency devaluation under a fixed exchange rate.[24]

EXCHANGE RATE OVERSHOOTING   The economy's adjustment to the new long-run equilibrium following an expansionary monetary policy reveals an interesting and important phenomenon known as exchange rate overshooting. **Overshooting** happens when a variable responds to a disturbance more in the short or medium run than it does in the long run. Overshooting can occur whenever some variables adjust more quickly than others to a disturbance. Our model of the macroeconomy suggests that the exchange rate and interest rate adjust more quickly than do prices, which tend to be sluggish or "sticky" because of incomplete information and long-term contractual rigidities. In the case of a one-time permanent monetary expansion under a flexible exchange rate regime with perfectly mobile capital, overshooting happens as the domestic currency depreciates sharply in the medium run and then undergoes a partially offsetting appreciation as the price level adjusts.

To understand exchange rate overshooting, we begin from the interest parity condition and trace the effect of the expansionary monetary policy on each of the relevant variables. Equation 1 repeats the uncovered interest parity condition:

$$i - i^* = (e^e - e)/e \qquad [1]$$

For simplicity, we assume that the story begins at a point where $e^e = e$ and, therefore, $i = i^*$. The foreign interest rate, i^*, remains constant throughout the whole process. The monetary policy is recognized as permanent, so the expected exchange rate, e^e, moves immediately to its new long-run level, which equals the value that the actual exchange rate will have at the new long-run equilibrium (point 3 in Figure 11). In the medium run following the monetary expansion, i falls because P rises by less than M, resulting in a rise in the real money stock. But if $i < i^*$ at point 2, interest parity implies that it must be true that $e > e^e$ at point 2. (*Why?*) Since at point 2 e^e already equals the new long-run equilibrium value that e will reach at point 3, it follows that e is higher at point 2 than at point 3. The monetary expansion generates a medium-run depreciation of the domestic currency that exceeds the long-run depreciation. In other words, the domestic currency *appreciates* in the adjustment from point 2 to point 3.

Why does overshooting depend on the slow adjustment of the price level? If the monetary expansion pushed the price level immediately to P_2, the real money supply wouldn't rise, even in the medium run. The domestic interest rate wouldn't fall below the foreign interest rate, and a period of expected appreciation ($e > e^e$) wouldn't be necessary to maintain interest parity.

Again the outlook for expansionary monetary policy beginning from a point of long-run equilibrium is pessimistic. However, a more important issue concerns its ability to

---

24. See footnote 17.

Figure 12 Expansionary Monetary Policy versus Automatic Adjustment

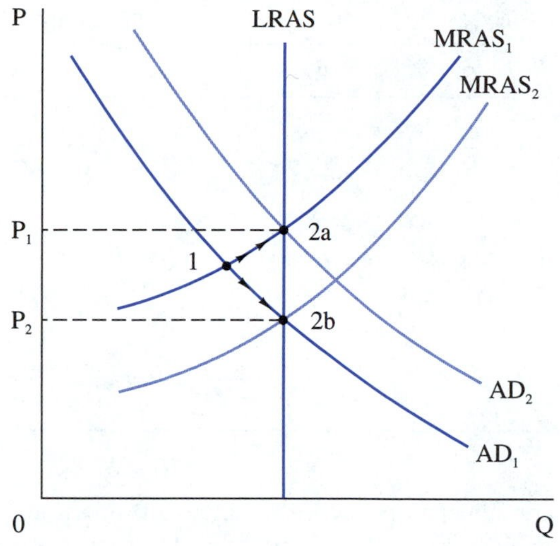

Beginning from point 1, expansionary monetary policy leads to a long-run equilibrium at point 2a with price level P_1. Automatic adjustment leads to a long-run equilibrium at 2b with price level P_2.

move the economy to equilibrium from a point of low output and employment to the left of the long-run aggregate supply curve. Figure 12 demonstrates that expansionary monetary policy can move the economy into equilibrium, but only at the cost of a rise in the price level. At point 1, the economy suffers from low output and employment. An expansionary monetary policy shifts the AD curve to the right. The price level rises, and output returns to its long-run level at point 2a. The alternate course involves reliance on the economy's automatic adjustment mechanism. In that case, below-full-employment output at point 1 eventually causes input prices to fall and individuals in the economy to adjust downward their price-level expectations. The medium-run supply curve shifts downward, restoring output to its long-run level at point 2b—at a price level lower than that in the case of expansionary monetary policy.

9.3 Summary of Long-Run Policy Effects under Flexible Exchange Rates

Table 5 summarizes the long-run effects of one-time permanent expansionary fiscal and monetary policies under a flexible exchange rate, flexible prices, and perfectly mobile capital.[25] Fiscal policy exerts no long-run effects on output, the price level, or the interest rate. An expansionary fiscal policy generates a nominal and real appreciation of the domestic currency that shifts the current account toward a deficit and reduces other expenditure, in particular net exports, by the amount of the initial fiscal expansion.

Monetary policy, in contrast, can affect output, although only if instituted after some disturbance has pushed the economy away from long-run equilibrium. Otherwise,

---

25. For contractionary policies, simply switch the signs of all nonzero entries in the table.

Table 5	LONG-RUN EFFECTS OF EXPANSIONARY POLICIES UNDER A FLEXIBLE EXCHANGE RATE						
		Effect on					
Policy	Q	P	i	e	R	CAB
Fiscal:						
Initiated on LRAS	0	0	0	−	+	−
Initiated to left of LRAS	0	0	0	−	+	−
Monetary:						
Initiated on LRAS	0	+[a]	0	+[a]	0	0
Initiated to left of LRAS	+	+	0	+	−	+

[a]Proportional to initial policy.

expansionary monetary policy leads only to a proportional increase in the price level and the nominal exchange rate, with no long-run effect on output, the real exchange rate, or the current-account balance.

10 SUPPLY SHOCKS

So far, we've considered how the macroeconomy responds to shifts in the aggregate *demand* curve, shifts that may reflect either exogenous shocks or policy makers' efforts to influence the economy. We've assumed that the long-run aggregate supply curve remains stable throughout the adjustment process and that the medium-run aggregate supply curve shifts as input prices and price expectations adjust up or down in response to shifts in aggregate demand. Our discussion thus far has ignored the second major source of macroeconomic disturbances and the second major set of events to which policy makers must respond: **supply shocks**. Such shocks include any event that alters the economy's long-run equilibrium productive capacity.[26] Any newspaper suggests many possible examples, such as earthquakes, floods, pandemics, and wars. The OPEC oil embargoes of the 1970s, which dramatically increased the real price of petroleum, provide the most famous case examined by macroeconomists. For now, let's focus on the effects of a generic supply shock.

Point 1 in Figure 13 represents an economy in long-run equilibrium at the intersection of AD_0, $MRAS_0$, and $LRAS_0$. Output is at its full-employment level, Q_0; all prices have adjusted fully to long-run equilibrium in their respective markets, with an overall price level of P_1. Now suppose an adverse supply shock hits the economy and reduces its ability to produce goods and services. Both the medium-run and long-run supply curves shift to the left, although the relative magnitude of the two shifts depends on the exact nature of the shock.

If policy makers don't respond right away to the decline in supply, the economy moves to point 2, at the intersection of the original aggregate demand curve and the new medium-run aggregate supply curve, $MRAS_1$. The price level rises to P_2. The increase in

---

26. Temporary supply shocks that shift the medium-run supply curve to the left but leave the long-run supply curve unaffected also are possible. We restrict our attention to supply shocks that influence the economy's long-run ability to produce goods and services.

Figure 13 **An Adverse Supply Shock and Potential Policy Responses**

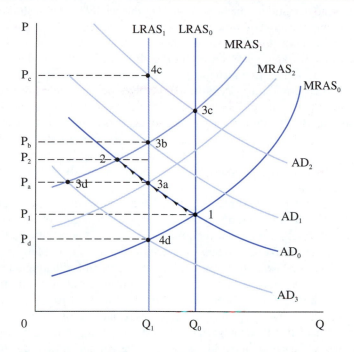

An adverse supply shock shifts the medium- and long-run aggregate supply curves to the left. Policy makers can choose from several policy options. First, they can leave AD unchanged at AD_0, so the new long-run equilibrium occurs at point 3a. Second, they can expand AD to AD_1 to speed the economy's return to full employment at point 3b, but such a policy raises prices. Third, policy makers can expand AD by more (to AD_2) and push output back to its preshock level, but only temporarily. The long-term cost of this aggressively expansionary policy is a much higher price level at point 4c. Finally, policy makers can contract AD to AD_3 and restore long-run equilibrium at point 4d. This keeps prices down but may require an extended period of exacerbated unemployment (at 3d). Regardless of policy makers' choice, the new long-run, full-employment output is at the lower Q_1.

---

price cuts the quantity demanded of domestic goods and services, along AD_0, to match the curtailed supply. This combination of rising prices and declining output often is called **stagflation**, a combination of stagnating real output and a rising price level or inflation.

What happens next depends on if and how policy makers respond. We can outline four basic possibilities, ranging from the most passive to the most aggressive responses. First, macroeconomic policy makers can choose to follow scenario (a): do nothing to alter aggregate demand. From point 2, to the left of the new long-run aggregate supply curve, $LRAS_1$, input prices would fall in response to the less-than-full-employment level of output. The medium-run aggregate supply curve eventually would shift down with input prices, and a new long-run equilibrium would occur at point 3a. Output would be lower than prior to the supply shock, but this is inevitable. The price level (P_a) would be higher.

A more active response by policy makers would involve scenario (b): an expansionary policy to shift aggregate demand to the right to AD_1, rather than waiting for unemployment and falling input prices to shift the medium-run aggregate supply curve down. An expansionary policy would restore long-run equilibrium at point 3b. Again, real output is lower than before the shock. The price level rises to P_b, higher than in scenario (a), the case in which policy makers chose to avoid an expansionary policy.

Policy makers also might follow scenario (c): an even more aggressively expansionary policy in an attempt to restore real output to its pre-supply-shock level. By shifting aggregate demand all the way up to AD_2, they could accomplish this goal at point 3c, but only temporarily. The new postshock, full-employment output is Q_1, not Q_0, so policy makers' attempt to keep output at Q_0 eventually pushes the price level up to P_c as the medium-run aggregate supply curve shifts up. Point 4c denotes the new long-run equilibrium under this scenario.

A final possibility, scenario (d), involves policy makers pursuing policies designed to prevent the supply shock from generating a rise in the price level. For example, beginning from point 2, they could *cut* aggregate demand to AD_3. In the medium run, output would fall even further, to point 3d. Eventually, as input prices and price expectations adjusted, the MRAS curve would shift down and the economy would reach a new long-run equilibrium at point 4d, with prices at P_d, slightly below the preshock value.

The four policy scenarios just outlined suggest the menu of possibilities that policy makers faced in the aftermath of the OPEC oil embargoes of 1973–1974 and 1979–1980. The first shock, during which oil prices quadrupled, occurred shortly after the breakdown of the Bretton Woods system of pegged exchange rates. Many economists believe that exchange rate flexibility played an important role in facilitating adjustment to the shocks. Under a fixed-rate system, countries' abilities to choose among the various policy responses would have been constrained by the need to intervene in foreign exchange markets to prevent appreciations or depreciations of their currencies. Alternatively, a system of fixed exchange rates would have ruled out monetary policy as a tool for shifting aggregate demand in response to the supply shocks. But because exchange rates were flexible, most countries responded with monetary policies, although the degrees of expansion pursued by different countries varied substantially, as we'll see in the upcoming chapter.

CASE 1: UNEMPLOYMENT—STRUCTURAL AND CYCLICAL

Economists make an important distinction between two types of unemployment: structural and cyclical. Structural unemployment refers to individuals who lack jobs for long periods of time, despite looking for work, because of mismatches between their location or skills and the location or skill requirements of available job openings. This type of unemployment doesn't directly depend on the stage of the business cycle. A steel worker might be unemployed in Gary, Indiana, even during an economic boom when lots of job openings exist for accountants in New York, construction workers in Phoenix, and nurses in Seattle. In terms of our aggregate demand–aggregate supply model, the structural unemployment rate is the one that corresponds to "full-employment" real output—on the LRAS curve. Cyclical unemployment, on the other hand, counts individuals who lack jobs because the economy currently operates at less than its full-employment level of real output, or to the left of its long-run aggregate supply curve.

Actual unemployment rates vary significantly across countries. This variation reflects differences both in structural unemployment rates and in the timing of countries' economic booms and recessions. Figure 14 reports 2002 unemployment rates for 20 developed countries. On the left-hand side of the figure, the length of the upper bar for each country reflects its actual unemployment rate in 2002, including both the structural and cyclical components. These rates vary from about 3 percent (the Netherlands) to about 11 percent (Spain), with most countries in the 4 to 8 percent range. Still on the left-hand side of the figure, the length of the lower bar for each country reflects its rate of structural unemployment.

Figure 14   **Actual and Structural Unemployment, 2002**

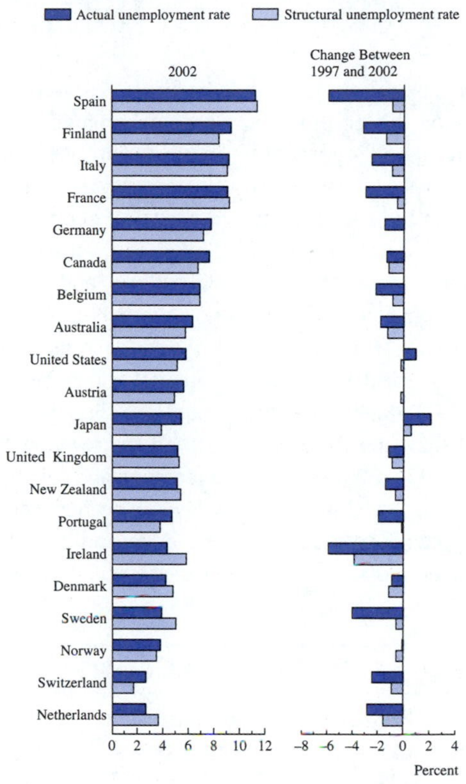

On the left-hand side of the figure, the upper bar for each country represents the overall unemployment rate, and the lower bar the structural unemployment rate. On the right-hand side of the figure, the two bars report the change in the overall and structural unemployment rates, respectively, between 1997 and 2002.

Source: Data from Organization for Economic Cooperation and Development and International Monetary Fund.

Note that structural unemployment accounts for the vast majority of the total for every country. The cyclical component of unemployment (the difference in length between the upper and lower bars) rarely makes up more than 1.5 percent.

The economies in the figure are split roughly evenly between those that exhibited positive cyclical unemployment in 2002 (such as Finland, Australia, and Japan) and those such as Ireland and Sweden that exhibited negative cyclical unemployment. The former operated to the left of their LRAS in 2002, and the latter operated to the right.

Many Western European economies have had high rates of structural unemployment for several decades. Policy makers have started to focus on policies to bring those rates down. Such policies include job training, imposing job-search requirements for receipt of public-assistance and unemployment benefits, eliminating labor-market inflexibilities such as restrictions on firms' abilities to reassign workers or reduce their workforces, and shifting wage bargaining from the national to the local or firm level. The right-hand side of Figure 14 documents the results of those policies. The lengths of the two bars for each country report the change in the actual and structural unemployment rates, respectively, between 1997 and 2002. Since the late 1990s, countries such as Spain and Ireland succeeded in reducing their structural unemployment rates substantially. Others, including, Germany and Japan, experienced either no change or even an increase in their rates of structural unemployment.

CASE 2: THE UPS AND DOWNS OF BUSINESS CYCLES

Business cycles are the recurrent expansions and contractions in economic activity, or the economy's recurrent fluctuations around its long-run aggregate supply curve. How have the business cycles experienced by industrial countries changed over time in terms of severity or duration? Table 6 addresses this question using data from a recent study by the International Monetary Fund. The table describes the average characteristics of both recessions and economic expansions in 16 developed countries during 4 periods, the pre-World War I era (1881–1913), the interwar years (1919–1938), the Bretton Woods and pre-OPEC period (1950–1972), and the recent post-Bretton Woods, post-OPEC years (1973–2000).[27]

What are the broad trends? Although the oil shocks of the 1970s reversed the longer-term patterns to a degree, recessions appear to have become milder and shorter over the past 120 years. Expansions have become longer. Industrial countries spend fewer years in recession and more in expansion. Why the changes? Economists who study business cycles have pointed to several reasons. The developed economies shifted out of the agriculture and manufacturing sectors, both subject to cyclical fluctuations, and into service sectors that are less so. Most governments put in place automatic stabilizers, or fiscal policies (such as progressive tax rates, unemployment benefits, and public assistance) that apply an automatic counter-cyclical fiscal policy by expanding spending and cutting tax revenue when the economy begins to enter a recession and cutting spending and increasing tax revenue when the economy enters a boom. Experts also believe that the development of better integrated and regulated financial markets, along with bank deposit insurance (which

Table 6   CHARACTERISTICS OF RECESSIONS AND EXPANSIONS, 1881–2000

	Prewar 1881–1913	Interwar 1919–1938	Bretton Woods 1950–1972	Post-Bretton Woods 1973–2000
Recessions				
Average decline in output (%)	−4.3	−8.1	−2.1	−2.5
Proportion with a decline of				
< 2 percent	29.4	23.5	50.0	57.5
2–4 percent	33.3	17.6	44.4	30.0
> 4 percent	37.3	58.8	5.6	12.5
Length				
Average (years)	1.3	1.8	1.1	1.5
Proportion that were				
> 2 years	79.4	60.8	94.4	60.0
2–3 years	16.7	15.7	5.6	32.5
> 3 years	3.9	23.5	0.0	7.5
Proportion of years in recession	24.7	29.4	5.2	13.4
Expansions				
Average increase in output (%)	19.8	34.6	102.9	26.9
Length (years)	3.6	3.7	10.3	6.9
Proportion of years in expansion	75.3	70.6	94.8	86.6

Source: Data from International Monetary Fund.

---

27. The 16 countries are Australia, Canada, Denmark, Finland, France, Germany, Italy, Japan, the Netherlands, Norway, Portugal, Spain, Sweden, Switzerland, the United Kingdom, and the United States.

discourages banking crises), have contributed to the reduced amplitude of developed-country business cycles. One pattern that has persisted throughout the 1881–2000 period is the international synchronization of most business cycles. Developed economies tend to experience booms and recessions as a group. In particular, when the dominant economy (the United Kingdom during 1881–1913 and the United States since) booms, other economies tend to experience expansions as well; and when the dominant economy enters a recession, other follow.

SUMMARY

The introduction of price flexibility in this chapter has three major implications:

1. Our model economy now contains an automatic adjustment mechanism to bring output to its long-run equilibrium level at full employment, unlike the situations of chronic internal imbalance in earlier chapters.
2. The effective tools of macroeconomic policy (fiscal and exchange rate policy under fixed exchange rates, and monetary policy under flexible exchange rates) can permanently increase output *only* if the economy is operating temporarily to the left of the long-run aggregate supply curve and then *only* by raising the price level.
3. Expansionary macroeconomic policy, if pursued beginning from a point of long-run equilibrium, can permanently affect only the price level, not the level of real output or employment.

Table 7 summarizes the policy results derived in the chapter.

LOOKING AHEAD

We've seen that macroeconomic policies' effectiveness depends critically on the exchange rate regime under which the economy operates. Recall from the chapters on short-run macroeconomic policy that countries manage their exchange rates in a variety of ways,

Table 7 **POLICY EFFECTIVENESS WITH FLEXIBLE PRICES AND CAPITAL MOBILITY**		
Policy	**Fixed-Rate Regime**	**Flexible-Rate Regime**
If instituted beginning at point of long-run equilibrium:		
Fiscal:		
Medium run	Effective[a]	Ineffective
Long run	Ineffective[a]	Ineffective
Monetary:		
Medium run	Ineffective	Effective[a]
Long run	Ineffective	Ineffective[a]
If instituted at point to left of long-run equilibrium:		
Fiscal:		
Medium run	Effective[a]	Ineffective
Long run	Effective[a]	Ineffective
Monetary:		
Medium run	Ineffective	Effective[a]
Long run	Ineffective	Effective[a]

[a]Results accompanied by changes in the price level.

ranging from a fixed to a purely flexible exchange rate. The upcoming chapter traces recent macroeconomic history, considers the major arguments regarding the choice of exchange rate regime, and explores several possible arrangements other than a simple fixed or flexible rate.

KEY TERMS

inflation

deflation

aggregate demand curve

aggregate supply

short run

medium run

long run

long-run aggregate supply curve

medium-run aggregate supply curve

perfectly mobile capital

automatic adjustment mechanisms

price adjustment mechanism

overshooting

supply shocks

stagflation

PROBLEMS AND QUESTIONS FOR REVIEW

1. Use the aggregate demand–aggregate supply model to analyze the following policy dispute concerning an open economy with perfectly mobile capital and a fixed exchange rate. The economy currently operates at a long-run equilibrium, including the balance of payments.
   a. *Policy maker 1:* "We need to expand real output and lower the unemployment rate. If only we had a flexible exchange rate, we could undertake an expansionary monetary policy that would have the desired effect. But since our exchange rate is fixed, there's no way we can expand our money stock."
   b. *Policy maker 2:* "There are two things wrong with your argument. First, it is possible to increase our money stock even though our exchange rate is fixed; all we have to do is devalue our currency. Second, if we follow such a policy, the increase in real output and decrease in unemployment will be a medium-run effect only. In the long run, all it will accomplish is a rise in the price level."
2. This question asks you to examine the relationship between an economy's openness and the effects of fiscal policy.
   a. Country A is a closed economy. It engages in no transactions with other countries, so its current-account and capital-account balances always equal zero. Country A pursues an expansionary fiscal policy of cutting taxes and increasing government purchases. Illustrate and explain the effects of the policy on real output and on the price level in the medium run and in the long run. What is the effect on the interest rate? What are the long-run distributional effects of the policy?
   b. Country B is an open economy. It engages in trade in goods, services, and financial assets. It operates under a flexible exchange rate regime and has perfectly mobile capital. Country B pursues an expansionary fiscal policy of cutting taxes and increasing government purchases. Illustrate and explain the effects of the policy on real output and on the price level in the medium run and in the long run. What is the effect on the interest rate? What are the long-run distributional effects of the policy?
   c. Compare the effects of expansionary fiscal policies in countries A and B. Assume that both countries follow identical, neutral monetary policies that can be ignored for purposes of this analysis. As an economy becomes more open, how do the effects, especially the distributional effects, of fiscal policy change?
   d. In the early 1980s, the United States followed an expansionary fiscal policy of lower taxes and increased government purchases. Policy makers seemed surprised by two characteristics of the period, in comparison with earlier experience. First, the U.S. trade balance moved sharply into deficit. Second, private investment remained relatively high. Given your answers to parts (a), (b), and (c), can you explain the two observations? Should they have come as a surprise?

One of the major events in the late-twentieth-century international economic system was the unification of Germany and the accompanying macroeconomic adjustment. The next two questions ask you to analyze two aspects of that process.

3. One aspect of unification that had to be dealt with was the East German currency, the ostmark, which had been nonconvertible. Black market prices suggested that the market value of the ostmark relative to other currencies was about 10 percent of its official East German exchange rate. As a part of unification, (West) Germany decided to intervene in the foreign exchange market to buy up the ostmarks. Policy makers had to decide at what price to purchase the currency. Consider three possibilities: (i) Buy the ostmarks at the black market price of approximately DM0.08 per ostmark, (ii) buy the ostmarks at the official East German exchange rate of DM1.00 per ostmark, or (iii) buy the ostmarks at an intermediate value of, say, DM0.50 per ostmark.

    a. Write the expression for a country's money stock as a function of the assets held by the central bank.

    b. What would be the effects of the three cases of intervention listed above on the German money stock? (*Hint:* Remember that the foreign exchange reserve component of the monetary base is expressed in units of the *domestic* currency, the DM in the case of West Germany. For example, if the U.S. Federal Reserve buys one pound sterling at an exchange rate of two dollars per pound, the foreign exchange reserve component of the U.S. monetary base rises by two dollars.)

    c. Assume that Germany decided to go with option (ii) and exchanged ostmarks for Deutsche marks at a one-for-one exchange rate. This might raise serious questions about inflation in historically inflation-conscious Germany. Illustrate and explain the logic behind this concern. Assume that unified Germany uses a flexible exchange rate and has perfectly mobile capital.

4. A second aspect of German unification concerned the supply or production side of the economy. East German factories were notoriously inefficient after years of central planning. Before unification, East German workers were paid in ostmarks. After unification, those same workers were to be paid in Deutsche marks. Again, a decision had to be made how to translate ostmark-denominated wages into DM-denominated wages. This question asks you to analyze the macroeconomic effects of a decision to translate wages on a one-for-one basis; in other words, a worker who previously made 100 ostmarks per week now would be paid 100 DM per week.

    a. Remember that the real value of DM is much higher than the real value of ostmarks; therefore, the one-for-one wage policy is equivalent to a large increase in real wages. Illustrate and explain the effects on real output and the price level of the change from ostmark wages to DM wages in the medium run. (*Hint:* How does a rise in real wages or other input prices affect the aggregate demand–aggregate supply model?)

    b. After unification, Germany had relatively high unemployment, particularly in the "new states" of former East Germany. Is this surprising, given your analysis in part (a)? Can you think of a wage policy (that is, an alternative to the one-for-one translation of ostmark wages into Deutsche mark wages) that might have resulted in less unemployment? Explain.

    c. Given the one-for-one translation of wages, what adjustments would you expect to occur in the long run? Explain.

5. The countries of USia and Germania have flexible price levels, flexible exchange rates, and perfectly mobile capital.

    a. The USia economy currently operates to the left of its long-run aggregate supply curve. USia has a large government debt, so policy makers decide to pursue expansionary monetary policy rather than fiscal policy. Illustrate, showing the initial position, the effect of the policy, and the new long-run equilibrium. Explain.

    b. The Germania economy currently operates to the left of its long-run aggregate supply curve. Residents of Germania, for historical reasons, have an aversion to inflation. Germania has just undertaken political unification with a less-developed neighbor, and the unification involved substantial expansion of government purchases of goods and services. Because of the expansionary fiscal policy, Germania's policy makers decide to hold the money stock constant rather than pursue expansionary monetary policy. Illustrate, showing the initial position, the effect of the fiscal policy, and the new long-run equilibrium. Explain.

    c. Using your answers to parts (a) and (b), what would you expect to happen to the exchange rate between USia's currency (the dollie) and Germania's currency (the markie) in the medium run? What would you predict about the two countries' current and capital accounts? Explain.

6. In 2003–2004, the world economy experienced a dramatic increase in the real price of oil, a negative supply shock.
   a. In a speech at the time, U.S. Treasury Secretary for International Affairs (and economist) John Taylor said, "In the past, in the face of an oil price shock, central bankers were faced with the vexing choice of whether to cushion the loss in output or resist the upward pressure on prices. In contrast, around the globe today, people have become more confident that central banks are not going to allow such shocks to feed into more long-term inflation. As a result, central banks can respond more to the output and employment effects" (*Financial Times,* October 20, 2004). Interpret Taylor's comments in terms of Figure 13 and the discussion of supply shocks and possible policy responses in section 10. What is the diagrammatic equivalent of Taylor's "vexing choice"? And how would the increased confidence in central banks' inflation-resistance to which Taylor refers be reflected in an analysis similar to that in Figure 13?
   b. Ben Bernanke, a member of the U.S. Board of Governors of the Federal Reserve (and economist) said at the time, "Central bankers have to be vigilant about the possibility of second round effects on prices and wages following an oil price shock. If you knew for sure that an oil price increase would not affect long-term inflation expectations, and that consequently prices and wages would remain stable following the shock, then perhaps you could ease policy a bit to try to return the economy to its potential growth path. But in practice, you don't know how well anchored inflation expectations are and so must be very cautious in responding" (*Financial Times,* October 20, 2004). Interpret Bernanke's comments in terms of Figure 13 and the discussion of supply shocks in section 10.

7. This question asks you to analyze the effects of a currency devaluation.
   a. Trustia is a country with perfectly mobile capital and a long history of price stability. The government pegs Trustia's currency to the currency of an important trading partner. Trustia's policy makers, especially its central bankers, always do exactly what they say they will do. Unfortunately, Trustia's economy has fallen into a recession. Policy makers decide that the appropriate response is a permanent, one-time devaluation of Trustia's currency, and they announce and enact such a policy. Illustrate and explain the devaluation's likely effects on Trustia's economy.
   b. Messia is another country with perfectly mobile capital but a long history of high inflation. The government pegs Messia's currency to the currency of an important trading partner. Messia's policy makers, especially its central bankers, rarely do what they say they will do, and the country has a long history of failed economic reforms. Unfortunately, Messia's economy has fallen into a recession. Policy makers postpone a devaluation as long as possible and deny publicly that they are even considering one. Finally, the central bank runs short of foreign exchange reserves and is forced to devalue. Illustrate and explain the likely effects of the devaluation on Messia's economy.
   c. Based on your answers to parts (a) and (b), is devaluation an effective policy tool for an economy operating under a fixed exchange rate and a high degree of capital mobility? Why or why not?

8. Mediate the following dispute between two macroeconomic policy makers. The economy they're discussing operates under a flexible exchange rate and has perfectly mobile capital.
   a. *Policy maker 1:* "To increase real output, we should use expansionary fiscal policy. After all, the primary problem with fiscal policy is crowding out. But because our country has perfectly mobile capital, expansionary fiscal policy can't push up the interest rate and discourage investment. Therefore, any increase in government purchases or any cut in taxes will go directly into increased real output."
   b. *Policy maker 2:* "You need to review the notes from your undergraduate macroeconomics course. Fiscal policy never works under a flexible exchange rate with perfectly mobile capital—an ideal combination to generate complete crowding out."

REFERENCES AND SELECTED READINGS

Barsky, Robert B., and Lutz Kilian. "Oil and the Macroeconomy Since the 1970s." *Journal of Economic Perspectives* 18 (Fall 2004): 115–134.
Argues that the effects of oil shocks on the U.S. economy have been modest; for all students.

Blinder, Alan S. "What Central Bankers Could Learn from Academics—and Vice Versa." *Journal of Economic Perspectives* (Spring 1997): 3–19.
An academic and former central banker's discussion of the relationship between models of monetary policy and actual central-banking problems; for all students.

Browne, L. E. "Does Japan Offer Any Lessons for the United States?" Federal Reserve Bank of Boston, *New England Economic Review* (2001), No. 3: 3–18.
Similarities and differences between Japan's economic downturns of the 1990s and the U.S. downturn of 2001.

Cooper, Richard N., and Jane Sneddon Little. "U.S. Monetary Policy in an Integrating World: 1960 to 2000." In *The Evolution of Monetary Policy and the Federal Reserve System over the Past Thirty Years,* edited by R. W. Kopcke and L. E. Browne, 77–130. Boston: Federal Reserve Bank of Boston, 2000.
History of international influences on U.S. monetary policy.

Croce, Enzo, and Mohsin S. Khan. "Monetary Regimes and Inflation Targeting." *Finance and Development* 37 (September 2000): 48–51.
The interconnection between monetary policy tools and targets and inflation.

Fuhrer, Jeffrey C., and Scott Schuh. *Beyond Shocks: What Causes Business Cycles?* Boston: Federal Reserve Bank of Boston, 1998.
Collection of papers on causes of business cycles; most are accessible to all students.

Isard, Peter. *Exchange Rate Economics.* Cambridge: Cambridge University Press, 1995.
Survey of the literature on exchange rates and the macroeconomy; for intermediate students.

Klitgaard, Thomas. "Exchange Rates and Profit Margins: The Case of Japanese Exporters." Federal Reserve Bank of New York, *Economic Policy Review* 5 (April 1999): 41–54.
How do exporting firms adjust their prices when exchange rates change?

Kose, M. Ayhan, et al. "International Business Cycles: World, Region, and Cross-Specific Factors." *American Economic Review* 93 (May 2003): 1216–1239.
What explains the pattern of international business cycles? For advanced students.

Kouparitas, Michael A. "Are International Business Cycles Different under Fixed and Flexible Exchange Rate Regimes?" Federal Reserve Bank of Chicago, *Economic Perspectives* (First Quarter 1998): 46–64.
Finds that increased post-Bretton Woods correlation among G-7 real outputs is due to common shocks and common policy responses to them; for intermediate students.

Mishkin, Frederic S. "Inflation Targeting in Emerging-Market Countries." *American Economic Review Papers and Proceedings* 90 (May 2000): 105–109.
Is inflation-targeting a viable policy approach for emerging-market economies?

Mishkin, Frederic S., and Adam S. Posen. "Inflation Targeting: Lessons from Four Countries." Federal Reserve Bank of New York, *Economic Policy Review* (August 1997): 9–110.
An argument in favor of inflation targeting, based on the experiences of New Zealand, Canada, the United Kingdom, and Germany; for all students.

Olivei, Giovanni P. "Exchange Rates and the Prices of Manufactured Goods Imported into the United States." Federal Reserve Bank of Boston *New England Economic Review* (First Quarter 2002): 3–18.
Do nominal exchange-rate changes affect the relative prices of foreign manufactured goods? For all students.

Organization for Economic Cooperation and Development. *OECD Economic Outlook.* Paris: OECD, biannual.
Excellent source for recent macroeconomic events, data, and forecasts.

Pollard, Patricia S. "A Look Inside Two Central Banks: The European Central Bank and the Federal Reserve." Federal Reserve Bank of St. Louis *Review* 85 (January/February 2003): 11–30.
How policy-making institutions affect the making of monetary policy; for all students.

Rogoff, Kenneth. "Globalization and Global Disinflation." Federal Reserve Bank of Kansas City *Economic Review* 88 (Fourth Quarter 2003): 45–78.
Overview of globalization's role in supporting 20 years of disinflation in much of the world; for all students.

Saint-Paul, Gilles. "Why Are European Countries Diverging in Their Unemployment Experience?" *Journal of Economic Perspectives* 18 (Fall 2004): 49–68.
Why some European countries have been able to reduce their chronically high unemployment while others haven't; for all students.

Sarno, Lucio, "Toward a New Paradigm in Open Economy Modeling: Where Do We Stand?" Federal Reserve Bank of St. Louis, *Review* 83 (May/June 2001): 21–36.
Survey of the newest theoretical models in open-economy macroeconomics; for intermediate and advanced students.

Session on "International Transmission of Business Cycles in an Increasingly Integrated World Economy." *American Economic Review Papers and Proceedings* 93 (May 2003): 51–69.
Several short papers on the interaction of business cycles across countries; level varies.

Tootell, Geoffrey M. B. "Globalization and U.S. Inflation." Federal Reserve Bank of Boston, *New England Economic Review* (July–August 1998): 21–34.
Argues against a big effect of foreign capacity on U.S. inflation; for all students.

THE AGGREGATE DEMAND CURVE

In this chapter, we used the aggregate demand curve to examine macroeconomic policies' effects on prices and output. This appendix demonstrates how to derive the aggregate demand curve from the IS-LM-BOP model of earlier chapters. The aggregate demand curve differs slightly under fixed and flexible exchange rate regimes, so we'll consider the two cases separately, beginning with the aggregate demand curve under a fixed exchange rate.

A.1 DERIVATION OF THE AGGREGATE DEMAND CURVE UNDER A FIXED EXCHANGE RATE

As in the chapter, we assume that capital is perfectly mobile among countries. This implies a horizontal BOP curve representing equilibrium in the balance of payments. At points above the BOP line, the balance of payments is in surplus; at points below it, the balance of payments is in deficit. With perfectly mobile capital, the economy will never actually be off its BOP line, but examining what would happen in such a case will help clarify the adjustment processes.

Panel (a) of Figure A.1 illustrates an initial equilibrium at the intersection of IS_0, LM_0, and BOP. The price level is P_0, and the equilibrium level of output is Q_0. Panel (b) represents that equilibrium price and output combination (P_0, Q_0) as a point on an aggregate demand curve.

Now suppose the price level rises from P_0 to P_1. The effects in the IS-LM-BOP diagram will include (1) a shift to the left of the IS curve because of the increase in the relative price of domestic goods and (2) a shift to the left of the LM curve due to the negative effect of the price rise on the real money stock. The more sensitive are the demands for imports and exports to changes in relative prices (that is, the higher are the price elasticities of the import and export demand curves), the larger will be the shift of the IS curve relative to that of the LM curve. IS_1 represents the low-elasticity case, in which the IS shift is relatively small. In this case, the new equilibrium occurs at the intersection of IS_1 and LM_1, implying a point corresponding to (P_1, Q_1) on the aggregate demand curve labeled *AD (fixed rate, low elasticity)* in panel (b). IS_2 represents the high-elasticity case, in which the IS shift is relatively large. In this case, the new equilibrium occurs at the intersection of IS_2 and LM_1, implying a point corresponding to (P_1, Q_2) on the

aggregate demand curve labeled *AD (fixed rate, high elasticity)* in panel (b). As panel (b) demonstrates, the higher the elasticity values, the flatter the aggregate demand curve under a fixed exchange rate. (*To test your understanding, explain the points on the aggregate demand curve corresponding to a fall in the price level to $P_2 < P_0$.*)

Note that at points (P_1, Q_1) and (P_1, Q_2) on the two fixed-exchange-rate aggregate demand curves in panel (b) the balance of payments is *not* in equilibrium, but in surplus and deficit, respectively. (*Why?*) To restore balance-of-payments equilibrium given the fixed exchange rate, the central bank will have to intervene appropriately in each case. Intervention will alter the money stock and shift the aggregate demand curve.

A.2 DERIVATION OF THE AGGREGATE DEMAND CURVE UNDER A FLEXIBLE EXCHANGE RATE

The derivation of the aggregate demand curve from the IS-LM-BOP framework under a flexible exchange rate is quite similar to that under a fixed exchange rate. In fact, we can use Figure A.1 again. We continue to assume that capital is perfectly mobile internationally. In panel (a), the initial equilibrium is at the intersection of IS_0, LM_0, and BOP; the price level is P_0 and the equilibrium output Q_0. This initial equilibrium is represented in panel (b) of Figure A.1 as a point on the *AD (flexible rate)* curve.

A rise in the price level to $P_1 > P_0$ shifts the IS curve to the left, because the relative price of domestic goods rises and consumers switch to imports. The LM curve also shifts to the left (to LM_1), because the rise in the price level reduces the real money stock. The new equilibrium output at price level P_1 is Q_3. This new equilibrium forms a second point on the flexible-rate aggregate demand curve in panel (b).

But how do we know exactly how much the IS curve shifts as a result of the rise in the price level? In particular, how can we be sure that IS_3 and LM_1 intersect *on* the BOP curve at output level Q_3? If the IS curve (such as IS_2) intersected LM_1 below the BOP line, the balance of payments would be in deficit. Under a flexible exchange rate regime, the domestic currency would depreciate and the relative price of domestic goods would fall. The change in relative prices would shift the IS curve to the right to IS_3. On the other hand, if the IS curve (such as IS_1) intersected LM_1 at a point above the BOP line, the balance of payments would be in

Figure A.1   **Derivation of Aggregate Demand Curve from IS-LM-BOP with Perfectly Mobile Capital**

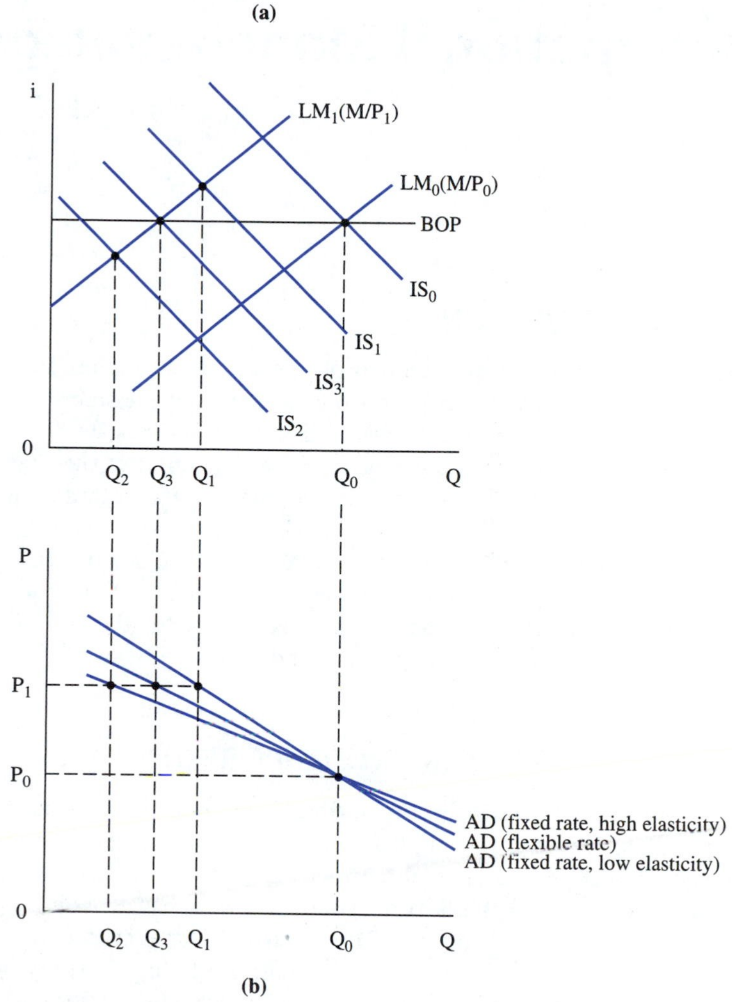

(a)

(b)

Real output and the price level are negatively related along an aggregate demand curve.

surplus. With a flexible exchange rate, the domestic currency would appreciate and domestic goods would become more expensive relative to foreign goods. The IS curve would shift to the left to IS_3. This exchange rate adjustment in response to the balance of payments will ensure that the new IS curve intersects LM_1 on the BOP line at output level Q_3. (*As an exercise, explain the shifts in the IS and LM curves in response to a fall in the price level to $P_2 < P_0$.*)

Note that, unlike the fixed exchange rate case, the balance of payments is in equilibrium at each and every point on the flexible-rate aggregate demand curve. The slope of the flexible-rate curve falls between the slopes of the fixed-rate curves for the low- and high-elasticity cases.

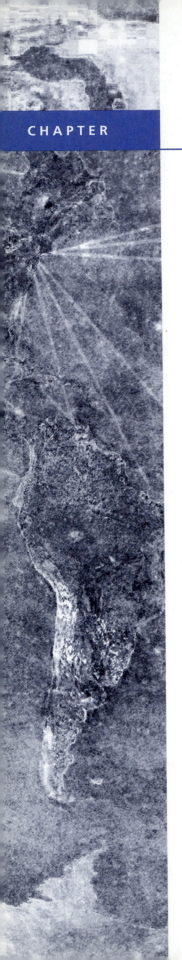

10

International Monetary Regimes

1 INTRODUCTION

We've encountered many examples of how a country's adjustment and the effects of its macroeconomic policy depend on the exchange rate regime. For the most part, we've concentrated on differences between fixed- and flexible-rate regimes and assumed that the regime was imposed exogenously. However, countries *choose* the systems to manage their currencies, and the choices countries make in this regard differ widely, as indicated in Table 1.

This chapter's goals are to (1) examine the considerations that go into the choice of exchange rate regime, (2) outline some of the available alternatives other than pure fixed or flexible exchange rates, and (3) evaluate the strengths and weaknesses of alternate regimes as well as historical experience under each.

2 WHAT DOES A MONETARY REGIME NEED TO DO?

Any country that engages in international trade must make some provision for handling transactions that involve more than one currency. Countries use a variety of arrangements, ranging from barter or countertrade, which eliminates currencies altogether, to a perfectly flexible exchange rate, which permits unrestricted exchange of one currency for another at a market-determined exchange rate. That different countries choose such different arrangements suggests that the decision involves trade-offs. We begin our study of alternative monetary regimes by examining some desirable goals that a hypothetical "ideal" regime would achieve.

An international monetary regime should promote efficient functioning of the world economy by *facilitating international trade and investment* according to the patterns of comparative advantage. The regime also should *support international borrowing and lending* that produce gains from intertemporal trade. Regimes that depend on trade restrictions or capital controls don't perform well in the long run. Such restrictions reduce the world economy's output by encouraging inefficient production and by preventing resources and investment funds from flowing to their most productive uses. The ideal regime would allow trade and finance to proceed just as if the entire world used a single currency.

A successful international monetary regime should also *promote balance-of-payments adjustment* to prevent the disruptions and crises associated with large, chronic BOP imbalances. This means that the system needs to either contain automatic adjustment mechanisms for restoring BOP equilibrium or encourage policy makers to take steps to correct balance-of-payments problems promptly. A related requirement is that the system *provide countries with liquidity* sufficient to finance temporary BOP deficits. Under any

Table 1 **NUMBER OF IMF COUNTRIES USING VARIOUS EXCHANGE RATE ARRANGEMENTS, 2003**

Exchange Rate Arrangement	Number of Countries
Less-Flexible Regimes:	
Exchange arrangements with no separate legal tender	41
Currency board	7
Other conventional fixed peg (including de facto peg under managed floating)	41
Pegged exchange rates within horizontal bands	4
Crawling peg	5
Exchange rates within crawling bands	5
More-Flexible Regimes:	
Managed floating with no preannounced path for exchange rate	50
Independently floating	34
Total:	187

Source: International Monetary Fund.

arrangement other than a perfectly flexible exchange rate, some temporary imbalances are inevitable. Adequate provisions for handling those imbalances play a vital role in avoiding and resolving crises.

Individuals and firms that engage in international trade and financial transactions face many types of uncertainty. An ideal international monetary regime would *avoid adding to this uncertainty*, which may discourage international transactions and cause countries to forgo gains from trade. Proponents of fixed exchange rates often present this criterion as an argument for using fixed rather than flexible exchange rates. As we'll see later in the chapter, however, fixed exchange rates don't necessarily involve less uncertainty than flexible ones.

We've learned that the choice of monetary regime interacts with the policy-making process to determine the effectiveness of various macroeconomic policies. The ideal monetary system would *enhance policy effectiveness* and provide policy makers with a number of policy instruments at least equal to the number of targets. The system would also *minimize the possibility of policy mistakes and cushion their negative impact*. It would encourage policy makers to take correct and timely policy actions and *shield the policy-making process from undue political pressure*.

The very definition of money demonstrates that confidence provides an essential ingredient in a successful monetary system. Money can function only as long as the public has confidence in the monetary unit and its acceptance as payment for goods and services. Mere expectations of disruptions in the world monetary system can themselves cause volatility, disorder, and poor economic performance, so the ideal monetary system would *generate confidence in its stability and continuity*.

Finally, any international monetary system involves costs to operate. The relevant costs include those of negotiating international agreements, maintaining international organizations such as the International Monetary Fund, and holding stocks of foreign exchange reserves, as well as the costs to individuals and firms of handling multiple currencies. Other things being equal, an international monetary system with *lower administrative and operating costs* is superior to one involving higher costs.

The list of attributes desirable for an international monetary regime is quite long. The following passage by Barry Eichengreen, a leading expert on international monetary history, summarizes the goals:

> The international monetary system is part of the institutional framework that binds national economies together. An ideally functioning system permits producers to specialize in goods in which the nation has a comparative advantage and savers to search beyond national borders for profitable investment opportunities. It does so by combining the virtues of stability and flexibility. Stability in the market for foreign exchange minimizes the volatility of import and export prices, permitting producers and consumers to exploit fully the advantages of international specialization. Flexibility in the operation of the international monetary system permits the divergent objectives of national economic authorities to be reconciled with one another.[1]

No system satisfies all these attributes perfectly. Rather, the choice of international monetary system implies trade-offs among the various criteria. We now turn to a brief examination of the major monetary regimes and to the question of how each fares in terms of the preceding criteria. We begin with the gold standard.

3 THE GOLD STANDARD, 1880–1913: PANACEA OR ROSE-COLORED GLASSES?

3.1 What's a Gold Standard?

Use of precious metals, especially gold, as money dates back many centuries. Gold's characteristics make it well suited for this purpose. It's scarce, durable, easily measurable, mintable into uniform coins, and transportable (at least in the quantities required for most economic transactions—don't try to carry a gold bar in your pocket).

The precise way gold functioned as money evolved as national governments assumed larger roles in the money-supply process. At first, unminted gold circulated as dust or bullion. Market forces determined the relative price between gold and goods. For example, gold discoveries led to a fall in gold's relative price and a rise in the relative price of goods, as gold became more abundant relative to goods. Gradually, sovereigns started to mint gold into coins of a specified weight and to certify the coins' value. The value of these "full-bodied" coins equaled the value of their gold. Coining gold offered clear advantages, because it eliminated the need to weigh and measure at each transaction.

As economies grew and the number and size of economic transactions increased, use of currency or paper money as a substitute for gold began to spread. Paper money was lighter and easier to transport, and each unit of it could represent a unit of gold held in safekeeping by the issuer of the currency. Currency was **convertible**; that is, holders of currency could convert it into gold on request, and vice versa. This type of **gold standard**, in which currency backed by gold circulated as money, evolved independently in many countries. While the gold standard involved no explicit international agreement, the major trading economies—including Britain, Germany, the United States, and Japan—operated under such a standard by around 1880, providing the basis for an international monetary regime that would last until World War I.

Simple rules governed the gold standard. First, each government defined the value of its currency in terms of gold; for example, the United States defined the dollar value of an

---

1. Barry Eichengreen, "Editor's Introduction," in *The Gold Standard in Theory and History,* edited by Barry Eichengreen (New York: Methuen, 1985), p. 1.

ounce of gold as $20.67, and Britain defined the pound price of gold as £4.24 per ounce. The U.S. government committed itself to buy or sell gold at $20.67 per ounce, while the British government likewise stood ready to exchange pounds for gold, and vice versa, at £4.24 per ounce. Each government held gold reserves to back its commitment. Together, the two governments' commitments defined an implicit or **mint exchange rate** between dollars and pounds of ($20.67/oz.)/(£4.24/oz.), or about $4.87/£1.

Under a gold standard, the mint exchange rate fixes the market exchange rate between two currencies, not through direct intervention by the countries' monetary authorities, but by private arbitrage.[2] Suppose that the dollar price of pounds in the foreign exchange market rose above the mint exchange rate of $4.87/£1, say, to $5 per pound. Arbitrageurs would find it profitable to use dollars to buy gold in the United States at the official rate of $20.67 per ounce, ship it to Britain, sell it at the official rate of £4.24 per ounce, and exchange the pounds for (£4.24) · ($5.00/£1) = $21.20 in the foreign exchange market. The arbitrageurs would earn a profit of $21.20 − $20.67 = $0.53 on each ounce of gold, ignoring transportation and other transaction costs. The arbitrage process would raise the demand for dollars in the foreign exchange market and push the market exchange rate downward toward the mint rate of $4.87 per pound.

A fall in the dollar price of pounds to, say, $4.50 would cause arbitrageurs to ship gold from Britain to the United States at a profit of £0.35 per ounce. (*Why?*) Because of the transaction costs involved in shipping gold in response to deviations between the mint and market exchange rates, arbitrage couldn't keep the two rates identical continuously. However, it did keep the market rate within a band around the mint rate. The costs of gold shipments determined the width of the band, and the boundaries of the band were called *gold points*.

The combination of (1) government purchases and sales of gold to keep each currency's price fixed in terms of gold and (2) private arbitrage to keep the market exchange rate approximately equal to the mint exchange rate ensured a fixed exchange rate between each pair of currencies under the gold standard. The viability of the gold standard required that each monetary authority issue no more currency than it could back with its stock of gold. If a central bank violated this rule, it faced the possibility of being unable to honor its promise to convert currency into gold on demand.

We can see how a gold standard can discipline monetary policy by considering a country that pursues an open market purchase to expand its money stock. Initially, the domestic real money stock rises and the interest rate falls. The decline in domestic relative to foreign interest rates makes foreign-currency-denominated assets more attractive. Asset owners sell the now-unattractive domestic-currency-denominated assets to the central bank for gold, a transaction the central bank is obligated to fulfill under gold-standard rules. New owners of gold then sell it to foreign central banks in exchange for foreign currency that they use to purchase foreign-currency-denominated assets—which pay a higher interest rate. The net effect: The country that raised its money stock experiences a capital outflow, and other countries a matching capital inflow.

These capital flows reequilibrate the foreign exchange market. The money stock of the country that conducted the expansionary monetary policy shrinks back to its original size as the country loses gold reserves. Other countries experience money-stock growth as they accumulate gold reserves. Once interest parity reestablishes itself, capital flows cease. The total world money stock remains unchanged, but it's been redistributed between the countries. Note two important results. First, both countries take part in the adjustment process. This makes adjustment under the gold standard *symmetrical*, as

---

2. Recall that arbitrage is an effort to make a profit by taking advantage of price differentials that exist in two submarkets at a given time.

opposed to the *asymmetrical* adjustment under other fixed exchange rate systems, in which the reserve country both controls its own money stock and determines money growth for all members of the group.[3] Second, the gold standard's rules link a country's money stock to its central bank's gold. This key characteristic of the gold standard—the tying of the money stock to the central bank's stock of gold—lies at the heart of arguments both in favor of and against use of a gold standard as an international monetary regime.

3.2 How's a Gold Standard Supposed to Work?

The primary arguments in favor of a gold standard rest on the belief that such a system contributes to price stability, particularly to avoiding inflation, and contains an automatic adjustment mechanism for maintaining balance-of-payments equilibrium. The price-stability argument stems from a gold standard's limit on money-stock growth. At the worldwide level, the money stock can't grow faster than the total world stock of gold. At the national level, each country's money stock can't grow faster than that central bank's stock of gold, because gold must back all currency. A country's central bank can't create gold but must either buy existing gold from the public or promote mining to enlarge the available supply.[4] Insofar as this limit on money growth works, the gold standard imposes **price discipline** on central banks, both individually and collectively. This discipline keeps central banks from creating continual increases in the price level through excessively expansionary monetary policy.

The automatic adjustment mechanism for the balance of payments under a gold standard provides an example of David Hume's specie-flow mechanism. *Specie* is a term for money in the form of precious metal. In the **specie-flow mechanism**, international flows of gold (money) correct BOP disequilibria. Suppose, for example, that the United States runs a balance-of-payments (or, more accurately, a current-account) deficit with Britain under a gold standard. The value of goods and services the United States imports from Britain exceeds that of U.S. exports to Britain. To cover the difference and settle its account, the United States must ship gold to Britain. This movement of gold reduces the U.S. money stock and increases Britain's. The fall in the U.S. money stock causes U.S. prices to fall, while the rise in the British money stock causes British prices to rise. The change in relative prices of American and British goods (or, equivalently, the real depreciation of the dollar) shifts demand away from British goods and toward American ones, correcting the original current-account imbalance. Under a gold standard, any such imbalance reduces the money stock of the deficit country and increases that of the surplus country. The resulting change in relative prices of the two countries' products, or the real exchange rate between their currencies, raises the deficit country's net exports and lowers those of the surplus country, moving the balance of payments back toward equilibrium.

Hume presented his specie-flow mechanism in 1752 as a counter to mercantilist arguments for restricting trade. Mercantilists saw trade policy primarily as a vehicle for accumulation of specie, which they viewed as the source of wealth and power. The route to this accumulation involved restrictive trade policies designed to create BOP surpluses that would be settled in gold. Hume's logic, along with that of classical economists David Ricardo and Adam Smith, exposed the fallacies of mercantilism. The specie-flow mechanism contributed by demonstrating the inherently short-run nature of balance-of-payments

---

3. For more on reserve-currency countries, see section 6 and Case One in the chapter on short-run macroeconomic policy under fixed exchange rates.

4. The other way of increasing the domestic stock of gold, as we'll see, is to run a balance-of-payments surplus.

surpluses. When a country succeeded in creating a BOP surplus through mercantilist policies, it indeed experienced a gold inflow. But this inflow swelled the money stock and raised prices, thereby encouraging imports, discouraging exports, and eliminating the BOP surplus. On the basis of this automatic adjustment mechanism, Hume argued that mercantilist policies, *even if* they'd been desirable, couldn't succeed in the long run.

The simple version of Hume's specie-flow mechanism emphasized price flexibility and focused on adjustment of the current-account balance rather than the overall balance of payments. However, we've seen that a similar adjustment mechanism works through the capital account. When the U.S. money stock falls and Britain's rises, U.S. interest rates rise relative to Britain's.[5] This causes the U.S. capital account to move toward surplus and corrects the original deficit in the U.S. balance of payments. Thus, although Hume's treatment of the specie-flow mechanism analyzed the effect of price flexibility in promoting adjustment through the current account, the same basic idea can be applied to adjustment in the capital account.

In summary, a gold standard requires that individual governments peg their respective currencies' values in terms of gold, that arbitrageurs keep the market exchange rate approximately equal to the mint exchange rate, and that adequate gold stocks back countries' money stocks. The gold standard imposes a degree of price discipline on the central bank by limiting money growth to gold-stock growth. The gold standard also contains an automatic adjustment mechanism in the form of Hume's specie-flow mechanism to solve balance-of-payments problems through symmetric changes in countries' relative money stocks. As under any fixed exchange rate regime, the link between the balance of payments and the money stock plays an essential role in automatic adjustment. Given these proposed advantages of a gold standard, let's examine the historical evidence on the actual operation of a gold-based international monetary regime.

3.3 How'd the Gold Standard Really Work?

A gold standard links the growth of the domestic money stock to that of the gold stock, so an accurate evaluation of its desirability depends on the pattern of growth in the gold stock, among other things. A smooth pattern of growth, which kept pace with full-employment output, would prevent shocks to the world economy. Consistently faster growth in gold than in output would put upward pressure on the price of goods relative to gold as countries accumulated gold reserves. Consistently slower growth in gold than in output would put downward pressure on the price of goods relative to gold and create a shortage of reserves for the growing economies. An erratic growth pattern in gold, on the other hand, could disrupt the world economy by generating business cycles.

Table 2 reports the growth rate of the U.S. monetary gold stock from 1880 to 1913, when the major economies operated under a gold standard. The annual rates of change ranged from a low of −7 percent to a high of 43 percent. Even if monetary authorities had closely followed the rule of creating no more money than they could back by gold, the rate of growth in the money stock would have been quite volatile.

But how closely did governments actually abide by the rules of the gold standard? Studies suggest that policy makers often disregarded the rules. If the growth of the gold stock proved insufficient to support the money growth that policy makers wanted, they could change the law to require less gold backing for each unit of currency issued or to

---

5. A rise in the money supply could cause expectations of inflation and a rise in the long-term nominal interest rate; however, short-term interest rates are of primary concern here. Section 4.4 in the chapter on the exchange rate in the long run treats the relationship between inflation and long-term interest rates.

Table 2   **ANNUAL GROWTH IN THE U.S. MONETARY GOLD STOCK, 1880–1913 (PERCENT)**

Year	Annual Growth in U.S. Monetary Gold Stock	Annual Growth of U.S. M2	Year	Annual Growth in U.S. Monetary Gold Stock	Annual Growth of U.S. M2
1880	43%	22%	1897	13%	7%
1881	33	20	1898	23	13
1882	7	8	1899	18	16
1883	6	6	1900	7	8
1884	2	0	1901	10	13
1885	6	3	1902	5	9
1886	4	8	1903	7	6
1887	9	7	1904	6	6
1888	7	3	1905	2	11
1889	−2	6	1906	9	8
1890	0	9	1907	10	5
1891	−3	4	1908	10	−1
1892	−3	9	1909	1	11
1893	−7	−4	1910	1	5
1894	0	0	1911	6	6
1895	−5	4	1912	9	7
1896	0	−2	1913	3	4

Source: U.S. Department of Commerce, *Historical Statistics of the United States: Colonial Times to 1970.*

exempt certain types of money creation (for example, bank deposits as opposed to currency) from gold backing. As under any fixed exchange rate regime, central banks could sterilize the effects of changes in the gold stock by engineering offsetting changes in domestic monetary policy.

In practice, the expediency of such policies limited the price discipline imposed by the gold standard. The U.S. money stock grew erratically even by today's standards, as documented in Table 2. The table also reveals that changes in the gold stock explain most changes in the U.S. money stock during the gold-standard era. The years of the most rapid gold-stock growth (1880–1881 and 1898–1899) correspond to those of fastest monetary growth. At the other extreme, during 1893 both the gold stock and the money stock suffered their biggest declines.

The gold standard in the United States doesn't appear to have promoted smooth, disciplined behavior of the money stock. However, the behavior of the money stock matters not in itself but for its implications for real output and the price level. Recall the ultimate goal of an international monetary system: smooth functioning of the world economy as reflected in steady growth of real output and stable prices. Table 3 reveals that wide variations in both real output and the price level matched the instability in the money stock, as the model of the preceding chapter would lead us to expect.

Overall, the gold-standard era exhibited greater instability in terms of money growth, prices, and real output than some analysts admit. Apparently, rose-colored perceptions of the "good old days" filter some popular views of the gold standard. Efforts to smooth and limit money growth by tying the money stock to gold had limited success, for two basic reasons. First, the gold stock itself grew erratically due to new discoveries, new extraction

Table 3   ANNUAL CHANGES IN U.S. REAL GNP AND PRICE LEVEL UNDER
THE GOLD STANDARD, 1890–1913 (PERCENT)

Year	Change in Real GNP (Q)	Change in GNP Deflator (P)	Year	Change in Real GNP (Q)	Change in GNP Deflator (P)
1890	7%	−2%	1902	1%	3%
1891	5	−1	1903	5	1
1892	10	−4	1904	−1	1
1893	−5	2	1905	7	2
1894	−3	−6	1906	12	2
1895	12	−1	1907	2	4
1896	−2	−3	1908	−8	−1
1897	9	0	1909	17	4
1898	2	3	1910	3	3
1899	9	4	1911	3	−1
1900	3	5	1912	6	4
1901	11	−1	1913	1	−1

Source: U.S. Department of Commerce, *Historical Statistics of the United States: Colonial Times to 1970.*

technologies, and changing incentives for mining. Second, unless inclined to abide by the restrictions placed on money growth by the gold stock, central banks can circumvent the rules and eliminate much of the discipline credited to the gold standard. This second weakness of a gold standard seems likely to pose an even bigger problem for a gold standard today than during the early days of the twentieth century. A gold standard compels policy makers to focus on *external* balance, but throughout the postwar period, governments have accepted increasing responsibility for *internal*-balance targets, such as full employment. Policy makers committed by law to the pursuit of full employment (as is, for example, the U.S. central bank, the Federal Reserve) seem unlikely to abide by the rules of a gold standard when those rules require behavior that may carry high short-run costs in terms of domestic economic targets.

4 THE INTERWAR YEARS, 1919–1939: SEARCH FOR AN INTERNATIONAL MONETARY SYSTEM

World War I disrupted all aspects of the world economy, including the gold standard. Economic policy in the large trading economies focused on financing the war. Fiscal authorities borrowed to pay armies, buy weapons, and later to finance reconstruction. Monetary policy makers printed money to cover the fiscal expenditures.[6] Except for the United States, countries abandoned their currencies' convertibility into gold, ushering in a period of flexible exchange rates. The dollar remained convertible into gold, but other governments stopped converting their currencies into either gold or dollars at fixed rates. Thus, the fixed mint exchange rates of the gold-standard era disappeared.

Few policy makers or economists viewed the flexible exchange rates as permanent, however. Discussion focused on when to reestablish the gold standard and how to

---

6. Other ways to finance government expenditures include raising taxes or borrowing from the public.

choose the new rate at which to peg each currency to gold. The demands of financing the war and reconstruction had produced high rates of inflation in most economies, especially outside the United States; so most policy makers recognized a return to prewar rates as infeasible. The war had shaken confidence in the gold standard, and the relative strengths of the United States and Britain in the world economy had changed. A handful of countries reestablished a partial gold standard in 1925, but with unsustainable exchange rates. British war-generated inflation, combined with the British government's determination to return the pound to gold convertibility at its prewar rate, led to severe monetary contraction, a dramatic real appreciation of the pound, and a prolonged British recession. Germany—saddled with a devastated economy and war reparations that it attempted to pay by printing massive quantities of money—suffered a hyperinflation in which the price level rose by a factor of almost 500 *billion* between 1919 and 1925.

Beginning in 1931, the brief return to a gold standard collapsed in the midst of the Great Depression. One by one, countries again suspended their currencies' convertibility into gold. International monetary cooperation took a back seat to countries' self-interested attempts to regain control of their economies through competitive devaluations, tariffs, exchange and capital controls, and a variety of other desperate and often counterproductive policies.

Pervasive political and economic instability characterized the period between World War I and World War II. Table 4 summarizes the erratic macroeconomic performance. The lack of a smoothly functioning international monetary system was but one symptom of the overall problem. Neither the breakdown of the gold standard nor the spread of trade restrictions can shoulder blame for all the interwar economic problems, but narrowly nationalistic policies did little to alleviate them.

The interwar years left a historical record that still serves as a reminder of the world economy's interdependence and of the costs of beggar-thy-neighbor policies. Only after the Great Depression did macroeconomic stability and internal balance become central goals of government policy. One result of the interwar and Depression experiences was

Table 4   **ANNUAL CHANGES IN U.S. REAL GNP AND PRICE LEVEL, 1919–1941 (PERCENT)**

Year	Change in Real GNP (Q)	Change in GNP Deflator (P)	Year	Change in Real GNP (Q)	Change in GNP Deflator (P)
1919	−4%	14%	1931	−8%	−9%
1920	−4	14	1932	−15	−10
1921	−9	−17	1933	−2	−2
1922	16	−8	1934	9	7
1923	12	2	1935	10	1
1924	0	0	1936	14	0
1925	8	1	1937	5	4
1926	6	−2	1938	−5	−1
1927	0	−2	1939	9	−2
1928	1	2	1940	9	−2
1929	7	0	1941	16	8
1930	−10	−3			

Source: U.S. Department of Commerce, *Historical Statistics of the United States: Colonial Times to 1970.*

the major economies' determination to unite to build stable and open international trade and monetary systems after World War II.[7]

5 BRETTON WOODS, 1945–1971: A NEGOTIATED INTERNATIONAL MONETARY SYSTEM

In the 1940s, few scholars or policy makers viewed flexible exchange rates as a viable basis for an international monetary regime. The Bretton Woods system established after World War II reinstated fixed exchange rates, but with three major changes from the prewar system:

1. The new regime represented a gold-exchange standard rather than a gold standard. This meant that a national currency—the U.S. dollar—played a central role along with gold.
2. The new system was an adjustable-peg exchange rate system rather than a fixed-rate system, because the Bretton Woods agreement contained provisions for altering exchange rates under certain, albeit vaguely specified, conditions.
3. The Bretton Woods system, unlike the gold standard, represented the outcome of international bargaining, even though the United States and Britain dominated the negotiations. Those negotiations created an international organization, the International Monetary Fund (IMF), as a multilateral body to support the new agreement.

5.1 What's a Gold-Exchange Standard?

The Bretton Woods system provides an example of a **gold-exchange**, or **gold-dollar**, **standard**. Nondollar currencies weren't convertible directly into gold, but were convertible, at a pegged exchange rate, into dollars, which in turn were convertible into gold at $35 per ounce.[8] That the U.S. dollar served as the key currency in the Bretton Woods gold-exchange standard implied a distinction between the policy rules followed by the United States and those followed by other countries.[9] The **key**, or **reserve, currency** was convertible into gold. Maintaining this convertibility, initially at $35 per ounce, defined the primary U.S. responsibility under Bretton Woods. Fulfillment of this responsibility required the United States to (1) stand ready to buy or sell gold in exchange for dollars at $35 per ounce at the request of other central banks and (2) create no more dollars subject to convertibility than the U.S. stock of gold could support. Other countries' central banks held responsibility for intervening in foreign exchange markets to buy and sell dollars, to keep the dollar values of their respective currencies at the agreed-upon pegged rates.

Notice the fundamental difference between a gold standard and a gold-exchange standard. Under a true gold standard, *each* currency is convertible into gold. Under a gold-exchange standard, *only* the reserve currency is convertible directly into gold. Other currencies, in turn, are convertible into the reserve currency at pegged exchange rates maintained through intervention by nonreserve-currency central banks.

---

7. This determination was evidenced by the negotiations for a postwar international monetary system that began in 1941 and continued throughout the war.

8. At the war's end, most currencies weren't convertible. The Bretton Woods agreement urged member countries to establish convertibility, at least for current-account transactions, as soon as possible. Most major economies accomplished this move by the late 1950s or early 1960s. In the upcoming chapter, we'll look into the costs that nonconvertible currencies impose on economies.

9. Section 6 in the chapter on short-run policy under a fixed exchange rate discusses the special status of reserve-currency countries.

5.2 How Was Bretton Woods Supposed to Work?

The gold standard had collapsed when policy makers no longer would subordinate their domestic, internal-balance goals to the gold standard's externally oriented rules. To fight unemployment during the Great Depression, governments resorted to abandoning their exchange-rate pegs, competitively devaluing, and imposing trade barriers. Negotiators at Bretton Woods, fresh from the interwar experience, recognized that any new international monetary system, if it was to succeed based on fixed exchange rates, would have to provide governments with some flexibility to address the domestic macroeconomic priorities for which electorates increasingly held governments responsible. The Bretton Woods agreement contained three important elements meant to incorporate this flexibility: an adjustable-peg exchange rate system, IMF lending facilities, and permission for countries to institute or continue to use exchange controls on some types of international transactions.

THE ADJUSTABLE PEG   The designers of Bretton Woods recognized that the pegged exchange rates selected at the close of World War II would require periodic adjustment as countries' economic situations evolved. The major economies found themselves in widely divergent circumstances and pursuing diverse policies at the end of the war. Some economies were growing rapidly, while others struggled to reconstruct their basic productive capacities. For all these reasons, the negotiators at Bretton Woods recognized the need for periodic devaluations and revaluations to correct chronic balance-of-payments imbalances. Rather than permanently fixing exchange rates, the Bretton Woods agreement explicitly left open the possibility of occasional currency realignments and allowed countries to devalue or revalue their currencies under specified conditions with the consent of the rest of the group.[10] The framers of the agreement hoped that by providing a cooperative framework for these changes, through the IMF, policy makers could avoid future episodes of the destructive competitive devaluations that had occurred during the Great Depression. A system of fixed exchange rates that embodies rules for periodic adjustment of rates as economic conditions change is called an **adjustable-peg system**.

Bretton Woods' adjustable peg required a central bank to intervene to buy or sell foreign exchange whenever short-run disturbances caused a temporary disequilibrium at the pegged rate for that central bank's currency. If, however, economic circumstances changed permanently or dramatically such that the pegged rate clearly differed from long-run equilibrium, intervention to maintain the rate could be undesirable or even infeasible. In such cases of **fundamental disequilibrium**, policy makers could change the pegged exchange rate, under the guidance of the IMF, to a rate that corresponded more closely to equilibrium.

IMF LENDING FACILITIES   A fixed exchange rate regime requires central banks to intervene in foreign exchange markets to maintain balance-of-payments equilibrium at the assigned exchange rates. This intervention alters the domestic money stock; in fact, we've seen that intervention's effect on the money stock represents the key step in the mechanism through which intervention restores balance-of-payments equilibrium.[11] However, these changes in the money stock may exacerbate problems of internal balance, particularly unemployment, and lead policy makers to circumvent the rules of the regime and cause crises. The Bretton Woods agreement recognized this possibility

---

10. Each exchange rate fluctuated in a band (of ±1 percent) around the pegged rate; minor exchange adjustments didn't require consent.

11. See section 7, especially Figure 16, in the chapter on money, the banking system, and foreign exchange.

and incorporated provisions for lending reserves (either gold or foreign currencies) to governments that faced temporary balance-of-payments deficits but for which immediate monetary contraction presented unacceptable domestic economic consequences.

The International Monetary Fund consists of member countries that promise to abide by the organization's Articles of Agreement, which define the rules, privileges, and obligations of membership. Each country joins the IMF by contributing a sum called the *quota*, which consists of gold (25 percent) and the country's domestic currency (75 percent). The IMF, in turn, could lend these funds to countries that needed its assistance to meet their Bretton Woods obligations. Countries could use their quotas to buy specific currencies they needed for foreign exchange market intervention. This allowed countries to maintain their exchange rate pegs while postponing monetary adjustment.

A country's economic size determined the size of its IMF quota and, therefore, of its routine borrowing privilege. Voting within the IMF also was determined by the size of a country's quota. The IMF divided each country's borrowing privileges into several classes called **tranches**. **Conditionality** referred to the IMF's requirement that countries follow certain policy prescriptions as a condition for borrowing. When a country borrowed small sums from the fund, the borrowing came from the lower tranches subject to no conditionality requirements. As the country's borrowing rose into higher and higher tranches, which generally reflected increasingly serious and persistent economic problems, the number of conditions the IMF imposed increased. The most common conditions included adjusting the exchange rate to make it more consistent with balance-of-payments equilibrium, lowering deficit spending by the public sector, and lowering money growth rates. These conditionality prescriptions were designed to eliminate the balance-of-payments problems that required borrowing from the fund, while the IMF lending itself provided short-term relief to countries with high domestic unemployment and large balance-of-payments deficits.

EXCHANGE AND CAPITAL CONTROLS   At the end of World War II, most national currencies weren't convertible; that is, they couldn't be exchanged freely for other currencies. Nonconvertibility reduces the world economy's efficiency by making international trade more costly, because it limits the usefulness or the liquidity of foreign-currency-denominated export receipts. To encourage the reestablishment of international trade after the war, the Bretton Woods agreement urged member countries to restore currency convertibility quickly. However, the agreement limited the call for convertibility to current-account or international trade transactions and avoided requiring convertibility of capital-account or financial transactions.[12] The logic of the distinction was based on negotiators' perceptions that private capital flows, which could move quickly across national boundaries in response to expected changes in exchange rates, might add instability to the world economy. If policy makers constantly had to worry about foreign exchange market participants' perceptions of their economy and policy, this might further constrain their ability to manage the economy while maintaining fixed exchange rates.[13]

Currency nonconvertibility for capital-account transactions severely limited private capital flows in the years following the war. This implied that current-account deficits had to be financed in one of two ways: central bank sales of foreign exchange, or official

---

12.   The chapter on the balance-of-payments accounts covers the distinction between current- and capital-account transactions.

13.   Case Four in the chapter on short-run policy under a fixed exchange rate provides more information about capital controls.

borrowing from either other countries or the IMF.[14] At the same time, each government had to worry about keeping enough foreign exchange reserves to maintain the credibility of its exchange-rate commitment.

As currencies gradually became convertible for capital-account transactions, private capital flows increased. This development enhanced countries' opportunity to reap gains from intertemporal trade. For some countries, private capital flows could offset current-account deficits or surpluses and reduce the need for foreign exchange intervention. For others, capital-account deficits or surpluses exacerbated their current-account counterpart and required larger-scale intervention that generated big swings in governments' foreign exchange reserves—and in domestic money stocks. Hints of an impending devaluation could cause immediate capital outflows and necessitate an actual devaluation, often one larger in magnitude than would have been required in the absence of the expectation-based capital outflow.[15]

5.3 How'd Bretton Woods Really Work?

Confidence in the international monetary system under Bretton Woods hinged on the credibility of two fundamental commitments: one tying countries' currencies to the dollar and the other tying the dollar to gold. Unfortunately, requirements for meeting the two commitments sometimes conflicted.

Immediately after World War II, reconstruction meant that the European and Japanese economies ran large current-account deficits. With private capital flows constrained by capital controls and currency nonconvertibility, those deficits required central banks to intervene on a large scale to maintain the countries' fixed exchange rates against the dollar. Such large-scale intervention was possible only if the central banks held sufficiently large stocks of foreign exchange reserves. This implied that the United States had to make available enough dollars to provide adequate world **liquidity** or reserves, because countries held the bulk of their reserves in U.S. dollars, the reserve currency.[16]

At the same time, continued confidence in the U.S. commitment to hold the price of gold at $35 per ounce required that the dollars in the hands of foreign central banks, and therefore subject to requests for conversion into gold, not exceed the value of the U.S. gold stock. The U.S. stock of gold reserves was large but finite. Figure 1 reports the U.S. gold stock during the Bretton Woods period, along with the dollar liabilities that the United States could have been asked by other central banks to convert into gold. As the figure makes clear, dollar liabilities to foreign central banks surpassed the U.S. gold stock by the early 1960s. With dollars in the hands of foreign central banks exceeding the value of the stock of gold reserves (valued at $35 per ounce), the United States clearly could no longer convert all dollars into gold on request.[17]

An obvious conflict existed between the need to *create large stocks of dollars* to provide adequate liquidity for intervention and the need to *limit the creation of dollars* so as not to jeopardize confidence in their convertibility into gold. If the United States created a large quantity of dollars for use as reserves, confidence in its ability to honor its commitment to convert dollars into gold at $35 per ounce on foreign governments'

---

14. Recall from the chapter on the balance-of-payments accounts that BOP = CAB + KAB = −OSB. If capital controls limit the private capital flow portion of KAB, then CAB < 0 requires either OSB > 0 or official (noncontrolled) capital inflows such that KAB > 0.

15. See Cases One, Two, Three, and Five in the chapter on short-run policy under a fixed exchange rate.

16. The remaining reserve stocks took the form of gold and a few other currencies, such as pounds.

17. As long as the Bretton Woods system enjoyed widespread confidence, the United States didn't have to redeem all dollars at the promised rate, but the belief that it *could* do so was crucial.

Figure 1 **The U.S. Gold Stock and Dollars Eligible for Conversion into Gold during Bretton Woods (Gold Valued at the Official Rate)**

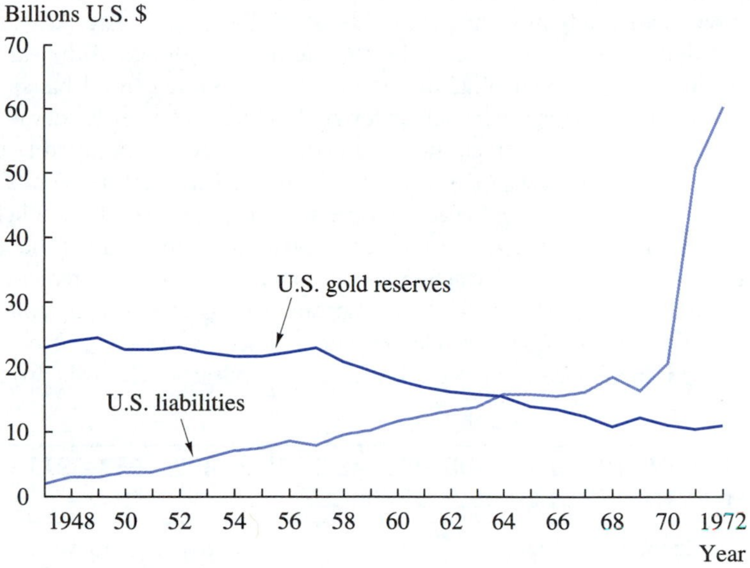

Billions U.S. $

During the 1960s, the number of dollars eligible for conversion into gold grew to exceed the value of official U.S. gold reserves.

Sources: *Economic Report of the President;* International Monetary Fund, *International Financial Statistics.*

---

request waned. Thus, it isn't surprising that during much of the Bretton Woods era, failure to meet one or the other of these two goals caused concern. In fact, one can argue that the evolution and eventual demise of the Bretton Woods system resulted from the interplay of these two problems.

During the early postwar years, the first problem prevailed as other countries experienced large current-account deficits and a chronic "dollar shortage" as they sought dollars to supplement their gold reserves. The European economies maintained protectionist policies and controls on private capital flows in an effort to hold their balance-of-payments deficits at manageable levels given their levels of dollar reserves.

In the mid-1960s, the United States pursued more expansionary monetary policy and itself ran balance-of-payments deficits. The reserve-currency country obviously lost its ability to honor its commitment to convert dollars into gold.[18] The expansionary U.S. monetary policy meant that foreign central banks had to buy large quantities of dollars from the foreign exchange market to prevent their own currencies from appreciating against the dollar. For a while, foreign central banks willingly accumulated dollar reserves that, unlike gold, paid interest. As long as no one expected a dollar devaluation against gold, the United States, as the reserve-currency country, could continue to conduct expansionary monetary policy

---

18. The classic explanation for U.S. expansionary macroeconomic policy during the mid-1960s goes as follows: The Johnson administration (1963–1968) incurred mounting fiscal expenditures as it financed both its Great Society programs (including the War on Poverty) and its defense buildup to support the expanding Vietnam War. Economists publicly warned Johnson of the need to raise taxes to finance the expenditures. But the president, aware of the growing unpopularity of the Vietnam conflict, insisted on printing money rather than raising taxes. The result was a succession of large increases in aggregate demand and, eventually, inflation and currency devaluation.

relatively unconstrained by its gold stock.[19] Intervention by foreign central banks swelled their money stocks and spread abroad the inflationary effects of U.S. expansionary policy.

Eventually, foreign governments and market participants began to anticipate a devaluation of the dollar (that is, a rise in the dollar price of gold). Foreign policy makers grew increasingly unwilling to hold large stocks of dollars, because they no longer viewed the dollar as "good as gold." The chronic dollar shortage of the early postwar years had turned into a "dollar glut" by the mid-1960s. Some central banks, especially France's, hurried to exchange their dollars for gold before the expected devaluation, and pressures rose as the U.S. gold stock dwindled. Countries strongly opposed to inflation, particularly West Germany and Japan, ceased to support the Bretton Woods system, which had exported the inflationary effects of excessively expansionary U.S. policies (see Table 5).

Finally, in August 1971, the United States announced that it no longer would convert dollars to gold at the official $35 rate on foreign central banks' request. By the end of 1971, a makeshift arrangement—the Smithsonian Agreement—had replaced Bretton Woods, fixing the price of gold at $38 per ounce (later to become $42 per ounce) and pegging foreign currencies against the dollar at higher rates. The shift from Bretton Woods to

Table 5 **INFLATION IN THE MAJOR INDUSTRIAL ECONOMIES, 1952–1973 (PERCENT CHANGE IN CONSUMER PRICES)**

Year	U.S.	Canada	Japan	France	Germany	Italy	United Kingdom
1952	2%	2%	4%	12%	2%	4%	9%
1953	1	−1	7	−1	−2	2	3
1954	0	1	6	0	0	3	2
1955	0	0	−2	1	1	3	5
1956	1	1	0	2	3	3	5
1957	4	3	3	4	2	1	4
1958	3	2	0	15	2	3	3
1959	1	1	1	6	1	0	0
1960	2	1	4	4	1	2	1
1961	1	1	5	3	2	2	3
1962	1	1	7	5	3	5	4
1963	1	2	8	5	3	7	2
1964	1	2	4	3	2	6	3
1965	2	2	7	3	3	4	5
1966	3	4	5	3	4	2	4
1967	3	3	4	3	1	3	3
1968	4	4	5	5	2	1	5
1969	5	5	5	6	3	3	5
1970	6	3	8	5	4	5	6
1971	4	3	6	6	5	5	10
1972	3	5	5	6	6	6	7
1973	6	8	12	7	7	10	8

Source: *Economic Report of the President.*

19. Gold's constraint on money expansion eroded further in 1968 when institution of a two-tier gold market allowed private traders to buy and sell gold at a market-determined price not linked to the official $35 per ounce price at which central banks continued to trade.

Smithsonian amounted to a dollar devaluation imposed unilaterally by the United States against all other member currencies. The Smithsonian Agreement also differed from Bretton Woods in that the United States made no promise to convert dollars into gold at the new $38 rate. In other words, the new system represented a **dollar standard** rather than a gold-dollar standard. The Smithsonian Agreement couldn't reestablish the stability and confidence enjoyed earlier under Bretton Woods. High rates of U.S. money growth continued, and foreign exchange market participants sold dollar-denominated assets in exchange for mark-denominated ones in anticipation of another dollar devaluation. By 1973, after several futile attempts to reestablish stable fixed exchange rates, the currencies of the major industrial economies floated against the dollar.

The Bretton Woods system met with difficulties for three basic reasons. First, as we've seen, U.S. responsibilities under the system sometimes conflicted, so at least some of them weren't carried out. Second, central banks faced conflicts between their international responsibilities under the agreement and the macroeconomic policies acceptable to their domestic political constituencies. Finally, as capital mobility increased, perceived conflicts between a country's international and domestic economic obligations could quickly trigger a capital outflow and a balance-of-payments crisis whenever market participants began to expect a devaluation.

5.4 How'd the Macroeconomy Perform under Bretton Woods?

The Bretton Woods system clearly had imperfections: It implied potentially contradictory responsibilities for the United States and imposed the effects of U.S. policy on foreign economies. Although the underlying agreement allowed for exchange rate adjustments by design, actual devaluations or revaluations were rare, and chronic BOP deficits and surpluses were common. Despite these problems, however, the world economy performed respectably during the Bretton Woods years.

Table 6 summarizes the behavior of U.S. real output and prices during the Bretton Woods era. Output grew, if not smoothly, and the international system's increased

Table 6 ANNUAL CHANGES IN U.S. REAL GNP AND PRICE LEVEL, 1946–1971 (PERCENT)

Year	Change in Real GNP (Q)	Change in GNP Deflator (P)	Year	Change in Real GNP (Q)	Change in GNP Deflator (P)
1946	12%	12%	1959	6%	2%
1947	−1	12	1960	2	2
1948	4	7	1961	2	1
1949	0	−1	1962	7	1
1950	10	1	1963	4	1
1951	8	7	1964	5	1
1952	3	2	1965	6	2
1953	4	1	1966	7	3
1954	−1	1	1967	3	3
1955	8	1	1968	5	4
1956	2	3	1969	3	5
1957	1	4	1970	0	5
1958	−1	3	1971	3	5

Source: *Economic Report of the President.*

openness led to rapid growth in world trade and investment. Inflation posed few problems during the early years once the immediate postwar adjustments passed. But it grew to be a bigger threat as U.S. expansionary policies produced growing BOP deficits and price increases.

6 POST-BRETTON WOODS, 1973– : ANOTHER SEARCH FOR AN INTERNATIONAL MONETARY SYSTEM

The breakdown of the Bretton Woods system of pegged exchange rates led less to a regime based on exchange rate flexibility than to a world in which individual countries unilaterally choose their own exchange rate arrangements. This represented less of a break with the past than is commonly acknowledged. Historically, the exchange arrangement used by the dominant economies has been treated as characteristic of each period, as if the entire world economy operated under a unified exchange regime. In fact, this rarely has been the case. During the gold-standard era, many countries never tied their currencies to gold, and others entered and exited the system according to prevailing domestic political constraints on economic policies. Under Bretton Woods, the regime was subject to negotiation, but the United States and Britain dominated those negotiations. Many countries, including large ones such as France, never liked the system. Many currencies never became fully convertible into dollars—a requirement for a true gold-exchange standard. Government leaders postponed exchange rate adjustments until crises arose—actions that clearly violated the spirit, if not the letter, of the Bretton Woods agreement.

If economic history has taught any lessons, one is certainly that national governments are reluctant to relinquish sovereignty in any area, including international monetary relations and international trade policy. Nations jealously guard the prerogative to manage their respective currencies and never freely relinquish that prerogative to the dictates of an international monetary regime. Nor do countries easily relinquish power over other aspects of macroeconomic policy making.

Despite the problems inherent in characterizing a world monetary regime based on the policy choices of a handful of large countries, we examine today's system as a managed float, the arrangement in use by the major industrial economies. A **managed float** refers to a system in which the forces of supply and demand in foreign exchange markets determine basic trends in exchange rates but central banks intervene when they perceive markets as "disorderly" or dominated by short-term disturbances. Some opponents call this arrangement a **dirty float**, referring to the fact that central banks' intervention actions dirty, or interfere with, market forces. Nonetheless, the period since 1973 represents the longest in modern economic history during which the major currencies have been allowed to float.

6.1 How's a Managed Float Supposed to Work?

A managed float attempts, by combining market-determined exchange rates with some foreign exchange market intervention, to capture the desirable aspects of both fixed and flexible exchange rates. The fundamental idea is to use intervention to avoid short-term exchange rate fluctuations that many policy makers think contribute to uncertainty. At the same time, central banks avoid long-term intervention so that the supply of and demand for various currencies determine long-run movements in exchange rates, thereby avoiding persistent fundamental misalignments and the resulting crises.

Figure 2 Responses to Permanent and Temporary Changes in Demand under a Managed Float

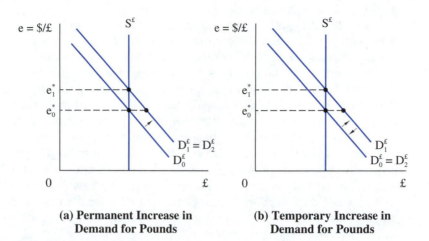

(a) Permanent Increase in Demand for Pounds

(b) Temporary Increase in Demand for Pounds

In panel (a), the demand for pounds increases permanently. The response under a managed float is to allow the exchange rate to move to a new equilibrium at e_1^*. In panel (b), the demand for pounds increases temporarily but then moves back down to its original level. Intervention would hold the exchange rate at its fundamental equilibrium level, e_0^*.

Figure 2 illustrates the ideal working of a managed float. For simplicity, we maintain the simple two-country (Britain/United States) framework.[20] Each panel depicts the demand for pound-denominated deposits along with the supply of such deposits. Initially the demand for and supply of pounds are given by $D_0^£$ and $S^£$, respectively. With no central bank intervention, the exchange rate or dollar price of pounds equals e_0^*, at which the quantity demanded of pounds equals the quantity supplied. At that rate, portfolio owners willingly hold the existing stock of pound-denominated deposits in their asset portfolios.

In panel (a) of Figure 2, a permanent increase in the demand for pound-denominated assets disturbs the foreign exchange market. A number of events could cause such an increase—for example, an increase in the interest rate on pound assets. Once the demand for pounds shifts to $D_1^£$, the old exchange rate, e_0^*, no longer represents an equilibrium. At e_0^*, the quantity demanded of pounds exceeds the quantity supplied. Individuals want to hold more than the available quantity of pound-denominated assets. How should the central banks react? Policy makers face two options: (1) allow the exchange rate to float in response to the forces of supply and demand, moving to a higher dollar price of pounds at e_1^*, or (2) intervene by selling pound-denominated assets from foreign exchange reserves to hold the exchange rate at e_0^*.

Under a managed float, the appropriate response to a *permanent* increase in the demand for pounds is to allow the exchange rate to move to a new equilibrium at e_1^*. Using intervention in an attempt to hold the exchange rate at e_0^* would require a fall in the U.S. money stock relative to Britain's to eliminate the payments imbalance. If the two countries are unwilling to allow balance-of-payments considerations to dictate their monetary policies, sterilization will result in a fundamental disequilibrium: a chronic U.S.

---

20. Sections 5 through 7 in the chapter on currency markets and exchange rates develop the basic demand and supply model of the foreign exchange market and apply the model under fixed and flexible exchange rates.

balance-of-payments deficit and British surplus.[21] The managed float breaks the link between the countries' BOPs and money supplies by allowing movements in the exchange rate to act as the adjustment mechanism when demand or supply conditions in the foreign exchange market change permanently.

Panel (b) of Figure 2 represents the case of a *temporary* increase in the demand for pounds (that is, demand shifts upward from $D_0^£$ to $D_1^£$ and then back down). Under a floating exchange regime, the dollar price of pounds would move upward from e_0^* to e_1^* and then back to e_0^*. Many analysts view this type of short-term exchange rate volatility as one of the primary drawbacks to a flexible exchange rate system. It can cause uncertainty about the profitability of international trade and financial transactions, because the future value of the exchange rate partially determines that profitability. (*Why?*) Proponents of intervention argue that uncertainty about exchange rates discourages specialization and trade and thereby reduces the efficiency of the world economy. Under an ideal managed float, the appropriate response to the temporary disturbance would be temporary intervention to hold the exchange rate at its underlying equilibrium level, e_0^*. This would require a sale of pounds by central banks, but only for the brief period during which demand was at $D_1^£$. As soon as the disturbance ended, demand would return to $D_0^£ = D_2^£$ and intervention could cease.

A managed float aims to limit exchange rate uncertainty by using intervention in foreign exchange markets to smooth short-run fluctuations in exchange rates, thereby achieving one of the proclaimed virtues of a fixed exchange rate. At the same time, a managed float allows market forces to determine long-run exchange rates, breaking the link between the balance of payments and the money stock and preventing chronic payments disequilibria, thereby achieving two virtues of a flexible exchange rate.

6.2 What Are the Problems with a Managed Float?

The major criticism of managed floating exchange rates is practical rather than theoretical. Figure 2 makes clear the correct policy response to each disturbance in the foreign exchange market because the nature of the disturbance is obvious—we labeled each up front as permanent or temporary. With this knowledge, a regime with rules that require intervention in the case of temporary disturbances and no intervention in the case of permanent disturbances performs satisfactorily. But in practice, of course, disturbances to the world economy have no labels to reveal their precise nature and time horizon.

Figure 3 illustrates the problem. Movement along the horizontal axis represents the passage of time, while the vertical axis measures the exchange rate. The jagged line to the left of t_0 depicts the historical movement of the exchange rate until today (time t_0). Let's assume that the dollar suddenly begins to appreciate rapidly against the pound just before t_0. Policy makers must decide whether to intervene to stop, or at least dampen, the appreciation. Under a managed float, intervention should occur only if the appreciation represents a short-term "blip" and not a fundamental change in the equilibrium exchange rate between dollars and pounds. But without knowing the future (that is, the path of the exchange-rate line to the right of t_0), how can policy makers distinguish between the two?

If line I turns out to be the future path of the exchange rate, the dollar appreciation will have been temporary and intervention the correct policy under the rules of a managed float. On the other hand, if the future exchange rate ends up following line II, the appreciation will have signaled the beginning of a trend, or a permanent change in the equilibrium exchange rate between dollars and pounds, and the appropriate policy

21. On the impact of sterilization, see sections 3.3 and 4.2 in the chapter on short-run policy under a fixed exchange rate.

Figure 3   **The Dilemma of a Managed Float: To Intervene or Not to Intervene?**

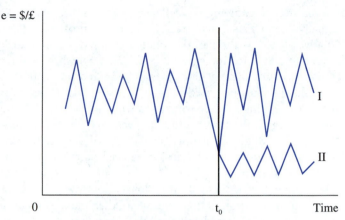

One interpretation of the "rules" of a managed float is to intervene in response to temporary disturbances in foreign exchange markets and to avoid intervention in response to permanent changes in the underlying equilibrium exchange rate. A practical difficulty arises because at the time of the disturbance (t_0), a policy decision must be made but policy makers cannot know the precise nature of the disturbance.

---

response will have been to allow the dollar to appreciate. In practice, central banks often intervene just enough to dampen or slow the exchange rate movement but not enough to stop it. Such policies are called **leaning against the wind**.

If central banks intervene often in foreign exchange markets, the heavily managed float will function much like an adjustable-peg exchange rate system. The primary advantage claimed for such active management of the exchange rate involves the greater reduction in exchange rate uncertainty than under a more flexible rate regime. For intervention to maintain the exchange rate successfully, monetary authorities must allow it to affect the money stock; that is, they mustn't sterilize.[22] If a currency depreciates in foreign exchange markets and the domestic central bank intervenes to stop the depreciation, the domestic money stock falls. This lowers domestic prices, raises interest rates, and may lower output. These changes help eliminate the balance-of-payments deficit that caused the initial depreciation. If the monetary authority sterilizes by making open market purchases to offset the intervention's impact on the money stock, the sterilization blocks the adjustment mechanism and the balance-of-payments deficit becomes chronic.

A managed float doesn't change the basic rule that *correction of a payments imbalance requires a change in either the exchange rate or the money stock*. When central banks engage in sterilized intervention to attempt to circumvent this basic rule, crises develop. Any advantage that pegged exchange rates may have in reducing uncertainty quickly disappears if they are accompanied by balance-of-payments crises that come from interference with the economy's adjustment mechanisms. In other words, pegged exchange rates generate confidence and stability only if the chosen rates are sustainable and consistent with policy makers' actions.

---

22. See footnote 21.

6.3 How's the Macroeconomy Performed in the Post–Bretton Woods Years?

For several years following the collapse of Bretton Woods in 1971, most policy makers and many economists considered the managed float a temporary measure. Gradually, alternatives faded as the world economy endured serious shocks, especially the OPEC oil embargo and price increase in 1973–1974, which brought rising price levels along with rising unemployment rates to most oil-importing countries.[23] Judging a return to fixed exchange rates not viable in the face of such shocks, policy makers turned their attention to defining specific rules as to when intervention should and should not occur or how "managed" the float should be. Eventually these attempts also failed. The *de facto* system, under which the major currencies float subject to central banks' case-by-case intervention decisions, finally received official sanction in 1975 and in a 1976 revision of the IMF agreement.

The United States pursued expansionary policies in the mid-1970s in an effort to end its OPEC-induced economic slowdown. Other industrial countries, particularly West Germany and Japan, feared inflation more and waited several years before joining U.S. expansionary policies. The U.S. monetary expansion of the mid-1970s, unaccompanied by expansions by trading partners, produced a substantial depreciation of the dollar against other currencies. Even intervention by the United States, West Germany, and Japan proved unable to stop the depreciation because of the continuing rapid U.S. money growth. In 1979, President Jimmy Carter appointed Paul Volcker, a respected financier with a strong anti-inflation reputation, chairman of the U.S. Federal Reserve Board. The appointment resulted in new Fed policies of lower monetary growth as well as renewed confidence in the dollar.

The effects of the slowdown in U.S. monetary growth hit the economy at about the same time as a second round of OPEC oil price increases in 1979–1980. Fearful of encouraging the inflation they had worked so hard to eliminate, U.S. policy makers didn't respond with expansionary monetary policies as they had after the 1973–1974 oil shock, and the economy underwent a severe recession that lasted through 1983. Money growth rates remained low, but fiscal policy grew more expansionary as tax rates fell and government spending rose during the Reagan administration. The dollar appreciated dramatically, which shifted demand away from U.S.-made goods and services toward foreign ones. (*Why?*) Gradually monetary policy loosened, but the dollar continued to appreciate into 1985, with virtually no intervention by the United States.

Although expansionary U.S. fiscal policies contributed to the recovery from the early 1980s recession, the resulting dollar appreciation also caused a significant redistribution of income. U.S. farmers found their overseas markets shrinking, while import-competing producers in U.S. industries such as automobiles, steel, and footwear endured increased competition from foreign rivals. Pressure mounted for protectionist policies, and Congress considered hundreds of bills ranging from import quotas for particular industries to across-the-board import tariffs.

In September 1985, the Reagan administration responded with the Plaza Accord. The Group of Five nations (known as G-5—the United States, Britain, Japan, Germany, and France) agreed to intervene in foreign exchange markets to bring about a depreciation of the dollar. The dollar actually had begun to depreciate in March, several months before the Plaza meeting. But in the months following the September accord, policy makers combined active intervention with public statements designed to "talk the dollar down" and with

---

23. Section 10 in the preceding chapter examines supply shocks and policy responses to them under alternative exchange rate systems.

expansionary U.S. monetary policy, primarily cuts in the discount rate. The value of the dollar continued to decline against trading-partner currencies, most notably those of Germany and Japan. By November 1986 it had reached postwar lows against the yen.[24]

By 1987, attention had turned to slowing the dollar's decline. Based on the Louvre Accord of February 1987, the Group of Seven countries (G-7 consists of the G-5 plus Canada and Italy) engaged in coordinated foreign exchange market intervention through 1987 and 1988, attempting to hold the dollar's value within secret bands.[25]

The extent of intervention in foreign exchange markets has varied since 1988. The dollar has experienced periods of both appreciation and depreciation against the currencies of most major trading partners. As the models of earlier chapters would lead us to expect, strong U.S. export performance accompanied the depreciations. During the recession of the early 1990s, exports proved one of the few sectors of the U.S. economy to grow strongly, although that growth slowed in 1992 as Germany and Japan entered recessions of their own and bought fewer U.S.-produced goods and services. Germany's expansionary fiscal policy (related to unification) and tight monetary policy caused both tensions between the United States and Germany and the near-breakdown in 1992–1993 of the European Union's efforts at monetary integration.[26]

By 1994, U.S. unemployment had fallen below many analysts' estimates of the full-employment level. Policy makers expressed concern about inflationary pressure, and the Federal Reserve tightened monetary policy. Most European economies experienced some recovery from their recessions, but European unemployment remained very high by U.S. standards. Large government budget deficits continued to constrain fiscal policy in both the United States and Europe.[27] Japan employed expansionary fiscal policy in an effort to emerge from its deepest slump since World War II, accumulating a rapidly rising level of government debt.

Throughout most of the early 1990s, the dollar depreciated, especially against the Japanese yen and the German mark.[28] All three central banks intervened periodically to buy dollars. However, intervention occurred more rarely than during the Plaza-Louvre period of the late 1980s. Macroeconomic policy in the major countries appeared less directed toward exchange rates, even when those rates exhibited dramatic movements. Table 7 reports the declining frequency and scale of U.S. foreign exchange market intervention in recent years.

During the late 1990s, attention centered on continuing macroeconomic problems in Asia, including both Japan's long slump and the severe financial crises facing South Korea, Indonesia, Malaysia, the Philippines, and Thailand, and on the European Union's plan to move to a single currency for most member countries.[29] After several years of non-intervention, U.S. and Japanese central banks intervened in foreign exchange markets during the summer of 1998 in an effort to stop or at least slow the yen's depreciation against the dollar.

---

24. For a discussion of the differential depreciation of the dollar against various currencies, see section 8 in the chapter on currency markets and exchange rates.

25. The G-7 countries never announced the band parameters, and financial market participants spent much time guessing about their values. Observing intervention activity by the central banks provided the major clues to the exchange rate values acceptable or unacceptable to the Group of Seven.

26. See section 8, as well as the cases on German unification and floating the pound in preceding chapters.

27. We'll see some of the reasons behind the constraints on European fiscal policy in section 8 on the European Monetary System.

28. Section 5 in the chapter on the exchange rate in the long run covers the long-run real depreciation of the dollar against the yen.

29. Section 8 examines the European Union's common-currency project.

Table 7 **U.S. INTERVENTION IN FOREIGN EXCHANGE MARKETS, 1989–2004**

Year	Total Intervention	Frequency (Days of Intervention)
1989	Sell $8.90 billion for DM; Sell $10.58 billion for ¥	97
1990	Sell $200 million for DM; Sell $2.18 billion for ¥	16
1991	Buy $1.34 billion with DM; Sell $520 million for DM; Sell $30 million for ¥	13
1992	Buy $1.27 billion with DM; Sell $250 million for ¥	8
1993	Buy $1.43 billion with ¥	5
1994	Buy $3.50 billion with DM; Buy $2.60 billion with ¥	5
1995	Buy $3.25 billion with DM; Buy $3.10 billion with ¥	8
1996		0
1997		0
1998	Sell $833 million for ¥	1
1999		0
2000	Sell $1.5 billion for €	1
2001		0
2002		0
2003		0
2004[a]		0

[a]Through third quarter.

Source: Federal Reserve Bank of New York. Updates available at http://www.newyorkfed.org.

The conjunction of a booming U.S. economy and slumping Asian ones placed policy makers in a difficult position. Based on the trajectory of the U.S. economy alone, the Federal Reserve almost surely would have tightened its monetary policy to prevent a rise in inflation as the U.S. unemployment rate fell below most estimates of its full-employment level. But tighter U.S. monetary policy would have risked generating further capital outflows from Asia. By late 1998, as the Asian situation failed to improve and threatened to spread to emerging markets in other regions, speculation shifted to the possibility of looser U.S. monetary policy—despite the historically low U.S. unemployment figures. European economies, many just starting to grow again after the early-1990s recession, hesitated to loosen their monetary reins for fear of unsettling markets as the European Union entered the critical period leading up to the January 1, 1999, adoption of the euro. Japan continued to pursue expansionary fiscal policy, but with little apparent effect. By the fall of 1998, Asia's lingering economic ills pushed central banks in other parts of the world to act. First the United States and then the countries of Western Europe (singly at first and later as a group) undertook expansionary monetary policies in an effort to prevent the Asian recessions from spreading.

Even after the worst of the Asian crisis passed, the U.S. economy continued to expand faster than its counterparts in Japan or Europe. The dollar appreciated, especially against the new euro. Finally, on September 22, 2000, after the euro had dropped by more than 25 percent of its initial value against the dollar, world central banks, including both the new European Central Bank and the U.S. Federal Reserve, intervened. Macro policy makers continued to confront a fast-growing U.S. economy, slow growth in Europe, and stagnation in Japan. During 2000, a sudden slowdown in the United States turned everyone's attention to that slowdown's effect on the rest of the world. Then on September 11, 2001, with many economies already on the brink of recession, analysts struggled to predict the economic implications of both terrorist attacks on New York and Washington and a long-term battle against terrorism around the world.

Despite the impact of the 2001 terrorist attacks and the economic demands of fighting terrorism at home and abroad, the U.S. economy has outperformed Japan and most of Western Europe, most notably Germany. Macroeconomic policy in the United States has been more expansionary than that in the European Union, especially on the fiscal side. The dollar has depreciated significantly against the euro, more than offsetting the euro's loss of value during the new currency's first several years. Policy makers in many Asian economies—most notably Japan, China, Korea, and Taiwan—have intervened often and on a large scale in efforts to prevent their currencies from appreciating against the dollar.

After experiencing several decades of sharp swings among the dollar, yen, and euro (as documented in Figure 4), policy makers and economists remain divided over the managed-float exchange rate system. On the one hand, many worry about exchange rate volatility, the resource-allocation effects of unpredictable changes in real exchange rates, and lack of effective policy coordination among the major players, especially the United States, the European Union, Japan, and—increasingly—China. On the other hand, most acknowledge both the difficulties of returning to a fixed-rate system in an environment of highly mobile capital and governments' reluctance to subordinate domestic economic interests to the requirements of external balance, as would be demanded under a fixed-rate regime.

Figure 4 Exchange Rates Between the Dollar, Deutsche Mark, Euro, and Yen, 1973–2003

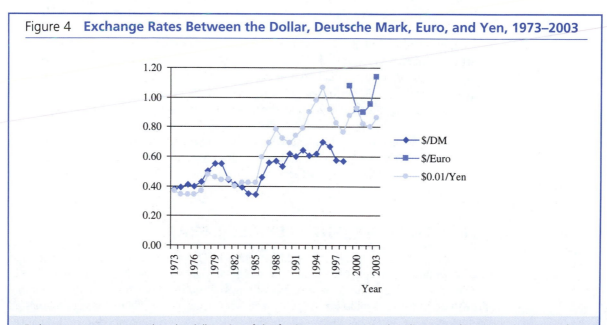

Exchange rates are reported as the dollar price of the foreign currency. Note that the yen exchange rate is measured as cents per yen ($0.01/¥) rather than dollars per yen ($/¥) to facilitate presentation on the same graphical scale with the DM and euro exchange rates. The euro replaced the Deutsche mark in 1999.

Source: *Economic Report of the President.*

Table 8   **ANNUAL CHANGES IN U.S. REAL GDP AND PRICE LEVEL, 1973–2003 (PERCENT)**

Year	Change in Real GDP (Q)	Change in GDP Deflator (P)	Year	Change in Real GDP (Q)	Change in GDP Deflator (P)
1973	5.8%	5.6%	1989	3.5%	3.8%
1974	−0.5	9.0	1990	1.9	3.9
1975	−0.2	9.5	1991	−0.2	3.5
1976	5.3	5.8	1992	3.3	2.3
1977	4.6	6.4	1993	2.7	2.3
1978	5.6	7.0	1994	4.0	2.1
1979	3.2	8.3	1995	2.5	2.0
1980	−0.2	9.1	1996	3.7	1.9
1981	2.5	9.4	1997	4.5	1.7
1982	−1.9	6.1	1998	4.2	1.1
1983	4.5	3.9	1999	4.5	1.4
1984	7.2	3.8	2000	3.7	2.2
1985	4.1	3.0	2001	0.8	2.4
1986	3.5	2.2	2002	1.9	1.7
1987	3.4	2.7	2003	3.0	1.8
1988	4.1	3.4			

Source: U.S. Department of Commerce.

In summary, the years since 1973 represent a period of widely varying degrees of management of exchange rates. Table 8 documents the yearly performance of U.S. real output and prices under the managed float.

Unfortunately, the history of international monetary regimes can't answer a fundamental question: Which exchange-rate arrangement is best? The answer to that question depends in complex ways on an individual country's circumstances. We can't rely on a comparison of past macroeconomic performance under the various systems, because each historical period brought unique challenges and shocks—from the Great Depression to world wars to OPEC embargoes to terrorist attacks—for the world economy. We can, however, analyze the facets of the different systems that worked well and those that apparently contributed to instability or other problems. In the next two sections, we summarize and briefly evaluate the main arguments for fixed versus flexible exchange rates as a basis for the international monetary system.

7 THE FIXED-VERSUS-FLEXIBLE DEBATE

Since the collapse of Bretton Woods in 1971–1973, policy makers, economists, and myriad pundits have engaged in dialogue and debate over the history and future course of the international monetary system. Was Bretton Woods responsible for the economic growth and relative stability of the 1950s and 1960s? Or was it a flawed system that lasted as long as it did only because of the period's otherwise strong economic performance? Do flexible exchange rates doom the world economy to an inflationary bias and lack of policy coordination? Or does exchange rate flexibility free the world economy from the constraints and overemphasis on external balance imposed by a fixed-rate regime? Even well-informed analysts and scholars differ in their answers to these questions.

7.1 Pros and Cons of Fixed Exchange Rates

We came across two major arguments for fixed exchange rates earlier in the chapter. Proponents of fixed exchange rates think that they impose price discipline by preventing central banks from engaging in excessively expansionary, and thus inflationary, monetary policies. Proponents also claim that fixed exchange rates reduce uncertainty about the future value of the exchange rate and thereby encourage international economic activity, such as trade and investment, that enhances the world economy's efficiency.

PRICE DISCIPLINE The price-discipline argument would be a solid one if a fixed exchange rate did indeed prevent inflationary monetary policies. Unfortunately, historical evidence suggests that central banks inclined to pursue overly expansionary policies tend to circumvent attempts at discipline. Under a fixed exchange rate, a country with a balance-of-payments deficit experiences a reduction in its money stock as the central bank intervenes to prevent a currency depreciation. Should the central bank be inclined to avoid this loss of control of the money stock (that is, the discipline of a fixed exchange rate), sterilization policies can offset the reduction in the money stock, resulting in a chronic deficit. In other words, a fixed exchange rate can impose price discipline only on central banks willing to submit to it. Also, a fixed exchange rate system based on a reserve currency, such as Bretton Woods, doesn't impose effective price discipline on the reserve-currency country, which conducts monetary policy for the entire system and exports any inflation it generates.[30]

Proponents of flexible rates counter the price-discipline argument by pointing out that voters can and do discipline governments that follow inflationary policies. Inflation did rise during the early years of the floating period; but voters have disciplined many governments for inflation, and governments have learned to control, at least to some extent, their inflationary tendencies.[31] Since the switch to flexible exchange rates, voters in the United States, Japan, several countries of Western Europe, and many developing countries have voted governments out of power for the inflation generated by their policies. Overall, experience suggests that avoiding inflation requires vigilance and discipline on the part of both voters and policy makers; a stable exchange rate regime can help under some circumstances, but can't substitute for sheer willpower and determination to avoid inflation.

REDUCED VOLATILITY AND UNCERTAINTY Exchange rate volatility and uncertainty can cause two problems. First, they may discourage beneficial international economic activity, such as trade and foreign investment, by making the domestic-currency value of future foreign-currency-denominated receipts and payments less certain. Second, volatile exchange rates can cause costly movements of resources as hard-to-predict exchange rate changes alter relative prices and shift demand back and forth between domestic and foreign goods. We've seen that such shifts in demand alter the performance of trade- and nontrade-oriented sectors of the economy, and these resource reallocations can generate political pressure for protection, exchange-rate manipulation, and other beggar-thy-neighbor policies.

Empirical evidence suggests that real exchange rates have exhibited more volatility since the shift to more flexible exchange rates. However, many analysts argue that exchange rate volatility actually exerts little negative effect on international trade and investment because of the availability of forward markets for hedging.[32] Proponents of fixed exchange rates counter by pointing out that forward contracts involve costs and may not be available for many currencies or for long-term economic activities such as foreign direct investment—although

---

30. On reserve-currency countries, see section 6 in the chapter on short-run policy under a fixed exchange rate.

31. See Table 2 in the preceding chapter.

32. Section 3.2 in the chapter on currency markets and exchange rates explains hedging.

innovative financial instruments to provide long-term hedges are evolving. Empirical studies that attempt to quantify exchange-rate uncertainty's effect on international trade, investment, or economic growth provide mixed rather than definitive results. Most economists agree that increased exchange rate flexibility doesn't appear to have exerted a dramatic negative effect on the growth of international trade and investment.

REAL EXCHANGE RATE ADJUSTMENT We've learned that changes in real exchange rates play a vital role in macroeconomic adjustment to the shocks that constantly impinge on economies. Under a fixed exchange rate regime, changes in real exchange rates ($R \equiv P/eP^*$) can occur in one of two ways: changes in countries' price levels or currency realignments. Proponents of fixed exchange rates claim that, by preventing unilateral devaluations and revaluations, a fixed-rate regime avoids the competitive devaluations that plagued the world economy during the Great Depression. Instead of such beggar-thy-neighbor policies, adjustment occurs when countries either allow their price levels to adjust or alter their pegged exchange rate in consultation with trading partners. Opponents of fixed rates point out that devaluations occurred too infrequently under Bretton Woods, resulting in chronic failure to adjust to shocks, and that price levels often adjust very slowly, leaving economies to endure extended periods of unemployment. They also note that Bretton Woods required countries to hand control of their money stocks over to the reserve-currency country—the United States.

EXCHANGE CRISES Countries that operate under a fixed exchange rate regime can avoid crises only if central banks play by the rules and allow adjustments in the money stock to correct any balance-of-payments disequilibria. When a government intervenes, sterilizes, and refuses to adjust the exchange rate, pressures build and crises develop. Balance-of-payments crises hardly reduce uncertainty, and they clearly discourage international trade and financial activities, at least in the short run. A fixed exchange rate regime builds confidence in the stability of exchange rates only when policy makers follow policies that facilitate adjustment. These policies include, first, not sterilizing the effects of the balance of payments on the money stock and, second, timely devaluations and revaluations when pegged exchange rates deviate too far from equilibrium. Both policies require a subordination of internal balance to external balance that may prove politically and economically painful. When market participants lose faith in a government's ability to withstand the domestic political pressures generated by this pain, a balance-of-payments crisis can develop as portfolio owners' willingness to hold the domestic currency drops because they expect an impending devaluation.[33]

Governments may attempt to avoid such crises by imposing capital controls that seek to limit the scale of payments imbalances, but controls can interfere with the economy's efficiency and tend to lose their effectiveness in the long run as individuals learn to circumvent them.[34] Sudden expectation-generated flows of short-term capital can clearly complicate policy makers' tasks. However, it's difficult to design controls that don't hamper beneficial trade and investment activities. Often, governments attempt to limit capital *outflows* while allowing or even encouraging *inflows*. But, of course, asset owners hesitate to purchase assets in a country if they fear that the government will restrict their ability to sell those assets; so controls on capital outflows can also discourage inflows. Most economists agree that capital controls are no substitute for appropriate exchange-rate adjustments, sound macroeconomic policies, or effective prudential regulation of banking and the financial sector.

---

33. See Cases One, Two, Three, and Five in the chapter on short-run macroeconomic policy under a fixed exchange rate and Case Three in the chapter on policy under a flexible exchange rate.

34. See Case Four in the chapter on macroeconomic policy under a fixed exchange rate.

7.2 Pros and Cons of Flexible Exchange Rates

CRISIS AVOIDANCE   The primary benefits claimed for flexible exchange rates are essentially the same as those for market-determined prices in any market: smooth, automatic, and continuous adjustment to equate quantity demanded with quantity supplied. Such adjustment under a flexible exchange rate has several advantages. It avoids large balance-of-payments deficits and surpluses, because the exchange rate moves in response to any tendency for either to develop. Needed adjustments in the real exchange rate can occur quickly through changes in the nominal exchange rate rather than slowly through changes in countries' potentially sticky price levels.[35] Flexible exchange rates also render many policy decisions unnecessary, thereby avoiding the potential for policy errors or delays. These characteristics, taken together, imply that floating rates may help avoid the crises that occur under fixed rates when expectations of an impending devaluation build.

The fact that flexible exchange rates respond to all disturbances in the foreign exchange market also is used as an argument *against* flexible rates—on the grounds that they produce unacceptable levels of volatility. Of course, this need not be true; exchange rates, like any other price, will be volatile only if the demand and supply conditions in the foreign exchange market are volatile. However, because expectations are so important in asset markets such as the foreign exchange market, the volatility of demand and supply conditions can be difficult to predict and to control.

POLICY INDEPENDENCE AND SYMMETRY   Flexible exchange rates allow each country to determine its monetary policy independently. Recall that a major problem during the late Bretton Woods years involved other countries' dissatisfaction with U.S. monetary policy, the inflationary effects of which were exported from the reserve-currency country through the rules of the adjustable-peg system. If one thinks, as some economists do, that policy makers will misuse their ability to control the money stock by creating excessive monetary growth and inflation, one could view the ability of flexible exchange rates to give policy makers such power as a *minus* rather than a *plus* for flexible rates. Flexible exchange rates do free up the money stock for use in pursuing domestic targets; but as we saw in the preceding two chapters, once we introduce price flexibility, monetary policy can affect only the price level in the long run and not real output.

On the other hand, a floating rate does permit a country to determine its own inflation rate, rather than forcing the country to accept the inflation rate chosen by the reserve-currency country. When domestic and foreign inflation rates differ, the exchange rate adjusts in the long run in accordance with purchasing power parity.[36] This allows countries to choose different rates of inflation, whereas a fixed exchange rate system such as Bretton Woods requires countries to either follow the same rate of inflation or realign their currencies. Evidence since the early 1970s indicates that flexible exchange rates *have* allowed countries to choose more divergent money-growth and inflation rates.

CONSISTENCY WITH CAPITAL MOBILITY   A country with a fixed exchange rate can avoid crises only as long as its policies convince foreign exchange market participants that no devaluation is forthcoming, because this confidence makes portfolio owners willing to hold assets denominated in the domestic currency. A loss of confidence in the future value of the domestic currency causes portfolio owners to sell assets denominated in that currency and requires the central bank to sell foreign exchange reserves to maintain the fixed exchange rate. If the loss of confidence is large enough in magnitude,

---

35.   On real exchange rate adjustment under fixed and flexible exchange rates, see sections 7 and 9 in the preceding chapter.

36.   See sections 3 and 4 on purchasing power parity in the chapter on the exchange rate in the long run.

the central bank may run short of reserves or ability to borrow and may be forced to devalue, possibly leading to a further loss of confidence in the currency.

Economies become particularly sensitive to such crises when capital is highly mobile, because portfolio owners can move quickly and easily in and out of different currency holdings. Therefore, a common policy for governments seeking to avoid exchange crises under a fixed exchange rate involves controls on capital flows.[37] But we've seen that capital mobility serves an important economic function: It allows capital owners to move their resources to locations where those resources will be most productive. In other words, capital mobility allows countries to take advantage of the gains from intertemporal trade. Capital controls can interfere with this capital-allocation process and generate efficiency losses for the world economy. By eliminating the major source of crises—expected currency devaluations—flexible exchange rates can eliminate one of the most important reasons that governments institute capital controls.

EXCESSIVE VOLATILITY AND REAL EXCHANGE RATES   While a perfectly flexible exchange rate gives policy makers control over the money stock, it requires them to accept market-determined movements in the exchange rate. Many economists doubt policy makers' ability to do this because of the exchange rate's broad impact on the domestic economy. Evidence suggests that, in the short and medium runs, changes in the nominal exchange rate (e) also affect the real exchange rate ($R \equiv P/eP^*$). This implies that movements in e lead to changing fortunes for the trade-sensitive sectors of the economy such as exporters and import-competing industries. Real appreciations, in particular, can cause dramatic increases in domestic political pressure for protectionism, as occurred in the United States in the early and mid-1980s. Domestic political pressures from trade-oriented sectors of the economy make policy makers sensitive to changes in the real exchange rate and may cause them to intervene in foreign exchange markets in an effort to maintain export competitiveness and domestic sectoral employment, even when the exchange rate is supposed to be flexible.[38]

The empirically demonstrated link between changes in real and nominal exchange rates in the short and medium runs also limits a flexible exchange rate's ability to insulate an economy from foreign monetary disturbances. If changes in the foreign money stock, for example, lead to proportional changes in the foreign price level and in the exchange rate in the long run, then foreign monetary policy exerts no real influence on the domestic economy because it doesn't alter the real exchange rate. (*Why?*) But in the short run, empirical evidence suggests that changes in the nominal exchange rate do alter the real exchange rate, as the foreign price level adjusts slowly to the change in the money stock, reducing the claimed insulation properties of a floating exchange rate.

Since the early 1970s, exchange rates, both nominal and real, often have exhibited high short-term volatility, much of which economists can't explain based on existing models.[39] Longer-run exchange rate movements, however, appear roughly consistent with relative purchasing power parity and with economic models' predictions concerning policy effects.

As the discussion makes clear, there's no "ideal" international monetary system. Both fixed and flexible exchange rate regimes have their advantages, and it's not surprising that various countries use different arrangements. During periods of stability when countries pursue consistent policy paths, either system can work quite well. During periods of instability in the world economy, both systems encounter problems and each has strengths and weaknesses in the face of different types of shocks.

---

37. See Case Four in the chapter on macroeconomic policy under a fixed exchange rate.

38. Large-scale interventions by Japan, China, and Korea provide recent examples.

39. Figure 4 illustrates the volatility in key nominal exchange rates.

7.3 Insulation from Economic Shocks

Three major classes of shocks disturb economies and require responses from policy makers: demand shocks that originate in the money market, demand shocks that originate in spending patterns, and supply shocks. Fixed and flexible exchange rates provide an economy with differing degrees of insulation from and ability to adapt to these various shocks. For an economy more prone to one type of shock than to others, these differences represent an important consideration in the country's choice of exchange rate regime.

SHOCKS TO THE DOMESTIC MONEY MARKET Fixed exchange rates tend to provide more insulation than flexible ones to economies subject to frequent shocks that originate in domestic money markets. Consider what happens when the domestic money stock falls (or, equivalently, domestic money demand rises). Under a fixed exchange rate, the balance of payments moves toward a surplus, and the central bank must intervene by buying foreign exchange to prevent an appreciation. The money stock rises and reestablishes equilibrium in the domestic money market. (*Analyze the effects using an aggregate demand–aggregate supply diagram.*) If, instead, the economy operated under a flexible exchange rate, the monetary shock would cause the domestic currency to appreciate, shift demand toward foreign and away from domestic goods, and require a fall in the domestic price level to bring the economy back to internal balance.[40] (*Analyze the effects using an aggregate demand–aggregate supply diagram.*) So, for economies prone to shocks to their domestic money market, fixed exchange rates can provide an advantage over flexible ones in the form of this insulating property.

Flexible exchange rates, in contrast, provide insulation against *foreign* monetary disturbances, but only in the long run. In the short and medium runs, adjustment in the price level lags behind changes in money stocks, leading to changes in the real exchange rate that affect output in both the domestic and foreign economies.

SHOCKS TO SPENDING ON DOMESTIC GOODS AND SERVICES Flexible exchange rates tend to provide more insulation to economies subject to frequent shocks that originate in output markets or spending patterns. Consider an economy that experiences a decline in demand for its exports. Under a fixed exchange rate, the decline in income reduces money demand, puts downward pressure on the interest rate, and causes a capital outflow. To keep the domestic currency from depreciating in response to the balance-of-payments deficit, the central bank must sell foreign exchange and reduce the domestic money stock. This accentuates the decline in aggregate demand and means that the price level must fall by more to restore full employment—a possibly slow and painful adjustment process. (*Analyze the effects using an aggregate demand–aggregate supply diagram.*) Under a flexible exchange rate, the balance-of-payments deficit depreciates the domestic currency rather than reduces the money stock. The depreciation shifts demand away from foreign goods toward domestic ones and mitigates the spending shock's negative impact on employment and output. A flexible exchange rate allows the economy to return to long-run equilibrium more quickly, because the exchange rate adjusts more quickly than the price level, and minimizes the shock's short-run recessionary impact. (*Analyze the effects using an aggregate demand–aggregate supply diagram.*) This implies that a flexible exchange rate regime can provide advantages to economies that face primarily spending shocks to their output markets.

SUPPLY SHOCKS As we saw in the preceding chapter, flexible exchange rates provide policy makers with more choices in their responses to supply shocks. When a country

---

40. Flexible exchange rates can speed the responsiveness of the price level to changes in the domestic money stock, as currency depreciation raises import prices and causes workers to demand higher wages in compensation. Therefore, monetary policy influences real output and employment for shorter periods.

experiences a permanent negative supply shock, of the kind examined in section 10 of that chapter, no policy can restore output permanently to its pre-shock level. A permanent negative supply shock reduces the economy's ability to produce goods and services and shifts its long-run aggregate supply curve to the left. Different macroeconomic policies can, however, influence how long the economy takes to adjust to its new long-run equilibrium, the extent of unemployment and reduced output during the adjustment period, and the shock's eventual impact on the price level.

A fixed exchange rate constrains policy makers to pursue macroeconomic policies consistent with balance-of-payments equilibrium and rules out expansionary monetary policy as a temporary device to cushion a supply shock's impact on the economy. Many economists believe that, had the OPEC oil shock of 1973–1974 occurred while the major industrial economies still operated under the fixed exchange rates of Bretton Woods, the shock's short-term impact on unemployment could have been much more severe. The economies generally responded to the OPEC shock with expansionary monetary policy that, while it contributed to inflation, did mitigate the short- and medium-run rise in unemployment.[41] This experience, coming at a time when negotiations to replace the Bretton Woods system were underway, discouraged countries from committing themselves to another fixed exchange rate system. In general, flexible rates have helped economies adjust to supply shocks and other disturbances that require changes in real exchange rates, albeit sometimes at a cost in terms of higher inflation.

In sum, different exchange rate regimes carry different implications for economies' adjustments to various types of economic shocks. Fixed exchange rates may mitigate domestic monetary shocks but exacerbate spending shocks. Flexible exchange rates may mitigate spending shocks and foreign monetary shocks but exacerbate domestic monetary ones. Floating rates provide policy makers with more flexibility in responding to supply shocks, but also give policy makers the option of following overly expansionary policies in vain attempts to avoid the inevitable decline in output following a permanent negative supply shock. Overall, governments' willingness and ability to coordinate their macroeconomic policies appear to depend more on the state of their domestic economies than on the exchange rate regime.

8 MONEY IN THE EUROPEAN UNION: FROM EMS TO EMU

In 1991, members of the European Union set out to accomplish an unprecedented feat: to have most, if not all, of the sovereign nation-states that belong to the EU using a common currency (since named the *euro*) and operating under a common monetary policy run by a common central bank, the European Central Bank. To understand the pros, cons, and risks of such a historic project, we need to know a bit about recent European monetary history.

8.1 History, 1979–1999

The major Western European currencies, as well as the U.S. dollar, have operated under a managed float since the early 1970s, but the European arrangement has been somewhat more complicated. Between 1979 and the euro's introduction in 1999, the currencies of most European Union members were *fixed* relative to one another and *floated* as a group against the dollar and other currencies, an arrangement called the **Exchange Rate**

---

41. Such a policy corresponds to following path "b" rather than path "a" or "d" in Figure 13 of the preceding chapter. Of course, flexible exchange rates also allow policy makers to choose the very inflationary path "c."

Mechanism (ERM) of the **European Monetary System (EMS)**.[42] A weighted basket or composite of the EU currencies called the **European Currency Unit (ECU)** floated against non-EU currencies. Within the ERM, each central bank intervened in foreign exchange markets to keep the value of its currency fixed within a prescribed band against the ECU and, thereby, against other EU currencies.[43]

We know that attempts to maintain fixed but adjustable exchange rates among countries that follow divergent macroeconomic policies are fraught with difficulties, especially when capital is highly mobile, as was increasingly the case in Europe. When individual countries follow divergent policies, those policies create pressures for exchange rate realignments, because rates threaten to move outside their defined bands. Foreign exchange market participants begin to anticipate those realignments and start to buy the currencies expected to face revaluation and to sell those subject to devaluation. Such speculative activity involves little risk because the official bands tell market participants which way the exchange rates must move. The process resembles buying or selling stock if you somehow knew the stock price could move only in one direction. Expectations become self-fulfilling prophecies as demand falls for already-weak currencies and rises for already-strong ones.

Given what we know about the difficulties of maintaining fixed exchange rates among economies that follow divergent economic policies and encounter diverse economic shocks, why did the European Union persist in its efforts? Proponents of European monetary integration hoped to accomplish several goals, some economic and some political. First, they hoped to improve European economic performance and make Europe more "competitive" with other industrial countries, especially the United States and Japan. For more than two decades, Europe had suffered much higher unemployment rates (an average of more than 10 percent), lower rates of job creation, and deteriorating technological leadership compared with its rivals.[44] Second, proponents hoped to present the United States with a more nearly equal macroeconomic counterpart in terms of economic size and voice in international negotiations. Third, within Europe, proponents believed that monetary integration would encourage intra-European trade and investment by lessening transaction costs associated with multiple currencies and exchange rate fluctuations. Fourth, proponents wanted to use the policy credibility of governments and other institutions with established policy-making reputations (for example, Germany's central bank, the Bundesbank) to help establish sound policies in countries that lacked such credible institutions (for example, Italy and Greece).[45] Finally, supporters of European economic and political integration hoped that monetary integration would contribute to the momentum toward more unified policy making in Europe.

Given this ambitious agenda and the problems that face fixed exchange rate systems, how did the European Monetary System survive for 20 years? During most of the post-1979 period, the pegged bilateral exchange rates within the EMS were adjustable and, in fact, periodically realigned, usually once or twice per year. In addition, EU rules required that member countries with BOP surpluses lend to countries that encountered difficulties as a result of BOP deficits. Throughout much of the 1980s, many EU members maintained

---

42. All EU member countries joined the EMS; however, not all joined the ERM, which required intervening to enforce the fixed intra-EU exchange rates. For example, Britain avoided joining the ERM until 1990 and dropped out in 1992 (see Case Three in the chapter on macroeconomic policy under flexible exchange rates).

43. Prior to 1993, the ERM bands allowed currencies to fluctuate up or down by 2.25 percent, or by 6 percent in some cases (Spain, Britain, Portugal, and Italy). After the European currency crises of 1993 (discussed later), the bands were widened to 15 percent, and Italy and Britain left the ERM. Italy reentered the ERM in 1996, and Greece in 1998. Finland entered in 1996. Sweden did not participate in the ERM.

44. Case One in the preceding chapter reports on European unemployment.

45. On Germany's reserve- or key-currency role within the EMS, see section 6 in the chapter on macroeconomic policy under a fixed exchange rate along with the two cases on German unification in preceding chapters.

some degree of capital controls that limited the magnitude of their BOP deficits and helped keep the required intervention and realignments manageable. But these capital controls imposed costs by preventing capital from flowing to its most productive location. The European program to complete an open internal market by 1992 required elimination of capital controls and made the currencies under the ERM adjustable-peg system more vulnerable to crisis. Increased capital mobility limited European governments' ability to realign their currencies without generating expectations-based crises. Beginning in 1987, facing the constraints of increasingly mobile capital, EU member countries began to place more emphasis on following convergent macroeconomic policies to reduce pressure for exchange rate realignments. The periodic exchange-rate adjustments stopped. The period between 1987 and mid-1992 was one of relative quiet on the monetary front in Europe, but the quiet didn't last.

8.2 Maastricht and Monetary Unification

The EMS was part of a long history of attempts to integrate the Western European economies. Like any international policy coordination effort, integration within the EMS encountered resistance when it threatened national sovereignty over macroeconomic policy. However, in 1991 at the Dutch town of Maastricht, the EU governments outlined an ambitious plan for **economic and monetary union (EMU)** that included "the irrevocable fixing of exchange rates leading to the introduction of a single currency" and the "definition and conduct of a single monetary policy and exchange rate policy the primary objective of both of which shall be to maintain price stability."[46] Proponents hoped to accomplish two goals: (1) Create a common currency to minimize transaction costs and establish a stable exchange rate system not susceptible to crises generated by expected currency realignments, and (2) Create a European system of central banks to give other EU countries a voice in monetary policy, dictated largely by Germany's Bundesbank under the pre-Maastricht EMS arrangements.[47]

The Maastricht plan turned out to be controversial in Europe and elsewhere. The timetable required ratification by all (then) 12 member countries, a process temporarily waylaid by Denmark's *no* vote in 1992. The uncertainty generated by the lengthy ratification process contributed to buildups of speculative pressure against some member currencies, especially the Italian lira, Spanish peseta, Portuguese escudo, and British pound.[48] EU governments pressured German policy makers to expand the German money stock to lower German interest rates and ease the devaluation pressures on non-Deutsche mark currencies. But German policy makers refused, not wanting to add more monetary expansion to their dramatic fiscal expansion to cover the costs of unification.[49] This forced other EU members—some already deep in recession—to intervene to support their currencies against the Deutsche mark. In September 1992, rather than continue to intervene and further contract their money stocks, Italy and Britain withdrew from the ERM and Spain devalued the peseta.[50] Denmark and Britain, in exchange for their ratification of Maastricht, won the right to "opt out" of its provisions for a common European currency.

---

46. The European Economic Community's Werner Report made a proposal similar in many respects to Maastricht back in 1971.

47. See section 6 in the chapter on macroeconomic policy under a fixed exchange rate and the cases on German unification and floating the pound.

48. See section 4.4 on exchange rate expectations in the chapter on macroeconomic policy under a fixed exchange rate.

49. For various perspectives see the cases on German unification and floating the pound.

50. See the cases cited in footnote 49.

A year of more-or-less constant crises followed. These crises forced several currency realignments, despite modest German monetary expansion. The EU reaffirmed each ERM member country's responsibility to intervene when its currency threatened to move outside its set trading band. Most members found themselves in recession and increasingly unwilling to constrain their monetary policies to maintain their exchange rates against the Deutsche mark. In 1993, the ERM exchange rate bands were widened to ±15 percent except for the guilder-mark rate, making the system resemble more closely a managed float. By 1994, Europe showed signs of recovery from recession, and the exchange crises of 1992–1993 abated. The wide ±15-percent bands remained in place, but most currencies (with the exceptions of the pound and lira, which remained outside the ERM) returned to their earlier, narrower bands until March 1995, when the peseta and escudo were again devalued.

The early 1990s, especially the economic implications of Germany's unification, confronted the European Union with a dramatic economic shock originating in the system's reserve-currency country. That this shock seriously damaged the EU's fixed exchange rate system, just as U.S. policy during the late 1960s had seriously damaged Bretton Woods, shouldn't surprise us. In 1995, EU members reconfirmed their intention to proceed with monetary unification and announced a new post-crises timetable. They announced that their new currency would be christened the **euro**.[51] As the countdown to the first key date began, attention focused on which countries would manage (or choose) to satisfy the economic criteria to participate.

MAASTRICHT CONVERGENCE INDICATORS   Prior to participation in the EU's common central bank, common monetary policy, and common currency, countries must conform to rules regarding exchange rate stability, inflation, interest rates, government budget deficits, and government debt. These rules are known as **convergence indicators**, because they measure whether the economies follow policies similar—or convergent—enough to make a common currency viable. This raised a politically controversial issue: Should the subset of countries that achieved policy convergence move ahead with plans for a common currency without the other EU members? The Maastricht plan's answer was yes. All countries that satisfied the criteria were to embark on currency unification as of January 1, 1999; other EU members could join later as they met the convergence criteria.

The Maastricht treaty requires each EU member country to meet five convergence criteria to participate in monetary unification:

1. Currency must have remained within its ERM trading band for at least two years with no realignment.
2. Inflation rate for the preceding year must have been no more than 1.5 percent above the average inflation rate of the three lowest-inflation EU members.
3. Long-term interest rate on government bonds during the preceding year must have been no more than 2 percent above the average interest rate of the three lowest-inflation EU members.
4. Budget deficit must not exceed 3 percent of GDP.
5. Government debt must not exceed 60 percent of GDP.

Most countries made substantial progress between 1993 and 1997 toward meeting the criteria, although in some cases the "progress" involved creative accounting. An EU conference in 1998 determined, based on 1997 data, which countries could participate initially in the monetary union. Of the 15 EU members, Denmark, Sweden, and Britain opted

51. Throughout years of discussion of a common currency, the unofficial name most often used was the *ecu*. When a last-minute decision resulted in *euro* instead, some commentators speculated that *ecu* had lost out because it sounded, especially to Germans, "too French."

out of participation in the common currency, at least temporarily. Of the remaining 12, only Greece was ruled to have made insufficient progress toward meeting the convergence criteria, in part because the drachma had only reentered the ERM in March 1998. The ruling admitting so many countries reflected a very flexible interpretation of the convergence criteria.

Throughout the early 1990s, most of the opposition to such a flexible interpretation came from Germany, which didn't want to tie itself to countries that lacked the policy discipline to meet the convergence criteria. Many German policy makers argued that Italy, in particular, shouldn't be admitted until it demonstrated further commitment to sustainable, sound, noninflationary macroeconomic policies. However, when the costs of unification and its early-1990s recession forced Germany itself to undertake some accounting wizardry to meet the criteria, German opposition to other countries' doing the same thing lost much of its force.

To get their government budget deficits below the 3 percent Maastricht limit, countries undertook a variety of one-time policies, implying that deficits were unlikely to stay below 3 percent in future years without further fiscal consolidation. Italy imposed a one-year "eurotax" to raise additional revenue. Spain froze public-sector wages to reduce its expenditure. France transferred the accumulated pension funds of state-owned France Telecom to the government account. Germany sold some of its government-owned oil reserves and raised its value-added tax.

Some economists and policy makers agreed that a lenient interpretation of the convergence criteria was appropriate. They argued that any delay in monetary union because of EU members' failure to meet the criteria strictly would provide opportunity for yet another period of instability to disrupt the schedule. Proponents of leniency also argued that EU member countries would find it much easier to meet the criteria once monetary unification occurred and that a union excluding more countries would be hardly worth the trouble. Opponents of leniency argued that it threatened the monetary union because a single currency ultimately couldn't work among countries following divergent and undisciplined macroeconomic policies.

As January 1, 1999, approached, the governments of many EU member countries had changed significantly from those that had negotiated the Maastricht agreement a decade earlier. Left-of-center parties controlled or shared power in 13 of 15 EU members, including 9 of the 11 initial euro participants. This political change, along with Europe's continued slow growth, raised questions about whether needed structural reforms and fiscal consolidation would move forward. With only weeks to go before the January 1, 1999, deadline for introduction of the euro, interest rates in participating countries still differed. Then, on December 3, 1998, the 11 countries announced simultaneous interest rate cuts designed to bring rates in all 11 to 3 percent, an event many commentators proclaimed "the birth of the euro."

EARLY POLICY CHALLENGES IN THE EURO AREA   As of January 1, 1999, the European Central Bank conducted monetary policy for the euro area. The bank faced challenging tasks. The brand-new institution had no reputation or credibility on which to draw and lacked established procedures. As its key date approached, most member countries struggled with high rates of structural unemployment, as we saw in Case One in the preceding chapter. To make policy decisions even harder, some countries, especially Spain and Ireland, boomed, while others, including the all-important Germany and France, had just started to recover from recessions. A single monetary policy appropriate for all wasn't easy to find; but, as we'll see in section 8.3, this represents the most important ongoing problem for any monetary union.

Policy makers at the European Central Bank faced a difficult policy-making environment. During the new currency's first three years, it depreciated significantly, especially against the U.S. dollar (see Figure 4). Euro-area economies were experiencing very different business-cycle conditions, illustrated by the countries' changes in real GDP, unemployment rates, and inflation rates, as shown in Figure 5. Ireland and the Netherlands boomed; their inflation rates exceeded the European Central Bank's 2 percent inflation target.[52] Other countries, most notably Germany, lagged. Should the ECB slow money growth, as appropriate for Ireland, or speed it up to give the German economy a short-run lift? More-expansionary monetary policy would run the risk of further euro depreciation, which policy makers worried might cause the public to lose confidence in the young currency, despite the short-run expansionary effects of a currency depreciation. On top of these problems, journalists and foreign policy makers seemed to pounce on every statement ECB officials made, eager to point out inconsistencies. Higher oil prices soon combined with the ECB's inflation-target rule made the bank's position even less comfortable: When the oil shock shifted the medium-run aggregate supply curve to the left, should the bank tighten monetary policy to meet its less-than-2-percent inflation target or loosen monetary policy in response to slowing output and rising unemployment?

Euro-area policy challenges weren't limited to the monetary side. The group experienced bitter disputes over fiscal policy, in particular over the Stability and Growth Pact. The pact represents an ongoing application of some of the convergence indicators. In particular, euro-area governments pledged to keep their government budget deficits below 3 percent of GDP, except in exceptionally severe economic conditions. Violations could—at least in theory—lead to fines of up to 0.5 percent of GDP. Soon France and Germany, with their slow growth and high unemployment, breached the 3-percent limit.[53] Smaller and newer members, who'd worked hard and made difficult policy moves to meet the rules, didn't appreciate the rules being ignored by the older, larger, and more politically powerful members. France in particular angered other members with its open flouting of the rules; Portugal and Germany, in contrast, seemed to at least try to meet their commitments under the pact.

Economists and policy makers debated whether the Stability and Growth Pact rules made good economic sense, needed fine-tuning, or were so deeply flawed that they should be abandoned completely. Pact proponents view the rules as an essential discipline on fiscal policy makers all too ready to overspend. Reformers argue that the pact should be more flexible; for example, allowing countries with low levels of accumulated government debt to run somewhat higher deficits than countries with bigger debts. Pact opponents claim that the rules force policy makers into pro-cyclical rather than counter-cyclical fiscal policy, cutting spending and raising taxes in economic downturns.

In late 2003, France and Germany succeeded—despite vocal opposition from Spain, the Netherlands, Austria, Finland, and the European Central Bank—in suspending the procedures to enforce the Stability and Growth Pact. The European Commission, the union's executive body, took the member states to the European Court of Justice, claiming that the suspension of the rules by their finance ministers was illegal. Later, the Commission reversed course and suggested rewriting the pact to allow bigger budget deficits when a country experienced "sluggish growth" and to provide each country with its own deficit ceiling, rather than a single 3-percent ceiling for all members regardless of their broader macroeconomic circumstances. Regardless of the outcome of the debate over specific reform proposals, the strict fiscal discipline embodied in the original Stability and Growth Pact failed when France and Germany faced no punishment for their multiyear violations of the clearly stated rules.[54] The long-term consequences for the EU economies remain to be seen. Having handed the tools of monetary policy over to the European Central Bank, several EU member

---

52. The ECB's target rate of less than 2 percent inflation refers to the average of Euro-area countries' rate of inflation, weighted by the sizes of the respective economies, illustrated in Figure 5 by the "Euro Area Average" line in panel (c).

53. Portugal had already been reprimanded for a deficit greater than the acceptable 3 percent.

54. In late 2004, European Union statisticians discovered that Greece had provided false budget-deficit figures both in 1998 to meet the Maastricht criteria to gain entry to the euro area and in every year since. See "Greece to Stay in Euro Despite False Data," *Financial Times*, November 16, 2004. The union also questions Italian budget figures.

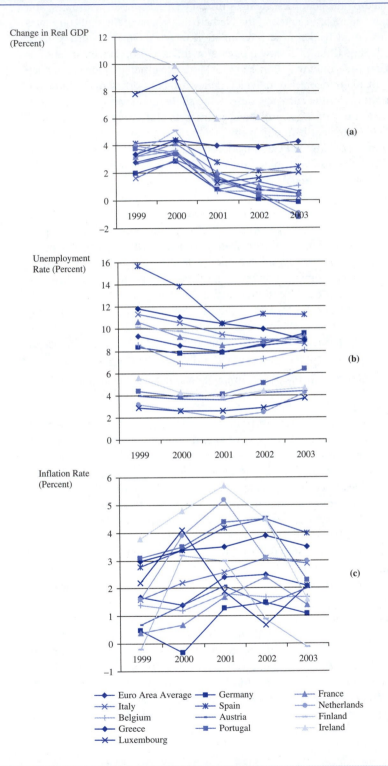

Figure 5 **Macroeconomic Conditions in the Euro Area, 1999–2003**

Euro-area countries exhibited very different rates of output growth, unemployment, and inflation during the euro's early years, complicating the European Central Bank's policy-making task.

Source: International Monetary Fund.

countries seem intent on maintaining national sovereignty over fiscal policy—even if some experts, including the head of the European Central Bank, think that such a strategy risks the viability of monetary union.

Besides the obvious political or sovereignty-related arguments by politicians and policy makers against monetary union, there are economic arguments both in favor of and against such ventures. Those arguments focus on the question, *Who should use a common currency, or how large is the optimal currency area?*

8.3 Who Should Use a Common Currency?

Two geographic regions that use a common currency experience both advantages and disadvantages compared with use of two distinct currencies. As the common-currency area grows, the costs of a common currency rise and the benefits decline. The geographical area or number of countries that maximizes the benefits minus the costs of using a single currency is called an **optimal currency area**. Economist Robert Mundell developed the theory of optimal currency areas in the early 1960s, but the issue took on new urgency and interest with recent events in the European Union.[55]

The potential benefits of using a common currency include reduced exchange rate volatility, reduced transaction costs, and enhanced policy credibility. As we noted earlier, uncertainty about future changes in exchange rates may discourage international trade and financial activity. A common currency—the ultimate fixed exchange rate—eliminates this uncertainty and allows firms to specialize according to comparative advantage and to plan imports and exports without worrying about losses due to future exchange rate movements and without having to hedge in forward markets. (*What do you think would happen to trade between New York and California if the two states used different currencies?*) A common currency also allows individuals and firms to avoid the transaction costs of exchanging one currency for another when engaging in travel or cross-border transactions. During the early 1990s in the European Union, if you began with one currency and exchanged it step-by-step for each of the other EU currencies *without buying any goods or services*, the transaction cost of the currency exchanges alone reduced the original sum by approximately half. A single currency eliminates those costs.[56] The higher the share of intragroup trade and investment within a set of countries, the greater these benefits from a single currency.

A common currency also can provide an advantage to policy makers by allowing them to credibly commit to a future course for monetary policy. This argument proved particularly relevant for the European case. There, the German Bundesbank's strong anti-inflation reputation, if effectively transferred to a European Central Bank, might allow historically high-inflation countries such as Italy and Greece to commit themselves to noninflationary policies. For this reason, much of the monetary-union debate in Europe centered on the proposed central bank's policy mandate. Inflation-conscious citizens and policy makers wanted to ensure it would follow policies similar to those of the Bundesbank rather than the Banque d'Italia! The European Central Bank's charter requires policy makers to follow an inflation target. The bank adjusts monetary policy to keep the average medium- to long-run inflation rate in member countries below 2 percent.

A common currency involves costs as well as benefits. Most important, countries lose the ability to pursue independent monetary policies. After all, a common currency represents the ultimate fixed exchange rate ($e \equiv €1/€1 \equiv 1$), and we know that a fixed exchange rate eliminates independent monetary policy as a macroeconomic policy

---

55. The Tavlas articles in the chapter references contain accessible discussions of optimal currency areas.

56. European banks' foreign-exchange trading revenues were predicted to drop by about 70 percent when the euro replaced national currencies.

instrument. A common currency also eliminates exchange devaluations or revaluations as a policy tool within the currency area. The entire region using a common currency binds itself to follow the same monetary policy.

Given the list of costs and benefits, how does a region determine whether a currency area would provide net benefits? The literature on optimal currency areas suggests that a region is likely to gain from a common currency if (1) a large share of members' trade occurs with other members, (2) the region is subject primarily to common shocks that affect the entire area similarly and not to shocks that affect subregions differentially, (3) labor is mobile within the region, and (4) a tax-transfer system exists to transfer resources from subregions performing strongly to those performing poorly. We've already seen why criterion (1) matters: The higher the share of intragroup trade, the greater the transaction-cost saving of a single currency. Criteria (2) through (4) all relate to how likely countries are to need different monetary policies.

If different shocks buffet subregions, policy makers in those subregions may need to follow different monetary policies or to allow their exchange rate to move to offset the shocks' short-run effects. For example, suppose the British economy booms while Germany's languishes. Germany might follow an expansionary monetary policy relative to that of Britain, thereby depreciating (or devaluing) the Deutsche mark and shifting demand toward German goods and services and away from British ones, at least in the short run. Such adjustment becomes impossible under a common currency.

When some subregions of a currency area grow quickly and others grow more slowly, movements of labor between subregions represent another possible adjustment mechanism. If cultural or institutional factors restrict such labor flows, then differential monetary policies and exchange rate realignment may be needed—ruling out a common currency. An alternative means of dealing with differential regional growth involves fiscal transfers from growing regions to stagnant ones. Suppose Florida booms while California suffers a recession. The U.S. federal tax and transfer system conducts an automatic transfer from Florida to California: Florida's tax payments rise with income, while California's fall; Florida's transfer-payment receipts (that is, unemployment benefits, welfare payments, and so forth) fall with rising income, and California's rise. These transfers partially offset the two states' differential economic performance and lessen the need for any exchange rate adjustment (impossible, of course, within the United States).

How does the European Union measure up to these standards for an optimal currency area?[57] Most empirical studies have compared Europe to the United States, which, after all, operates under a common currency. Members of the EU appear more subject to differential shocks than the regions of the United States. Labor is considerably less mobile between countries in Europe than between U.S. regions, perhaps because of greater language and cultural differences. In fact, labor is much less mobile even *within* countries in Europe than in the United States, but intra-European mobility does appear to be rising. Finally, the separate nation-states of the EU have no supranational tax and transfer system to reallocate resources across regions in response to differential shocks, although the EU does administer some development funds for less-developed or declining regions in the Union. All these findings have led many economists to question whether the EU really represents an optimal currency area, despite its relatively high level of intragroup trade. These questions take on even more significance as the EU extends its membership. Euro optimists argue that once the euro transition process is completed, the economies will become more alike and their business cycles more synchronized. Pessimists point out that the countries may specialize more heavily as intercountry trade becomes easier, making the countries even more different and more prone to subregion specific shocks.

---

57. The De Grauwe book in the chapter references contains a detailed discussion of the theory of optimal currency areas and its application to the European Union.

In the end, two considerations will play central roles in the success or failure of the European monetary union. First, most economists agree that many EU members must undertake significant structural reforms to improve the flexibility of their labor markets and to reduce the sizes of their welfare systems if the European economies are ever to grow faster and bring down high rates of structural unemployment. These policy changes are always politically difficult, but timing is important. To be politically feasible, the reforms need to be enacted when the respective economies are performing relatively well. Second, the countries must prove willing to subordinate some of their national policy-making sovereignty to the union.

CASE 1: MAPPING THE EURO ZONE

European Union

During 2004, membership in the European Union grew from 15 to 25 with the group's expansion into the formerly centrally planned economies of Central and Eastern Europe. Of the 15 pre-2004 EU members, lightly shaded in Figure 6, 12 use the union's common currency, the euro. Denmark, Sweden, and the United Kingdom, shaded lightly in blue in the figure, remain outside the euro area voluntarily, having won "opt out" rights during the debate over the Maastricht treaty that laid the groundwork for monetary union. These three union members can adopt the euro any time they choose, based on national referendums, so long as they meet the convergence criteria specified at Maastricht. But the opt-out three can also choose to remain outside the euro zone and continue to use their national currencies, the krone, krona, and pound, respectively.

The 10 members of the EU class of 2004, darkly shaded in blue in Figure 6, face a different set of choices. They are legally obligated to join the euro zone once they meet the Maastricht convergence criteria, although when that happens depends on each country's policy choices as well as

on economic conditions beyond the country's control. Some of the new EU members, such as Cyprus, Estonia, Lithuania, and Slovenia, are eager to adopt the euro as soon as possible and could do so as early as 2007. Others, such as Poland, the Czech Republic, and Hungary, will have to or have chosen to wait because of their ongoing struggles with budget deficits. EU accession involves substantial fiscal costs for new members as they must bring many aspects of their policy, law, and practice into line with union rules; so the Maastricht rule on keeping the government budget below 3 percent of GDP is particularly binding in the presence of these accession-related demands on spending. But the Maastricht spending ceiling can also provide useful discipline for governments to undertake necessary but politically difficult reforms. The European Central Bank has actively urged new members not to rush into adopting the euro, but to take time to ensure that long-term policies are in place to meet the convergence criteria on an ongoing basis—advice that either wasn't given to or wasn't heeded by original euro-zone members such as France, Germany, and Italy.

CASE 2: DO FLOATING RATES *REALLY* FLOAT?

Member countries report to the International Monetary Fund what type of regime they use for their respective currencies. Those reports indicate a dramatic shift from fixed to floating exchange rates since the early 1970s. For example, only 11 percent of countries reported that they pegged their exchange rate in 1999, compared with 97 percent in 1970.

But do governments actually allow the forces of supply and demand to determine their exchange rates, or do they

still control exchange rates while claiming to float? It's impossible to know for sure, since governments can use many policies to affect their exchange rates. Guillermo Calvo and Carmen Reinhart set out to try to find out.[58] They found that the exchange rates for supposedly floating currencies stay within 2.5-percent bands 80 percent of the time. And these countries' foreign exchange reserves varied by more than 2.5 percent in any given month

---

58. "Fear of Floating," National Bureau of Economic Research Working Paper W7993.

Figure 6   **Euro Status of EU Members, 2004**

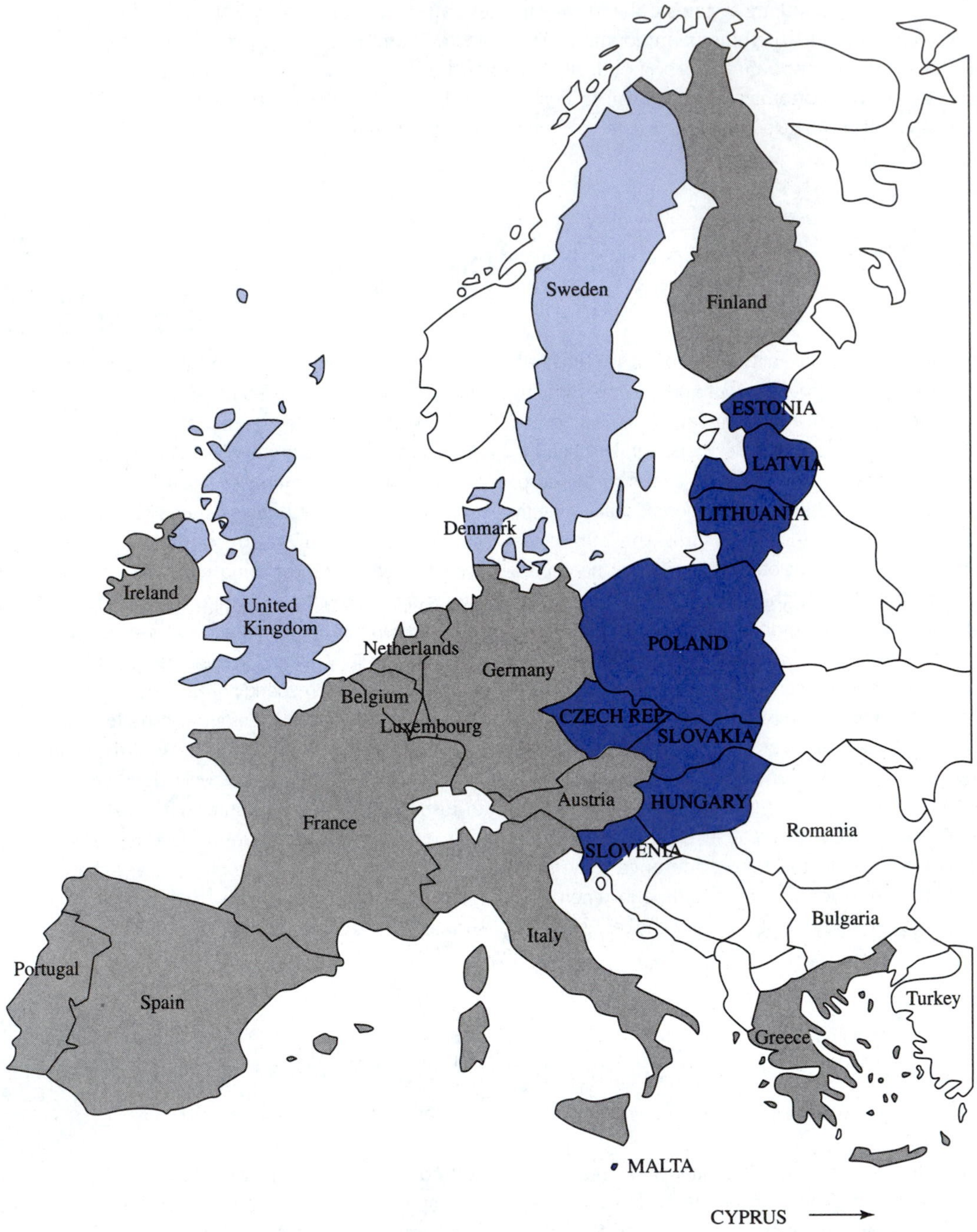

Of the 15 pre-2004 EU members (lightly shaded in the map), all but Denmark, Sweden, and the United Kingdom (lightly shaded in blue) use the euro. These three have euro-opt-out privileges, but can join the euro zone if they choose to do so based on national referendums. The 10 members added to the EU in 2004 (darkly shaded in blue in the map) have no euro-opt-out privilege, but are legally obligated to adopt the euro when they meet the Maastricht convergence criteria.

Table 9 *DE JURE* AND *DE FACTO* EXCHANGE REGIMES, 1990–2001 (PERCENT OF IMF MEMBERS)

	1990	1991	1992	1993	1994	1995	1996	1997	1998	1999	2000	2001
De Jure Regime												
Pegged	65.4	61.3	58.1	49.1	47.2	44.4	45.3	45.1	44.5	n.a.	n.a	n.a.
Floating	34.6	38.7	41.9	50.9	52.8	55.6	54.7	54.9	55.5	n.a.	n.a.	n.a.
De Facto Regime												
Pegged	79.9	76.4	69.4	68.7	64.3	65.4	66.5	66.7	64.0	59.7	58.6	55.9
Floating	20.1	23.6	30.6	31.3	35.7	34.6	33.5	33.3	36.0	40.3	41.4	44.1

Source: International Monetary Fund.

66 percent of the time. Both these observations suggest that many countries that claim to have floating exchange rates—including some developed industrial economies, but not including the United States—in fact intervene extensively to limit their exchange rates' movements.

Several other studies have confirmed Calvo and Reinhart's basic finding using different methodologies. As a result, in 1999 the International Monetary Fund altered how it reports member countries' exchange rate regimes. Table 9

documents for 1990–1998 the discrepancy between the percent of IMF member countries that reported following a fixed or flexible regime (the *de jure* regime) and the percentage that appeared actually to follow a fixed or flexible regime (the *de facto* regime). One of the Fund's main tasks is to advise member countries on their macroeconomic policies, so knowledge by the Fund of the policies in actual use constitutes an essential piece of background information for that policy advice.

CASE 3: WHEN IS A CENTRAL BANK NOT A CENTRAL BANK?

We've implied thus far that all economies, at least market-oriented ones with fixed exchange rates, have a central bank that both conducts open-market operations and intervenes in foreign exchange markets. In fact, some countries have a *currency board* instead of a central bank. A currency board intervenes in foreign exchange markets as needed to maintain its fixed exchange rate but doesn't conduct open-market operations. In other words, a currency board is a central bank that can't conduct expansionary monetary policies to cover the government's fiscal expenditures. A true currency board owns no domestic government bonds, so the board's foreign exchange reserves must back the entire domestic money stock.[59]

Whenever a balance-of-payments deficit arises, the currency board sells foreign exchange reserves and the domestic money stock falls. When the balance of payments moves into surplus, the currency board buys foreign exchange and the domestic money stock rises. In other words, operating under a currency-board system means allowing the balance of payments to determine changes in the money stock, with no opportunity to sterilize intervention's effects.[60] If the currency board "follows the rules," the system prevents overly expansionary (and thus inflationary) monetary policy. Many developing economies and countries in transition from central planning find this policy-commitment element of a currency board advantageous, since their governments

59. Section 2.3 in the chapter on money, the banking system, and foreign exchange outlines how central-bank assets, usually government bonds *and* foreign exchange, form the basis for the country's money stock.

60. Some currency boards, including Hong Kong's, give it some characteristics of a central bank. This generated controversy in 1997 when many analysts claimed that the Hong Kong Monetary Authority's attempts to behave like a central bank rather than a currency board produced expectations of a devaluation of the Hong Kong dollar.

typically lack policy credibility. Countries with currency boards include Bosnia, Brunei, Bulgaria, Djibouti, Estonia, Hong Kong, and Lithuania. All but Brunei, Djibouti, and Hong Kong introduced their boards during the 1990s, as part of economic reform programs.

Currency boards are somewhat controversial. Many economists recognize the system's potential benefits for historically inflation-prone economies trying to establish sounder macroeconomic policies. However, such a system can limit policy makers' options for responding to shocks. When a financial crisis such as the one in Asia during the late 1990s strikes, for example, a currency board, unlike a central bank, can't act as a lender of last resort to banks on the verge of failure. And the interest rate increases implied by a balance-of-payments deficit under a currency board can weaken poorly regulated or supervised banks.

Hong Kong has long experience with a currency board. Despite the former colony's historically strong banks and its large stock of foreign exchange reserves, the Hong Kong Monetary Authority's 1997 and 1998 defense

of the HK$7.8 = US$1 peg, in effect since 1983, imposed substantial costs on the economy. As the currency board sold dollars to defend the peg, the domestic money stock fell and interest rates rose dramatically, with negative consequences for banks, the stock market, and property prices. *(As of February 1998, Hong Kong interest rates were approximately 5 percent above comparable U.S. ones. What did this imply about market participants' exchange rate expectations at the time?)* As Hong Kong's economy has continued to lag following the Asian financial crisis, some analysts think it's time to end the rigid peg to the U.S. dollar. Other experts point out the lack of a good alternative. As a small, very open financial center, Hong Kong would be unlikely to tolerate well the fluctuations that could come with a flexible exchange rate. And a peg to China's yuan would be highly risky with little immediate benefit given the erratic course of China's financial-sector reforms, its dangerously weak banking sector, and the need eventually to delink the yuan itself from the U.S. dollar.

CASE 4: IS GROWTH FIXED OR FLEXIBLE?

Do countries with a particular type of exchange rate regime experience faster or slower long-run economic growth? Economists recently tackled this question using 183 countries' *de facto* exchange rate regime (see Case Two) and their output experience since 1974.[61] The study revealed that countries with fixed exchange rates grew more slowly than those with more flexible regimes. The difference stemmed mainly from nonindustrialized economies; industrialized countries' choice of exchange regime had little impact on their growth. On average, fixed-rate countries grew about

three-quarters of 1 percent slower than did flexible-rate countries. Over the quarter century following the end of Bretton Woods, this would amount to a 20–25 percent higher output by 2000 in a flexible-rate country than in a fixed-rate one, other characteristics held constant. The same study found that, in addition to suffering lower growth rates, countries with fixed exchange rates experienced greater output volatility; once again, the exchange rate mattered for nonindustrialized countries but not for industrialized ones.

CASE 5: SU CURRENCY ES MI CURRENCY

In common-currency projects such as the European Union's euro, countries join together to create a brand-new currency. Sometimes, however, a country chooses to adopt as its domestic legal tender another country's existing currency. This general process is widely known as *dollarization*, although in

principle the currency adopted need not be the U.S. dollar. Such practices aren't new; for example, Panama has used the U.S. dollar since 1904. But interest in dollarization is rising. Ecuador adopted the U.S. dollar in 2000, after 116 years of the sucre as the national currency; El Salvador followed.

61. Eduardo Levy-Yeyati and Federico Sturzenegger, "To Float or to Fix: Evidence on the Impact of Exchange Rate Regimes on Growth." *American Economic Review* 93 (September 2003), pp. 1173–1993.

Why might a country choose to abandon its national currency and adopt that of another country, thereby handing over its monetary policy to the other country's monetary authority? Typically because domestic policy makers have shown themselves—usually through long periods of high inflation—unable to conduct monetary and exchange-rate policies consistent with stability and credibility. In such circumstances, "signing on" to another country's more stable policies and institutions may help stabilize the domestic economy and rebuild confidence, but not without some costs.

Some analysts believe that dollarization promotes trade and financial integration, but the empirical evidence on this question appears mixed. If, by dollarization, a country can convince market participants that no possibility of a devaluation exists, then the country may enjoy lower interest rates as lenders no longer demand a premium to cover the fear of devaluation. For countries with high levels of debt, this possibility of lower borrowing costs serves as a powerful incentive for dollarization. But even dollarized economies can still face high interest rates to borrow if they follow unsustainable fiscal policies, because lenders must bear the risk of debt default even if not of devaluation.

Dollarization eliminates all possibility of a devaluation, even the small possibility preserved under a currency board.

Escaping dollarization would require reintroducing a national currency; and such an effort would likely encounter resistance and skepticism, especially during a crisis. Dollarization also eliminates the monetary authority's ability to act as a lender of last resort to banks during a banking crisis, because the domestic authorities can't create dollars. However, banking crises may be less likely to occur if dollarization increases public confidence in the banking system, and the government can still lend directly to banks in trouble.

Not all dollarization results from formal government policy decisions. In many economies, for example in Latin American countries such as Argentina, U.S. dollars handle many economic transactions, constitute large shares of bank reserves, and represent the currency of denomination for contracts such as wage agreements and borrowing and lending. With such informal dollarization already well advanced, formal dollarization provides both fewer benefits and fewer costs.

Policy makers in the country whose currency is being adopted by others aren't always enthusiastic about dollarization. After all, those policy makers' responsibility is to conduct policy appropriate for their own economy. But dollarizers experience those same policies, whether appropriate or not.

SUMMARY

International trade and financial transactions require some means of exchanging one currency for another, known as an *international monetary regime*. The major types of regime include fixed exchange rates (including Europe's common currency), flexible exchange rates, and managed floating. Each arrangement has benefits and costs, so the choice involves trade-offs that depend on the individual country's economic situation.

The strengths claimed for fixed exchange rates include discipline against inflationary policies and reduction in exchange rate uncertainty. Flexible exchange rates, on the other hand, promote adjustment and eliminate the need for foreign exchange market intervention, thereby allowing each country to determine its own monetary policy independently.

Since 1973, the major currencies have operated under a managed float that attempts to capture the benefits of both fixed and flexible exchange rates. Ideally, a managed float would allow the forces of supply and demand to determine the long-run paths of exchange rates while using intervention to smooth out short-term fluctuations. In practice, the lack of information concerning the nature of disturbances when policy decisions must be made makes it difficult to choose the appropriate extent of intervention.

LOOKING AHEAD

We've focused so far on developing general models that provide basic insights into macroeconomic policies, events, and performance for virtually any country. However, some countries face special challenges in designing and implementing sound macroeconomic policies. Two such groups are developing economies and countries in transition from central planning to more market-oriented economic systems. In the upcoming final chapter, we'll turn our attention to the macroeconomic problems and prospects facing these countries.

KEY TERMS

convertible currency

gold standard

mint exchange rate

price discipline

specie-flow mechanism

gold-exchange (gold-dollar) standard

key (reserve) currency

adjustable-peg system

fundamental disequilibrium

tranches

conditionality

liquidity

dollar standard

managed (dirty) float

leaning-against-the-wind policies

Exchange Rate Mechanism (ERM)

European Monetary System (EMS)

European Currency Unit (ECU)

economic and monetary union (EMU)

euro

convergence indicators

optimal currency area

PROBLEMS AND QUESTIONS FOR REVIEW

1. Explain the determination and maintenance of the exchange rate between the German Deutsche mark and the French franc
    a. Under the gold standard.
    b. Under the Bretton Woods gold-dollar standard.
    c. Under the Exchange Rate Mechanism of the European Monetary System.
    d. Under the post-2002 EU common currency.

2. In October 1, 2003, testimony before a U.S. Congressional subcommittee, U.S. Undersecretary for International Affairs John Taylor said, "We also recognize that, especially in the case of small open economies, there are benefits from a hard exchange-rate peg, whether dollarizing, as with El Salvador, joining a currency union, as with Greece, or using a credible currency board, as in Bulgaria or Hong Kong" (*Wall Street Journal*, October 31, 2003). What do these exchange regimes have in common? Why might they be of interest to small open economies?

3. Comment on the following statement: "A fixed exchange rate regime cannot work as long as policy makers place more importance on internal than on external balance."

4. What is the practical shortcoming of the following rule for policy makers under a managed floating exchange rate system: "Intervene in foreign exchange markets to offset the effects of temporary disturbances, and allow the exchange rate to change in response to permanent disturbances."

5. Some analysts argued that a common European currency could not work unless all members satisfied the Maastricht convergence indicators *prior* to joining. Others argued that EU member countries should adopt a common currency first and *then* satisfy the convergence indicators. What are some of the pros and cons of each argument?

6. When a central bank follows an inflation target rule, it loosens monetary policy if inflation falls below the target range and tightens monetary policy if inflation rises above the target range. Explain how such a policy response might exacerbate unemployment after a negative supply shock.

7. Some economies, especially those with histories of high inflation, operate under crawling-peg exchange rate regimes. Under a crawling peg, the domestic currency is devalued by a pre-announced amount on a regular schedule (for example, 1 percent per month). Suppose country A operates under such a regime.
    a. What relationship would you expect to hold between the domestic interest rate, i, and the interest rate of the foreign country, i*? Why?
    b. To keep the *real* exchange rate constant, what relationship would need to hold between P and P*?
    c. If the domestic inflation rate exceeded the foreign one by more than the crawling devaluation, what would happen to the real exchange rate? What would happen to the country's current-account balance? How might this contribute to the probability of a crisis?

8. One possible international monetary regime consists of a world central bank conducting monetary policy and issuing a single currency used throughout the world. What would be the advantages of such a system? The disadvantages?

REFERENCES AND SELECTED READINGS

Antinolfi, Gaetano, and Todd Keister. "Dollarization as a Monetary Arrangement for Emerging Market Economies." Federal Reserve Bank of St. Louis *Review* (November/December 2001): 29–40.
Accessible review article on the subject of Case Five.

Bayoumi, Tamim, et al. *Modern Perspectives on the Gold Standard.* Cambridge: Cambridge University Press, 1996.
Analyses of the pros and cons of a gold standard; for intermediate students.

Berg, Andrew, et al. "Monetary Regime Options for Latin America." *Finance and Development* 40 (September 2003): 24–27.
Introduction to the pros and cons of exchange rate choices for historically high-inflation countries.

Blanchard, Olivier, and Francesco Giavazzi. "Current Account Deficits in the Euro Area: The End of the Feldstein-Horioka Puzzle?" *Brookings Papers on Economic Activity* 2 (2002): 147–210.
What the euro experience can tell us about the reasons for the patterns of capital flows; for intermediate and advanced students.

Bubula, Andrea, and Inci Otker-Robe. "The Continuing Bipolar Conundrum." *Finance and Development* 41 (March 2004): 32–35.
Introduction to the problems caused by fixed but adjustable exchange rates.

Calvo, Guillermo A., and Carmen M. Reinhart. "Fixing for Your Life." *Brookings Trade Forum* (2000): 1–58.
Fixed exchange rates as a source of stability and credibility.

Chang, Roberto. "Policy Credibility and the Design of Central Banks." Federal Reserve Bank of Atlanta, *Review* (First Quarter 1998): 4–15.
Accessible overview of the theory and evidence on inflation and central-bank independence.

Chang, Roberto, and Andrés Velasco. "Exchange-Rate Policy for Developing Countries." *American Economic Review Papers and Proceedings* 90 (May 2000): 71–75.
Issues relevant to developing countries' choice of exchange-rate regime.

Chriszt, Michael. "Perspectives on a Potential North American Monetary Union." Federal Reserve Bank of Atlanta *Economic Review* (Quarter Four 2000): 29–38.
What are the chances of an eventual North American monetary union similar to the one in Western Europe?

Cooper, Richard N., and Jane Sneddon Little. "U.S. Monetary Policy in an Integrating World: 1960 to 2000." In *The Evolution of Monetary Policy and the Federal Reserve System over the Past Thirty Years,* edited by R. W. Kopcke and L. E. Browne, 77–130. Boston: Federal Reserve Bank of Boston, 2000.
History of international influences on U.S. monetary policy.

Corden, W. Max. *Too Sensational: On the Choice of Exchange Rate Regimes.* Cambridge, Mass.: MIT Press, 2002.
The economics of exchange-rate-regime choice; for intermediate students.

De Grauwe, Paul. *Economics of Monetary Union,* fifth edition. Oxford: Oxford University Press, 2003.
Comprehensive and accessible introduction to the macroeconomics of Europe's monetary union; for all students.

Duarte, Margarida. "The Euro and Inflation Divergence in Europe." Federal Reserve Bank of Richmond *Economic Quarterly* 89 (Summer 2003): 53–70.
Overview of the extent to which use of a common currency has affected the variation among European inflation rates.

Dueker, Michael J., and Andreas M. Fischer. "The Mechanics of a Successful Exchange Rate Peg: Lessons for Emerging Markets." Federal Reserve Bank of St. Louis, *Review* (September/October 2001): 47–56.
Why did Austria's peg to the Deutsche mark work while Thailand's peg to the dollar failed?

Eichengreen, Barry. *Globalizing Capital.* Princeton: Princeton University Press, 1996.
The history of capital flows in the world economy.

Enoch, Charles, and Anne-Marie Gulde. "Are Currency Boards a Cure for All Monetary Problems?" *Finance and Development* (December 1998): 40–43.
Introductory overview of what currency boards can and cannot accomplish.

Fischer, Stanley. "Exchange Rate Regimes: Is the Bipolar View Correct?" *Finance and Development* 38 (June 2001): 18–21.
Accessible overview of why softly pegged exchange rates—that is, those subject to devaluation or revaluation—may be disappearing.

Frankel, Jeffrey A., et al. "Verifiability and the Vanishing Intermediate Exchange Regime." *Brookings Trade Forum* (2000): 59–124.
Are regimes between a common currency and a float viable in a world of mobile capital?

Friedman, Milton. "The Case for Flexible Exchange Rates." In *Essays in Positive Economics.* Chicago: University of Chicago Press, 1953.
One of the first serious calls for a change to a flexible exchange rate regime; for all students.

Fuhrer, Jeffrey J. "Central Bank Independence and Inflation Targeting." Federal Reserve Bank of Boston, *New England Economic Review* (January–February 1997): 19–36.
A skeptical view of central-bank independence and inflation targeting; for all students.

Ghosh, Atich R., et al. *Exchange Rate Regimes: Choices and Consequences.* Cambridge, Mass.: MIT Press, 2002.
The theory and empirical evidence on alternate exchange rate regimes; for intermediate students.

Gulde, Anne-Marie. "The Role of the Currency Board in Bulgaria's Stabilization." *Finance and Development* 36 (September 1999): 36–39.
An example of use of a currency board during transition.

International Monetary Fund. *Exchange Arrangements and Foreign Exchange Markets.* Washington, D.C.: IMF, 2003.
Excellent data and information source on exchange rate regimes.

Isard, Peter. *Exchange Rate Economics.* Cambridge: Cambridge University Press, 1995.
Intermediate to advanced-level survey of the literature on exchange rate regimes.

James, Harold. *International Monetary Cooperation since Bretton Woods.* Oxford: Oxford University Press, 1996.
A comprehensive official history commissioned on the 50th anniversary of Bretton Woods.

Karacadag, Cem, et al. "From Fixed to Float: Fear No More." *Finance and Development* 41 (December 2004): 20–23.
What concrete steps can countries take to move from a fixed exchange rate to a floating one without triggering a crisis? For all students.

Kopcke, Richard W. "Currency Boards: Once and Future Monetary Regimes?" Federal Reserve Bank of Boston, *New England Economic Review* (May/June 1999): 21–38.
What currency boards can and cannot do, and in what circumstances.

Krueger, Anne O. "Conflicting Demands on the International Monetary Fund." *American Economic Review Papers and Proceedings* 90 (May 2000): 38–42.
Introduction to the myriad pressures on the IMF in its assistance of developing economies.

LeBaron, Blake, and Rachel McCulloch. "Floating, Fixed, or Super-Fixed? Dollarization Joins the Menu of Exchange-Rate Options." *American Economic Review Papers and Proceedings* 90 (May 2000): 32–37.
Introduction to the pros and cons of dollarization.

Levy-Yeyati, Eduardo, and Federico Sturzenegger. "To Float or to Fix: Evidence on the Impact of Exchange Rate Regimes on Growth." *American Economic Review* 93 (September 2003): 1173–1193.
Empirical evidence on the relationship between countries' regime choices and their growth; for advanced students.

Little, Jane Sneddon, and Giovanni P. Olivei. "Rethinking the International Monetary System: An Overview." Federal Reserve Bank of Boston, *New England Economic Review* (November/December 1999): 3–28.
An introduction to the challenges facing the international monetary system.

Little, Jane Sneddon, and Giovanni P. Olivei. "Why the Interest in Reforming the International Monetary System?" Federal Reserve Bank of Boston, *New England Economic Review* (September/October 1999): 53–84.
How recent challenges facing the international monetary system created a move toward reform.

López-Córdova, J. Ernesto, and Christopher M. Meissner. "Exchange Rate Regimes and International Trade: Evidence From the Classical Gold Standard Era." *American Economic Review* 93 (March 2003): 344–353.
Evidence that exchange-rate stability under the gold standard increased trade; for advanced students.

Masson, Paul, and Catherine Pattillo. "A Single Currency for Africa?" *Finance and Development* 41 (December 2004): 9–15.
Introduction to monetary relations in Africa.

Mundell, R. A. "A Reconsideration of the Twentieth Century." *American Economic Review* 90 (June 2000): 327–340.
A Nobel Prize winner's look back at the century's exchange rate regimes.

Obstfeld, Maurice, and Kenneth Rogoff. "The Mirage of Fixed Exchange Rates." *Journal of Economic Perspectives* 9 (1995): 73–96.
Argues that permanently fixed exchange rates have become infeasible for all but a few countries; accessible to all students.

Pakko, Michael R., and Howard J. Wall. "Reconsidering the Trade-Creating Effects of a Currency Union." Federal Reserve Bank of St. Louis, *Review* (September/October 2001): 37–46.
Cautions whether a common currency really increases countries' intra-group trade.

Pollard, Patricia S. "A Look Inside Two Central Banks: The European Central Bank and the Federal Reserve." Federal Reserve Bank of St. Louis *Review* 85 (January/February 2003): 11–30.
Introduction to the structure of central banks and how it affects policy making.

Pollard, Patricia S. "The Creation of the Euro and the Role of the Dollar in International Markets." Federal Reserve Bank of St. Louis, *Review* (September/October 2001): 17–36.
How will the euro affect international use of the dollar? For all students.

Reinhart, Carmen M. "The Mirage of Floating Exchange Rates." *American Economic Review Papers and Proceedings* 90 (May 2000): 65–70.
Evidence that many countries that claim to allow their exchange rate to float do not.

Soltwedel, Rüdiger, et al. "European Labor Markets and EMU: Challenges Ahead." *Finance and Development* 37 (June 2000): 37–40.
How much of a barrier does Europe's labor immobility create for the monetary union?

Symposium on "Global Economic Integration: Opportunities and Challenges." Federal Reserve Bank of Kansas City, 2000.
Challenges of creating and managing an open international financial system.

Symposium on "Rethinking the International Monetary System." Federal Reserve Bank of Boston, 1999.
Thoughts on the international monetary system in the wake of the late-1990s financial crises.

Tavlas, George S. "On the Exchange Rate as a Nominal Anchor: The Rise and Fall of the Credibility Hypothesis." *The Economic Record* 76 (June 2000): 183–201.
Problems with use of a pegged exchange rate as a nominal anchor; for intermediate students.

Tavlas, George. "The 'New' Theory of Optimum Currency Areas." *The World Economy* (1993): 663–685.
Excellent, detailed survey of the current state of the literature on optimum currency areas; for all students.

Tavlas, George. "The Theory of Optimum Currency Areas Revisited." *Finance and Development* 30 (June 1993): 32–35.
Accessible overview of the renewed interest in optimal currency areas.

Taylor, Alan M. "Global Finance: Past and Present." *Finance and Development* 31 (March 2004): 28–31.
Introduction to the history of exchange rate choices and the constraints on policy makers' choices.

Velde, François R., and Marcelo Veracierto. "Dollarization in Argentina." Federal Reserve Bank of Chicago, *Economic Perspectives* (First Quarter 2000): 24–37.
The experience of an early unofficial adopter of the dollar, written prior to Argentina's latest crisis.

11 CHAPTER

Macroeconomics of Development and Transition

1 INTRODUCTION

The models we developed in earlier chapters capture the fundamental knowledge that economists have acquired about how the international macroeconomy and monetary system work. Those models provide insight into macroeconomic events and policy options for *any* country, and we've used many diverse countries as examples and cases. However, we should remember that not all countries' macroeconomies are alike. The United States, Germany, Slovenia, Afghanistan, Turkmenistan, Brazil, Singapore, India, Iraq, and Ethiopia each face different macroeconomic challenges, policy options, and potentials. Important macroeconomic differences arise from countries' unique histories, economic and political systems, legal institutions, economic shocks, sizes, trading relationships, resource endowments, and many other factors.

Two groups of economies that exhibit distinctive macroeconomic characteristics and encounter special macroeconomic situations as a result are the developing economies and the countries in transition from central planning. Having now mastered the basic models, we're ready to focus on the unique macroeconomic challenges that face developing and transitional economies.[1]

Macroeconomists have turned more attention to these countries over the past few years for several reasons. The internationalization of output and finance markets, represented by rapidly growing trade in goods, services, and financial assets, creates more numerous and more important linkages between developed and developing economies. These linkages sometimes grow largely unnoticed until a dramatic event—such as the OPEC oil shocks of the 1970s, the debt crisis of the 1980s, the Asian financial crisis of the late 1990s, or the Turkish and Argentine crises of 2001—thrusts them onto newspapers' front pages. As many developing economies grow and integrate themselves further into the world economy, macroeconomic interdependence becomes more pronounced. Events in Mexico following the December 1994 peso devaluation provide one example in which macroeconomic events in a single developing economy exerted dramatic influence on other countries, both developed and developing.[2] Events in Asia after the July 1997 devaluation of the Thai baht provide another. A second reason for macroeconomists' increased attention to development-related issues comes from the emergence of a large group of "new" developing countries in the wake of the political and economic revolutions that swept the Soviet bloc in

---

1. Note that division of the problems facing developing and transitional economies into *micro*economic ones and *macro*economic ones is highly artificial.

2. Case Three in the chapter on short-run macroeconomic policy under a fixed exchange rate covers the Mexican crisis.

1989–1991. Those economies faced the need not only to establish sound day-to-day macroeconomic policies, but also to design economic and political institutions that would make such policies possible, sustainable, and credible.

We turn first to developing economies in general, and then to the newest group of developing economies—those making the transition toward market-oriented economic systems after decades of central planning.

2 DEVELOPMENT AND THE MACROECONOMY

An improvement in the economic well-being of a country's residents represents the fundamental goal of economic development. Per-capita GDP is the most common, albeit imperfect, measure of development status. Based on 2002 per-capita income, the World Bank classifies countries with annual incomes below $9,075 as developing countries, which the bank further divides into upper-middle-income ($2,936–$9,075), lower-middle-income ($735–$2,936), and low-income (<$735) countries. Table 1 reports average income for each country group, as well as regional averages for all low- and middle-income countries.

While developing economies share some important characteristics, significant differences exist *among* developing economies. Much of sub-Saharan Africa, where economic development has progressed least, continues to exhibit very low per-capita incomes and low or negative growth rates, along with high illiteracy and short (and falling) life expectancies compared with other countries. In East Asia, many developing countries still have low per-capita incomes; but until the financial crisis of the late 1990s, growth rates had been very high, and life expectancy almost equals that in developed economies. A handful of developing countries, most notably in Latin America, have accumulated such large amounts of external debt that, even after substantial debt rescheduling and forgiveness by creditors, that fact continues to dominate their macroeconomies. The fragility of their macroeconomic reforms and prospects was further highlighted by their negative reactions to the volatility in world financial markets generated by the Asian crisis and by another round of crises in 2001 centered on Argentina. And, as we'll see later in the chapter, the formerly centrally planned economies of Eastern Europe and Central Asia enjoy high incomes relative to those in many developing economies, as well as relatively high life expectancy and literacy rates, but nevertheless experienced dramatically negative growth rates during the transitional 1990s.

Table 1	PER-CAPITA INCOME, 2002 (DOLLARS)

Country Group	Per-Capita Income
Low Income	$430
Middle Income	1,850
Lower Middle Income	1,400
Upper Middle income	5,110
Low and Middle Income	1,170
East Asia and Pacific	960
Europe and Central Asia	2,160
Latin America and Caribbean	3,280
Middle East and North Africa	2,240
South Asia	460
Sub-Saharan Africa	450

Source: World Bank.

2.1 Developing Countries' Pre-Reform Macroeconomic Characteristics

We must keep in mind the important differences among developing economies; still, we can highlight a set of macroeconomic characteristics historically shared by many of these countries prior to their recent reforms. Common characteristics include the following:

1. Pervasive government involvement in the economy, including widespread government ownership of infrastructure, industry, and land, as well as extensive state control of day-to-day economic activity.
2. Poorly developed financial institutions.
3. Government finance through money creation rather than taxes or domestic borrowing.
4. Fixed exchange rates, accompanied by capital controls or direct government control of foreign exchange transactions.
5. Extensive foreign borrowing to cover current-account deficits.

Much of the reform undertaken by many developing countries during the 1980s and 1990s involved undoing or altering this web of characteristics, which most economists agree combined to hinder both macroeconomic performance and economic development. We can easily see, based on insights from the macroeconomic models developed in earlier chapters, how these five characteristics would interact to affect economic performance adversely.

GOVERNMENT OWNERSHIP AND CONTROL   Government directly owned and controlled much of the productive capacity in many developing countries. This created a variety of microeconomic and macroeconomic problems.[3] The state typically maintained its ownership and control through political power rather than by good economic performance that survived the test of the marketplace, so many state-owned enterprises exhibited low productivity, technological backwardness, and production patterns that ignored consumer preferences.

When government owned large sectors of the economy and engaged in detailed management of business enterprises, policy decisions often hinged more on politics than on economics. Plant managers, who realized that their fate depended more on political connections than on economic performance, had little incentive to enhance the productivity and efficiency of their plants. Wages often were set to reward the politically faithful with high-paying jobs, even if those wages outstripped labor productivity and resulted in uncompetitive products. As a result, many state-owned enterprises required constant government subsidies to keep them in operation. The inefficient enterprises also required protection from foreign competition, so economies with extensive state ownership and control often passed up substantial portions of the potential gains from international trade. After all, if state-owned domestic producers ignored consumer wants, consumers would try to import goods from abroad (or emigrate) to satisfy those wants. To maintain its control, the state had to stifle those attempts to circumvent its rules.

POORLY DEVELOPED FINANCIAL MARKETS AND INSTITUTIONS   In a context of such extensive state ownership and control, private capital markets could perform few of the functions they serve in industrial economies where government plays a more limited

---

3. In addition to the problems discussed here, many economists think that a pervasive state role in the economy creates additional opportunities for corruption.

role. As a result, capital markets and financial services tended not to evolve in developing economies even when they weren't restricted legally. The absence of well-developed financial markets then provided a rationale for still *more* government involvement to allocate capital and make investment decisions—tasks performed largely by private capital markets in the major industrial economies. Developing-country governments' poor policy records, bad reputations, and lack of credibility made it difficult for them to borrow by selling long-term bonds. At the same time, widespread state ownership of industry precluded a stock market as a means of raising private funds to finance investment. This left only bank loans as a source of domestic finance; since the state typically controlled the banking sector, government often determined which enterprises received financing and which didn't.[4] Government bureaucrats also used credit terms, such as the interest rate charged on loans, to subsidize favored activities and tax unfavored ones.

MONEY-FINANCED FISCAL EXPENDITURES   The state's broad role in the typical pre-reform developing economy dictated high levels of fiscal expenditure. And, as in *all* economies, these expenditures had to be paid for. Developing countries often had poorly functioning tax systems for several reasons: Low incomes translated into a small tax base. High-income elites typically enjoyed a close political relationship to the government, thereby insulating themselves from pressures to pay taxes. And tax compliance and enforcement tended to be weak.[5] These characteristics combined to render tax finance of government expenditure infeasible.

An alternative means of finance was government borrowing from the domestic population. But, as we mentioned, governments with poor policy records and credibility problems found it difficult to borrow by selling long-term bonds to the domestic population. The basic reason was that governments could, after selling bonds, create excessive money growth and inflation, which would erode the real rate of return earned by those who bought the bonds. In fact, if the rate of inflation exceeded the nominal interest rate paid on the bonds, investors actually earned *negative* real rates of return—quite a deterrent to buying bonds.[6] This left just one source of domestic financing for government expenditure: money creation. In effect, the central bank printed money that the government then used to buy goods and services. This combination of expansionary fiscal policy and expansionary monetary policy, of course, produced inflation, along with a bigger "inflation tax," which further reduced governments' credibility and future ability to borrow.

To keep the required interest payments low on whatever borrowing the state undertook, policy makers had an incentive to keep interest rates artificially low. This discouraged domestic saving and encouraged capital flight, as domestic savers attempted to earn higher and more secure real rates of return by placing their funds in foreign assets.[7] Low interest rates combined with government control over bank lending allowed politically favored sectors to receive handsome subsidies in the form of cheap loans. But low interest rates also resulted in a shortage of capital to finance investment and more opportunity for the state to allocate the scarce capital on political criteria.

---

4.   On banking crises and their potential macroeconomic effects, see section 3 in the chapter on money, the banking system, and foreign exchange.

5.   Poorly developed tax systems cause many developing countries to rely heavily on taxes on imports and exports. This imposes an additional cost on the economy by discouraging international trade and forcing the economy to forgo part of the potential gains from trade.

6.   Recall the Fisher relationship from the chapter on the exchange rate in the long run: The nominal interest rate, i, can be divided into two components: the real interest rate, r, and the rate of inflation, $i = r + \dot{P}$. Government policies that force banks to lend to state-favored borrowers at a nominal rate of interest less than the rate of inflation are referred to as *financial repression*.

7.   A high rate of private saving is one of the important characteristics that distinguished the East Asian economies from most other developing countries.

GOVERNMENT CONTROL OVER FOREIGN EXCHANGE In an attempt to keep domestic funds in the domestic economy rather than allowing them to escape as capital flight, governments often used capital controls and foreign exchange controls. Regulations commonly required exporters who earned foreign currencies to sell them immediately to the government in exchange for domestic currency. More generally, exchange controls rendered the domestic currency nonconvertible for current-account or capital-account transactions or both. These policies gave the state even more control over the economy. By choosing to whom to allocate scarce foreign exchange and what exchange rate to charge for it, government could tax or subsidize each transaction. Controls also restricted the domestic population's opportunity to circumvent the government's inflation tax by using a foreign currency instead of the domestic one in everyday domestic transactions.[8] Despite governments' best efforts, black markets in foreign exchange usually developed and limited official attempts to control access to loans and foreign exchange in the long run.

EXTERNAL DEBT Finally, we come to the characteristic that put developing countries on newspaper front pages around the world during the 1980s: external debt. Here we note the relationship between the macroeconomic aspects of external debt and the other macroeconomic characteristics of developing countries.

Consider one of the fundamental macroeconomic relationships, the link between domestic investment, saving, the government budget, and the current-account balance. For every economy, by definition:[9]

$$I = S + (T - G) - CAB \qquad [1]$$

Equation 1 implies that a country can finance domestic investment (I) in three ways: through domestic private saving (S), through government saving in the form of a budget surplus $(T - G > 0)$, or through a current-account deficit $(CAB < 0)$ and the matching borrowing from abroad. We argued earlier that the typical pre-reform developing country exhibited a low rate of private saving, high government expenditure, and low tax revenues. Together, these characteristics limited the feasibility of the first two forms of finance.

Developing countries still could take advantage of domestic investment opportunities, but they had to run current-account deficits and borrow abroad to finance them. This is just the intertemporal-gains-from-trade argument again: If developing economies have good domestic investment opportunities but little current income with which to finance them, those countries can borrow from foreigners who have investment funds available but few good domestic investment opportunities. Both parties can gain, but only so long as the borrowing finances investment projects that prove productive enough to generate an economic return sufficient to repay the loan.

Unfortunately, many developing economies in the 1970s borrowed to finance projects that failed this criterion. The projects failed for several reasons. Many were chosen by governments on a political rather than economic basis. Some borrowed funds supported grossly inefficient state-owned enterprises; others paid for military buildups; still others went toward unproductive "prestige projects" such as national airlines, steel mills, and new capital cities. Other projects failed because economic conditions changed between the time the projects were undertaken and the time repayment came due. The industrial-country recession of the early 1980s caused primary-product prices to plunge,

---

8. This phenomenon is called *currency substitution* or, more specifically, informal *dollarization;* see Case Five in the preceding chapter.

9. Section 7 in the chapter on the goods market develops this relationship.

real interest rates to soar, and the dollar to appreciate dramatically against most developing-country currencies. As a result, many borrowers suffered a decline in export earnings from which to make payments, a rise in interest payments, and a rise in the domestic-currency value of their outstanding foreign-currency-denominated loans. This unfortunate combination led many developing countries to the brink of default.

Only years of negotiations ended the 1980s debt crisis—centered on the big Latin American borrowers, Mexico, Brazil, and Argentina—with no major defaults and minimal long-term damage to the international monetary system. That debt crisis left a painful legacy and continuing economic problems for many developing countries. It did, however, have some positive effects as well. The crisis reminded developed and developing countries once again of their interdependence. The crisis also forced many developing countries to undertake much-needed and long-delayed economic and political reforms.

2.2 Reform

In a contest to select the top three trends in the international macroeconomy over the past 25 years, policy reform in the developing countries would be a strong candidate for inclusion. One by one, following decades of dismal economic performance, many countries changed some or all of the five key pre-reform macroeconomic characteristics we listed earlier.[10] The reforms differed from country to country in their timing and breadth, but the most common changes fall into two groups. **Stabilization reforms** refer to policy changes that aim to achieve macroeconomic *stability*. The most basic elements of this stage of reform include cutting excessive government spending and reducing excessive money growth. Together, these changes help reduce inflation and stabilize the value of the domestic currency. The other major component of reform, **structural reform**, or **structural adjustment**, refers to changes in the basic *structure* of the economy. The most important element involves reducing the extent of government involvement in the economy and increasing the role for markets. Structural reforms attempt to provide stronger incentives for productive economic activities, including production, saving, investment, and international trade based on comparative advantage. Note, however, that stabilization and structural reforms can't really be separated. After all, the primary forces that cause macroeconomic instability—excessive fiscal spending and money growth—follow directly from state ownership and control of the economy, and reducing state ownership and control requires structural reform.

Although the correspondence is rough and inexact, we can usefully think of stabilization reform as improving control over the aggregate *demand* curve (especially, stopping continual large rightward shifts that lead to persistent high inflation) and of structural reform as encouraging rightward shifts of the long-run aggregate *supply* curve, which represents the economy's basic productive capacity. Historically, many developing countries suffered a combination of (1) inefficient state management of the economy that mired supply far to the left of its potential position based on the countries' resources, and (2) excessively expansionary fiscal and monetary policies that continually shifted aggregate demand to the right and, given the economies' low productivities, generated persistent inflation and currency devaluations. Panel (a) of Figure 1 illustrates these effects. The fundamental policy reforms undertaken by many developing economies during the past 25 years attempt to undo this disastrous combination and move the economies to a situation more similar to that in panel (b) of Figure 1. The precise approach to reform and the relative emphasis on its many diverse aspects vary greatly from country to country; however, we can note some common themes.

---

10. In some cases, countries instituted reforms at least in part because of pressure from creditors and international organizations such as the International Monetary Fund.

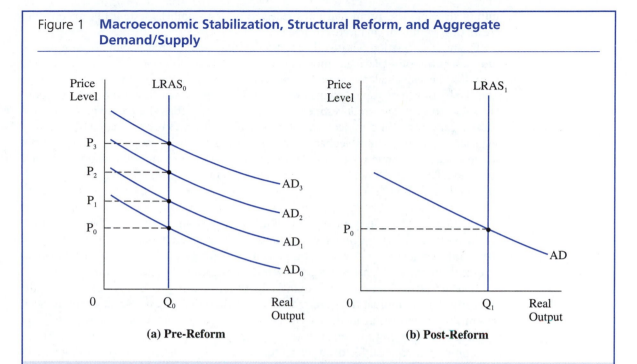

Figure 1 **Macroeconomic Stabilization, Structural Reform, and Aggregate Demand/Supply**

Panel (a) represents the typical macroeconomic situation in developing economies before reform. Overly expansionary fiscal and monetary policies shift aggregate demand (AD) continually to the right. Structural inefficiencies hold the long-run aggregate supply curve (LRAS) to the left of its potential position. This combination produces low levels of real output and rising prices. Reform shifts the situation to the one depicted in panel (b). Macroeconomic stabilization stops the continual rightward shift of AD, and structural reform allows LRAS to move to the right. This new policy combination produces higher real output and steady prices.

PRIVATIZATION AND DEREGULATION The most basic structural reform involves reducing the role of the state in the ownership and day-to-day control of the economy. Many state-owned enterprises have been privatized, sold to private investors. The goal is to confront the enterprises with a competitive economic environment, thereby forcing them to become more productive, efficient, and responsive to consumer preferences. Managers and workers in this new environment face stronger incentives to improve production techniques, minimize costs, adopt new technologies, and otherwise improve the enterprises' economic performance.

Privatization, as essential as it is to reform, can be a slow and difficult process. Emerging capital markets and investors find it hard to estimate reasonable prices for the enterprises up for sale, because their earlier performance under state ownership often provides a poor guide to their potential profitability. Foreign purchases of formerly state-owned enterprises can generate resentment of reform among the domestic population. Workers who held subsidized-wage jobs in the state-owned enterprises may oppose reforms that ultimately must limit wages to those justified by labor productivity. Some of the enterprises, established for political reasons, simply have no economic future and eventually must be closed or allowed to go bankrupt to avoid a continual drain on the government budget.

FINANCIAL INTEGRATION Historically, many developing countries deliberately isolated themselves from world capital markets. Authorities prohibited or strictly regulated foreign investment in the domestic economy and tried to prevent any outflow of domestic funds. This isolation gave the domestic government a near monopoly over capital allocation. As a result, economically promising investment projects often went unfunded, while less promising ones received not only initial funding but an ongoing stream of government-financed subsidies.

Financial integration with world capital markets—the macroeconomic counterpart of trade liberalization—plays an important role in undoing this legacy by replacing state control of the capital-allocation process with more efficiently functioning markets.[11] These markets, by providing capital owners with vehicles to move their funds around the world, allow investors to compare investment projects across countries and to invest in the most economically promising projects. Governments lose their ability to channel funds into politically motivated "white-elephant" projects. Governments also acquire an external check on their macroeconomic policies. If a government strays too far from the reform path and begins to follow policies not conducive to strong economic performance, investors can shift their funds away from that economy, signaling to the government the riskiness of its path.[12]

The changes associated with financial market integration also encourage domestic saving and create domestic sources of funds to finance investment projects. Even given their low incomes, developing-country populations can generate impressive levels of saving—*if* convinced that government won't expropriate those savings, erode them through inflation, or force them into instruments that pay low or even negative real rates of return.

Like privatization, financial market integration can prove politically difficult. Enterprises favored under the government capital-allocation regime may attempt to block reform that would result in their evaluation on economic rather than political criteria. Opening the economy to foreign investment may generate resentment, particularly in economies with colonial histories. Powerful banking interests, accustomed to monopoly access to domestic depositors and borrowers, may generate political pressure to keep their protected position. And policy makers may not always appreciate the check on their policies provided by investors' ability to shift funds in response to policy changes.

FISCAL CONSOLIDATION AND TAX REFORM Fundamental reforms of macroeconomic policy include reducing the level of government expenditure and shifting the finance of continuing expenditure away from money creation and toward taxes or government borrowing. The basic goal is reduction of the rate of growth in aggregate demand in order to reduce the exorbitant rates of inflation common in many pre-reform developing economies. Reducing government expenditure requires curtailing the role of government to include only those activities not well suited to markets—such as national defense, law enforcement, provision of a social safety net, and some infrastructure projects. Government also must cut ongoing subsidies to enterprises that continue under state ownership.

To reduce inflation, post-reform government expenditures must be financed more through taxes and government borrowing and less through money creation. Other aspects of reform help accomplish this shift, at least in the long run. For example, as reform improves policy making and economic performance, the government's policy-making reputation may improve to the extent that the domestic population would willingly purchase government bonds. Integration with world financial markets helps ensure that the rates of return on such bond offerings will be competitive with those available on foreign assets.

As with other aspects of reform, fiscal consolidation won't be universally popular. The country's elites may have adjusted to high inflation and learned to circumvent government controls; so they may actually prefer continued inflation to either paying taxes to finance government expenditures or forgoing government services or subsidies. And, of course, enterprises that lose their government subsidies may oppose reform.

11. See Case Four in the chapter on short-run policy under a fixed exchange rate.

12. Some analysts worry that capital markets may *overreact* to a government's policy missteps, such as Mexico's (1994) or Thailand's (1997) devaluation, thereby worsening macroeconomic performance.

CURRENCY CONVERTIBILITY   A country can't enjoy the full gains from trade in goods and services or from intertemporal trade unless its currency is convertible. As long as the state maintains control over foreign exchange and sets artificial exchange rates for those transactions, international activity can't be based on comparative advantage. Potential exporters, for example, have little incentive to produce for export if they know they must sell any foreign currency they earn to the government at artificially low prices. On the other hand, government-favored elites will import luxury consumption goods from abroad if provided with the requisite foreign exchange at reduced rates.

Currency convertibility implies that the exchange rate, if fixed, can't be set too far from equilibrium in the foreign exchange market. Convertibility means that international traders and investors can demand that the central bank buy and sell foreign exchange at the pegged rate in amounts sufficient to cover the desired international trade and financial activities. If the pegged exchange rate strays too far from equilibrium, the excess demand for foreign exchange will eventually exceed the central bank's ability to intervene and maintain the peg. If the central bank runs short of reserves, market participants may come to expect a devaluation and precipitate a currency crisis.

One way to avoid such crises is to operate under a flexible rather than a fixed exchange rate regime. Reforming developing countries often hesitate to make this move for two reasons. For very small developing economies, transactions in the domestic currency may be so infrequent and small that the "foreign exchange market" bears little resemblance to the active and competitive markets for dollars, yen, and euros. Forward and futures markets, in particular, may be thin or nonexistent, leaving individuals and firms with little opportunity to hedge foreign exchange risks under floating rates.

Perhaps more important, a fixed exchange rate, *if* crises can be avoided, can provide price discipline as part of the reform process by forcing the central bank to shrink the money stock when the balance of payments shifts to deficit (such policies are called using the exchange rate as a *nominal anchor*). However, we saw in earlier chapters that governments can circumvent such discipline if they're so inclined. Reforming governments may lean too heavily or too long on the exchange rate as the anchor of a disinflation program. If they refuse to devalue even when domestic inflation persistently outpaces foreign inflation, the result is a real currency appreciation.[13] This leads to declining exports, rising imports, and a growing current-account deficit that must be financed with either external borrowing or sales of foreign exchange reserves. (*Why?*) If foreign-exchange-market participants view this trend as unsustainable, a currency crisis erupts.

Another potential disadvantage of fixed exchange rates comes from interaction between the exchange rate regime and the production structure of the economy. For many developing economies, such as those in Africa, a mere handful of goods—often primary products—account for virtually all export revenues. World demand for these primary products moves with business-cycle conditions in the major industrial countries, so a recession there can severely reduce demand for a developing country's two or three export products. We learned in section 7.3 of the preceding chapter that a fixed exchange rate can exacerbate the macroeconomic impact of negative shocks to export demand. This happens because the initial decline in demand pushes down the domestic interest rate and leads to a balance-of-payments deficit. To hold the pegged exchange rate, the central bank must place further contractionary pressure on the economy by intervening in the foreign exchange market to sell foreign exchange and shrink the money stock. Under a flexible exchange rate, on the other hand, the balance-of-payments deficit would cause the domestic currency to depreciate, lowering the relative price of domestic goods and services, and improving the competitiveness of the country's products on world markets. (*Illustrate these results in an aggregate demand–aggregate supply diagram.*)

---

13. Recall that the real exchange rate, or the relative price of domestic goods and services, equals $R \equiv P/eP^*$.

Increased recognition of the limits on the discipline that fixed exchange rates can impose, of the crisis-generating potential of fixed rates with mobile capital, and of the interaction between fixed exchange rates and negative export-demand shocks has led growing numbers of developing economies to adopt more flexible exchange rate regimes as part of their reform packages.[14] Early empirical evidence from these economies suggests that a flexible exchange rate *can* work for developing countries—as long as they follow fiscal and monetary policies consistent with macroeconomic stability.

INVESTMENT FINANCE AND DEBT   The debt crisis of the 1980s reminded debtors and creditors alike of the fundamental rules for sound debt management: (1) To avoid insolvency crises, an investment project must produce a rate of return sufficient to cover loan payments; (2) To avoid illiquidity crises, loan maturity and project maturity must match so that returns from the project come in time to make loan payments; and (3) Uncertainty regarding future economic events, both domestic and international, constrains the prudent amount of debt accumulation any country can undertake.

Ideally, the aspects of reform already discussed can go a long way toward preventing a repeat of the 1980s debt crisis. With the state playing more limited roles in the economy of most developing countries, future borrowed funds are less likely to be wasted on unproductive, politically motivated projects. Privatization facilitates the growth of stock markets and equity finance, in which the debtor's obligation to the creditor varies with economic outcomes. This helps avoid the problem that arose in the 1980s when debtors—because their debt took the form of bank loans—owed fixed repayment schedules regardless of their investment projects' outcomes. Active capital markets help potential investors evaluate more accurately the return likely from various projects. Removal of capital controls and foreign exchange controls allows investors to express confidence or lack thereof in policy makers' decisions by "voting with their funds." Governments' improved reputations encourage domestic saving and make long-term government bonds a more feasible means of public finance. Early evidence indicates that the nature of developing-country borrowing has shifted away from the pre-reform pattern of predominantly bank loans to developing-country governments and toward debt and equity flows from private lenders to private borrowers. Still, the Asian financial crisis makes clear that accumulation of too much debt, regardless of the specific identities of the debtor and creditor, can plunge otherwise-healthy economies into crisis.

2.3 Lingering Risks

Current concerns about developing countries' macroeconomies differ between two groups of economies: (1) those that cling to pre-reform characteristics and policy choices and remain relatively isolated from the world economy, and (2) those that are "emerging" or reforming and integrating themselves into the world economy.

Among the first group, countries still haven't embarked on meaningful stabilization and structural reform programs. As other developing countries do reform their macroeconomies, those that fail to do so run the risk of becoming even more economically isolated. International investors, faced with a choice between reforming and nonreforming countries as hosts for investment, are likely to choose those with the strongest reform programs. Empirical evidence already strongly supports these predictions.

The lowest-income countries, in particular, remain deeply indebted and largely isolated from participation in world markets. Many have lagged in instituting macroeconomic reforms, and several continue to suffer from wars, both civil and with

---

14. However, recent evidence suggests many governments who claim to allow their exchange rates to float in fact don't. See, for example, Case Two in the preceding chapter.

neighbors. Foreign investors, with the exception of official lenders such as the World Bank, show little interest in investing in these economies.

The largest cluster of such countries lies in sub-Saharan Africa, where real per-capita GDP *fell* by an average of 1.1 percent per year during 1981–1990 and by 0.2 percent per year during 1991–2000. Inflation in the region has averaged more than 10 percent since 1971.[15] Government involvement in the economies remains high, and many continue to finance large-scale losses incurred by state-owned enterprises. Money growth rates are erratic. Real interest rates sometimes are negative as a result of high inflation along with government ceilings on nominal interest rates. Some countries continue to run large current-account deficits (a regional total of almost $8 billion in 2002), which implies that they continue to add to already-large external debts. In 2002, after several programs of debt forgiveness by creditors, total external debt for sub-Saharan Africa equaled over $200 billion, equal to about two-thirds of the region's total GDP. Net foreign direct investment inflows to sub-Saharan Africa in 2002 totaled about $8 billion (2.5 percent of GDP); most went to South Africa and to the oil industries of Angola, Nigeria, and Chad. Portfolio investment in the region equaled about $2.5 billion in 2002, but again, most went to South Africa. Not all these problems result from poor macroeconomic policy. The countries suffered dramatic declines in prices for their highly concentrated primary-product exports during the industrial-country recession of the early 1990s and again in the late 1990s. But failure to undertake and maintain strong macroeconomic reforms exacerbated the negative shocks' impact on the economies.

For the "emerging" developing economies, the important policy challenges include building popular support to stay on the reform path even during economic downturns and periods of stressful volatility. Evidence suggests that erratic reform fails to build credibility and imposes larger cumulative costs on the economy than more-determined, steady approaches. The Mexican, Asian, and Argentine crises brought the financial sector to the forefront of debates over emerging markets' reform agendas. In many reforming developing countries, banks and other financial-sector institutions remain weak and vulnerable. They often lack effective, honest, transparent, and watchful government regulation. Even senior bank staff often lack experience in international markets, having become accustomed to a protected domestic market insulated from market forces. Banks and other firms may overborrow in international capital markets newly open to them, relying on implicit guarantees of government bailouts if they run into trouble. Weak corporate governance and accounting standards deter foreign investment and hinder fund flows even to firms with the best economic prospects.

Developing countries remain, as a group, heavily dependent on external sources of finance for investment. These capital inflows continue only as long as the recipient countries maintain macroeconomic stability and provide attractive real rates of return. Fortunately, the same policies conducive to establishing *foreign* investor confidence also promote *domestic* saving and discourage capital flight, so there is long-term potential for building domestic saving into a viable source of investment finance. In the meantime, the need to maintain foreign investor confidence constrains policy makers' options. This can help hold countries on the reform path, but it also can make economies prone to expectation-generated crises similar to those suffered by Mexico, the economies of East Asia, and Argentina.

3 TRANSITION AND THE MACROECONOMY

Prior to the revolutions of 1989–1991, most analysts considered the centrally planned economies of the Soviet bloc to be developed industrialized economies. In one sense, this analysis was correct, because we'll see that industrialization—in fact, *over*industrialization— was a key characteristic of many of these economies. Yet in other senses the analysis was

---

15. World Bank, *Global Economic Prospects 2004*.

wrong or misleading, due in part to the lack of reliable economic statistics. The revolutions raised the Iron Curtain to reveal economies with low levels of productivity; drastic shortages of consumer goods; outmoded technologies; severe environmental problems; and a dramatic lack of political, legal, and economic institutional infrastructure suited to a market economy. These characteristics gave the transitional economies much in common with developing ones despite, in some cases, the presence of huge industrial plants, sophisticated military capabilities, relatively high per-capita incomes, and high literacy rates.

3.1 Centrally Planned Economies' Pre-Reform Macroeconomic Characteristics

Substantial differences existed *among* the pre-reform transitional economies, and these differences carried important implications for the countries' post-reform prospects. For some, such as Poland and Hungary, the histories of central planning were relatively short, and central planning never fully enveloped their highly productive agricultural sectors. For others, such as most of the states of the former Soviet Union, the history of central planning was much longer, and that planning encompassed and often devastated agriculture.

A few countries, such as China, embarked on market-oriented economic reforms with no explicit political revolution. Another, the former East Germany, ceased to exist as an independent state in the reform process.[16] Each of the 15 republics of the former Soviet Union became a new independent state. And Czechoslovakia and Yugoslavia each split into smaller states, peacefully in the former case and violently in the latter.

For some countries, such as China, dramatic increases in international trade have been a hallmark and important engine of the reform process. For others, such as Bulgaria and some of the former Soviet republics, the events of 1989–1991 brought trade to a virtual— albeit temporary—halt as the regional trade bloc of centrally planned economies, the Council for Mutual Economic Assistance, dissolved along with Soviet control.

The transitional economies also differ substantially in the extent to which they have in place legal and institutional frameworks to support a market-based economy. Vital elements of these frameworks include many items taken for granted in the major industrial economies: laws to protect private property, laws to enforce contracts, accounting rules and standards, orderly bankruptcy procedures, independent judiciaries, and economic policy-making institutions such as central banks.

Despite the important differences among transitional economies, we can make substantial progress toward understanding the macroeconomics of the process by focusing on a few key characteristics of the "typical" pre-reform centrally planned economy. It will soon become obvious why we treat these economies in the same chapter as more traditional developing ones. Common macroeconomic features include the following:

1. Extensive state ownership of productive assets; state control over all aspects of economic activity, prices, and trade; and state resource allocation according to a central economic plan.
2. Overly industrialized economic structure, with underdeveloped financial and services sectors.
3. Government-set prices and investment-funding procedures that encourage capital- and military-goods production and discourage consumer-goods production.
4. Extensive money finance of government expenditure, especially subsidies to large state-owned enterprises.
5. Capital and exchange controls to maintain highly artificial fixed exchange rates.

---

16. The article by the authors in the chapter references takes an economic approach to explaining the German choice to unify.

GOVERNMENT OWNERSHIP AND CONTROL   Until the mid-1980s, more than 95 percent of production in the Soviet Union was in state hands.[17] This figure put the Soviet Union at the upper end of the spectrum of state ownership (Hungary, for example, represented the lower end of the spectrum), but the predominant economic role of the state defined centrally planned economies. The state owned virtually all productive resources. Planners decided what would be produced, in what quantities, by which enterprises, using which inputs, on what schedule, to whom the output would be distributed, and at what "prices."

State planners allocated capital and other resources according to the economy's central plan. State-owned enterprises received government "credits" that they used to buy nonlabor inputs at state-determined prices. Different enterprises paid different prices for inputs, according to whether the government wanted to tax or subsidize the enterprise's activity. Enterprises that were "profitable" returned the profit to the state as tax revenue; enterprises that earned losses typically had their debt forgiven. The fact that losses didn't force enterprises into bankruptcy, because the state simply provided more loans and credits regardless of economic performance, meant that firms faced a **soft budget constraint**. In other words, profitability wasn't a requisite for continued operation under such a system. Workers received government-set wages, usually paid in cash, but the typical shortages of consumer goods implied that much of the cash went unspent. Officially recorded unemployment hovered close to zero—because planners assigned workers to jobs and prevented residential relocation or job changes.

The state's control also extended to international trade, handled through state trading companies rather than directly by individual enterprises. Comparative advantage, which rests on a comparison of relative prices across countries, can't determine trade patterns when prices are set bureaucratically without regard to market forces. Planners often attempted to keep the economy from relying on imports, especially from market-oriented economies; and state trading companies chose "surplus" goods to export in exchange for the necessary imports.[18]

OVERINDUSTRIALIZATION   Policy makers in some centrally planned economies used their power over prices and resource allocation to encourage production of capital and military goods and discourage production of consumer goods and services. Among other tools to accomplish this, governments provided the favored sectors with cheap energy, access to cheap foreign exchange for their imports, and heavy subsidies to cover wages and other input costs. As a result, in the late 1980s, industry accounted for twice as large a share of output in the former Soviet Union as in the United States, while Soviet service-sector output fell short of a third of the corresponding U.S. figure. Among the major transitional economies, China appears to have recognized its overemphasis on industry relatively early; it shifted policy in 1978 to create market-like incentives for agricultural production and to build a better-balanced productive structure.

In addition to their heavy emphasis on industry, centrally planned economies typically exhibited a prevalence of very-large-scale state-owned enterprises that held monopoly positions for their respective products.[19] The sheer size of the firms surpassed

---

17.   David Lipton and Jeffrey D. Sachs, "Prospects for Russia's Economic Reforms," *Brookings Papers on Economic Activity* 2 (1992), p. 219.

18.   In contrast to their disregard of comparative advantage, planners placed heavy emphasis on regional specialization and economies of scale. This produced a set of heavily dependent supplier–customer relationships that the events of 1989–1991 destroyed. This breakdown contributed to dramatic short-term declines in output and continues to constrain prospects for many transitional economies, particularly the former Soviet republics.

19.   Chinese policy during the disastrous "Great Leap Forward" of the late 1950s and early 1960s represents a dramatic exception; the government mandated what amounted to tiny backyard steel mills.

any possible economies of scale, and their protected monopoly status provided them little incentive to produce high-quality products or adopt new technologies.

PRICE CONTROLS AND SHORTAGES   State planners set prices administratively for both goods and resources, often ignoring supply and demand. The result, of course, was a situation of chronic shortages of goods that consumers and firms wanted and surpluses of goods that no one wanted. Shortages of consumer goods implied that citizens had to stand in line, often daily, to acquire even basic goods such as food. Workers hoarded their cash wages because of the lack of goods to purchase with them; and these hoarded funds (called **monetary overhang**) gave the government a further incentive to levy an inflation tax that eroded the savers' purchasing power. Existence of a large monetary overhang also meant that lifting price controls once reform became inevitable would likely lead to a dramatic price increase because of the pent-up money balances.

Price controls resulted in shortages of productive inputs for which state planners had set prices too low. This led to production bottlenecks as downstream firms ran short of vital inputs. To avoid these bottlenecks that could cause firms to fall short of their state-assigned output targets, firms hoarded inputs and inventories and attempted to vertically integrate and be as self-sufficient as possible.

MONEY-FINANCE OF FISCAL EXPENDITURES   Unproductive state-owned enterprises relied on massive government subsidies to keep them in operation. These subsidies, along with other extensive state functions, led to high rates of government expenditure. Tax systems often were poorly developed and overly reliant on the state-owned enterprises for revenues. Governments found it difficult to borrow because of their isolation from world capital markets, their poor credibility, and the domestic population's distrust of government promises to repay debts and avoid inflation that produces negative real rates of return. As a result, governments relied heavily on money finance of government expenditures. In essence, the central bank printed money to keep the state-owned enterprises in operation—an ideal recipe for inflation that price controls, in turn, attempted to suppress.

CAPITAL AND EXCHANGE CONTROLS   Government control over prices in centrally planned economies extended to the price of foreign exchange or the exchange rate. Currencies typically were nonconvertible, and governments maintained monopoly control over foreign-exchange transactions. International trade was channeled through state-trading companies, so the government controlled access to any foreign exchange acquired through exports. Planners then allocated the scarce foreign exchange by selling it at different prices to cover imports according to their different priorities under the central plan.

Currency nonconvertibility, along with price controls' distortion of comparative advantage, caused centrally planned economies to forgo most of the potential gains from trade. In particular, nonconvertibility imposed **bilateralism** on trade. Suppose Czechoslovakia exported tractors to the Soviet Union and received payments in rubles, the Soviet currency. The rubles couldn't be sold on the foreign exchange market for dollars, pounds, yen, or any other foreign currency; so to use the rubles, Czechoslovakia had to import a good from a country willing to accept rubles as payment—that is, the Soviet Union. Therefore, each pair of countries ended up importing and exporting approximately equal values of goods from one another, a pattern that foreclosed many opportunities for mutually beneficial trade.

Governments also restricted capital inflows and outflows, as well as use of foreign currencies, under central planning. The domestic population hoarded cash because government restrictions prohibited buying foreign assets and because domestic assets might be nonexistent or vulnerable to confiscation, inflation, or other risks. The state represented most enterprises' only potential source of investment funds. Many centrally planned economies reported high rates of investment, but the actual productivity of such investment often was low. Government planners, with little knowledge of actual production processes in different sectors of the economy, often provided inappropriate resources and funded inappropriate investments. In the Soviet Union, in particular, newly available evidence suggests that the domestic population was asked to forgo consumption goods in order for the economy to invest in ways that ultimately failed to enhance productivity.

3.2 Reform

Transforming the centrally planned countries into functioning market-oriented economies represents a task of a magnitude unprecedented in modern economic history. One reason for this assessment is that so many types of reform—economic, political, social, legal, and institutional—are needed. A high degree of consensus exists on the basic outline of economic reform. Most lingering controversies concern issues of timing. For example, is it better to attempt dramatic and immediate reforms on all margins simultaneously (the so-called **big-bang approach**, often associated with Poland), or to reform more slowly and take the different elements of reform one-by-one (the **gradualism approach**, often associated with China)? One right answer probably doesn't exist. For example, big bangs may be required in cases of large-scale breakdown of political authority, as in the former Soviet Union, but not in cases of more subtle political transformation, as in China. In the following discussion, we mention several timing dilemmas that confront reformers. No historical counterpart exists of so many countries undertaking such a broad array of reforms, so economists' ability to answer important questions about the optimal timing of reform is limited. All we can do is apply sound economic theory, watch as countries take different approaches, and try to learn what works, what doesn't, and why.

Regardless of approach—big-bang or gradual—successful reforms must include both macroeconomic stabilization and structural reform. Stabilization seeks to halt excessive fiscal spending and money growth in order to prevent the continual rightward shifts of the aggregate demand curve that generate chronic high inflation. Structural reform seeks to shift the long-run aggregate supply curve to the right in several ways. One is the elimination of gross productive inefficiencies and enhancement of market incentives; these move the economy onto its production possibilities frontier from the interior point associated with central planning. The second and third changes that can shift the supply curve involve improved knowledge and access to more productive technologies along with increased investment; these two processes should shift a country's production possibilities frontier outward.

PRIVATIZATION   Privatization represents a central task of structural reform. Just as state ownership of productive assets defines central planning, private ownership defines a market-oriented or price-based economic system. Privatization means the sale of state-owned enterprises to private owners, who then run the enterprises on a market basis; that is, buying inputs and selling outputs at market-determined prices, deciding what and how much to produce, what production techniques to use, and so on. These changes play several key roles in reform. Together, they harden the soft budget constraint faced by firms; profitability becomes a requisite for continued operation. This contributes to macroeconomic stabilization because it eliminates enterprise losses as a continual drain on the government's budget and reduces the incentive to print money to cover those losses. Privatization can help absorb some of an economy's monetary overhang as individuals spend accumulated cash to buy shares in privatized enterprises. And the revenues raised through privatization contribute, albeit on a one-time basis, to reduction of the government budget deficit. By giving investors a clear financial stake in the firm's future, privatization also enhances productivity incentives and avoids the tendency, prevalent in years just prior to reform, for workers to "decapitalize" firms by paying themselves exorbitant wages and counting on government subsidies to cover the shortfall.

Privatization has proven to be one of the more politically difficult and slow-moving reforms for most countries, especially in the large-enterprise sector. Some of the reasons are easy to see: Who should be eligible to buy the enterprises? Before other reforms, especially price liberalization, are in place, how can potential investors evaluate enterprises' potential values? What if the new owners are foreign? What if the new owners decide to cut employment? Despite these problems, countries have made progress. Estonia, Hungary, and the Czech and Slovak Republics have almost completed privatization programs. Others, such as Albania and Tajikistan, have made substantial progress in privatizing small-scale enterprises but lag in dealing with large-scale ones, where ownership and employment issues are more politically sensitive. Figure 2 documents countries' cumulative progress in privatization as of 2004, including the distinction between small- and large-scale enterprises. Note that only one country, Bulgaria, has made more progress in the large-enterprise sector than in the small-enterprise one; Bulgaria undertook several large privatizations during 2004 in its energy, telecommunications, and shipbuilding industries. The European Bank for Reconstruction and Development, created to assist countries in their transition from centrally planned to market economic systems, ranks countries' progress on a four-point scale with pluses and minuses, much like grades in school.

In practice, privatization results have, in some cases, disappointed. First, before many of the positive effects of privatization could happen, some transitional economies (especially the former Soviet Union) experienced sudden drops in output as the government's coordination role in the economy—no matter how ineptly performed—disappeared with no short-term replacement. Basic input-supply relationships broke down, because enterprises had little experience interacting directly with one another without the state as an intermediary. Output declined by an average of about 20 percent before the reform process even began. Even more important, privatization often failed to produce restructured, competitive firms with effective and honest corporate governance.

GOVERNANCE AND RESTRUCTURING   Central planning produces an economy in which the quantities supplied and quantities demanded for various goods and resources don't match. This is reflected in many ways, such as overindustrialization, queues for consumer goods, and the existence of large monetary overhangs. Sectoral restructuring occurs when market-determined prices begin to allocate resources so that the economy produces those goods that consumers and firms want.

Many large state-owned enterprises existed largely on government subsidies and produced poor-quality versions of goods no one wanted. These enterprises must be allowed to either adapt or die as part of the reform process, because they represent a huge drain on the economy and a major barrier to stabilizing fiscal expenditures. In other words, the previously soft budget constraint facing state-owned enterprises must become a hard one—an essential step in both long-term macroeconomic stabilization and structural reform.

Many of the transitional economies suffered from poorly developed service and financial sectors, the mirror image of their overindustrialization. A shift toward markets means improvements in retailing and distribution, as well as creation of private financial and banking sectors to replace state control over financial activity in the economy. The new financial sectors often suffer from a lack of expertise, vulnerability to fraud, and lack of transparent accounting standards, regulation, and supervision.

Figure 2   **Transitional Economies' Progress in Privatization, 2004**

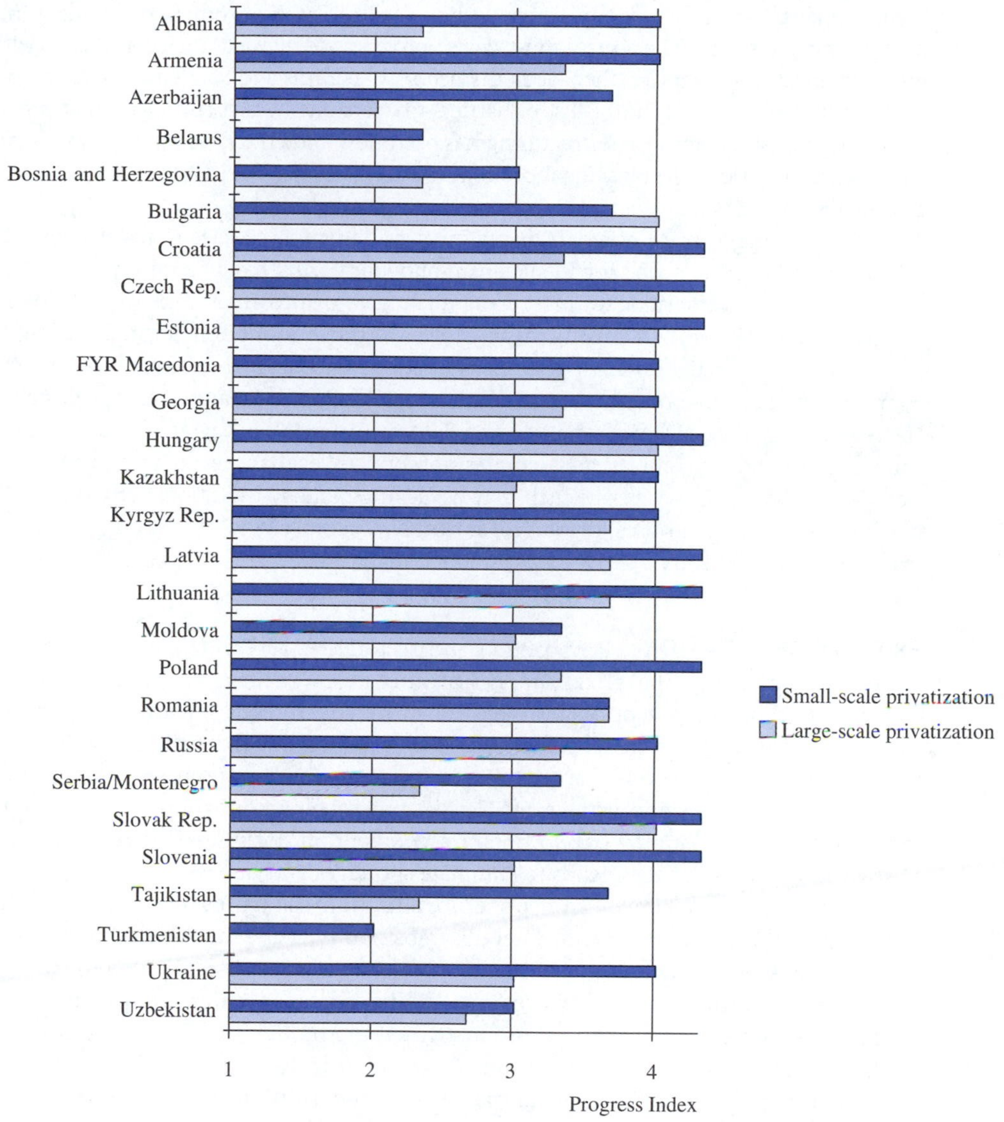

Small-scale privatization
Large-scale privatization

Progress Index

Note: For large-scale privatization: 1 = little private ownership; 2 = comprehensive scheme almost ready for implementation, some sales completed; 3 = more than 25 percent of large-scale enterprise assets in private hands or in the process of being privatized (with the process having reached a stage at which the state has effectively ceded its ownership rights), but possibly with major unresolved issues regarding corporate governance; 4 = more than 50 percent of state-owned enterprise and farm assets in private ownership and significant progress on corporate governance of these enterprises; 4+ = standards and performance typical of advanced industrial economies, more than 75 percent of enterprise assets in private ownership with effective corporate governance. For small-scale privatization: 1 = little progress; 2 = substantial share privatized; 3 = comprehensive program almost ready for implementation; 4 = complete privatization of small companies with tradable ownership rights; 4+ = standards and performance typical of advanced industrial economies, no state ownership of small enterprises, effective tradability of land.

Source: Data from European Bank for Reconstruction and Development, *Transition Report 2004.*

A need for sectoral restructuring in *any* economy, centrally planned or otherwise, presents a difficult task. Workers in industries that must shrink have strong incentives to oppose reform, especially when they have been the longtime recipients of heavily subsidized wages. Some workers, especially older ones, may lack the skills to move to other employment in the growing private sector. The society must devise programs to alleviate the economic hardship imposed on such workers lest they block the necessary reforms and condemn the economy to continuing stagnation. Given this list of barriers to overcome, it isn't surprising that progress on governance and enterprise restructuring has been slow and erratic, as reported in Figure 3. However, as of 2004, all transitional economies except former Soviet republics Belarus and Turkmenistan had begun to address governance and restructuring.

The other major piece of restructuring involves designing policies to foster competitive markets and limit the scope for inefficient monopolies. This has proven one of the most difficult elements of transition for most economies. State-owned enterprises were deliberately created as monopolies, so privatization can leave those monopolies intact unless it is accompanied by effective antitrust policies. Figure 4 documents that this area is one in which many transitional economies have made little progress. But all countries except Bosnia and Herzegovina, Serbia and Montenegro, and Turkmenistan have begun the task. Effective competition policy is complex and requires appropriate legal and economic institutions as well as a pool of expertise, all of which may be lacking in many transitional economies. And, of course, existing enterprises, privatized or not, have an incentive to lobby against policies that would promote entry by new rivals into their markets.

PRICE LIBERALIZATION Privatization and sectoral restructuring can't occur without large doses of price liberalization. Private investors will be hesitant to purchase enterprises whose output prices are held down by government price controls, because such enterprises will earn losses rather than profits. And sectoral restructuring, or shifting resources toward the goods wanted by consumers and firms, requires that producers know what consumers and firms want. Prices convey this information by signaling how much buyers are willing to pay to obtain a good. From consumers' perspective, price liberalization represents the means to eliminate shortages and queues.

All these salutary effects from price liberalization can't prevent controversy from surrounding this aspect of reform. After all, transition typically means that some workers lose their jobs in antiquated, unproductive state-owned enterprises. For those who keep their jobs, the artificially high wages paid under central planning must give way to market-determined wages based on productivity if the products are to compete in world markets. In this context, a rise in consumer-goods prices due to price decontrol is bound to prove unpopular, even if it does fill previously empty store shelves with goods.

Note, however, that price decontrol leads to a one-time price increase, *not* to ongoing inflation. In the former Soviet Union, prices rose by between 350 and 400 percent on decontrol.[20] When—as in Russia—authorities decontrol prices *before* they stabilize the macroeconomy and control inflation, they risk the populace mistakenly attributing the inflation to price decontrol. Such mistaken attribution can lead to a loss of popular support for reform. Does this mean that price liberalization should always wait until *after* authorities can control inflation? Not necessarily. In Russia, policy makers feared that the growing shortages of consumer goods posed a greater threat to support for reform than did further inflation; and the only way to fill store shelves was to liberalize prices.

By 2004, most transitional economies had liberalized most prices, as reported in Figure 5. Laggards on this margin of reform include Turkmenistan and Uzbekistan.

---

20. Stanley Fischer, "Stabilization and Economic Reform in Russia," *Brookings Papers on Economic Activity* 1 (1992), p. 78.

Figure 3   **Transitional Economies' Progress in Governance and Restructuring, 2004**

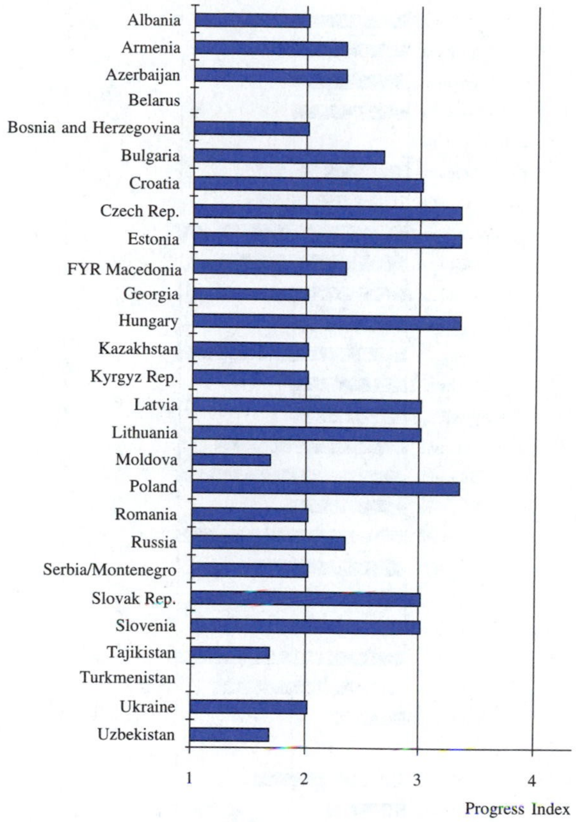

Note: 1 = soft budget constraints (lax credit and subsidy policies weakening financial discipline at the enterprise level), few other reforms to promote corporate governance; 2 = moderately tight credit and subsidy policy but weak enforcement of bankruptcy legislation and little action taken to strengthen competition and corporate governance; 3 = significant and sustained actions to harden budget constraints and to promote corporate governance effectively (for example, privatization combined with tight credit and subsidy policies and/or enforcement of bankruptcy legislation); 4 = substantial improvement in corporate governance and significant new investment at the enterprise level; 4+ = standards and performance typical of advanced industrial economies: effective corporate control exercised through domestic financial institutions and markets, fostering market-driven restructuring.

Source: Data from European Bank for Reconstruction and Development, *Transition Report 2004.*

FISCAL CONSOLIDATION   Extensive state control of the economy translates into extensive government expenditures. Macroeconomic stabilization, essential as a foundation for longer run structural reforms, requires that these expenditures be brought under control. There are two major parts of this task. The first is simply reduction in government expenditure, with much of the reduction coming from curtailed subsidies to unproductive state-owned enterprises. Military spending and unproductive investment expenditures are other candidates for cuts. The second part of fiscal consolidation involves shifting from money finance of expenditure to taxes and government borrowing. This requires both strengthening the tax system (often *ad hoc,* corrupt, and politicized under central planning) by making it simple, transparent, and enforceable, and improving the government's credibility to the point that it becomes able to issue bonds to finance its expenditure.

Figure 4   **Transitional Economies' Progress in Competition Policy, 2004**

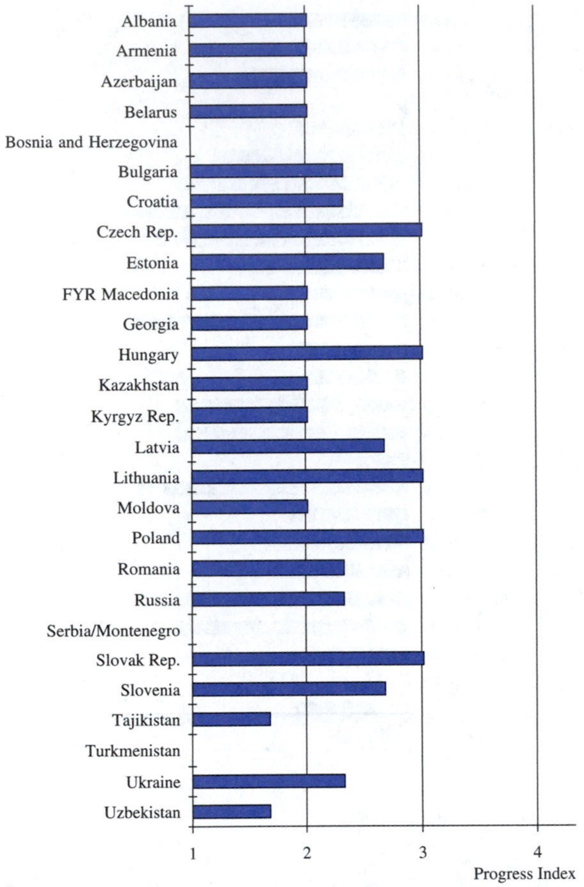

Note: 1 = no competition legislation and institutions; 2 = competition policy legislation and institutions set up, some reduction of entry restrictions or enforcement action on dominant firms; 3 = some enforcement actions to reduce abuse of market power and to promote a competitive environment, including breakups of dominant conglomerates, substantial reduction of entry restrictions; 4 = significant enforcement actions to reduce abuse of market power and to promote a competitive environment; 4+ = standards and performance typical of advanced industrial economies: effective enforcement of competition policy, unrestricted entry to most markets.

Source: Data from European Bank for Reconstruction and Development, *Transition Report 2004.*

The whole process of fiscal consolidation involves not only changes in policy makers' day-to-day behavior but changes in the fundamental structure of policy-making institutions. Most notably, the money-supply process must be reoriented toward monetary control as a tool of macroeconomic policy rather than a passive accommodator of fiscal expenditure. This presented a particular challenge to the former Soviet republics, where runaway inflation during the early 1990s threatened to drive the economies back to barter; Russia continued well into the transition years to succumb periodically to the temptation to print money to cover wages at its unreformed state-owned enterprises and other fiscal expenditures.

Figure 6 illustrates 2003 government budget balances, as a percent of GDP, in the transitional economies. Positive numbers (there are only four: Estonia, Moldova, Russia, and Tajikistan) reflect budget surpluses, and negative numbers reflect budget deficits.

Figure 5   **Transitional Economies' Progress in Price Liberalization, 2004**

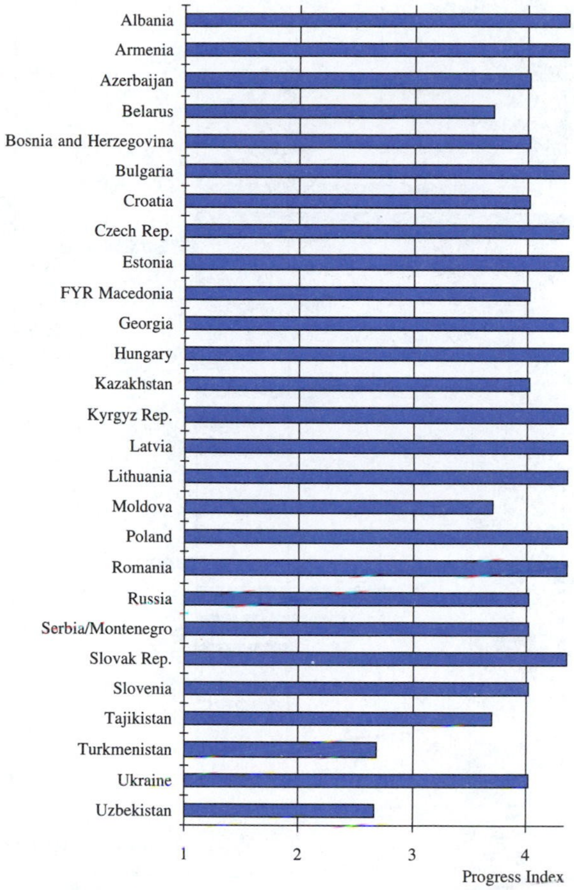

Country	Progress Index
Albania	4.3
Armenia	4.3
Azerbaijan	4.0
Belarus	3.7
Bosnia and Herzegovina	4.0
Bulgaria	4.3
Croatia	4.0
Czech Rep.	4.3
Estonia	4.3
FYR Macedonia	4.0
Georgia	4.3
Hungary	4.3
Kazakhstan	4.0
Kyrgyz Rep.	4.3
Latvia	4.3
Lithuania	4.3
Moldova	3.7
Poland	4.3
Romania	4.3
Russia	4.0
Serbia/Montenegro	4.0
Slovak Rep.	4.3
Slovenia	4.0
Tajikistan	3.7
Turkmenistan	2.7
Ukraine	4.0
Uzbekistan	2.7

Progress Index

Note: 1 = most prices formally controlled by the government; 2 = some lifting of price administration, state procurement at nonmarket prices for the majority of product categories; 3 = significant progress on price liberalization, but state procurement at nonmarket prices remains substantial; 4 = comprehensive price liberalization, state procurement at nonmarket prices largely phased out, only a small number of administered prices remain; 4+ = standards and performance typical of advanced industrial economies: complete price liberalization with no price control outside housing, transport, and natural monopolies.

Source: Data from European Bank for Reconstruction and Development, *Transition Report 2004*.

FINANCIAL INTEGRATION   A system of central planning, with its artificial prices, requires isolation from world markets where demand and supply determine prices. This holds true not only for goods markets, but for capital and foreign exchange markets as well. Uncontrolled contact with world markets makes the central plan's artificial prices unsustainable. Once reform begins, building contacts with world markets serves an important function by helping align prices to their market levels.

Removing capital controls means allowing domestic residents to invest abroad and allowing foreign investors to invest in the domestic economy. Under a market-oriented system, funds to finance investment flow toward projects that offer the most attractive mix of real rate of return and risk, regardless of location. If domestic residents distrust their government, they can place their funds in foreign assets instead. Enterprises attract

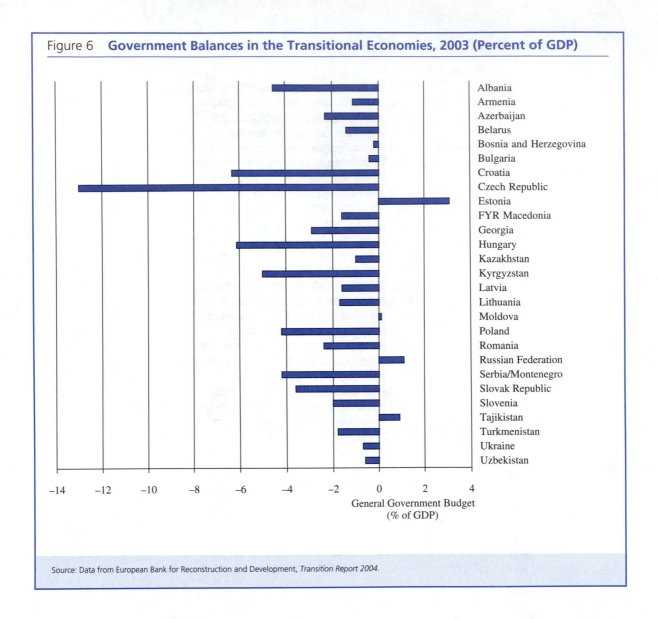

Figure 6   **Government Balances in the Transitional Economies, 2003 (Percent of GDP)**

General Government Budget
(% of GDP)

Source: Data from European Bank for Reconstruction and Development, *Transition Report 2004.*

capital by promising to use it productively rather than through their priority in the government's central plan.[21] The banking sector presents significant reform challenges. In the former Soviet Union, for example, the primary assets owned by banks consisted of loans to unproductive state-owned industrial enterprises that eventually must go bankrupt; yet many analysts believed the banks needed to be saved in order to help in the privatization process.

Reform of banks and nonbank financial institutions has proceeded slowly (see Figure 7). Only Croatia, Estonia, and Hungary had achieved a grade of 4 by 2004; Belarus, Tajikistan, Turkmenistan, and Uzbekistan had hardly begun reforms in this crucial sector. Many banks remain state-owned or subject to state interference. Most lack the expert staff, modern

---

21.   Some estimates suggest that half to three-quarters of capital investment in Czechoslovakia, Hungary, and Poland under central planning was wasteful in the sense that it would be useless in a market economy. See Rudiger Dornbusch and Holger Wolf, "Economic Transition in Eastern Germany," *Brookings Papers on Economic Activity* 1 (1992), p. 252.

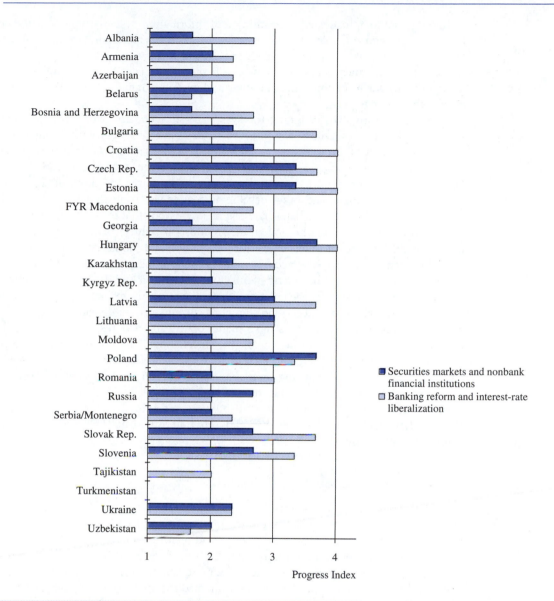

Note: For banking reform and interest-rate liberalization: 1 = little progress beyond establishment of a two-tier system; 2 = significant liberalization of interest rates and credit allocation, limited use of directed credit or interest-rate ceilings; 3 = substantial progress in establishment of bank solvency and of a framework for prudential supervision and regulation, full interest-rate liberalization with little preferential access to cheap financing, significant lending to private enterprises and significant presence of private banks; 4 = significant movement of banking laws and regulations toward BIS standards, well-functioning banking competition and effective prudential supervision, significant term lending to private enterprises, substantial financial deepening; 4+ = standards and performance norms of advanced industrial economies: full convergence of banking laws and regulations with BIS standards, provision of full set of competitive banking services.

For securities markets and nonbank financial institutions: 1 = little progress; 2 = formation of securities exchanges, market makers, and brokers, some trading in government paper and/or securities, rudimentary legal and regulatory framework for the issuance and trading of securities; 3 = substantial issuance of securities by private enterprises, establishment of independent share registries, secure clearance and settlement procedures, and some protection of minority shareholders, emergence of nonbank financial institutions (for example, investment funds, private insurance and pension funds, leasing companies) and associated regulatory framework; 4 = securities laws and regulations approaching IOSCO standards, substantial market liquidity and capitalization, well-functioning nonbank financial institutions and effective regulation; 4+ = standards and performance norms of advanced industrial economies: full convergence of securities laws and regulations with IOSCO standards, fully developed nonbank intermediation.

Source: Data from European Bank for Reconstruction and Development, *Transition Report 2004*.

technology, and sophisticated accounting and information systems typical of financial institutions in industrial market economies. Regulation and supervision are lax; bankruptcy provisions to eliminate "zombie" banks don't exist or aren't enforced effectively.[22] Several transitional economies, including Russia, Albania, the Czech Republic, and Romania, endured crises due to fraudulent financial institutions and pyramid schemes that cost many citizens their savings.

Reform also involves changing the system of state control over foreign-exchange allocation. The domestic currency must be made convertible, particularly for current-account transactions. This openness to international markets allows world market prices to bring artificial domestic prices into line. Governments can choose between fixed and flexible exchange rate regimes, each of which carries advantages and disadvantages, just as is the case for developed and other developing economies. Transitional economies often select some type of pegged exchange rate regime in the hope that the exchange-rate anchor will provide credibility for the government's effort to reduce excessive growth of the money stock. If unaccompanied by fiscal consolidation and monetary restraint, however, a fixed exchange rate can lose credibility and become prone to balance-of-payments and currency crises. As long as high rates of inflation continue, failure to devalue the domestic currency sufficiently to offset the inflation differential results in real currency appreciation, rising imports, dwindling exports, and a growing current-account deficit to finance.

Most transitional economies have made significant progress in reforming their foreign-exchange systems and in liberalizing international trade (see Figure 8). Some, such as Belarus, Turkmenistan, and Uzbekistan, however, have hardly started the needed changes. Others, after liberalizing trade, have encountered domestic political pressures for protection and reinstituted tariffs, quotas, and other trade restrictions. On the foreign-exchange front, crises have caused several countries, most notably Russia in late 1998, to abandon reforms at least temporarily and take large steps backward toward arrangements consonant with central planning rather than with a market-oriented economy.

3.3 Transition Prospects

Initial prospects for the transitional economies differed substantially—depending on the degree of their economic problems, the wisdom and perseverance of their reforms, their political stability to endure the reform process, and their luck in avoiding adverse domestic and international shocks during transition. Each country faced unique advantages and disadvantages. Russia, for example, inherited a more complete set of economic institutions than did the other Soviet republics, but also inherited the Soviet army payroll and the bulk of outstanding Soviet external debt, on which it defaulted in late 1998.

By 1992, Poland began to experience positive real GDP growth; other early reformers joined it during the next few years. This contrasted sharply with the experience of late or timid reformers. In Russia, legislative opposition to fiscal consolidation, along with rising military expenditures in 1994, damaged the earlier progress made toward macro stabilization, and the run-up to the June 1996 presidential election, along with massive corruption, stalled reform. Armed conflict complicated reform efforts in Armenia, Georgia, and the former Yugoslavia. As of 1995, reforms had barely begun in Azerbaijan, Belarus, Tajikistan, Turkmenistan, and Uzbekistan.

By 1995, small private capital flows into the transitional economies had begun, along with some repatriation of flight capital. Both trends, however, applied primarily to those

---

22. The term "zombie" has been suggested for banks that are dead by any market-oriented economic criteria but that nonetheless continue to operate because governments keep them alive for political reasons.

Figure 8   **Transitional Economies' Progress in Trade and Foreign-Exchange Reform, 2004**

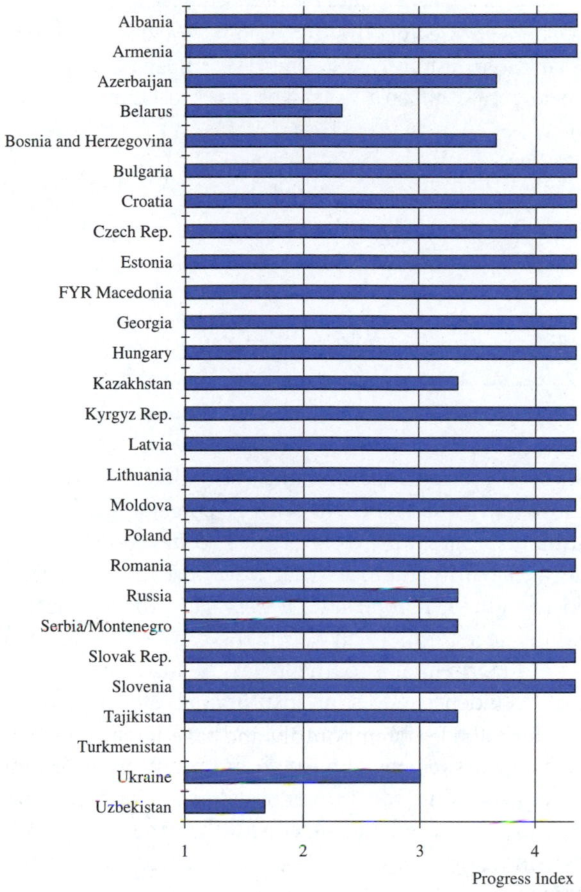

Note: 1 = widespread import and/or export controls or very limited legitimate access to foreign exchange; 2 = some liberalization of import and/or export controls, almost full current-account convertibility in principle but with a foreign exchange regime that is not fully transparent (possibly with multiple exchange rates); 3 = removal of almost all quantitative and administrative import and export restrictions, almost full current-account convertibility; 4 = removal of all quantitative and administrative import and export restrictions (apart from agriculture) and all significant export tariffs, insignificant direct involvement in exports and imports by ministries and state-owned trading companies, no major non-uniformity of customs duties for nonagricultural goods and services, full current-account convertibility; 4+ = standards and performance norms of advanced industrial economies: removal of most tariff barriers, membership in WTO.

Source: Data from European Bank for Reconstruction and Development, *Transition Report 2004.*

countries most advanced in the reform process—particularly the Czech Republic, the Slovak Republic, Hungary, and the Baltic states. And flows were modest compared with experts' earlier predictions. The same held true for foreign direct investment, which potentially plays a vital role in transition by transferring new technology, worker training, and managerial know-how. Opaque legal systems and uncertain governance structures appeared as responsible as macroeconomic instability for the dearth of investment inflows.

Table 2 reports the year in which each transitional economy first achieved positive real GDP growth. By 2000, all had reported positive growth in at least one year. But as of 2003, only ten had reached or surpassed their respective estimated real GDPs from 1989: Poland, Albania, Slovenia, Hungary, the Slovak Republic, the Czech Republic,

Table 2	**YEAR OF FIRST POST-TRANSITION POSITIVE REAL GDP GROWTH**							
1992	1993	1994	1995	1996	1997	1998	1999	2000
Poland	Albania	Bulgaria	Georgia	Azerbaijan	Moldova	Turkmenistan		Ukraine
	Czech Rep.	Croatia	Estonia	Belarus	Russia			
	Romania	Hungary	Lithuania	Kazakhstan	Tajikistan			
	Slovenia	Latvia	Bosnia	Kyrgyzstan				
		Slovak Rep.		Uzbekistan				
		Armenia		Macedonia				
		Serbia/ Montenegro						

Source: Data from European Bank for Reconstruction and Development, *Transition Report 2004*.

Uzbekistan, Turkmenistan, Estonia, and Belarus. Former Soviet republics Georgia and Moldova had 2003 real GDPs only 41 percent of their respective 1989 levels.

Continued progress in reform seems to have slowed recently in some of the central European and Baltic countries that have already achieved accession to the European Union.[23] In southeast Europe, after a slow start, the prospect of EU accession is supporting and speeding up reform, as had been the case earlier in the central European and Baltic economies.[24] Reform in most of the former Soviet republics outside the Baltics remains slow and erratic. Confidence in Russian institutional reform was dealt a setback in late 2004 with the renationalization of the oil firm Yukos; but Russia, along with the other former Soviet oil exporters, continues to benefit in the short term from record-high oil prices.

Generally speaking, most transitional economies' macroeconomic *stabilization* efforts have been more sustained and successful than their *structural* reforms. Continued success in the transition process depends on countries' abilities both to *maintain* the progress made in macroeconomic stabilization and to *move forward* on the difficult issues of institutional and structural reform.

CASE 1: THE HIPC INITIATIVE

During the developing-country debt crisis of the 1980s, large developing countries—Mexico, Argentina, Brazil, and Chile—took center stage as their debt threatened developed-country commercial banks and, therefore, the stability of the international financial system. More recently, attention during the financial crises of the 1990s centered on the debt of (relatively) high-income developing economies—Korea, Thailand, Indonesia, Turkey, and, again, Mexico, Brazil, and Argentina. However, the 41 countries classified by the International Monetary Fund and the World Bank as *Heavily Indebted Poor* Countries (HIPCs) include none of the countries mentioned. Instead, the list includes mostly small economies,

---

23. The Czech Republic, Estonia, Hungary, Latvia, Lithuania, Poland, the Slovak Republic, and Slovenia joined the EU in May 2004.

24. Bulgaria, Croatia, and Romania hope to join the European Union within the next few years.

Table 3   **DEBT INDICATORS FOR HIPC COUNTRIES, 2002**

Country	Present Value of Debt as Percent of GNP	Public and Publicly Guaranteed Debt Service as Percent of GNP	Public and Publicly Guaranteed Debt Service as Percent of Exports	Country	Present Value of Debt as Percent of GNP	Public and Publicly Guaranteed Debt Service as Percent of GNP	Public and Publicly Guaranteed Debt Service as Percent of Exports
Africa:				Mozambique	27	1.1	23.9
Benin	36	1.9	8.5	Niger	26	0.7	n.a.
Burkina Faso	16	1.4	14.8	Rwanda	40	1.1	13.2
Burundi	110	2.6	47.1	São Tomé & Principe	n.a.	n.a.	n.a.
Cameroon	58	3.2	n.a.	Senegal	53	3.6	11.4
C. African R.	78	0.0	n.a.	Sierra Leone	131	2.8	n.a.
Chad	37	1.2	n.a.	Sudan	103	0.0	0.0
Congo, D. R.	171	7.5	n.a.	Tanzania	19	1.4	7.8
Congo	228	0.5	0.5	Togo	92	0.1	0.2
Côte d'Ivoire	91	4.5	8.6	Uganda	22	1.0	7.6
Ethiopia	66	1.6	8.9	Zambia	127	6.4	19.9
Gambia	77	5.3	n.a.	*Asia*:			
Ghana	73	2.8	6.6	Lao, PDR	87	2.2	n.a.
Guinea	47	3.9	12.4	Myanmar	n.a.	n.a.	n.a.
Guinea-Bissau	235	6.1	n.a.	*W. Hemisphere*:			
Madagascar	33	1.5	9.1	Bolivia	23	2.8	13.1
Malawi	51	1.5	5.7	Guyana	n.a.	n.a.	n.a.
Mali	47	2.4	5.8	Honduras	49	2.6	6.5
Mauritania	66	5.8	n.a.	Nicaragua	77	2.6	10.7

Source: International Monetary Fund and World Bank.

many in Africa, for which the present value of debt averages at least 120 percent of GNP or 400 percent of annual export revenues. Table 3 provides country-by-country debt information for the HIPCs.

The HIPCs' external debt totals about $150 billion, or about 90 percent of their collective GDPs. Approximately 600 million people live in these countries, and more than half live on less than one dollar per day. The countries' circumstances vary, but most suffer from low growth rates due to some combination of unstable macroeconomic policies, war, civil unrest, weak governance, failure to undertake price liberalization and other economic reforms, and unfavorable movements in their terms of trade. Plus, the sheer size of their debt places a drag on economic performance for several reasons—a phenomenon known as *debt overhang*. If the benefits of improved economic performance go to creditors rather than the domestic economy, this may reduce the incentives for reform. High

levels of debt can also discourage both domestic and foreign investment in the economy.

In 1996, the World Bank and International Monetary Fund responded with the Heavily Indebted Poor Country Initiative, which was enhanced and fine-tuned in 1999. The initiative has three main goals:

- Reduce the countries' debt to sustainable levels (that is, levels at which the countries could meet their future debt-service obligations without further debt relief or other outside assistance). The initiative's debt-relief targets lower the net present value of debt to 150 percent of export earnings (because exports are how the countries earn foreign exchange to pay their foreign-currency-denominated debt) or to 250 percent of government tax revenue (because the bulk of many countries' debt is owed by the public sector).

- Encourage anti-poverty programs, especially increased resources devoted to primary education and preventive health care, based on a Poverty Reduction Strategy Paper prepared by each country. The funds saved through the initiative's debt relief are to be focused on poverty reduction and on the types of educational and health services that benefit primarily the poorest segment of the population.

- Encourage and reward successful macroeconomic and structural reforms that support growth and reduce the likelihood of future debt problems. Empirical evidence from earlier episodes of debt relief indicates that reforms are necessary both for successful debt reduction and for growth.[25] Important reforms include macroeconomic stabilization (for example, control of fiscal deficits), as well as structural reforms (for example, building institutions to facilitate the rule of law and systems of governance that credibly support individuals' saving and investment in the economy).

The first group of countries to qualify for HIPC debt relief included Bolivia, Burkina Faso, Côte d'Ivoire, Guyana, Mali, Mozambique, and Uganda; their debt-service relief totaled almost $7 billion (or $3.4 in net present value terms). Despite support and political pressure for debt relief by groups such as Jubilee 2000, evidence indicates that debt relief is no panacea. In fact, the HIPCs that received $33 billion in debt relief between 1987 and 1997 undertook net new borrowing of $41 billion during that same period.[26] William Easterly (2001, p. 136), author of many empirical studies of development and growth, summarizes:

> Our heart tells us to forgive debts to the poor. Alas, the head contradicts the heart. Debt forgiveness grants aid to those recipients that have best proven their ability to misuse that aid. Debt relief is futile for countries with unchanged government behavior. The same mismanagement of funds that caused the high debt will prevent the aid sent through debt relief from reaching the truly poor. A debt relief program could make sense if it meets two conditions: (1) it is granted where there has been a proven change from an irresponsible government to a government with good policies; (2) it is a once-for-all measure that will never be repeated.

China

CASE 2: MONETARY-POLICY TRANSITION IN CHINA

Ten years ago, monetary policy in China, like that in most centrally planned economies, consisted of passively accommodating the spending demands embodied in the central plan. Monetary policy played little independent role as a tool for controlling the overall direction of the macroeconomy. In fact, the People's Bank of China, the central bank, couldn't conduct open market operations—the main tool central banks in industrial market economies use to control their money stocks—because it couldn't participate in the government-bond market.[27] If central planners, primarily the National Development and Reform Commission in China, wanted more steel or cement or aluminum, state-owned banks provided generous funds to firms in those industries. If planners wanted less steel or

cement or aluminum, banks received "administrative guidance" not to provide investment funds to those sectors; and the firms had no alternative sources of funds.

Analysts sensed a possible change in emphasis toward more market-oriented monetary-policy tools in late 2003 when Chinese policy makers announced the first of two increases in the required reserve ratio, the portion of deposits banks are required by law to hold rather than loan out. The People's Bank of China announced the change as a response to concerns about too much bank lending and the implications for money growth and inflation. The state still used "administrative measures," such as moratoriums on all new bank loans, in efforts to reduce the rate of growth of the money stock.[28] But these command-and-control policies

---

25. See the Easterly book in the chapter references.

26. Easterly (2001), p. 128.

27. "Beijing Wields Sophisticated Armoury to Curb Growth," *Financial Times*, November 26, 2003.

28. "China Orders Banks to Suspend Making New Commercial Loans," *Wall Street Journal,* April 29, 2004.

were less effective than in the past, in part because informal, nonstate sources of investment funds had emerged with economic reform and liberalization. With widespread alternative sources of funds available, the state's administrative dictates that state-owned banks stop lending to particular overheated sectors of the economy—property, cement, automobiles, and steel—no longer sufficed to choke off investment funds to those sectors.

In late 2004, the central bank raised state-set interest rates for the first time in nine years. The bank now routinely engages in open market operations to affect the rate of growth of the money stock. The transition from central planning to a market-oriented system requires such changes in policy makers' toolkits as well as changes in the overall structure of the economy and its economic institutions.

CASE 3: OWNERSHIP MATTERS

Privatization involves the transfer of ownership of firms or other productive assets from the state to private investors. A comparison of Figures 2 and 3 reveals that transitional economies have made much more progress in privatization, even in the challenging large-scale sector, than in "governance and restructuring," which measures the extent to which firms operate in a competitive market-oriented environment, both internally and externally. How can a privatized firm lack restructuring and effective corporate governance?[29] Part of the answer lies in the various ways firms can be privatized.

Governments privatize enterprises in different ways for several reasons. In some cases, governments have been so eager to earn privatization revenues and to rid themselves of the budget drain of loss-making enterprises that they sold quickly to virtually anyone who made an offer. In other cases, workers and managers threatened to block privatization unless they maintained control over their enterprises, leading to sales to "insiders." Still another possibility is "mass privatization" in which governments issue vouchers to large groups of citizens, who can then use the vouchers to purchase stakes in various enterprises available for sale.

Foreigners may or may not be allowed to participate in privatization. The main advantages of including foreigners are two. By enlarging the pool of potential buyers, governments may be able to obtain a better price. And foreign owners may bring expertise, management skills, and access to new technology and finance badly needed by formerly state-owned enterprises. On the other hand, selling formerly state-owned enterprises to foreigners can be politically controversial, especially among workers and managers who fear losing their

jobs or their above-productivity wages. Even if excluded from initial privatizations, foreigners may be able to acquire firms later. In 1998, about 58 percent of all developing countries' privatization proceeds came from foreign investors.[30]

The privatization programs in the non-Baltic former Soviet republics including Russia (now members of the Commonwealth of Independent States), former Yugoslav republics, and Poland benefited primarily insiders, through insider-oriented voucher programs or management-employee buyouts. Generally, methods of privatization that place enterprises in insiders' hands, while sometimes necessary for political reasons, can leave lingering governance and restructuring problems, since they provide no outside shareholders to judge managers' and workers' operational and financial performance. These problems are made worse if the privatization scheme makes no provision for outsiders to acquire the firm if they think they can improve its performance. Despite the problems of insider control, these programs represented substantial improvements over state ownership. And, given managers' and workers' effective pre-privatization control over the enterprises, some reformist governments felt they faced little choice if privatization was to be politically feasible. These programs tended to treat all enterprises the same—whether commercially viable, potentially viable, or nonviable.

Eastern European and Baltic transitional economies faced less political pressure for insider-dominated privatization. Estonia and Hungary sold to outside owners. The Czech Republic, Latvia, and Lithuania provided vouchers to all citizens, with little or no preference to enterprise insiders. In both cases, the enterprises judged to

---

29. For more information, see Chapter Three in the World Bank's *World Development Report 2002*.

30. World Bank, *Global Development Finance 2000,* p. 191.

be most commercially viable were singled out for sale to outsiders. Buyers of such enterprises often are called *strategic investors,* chosen for their ability to exert effective control over managers and to access finance for the firm.

One benefit of privatization is the revenue it generates for governments. The sums represent a combination of the *number* of enterprises privatized, the economic viability and therefore the *value* of those enterprises, and the *method* of privatization, which affects the prices the enterprises bring. While privatization revenues certainly prove helpful to governments struggling with large budget deficits, it's important to keep in mind that they represent one-time inflows of funds. Such revenues, because of their one-time nature, can't be counted on as a source of funding for ongoing government expenditures.

Among the privatized assets are infrastructure facilities (such as power and telecommunications); manufacturing; oil, gas, and mining operations; and banking and other financial services. Countries engaging in recent privatizations include not just the Eastern European and Central Asian economies in transition from central planning, but Latin America and the Caribbean, plus East Asia. Countries in East Asia, especially Indonesia, Thailand, Malaysia, and South Korea, faced renewed privatization tasks to undo nationalizations within the financial sector undertaken during the financial crisis of 1997–1998.

It's still early to draw firm conclusions about the success or failure of various approaches to privatization.

However, some patterns have emerged. In the transitional economies outside the Commonwealth of Independent States (comprised of the non-Baltic former Soviet republics), privatized firms have restructured more thoroughly and performed better than nonprivatized ones. This has not been the case in the Commonwealth of Independent States, where state subsidies and continuing softness of budget constraints have allowed even privatized firms to avoid restructuring, with negative consequences for their performance. Strategic foreign investors have produced the best performance results. And firms with relatively concentrated ownership have outperformed those with more dispersed ownership, especially in states where the legal framework for good corporate governance (such as protection of minority shareholders) is weak.

In the end, the same things matter for successful privatization that matter for strong economic performance more generally: open competition, hard budget constraints, open international trade, unrestricted entry for new firms, lack of corruption, transparent accounting and legal standards, and a healthy financial sector to provide investment funds based on sound economic criteria. It's a recipe for growth taken for granted in industrial market economies and, increasingly, in a subset of developing and transitional economies; but it's yet to spread to other areas of the world economy, where the recipe could do much to alleviate poverty.

SUMMARY

The developing and transitional economies share two major tasks in their pursuit of improved economic performance: macroeconomic stabilization and structural reform. Macroeconomic stabilization includes reformed fiscal and monetary policies that reduce the rate of inflation and stabilize the value of the domestic currency. Structural reform includes reduction of the government's role in the day-to-day management of the economy and development of the institutional infrastructure necessary for a market economy to function and grow. Most developing and centrally planned economies have embarked on these tasks. The timing and boldness of reforms differ significantly across countries; early evidence indicates that early, bold, and persistent reform contributes to improved economic performance. Most reforming economies have made greater progress toward macroeconomic stabilization than toward structural reform, and many continue to have weak and vulnerable financial sectors, leaving them vulnerable to crises.

KEY TERMS

stabilization reforms
structural reform (structural adjustment)
privatization
soft budget constraint

monetary overhang
bilateralism
big-bang approach
gradualism approach

PROBLEMS AND QUESTIONS FOR REVIEW

1. Describe several macroeconomic characteristics typical of pre-reform developing economies. Briefly explain each characteristic's likely effect on macroeconomic performance.
2. What are the two key types of economic reform for developing and centrally planned economies? Relate the two to the aggregate demand–aggregate supply model.
3. Describe how reform in developing economies alters the characteristics you listed in problem 1. How is each element of reform likely to affect a country's macroeconomic performance?
4. Describe several macroeconomic characteristics typical of pre-reform centrally planned economies. Briefly explain each characteristic's likely effect on macroeconomic performance.
5. Describe how reform in transitional economies alters the characteristics you listed in problem 4. How is each element of reform likely to affect a country's macroeconomic performance?
6. Consider several aspects of recent macroeconomic policy in Zimbabwe.
   a. In 1998, the authoritarian president, Robert Mugabe, expropriated most of the country's commercial farms and turned them over to army veterans and political cronies in a bid to maintain power. Within five years, the economy's real output had fallen by almost half.[31] Illustrate how such a policy would affect the country's macroeconomy using an aggregate demand–aggregate supply diagram.
   b. In 2003, President Mugabe demanded that banks lower their interest rates, which were 95 percent. The rate of inflation was approximately 600 percent. What does this imply about the real interest rate and incentives to save?
   c. During 2004, the Zimbabwean dollar's value fell by about 85 percent relative to that of the U.S. dollar. How would you describe the country's likely monetary policy? Illustrate how such a policy would affect the economy using an aggregate demand–aggregate supply diagram.
7. Consider the hypothetical transitional economy of Russokia, which lacks effective corporate governance laws. The government removes capital controls and privatizes many of the country's state-owned enterprises into the hands of political cronies. There's uncertainty about how long the current government will be in power. What would you expect to happen? If you're right, how would you expect events to affect political support for reform and the country's rate of economic growth?
8. In June 1998, the OECD's *Economic Outlook* (p. 151) reported about Bulgaria that "Since mid-1997, a currency board has pegged the lev to the DM. The restoration of confidence in the government and the currency has been reflected in a much higher domestic and international demand for lev-denominated assets. In this context, between 1 July 1997 and 1 February 1998, the foreign exchange assets of the currency board more than doubled to over DM4 billion and interest rates on government paper have actually fallen to levels close to those on German treasury bonds." Explain.

REFERENCES AND SELECTED READINGS

Ahearne, Alan G., et al. "Countering Contagion: Does China's Experience Offer a Blueprint?" Federal Reserve Bank of Chicago *Economic Perspectives* (Fourth Quarter 2001): 38–52.
Skeptical look at China's attempts to insulate itself with capital and currency controls; for all students.

Bhattacharya, Rina, and Benedict Clements. "Calculating the Benefits of Debt Relief." *Finance and Development* 41 (December 2004): 48–50.
Theory and empirical evidence on debt relief such as that provided by the HIPC initiative; for all students.

Campos, Nauro F., and Fabrizio Coricelli. "Growth in Transition: What We Know, What We Don't, and What We Should." *Journal of Economic Literature* 40 (September 2002): 793–836.
Survey of the state of economists' knowledge about transition; for intermediate students.

Chiodo, Abbigail, and Michael T. Owyang. "A Case Study of a Currency Crisis: The Russian Default of 1998." Federal Reserve Bank of St. Louis *Review* 85 (January/February 2003): 11–30.
Accessible analysis of what went wrong in Russia in 1998.

Clements, Benedict, et al. "Foreign Aid: Grants versus Loans." *Finance and Development* 41 (September 2004): 46–49.
Institutional implications of aid in the form of grants rather than loans; for all students.

De Nicoló, Gianni, et al. "Bridging the 'Great Divide.'" *Finance and Development* 40 (December 2003): 42–45.
What can be done to improve the financial systems of the seven poorest former Soviet states? For all students.

---

31. "Inflation at 700% and Halved Output Predicted," *Financial Times,* November 21, 2003.

Easterly, William. *The Elusive Quest for Growth.* Cambridge, Mass.: MIT Press, 2001.
Readable account of recent development experience.

Edwards, Sebastian. *Crisis and Reform in Latin America.* New York: Oxford University Press for the World Bank, 1995.
Readable account of Latin American developments from 1982 through 1994.

European Bank for Reconstruction and Development. *Transition Report.* London: EBRD, annual.
Excellent annual survey of transitional economies and reform.

Goldsbrough, David, et al. "Prolonged Use of IMF Loans: How Much of a Problem Is It?" *Finance and Development* 34 (December 2002): 34–37.
How many countries continually borrow from the IMF, and how does it affect them? For all students.

Goldstein, Morris. *The Asian Financial Crisis: Causes, Cures, and Systemic Implications.* Washington, D.C.: Institute for International Economics, 1998.
Accessible survey of the Asian crisis.

"IMF at 60." *Finance and Development* 41 (September 2004): 8–29.
Series of short papers on the evolution of the International Monetary Fund; for all students.

International Monetary Fund. *Evaluation of Prolonged Use of IMF Resources.* Washington, D.C.: International Monetary Fund, 2002.
Analysis of the prevalence and effects of a country's long-term reliance on IMF funds; for all students.

International Monetary Fund. *World Economic Outlook.* Washington, D.C.: International Monetary Fund, biannual.
Overview of current economic events and prospects relevant to the developing economies, with data.

Kose, M. Ayhan, et al. "Taking the Plunge Without Getting Hurt." *Finance and Development* 41 (December 2004): 44–47.
The effects of openness on growth and volatility; for all students.

Krueger, Anne O. "Whither the World Bank and the IMF?" *Journal of Economic Literature* (December 1998): 1983–2020.
The former Chief Economist of the World Bank, now at the IMF, addresses the current role for the two institutions.

Kutan, Ali M., and Josef C. Brada. "The Evolution of Monetary Policy in Transition Economies." Federal Reserve Bank of St. Louis, *Review* 82 (March/April 2000): 31–40.
Overview of how the monetary policy-making process has changed during transition.

Lipschitz, Leslie, et al. "The Tosovsky Dilemma: Capital Surges in Transition Countries." *Finance and Development* 39 (September 2002): 30–33.
How can transitional economies handle capital flows without costly controls or crises? For all students.

Rajan, Raghuran. "How Useful Are Clever Solutions?" *Finance and Development* 31 (March 2004): 56–57.
Prospects for solution of developing economies' inability to borrow in their own currencies; for all students.

"Reform: What Pace Works Best?" *Finance and Development* 41 (September 2004): 34–41.
Accessible debate over the pros and cons of fast versus slow reform.

Reinhart, Carmen. "Debt Intolerance." *Brookings Papers on Economic Activity* 1 (2003): 1–74.
Evidence on the low level of debt tolerance in emerging market economies; for intermediate and advanced students.

Rodrik, Dani. "Understanding Economic Policy Reform." *Journal of Economic Literature* (March 1996): 9–41.
The politics of economic reform.

Schneider, Friedrich, and Dominik H. Enste. "Shadow Economies: Size, Causes, and Consequences." *Journal of Economic Literature* 38 (March 2000): 77–114.
Intermediate/advanced discussion of underground economies.

Session on "The Future of the International Monetary Fund and World Bank." *American Economic Review Papers and Proceedings* 93 (May 2003): 31–50.
Short papers on the roles of the primary international financial institutions; level of papers varies.

Session on "New Approaches to Resolving Emerging-Market Financial Crises." *American Economic Review Papers and Proceedings* 93 (May 2003): 70–84.
Series of short papers on dealing with crises; level of papers varies.

"Symposium on International Financial Architecture." *Journal of Economic Perspectives* 17 (Fall 2003): 51–118.
Pros and cons of various structures for the international financial system; for all students.

"Symposium on New Bankruptcy Arrangements for Sovereign Debt." *Brookings Papers on Economic Activity* 1 (2002): 229–249.
What are the options for handling sovereign insolvency? For intermediate and advanced students.

World Bank. *Bureaucrats in Business: The Economics and Politics of Government Ownership.* New York: Oxford University Press, 1995.
Detailed case studies of state-owned enterprises, privatization, and reform; for all students.

World Bank. *Global Development Finance.* Washington, D.C.: World Bank, annual.
Overview and data on capital flows to developing and transitional economies.

World Bank. *Global Economic Prospects and the Developing Countries.* Washington, D.C.: World Bank, annual.
Overview of current issues facing developing and transitional economies.

World Bank. *World Development Report.* Oxford: Oxford University Press, annual.
Devoted to examination of various aspects of development; accessible to all students. Also contains a large collection of data.

Yarbrough, Beth V., and Robert M. Yarbrough. "Unification and Secession: Group Size and 'Escape from Lock-In.'" *Kyklos* (1998): 171–195.
Simple model of German unification as a means of achieving reform in the former East Germany.

Country or Economy Index

A

Albania, 366, 374, 375
Angola, 268, 361
Argentina, 6, 7–8, 105, 128, 129, 132, 135, 191, 195–196, 233, 347, 352, 356, 361, 376
Armenia, 374
Australia, 295
Austria, 259, 339
Azerbaijan, 374

B

Bahrain, 42
Baltic Republics, 375
Bangladesh, 84
Belarus, 268, 368, 372, 374, 376
Bolivia, 378
Bosnia, 155–156, 346, 368
Brazil, 6, 7–8, 191, 202, 356, 376
Britain, 10, 42, 45, 156, 189, 225, 306, 312, 320, 324–325, 336, 337–338. *See also* United Kingdom
Brunei, 346
Bulgaria, 346, 362, 366
Burkina Faso, 378

C

Canada, 7, 10, 202, 244, 325
Cayman Islands, 42
Chad, 361

Chile, 193, 376
China, 8, 19, 73–74, 105, 106, 130, 132, 190, 196, 327, 346, 362, 363, 365, 378–379
Chinese Taipei *See* Taiwan
Congo, Democratic Republic of, 268
Côte d'Ivoire, 378
Croatia, 372
Cuba, 19
Cyprus, 343
Czechoslovakia, 362. *See also* Czech Republic; Slovak Republic
Czech Republic, 259, 343, 366, 374, 375, 379. *See also* Czechoslovakia

D

Denmark, 49, 336, 337–338, 343
Djibouti, 346
Dominican Republic, 133–134

E

East Germany, 108, 156, 362. *See also* Germany
Ecuador, 162, 346
El Salvador, 346
England *See* Britain; United Kingdom
Estonia, 259, 343, 346, 366, 370, 372, 376, 379

European Union, 7, 10, 82, 162, 188–189, 259, 325, 326, 327, 334–343, 376

F

Federal Republic of Germany *See* West Germany
Finland, 295, 339
France, 154, 156, 189, 225, 318, 320, 324–325, 338, 339, 343

G

Georgia, 374, 376
German Democratic Republic *See* East Germany
Germany, 7, 10, 42, 108, 109, 154, 156, 188–189, 225, 252, 259, 295, 306, 312, 324–325, 327, 335, 336, 337, 338, 339, 341, 343. *See also* East Germany; West Germany
Great Britain *See* Britain; United Kingdom
Greece, 235, 335, 338, 341
Guyana, 378

H

Herzegovina, 155–156, 368
Holland *See* Netherlands
Hong Kong, 9, 42, 45, 73–74, 105, 132, 137, 162, 190, 195, 346

Subject Index